D0520775

SKI NORTH AMERICA

THE ULTIMATE TRAVEL GUIDE

SKI NORTH AMERICA

THE ULTIMATE TRAVEL GUIDE

DAVID HOLYOAK

FIREFLY BOOKS

BOSS
HUGO BOSS

APR 1 2004

A FIREFLY BOOK

Published by Firefly Books Ltd., 2003

Copyright © 2003 Ultimate Sports Publications Ltd.

© 2001 by Bruce Tremper. Text on pages 18 to 23 and charts on pages 19 and 21 from *Staying Alive in Avalanche Terrain* by Bruce Tremper reprinted with permission of the publisher, The Mountaineers, Seattle, WA. www.mountaineersbooks.org.

First Printing, 2003

National Library of Canada Cataloguing in Publication Data

Holyoak, David
Ski North America: the ultimate travel guide / David Holyoak.
Includes index.
ISBN 1-55297-828-1 (pbk)
1. Ski resorts–Canada–Guidebooks. 2. Ski resorts–United States–Guidebooks. 3. Skis and skiing–Canada–Guidebooks. 4. Skis and skiing–United States–Guidebooks. I. Title.
GV854.8.N58H64 2003 796.93'025'71
C2003-900780-4

Publisher Cataloging-in-Publication Data (Library of Congress standards)

Holyoak, David.
Ski North America: the ultimate travel guide / David Holyoak.
[312] p.: col. ill., photos., maps ; cm.
Includes index.
Summary: A guide to the top 40 ski resorts in North America
ISBN 1-55297-828-1 (pbk.)
1. Ski resorts – United States – Directories. 2. Ski resorts – Canada – Directories. 3. Skis and skiing – North America. I. Title.
796.9/3/097 21 GV854.4.H761 2003

First published in Canada in 2003 by
Firefly Books Ltd.
3680 Victoria Park Avenue
Toronto, Ontario M2H 3K1

First published in the United States in 2003 by
Firefly Books (U.S.) Inc.
P.O. Box 1338, Ellicott Station
Buffalo, New York 14205

www.fireflybooks.com

EDITOR/AUTHOR David Holyoak

PROJECT MANAGER Richard Watts

EDITORIAL CONTRIBUTORS Eric Kendall, Sarah Hudson, James Harrison, Robin Neillands, David Murdoch and Mike Allaby

DESIGNERS Duncan Kitson and Paul Kellett

CARTOGRAPHER Tim Williams

PRODUCTION Clive Sparling

PROOFREADER Vanessa Morgan

SPECIAL THANKS TO:
Richard Watts and each of the contributors named above.

Guy Chambers, Craig Johnson, Jim Odoire, Sam Stoyel, Charlie Witheridge and all at Black Diamond.

ACKNOWLEDGEMENTS:
And thanks to the skiers, boarders, photographers, and staff at each resort. (please see page 304 for a full list)

AND TO:
Bruce Tremper, Director, Utah Avalanche Institute, and to Mary Metz and Tim Warne at Mountaineers Books.

Françoise Vulpé at Firefly Books Ltd.

Family, friends, and everyone else who has helped in any way.

ULTIMATE SPORTS

Planned and produced by
Ultimate Sports Publications Limited.
42-44 Dolben Street
London SE1 0UQ
United Kingdom

Tel: +44 (0)20 7630 0344
Mobile: +44 (0)7775 894120
Fax: +44 (0)20 7620 2298
E-Mail: info@ultimate-sports.co.uk
www.ultimate-sports.co.uk

All rights reserved. No part of this publication may be reproduced, stored in a retrieval system or transmitted in any form or by any means, electronic, mechanical, recording or otherwise without the prior permission in writing of the copyright holder, Ultimate Sports Publications Limited.

All requests for permission should be addressed in writing to David Holyoak, Ultimate Sports Publications Limited, c/o 8 Grange Road, Barnes, London SW13 9RE.

Database right Ultimate Sports Publications Limited.

Although every care has been taken in compiling this publication, using the latest information available at the time of going to press, some details are liable to change and cannot be guaranteed. Neither Ultimate Sports Publications Limited nor the Editor/Author accept any liability whatsoever arising from errors or omissions, however caused

The representation of a road or pathway in this guide is no proof of the existence of a right of way. Likewise the frontiers shown do not imply any recognition or official acceptance on the part of the publishers. The representation of any or all specifically marked mountain trails, lifts, paths or pistes, does not necessarily guarantee their existence.

Skiing and snowboarding can be dangerous and addictive activities. You ski and ride in the mountains at your own risk. Neither the publishers nor the Editor/Author accept any responsibility or liability for accident, injury or loss of life or limb as a result of using all or any of the information contained in this guide.

Reprographics by News SPA Italy.
Printed in Spain by Mateu Cromo Artes Graficas.

► HIGHLAND BOWL, ASPEN COLORADO
◄◄ ROLO'S, MIKE WIEGELE'S HELISKIING

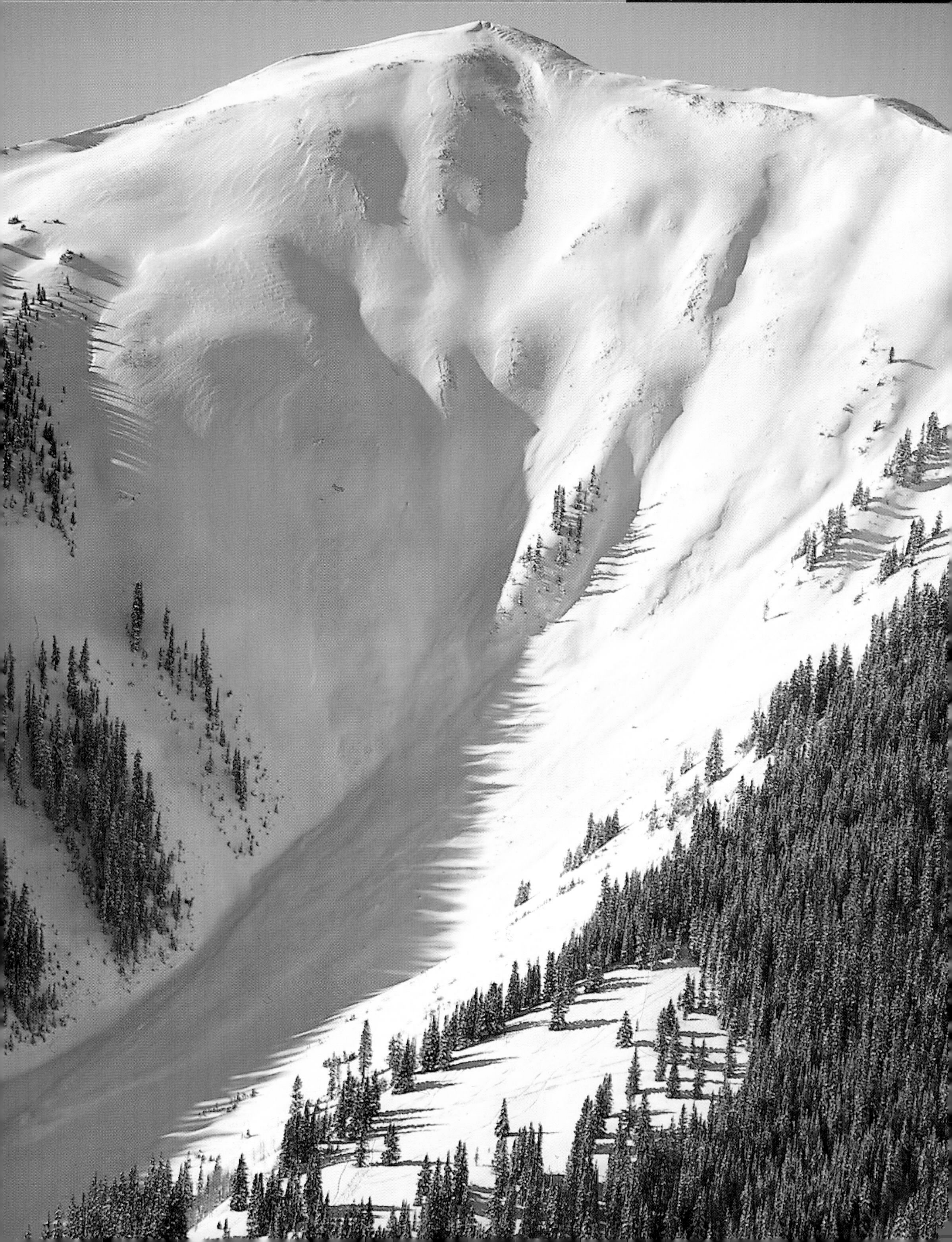

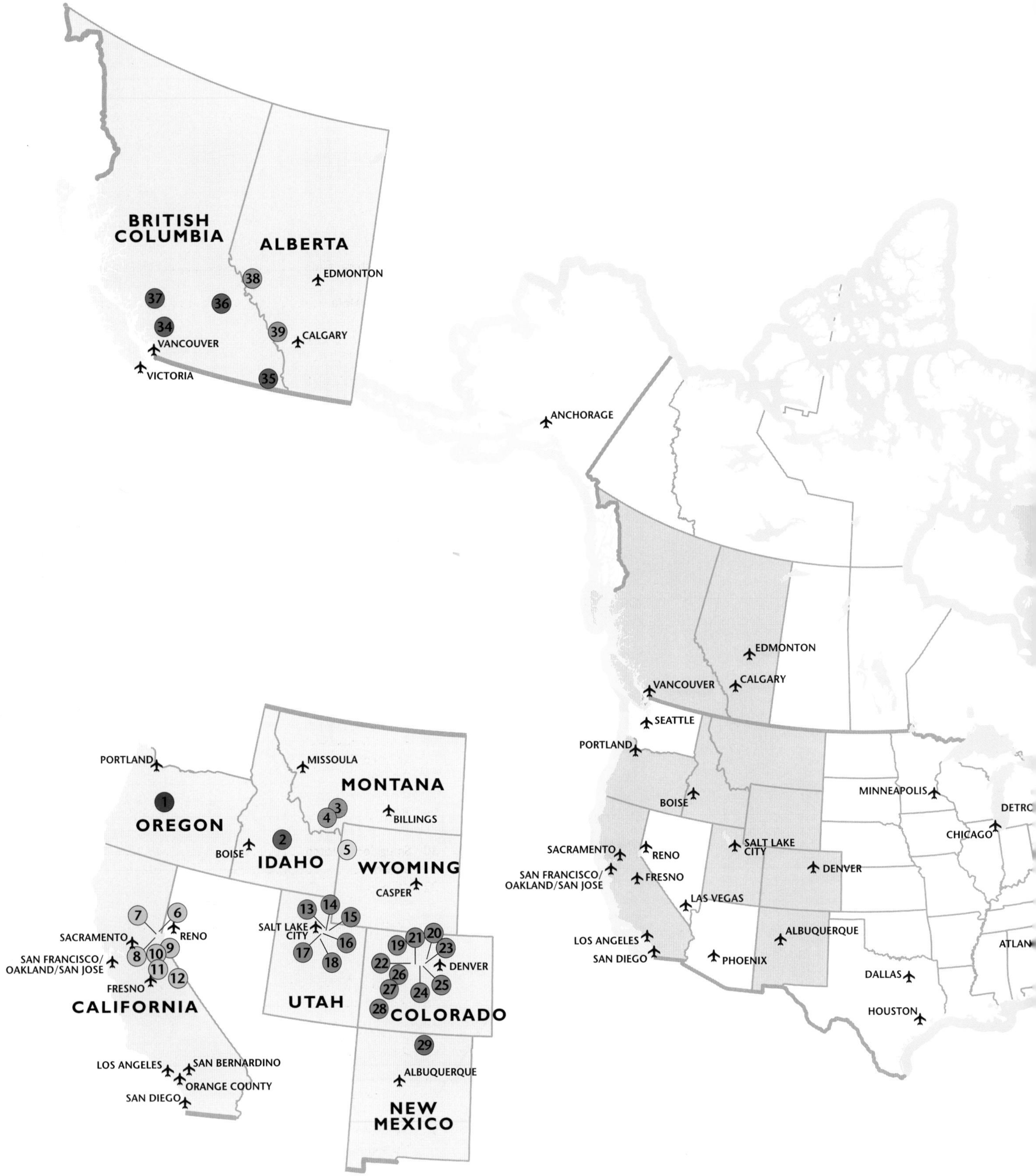
BRITISH COLUMBIA
ALBERTA
EDMONTON
CALGARY
VANCOUVER
VICTORIA
34
35
36
37
38
39
ANCHORAGE
EDMONTON
VANCOUVER
CALGARY
SEATTLE
PORTLAND
BOISE
MINNEAPOLIS
DETRO
CHICAGO
SACRAMENTO
RENO
SALT LAKE CITY
DENVER
SAN FRANCISCO/ OAKLAND/SAN JOSE
FRESNO
LAS VEGAS
LOS ANGELES
SAN DIEGO
ALBUQUERQUE
PHOENIX
ATLAN
DALLAS
HOUSTON
PORTLAND
MISSOULA
MONTANA
BILLINGS
OREGON
BOISE
IDAHO
WYOMING
CASPER
SACRAMENTO
RENO
SAN FRANCISCO/ OAKLAND/SAN JOSE
FRESNO
CALIFORNIA
SALT LAKE CITY
UTAH
DENVER
COLORADO
LOS ANGELES
SAN BERNARDINO
ORANGE COUNTY
SAN DIEGO
ALBUQUERQUE
NEW MEXICO
1
2
3
4
5
6
7
8
9
10
11
12
13
14
15
16
17
18
19
20
21
22
23
24
25
26
27
28
29

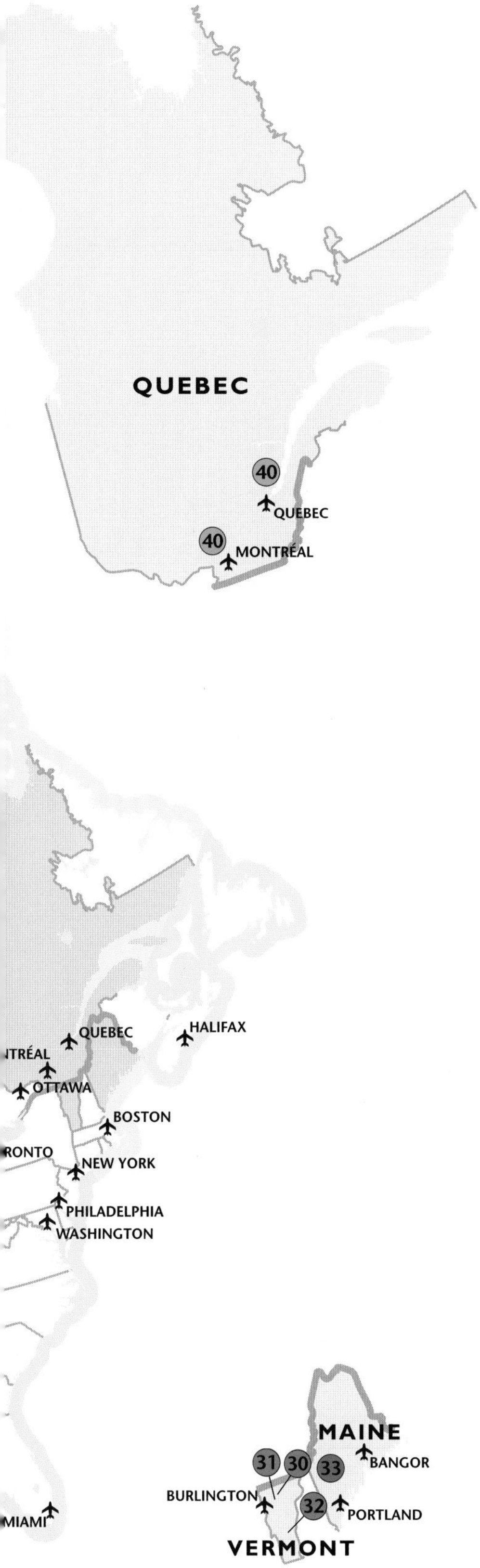
QUEBEC
40
QUEBEC
40
MONTRÉAL
QUEBEC
HALIFAX
NTRÉAL
OTTAWA
BOSTON
RONTO
NEW YORK
PHILADELPHIA
WASHINGTON
MAINE
31
30
33
BANGOR
BURLINGTON
32
PORTLAND
MIAMI
VERMONT

CONTENTS

INTRODUCTION

WELCOME TO SKI NORTH AMERICA—THE ULTIMATE TRAVEL GUIDE—AND TO FORTY OF THE TOP SKI AND SNOWBOARD DESTINATIONS IN THE UNITED STATES AND CANADA.

Skiing and boarding are addictive and expensive pastimes. With so many destinations to choose from worldwide, the choice of resort is never easy, and it's made more difficult if you don't have easy access to reliable, accurate information.

Most established ski guidebooks cover as many as 150 resorts in up to a dozen countries, concentrating on Europe and North America. Because of their large scope and small page size, the information is limited and the use of photography, whether to inspire or inform, is minimal.

Ski North America is different: the Ultimate Sports format gives you the information you need to choose the right resort and to get the most from it once you arrive. We've presented the facts in a user-friendly way, and used the photography to tell the story as well, with accurate, informative captions and big landscapes that really show the terrain. For the first time, you can see what's being described, and, with the help of the official trail maps, you'll know where you're going before you even get there. The images also reflect the way we feel about the mountains, the snow, and skiing and boarding, without feeling the need to invert, ski fake, or leap from a cliff more than once every few pages.

Our regional focus allows us to present each ski resort in full detail. Forty destinations are covered in 270 pages, giving the resorts the space they deserve and added value to the reader. To help make resort comparison easier, there are panels summarizing key information throughout the chapters. We tell you how to get there, about the ski village or town, accommodations, après ski, and other activities. But mostly it's about what really counts: the ski area, the lifts, and the best itineraries for beginners, intermediates, advanced, and expert skiers and riders.

There are also separate sections for boarders and freestyle skiers, including details of all the main terrain parks.

Before you get down to the resorts themselves, there are sections on climate, snow, avalanches and mountain safety. In the light of over 50 fatalities in North America last season (2002/03), these pages should help you understand the essentials and ensure you have the necessary training, equipment, and experience before heading out in search of backcountry adventure.

Working with a network of local skiers, boarders, and journalists we have spent two years carefully researching this guide with the aim of building an objective and accurate picture of the main North American ski resorts. Just compiling our "Top 40" involved choices that someone, somewhere, will disagree with—but we hope we reached a fair representation. For comparison, we've included all but two of *Ski Magazine's* "top 30 North American resorts" based on that magazine's Reader Resorts Survey 2003, and also a further ten resorts including three of Ski Mag's "top five" eastern resorts, and two of the world's best heliskiing operations for those in search of the ultimate deep snow thrills. Next season we will be researching a further ten North American ski and snowboard resorts.

We hope you enjoy reading Ski North America and find it helpful when making your choice of ski resort. Please remember that this is evolving book, which will be updated and extended for future seasons. We welcome your feedback—it will help us to make this ski guide even more effective in years to come.

As Warren Miller, film-maker, said, "The best resort in the world is the one you are skiing that day." This book should help make certain of it.

David Holyoak
June, 2003

◄ KERMIT GLACIER, MIKE WIEGELE'S HELISKIING

MOUNTAIN FACTS

RESORT	STATE	BASE FEET (M)	SUMMIT FEET (M)	ELEVATION FEET (M)	SNOWFALL INCHES (CM)	TOTAL AREA ACRES (HA)	SNOWMAKING ACRES (HA)	NUMBER OF TRAILS	TRAIL DENSITY	SKIER DENSITY
Mount Bachelor	Oregon	6,300 (1,890)	9,065 (2,719)	2,765 (829)	350 (889)	3,683 (1,473)	- -	71	52	5
Sun Valley	Idaho	5,750 (1,752)	9,150 (2,788)	3,400 (1,036)	346 (866)	2,054 (831)	630 (255)	78	26	14
Big Sky	Montana	6,800 (2,073)	11,150 (3,398)	4,350 (1,326)	400 (1,016)	3,600 (1,457)	360 (146)	150	24	6
Yellowstone Club	Montana	6,800 (2,073)	9,856 (3,005)	3,056 (931)	400 (1,016)	2,000 (809)	- -	30	67	-
Jackson Hole	Wyoming	6,311 (1,923)	10,450 (3,185)	4,139 (1,262)	402 (1,021)	2,500 (1,012)	160 (65)	76	33	5
Northstar at Tahoe	Callifornia	6,330 (1,899)	8,610 (2,583)	2,280 (684)	350 (889)	2,420 (968)	1,210 (490)	70	35	9
Squaw Valley	California	6,200 (1,889)	9,050 (2,758)	2,850 (868)	453 (1,150)	4,000 (1,619)	400 (162)	100	40	12
Alpine Meadows	California	6,835 (2,083)	8,637 (2,633)	1,802 (549)	495 (1,257)	2,000 (810)	140 (57)	100	20	8
Heavenly	California	6,223 (1,866)	10,067 (3,020)	3,844 (1,153)	360 (914)	4,800 (1,920)	3,312 (1,340)	85	56	6
Sierra-at-Tahoe	California	6,640 (1,992)	8,852 (2,655)	2,212 (663)	480 (1,219)	2,000 (800)	80 (32)	46	43	7
Kirkwood	California	7,800 (2,377)	9,800 (2,987)	2,000 (610)	500 (1,270)	2,300 (932)	55 (22)	65	35	8
Mammoth Mountain	California	7,953 (2,424)	11,053 (3,369)	3,100 (945)	384 (975)	3,500 (1,400)	477 (193)	150	23	14
The Canyons	Utah	6,800 (2,040)	9,990 (2,997)	3,190 (957)	355 (901)	3,500 (1,400)	160 (64)	118	30	7
Park City	Utah	6,900 (2,103)	10,028 (3,056)	3,128 (953)	350 (890)	3,300 (1,335)	500 (202)	100	33	8
Deer Valley	Utah	6,570 (2,002)	9,570 (2,916)	3,000 (914)	300 (762)	1,750 (700)	500 (202)	88	20	23
Alta	Utah	8,530 (2,600)	10,550 (3,216)	2,020 (618)	500 (1,270)	2,200 (890)	50 (20)	23	96	5
Snowbird	Utah	7,760 (2,365)	11,000 (3,352)	3,240 (987)	500 (1,270)	2,500 (1,000)	200 (80)	85	29	7
Sundance	Utah	6,100 (1,859)	8,250 (2,514)	2,150 (655)	300 (762)	450 (182)	450 (182)	41	11	11
Steamboat	Colorado	6,899 (2,103)	10,568 (3,221)	3,668 (1,118)	360 (915)	2,939 (1,189)	438 (174)	142	21	11
Winter Park	Colorado	9,000 (2,743)	12,060 (3,675)	3,060 (932)	367 (914)	2,886 (1,168)	294 (119)	134	22	12
Vail	Colorado	8,120 (2,475)	11,570 (3,527)	3,450 (1,052)	346 (866)	5,289 (2,140)	380 (154)	193	27	10
Beaver Creek	Colorado	8,100 (2,469)	11,440 (3,487)	3,340 (1,018)	310 (787)	1,625 (658)	605 (245)	146	11	15
Keystone	Colorado	9,300 (2,835)	12,200 (3,719)	2,900 (884)	230 (584)	1,861 (754)	859 (348)	116	16	19
Copper Mountain	Colorado	9,712 (2,960)	12,313 (3,753)	2,601 (793)	280 (710)	2,433 (985)	380 (153)	122	20	13
Breckenridge	Colorado	9,600 (2,926)	12,142 (3,963)	3,398 (1,036)	300 (761)	2,208 (894)	560 (227)	145	15	17
Aspen Snowmass	Colorado	8,104 (2,473)	12,510 (3,813)	4,406 (1,343)	300 (762)	4,805 (3,027)	608 (246)	315	15	11
Crested Bute	Colorado	9,100 (2,858)	12,162 (3,707)	3,062 (933)	298 (745)	1,058 (428)	300 (121)	85	12	17
Telluride	Colorado	8,725 (2,660)	12,260 (3,738)	3,530 (1,978)	309 (789)	1,700 (680)	204 (82)	84	20	12
Taos	New Mexico	9,207 (2,806)	12,481 (3,804)	3,274 (998)	312 (792)	1,294 (524)	647 (262)	72	18	12
Smugglers' Notch	Vermont	1,030 (283)	3,640 (1,110)	2,610 (796)	284 (721)	1,000 (405)	141 (57)	72	14	7
Stowe	Vermont	1,280 (390)	3,640 (1,340)	2,360 (719)	260 (660)	480 (194)	350 (142)	48	10	26
Killington	Vermont	1,091 (332)	4,241 (1,292)	3,150 (960)	250 (625)	1,182 (478)	827 (335)	200	6	44
Sugarloaf	Maine	1,417 (425)	4,237 (1,271)	2,820 (846)	216 (548)	1,400 (560)	490 (196)	129	11	16
Whistler-Blackcomb	British Columbia	2,214 (675)	7,494 (2,284)	5,280 (1,609)	360 (914)	7,071 (2,862)	565 (229)	200	35	8
Fernie	British Columbia	3,500 (1,050)	6,316 (1,894)	2,816 (844)	348 (870)	2,504 (1,000)	25 (10)	107	23	5
Jasper	Alberta	5,534 (1,686)	8,534 (2,601)	3,000 (915)	160 (400)	1,500 (608)	15 (6)	75	20	8
Banff Lake Louise	Alberta	5,400 (1,646)	8,650 (2,637)	3,250 (991)	140 (356)	7,358 (2,978)	1,871 (757)	216	34	5
Mount Tremblant	Quebec	870 (261)	3,000 (900)	2,130 (639)	15 (380)	610 (244)	464 (188)	92	7	45
Le Massif	Quebec	118 (36)	2,645 (806)	2,527 (770)	253 (643)	240 (98)	168 (68)	36	7	27
Mont-Sainte-Anne	Quebec	575 (225)	2,625 (800)	2,050 (625)	160 (406)	428 (171)	342 (138)	56	8	44
Stoneham	Quebec	695 (212)	2,075 (632)	1,863 (420)	140 (350)	326 (130)	280 (113)	32	10	44
AVERAGE		5,909 (1,801)	8,869 (2,703)	2,960 (902)	326 (828)	2,457 (994)	514 (208)	105	26	15
United States		6,766 (2,062)	9,776 (2,980)	3,010 (917)	353 (897)	2,446 (990)	527 (213)	105	28	12
Canada		3,515 (1,071)	6,732 (2,052)	3,21 (980)	232 (589)	3,809 (1,541)	588 (238)	138	24	14
Eastern United States		1,205 (367)	3,940 (1,201)	2,735 (834)	253 (643)	1,016 (411)	572 (231)	112	10	23
Colorado		8,666 (2,641)	11,928 (3,636)	3,262 (994)	310 (787)	2,680 (1,084)	463 (187)	148	18	14
California		6,854 (2,089)	9,438 (2,877)	2,584 88)	432 (1,097)	3,003 (1,215)	823 (333)	88	36	9
Utah		7,110 (2,167)	9,893 (3,015)	2,783 (848)	384 (975)	2,283 (924)	310 (125)	76	36	10

EASY	INTERMEDIATE	ADVANCED /EXPERT	LONGEST TRAIL MILES (KM)	LIFTS	RIDERS PER HOUR	CABLE CAR	GONDOLA	HIGH SPEED 6-CHAIRS	HIGH SPEED QUADS	FIXED QUADS	TRIPLE CHAIRS	DOUBLE CHAIRS	SURFACE LIFTS	MAGIC CARPETS
15%	25%	60%	1.5 (1.6)	13	20,100	-	-	-	7	-	3	-	3	-
42%	40%	18%	3.0 (4.8)	20	28,180	-	-	-	7	-	5	5	3	-
17%	25%	58%	6.0 (9.6)	18	22,000	1	1	-	3	1	4	5	3	-
15%	55%	30%	- -	5	-	-	-	-	3	-	1	1	-	-
10%	40%	50%	4.5 (7.2)	12	12,096	1	1	-	2	4	1	1	-	2
25%	50%	25%	3.0 (4.8)	14	21,800	-	1	-	5	-	2	1	4	1
25%	45%	30%	3.2 (5.1)	33	49,000	2	1	3	4	1	8	9	4	1
25%	40%	35%	2.5 (4.0)	14	16,000	-	-	1	1	-	4	5	3	-
20%	45%	35%	5.5 (8.8)	29	29,000	1	1	1	5	-	8	5	6	2
25%	50%	25%	2.5 (4.0)	10	14,920	-	-	-	3	-	1	5	-	1
15%	50%	35%	2.5 (4.0)	14	17,905	-	2	-	1	1	7	1	2	-
25%	40%	35%	3.0 (4.8)	27	50,000	-	3	1	8	1	7	5	2	-
14%	44%	42%	2.5 (4.0)	18	25,700	-	2	-	5	4	2	1	3	1
18%	44%	38%	3.5 (5.6)	14	27,200	-	-	4	1	-	5	4	-	-
15%	50%	35%	2.0 (3.2)	19	40,700	-	1	-	9	-	7	2	-	-
25%	40%	35%	3.2 (5.1)	13	11,200	-	-	-	1	-	3	4	5	-
27%	38%	35%	2.5 (4.0)	13	16,800	1	-	-	3	-	7	-	2	-
20%	40%	40%	2.5 (4.0)	4	5,000	-	-	-	1	-	2	-	1	-
13%	27%	60%	3.0 (4.8)	20	32,158	-	1	-	4	1	6	6	2	-
9%	21%	70%	6.1 (9.8)	22	35,030	-	-	-	8	-	4	7	3	-
18%	29%	53%	3.0 (4.8)	33	53,381	-	1	-	14	1	3	5	9	-
34%	39%	27%	3.0 (4.8)	13	24,739	-		-	6	-	3	4	-	-
16%	37%	47%	3.0 (4.8)	21	35,175	-	2	1	5	1	1	4	2	5
21%	25%	54%	2.8 (4.5)	21	30,630	-	-	-	1	4	5	5	6	-
13%	32%	55%	3.5 (5.6)	27	36,880	-	-	2	6	-	1	6	5	7
14%	40%	46%	5.0 (8.0)	40	51,623	-	1	-	12	2	4	14	4	3
14%	32%	54%	2.6 (4.2)	14	18,160	-	-	-	3	-	3	3	3	2
24%	38%	38%	4.6 (7.4)	16	21,186	-	2	-	7	-	2	2	2	1
24%	25%	49%	5.8 (9.3)	12	15,500	-	-	-	-	4	1	5	2	-
22%	53%	25%	2.5 (4.0)	8	7,053	-	-	-	-	-	-	6	2	-
16%	59%	25%	3.7 (6.0)	5	12,326	-	1	-	1	-	-	-	3	-
30%	39%	31%	6.2 (10)	31	52,361	-	3	-	6	6	6	4	5	1
27%	30%	43%	3.5 (5.6)	15	21,805	-	-	-	4	-	1	8	2	-
20%	55%	25%	7.0 (11)	33	59,007	-	3	-	12	-	5	1	12	-
30%	40%	30%	3.0 (4.8)	10	13,716	-	-	-	2	2	2	-	3	1
16%	25%	59%	3.5 (5.6)	8	11,934	-	-	-	1	1	1	3	2	-
23%	38%	39%	5.0 (8.0)	28	36,920	-	2	1	5	8	2	5	5	-
16%	32%	52%	3.8 (6.1)	13	27,230	-	1	-	6	1	2	-	-	3
20%	36%	44%	2.3 (3.7)	5	6,500	-	-	-	2	-	-	1	2	-
23%	46%	31%	3.6 (5.8)	13	18,650	-	1	-	1	2	1	2	5	1
20%	23%	57%	2.0 (3.2)	9	14,200	-	-	-	1	2	-	1	5	-
21%	39%	41%	3.5 (5.6)	17	26,094									
20%	39%	41%	3.5 (5.6)	18	26,738									
21%	38%	41%	4.5 (7.2)	18	29,761									
24%	45%	31%	4.0 (6.4)	15	23,386									
18%	32%	50%	3.7 (6.0)	23	33,896									
23%	46%	31%	3.2 (5.1)	20	28,375									
20%	43%	38%	2.7 (4.3)	14	21,100									

TOP TEN RANKINGS

BIGGEST SKI AREA

1	Banff Lake Louise, ALB	7,358
2	Whistler Blackcomb, BC	7,071
3	Vail, CO	5,289
4	Aspen Snowmass, CO	4,805
5	Heavenly, CA	4,800
6	Squaw Valley, CA	4,000
7	Mount Bachelor, OR	3,683
8	Big Sky, MT	3,600
9	Mammoth Mountain, CA	3,500
10	The Canyons, UT	3,500

Total acres (inbounds)

LIFT CAPACITY

1	Whistler Blackcomb, BC	59,007
2	Vail, CO	53,381
3	Killington, VT	52,361
4	Aspen Snowmass, CO	51,623
5	Mammoth, CA	50,000
6	Squaw Valley, CA	49,000
7	Deer Valley, UT	40,700
8	Banff Lake Louise, ALB	36,920
9	Breckenridge, CO	36,880
10	Keystone , CO	35,175

Lift riders per hour

MOSTLY EASY

1	Sun Valley, ID	42%
2	Beaver Creek, CO	34%
3	Killington, VT	30%
4	Fernie, BC	30%
5	Snowbird, UT	27%
6	Sugarloaf, ME	27%
7	Mammoth, CA	25%
8	Squaw Valley, CA	25%
9	Northstar at Tahoe, CA	25%
10	Sierra, CA	25%

As a percentage of total trails

BIGGEST VERTICAL

1	Whistler Blackcomb, BC	5,280 (1,609)
2	Aspen Snowmass, CO	4,406 (1,343)
3	Big Sky, MT	4,350 (1,326)
4	Jackson Hole, WY	4,139 (1,262)
5	Heavenly, CA	3,844 (1,153)
6	Steamboat, CO	3,668 (1,118)
7	Telluride, CO	3,530 (1,978)
8	Vail, CO	3,450 (1,052)
9	Sun Valley, ID	3,400 (1,036)
10	Beaver Creek, CO	3,340 (1,018)

Vertical elevation - feet (m)

MOST TRAILS

1	Aspen Snowmass, CO	315
2	Banff Lake Louise, ALB	216
3	Whistler Blackcomb, BC	200
4	Killington, VT	200
5	Vail, CO	193
6	Big Sky, MT	150
7	Mammoth Mountain, CA	150
8	Beaver Creek, CO	146
9	Breckenridge, CO	145
10	Steamboat, CO	142

Total number of trails

MOSTLY INTERMEDIATE

1	Stowe, VT	59%
2	Whistler Blackcomb, BC	55%
3	Smuggler's Notch, VT	53%
4	Northstar at Tahoe, CA	50%
5	Sierra-at-Tahoe, CA	50%
6	Deer Valley, UT	50%
7	Kirkwood, CA	50%
8	Mont-Sainte-Anne, QUE	46%
9	Squaw Valley, CA	45%
10	Heavenly, CA	45%

As a percentage of total trails

MOST SNOW

1	Alta, UT	500 (1,270)
2	Kirkwood, CA	500 (1,270)
3	Snowbird, UT	500 (1,270)
4	Alpine Meadows, CA	495 (1,257)
5	Sierra-at-Tahoe, CA	480 (1,219)
6	Squaw Valley, CA	453 (1,150)
7	Jackson Hole, WY	402 (1,021)
8	Big Sky, MT	400 (1,016)
9	Mammoth Mountain, CA	384 (975)
10	Winter Park, CO	367 (914)

Average annual snowfall - inches (cm)

LONGEST TRAIL

1	Whistler Blackcomb, BC	7.0 (11)
2	Killington, VT	6.2 (10)
3	Winter Park, CO	6.1 (9.8)
4	Big Sky, MT	6.0 (9.6)
5	Taos, NM	5.8 (9.3)
6	Heavenly, CA	5.5 (8.8)
7	Aspen Snowmass, CO	5.0 (8.0)
8	Banff Lake Louise, AB	5.0 (8.0)
9	Telluride, CO	4.6 (7.4)
10	Jackson Hole, WY	4.5 (7.2)

Longest trail - miles (km)

MOSTLY ADVANCED & EXPERT

1	Winter Park, CO	70%
2	Steamboat, CO	60%
3	Mount Bachelor, OR	60%
4	Jasper, ALB	59%
5	Big Sky, MT	58%
6	Stoneham, QUE	57%
7	Breckenridge, CO	55%
8	Crested Bute, CO	54%
9	Copper Mountain, CO	54%
10	Vail, CO	53%

As a percentage of total trails

Notes: 1. Top Ten Rankings are mostly compiled from the Mountain Facts set out on pages 10 and 11 and are presented for convenience only.
2. Skier Density is calculated as ski area (acres) divided by lift rider capacity per hour. Resorts with low skier density are likely to be less crowded and vice versa.
3. Yellowstone Club, Mike Wiegele's & TLH Heli-skiing are purposely excluded from these Top Ten rankings as they are not directly comparable to other resorts.

LOW SKIER DENSITY

1	Jackson Hole, WY	5
2	Banff Lake Louise	5
3	Alta, UT	5
4	Fernie, BC	6
5	Mount Bachelor, OR	6
6	Heavenly, CA	6
7	Big Sky, MT	6
8	Snowbird, UT	7
9	Smuggler's Notch, VT	7
10	The Canyons, UT	7

Lift riders per hour per acre

HIGH SKIER DENSITY

1	Mont Tremblant, QUE	45
2	Killington, VT	44
3	Mont-Sainte-Anne, QUE	44
4	Stoneham, QUE	44
5	Le Massif, QUE	27
6	Stowe, VT	26
7	Deer Valley, UT	23
8	Keystone , CO	19
9	Crested Bute, CO	17
10	Breckenridge, CO	17

Lift riders per hour per acre

ACCESS

1	Stoneham, QUE	15 (24 km)
2	Mont-Sainte-Anne, QUE	25 (40 km)
3	Snowbird, UT	29 (47 km)
4	Alta, UT	33 (53 km)
5	Park City, UT	37 (59 km)
6	Deer Valley, UT	37 (59 km)
7	Northstar at Tahoe, CA	40 (64 km)
8	The Canyons, UT	40 (64 km)
9	Squaw Valley, CA	42 (67 km)
10	Alpine Meadows, CA	45 (72 km)

Distance from main airport - miles (km)

SERVICE

1	Deer Valley, UT
2	Beaver Creek, CO
3	Sun Valley, ID
4	Whistler Blackcomb, BC
5	Aspen Snowmass, CO
6	Vail, CO
7	Steamboat, CO
8	Mont Tremblant, QUE
9	Telluride, CO
10	Northstar at Tahoe, CA

EATING ON THE MOUNTAIN

1	Deer Valley, UT
2	Sun Valley, ID
3	Mont Tremblant, QUE
4	Aspen Snowmass, CO
5	Whistler Blackcomb, BC
6	Beaver Creek, CO
7	Vail, CO
8	Snowmass, CO
9	Park City, UT
10	Telluride, CO

SCENERY

1	Heavenly, CA
2	Lake Louise, ALB
3	Telluride, CO
4	Jackson Hole, WY
5	Sundance, UT
6	Jasper, ALB
7	Steamboat, CO
8	Aspen Snowmass, CO
9	Whistler Blackcomb, BC
10	Alta, UT

DINING

1	Aspen Snowmass, CO
2	Deer Valley, UT
3	Mont Tremblant, QUE
4	Stowe, VT
5	Sun Valley, ID
6	Whistler Blackcomb, BC
7	Vail, CO
8	Beaver Creek, CO
9	Park City, UT
10	Telluride, CO

CHALLENGING

1	Jackson Hole, WY
2	Alta, UT
3	Snowbird, UT
4	Crested Butte, CO
5	Whistler Blackcomb, BC
6	Taos Ski Valley, NM
7	Mammoth Mountain, CA
8	Aspen Snowmass, CO
9	Telluride, CO
10	Squaw Valley, CA

APRÈS SKI

1	Aspen Snowmass, CO
2	Whistler Blackcomb, BC
3	Vail, CO
4	Killington, VT
5	Heavenly, CA
6	Mont Tremblant, QUE
7	Breckenridge, CO
8	Park City, UT
9	Stowe, VT
10	Sun Valley, ID

An American Classic
40 Years in the Making.

WWW.K2SKIS.COM

CLIMATE

NORTH AMERICA IS BIG AND SO TOO ARE ITS WEATHER SYSTEMS. THERE ARE MANY DEPRESSIONS CAPABLE OF DELIVERING VERY HEAVY SNOW ALTERNATING WITH HIGH-PRESSURE SYSTEMS THAT BRING CLEAR SKIES AND LOW TEMPERATURES.

North America has a continental climate. This means the climate is generally dry, with cold winters and hot summers, but with the wide variation that is to be expected over a continent extending from the Arctic Circle to the tropics.

This variation is only partly due to the range of latitude the continent spans. The overall shape and elevation also influence the climate. Although large, North America is compact. The only extensive areas of open water are Hudson Bay and the Great Lakes. There are no deep indentations along the western coast. The western mountain ranges run north-to-south, thus forming an effective barrier to weather systems moving from west to east. To the east of these mountains the land slopes very gradually to the Great Plains. Dodge City, Kansas, equidistant between the Pacific and Atlantic, is still 2,594 feet (791 m) above sea level. Temperature decreases with height, making the western side of North America cooler than it would be were its elevation lower.

AIR FLOWS

The North American climate is produced by the type of air that crosses it. Cold, dry, continental polar air lies over northern Canada and sometimes moves south in winter, producing cold waves that reach almost as far as the Gulf of Mexico. Hot, dry continental air lies over Mexico. It tends to move north in summer. Cool, moist maritime polar air enters the continent from both the Atlantic and Pacific. The Atlantic air enters over Labrador and moves south as far as Maine. Pacific air crosses the Rocky Mountains, losing most of its moisture on the western side of the range and producing dry conditions over the Great Plains. Maritime tropical air from the Gulf and Pacific brings warm, moist conditions to the Gulf states and to southern California in winter.

The interior of the continent cools fairly rapidly during the autumn. This chills the air, increasing its density and causing it to subside. Consequently, a large area of high pressure forms, centered approximately over Utah. High pressure also forms over northwestern Canada. Pressure is low over the Aleutian Islands and in the northeast. Air circulating counterclockwise around the low-pressure center in the northwest and clockwise around the high-pressure center further south drives weather systems across the continent. There are many depressions, capable of delivering heavy snow and moving quite fast along a generally easterly or northeasterly track. The depressions alternate with high-pressure systems (anticyclones) that bring clear skies and low temperatures.

TEMPERATURE AND THE CHINOOK EFFECT

Obviously, the average temperature must remain below freezing in order for snow to fall and then remain on the ground. In January, the mean temperature is cold enough for snow over the whole of Canada, except for the coastal fringe of British Columbia, and in the northwestern and northeastern United States and in the central part of the continent to about the latitude of Omaha, Nebraska.

Snow tends not to survive the winter immediately to the east of the Rocky Mountains. This is due in part to the fact that the climate is dry. Calgary, Alberta, for example, receives an average of only 2.3 inches (5.9 cm) of rain over the four months from November to February. It is also due to the chinook winds that from time to time bring dry, much warmer air down from the mountains. The effect is so dramatic that the chinook is sometimes called the "snow eater."

The chinook (named after the Native American people who once lived along the lower reaches of the Columbia River) occurs when stable air is lifted over the Rocky and Cascade Mountains. The air subsides on the lee side of the mountains, warming by compression as it does so. It brings winds that sometimes gust to 100 mph (160 kph), but more significantly it rapidly raises the temperature. A chinook has been known to raise the temperature from -4°F (-20°C) to 45°F (7°C) in two minutes, and a rise of 40°F (22°C) in 15 minutes is quite common. A chinook can clear snow faster than a snowplow!

THE LAKE EFFECT

There are ski resorts in almost every state and province that have mountains. Obviously, most of the best skiing is to be found in the Rocky Mountains, especially in Colorado, which has the highest peaks and therefore abundant snow despite the state's semi-arid climate. The heaviest snowfalls are often not there, however, but in the northeastern United States and Appalachian Mountains. This is "lake effect" snow and it provides excellent conditions for winter sports.

During the autumn, large bodies of water cool down much more slowly than does the

THE CHINOOK EFFECT

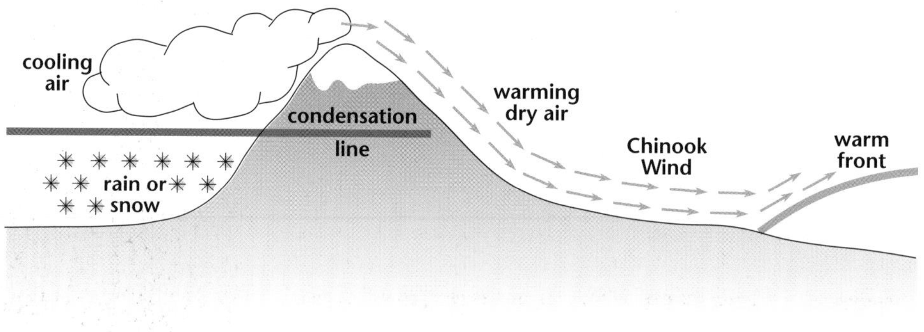

THE LAKE EFFECT

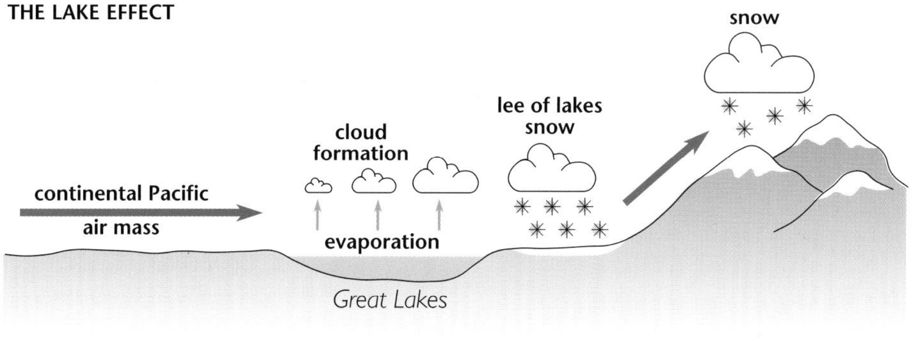

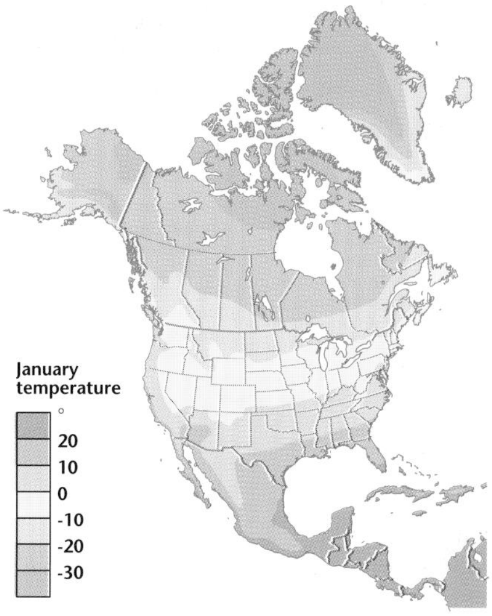

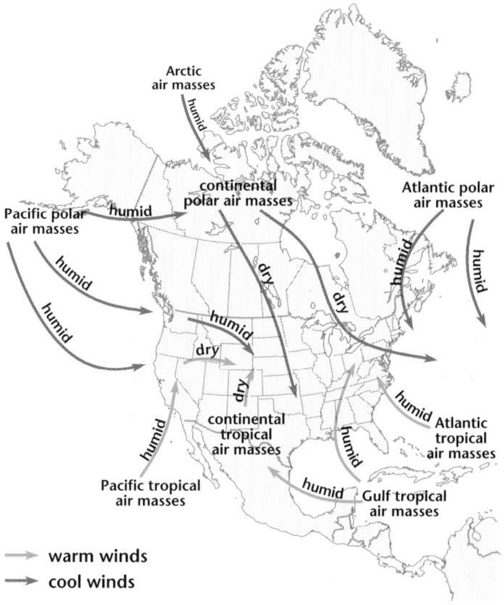

surrounding land. Even at the end of winter, when the lakes have cooled, the water is still much warmer than the land and the lakes do not freeze over. It is in late autumn and early winter, however, that the difference in temperature between the land and the surface water of the lakes is most marked, and that is when the heaviest snowstorms occur—notoriously, around Thanksgiving.

Cold, dry air crosses the continent from the west. When it crosses the lakes, contact with the relatively warm water raises the temperature of the lowest layer of air, and because the air is then warmer, large amounts of water evaporate into it. The warm air rises in discrete amounts, like huge bubbles, and mixes with the overlying colder air. This moistens the upper air and the moistened layer becomes progressively deeper as the air continues across the lakes. Some of the moisture soon condenses again to form steam fog on the water surface, and some condenses near the top of the mixed layer to form stratocumulus cloud. More than half of the moisture mixes into the air beyond the lakes.

Droplets in the stratocumulus cloud start to freeze, and snowflakes begin to develop. These drift with the cloud to the downwind shore. Beneath the cloud, the moist, warm air crosses the land beyond the lakes, but when it reaches the hills to the east of the lakes and is forced to rise, its moisture condenses, snowflakes form, and there is a snowstorm.

The average annual snowfall to the east of the Great Lakes is up to three times greater than that in the same latitude to the west. North Dakota usually expects about 40 inches (1 m) of snow during the winter. Parts of New England, the Adirondacks, and the eastern Appalachians, however receive 130 inches (3.3 m.) The heaviest snowfalls occur in areas known as "snowbelts," up to about 50 miles (80 km) to the east of the Great Lakes. Look for good snow in Wisconsin, Michigan, Pennsylvania, New York, and the Adirondack and Appalachian Mountains, but of course skiers need good mountainous terrain and not all of these states are ideal for skiing.

▼ ABUNDANT SNOW
Snowfall in the Rocky Mountains makes it an ideal location for ski resorts such as Telluride, situated in the San Juan Range, southwest Colorado.

AVERAGE TEMPERATURES °F (°C)

	N	D	J	F	M	A	M
New Mexico	45 (7)	36 (2)	34 (1)	39 (4)	46 (8)	55 (13)	64 (18)
Colorado	39 (4)	32 (0)	32 (0)	34 (1)	39 (4)	48 (9)	57 (14)
Utah	41 (5)	32 (0)	30 (-1)	34 (1)	41 (5)	50 (10)	59 (15)
California	45 (7)	37 3)	37 (3)	43 (6)	46 (8)	54 (12)	63 (17)
Montana	41 (5)	30 (-1)	27 (-3)	28 (-2)	36 (2)	46 (8)	57 (14)
Wyoming	46 (8)	39 (4)	36 (2)	37 (3)	45 (7)	54 (12)	63 (17)
Oregon	41 (5)	34 (1)	34 (1)	39 (4)	45 (7)	50 (10)	57 (14)
Idaho	50 (10)	39 (4)	37 (3)	43 (6)	54 (12)	63 (17)	72 (22)
Alberta	27 (-3)	16 (-9)	16 (-9)	23 (-5)	30 (-1)	37 (3)	46 (8)
British Columbia	30 (-1)	19 (-7)	18 (-8)	25 (-4)	32 (0)	41 (5)	50 10)
Maine	36 (2)	21 (-6)	16 (-9)	21 (-6)	32 (0)	48 (9)	61 (16)
Vermont	39 (4)	28 (-2)	23 (-5)	25 (-4)	34 (1)	43 (6)	54 (12)
Quebec	36 (2)	21 (-6)	16 (-9)	18 (-8)	30 (-1)	43 (6)	55 (13)
Western Region	43 (6)	54 (12)	34 (1)	37 (3)	45 (7)	52 (11)	61 (16)
Eastern Region	34 (1)	21 (-6)	18 (-8)	23 (-5)	32 (0)	43 (6)	54 (12)
Average	39 (4)	30 (-1)	27 (-3)	32 (0)	39 (4)	48 (9)	59 (15)

SNOW

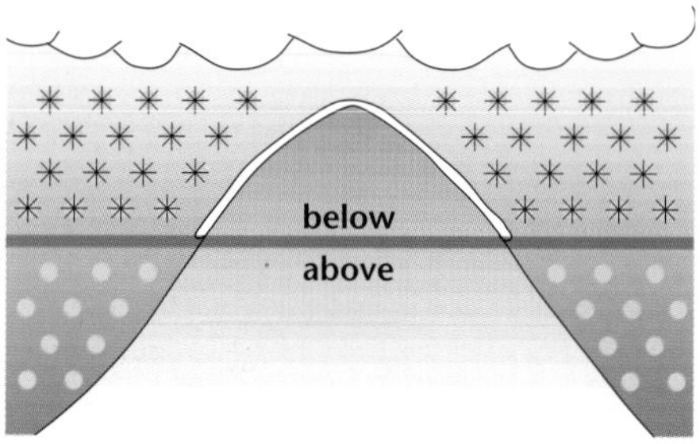

SNOW FALLS IN SOFT CRYSTALS OF INFINITE VARIETY, BUT AS THE PIONEERING AVALANCHE RESEARCHER MONTY ATWATER WRITES, "SNOW SEEMS AVERSE TO BEING STUDIED. WHEN IT IS POKED OR DISTURBED OR MANHANDLED IN ANY WAY, IT CHANGES, QUICKER THAN A CHAMELEON, FROM ONE KIND OF SNOW TO ANOTHER, LEAVING THE OBSERVER BAFFLED."

Snow falls in winter, but snowflakes form throughout the year. Most of the rain that falls in middle latitudes, even in summer, is melted snow.

HOW ICE CRYSTALS ARE FORMED

Air temperature decreases with height, and the amount of water vapor air can hold is proportional to the temperature—the warmer the air, the more moisture it can hold. As air rises its temperature falls and if it falls to below the "dewpoint" temperature some of the water vapor will condense into droplets and a cloud will form. If the temperature falls below freezing, the moisture will form ice crystals.

This sounds straightforward, but it is not quite so simple. Water vapor will not condense unless there are minute particles—cloud condensation nuclei—on which the droplets can form. These are usually abundant, but even so it is common for air to be slightly supersaturated. Ice crystals will not form unless there are freezing nuclei present, such as fine clay particles, onto which water can freeze. These are much less plentiful than condensation nuclei and most do not initiate freezing at temperatures above about 14°F (-10°C.) Consequently, clouds usually contain a mixture of ice crystals and supercooled water droplets—liquid droplets that are several degrees below freezing temperature. Once ice crystals begin to form, they do so at the expense of the supercooled droplets. Water evaporates from the droplets and is deposited on the ice crystals.

Where the cloud temperature is between about 14°F (-10°C) and -4°F (-20°C) there are approximately equal amounts of water droplets and ice crystals. Ice crystals predominate where the temperature is below -20°C (-4°F) and there is almost no ice in a cloud warmer than 14°F (-10°C.) If the temperature is 75°F (24°C) at the surface, it will be 14°F (-10°C) at about 20,000 feet (6 km.) That is about one-third of the way from the top of an average cumulonimbus cloud capable of delivering a heavy shower.

FROM ICE CRYSTALS TO SNOWFLAKES

Because the shape of its molecule determines the way it crystallizes, water invariably freezes into a hexagonal crystal. This grows larger as more water freezes onto it, but it preserves its hexagonal shape. Ice crystals vary in shape, but whatever their shape they always have six sides. Crystals are classified according to their shape. The International Commission on Snow and Ice has developed a classification system that recognizes seven crystal types—plates, stellars, needles, columns, capped columns, spatial dendrites, and irregulars, with a standard symbol to designate each of them, as well as three more symbols for graupel (soft hail), sleet (minute ice crystals, not the mixture of rain and snow that is called sleet in the United Kingdom), and hail.

Ice crystals initially take the form of flat hexagons, but the wind sweeps them thousands of feet up or down, and with each change of temperature the crystals change form and as they drift this way and that, they collide. When large ice crystals collide they often shatter. Such collisions release tiny splinters of ice that act as freezing nuclei for the formation of more crystals. When large crystals collide with smaller ones they tend to stick together. This is how ice crystals grow into snowflakes, and with so much evolution it is generally accepted that no two snowflakes are alike.

The process works best if the temperature is above about 23°F (-5°C), so there is a plentiful supply of supercooled water droplets. Water droplets also collide with the ice crystals, forming a thin layer of water that freezes when another ice crystal arrives, so the water acts as an adhesive. Really big snowflakes form at this temperature, from smaller snowflakes that join by interlocking and thereby preserving the six-sided symmetry. Colder clouds produce smaller snowflakes. Powder snow—the consistency that is best for skiing—forms in very cold cloud.

NO TWO SNOWFLAKES ARE ALIKE

"The nuclei around which water molecules freeze are exceedingly small: it takes as many as ten million of them to form a single raindrop, and perhaps a million frozen ice crystals to make one snowflake. The flakes they form are legion: a million billion may fall on a single acre of land during a ten-inch accumulation."

Wilson Alwyn Bentley, a Vermont farmer, published a photographic portfolio with 2,453 microphotographs of individual snowflakes, taken between 1884 and 1931. He also knew he had barely begun his list. Indeed, since a single cubic foot of snow may contain as many as ten million individual flakes, and since over time enough snow has fallen on the earth to cover it to a depth of 50 miles, the claim of the eternal snowflake idiosyncrasy seems mathematically unfathomable.

McKay Jenkins: *White Death*

THE SNOW PACK

If the snow falls through air that is warmer than freezing it will start to melt. If it falls for more than about 820 feet (250 m) through air warmer than about 35°F (2°C) the snow will melt and fall as rain. If it falls as snow it will

▲ SNOW SCULPTURE
"Colorado Pack" clinging to a fence line in the resort of Telluride. "Colorado Pack" is made up of freshly fallen powder snow with interlocking snowflakes, and has considerable cohesion.

not settle unless the ground temperature is below about 39°F (4°C.)

Once snow has fallen, it packs together under its own weight and becomes denser. The character of the pack depends on the amount of liquid water that is trapped between crystals. Wet snow contains 3–6 percent of water. This makes it dense and heavy. It is excellent for making snowballs, but not as good for skiing. Wet snow of this type falls on the windward side of coastal mountain ranges, for example in Alaska and on the western side of the Rocky Mountains, and also in the Alps. Some Californian snow is nicknamed "Sierra cement"!

Powder snow, which is much drier and therefore lighter, falls further inland, for example on the eastern side of the North American coastal ranges. This is the type of snow found in Alberta, Utah, Wyoming, and Colorado. "Colorado pack" is made from powder snow. Freshly fallen powder snow is very light and loosely textured, but the spikes on the snowflakes interlock, so the snow has considerable cohesion. Skiing across it has the effect of packing it very hard in some places, but throwing it into much softer heaps in others. In this condition it is sometimes called "crud."

During the day the snow surface may warm to above freezing. The snow will start to melt, so a thin layer of water covers the surface, but as the temperature falls again this water will freeze to form a crust of ice. Freezing rain—rain comprising supercooled raindrops that freeze on contact with a cold surface—falling on fallen snow will produce a similar crust. The crust may be so thin that it will not support the weight of a person or so thick that skiers pass over the top of it. Between these conditions the crust may be thick in some places but thin in others, making skiing difficult. This is also called "crud." Toward the end of a prolonged dry spell when the surface has been thawed and frozen several times, the old snow is called "sugar snow" because of its texture.

Physical changes can also take place near the base of a snowpack. Even when it is densely packed, a layer of snow contains tiny pockets of air between the individual crystals. At the base of the pack crystals may sublime—change directly into water vapor—into these air pockets. The water vapor is then immediately deposited once more as ice crystals. These crystals are called "hoar"—not to be confused with hoarfrost. They are dense, but they pack loosely and can flow like a liquid. The process of sublimation and deposition may then spread upward until a substantial part of the base of the pack has been transformed. The snow is now in a potentially dangerous condition because the pack is no longer securely bonded to the ground beneath it. It can move, triggering an avalanche.

SNOW ISN'T WHITE

"It should also be remembered snow isn't white. Snowstorms are made up of billions of tiny, clear prisms, each of which breaks up the light that strikes it into the entire color spectrum; snowflakes are, like the water that forms them, actually clear. Refracting all the light that passes through them, snowflakes flood the visual field not with one color but with all colors. The confused eye, unable to handle such a burst of sensory overload, turns the colors back into whiteness, often with serious side effects. Blinded by so much whiteness—a so-called whiteout—a skier or hiker can quickly become completely disoriented. Losing any sense of horizon, those caught in a whiteout can become overwhelmed by vertigo, a state in which the confusion between the eye and the inner ear becomes so acute that one's very sense of footing becomes unreliable."

McKay Jenkins: *White Death*

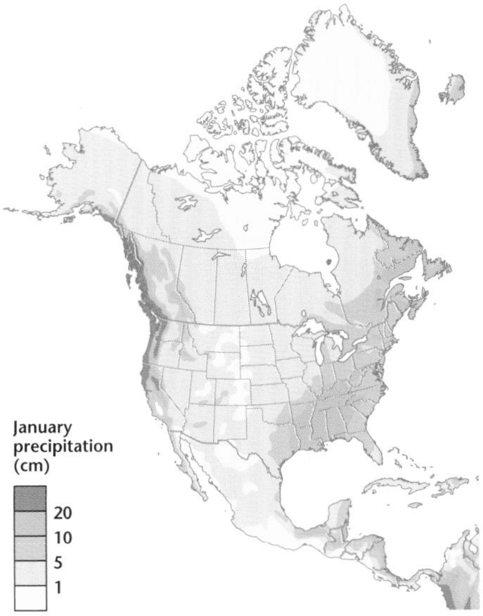

AVERAGE SNOWFALL

	inches	cm
California	432	1,097
Wyoming	402	1,021
Montana	400	1,016
Utah	384	975
British Columbia	356	904
Oregon	350	889
Idaho	346	878
New Mexico	312	792
Colorado	310	787
Vermont	264	670
Maine	216	663
Alberta	150	381
Quebec	150	381
Western North America*	344	874
Eastern North America*	210	533
Whole of North America*	313	795

*Average snowfall of 40 ski areas across 13 states and provinces.

AVALANCHES & MOUNTAIN SAFETY

NORTH AMERICAN SKI RESORTS ARE STRONG ON SAFETY. SINCE 1980 LESS THAN ONE PERCENT OF AVALANCHE FATALITIES HAVE OCCURRED WITHIN THE SKI AREA BOUNDARIES ON OPEN RUNS, BUT IN THE BACKCOUNTRY FATALITIES ARE RISING.

Many, it seems, are fascinated by avalanches, the majority of which are triggered by recreational, snowmobilers, skiers, and snowboarders—often experienced ones at that. And in the same way that a great white shark is best viewed onscreen or from a safe distance, so too is it safest to keep well away from the White Death, the jaws of which are just as cruel and may deliver fatal consequences if you venture unprepared to ski or ride off-piste in the backcountry.

Throughout this book we focus on the ski resort, providing information on skiing for beginners, intermediates, advanced and experts. As you climb the ladder of ability you are more likely to spend time off-piste, away from the crowds (and safety!) in search of that perfect powder day. You also start to play the law of averages and run the risk of being caught in a slide.

WHAT HAPPENS WHEN YOU GET CAUGHT IN AN AVALANCHE?

In November 1978, Bruce Tremper—then 24 years old and fresh out of college—was helping to build chairlifts at the Bridger Bowl Ski Area in Montana. Having learned about avalanches and skied the backcountry since he was 10 years old he naturally enough considered himself to be something of an expert, i.e. a typical avalanche victim. Over a foot (30 cm) of light snow had fallen the night before and the wind was blowing hard, loading up the steep slopes beneath the upper section of the chairlift with thick slabs of wind-drifted snow.

Hard slab avalanche in the Monashee Mountains, Canada.

Working alone (first mistake) and not wearing a beacon (second mistake), he found himself part of the way down the slope without backcountry skis or skins (third mistake) and faced with an exhausting pig wallow to climb back up, through chest-deep snow. Aware of the risky conditions he noticed that only a 15-foot (4.5 m) wide couloir separated him from the safe slopes on the other side. Thinking that a good skier like him should be able to get up enough speed and zip across it before anything too bad happened (fourth mistake), he attempted to ski to safety.

". . . I did my ski cut according to the book. I built up speed and crossed the slope at about a 45-degree angle so that, in theory, my momentum would carry me off the moving slab, in case it did break on me. Since I had never been caught in an avalanche before, I had no idea how quickly the slab—after it shatters like a pane of glass—can pick up speed. I heard a deep, muffled thunk as it fractured. Then it was like someone pulled the rug out from under me . . . the blocks of shattered slab were moving around me like a herd of tumbling cardboard boxes blowing in the wind. Nothing seemed to work. Even though only two or three seconds had elapsed, the avalanche, with me as its unintended passenger, was already moving at a good 20 miles per hour (32 km/h) . . . ."

Looking downhill he saw a line of small trees coming toward him, and when the avalanche slammed him into the smallest one he held on with all his strength.

" . . . The snow pounded me like I was standing under a huge waterfall, and it felt like my neck would snap as each block of wind slab smashed into my head. The tree snapped off, and I rocketed down the slope again. Then the tumbling started, over and over again like being in a giant washing machine filled with snow. Hat and mittens, instantly gone. Snow went everywhere, down my neck, up my sleeves, down my underwear, even under my eyelids, something I would never have imagined. With every breath, I sucked in a mixture of snow and air that formed a plug in

PARTS OF AN AVALANCHE SLIDE PATH

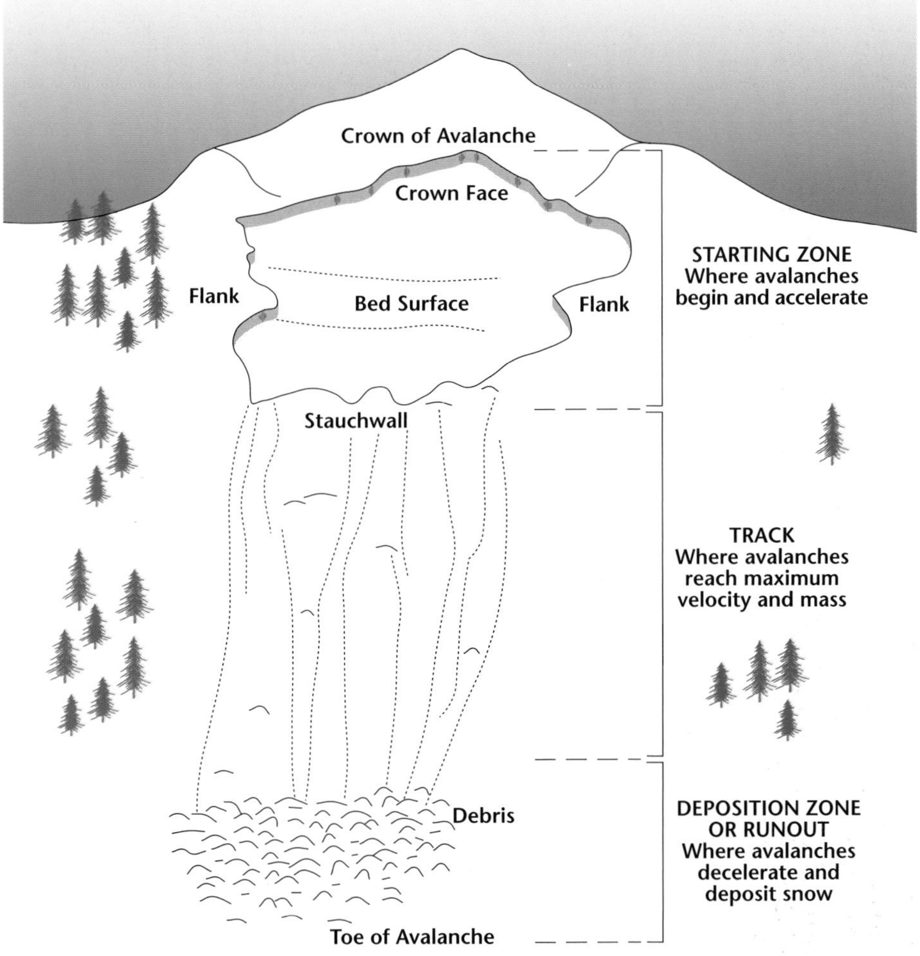

WHAT TO EXPECT IF CAUGHT

FRACTURE
You may hear a muffled WHOOMPH sound; sometimes a loud CRACK. You notice cracks around you.

1 TO 2 SECONDS
The slab starts to move. It feels as if someone pulled the rug from out under you. Most people invariably fall down. The slab shatters into blocks. The slab quickly picks up speed and after two seconds is moving at about 10 mph (16 km/h). In other words, in order to escape off the slab you need to take action now. After this it will be too late. If you haven't preplanned your escape route, you probably won't be able to make it.

2 TO 5 SECONDS
After five seconds, the avalanche is moving at 10–30 mph (16–48 km/h). The blocks are now tumbling furiously. Skiing, snowboarding, and snowmobiling become impossible. Ski bindings release. This is your last opportunity to grab a tree but you're definitely moving fast enough to cause injury or death.

5 TO 10 SECONDS
The avalanche is traveling 40–80 mph (64–128km/h). You are being tumbled hard and do not know which way is up. With every breath, you suck in a snow-air mixture that forms a plug of ice in your throat. Breathing is difficult. Hats, mittens, and goggles are gone. Impacts with trees or rocks cause injury or death. You must swim hard to stay on the surface.

10 TO 15 SECONDS
The avalanche slows down. Continue swimming hard. This is your last chance to form an air pocket in front of your face.

AVALANCHE STOPS
Debris instantly sets up like concrete. You are frozen in place and cannot move. Completely buried victims cannot dig themselves out or form an air pocket.

4 MINUTES
As you rebreathe the carbon dioxide that builds up in the snow around your mouth, you begin to lose consciousness.

15 MINUTES
Most buried victims will still be alive but unconscious, and some may have already suffered brain damage.

25 MINUTES
50 percent of completely buried victims will be dead.

35 MINUTES
73 percent of completely buried victims will be dead. Anyone who survives after this time must have an air pocket.

90 MINUTES
81 percent of victims are dead.

130 MINUTES
97 percent of victims are dead. Anyone who survives after this time must have an air channel to the surface.

► **A hard slab avalanche in Bennet's Bowl, Loveland Ski Area, Colorado.**

my mouth and down into my throat. I coughed it out but the next breath rammed it full of snow again. Just when I needed to breathe the most I couldn't—I was drowning to death high in the mountains, in the middle of winter, and miles from the nearest water."

Most skiers have heard that when caught in an avalanche you should attempt to swim, but how good a swimmer are you? How well can you swim wearing ski boots and skis? As the avalanche slowed from about 60 mph (90 km/h) to around 40 mph (64 km/h), Bruce Tremper found himself on the surface and able to breathe once again—but he soon discovered that his body tended to sink like a rock unless he swam hard.

". . . So I swam. But something was pulling one of my legs down. This was in the days before ski brakes and I had safety straps attaching my skis to my boots. I could swim but my skis couldn't. One safety strap had torn free but the other one remained attached, and it felt like a boat anchor tied to my leg. The ski was beneath me in the slower-moving debris, and as the surface debris moved faster it tipped me forward, shoving my face in the snow again and again. I struggled hard to pull that ski up through the debris with my furious swimming. Eventually, the swimming worked, and when the avalanche finally came to a stop I found myself upright and buried only chest deep, breathing hard, very wet and very cold."

With the avalanche debris set like concrete around him as soon as it came to a halt, Bruce Tremper was trapped in a body cast from the chest down. Fortunately he had a shovel but it still took him 10 minutes to chip away at the rock-hard snow before he could finally free his legs. On one foot the heel section of the binding hung from a 6-inch (15-cm) section of the top layer of the ski, but the rest of the ski was missing and although the other ski was still attached, the tip and the tail were broken. Clearly luck played a big part in allowing him to survive but it is also clear that someone with less experience might not have been able to swim that last section to avoid becoming completely buried. Ask yourself the question, how would you have coped in these extreme circumstances?

WHAT HAPPENS WHEN YOU GET BURIED IN AN AVALANCHE?

If they do not die as a result of trauma by hitting trees and rocks on the way down—around a quarter of avalanche victims die from trauma impact injuries—completely buried victims begin a desperate race against time, and the statistics show that only 28 percent survive.

You may have heard that you should spit and see which way the saliva runs across your face to try and figure out which way is up, then dig in that direction, but it doesn't matter which way is up because typically you are entombed, as if frozen in concrete and unable even to move your fingers, so it is highly unlikely that you can dig yourself out. In the vast majority of cases there are only two ways to get out of the snow—to be dug out (are you wearing a beacon?) or to melt out.

It was once believed that you had just a 50 percent chance of being dug out alive if found and rescued within 30 minutes, but as rescue times have become shorter and shorter it seems you need to be dug out much faster than that to have a good chance of survival. Statistics now show that 92 percent of completely buried victims can be revived if recovered, within the first 15 minutes, but only 27 percent are alive after 35 minutes. Most contemporary research shows that around half of the victims are dead within the first 25 minutes. Bear in mind also that brain damage starts well before death—perhaps at 10 minutes for the average victim—and there are plenty who emerge unconscious and blue-faced when dug out after only five minutes.

The fact is that if you are completely buried the odds of survival are slim, unless your partners escape or survive the slide, *and* you are wearing a beacon *and* your partners have been regularly practicing with theirs (and their shovels and probes), you are not far beneath the surface, *and* last but not least, you have luck on your side. Statistics show that only around one in ten victims is rescued alive by their partners from a complete burial.

THE NUMBER OF FATALITIES IS STEADILY RISING

Since 1980, less than one percent of avalanche fatalities in North America have occurred within the ski area boundaries on open runs. The vast majority of incidents occur in the backcountry where no avalanche control is done, save to protect adjacent highways.

However, the number of avalanche fatalities in North America has risen steadily since the 1950's with the 5-year average moving up from close to zero in the early 1950's to around 26 deaths per annum in the U.S. and around 15 deaths in Canada by 1995–2000; and it's still rising. In the 2002–2003 season there were 54 recorded incidents in North America involving 151 people (73 were snowmobilers), 82 of whom were completely buried, 58 killed and 14 injured. Not a big number when compared to the total numbers of people participating in winter sports, but for those caught and

THE RELATIONSHIP BETWEEN STEEPNESS AND AVALANCHE RISK

STEEPNESS		SKI AREA RATING	AVALANCHE ACTIVITY	PERCEIVED DANGER
10–25°	●	Beginner to intermediate. Green trails.	Slush flows in arctic climates. Infrequent wet avalanche runouts. Dry slabs in extremely unusual situations.	What is this, a golf course?
25–30°	■	Intermediate slopes. Blue trails.	Infrequent slabs in unstable conditions. Those that do occur tend to be large.	Okay, but not steep enough to have fun.
30–35°	◆	Advanced slopes. Black diamond trails.	Slabs increasing rapidly in frequency as you approach 35 degrees. Usually requires fairly unstable conditions.	Starting to get steep enough to have fun.
35–45°	◆◆	Expert slopes. Double black diamond trails.	This is prime avalanche terrain with the bull's eye at around 38 degrees. Frequent slab avalanches, some large.	Perfect! But this is where most avalanches happen.
45–55°		Extreme terrain. Couloirs in cliffs. Usually roped off.	Frequent smaller slabs and sluffs reduce the number of larger slabs.	Whoa, this is getting steep. I'm scared.
55–90°		Alpine climbing terrain. Cliffs and very steep couloirs.	Frequent smaller slabs and sluffs dramatically reduce the number of larger slabs.	Wow it's a cliff! Give me a rope!

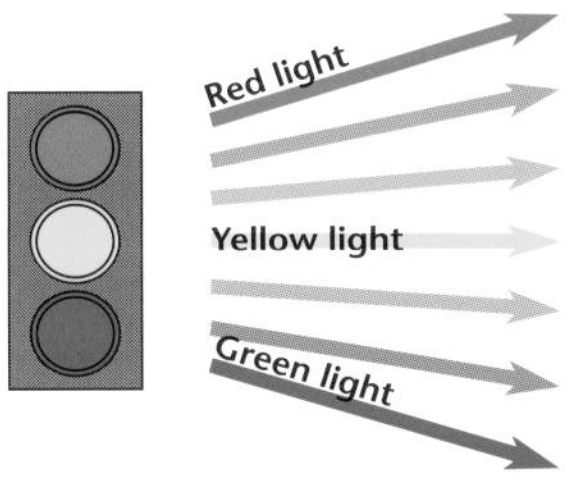

MORE DANGEROUS TERRAIN
- Steep 30° to 50°, especially 35° to 45°
- Leeward or cross-loaded
- Few anchors
- Bad consequences

SAFER TERRAIN
- Gentle 0° to 25° or very steep 55° to 90°
- Windward
- Thick anchors
- No bad consequences

NORTH AMERICAN AVALANCHE FATALITIES

	1997	1998	1999	2000	2001	2002	2003	TOTAL
Colorado	1	6	6	8	4	8	6	39
Alaska	4	3	12	5	4	11	4	43
Utah	6	2	5	2	6	3	1	25
Montana	1	7	2	2	7	10	4	33
California	-	1	1	-	2	1	1	6
Washington	5	2	4	1	3	-	1	16
Wyoming	2	1	2	-	7	1	7	20
Idaho	3	3	-	2	-	1	3	12
Oregon	-	1	-	-	-	-	-	1
Nevada	-	-	-	-	-	-	1	1
New Hampshire	-	-	-	1	-	-	2	3
New York	-	-	-	1	-	-	-	1
U.S.	22	26	32	22	33	35	30	200
Alberta	1	5	1	2	1	4	3	17
British Columbia	13	9	6	5	11	9	25	78
Quebec	-	1	9	3	-	-	-	13
CANADA	14	15	16	10	12	13	28	108
TOTAL	36	41	48	32	45	48	58	308

Hard slab avalanche debris in the Monashee Mountains, Canada.

AVALANCHE DANGER DESCRIPTORS

DANGER LEVEL (AND COLOR)	AVALANCHE PROBABILITY AND TRIGGER	DEGREE AND DISTRIBUTION OF DANGER	RECOMMENDED ACTION IN THE BACKCOUNTRY
LOW (GREEN)	Natural avalanches very unlikely. Human-triggered avalanches unlikely.	Generally stable snow. Isolated areas of instability.	Travel is generally safe. Normal caution is advised.
MODERATE (YELLOW)	Natural avalanches unlikely. Human-triggered avalanches possible.	Unstable slabs possible on steep terrain.	Use caution in steeper terrain on certain aspects.
CONSIDERABLE (ORANGE)	Natural avalanches possible. Human-triggered avalanches probable.	Unstable slabs probable on steep terrain.	Be increasingly cautious in steeper terrain.
HIGH (RED)	Natural and human-triggered avalanches likely.	Unstable slabs likely on a variety of aspects and slope angles.	Travel in avalanche terrain is not recommended. Safest travel on windward ridges of lower-angled slopes without steeper terrain above.
EXTREME* (BLACK)	Widespread natural or human-triggered avalanches certain.	Extremely unstable slabs certain on most aspects and slope angles. Large, destructive avalanches possible.	Travel in avalanche terrain should be avoided, and travel confined to low-angled terrain well away from avalanche path runouts.

*Please note that in Canada the Extreme Danger Level is shown as red with a black border.

completely buried the picture is bleak.

The increase is largely attributable to a significant rise in the numbers of people heading off into the backcountry, assisted by improvements in equipment which make it easier for skiers, boarders, and snowmobilers to venture into avalanche terrain. What is also interesting is that although most victims are experienced and skilled, their avalanche skills invariably lag far behind their sports skills.

Eighty percent of all incidents in the U.S. happen in just five states Alaska, Colorado, Montana, Utah and Wyoming and in 90 percent of cases the avalanche is triggered by the victim or by someone in the victim's party, but the biggest increase is over the boarder in British Columbia.

According to Bruce Tremper: "Almost all avalanche fatalities in North America involve recreationists, most notably snowmobilers, climbers, backcountry skiers, and boarders, in that order. Almost all are very skilled in their sport, male, fit, educated, intelligent, middle class, and between the ages of 18 and 40." Does this sound like you?

Most times when people venture into the backcountry nothing happens, again and again, except they gain in confidence and look forward to the next time. And since snow is stable about 95 percent of the time you get the 95 percent-success rate even if you know zero about avalanches. And in most cases, the average person has no idea they've even had a close call.

WET AVALANCHES

Most avalanche professionals make a hard separation between wet snow avalanches and dry snow avalanches, because they are so different. Much of their mechanics are different, they move differently, and it's only natural for us to think of them as two altogether separate beasts. But really there's a continuum between wet and dry avalanches.

Like dry snow avalanches, wet avalanches can occur as both sluffs and slabs. Wet avalanches usually occur when warm air temperatures, sun or rain cause water to percolate through the snowpack and decrease the strength of the snow, or in some cases, change the mechanical properties of the snow. Once initiated, wet snow tends to travel more slowly than dry snow—like a thousand concrete-carrying trucks dumping their loads at once, rather than the hovercraft-like movement of a dry avalanche.

A typical wet avalanche travels at 10 to 20 mph (15 to 30 km/h), but on steeper terrain they can go nearly as fast as a dry avalanche. Probably because not as many recreationists are out on wet snowy days, wet avalanches don't account for nearly as many avalanche fatalities as dry snow avalanches. However, they still account for a sizeable percentage of avalanche fatalities in maritime climates (mountains bordering oceans), especially to climbers.

DRY AVALANCHES

These are the stunningly beautiful ones that roar down the mountain, light and fluffy, like clouds of powder, but beneath the misty powder cloud is a rushing mass of snow—the "core" of the avalanche—that is a fluidized mix of air (70 percent) and ice particles (30 percent). As the snow rushes through the air it kicks up an envelope of powder, appropriately enough called a "powder cloud," which comprises only about one percent snow and 99 percent air, and this is the part of the avalanche that gives it its beauty.

In front of the powder cloud is the invisible "air blast" that pushes out in front of the moving snow. The air blast carries only about one tenth of the impact of the core, but it can travel fast enough to explode your lungs if are caught by the full impact of the blast.

The avalanche is slowed down mainly by friction with the rocks, vegetation, and the snow surface it runs on. The snow nearest the bed travels more slowly than the snow above. Often, if you look close enough, you can see avalanches come down in waves. One wave shoots out, is slowed by friction with the ground and air, and then the next wave—traveling on the back of the first wave—shoots out ahead of the first wave, and so on. It looks like pulses of snow being spat out the front of the avalanche about once every few seconds.

The extreme violence inside the flowing debris grinds up all the snow into finer and finer particles, and even if the snow started out light and fluffy, it can become very dense by the time it finally comes to a stop. A large avalanche that starts out with a density of 5 to 10 percent (volume of snow versus air) can often end up as 30 to 40 percent at the bottom. This means that when everything comes to a stop, the dense snow packs very tightly.

Also, small grains sinter (coalesce) much more quickly than large grains, and the tiny grains making up avalanche debris can sinter as much as ten thousand times faster than the larger grains of the initial slab.

Finally, all of the kinetic energy liberated on the way down heats up the snow a little and creates small drops of liquid water on the surface of the ice grains. Combining all these factors, it's easy to see why avalanche debris seizes up like concrete the instant it comes to a stop. The avalanche victim is frozen in place.

LOOSE SNOW AVALANCHES

Loose snow sliding down a mountain is called a loose snow avalanche. Small loose snow avalanches are called "sluffs." Few people are killed by loose snow avalanches because they tend to be smaller, and they tend to fracture beneath you as you cross a slope, rather than above you, as slab avalanches often do. Most of the people killed in loose snow avalanches are climbers, or extreme skiers and boarders in very steep terrain.

SLAB AVALANCHES

If you're looking for the killer, then this is your man. This is the White Death, the Snowy Torrent, the Big Guy in the White Suit. Dry slab avalanches account for nearly all of the avalanche deaths in North America.

A "slab" is a cohesive plate of snow that slides as a unit on the snow underneath. A slab doesn't have to be hard, it just has to be relatively stronger than the snow underneath.

A typical slab is about half the size of a football field, about one to two feet (30–60 cm) deep, and usually reaches speeds of 20 mph (32 km/h) within the first three seconds, quickly accelerating to around 80 mph (128 km/h) after the first, say, six seconds. The bonds holding a slab in place fracture at about 220 mph (352 km/h) and the slab appears to shatter.

Dry slab avalanches can lie teetering on the verge of catastrophe, sometimes for days or even months. The weak layers beneath the slabs are extremely sensitive and the rapid addition of the weight of just one person can easily initiate a fracture on a slope that would not have avalanched otherwise. A slope can sometimes be a giant booby trap—seemingly waiting for just the right person to come along. The crack often forms well above the victim, leaving little room for escape.

CORNICE FALL AVALANCHES

Cornices are the fatal attraction of the mountains, their beauty matched only by their danger. Cornices are elegant, cantilevered snow structures formed by wind drifting snow on to the lee (downwind) side of an obstacle, such as a ridgeline. Similar to icefall avalanches, the weight of a falling cornice often triggers an avalanche on the slope below, or the cornice breaks into hundreds of pieces and forms its own avalanche—or both. Again like ice avalanches, statistically cornice fall avalanches don't kill very many people. And similar to slab avalanches, the skiers who get into trouble almost always trigger the avalanche, in this case by traveling too close to the edge of the cornice. Cornices have a nasty habit of breaking farther back than you expect. Never walk up to the edge of a drop-off without wearing a rope or first checking out the drop-off from a safe place.

ICE AVALANCHES

When glaciers flow over a cliff they form the ice equivalent of a waterfall—an icefall. Falling blocks of ice can trigger an avalanche of ice, which often entrains snow below it, or triggers slabs. Especially in big mountains, ice avalanches can be large and travel long distances. Despite this, ice avalanches kill few people compared to dry slabs that people trigger themselves. Most of the deaths from ice avalanches occur to climbers in big mountains who happen to be in the wrong place at the wrong time.

SAFETY EQUIPMENT

- Buy a beacon, collapsible probe, and a shovel—and practise with them.
- Carry a compass and inclinometer.
- Take an avalanche awareness class, or better still a multi-day class.

SAFETY TRAVEL

- Ski in groups.
- Appoint a group leader (and an alternative) to be responsible for making decisions in an emergency.
- Go one at a time and always think about who will do the rescue if something goes wrong.
- Be wary of cornices. Never walk up to the edge of a drop-off.
- Travel gently. Wider skis are better than narrow skis, and a snowboard is better yet.
- Remember that the avalanche doesn't know (or care) you're an expert.

USEFUL WEBSITES

Avalanche.org	www.avalanche.org
American Avalanche Association	www.americanavalancheassociation.org
Canadian Avalanche Association	www.avalanche.ca
National Ski Patrol	www.nsp.org
Avalanche Information in Europe	www.lawine.org

STAYING ALIVE IN AVALANCHE TERRAIN

Bruce Tremper, Director of the Utah Avalanche Center, is one of the world's leading avalanche professionals, and the author of *Staying Alive in Avalanche Terrain*, first published by Seattle-based The Mountaineers Books in 2001 and reprinted in 2002.

Some 284 pages long and packed with informative photographs, diagrams, and statistics, it covers most of what you will ever need to know about avalanches, how they work, terrain, weather, the snowpack, stability, hazard evaluation, advice on route finding, safe travel and rescue, and about the all-important human factor that contributes to the making of mistakes.

We are grateful to Bruce Tremper and The Mountaineers Books Company for allowing us to extract passages from *Staying Alive in Avalanche Terrain.* At US$17.95 we consider it essential reading for any skier pushing the limits inbounds or skiing off-piste in the backcountry.

ISBN: 0-89886-834-3
The Mountaineers Books
1001 SW Klickitat Way, Suite 201
Seattle, WA. 98134
mbooks@mountaineersbooks.org
www.mountaineersbooks.org

CANADA
UNITED STATES
MEXICO
PACIFIC OCEAN
GULF OF MEXICO
Vancouver Island
Seattle
Olympia
Mt. Rainier 14,410 ft (4,392 m)
Portland
Salem
Columbia
CASCADE RANGE
Coastal Ranges
Great Sandy Desert
Columbia Plateau
Bitteroot Range
ROCKY MOUNTAINS
Missouri
Helena
Madison Range
Yellowstone
Sawtooth Range
Boise
Snake
Teton Range
Bismarck
GREAT PLAINS
Black Hills
Pierre
Sacramento
SIERRA NEVADA
Great Basin
Reno
Carson City
Sacramento
San Francisco
Great Salt Lake
Salt Lake City
Wasatch Range
Front Range
Platte
Cheyenne
Denver
Mt. Elbert 14,420 ft (4,395 m)
Mt. Whitney 14,495 ft (4,418 m)
Colorado
San Juan Mts
Sangre de Christo Mts.
Las Vegas
Grand Canyon
Mojave Desert
Colorado Plateau
Santa Fe
Los Angeles
San Bernardino Mts.
San Diego
Gila
Phoenix
Sonoran Desert
Llano Estacado
El Paso
Pecos
Minneapolis
St. Paul
Mississippi
Lake Superior
Upper Peninsula
Lake Michigan
Lake Huron
Lower Peninsula
Lake Erie
Milwaukee
Madison
Lansing
Detroit
Cleveland
Chicago
Pittsburgh
Des Moines
Omaha
Lincoln
CENTRAL LOWLANDS
Indianapolis
Columbus
Springfield
Cincinnati
Louisville
Frankfort
St. Louis
Kansas City
Topeka
Jefferson City
Ohio
Cumberland
Ozark Plateau
Nashville
Oklahoma City
Arkansas
Memphis
Tennessee
Little Rock
Birmingham
Atlanta
Alabama
Red
Dallas
Montgomery
Jackson
COASTAL PLAIN
Colorado
Brazos
Baton Rouge
New Orleans
Edwards Plateau
Austin
Houston
San Antonio
Rio Grande
Tallahassee

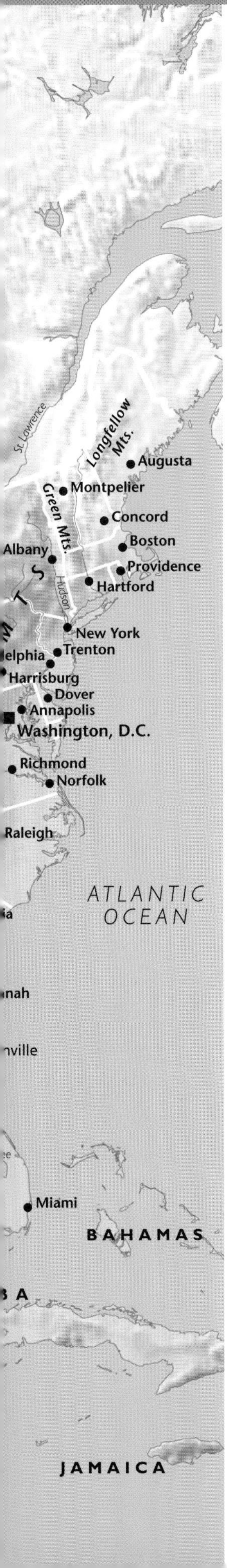

UNITED STATES

LIKE THE NORTH AMERICAN CONTINENT ITSELF, SKIING IN THE U.S. IS BIG! THERE ARE AN ESTIMATED 600 OR MORE SKI AREAS RANGING FROM THE VERY SMALL LOCAL SKI HILL—JUST A FEW ACRES AND A TOW ROPE—TO THE BIGGEST U.S. RESORTS OF VAIL (5,289 ACRES/2,140 HA), ASPEN SNOWMASS (4,805 ACRES/1,945 HA), HEAVENLY (4,800 ACRES/1,920 HA) AND SQUAW VALLEY (4,000 ACRES/ 1,619 HA).

Our selection focuses not just on the biggest, but on the best. There is big vertical in the U.S., with three resorts—Aspen Snowmass, Big Sky and Jackson Hole—offering over 4,000 vertical feet (1,219 m) of challenging skiing. To European diehards this may not quite measure up to the Alps but North America includes some amazing opportunities for top-level skiers.

Almost half of the U.S. resorts featured here have between 40 percent and 70 percent of trails designated for advanced and expert skiers, reflecting the general policy of making everything within the resort boundaries "skiable" and largely dispensing with the need for guides and additional safety precautions, unlike the European situation where "off-piste"— even the area between the marked trails—is unpatrolled and skied at your own risk.

Much of the skiing is at high altitude. Around a dozen resorts, mostly in Colorado, have a base area above 8,000 feet (2,438 m) and a ski area rising to around 12,000 feet (3,658 m). That's high enough to leave flatlanders short of breath even before they exert themselves, so you should consider your fitness level, allow time to acclimatize and make sure you drink plenty of fluids (no, not beer) when visiting these resorts. Remember too that temperature decreases with altitude: be ready for bitter temperatures up top, particularly with wind chill thrown in.

Snow is seldom a problem: the majority of our featured resorts average more than 25 feet (8 m) of snowfall per season. Alta and Snowbird in Utah, and Kirkwood, California, share top place with around 500 inches (1,270 cm). Colorado boasts the driest, lightest powder and Grand Targhee reminds you that their snow is "...from heaven, not from hoses".

By contrast, many resorts, particularly those on the east coast, get the season started with artificial snowmaking and continue to supplement natural snowfall through the season. Other than during exceptionally mild periods this ensures good snow cover though it's not without drawbacks: man made snow is between two and five times wetter than natural snow, making it more icy and less fun to ski on, while the 150,000 gallons (567,750 liters) of fresh water needed to cover an acre to a depth of one foot (30 cm) makes snow production potentially damaging environmentally.

It's also worth remembering that all the snow-making facilities in the world are worth nothing without big water reserves, as many east coast resorts found during the 2001/02 season, when it was cold enough to make snow day and night, but drought conditions brought things to a grinding halt.

Investment in the latest high-speed lift systems has further reduced lift lines. One of the great attractions of skiing in the U.S. is the relative scarcity of other skiers, along with lift systems organized to keep lines to a minimum. Even during holiday periods and in resorts close to big cities, anyone with European lift-line experience will find the U.S. a walk in the park. Good grooming, high levels of friendly service and exceptional standards of ski tuition (with daycare for young children) are other areas where U.S. resorts stand out.

A couple of aspects about skiing in the U.S. can take international visitors by surprise: many of America's resorts lack real communities at the base of the mountain, meaning ambience (and sometime even accommodation) is lacking; you may have to shuttle from a nearby town each day to ski. But many of the individual ski areas are also relatively small, so unless choosing one of the bigger U.S. resorts, the ideal solution is to select a number of resorts to visit, moving on by car at the end of the ski day to maximize variety on and off slope. It's the perfect way to get a taste of the continent's magnificent mountain diversity too and a chance to see some of the U.S.'s famous national parks en route to your next destination, if you can tear yourself away from the skiing.

Also noteworthy are American liquor laws that require you to be over 21 to consume alcohol legally; sometimes children under 21 aren't permitted to accompany their parents in bars, creating a more restrictive après-ski scene for families than in Europe.

SET IN CENTRAL OREGON, MOUNT BACHELOR IS OREGON'S PREMIER SKI RESORT. SKIERS AND SNOWBOARDERS TRAVEL HERE FOR THE QUALITY SNOW CONDITIONS OF THE CASCADE MOUNTAINS AND CROSS-COUNTRY SKIERS AND SNOWSHOEING FANS VACATION IN THE CASCADES FOR THE NUMEROUS TRAILS AND SPECTACULAR MOUNTAIN VIEWS.

MOUNT BACHELOR

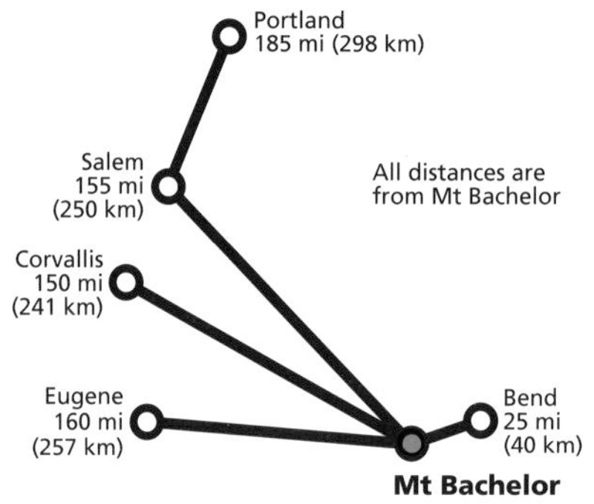

With 350 inches (889 cm) annual snowfall, 71 marked trails, countless unmarked chutes, glades, and tree trails, along with some of the world's fastest lifts, Mount Bachelor is the finest ski area in Oregon. All levels of skiers will enjoy the diversity and beauty this mountain has to offer. Nordic skiers have 35 miles (56 km) of groomed trails to explore, not to mention thousands of acres of open wilderness. The ski season at Mount Bachelor runs from mid-November to Memorial Day Weekend in May.

Generally considered inexpensive by U.S. standards, Mount Bachelor is a daytime ski area. In nearby Bend, Redmond, Sisters, and Sunriver there are fine hotels, lodgings, cabin rentals, and bed and breakfast establishments. The drive to the mountain, while straight and only 20 minutes, is the sacrifice you make for affordable lodgings and great skiing.

GETTING THERE

Mount Bachelor is situated 25 miles (40 km) southwest of Bend. The closest airport is Redmond, approximately 20 miles (32 km) from Bend. Direct flights from San Francisco, Seattle, and Portland to Redmond are available. The nearest regional hub is Portland International Airport. A shuttle service from

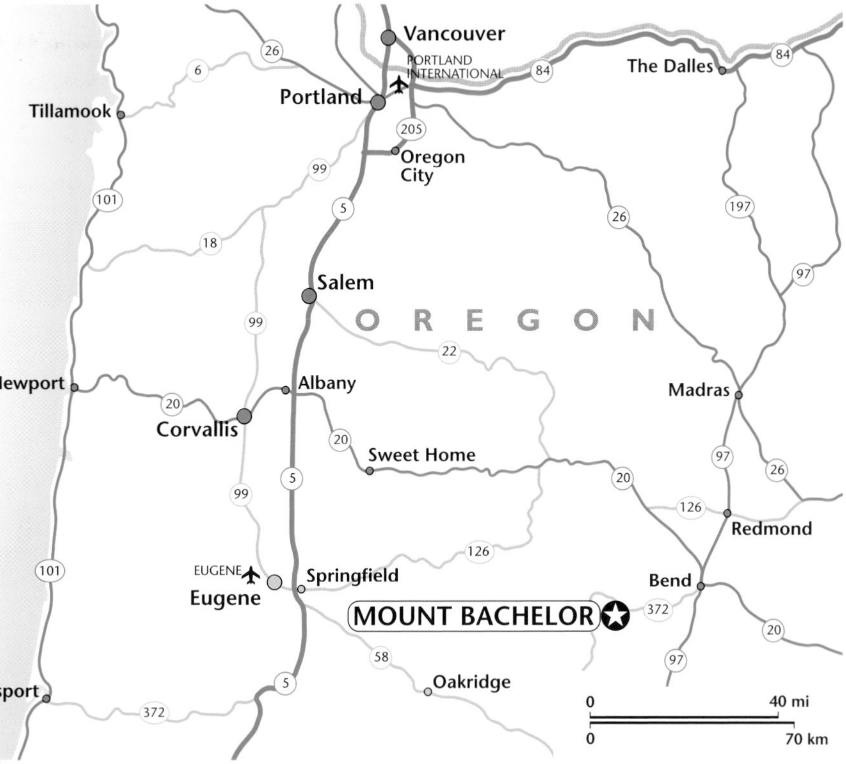

Portland to Bend is also available. If driving, Portland is around three hours away, and both Salem and Eugene are approximately two hours away. From Thanksgiving through spring, the Mount Bachelor Super Shuttle takes you from Bend to the mountain, and departs from the Bend Park-N-Ride on the corner of Simpson and Colorado Streets (US$3 each way). The service starts on November 23 and runs weekends only until December 21, then daily from December 21 through April 20. The free Interlodge Shuttle runs weekends and holidays between the Sunrise and West Village Lodges.

THE VILLAGE

The nearest town to the mountain is Bend, which has recently undergone significant remodeling. There are plenty of accommodations in Bend, Sunrise, Sisters, and Redmond, and a shuttle service is on hand to take you to and from the mountain for the day's skiing.

ACCOMMODATIONS

Mount Bachelor does not have any on-mountain accommodations, but condos, resorts and hotels are all within 20–45 minutes' drive. The best places to stay are Bend, Redmond, Sunriver or Sisters. For information contact the Central Oregon Visitors' Association on 800-800-8334 or visit the website www.visitcentraloregon.com.

Two of the best hotel resorts are Mount Bachelor Village Resort and the Inn of the Seventh Mountain. Mount Bachelor Village Resort (800-452-9846) has good executive hotel rooms, river ridge condos (US$115–380), and ski house condos (US$130–195). You can even take a virtual tour of them online at www.mtbachelor.com. Inn of the Seventh Mountain (800-452-6810, www.seventhmountain.com) is near Bend, encircled by peaks, lakes, and meadows.

◄ **PINE MARTEN LODGE**
One of three lodges on the mountain, it's impossible not to love the views, surroundings, and good food at Pine Marten.

MOUNTAIN FACTS

Base	6,300 feet (1,920 m)
Summit	9,065 feet (2,763 m)
Elevation	2,765 feet (843 m)
Easy	15%
Intermediate	25%
Advanced/Expert	60%
Number of trails	71
Longest trail	1.5 miles (2.4 km)
Ski area	3,683 acres (1,490 ha)
Cross-country	35 miles (56 km)

SNOWFALL

Annual snowfall	350 inches (889 cm)
Snowmaking	Pine Marten quad area

SKI LIFTS

High-Speed Quads	7
Triple Chairs	3
Surface Lifts	2
Total	12
Riders per hour	20,100

SKI SEASON
Mid-November to late May

▼ **WEIGHTY WINTER**
You can find this scene even in May as Mount Bachelor has one of the longest seasons.

DAYCARE

Mount Bachelor Daycare Centers cater for children aged six weeks to 10 years at West Village and Sunrise Lodges, open weekdays 8:30 AM–4:00 PM, or from 7:30 AM at weekends. Lunch is offered for US$5, but children can bring their own and parents can join them from noon–1:00 PM. Reservations required.
Call 800-829-2442 or 541-382-1709.

ACCOMMODATIONS

MOUNT BACHELOR VILLAGE RESORT
INN OF THE SEVENTH MOUNTAIN

For more information contact the Central Oregon Visitors' Association.
Tel: 800-800-8334
www.visitcentraloregon.com.

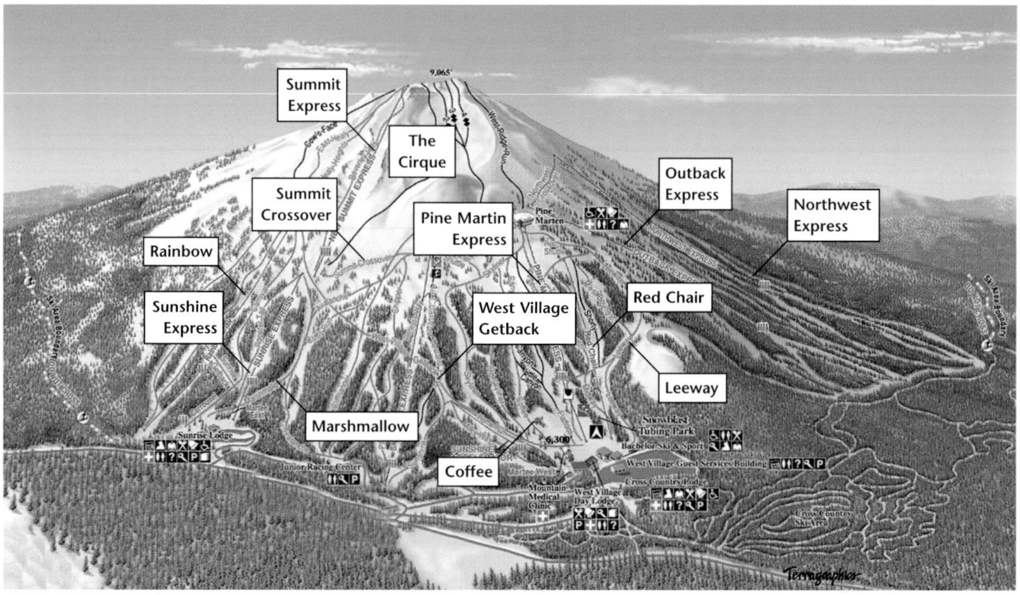

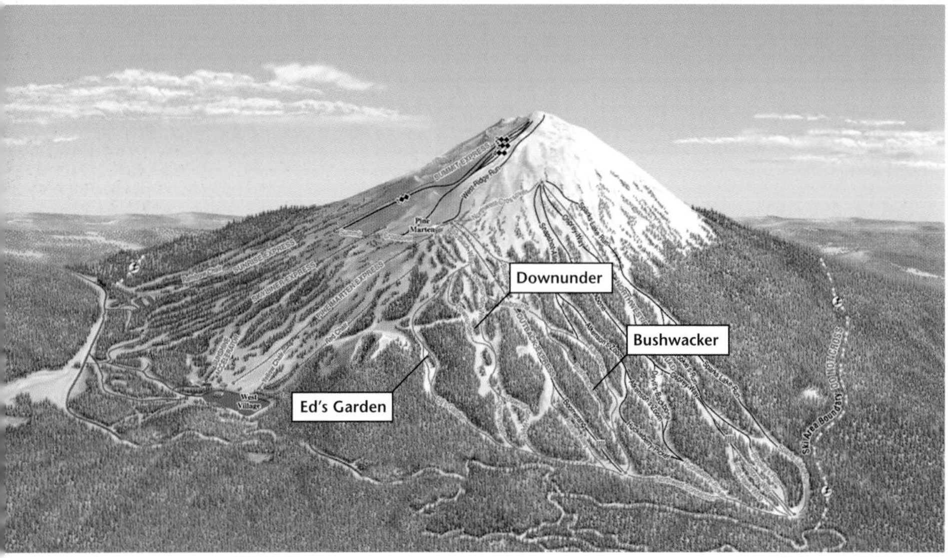

SKI AREA

Mount Bachelor is well regarded for beginners (15 percent) and intermediates (25 percent) but most of the 3,683-acre (1,490-ha) ski area is for advanced skiers, including several double black diamond trails for experts. The east side of the mountain has excellent cruising trails favored by intermediates and beginner skiers. The New Summit Express, Outback Express, and Northwest Express lifts access the most difficult terrain. Steep bowls in The Cirque, gladed tree trails, and deep chutes leading into tight trees are the benchmarks of these lifts. Mount Bachelor is also keenly building its reputation as a good location for snowboarders with the Superpipe and the Air Chamber Terrain Park.

In 2002/3 eight Super Wizard Snowguns were installed in the Pine Marten Express lift area to assure good coverage for early-season runs. Cross-country skiers will find plenty of room to roam too with more than a dozen trails totaling 35 miles (56 km). All trails are well maintained and wind through the scenic Deschutes National Forest. There's a cross-country trail map on www.mtbachelor.com.

SKI LIFTS

The network of 12 mostly high-speed lifts gives excellent access to all of Mount Bachelor's terrain in a single day. In fact, for three of the last four years, readers of *SKI Magazine* have rated the Mount Bachelor lifts No.1 in North America. Due to the cone-shaped peak of the mountain, the lifts are spread outward around the base and gather toward the center, and because seven of the lifts are high-speed quads, there is rarely a lift line anywhere. In addition to the quads there are three triple chairlifts and two surface lifts. The most recent addition, the Northwest Express quad, gives access to the best powder and tree skiing. The trails are long and everyone will find something they like, whether it's bumps, groomed or ungroomed, trees or glades. The Pine Marten Express quad is the link to the entire

▶ CROSS-COUNTRY
The 35 miles (56 km) of cross-country trails wind through the scenic Deschutes National Forest.

mountain. From the top you can ski or ride to the expert area on the northwest of the mountain, or east to Skyliner Express or the Sunrise area. The lifts are open Monday to Friday 9:00 AM–4:00 PM and Saturday to Sunday and holidays 8:00 AM–4:00 PM.

LIFT PASSES

Lift passes are available for all ages and abilities, and there are also several special options. Day passes in high season cost US$47 for adults, US$28 children (6–12), US$39 teenagers (13–18), and US$27 seniors (65–69), while children aged five and under and seniors aged 70 and over ski free. A weekly pass costs US$235 for adults, US$140 for children, and US$195 for teens. Other options are available for limited lift access, half-day tickets, and express passes. Photo I.D. is required for age requirement discounts. Tickets can be purchased on-mountain, online, at Central Oregon's participating retailers, and at the lodges.

SKI SCHOOLS AND GUIDING

The Ski School centers are at the West Village and Sunrise Lodges. Reservations can be made on 800-829-2442, or online at the e-center. Full-day lessons are 10:00 AM–3:00 PM; half-day lessons 1:00–3:00 PM. Telemark and snowboard lessons are also available. For children there are several levels of classes for all ages, including instruction, lift ticket, and lunch. The levels are clearly defined to enable kids to join the class best suited to their abilities. The minimum age for lessons is four years. For adults there are nine levels to determine the right class for you. Private or group lessons are available. Adult snowboard lessons have five levels, but require some experience of snowboarding. Adaptive ski programs for persons with disabilities can be reserved on 541-382-2607. The Mount Bachelor Learning Center has specially trained instructors, skilled in all levels of adaptations.

BEGINNERS

About 15 percent of trails are for beginners. The best area for beginners is on the east side of the mountain, where the bulk of the easier cruising trails can be found. However, green trails can be found at every chair except New Summit Express, Outback Express and Northwest Express. The greens are all well marked on trail maps, along with a special yellow area indicating the easiest descent. A good itinerary for a beginner is to ride the Sunrise Express quad and follow Marshmallow down the mountain, then take the Rainbow triple chair and the West Village Getback trail down to West Village Day Lodge. Then ride the Pine Marten Express quad to Pine Marten Lodge, and take the Skyliner route back down the mountain to the bottom of the quad. Then you should go up the lift again and this time take Leeway back down to West Village Day Lodge for a well-earned rest.

▲ SPLENDID SIGHT
Mount Bachelor (over 9,000 ft/2,700 m) will quite take your breath away when you first see it.

INTERMEDIATES

About 25 percent of the terrain is suitable for intermediates. For a good day's intermediate skiing, park at the West Village Lodge, warm up on Old Skyliner, Coffee, and the Canyons. Then take a screamer down Ed's Garden to the Outback Express quad. Follow that with another screamer on Downunder. Then Downunder West. Then Bushwacker, and so on until you have skied each trail on the Outback Express. Then start over again with Ed's Garden.

▲ EYES DOWN
There are plenty of chances to find yourself careering over rocky outcrops, but will you still be standing afterward?

ADVANCED AND EXPERT

Around 60 percent of the trails are designated for advanced and expert skiers and riders. The trails in The Cirque are considered the most challenging, are difficult to get to (hiking required), steep, difficult to get out of, and susceptible to the weather. The glades around the Outback Express quad and the black diamond trails on the new Northwest Express quad are best for advanced and expert skiers. The unnamed chutes to the west of Northwest Express are tight and deep, and all lead into thick trees. If powder's your thing, the back of the mountain (accessed only from the New Summit Express quad) keeps powder the longest, but is rarely open. The trees and glades around the Red Chair boast steep but short lines.

On a fresh powder day, park at the base of the Skyliner Express quad before Mount Bachelor opens, and get in line with the locals who will be waiting. Use the green Summit Crossover trail to warm up your legs, then ride the New Summit Express quad to the peak. Conditions vary so you must be on your game and alert. Shoulder your gear and hike 15 minutes to the peak above The Cirque. Dropping straight down Chute 1, snow flying into your mouth as you gasp for breath, avoid smashing into The Pinnacles on your left. Once clear of The Pinnacles, keep cutting to your left to join into Chutes 2, 3, and 4. Just below Pine Marten Lodge run the tight trees around Tippy Toe. Although by now many will be on the hill, Tippy Toe will be relatively untracked. End at the base of Pine Marten Express quad ready for more.

Skiing from the summit down to the base of Northwest Express quad also provides varied and changing conditions on a 1.5-mile (2.5 km) trail. There is no out of bounds skiing allowed at Mount Bachelor. Except for crowded areas, jumping and fast skiing is allowed if in control.

BOARDING & FREESTYLE

Snowboarders are welcomed at Mount Bachelor. Check out the Superpipe, a 400-foot (120-m) long Olympic-quality run with 17-foot (7-m) walls. A new HPG R17 Superpipe cutter will groom and contour the walls and keep it in shape for all your best moves. Boarders can also enjoy the 6,300 feet (1,890 m) of sculpted trails in the Air Chamber Terrain Park, next to the Skyliner Express lift, with a variety of hits, spines, tabletops, jumps, and rails to complement the light, dry powder. The layout of Mount Bachelor creates easy traverses between lifts for any type of snow rider.

EATING ON THE MOUNTAIN

There are seven restaurants on the mountain spread around the three lodges: Sunrise, Pine Marten, and West Village, with a range of food from cafeteria-style through Pacific Northwest cuisine to Italian.

Pine Marten Lodge features some of the highest restaurants in the Northwest, with spectacular views. Scapolo's for open-hearth pizzas; Pinnacles Espresso and Smoothie Bars for coffee, pastries, and smoothies; the Pine Marten Grill for burgers and fries; and The Skiers' Palate for a fine dining experience, although dress code is ski-boot friendly. At West Village Lodge, the Village Café is good for breakfast, pizza, pasta, and traditional American fare, while The Lower Castle Keep Restaurant is a large family dining facility offering table service for lunch. The Upper Castle Keep Lounge has a full-service bar and restaurant offering a lunch menu to those aged 21 years and over, while The Espresso Bar is good for coffee and pastries, and over at Sunrise Lodge the Sunrise Café offers Mexican and traditional American fare.

► BOARDING
Snowboarders can easily cross the mountain and also have the fabulous Air Chamber Terrain Park with loads of stimulations.

◄ DEEP DELIGHTS
Fine, dry powder settles in the trees to create the perfect opportunity to test your deep snow skills.

APRÈS SKI

With seven restaurants and three bars on the mountain, there's a reasonable choice for après ski. On-mountain, the Upper Castle Keep Lounge is the place to be. Pitchers of beer and giant plates of nachos keep the party going until the mountain closes. Off-mountain, the Bend Brewing Company and Deschutes Brewing in Bend serve handcrafted ales in a raucous atmosphere. Both have the best pub food in town. Bend has more restaurants than any other city in Oregon, with everything from drive-through fast foods and casual restaurants to elegant resort dining. Many ethnic restaurants are among the favorites. The minimum age in Oregon for consuming alcohol is 21. Children can only accompany parents in bars and other places serving alcohol in certain situations, usually only in bars serving food and if eating a meal. Most bars will close at 2:30 AM.

OTHER ACTIVITIES

Experience the snow like never before! At Snowblast Tubing Park rubber meets snow for an exhilarating ride full of twists, turns, and rolls. The new handle-tow tubing lifts are built with the latest technology and will pull you up the slope comfortably and quickly. Once at the top there are eight sculpted lanes to choose from. It's easygoing fun for everyone, regardless of age and tubing ability. The park is open daily 10:00 AM–4:00 PM.

Exploring Mount Bachelor in a pair of snowshoes is a whole new way to experience the beautiful Deschutes National Forest. Snowshoers can use the groomed trails with the purchase of a Trail Pass. If you want to go on a guided snowshoe tour, meet outside the West Village Bachelor Ski & Sport Shop for a one-hour, one-mile snowshoe walk. Dress warmly, snow boots are recommended. Tours and walks are free, but donations to the Northwest Interpretive Association are gladly accepted.

Ride through the Deschutes National Forest on an Oregon "Trail of Dreams" dogsled ride. All rides start at the Sunrise Lodge lower parking lot. Learn about this unique sport and have the adventure of a lifetime. Standard rides last about an hour, maximum weight 450 lbs (202 kg).

For shoppers, there's the Mount Bachelor Ski & Sport in West Village, and Sunrise Lodges for clothing and equipment. Bend River Mall houses The Bon Marché and Sears department stores, and there are charming boutiques in Redmond, Sisters, and Sunriver. And when you've had enough shopping there are art galleries, museums, performing arts, concerts, theaters, and all kinds of events taking place in the Bend, Sunriver, Redmond, and Sisters areas. Check www.visitcentraloregon.com for details.

USEFUL PHONE NUMBERS

Reservations and Information	800-829-2442
Snow Report	541-382-7888
Corporate Office	541-382-2442
Snowshoe Tours	541-388-5664

USEFUL WEBSITES & E-MAIL ADDRESSES

Official Website	www.mtbachelor.com
Official E-mail	info@mtbachelor.com
Tourist Information	www.visitcentraloregon.com
Dogsled Rides	www.SledDogRides.com

EATING ON THE MOUNTAIN

PINE MARTEN LODGE
PINE MARTEN GRILL
SCAPOLO'S
PINNACLES ESPRESSO BAR
THE SKIERS' PALATE

WEST VILLAGE LODGE
VILLAGE CAFÉ
LOWER CASTLE KEEP RESTAURANT
UPPER CASTLE KEEP LOUNGE
ESPRESSO BAR

SUNRISE LODGE
SUNRISE CAFÉ
SUNRISE BAR

BARS

ON-MOUNTAIN
UPPER CASTLE KEEP LOUNGE, IN WEST VILLAGE LODGE

BEND
BEND BREWING COMPANY
DESCHUTES BREWING

STAY AT SUN VALLEY AND YOU'LL FEEL ECHOES OF A PRE-WAR, 'HIGH SOCIETY' ERA IN A RESORT THAT STILL BOASTS VERY CHI-CHI LODGES TODAY. SPRINKLE SOME BALMY WEATHER, ABSENCE OF CROWDS, PLUS A MOUNTAIN THAT CLAIMS THE MOST CONSISTENT PITCH IN THE U.S. AND YOU HAVE A DREAM FOR INTERMEDIATE SKIIERS.

SUN VALLEY

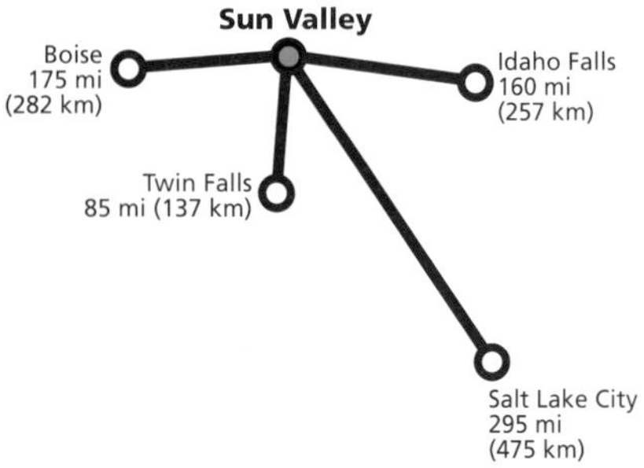

Step into Sun Valley, America's oldest purpose-built ski resort, and you can feel the echoes of an era when Hollywood stars, writers, socialites, and European nobility were lured here to ski and play. On December 23, 1936, the Sun Valley Lodge opened for its first winter season, complete with the world's first chairlift. Railroad tycoon Averell Harriman wanted to develop America's first grand destination ski resort to promote his Union Pacific Railroad, and Sun Valley was selected for its balmy weather, mostly treeless and wind-sheltered slopes, and pure snow quality. A gracious mock-alpine resort was built to lure the likes of Errol Flynn and Ernest Hemingway and put Sun Valley on the map—which they did. Sixty years on those skiing enticements are still evident and stars like Arnold Schwarzenegger still have hideaways here.

▼ BALDY ON TOP
Rightly regarded as one of the finest single ski mountains in the United States, Bald Mountain has a steep and near-perfect gradient from summit to base.

GETTING THERE

Sun Valley Resort is located in South Central Idaho in the Northern Rockies. It's pretty remote and can be difficult to get to. The nearest international airport is Salt Lake City, Utah, or Seattle, Washington. From Salt Lake it's a four to five hours' drive. However, there are now direct, non-stop daily flights from Los Angeles International Airport, via Horizon Air, to Friedman Memorial Airport—a regional airport in Hailey, only 11 miles (18 km) south of Sun Valley—but bad weather sometimes closes it, and it cannot handle big jets, so most visitors still come via Twin Falls, about 90 minutes away.

THE VILLAGE

Sun Valley Resort is actually part of the larger, old cowboy town of Ketchum. The self-contained, pedestrianized village is 1930s Tyrolean style and at the heart of the resort is the Sun Valley Lodge with alpine-style rooms, restaurants, stores and outdoor ponds, ice rink, and steaming pools. It was in this lodge that Hemingway wrote most of *For Whom The Bell Tolls*. Ketchum by contrast is mostly redbrick buildings in the Old Western style, housing many gourmet restaurants, bars and nightspots as well as art galleries and a theater. It's a lively and casual community with real small town friendliness and a vigorous local artists' colony. A free continuous shuttle-bus service links Sun Valley Resort to both Dollar and Bald Mountains and throughout the Woods River Valley including Ketchum, Hailey, and Bellavue.

▲ COZY MOUNTAIN GETAWAYS
Sitting on the Big Wood River, the River Run Plaza is the choicest of the lodges on Bald Mountain.

ACCOMMODATIONS

There is a total bed base of 6,000 with a large variety of accommodations to choose from. There are two hotels at Sun Valley Resort with many others in Ketchum itself. The Sun Valley Lodge was built in 1936 and remains world class today. It's a beautifully kept property with a mid-20TH-century feel enhanced by the uniformed doormen, the large second-floor "drawing room" with piano in the center, overstuffed chairs and sofas in the middle, fireplaces at either end, and an immense hot tub-style swimming pool that dates to the early days of the resort. If you are going to spoil yourself this is

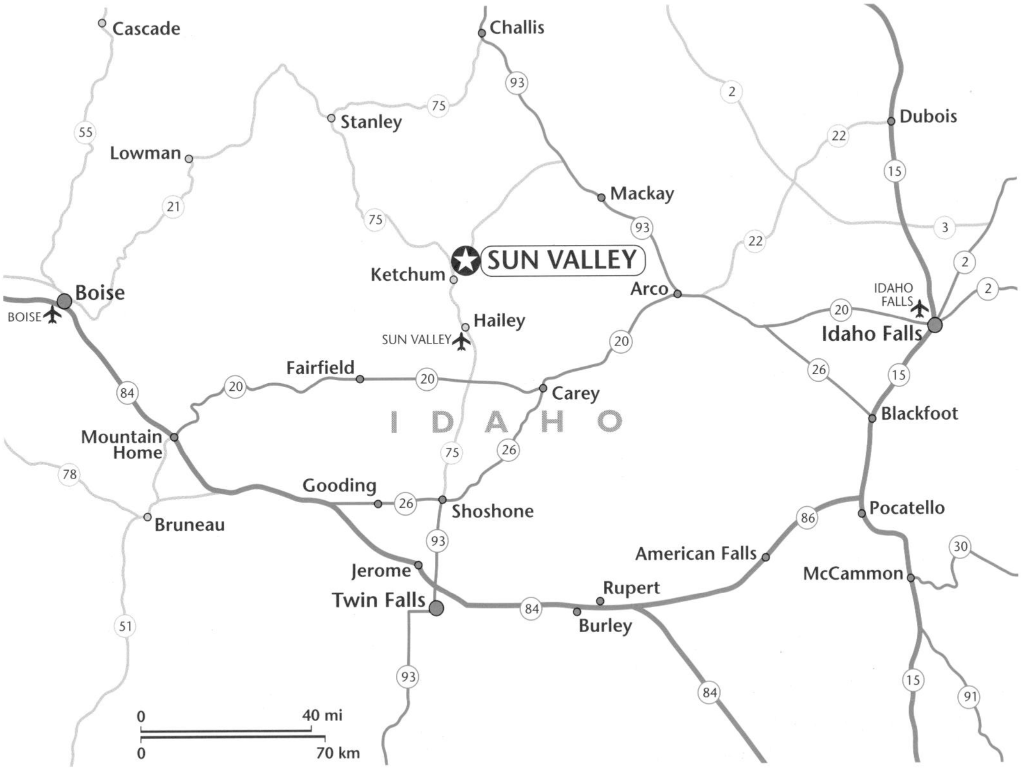

MOUNTAIN FACTS

Base	5,750 feet (1,752 m)
Summit	9,150 feet (2,788 m)
Elevation	3,400 feet (1,036 m)
Easy	42%
Intermediate	40%
Advanced	18%
Number of trails	78
Longest trail	3 miles (4.8 km)
Ski area	2,054 acres (831 ha)

SNOWFALL

Annual snowfall	346 inches (866 cm)
Snowmaking	630 acres (255 ha)

SKI LIFTS

Gondolas	-
High-Speed Quads	7
Fixed Grip Quads	-
Triple Chairs	4
Double Chairs	5
Surface Lifts	3
Total	19
Riders per hour	28,180

SKI SEASON
Late November to early April

▲ **GROOMED TO PERFECTION**
A cold climate and mainly northerly aspect preserve the generally modest snowfall, but Sun Valley has one of the largest automated snow-making systems, covering 630 acres (255 ha) and a fleet of snowcats to smooth the trails and keep you gliding.

the place to stay. The Sun Valley Inn is a short walk from the Lodge, and a bit less expensive, but shares most amenities. Condos and suites are available, as are packages.

The luxurious Knob Hill Inn has a Tyrolean feel and the Best Western lodges offer excellent amenities. Ski View Lodge, near downtown Ketchum, is close to everything with Bald Mountain views behind. There are self-catering rustic cabins to rent too. Staying here is not cheap by other U.S. resort standards, but if you're prepared to consider the wider Wood River Valley area you'll find something to suit. Central Reservations is the best starting point for all lodgings enquiries.

ACCOMMODATIONS

SUN VALLEY LODGE
SUN VALLEY INN
CONDOMINIUMS
APARTMENTS
COTTAGES
Tel: Reservations 800-786-8259 or
E-Mail: reservations@sunvalley.com

KNOB HILL INN
800-526-8010
www.knobhillinn.com

BEST WESTERN KENTWOOD LODGE
800-805-1001
www.bestwestern.com

BEST WESTERN TYROLEAN LODGE
800-333-7912
www.bestwestern.com

PENNAY'S AT RIVER RUN PLAZA
888-275-4423

SKI VIEW LODGE
208-726-3441

SKI AREA

Skiing is split over two mountains: Bald Mountain (known as "Baldy" to the locals) and Dollar/Elkhorn. Most of the 78 trails on Baldy are generously wide and slanted towards intermediate skiers. It's consistently rated as one of the best ski mountains in the U.S. because of its steep and near-perfect gradient from peak to base—a vertical drop of 3,400 feet (1,036 m) to the edges of the Sawtooth National Forest. All in all there are 2,054 acres (831 ha) of skiable terrain serviced by 19 lifts. There are no flats either, which is good news for boarders. Baldy's mountain bases are at River Run on the south and Warm Springs on the north and both are over a mile from the Sun Valley Village.

Much nearer, and just a short walk from Sun Valley Lodge, is Dollar Mountain, a treeless, sunny and beginner-friendly mountain. It is only 6,638 feet (2,023 m) high with 10 trails and 628 feet (191 m) of gentle vertical slopes. Its day lodge—Dollar Cabin—houses a cafeteria-style restaurant and a ski school. On the other side of this mountain, Elkhorn Face offers slightly more challenging novice trails spreading out from a steeper-pitched bowl.

The only, but big, problem with the ski area is the distance between the two mountains. The fact that they are not interlinked means that if you're in a mixed-ability ski group it will be tough trying to meet up and ski together. But if you're happy to stick to your slopes then you will find calm, sunny skiing protected from north winds by the Sawtooth Range, so you get plenty of sunshine without the biting chills. Snow records in the region are okay—the average is 150–200 inches (380-500 cm) per season. Not as much as most other Rocky Mountain resorts, but any shortfall in snow is augmented by a computer-controlled snowmaking system covering 630 acres (255 ha), around 30 percent of the ski area.

LIFT SYSTEM

The two mountains combined have a total of 19 lift's—seven high-speed quads (including one rising 3,144 vertical feet/958 m in 10 minutes), four triples, five doubles, three surface lifts—together a capacity of 28,180 skiers per hour. Dollar's lift capacity is about 5,000 skiers, while Baldy's is 23,180. Lifts are open from 9:00 AM to 4:00 PM. The season runs from Thanksgiving Day through to early April. Relatively speaking, Sun Valley has virtually no lift lines, except during peak season and even then they are nothing compared to ski resorts near metropolitan areas.

LIFT PASSES

A full-day adult ticket is US$65 and there are discounts for children. Children 15 and under can ski free most of the season when staying in a Sun

▼ **COMFORTABLE ASCENT**
The Challenger Quad rises 3,142 feet (958 m) to the Lookout Restaurant in 10 minutes.

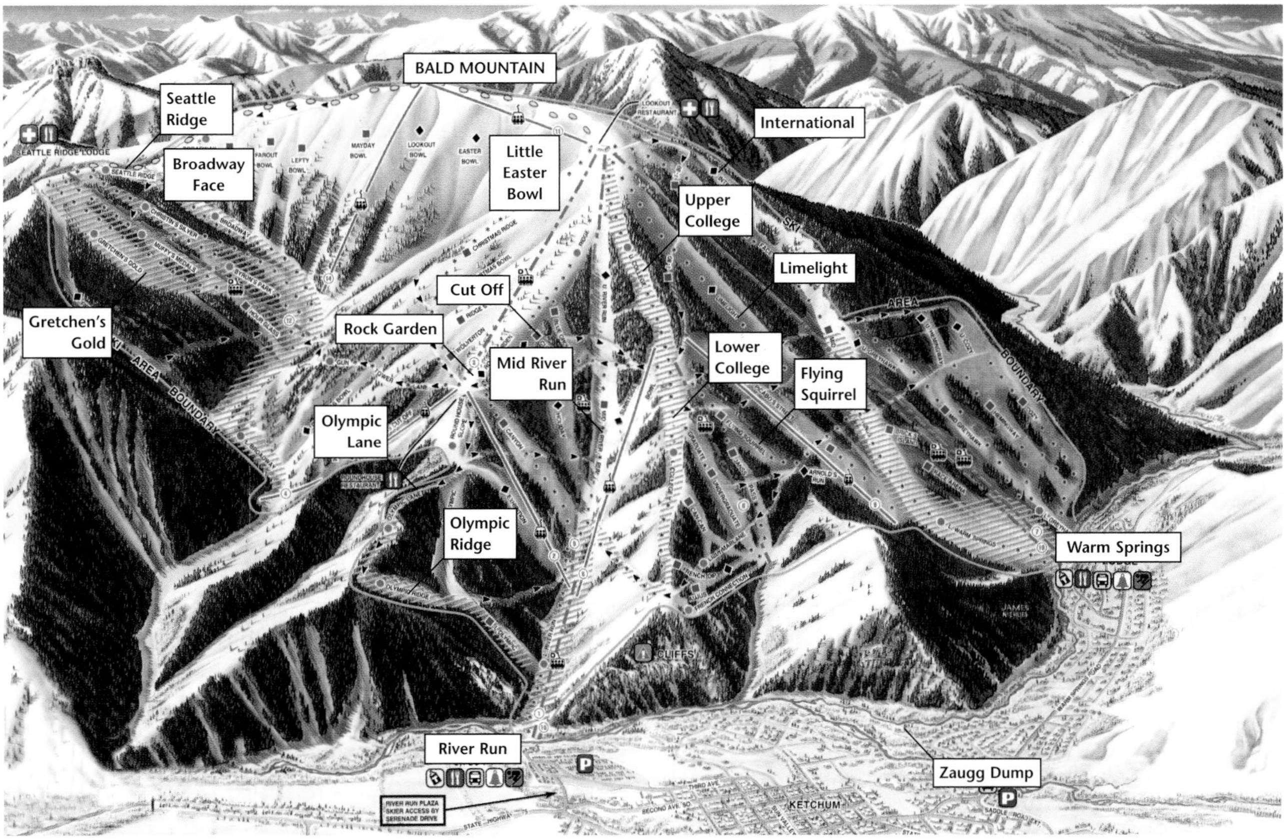

Valley accommodation, but restrictions apply (i.e. one child per parent, usually low season and so on). Beginners ski at Dollar Mountain and being a smaller mountain this is less expensive than Baldy. Lift passes can be bought at River Run Plaza, Warm Springs Lodge, and Dollar Mountain. There are also various weekly packages available. Visit Sun Valley online at www.sunvalley.com for details.

SKI SCHOOL

The Sun Valley Ski and Snowboarding School has some 240 experienced instructors. The minimum age for young children's classes is four. An adult one-day (two-hour) lesson will cost US$44; five consecutive days (10 hours) US$160; children's one-day (four hours) costs US$85 including lunch; five consecutive days (20 hours) including lunch is US$360, and an all-day private lesson for one person is US$425. Many other clinics and configurations are available. Lift tickets are not included in the lesson price. There is also the Sun Valley Nordic Ski School with 25 miles (40 km) of beautifully groomed tracks and five miles (8 km) of snowshoe trails.

BEGINNERS

Dollar Mountain is all treeless and great for novices and beginners, with plenty of practice slopes (as well as Sun Valley Ski School), and the New Bowl providing a good straight trail. The base of River Run on Baldy is groomed for those beginners wishing to move on. But be warned, what Sun Valley designate as easiest trails (42 percent of them) are actually pretty challenging and more like blue. Again, the problem is that if you go for Dollar and your friends and family are intermediates-to-expert and head for Baldy, you won't be seeing them at lunch or at après ski. If you feel you're ready for Baldy, try the Upper College linked to the Lower College trail first.

INTERMEDIATES

You can choose between 40 percent of blue ("more difficult") trails including the longest trail at three miles (4.5 km) and any blues on River Run side, Upper and Lower College, Seattle Ridge, and Flying Squirrel are recommended. From Lookout Restaurant intermediate skiers can choose Cutoff or Blue Grouse to Mid River Run to get back to the River Run Lift. From there it is a nine-minute lift ride back to the top. Easier trails are Olympic Ridge and Olympic Lane, and from Seattle Ridge Lodge you can try all the well-groomed trails designated as slow skiing (the exception being the difficult Fire Trail). Catch the Seattle Ridge chairlift, a five-minute ride from the bottom of the ridge back to the top. Here you'll also find Gretchen's Gold—named after local girl Gretchen Fraser who captured America's first Olympic alpine ski medals (a gold for slalom and a silver for the combined in the 1948 St. Moritz

LIFT PASSES

Daily Ticket Prices (high season):

BALD MOUNTAIN	
Adult:	
Full Day	US$65
Five Days	US$360
Child:	
Full Day	US$36
Five Days	US$165
DOLLAR MOUNTAIN	
Adult:	
Full Day	US$25
Child:	
Full Day	US$20

▲ **CORDUROY SLOPES**
Sun Valley has 817 acres (330 ha) of groomed terrain but nearly three times that of skiable acreage. While the snowfall may be variable, you'll get quality turns from top to bottom with no flats to frustrate boarders and plenty of bowls.

Winter Olympic Games). Perhaps the most ideal spot is Warm Springs, named for the warm bubbling water at the base of the lift. This area is cool for intermediates who are happy being intermediates. The slopes also get great afternoon sunshine. The top of the area is home to Warm Springs Face, and most difficult trails International and Limelight. Halfway down, you can decide which of the more difficult trails you want but Hemingway is a good route. The Bowls along the top of Bald Mountain tend to be difficult, but intermediate skiers can begin at the left of the mountain and move to the right as they feel more comfortable—try Broadway Face to start with. The Bowls are easily served by the Mayday chairlift, a seven-minute ride back to the top.

ADVANCED & EXPERT

There are no double black diamonds but enough black diamond ("most difficult") trails to give you long and demanding tests. The moguls on Exhibition on River Run are tough (catch the Exhibition chair) as is Olympic. Also on River Run advanced skiers can tackle the Rock Garden or Upper Holiday trails for moguls galore. The bowls are largely "most difficult"—Little Easter Bowl especially—and the trails kick off in wide-open bowls moving down into gladed trails.

Out of bounds is not patrolled, but for adrenaline seekers heliskiing is available in the surrounding mountains, usually north of Ketchum. A great way to enjoy the pockets of good powder snow in the backcountry is with a one-lift tour. Sun Valley Heli-Ski is permitted to drop expert and advanced skiers and boarders in over 750 square miles (1,200 sq km) of terrain. The one-lift helicopter tour combines a helicopter flight into the backcountry with a full day of adventure. It can be pretty hairy and avalanche warnings need to be checked.

BOARDING & FREESTYLE

There are no special areas for boarders and freestyle skiers, but Baldy's long trails are perfectly pitched for turning perfect arcs. Superbly groomed black diamonds make carving a dream. Head out for the mile-long ridge trails that lead to several advanced and intermediate bowls. If it's a powder day then the bowls will be great. Challenger

▼ **ROLLERCOASATER RIDES**
With extremely consistent gradients, and groomed black diamonds, Sun Valley is good for pure carving.

followed by The Lookout Chair will get you there quick. If you're an intermediate planning to sample the Warm Springs terrain, watch out for the cat track that makes up the intermediate entrance. Novices and beginner boarders should stick to Dollar Mountain.

EATING ON THE MOUNTAIN

The day lodges at Seattle Ridge, River Run, and Warm Springs have excellent restaurants in ritzy surroundings with a plethora of fireplaces, cozy seating, fine dining, and welcoming staff. Seattle Ridge, atop Baldy Mountain, is probably the finest with its spectacular views and sun-drenched outdoor deck. At the timber, stone, and glass Warm Springs you can sip your Sun Valley ale and take in uninterrupted views of the Wood River Valley and Pioneer Mountains.

The Roundhouse, Sun Valley's first day lodge, also has on-mountain sit-down dining service, while Lookout and Dollar Cabin serve deli and cafeteria-style lunches. A special lunch (or dinner) experience is to take a horse-drawn sleigh, cross-country ski, snowshoe or drive out to Trail Creek Cabin, about 1.5 miles (2.4 km) east of Sun Valley Lodge. For cheap and cheerful, Irving's Red Hots serving hot dogs and chips at the base of Warm Springs is something of an institution.

APRÈS SKI

There are around 107 restaurants, most of them in Ketchum, which makes it a lively place in the evenings. The bars are said to "wail" by some boarders, but gourmands will not be disappointed. In Sun Valley Village, the Sun Valley Lodge dining room has elegant dining and the bar serves some of the finest wines around. The Ram, attached to the Sun Valley Inn is a casual venue with a pianist. Gretchen's, also in the Sun Valley Lodge, is quiet, family-oriented, and cozy for breakfast, lunch, snacks, or dinner.

Restaurants to savor in Ketchum include Evergreen Bistro with gourmet dining; Chandler's likewise; Sushi on Second for Japanese; and Globus for Asian cuisine. The cheery Pioneer Saloon is famous for its steaks, prime rib, and mounted elk and moose on the walls, and is a very popular eatery and watering hole. There are about 20 other bars in the area for après-ski chilling out, including the Duchin Room in Sun Valley Lodge, where the older crowd dance to live music courtesy of the Joe Foss Trio who have been doing it for over 20 years. The younger crowd hang out in Ketchum at Apples, and at the Western-themed Whiskey Jacques as well as Grumpy's for beer and burgers.

▲ SUN VALLEY SERENADE
Since 1936 Sun Valley has lured European nobility, Hollywood film stars, and Olympic medallists to its enchanting Lodge.

OTHER ACTIVITIES

Sun Valley has two ice rinks (one indoor, one outdoor), two glass-enclosed heated pools, bowling, and the previously mentioned Nordic and Snowshoe Center with miles of trails. Between Ketchum and Sun Valley there are many, many eye-catching stores and art galleries. To rent or buy ski equipment go to Pete Lane's. For those into nostalgia and trying to spot places on the mountain, check the schedule for the movie times of nonstop reruns for *Sun Valley Serenade*—which was filmed here—and for Warren Miller movies at the Opera House in Sun Valley (www.sunvalley.com and visitsunvalley.com). But ultimately it's the skiing and serenity that are going to draw you to Sun Valley.

USEFUL PHONE NUMBERS

Tourist Information Center	800-634-3347
Central Reservation Center	800-634-3347
Restaurant Reservations	208-622-2135
Ski Patrol & Rescue Service	208-622-6151
Sun Valley Heli-Skiing	800-872-3108
Snow Report	800-635-4150
A1 Taxi	208-726-9351

USEFUL WEBSITES

Official web site	www.sunvalley.com
Sun Valley Visitors' Bureau	www.visitsunvalley.com
Sun Valley Backcountry	www.svtrek.com
Sun Valley Heli-Skiing	www.svheli-ski.com
Vacation Planner	www.summitnet.com
Virtual Map of Sun Valley	www.sunvalleymap.com
Weather Reports	www.wunderground.com
Snow Report & Web Cams	www.rsn.com/cams/svalley

EATING ON THE MOUNTAIN

SEATTLE RIVER LODGE
ROUNDHOUSE
LOOKOUT
RIVER RUN LODGE
WARM SPRINGS LODGE
TRAIL CREEK CABIN
DOLLAR CABIN
IRVINGS' RED HOTS

RESTAURANTS & BARS

SUN VALLEY RESORT
GRETCHEN'S @ SUN VALLLEY LODGE
THE DINING ROOM @ SUN VALLEY LODGE
THE DUCHIN @ SUN VALLEY LODGE
THE RAM @ SUN VALLEY INN
TRAIL CREEK CABIN

KETCHUM
EVERGREEN BISTRO
CHANDLERS
SUSHI ON SECOND
GLOBUS
PIONEER SALOON
APPLES
WHISKEY JACQUES
GRUMPY'S

FAR FROM THE CROWDS IN SOUTHWEST MONTANA, BLUE SKY IS THE PLACE TO GO FOR KEEN SKIERS WANTING CHUTES AND GULLIES, PLUS SOME OF THE UNITED STATES' TOUGHEST IN-BOUNDS SKIING ON UPPER LONE PEAK'S STEEP, EXPOSED SLOPES. WITH 150 TRAILS AND 4,350 FEET (1,326 M) ELEVATION FROM TOP TO BOTTOM, BIG SKY OFFERS MORE VERTICAL THAN MOST OTHER RESORTS.

BIG SKY

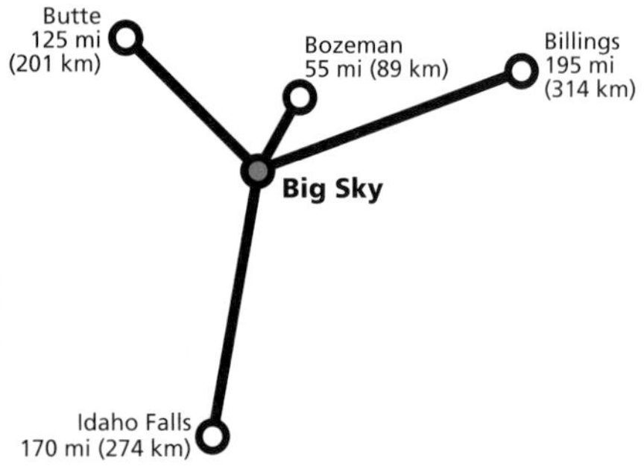

Big Sky, Montana, used to be considered an intermediate's deserted paradise by the few who had heard of the resort. But all that changed in 1995 when the tram (a small cable car) was built to the top of Lone Mountain, the highest peak in the region, opening up a hill from which there is no easy way to descend. Overnight it became a yardstick by which experts can measure themselves while it remains short of waiting lines even by U.S. standards; it's still Montana, after all.

Big Sky is right up there in every sense: just a few hundred miles further north is Canada; Lone Mountain, the resort's highest point, towers 11,166 feet (3404 m) above sea level, and the area's skiing puts the resort at the top of the league for keen intermediates, advanced and expert skiers.

But the telling word is keen. It's a long way to Montana from most places and Big Sky as a resort is not big on anything other than skiing. There are saving graces, specifically Yellowstone, the oldest National Park in the U.S. and a unique winter destination in its own right, just down the road. Within the resort accommodation standards are high even if the architecture—which features a 10-story hotel block —doesn't take your fancy.

With around 400 inches (1,016 cm) falling throughout the season, snow is seldom a problem although cold and wind can be. They say that the highest elevations rocks "float" thanks to the scouring gales that blow there. But if you're a Big Sky type of skier, that won't put you off, nor should it: you're going there for some of the most challenging and extensive terrain in North America.

GETTING THERE

Big Sky is in the Madison Mountain Range—part of the Rocky Mountains in southwest Montana. The local airport is at Bozeman, 50 miles (80 km) north on Interstate 191, which runs alongside the Gallatin River toward Yellowstone National Park 18 miles (29 km) to the south. Transfer time is one hour, although with the state's unique "reasonable and prudent" unrestricted daytime speed limit, it could be even quicker. Reasonably priced shuttle transfers

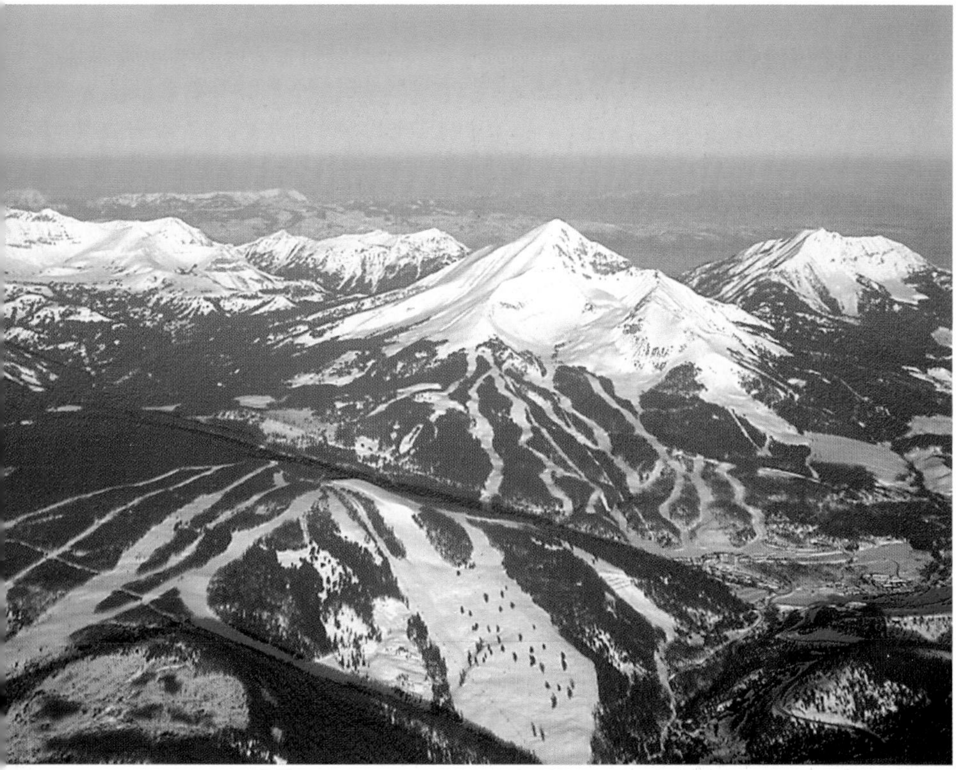

◄ PEAK PERFORMANCE
Lone Mountain's peak has classic mountain proportions with no initial easy way down. From the top, both sides drop into heart-thumping cliffs and chutes yielding finally into a rugged bowl above the tree line. The longest trail stretches some 6 miles (9.6 km).

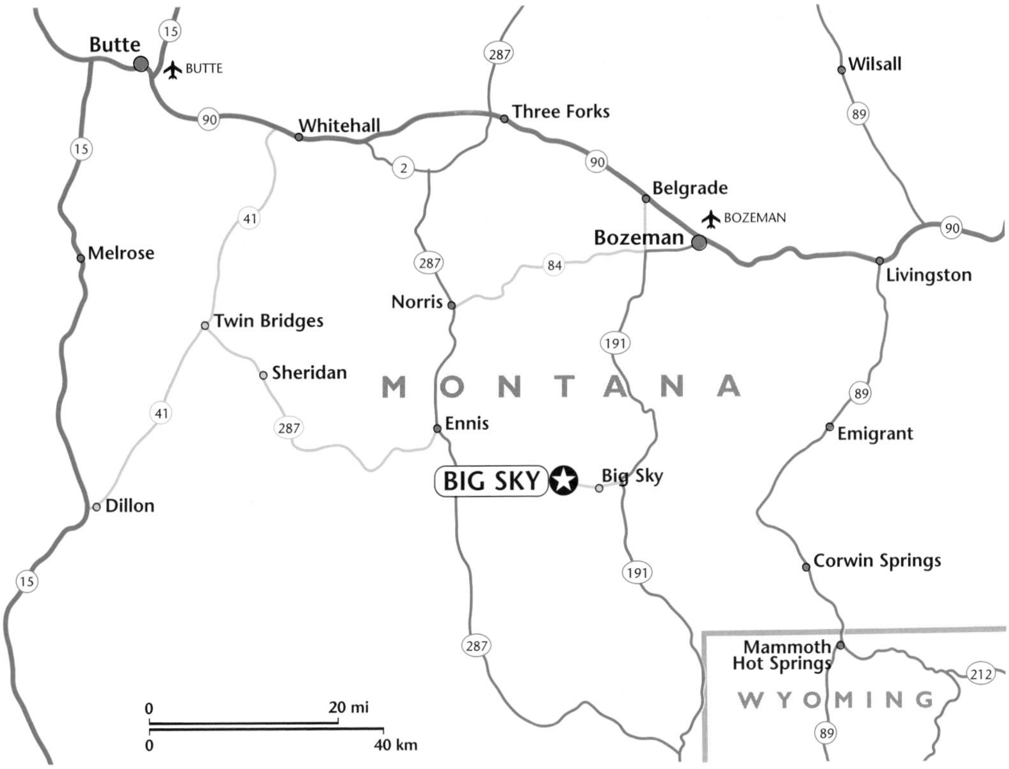

are available. Bozeman airport has a direct service from several international U.S. airports including Denver and Los Angeles. The closest international airport is Salt Lake City, approximately six hours away by road. There is no rail link to Big Sky.

THE VILLAGE

Several areas make up Big Sky resort: the Canyon, the Meadow Village, and the Mountain Village, all connected by a free shuttle. The Mountain Village is the center of the resort, made up of the 10-story Summit and the seven-story Shoshone buildings. A pedestrian plaza connects the Mountain Village buildings and the Mountain Mall, and exits near the base area at the foot of several major lifts.

The Mall contains most of the resort's shopping and eating outlets, meaning you never need brave the weather other than to ski. This is useful on stormy days but can leave the impression that you've spent a week underground, other than when skiing. Part of the US$400 million earmarked for resort development will go specifically to tackle the pedestrian area at some time in the future.

ACCOMMODATIONS

With just three hotels, choice is limited within the Mountain Village, which for practical purposes is the resort. The newest luxury hotel is the 10-story 213-room Summit, complete with all amenities. The Mountain Inn is a recently completed 90-room economy hotel within walking distance of the lifts. The Shoshone Condominium Suites and the Huntley Lodge provide the rest of Big Sky's most central accommodations; there are also budget and luxury condominiums, cabins and townhouses, some of which are within easy walking distance of the lifts. Standards are high, but the atmosphere within the main buildings is more of an international business center than of alpine charm, despite some impressive log fires and Native American Indian artifacts.

◄ SIGNATURE PEAK
Big Sky actually has three mountains—Lone Mountain, the resort's signature peak; adjacent Andesite Mountain; and Flat Iron Mountain on the eastern shoulder of Andesite.

MOUNTAIN FACTS

Base	6,800 feet (2,073 m)
Mountain village	7,500 feet (2,286 m)
Summit	11,150 feet (3,398 m)
Elevation	4,350 feet (1,326 m)
Easy	17%
Intermediate	25%
Advanced	37%
Expert	21%
Number of trails	150
Longest trail	6 miles (9.6 km)
Ski area	3,600 acres (1,457 ha)

SNOWFALL

Annual snowfall	400 inches (1,016 cm)
Snowmaking	360 acres (146 ha)

SKI LIFTS

Tram	1
Gondola	1
High-Speed Quads	3
Fixed Grip Quads	1
Triple Chairs	4
Double Chairs	4
Surface Lifts	3
Total	17
Riders per hour	22,000

ACCOMMODATIONS

HUNTLEY
SHOSHONE
SUMMIT
ARROWHEAD
BEAVERHEAD
BIGHORN
CEDAR CREEK
THE LAKE
LONE MOOSE
POWDER RIDGE
SADDLE RIDGE
SKYCREST
SNOWCREST
STILL WATER

SKI SEASON
Late November to mid April

SKI AREA

Big Sky's skiing takes place on two main mountains, Lone Peak and Andesite; total trail length is 85 miles (137 km). The truly unique element of the resort is the huge amount of lift-accessible terrain from the top of the Peak. From 11,150 feet (3,398 m) down to the treeline there are 1,200 acres (485 ha) of steep, exposed slopes that offer a huge variety of expert challenges. There is no way down for anyone other than advanced and expert skiers, apart from the tram. With its capacity limited to just 15 people every four minutes, the summit and all routes down invariably feel deserted, adding to the thrill. All of this advanced terrain is marked either black diamond, or double black diamond; much of it consists of chutes and gullies. Natural hazards are unmarked, although general warnings about the terrain and the obstacles you might encounter are displayed at the tops of lifts. The slopes are too severe for any grooming to take place on the upper mountain. Combined with advanced trails lower down the mountain, this area accounts for over half the resort's terrain, with 21 percent of the trails rated expert and 37 percent advanced.

The total vertical drop back down to the village at 7,500 feet (2,286 m) is 4,350 feet (1,326 m). The latter half of this is mostly intermediate terrain, marked with blue squares, interspersed with advanced glade trails. Obstacles are marked and grooming takes place on many but not necessarily all trails, depending on snow conditions; notice boards list the slopes that are groomed. The aim is to provide some well-groomed trails but to avoid spoiling natural snow conditions for skiers who enjoy skiing pristine trails. This works particularly well at Big Sky thanks to frequent snowfall and few skiers.

▼ AMPLE ANDERSITE
From the summit of Lone Mountain, the more wooded and well-linked slopes of Andesite Mountain lie some 2,365 feet (725 m) below. Andesite has several expert tree trails as well as plenty of wide, groomed trails for intermediates and beginners.

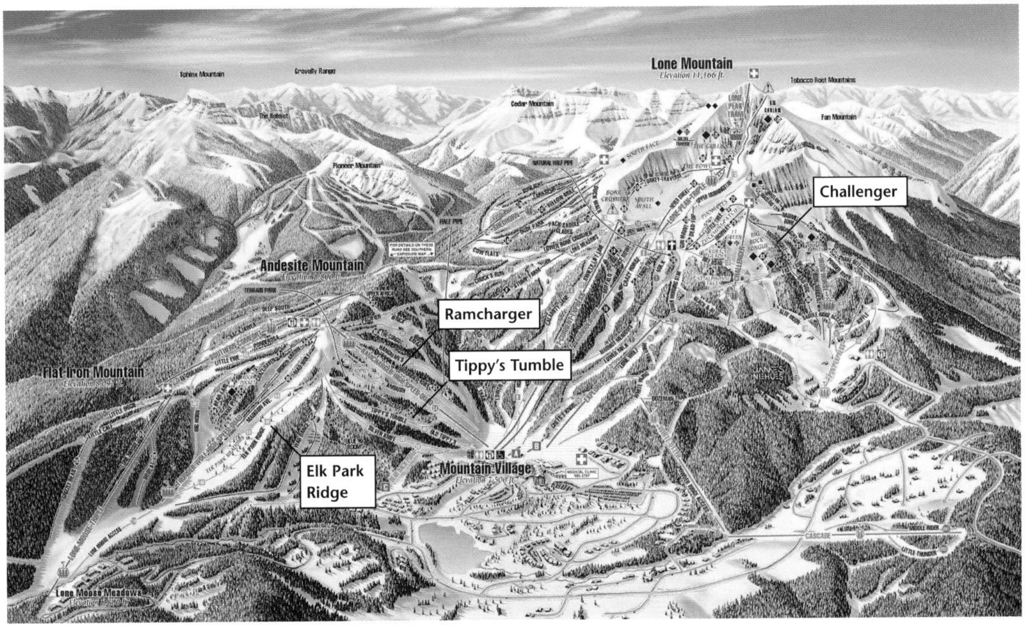

The layout of the resort, dictated by the steep upper slopes of Lone Mountain, effectively segregates skiers according to their skills. Beginners enjoy a slow skiing zone served by a magic carpet and a chair right out of the base area. There's no question of intermediates skiing the upper mountain and they are unlikely to come across any nasty surprises lower down. Both intermediates and beginners can access all the relevant terrain without circuitous lift journeys, while advanced and expert skiers can head for the upper mountain and remain there for the day. For families and mixed groups this could prove disruptive, though with the best lunch options located back at base, meeting up again isn't hard.

If there is a serious criticism about the skiing on offer, it's that strong intermediates and advanced but not adventurous skiers may find the gap between the lower and upper mountain too big.

SKI LIFTS

Big Sky has 17 lifts serving over 3,600 skiable acres (1,457 ha.) With the high proportion of trails emanating from just one point—the top of the single-span tram on Lone Peak—the rest of the area is more densely supplied than the figures imply. The lift system includes three high-speed quads and one gondola. Terrain of every aspect is covered, including steep, north-facing ground from the Challenger lift. Lifts run from 9:00 AM till 4:00 PM and with the capacity to carry 22,000 people per hour, the system is still a long way from becoming overloaded. Even on the slower lifts, lines are scarce although there is sometimes a wait at the tram.

There are plans to build a new high-speed lift to access the north-facing terrain on the other side of the ridge from the A-Z chutes. This is rolling terrain, protected from the sun, which is currently used for snowcat skiing. There will also be a new lift replacing Southern Comfort that accesses expansive beginner terrain.

LIFT PASSES

A one-day lift pass costs US$58; children aged 10 and under ski for free, and juniors (11-17) and college students ski for US$43. Ski school participants can buy packages that include access to the lower mountain lifts. Tickets are available at both the Summit and Huntley/Shoshone concierge desks, and at the ticket sales offices in the Snowcrest Lodge. No photo I.D. is required.

▼ SHARP EXIT
Before the Lone Peak Tram was built in 1995, the mountain offered mainly intermediate terrain (unless you were an adrenaline-seeking peak hiker). Now two seriously daunting couloirs await any expert skiers taking the tiny 15-person cable car. For these couloirs you have to check in with the ski patrol and ski down with a partner. Alternatively you can turn left at the top station and make your way down the steep but manageable main trail or ski around to the Lenin and Marx chutes with a 38-degree slope.

▲ **FEARLESS FREE-SKIING**
The south face of Lone Mountain has the steepest open terrain with double black diamond chutes and bowls above the tree line.

VILLAGE TRANSPORT

Free skier shuttle is provided by the Snow Express buses that circulate the Meadow, Mountain, and Canyon areas approximately every 30 minutes.

SKI SCHOOLS AND GUIDING

Big Sky Snowsports School, based at the Snowcrest Lodge, provides ski, snowboard, and telemark lessons as well as guiding services. Classes run from 9:00 AM to 4:00 PM with a maximum group size of ten. Children as young as three are taught and lunchtime supervision is available to allow parents full days to themselves. A 45-minute introductory lesson for three to four year-olds—Small Fry Try—costs US$31. For kids aged four to six, the Mini Camp morning lesson costs US$42, lunch US$10, and afternoon lesson US$33. Ski Camp for ages six to 14 is slightly cheaper, and half-day adult group lessons cost US$38 per person; private lessons cost from US$175 for two hours to US$420 for a full day. Thanks to the terrain on offer, Big Sky also attracts specialist "steep and deep" and extreme ski clinics whose dates are advertised on the resort website.

BEGINNERS

Just because Big Sky has developed an extreme reputation doesn't mean to say you can't learn there, although it would be a long way to travel just to give skiing a try. Of the total terrain, 17 percent is specifically for novices. Given the size of the resort, that amounts to more acreage than many U.S. resorts with a higher proportion of easy trails.

Complete beginners start by riding the magic carpet in the base area, then the Explorer chair that serves two main beginner trails. The next step is to ride the Gondola and take Mr. K down for a long, wide-open ride. You can then progress to trails under the Southern Comfort lift on the south side of Andesite.

INTERMEDIATES

Before the opening of the top half of the mountain, intermediate terrain was Big Sky's bread and butter. It still accounts for a quarter of the resort's skiing and has benefited from recent lift improvements too. The obvious start to any day is to head for Andesite mountain on the Ramcharger lift to gain access to two long cruisers, Big Horn and Elk Park Ridge. This is the longest intermediate trail, wide open and groomed, which runs all the way down the east ridge of Andesite. It varies in pitch and is a perfect carving slope.

On the front of Andesite are plenty of trails—Ambush, Tippy's Tumble, Hangman's, and Silver Knife—as well as glade skiing, with trails cut among the trees. A popular trip is to the top of Lone Mountain to enjoy the view over three states, Yellowstone National Park and, on clear days, the Tetons of Jackson Hole fame. Riding the tram down gets you back to intermediate terrain on Upper Morning Star.

ADVANCED & EXPERT

A glance at the trail map might make advanced skiers head straight to the top of Lone Mountain. In fact there's just one single black diamond trail to be found there—the Liberty Bowl. The rest of Big Sky's advanced terrain is in the trees on Andesite and on Challenger. For a long bump trail, head toward Mad Wolf from the top of Andesite; the best powder is usually in the Bavarian Forest at the bottom of Liberty Bowl, or in the north-facing Rice Bowl off Swift Current.

Experts can head straight to the top to ski the gullies as a warm up, then try the 1,450 feet (441 m) Big Couloir straight down the cliff-like face of Lone Peak. To gain access you must check in with ski patrol, have an avalanche transceiver, and a partner. Other limited-access areas include the A-Z chutes, Bonecrusher, and new terrain called Elvis and Graceland from the top of Challenger. Although the

◄ MOUNTAIN VILLAGE VIEWS
The seven-story Shoshone Condominium Hotel is attached to the Yellowstone Conference Center and Huntley Lodge and has ski-in, ski-out to the core base area. You get a luxury stay combining the service of a hotel with the comforts of a condominium, including a fully equipped health club, steam room, saunas, indoor/outdoor jacuzzi, and outdoor swimming pool.

rest of the double black diamond offerings may not be as seriously exposed, they all deserve their rating. No skier in this league is likely to be disappointed.

Out of bounds lines may not be crossed—it's private property—and there's no heli-skiing available, but Montana Backcountry Adventures (www.skimba.com) offers cat-skiing near Moonlight Basin Ranch on the north side of the mountain. The Ski School offers guide services for all the Big Sky terrain including the most extreme routes.

BOARDING & FREESTYLE

Strong freeriders can get all over the mountain, though there is some traversing involved to reach the best spots. There is a halfpipe on Ambush, and a terrain park above it in Ambush Meadows for boarders and freestyle skiers.

EATING ON THE MOUNTAIN

There are only two on-mountain restaurants, including the Dug Out on top of Andesite. There are a further 14 options in Mountain Village, where the majority of skiers eat lunch. There are no fast-food franchises in Big Sky.

APRÈS SKI

The skiing, not the après ski, is what you visit Big Sky for. There are no nightclubs but Chet's bar has a "high energy show" featuring the Crazy Austrian brothers playing their classic cover songs; there's also poker and pool. Other bars in the Mountain Village include the Alpine Lounge, Moose River Hummer, Jack Creek Saloon, and Carabiner. Twenty-one is the minimum age for drinking alcohol but children can accompany parents in bars before 10:00 PM. Many popular drinking places are also restaurants, such as Dante's Inferno. The hotel dining rooms offer some of the best eating—try Southwestern cuisine from the Peaks Dining Room in the Summit Hotel, or wild game in the Huntley Dining Room.

OTHER ACTIVITIES

Snowmobiling, cross-country skiing, dogsledding, horseback riding are the main alternatives to skiing.

USEFUL PHONE NUMBERS

Big Sky Central Reservations	800-548-4486
Ski School	406-995-5743
Handprints Daycare Center	406-995-3332
4x4 Stage Airport Shuttle Service	406-388-2293
Mountain Taxi Shuttle Service	406-995-4895
Karst Stage Coach Shuttle Service	406-388-2293

USEFUL WEBSITES

Official Website	www.bigskyresort.com
Karst Stage Airport Shuttle Service	www.karststage.com
Weather Reports	www.wunderground.com
Snow Report & Web Cams	www.rsn.com/cams/

▼ BIG SKY FOR BOARDERS
Good hits and jumps await freestyling boarders on the lower slopes of Crazy Horse trail on Lone Mountain (reachable from Gondola One) while Andersite Mountain also offers a terrain park as well as a half-pipe with its own rope tow by Ambush Meadows.

THE YELLOWSTONE CLUB

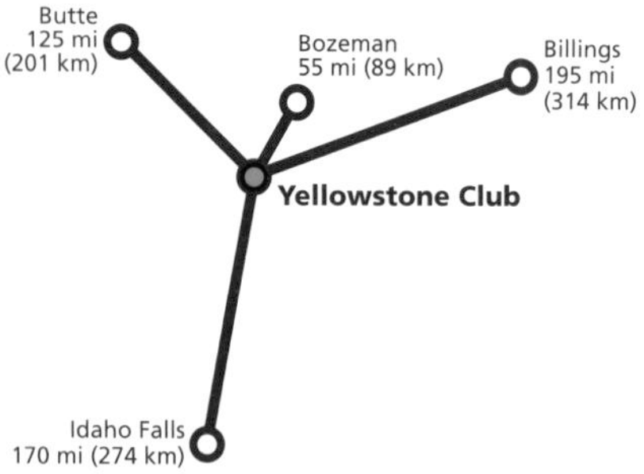

If Vail, Aspen, St. Moritz, and all the other glitzy resorts are simply too common but you have plenty of cash to spare, you might like to try the Yellowstone Club.

"One of a kind" is probably the only way to describe it. Thanks to its unique vision, it will probably remain that way for years to come. The premise is simple, and on the face of it, not controversial: to offer a limited membership club, based at a purpose-built ski resort in the depths of Montana.

Such a scheme was never going to be cheap and neither is the membership fee. Along with a number of environmental concerns about where and how the resort is being built, the exclusivity issue has resulted

▼ PRIVATE POWDER
Exclusive it may be, but Yellowstone Club has 2,000 acres (809 ha) of well-groomed snow.

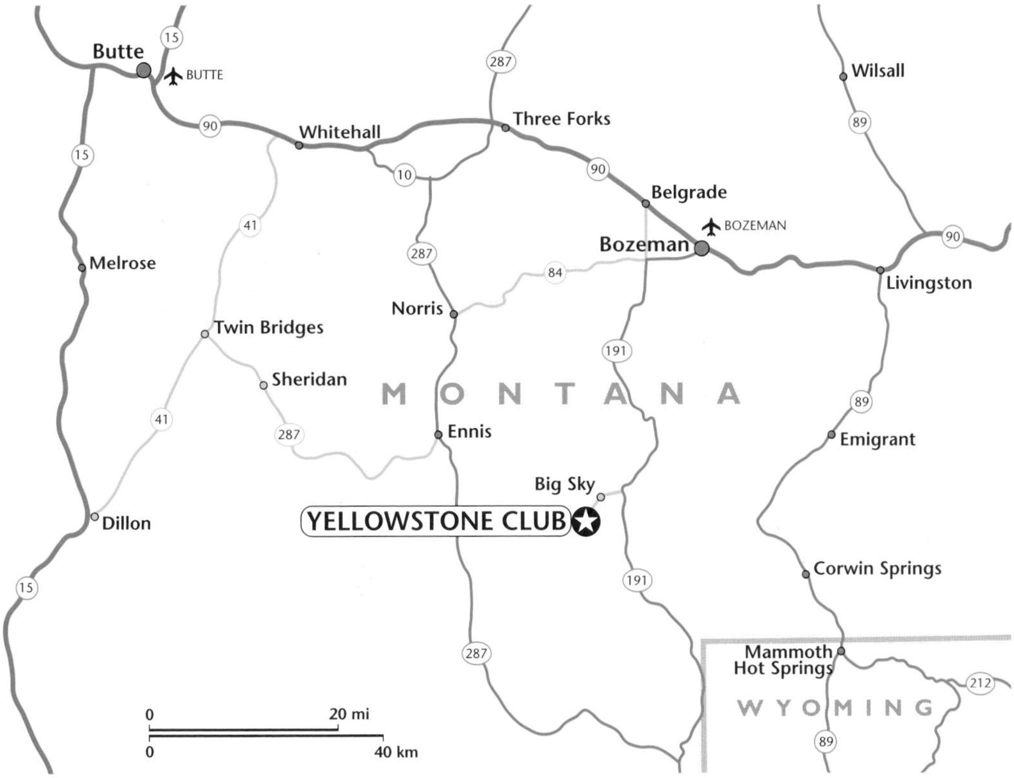

MOUNTAIN FACTS

Base	6,800 feet (2,073 m)
Summit	9,860 feet (3,005 m)
Elevation	3,056 feet (931 m)
Easy	15%
Intermediate	55%
Advanced/Expert	30%
Number of trails	30
Ski area	2,000 acres (809 ha)

SNOWFALL

Annual snowfall	400 inches (1,016 cm)

SKI LIFTS

High-Speed Quads	4
Fixed Grip Triple	1
Fixed Grip Double	1
Tranverse Lift	1
Total	7

in a few hackles being raised, mainly of those for whom joining the club will never be an option.

Whatever your feelings about private ownership of mountains—a more common occurrence in the U.S. than Europe—you can't argue with the quality of ski experience the club aims to provide. "Private Powder" might be its slogan, but the exceptional snow conditions are just one component of a complete package that could become a yardstick for best practice in the provision of quality skiing. Precisely the aspect that attracts so much criticism—a limited membership providing exceptional ski facilities—is simply the logical response to the problem with so many of the world's great ski domains: too many people cluttering the slopes.

The club is in fact the tip of the iceberg. Some other U.S resorts limit the numbers of lift tickets sold (an unimaginable concept in Europe) to maintain the quality of skiing; in effect, the club just takes that practice to the extreme. Not only should it make for more fun but it's safer too, and allows the Yellowstone Club to pursue its goal of being a truly family-oriented resort. Given space and resources, this might be the way of the future.

MEMBERSHIP

There is no easy way to say this: membership (covering your immediate family) costs US$250,000 to sign up, with annual fees of US$16,000. Members will then need to buy land and build a house, probably costing several million dollars. As an alternative to building your own home, there will be a range of condos at the resort base costing from just under US$1 million to US$3 million. The total membership won't exceed 900 families, with the majority of places still available.

As well as the skiing, membership covers use of the summer facilities including a Tom Weiskopf-designed golf course, fly-fishing streams, hiking, biking, and horse-riding trails.

Along with the ready cash, prospective members must pass a financial review and be vetted by the membership committee—the founder of the Yellowstone Club, Tim Blixseth, and his wife, who are looking for down-to-earth (albeit seriously rich) people.

GETTING THERE

The Yellowstone Club is adjacent to Big Sky, a ski resort to which it will be linked (for club members only) in future to form the biggest ski domain in the United States. The two resorts share part of the Madison Mountain Range in the Rocky Mountains of southwest Montana.

Yellowstone National Park, from where the Club takes its name, is just 18 miles (29 km) to the south. Bozeman is the nearest city (and local airport), 55 miles (89 km) north—a brief helicopter ride.

▼ WESTERN CHARM
Rustic five-star simplicity is the order of the day. Before spending those large sums of money prospective members are invited to stay in mid-mountain log cabins. No one is expected to chop their own firewood.

THE VILLAGE

The club is still being built, and members recruited, though the ski facilities are already well developed. Currently there is no village and barely even an identifiable resort center. Due to the private nature of the Club, no sign advertises what lies at the end of the winding mountain road off the Big Sky resort access road. The first building you reach is the gatehouse, through which you will not pass unless you are on the list. Then you reach the Buffalo Bar & Grill, at the base of the resort. Halfway up the mountain are a lodge and log cabin visitors' accommodations.

ACCOMMODATIONS

As part of their membership deal, each member contracts to buy a plot of land and build their own house on it. These will tend toward the trophy-home end of the scale, with ample space for guests—who can take advantage of all the club's services when visiting with a member.

Prospective members currently stay in mid-mountain log cabins. Rustic five-star simplicity and western charm is the order of the day. You don't have to chop your own firewood. For many skiers, these beautifully furnished, stunningly situated, intimate log cabins would be a dream hideaway for a week or a month, and that's before you find out about the skiing on your doorstep.

SKI AREA

Unless you fall into the appropriate income bracket, you might want to avert your gaze at this point. The heart of the project, the skiing, has not been skimped on. When they've finished the entire project a few years from now, four thousand acres will have been shaped into ski terrain that looks and feels natural, although it's anything but: having gone through hoops to get here, the club's members don't expect to snag their skis on rocks or tree stumps. But there are plenty of advanced, even intimidating challenges, with rocks, trees, and chutes to test the expert.

Although the grooming at Yellowstone is such a talking point, a significant advantage at the club is that the ungroomed terrain can remain untracked not just for a couple of hours, but sometimes for days, with some stashes staying in shape almost indefinitely. Given the abundant snowfall and the limited number of skiers, you're likely to find fresh powder or untracked spring snow on any given day through the season.

Most of the runs are cut through forest, and on the back of the mountain, Ching Forest remains intact for glade skiing. Only the steepest terrain, off Pioneer Ridge, is unforested.

SKI LIFTS & PASSES

There are four quads, which on some days will represent more than one lift per skier. Nevertheless, more are planned. There is no lift pass. Not having to go through turnstiles is just one more advantage of the US$16,000 per year membership dues.

SKI SCHOOLS AND GUIDING

There are staff members at every turn. Lessons will be available to suit you and your family's needs, while ski patrol can offer impromptu guiding services—and will be discreetly watching out for you when you venture off alone.

▼ FINE TERRAIN
From knee-deep bowls of powder and perfectly formed runs, to exhilarating chutes, Yellowstone has it all—the grooming, too, is perfection.

BEGINNERS

With such impeccable grooming and so few skiers around, novices should build confidence rapidly, with plenty of appropriate terrain.

INTERMEDIATES

One of the club's many strong points is the amount of intermediate terrain. The whole mountain, including the gentle gladed and open areas on the far side of Pioneer Ridge, is accessible, giving the opportunity to experiment with tree skiing and deep snow without having to deal with intimidating terrain—or spectators. On piste, many of the runs represent the ultimate carving opportunity, with few moving obstacles and a perfect corduroy surface.

ADVANCED

"Private Powder" is what you come for and it's what you get. The snow in this region is good (see Big Sky), even before you start hoarding it. After fresh snowfall, some groomed runs are left untouched to provide the ultimate ego-powder and employees aren't allowed to ski untracked runs before members; after all, people will have paid a lot for the privilege and this is gun country...

At the top end of the scale, a series of chutes from Pioneer Ridge remain ungroomed and even have their original rocks and trees. These runs are threatening enough to provide a real challenge; if you don't like the look of the narrow entrances, you can continue along the groomed ridgeline and access the back of the mountain for some tree skiing.

The one thing you won't find in Yellowstone is a bump run. Unless they decide to build some, they'll never happen, with just a handful of skiers each day.

▲ **UNPARALLELED BEAUTY**
With pristine views from the Andesite Mountain the two- or four-acre homesites have ample space for guests. Many have their own ski-in and ski-out access.

◄ **NO CROWDS**
With abundant snowfall and limited numbers of skiers it is easy to find powder, or untracked spring snow, on any given day through the season.

EATING ON THE MOUNTAIN

Yes, please. Every visitor to the club marvels at the amount of freshly groomed trails toward the day's end, and concludes that there are simply too few skiers to spoil the grooming. But it might be down to the fact that club members have trouble tearing themselves away from breakfast, never mind lunch, thanks to both the quality of what's on offer and the ambience and settings of the various restaurants. Even passionate skiers forget the powder to linger over the menu, or to order their own special, direct from the chef. This is the Yellowstone Club at its most persuasive, with the plastic trays and fast food that characterize North American on-mountain eating a very distant memory.

APRÈS SKI

It's probably safe to say that the Club will never resound to the thud of a nightclub, and for the moment après ski is limited to the same bars and restaurants used at lunch. But the company is guaranteed to be influential, and whatever you're drinking, it will be good.

USEFUL PHONE NUMBERS & WEBSITES

General Information	888-700-7748
Official website	www.theyellowstoneclub.com
Weather	www.weather.unisys.com
Avalanche Forecast	www.mtavalanche.com

MUSCULAR, RUGGED MOUNTAINS WITH STARK GRANITE WALLS; HIGH-ALPINE BOWLS; 4,139 VERTICAL FEET (1,262 M), AND 2,500 ACRES (1,012 HA) OF SOME OF THE MOST CHALLENGING INBOUNDS SKIING IN NORTH AMERICA; ALL SURROUNDED BY 120 SQUARE MILES (310 SQ KM) OF OPEN-GATE BACKCOUNTRY. JACKSON HOLE IS TO NORTH AMERICA WHAT CHAMONIX IS TO EUROPE: GOOD SKIERS AND BOARDERS ABOUND AND THE ALPINE LIFESTYLE RULES.

JACKSON HOLE

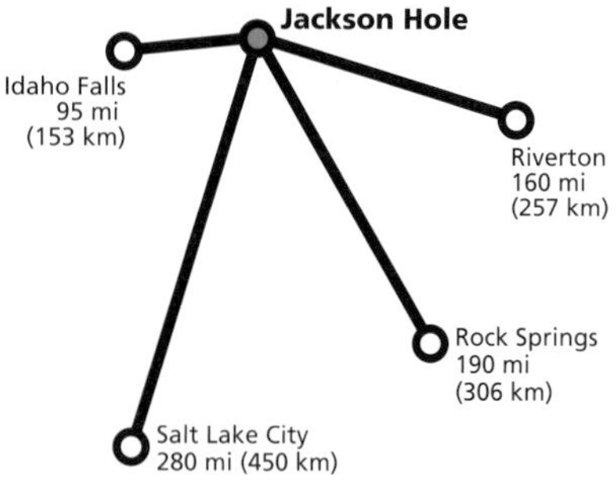

The resort of Jackson Hole has a big reputation to live up to: one of North America's biggest vertical drops, endless backcountry skiing, great snow (and a lot of it), and more advanced skiing—some of it verging on the extreme—than most visitors know what to do with.

First impressions are likely to confirm the reputation. From the moment you see the craggy Teton Range, you know you're going to be skiing mountains to be reckoned with. And then there's the town itself, a reasonably authentic slice of the west, with a gunslinging feel and plenty of quality accommodations and nightlife.

GETTING THERE

Jackson Hole's setting among the mountains of northwest Wyoming seems calculated to impress. Sweeping into the broad Snake River valley by plane gives a grandstand view of the Teton Range to the north. From touchdown at Jackson Hole airport, it's an easy 9 miles (14 km) to the town of Jackson Hole and a further 20 miles (32 km) to Teton Village resort at the base of the ski area—just thirty minutes by car or shuttle bus. Here the peaks rise dramatically from the high valley plain, from around 6,000 feet (1,829 m) above sea level to a lift-served maximum of over 10,000 feet (3,048 m.) The highest peak in the range, Grand Teton, reaches nearly 14,000 feet (4,267 m.)

There are no direct flights from outside the U.S. but there are connections from most of the major U.S. airports. The nearest international airport with good European connections is Salt Lake City, from where you can drive (about 280 miles/450 km) or fly to Jackson.

Yellowstone National Park's south entrance is just 55 miles (88 km) north of town and is responsible, along with Grand Teton National Park, for a busy summer season. That also accounts for the winter

◄ **WATERING HOLES**
Lit up below the dark grandeur of the Teton Mountains, Jackson Hole offers lively après ski and seriously good regional cooking.

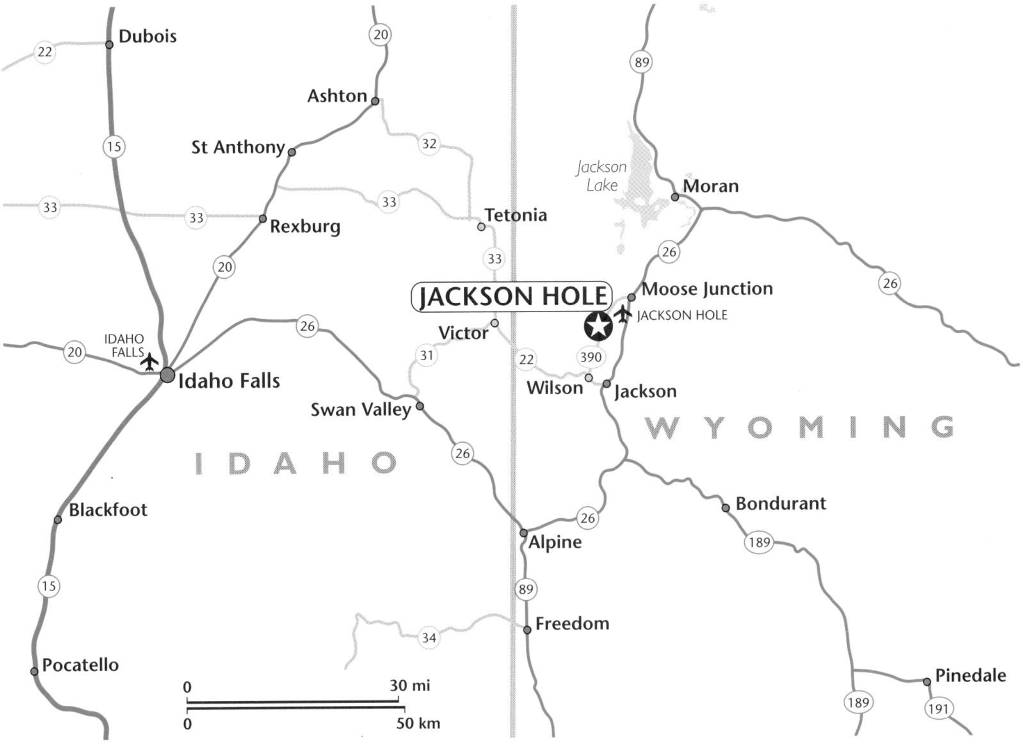

low season—a strange anomaly for one of the world's great ski resorts—and ensures there's always a good range of accommodations to choose from.

An hour and a half by car from Jackson on the other side of the Tetons is the cat-ski and powder mecca, Grand Targhee, an easy (and essential) day trip for visitors to Jackson Hole.

THE VILLAGE

Deciding where to stay in Jackson isn't easy. Slopeside in Teton Village seems sensible for any keen skier who wants to make the most of the skiing, but the town of Jackson Hole, with the majority of lodgings, dining and nightlife venues, is unique—as close to a real wild west town as you're ever likely to spit in.

The architectural style is right in the mood: western-style saloons and shop fronts, galleried wooden sidewalks and hitching posts. If you took a wrong turn in the morning, you feel you could easily spend your day branding cattle rather than making your mark on the slopes. But don't be fooled: Jackson is now home to more millionaires than cowboys, with luxurious ranches scattered over the surrounding area and a range of luxury hotel accommodations to match.

In-town is definitely the place for non-skiers, with plenty of diversions nearby, including snowmobile riding (outfitters offer full-day and half-day trips throughout the valley) and the National Elk Refuge which organizes sleigh rides through the giant herds of elk that make Jackson Hole their home during the winter months.

Twelve miles (32 km) away, Teton Village has some of the western feel of Jackson, despite being a purpose-built ski resort. It's the place to stay if you want to really maximize time on the slopes. Most accommodations are within a short walk of the lifts, and there are all the amenities you are likely to need within the village, including stores, restaurants, and après-ski venues. Nevertheless, one or more après ski visits to town are essential. There's a US$2 (infrequent) bus service for which you can buy a book of tickets, or it's a 15-minute cab ride.

The Village is currently undergoing expansion and renovation with over US$60 million spent on improving resort facilities since 1996. Along with

MOUNTAIN FACTS

Base	6,311 feet (1,923 m)
Summit	10,450 feet (3,185 m)
Elevation	4,139 feet (1,262 m)
Easy	10%
Intermediate	40%
Advanced/Expert	50%
Number of trails	76
Longest trail	4.5 miles (7.2 km)
Ski area	2,500 acres (1,012 ha)

SNOWFALL

Annual snowfall	402 inches (1,021 cm)
Snowmaking	160 acres (65 ha)

SKI LIFTS

Cable Car	1
Gondolas	1
High-Speed Quads	2
Fixed Grip Quads	4
Triple Chairs	1
Double Chairs	1
Surface Lifts	2
Total	12
Riders per hour	12,096

SKI SEASON
Early December to mid-April

▼ TETON VILLAGE
Three- and four-bedroom Moose Creek Townhomes are at the high rate for condos but offer top-of-the-range facilities.

▲ **AERIAL TRAM**
Jackson's 63-person lift is one of 11 lifts servicing Après Vous and Rendezvous mountains.

ACCOMMODATIONS

EXPENSIVE

AMANGANI RESORT
1535 North East Butte Rd., Jackson
307-734-7333

SNAKE RIVER LODGE AND SPA
Teton Village
307-732-6000

TETON MOUNTAIN LODGE
Teton Village
307-734-7111

SPRING CREEK RANCH
Top of Gros Venture Butte
1800 Spirit Dance Road
307-733-8833

MODERATE

RUSTY PARROT LODGE
P.O. Box 1657, Jackson
307-733-2000

INN AT JACKSON HOLE
3345 McCollister Drive,
Teton Village
307-733-2311

WORT HOTEL
Downtown Jackson
307-733-2190

BUDGET

HOSTEL X
Teton Village
307-733-3415

CONDOS AND HOUSES

JACKSON HOLE RESORT LODGING
307-733-3990

Check out www.jacksonhole.com for more options.

updated ski infrastructure, several new skier-oriented provisions have been made, including a kids' ranch building, retail space, ski rentals, lockers, and food and drink outlets. Three new hotels have also opened, with the Four Seasons Resort, Jackson Hole, planned to open in December 2003. It will be Teton Village's premier hotel and the first Four Seasons Resort in a ski resort anywhere in the world.

ACCOMMODATIONS

There are eleven hotels in Teton Village and many more in and around the town of Jackson Hole. In the Village there's a wide range from upmarket places right through to a hostel, just yards from the lifts, which makes the out-of-town motels around Jackson irrelevant to budget skiers, except in the busiest periods, and dispenses with the need for a rental car.

The recently renovated Best Western Inn has good quality accommodations, including loft suites complete with fireplace, and split level bedrooms and sitting rooms. It also houses the excellent (and improbable) Masa Sushi Japanese restaurant, which provides a welcome change to the red meat served in large portions almost everywhere else in town. The smaller Alpenhof Lodge has a Bavarian- style interior, serves good food, and has a private pool and hot tub.

In Jackson Hole, the centrally located Rusty Parrot Lodge is well recommended, with good dining and full facilities. Out of town, the Amangani Resort provides the most luxurious escape. There are also a wide range of self-catering accommodations in Jackson, in the Village, and between the two.

SKI AREA

Jackson has two main mountains: the big one, Rendezvous (10,450 feet/3,185 m) and the smaller Après Vous (8,481 feet/2,585 m). Lifts to both mountains start from the base area in Teton Village and several traversing trails connect the two mountains in both directions.

The ski area covers 2,500 acres (1,012 ha) and has one of North America's biggest verticals (4,139 feet/1,262 m). But more important than the size of the drop is how steeply it descends: much of the inbounds terrain makes even accomplished skiers think twice, with around 50 percent of the mountain designated advanced or expert, 40 percent for intermediates, and 10 percent (at best) for beginners. There are rock-lined chutes and steep bowls in this category as well as wide-open, rolling slopes, and groomed cruisers for intermediates. The longest trail is 4.5 miles (7.2 km).

Probably the most famous single trail at Jackson is Corbett's Couloir—there's a grandstand view of the leap into it from the aerial tram (cable car) passing overhead. In fact, Corbett's is just one of many opportunities to tackle truly steep and

▼ **CORBERT'S COULOIR**
Straight down below Corbet's Cabin near the peak of Rendezvous Mountain, lies the rock-lined long jump that is Corbet's Couloir—Jackson's most notorious descent.

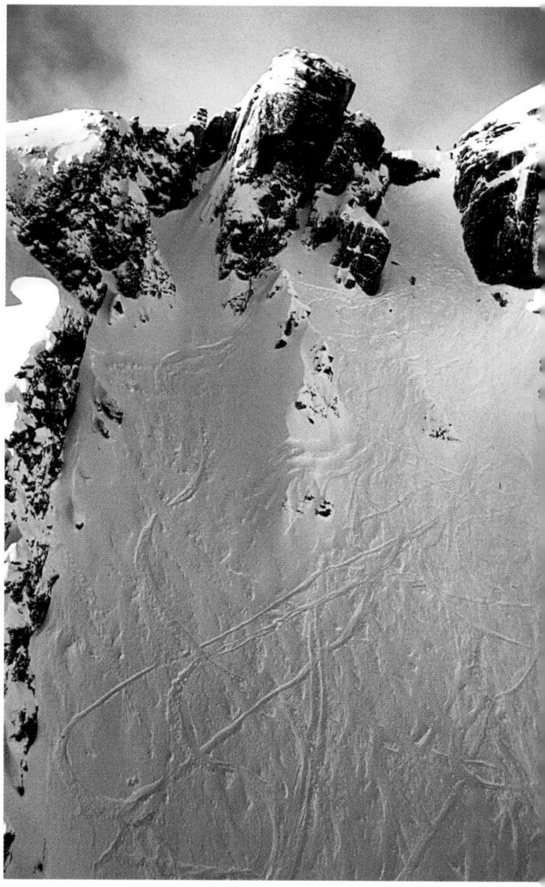

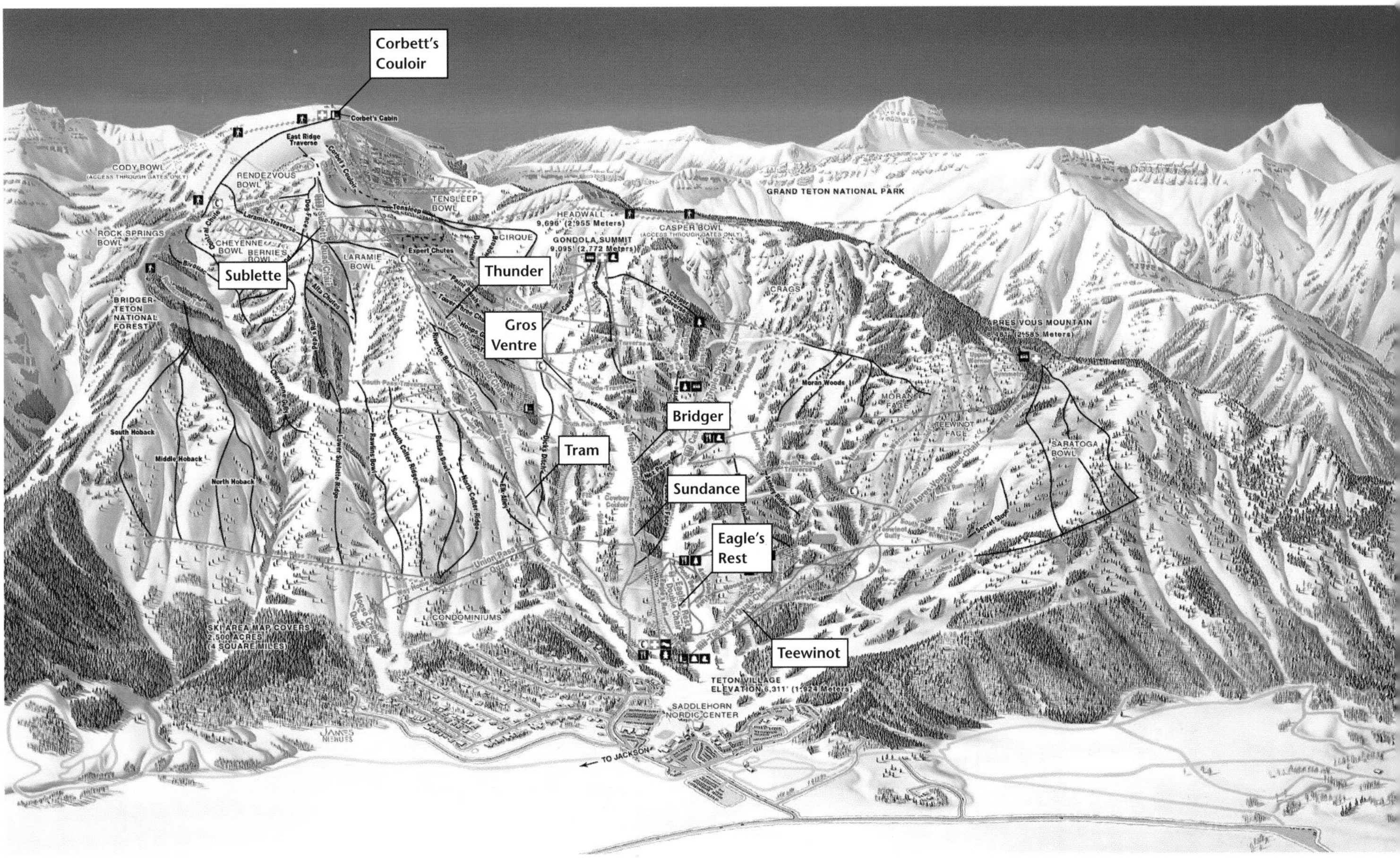

challenging terrain; virtually every part of the mountainside between the major trails can be skied, though in many cases, these areas are for extreme skiers only, particularly those willing to "get air" off the many cliffs.

Snow cannons cover 10 percent of the area, looking after conditions on the lower slopes—the base of the resort is quite low by Rockies standards—but the steeps rely on the average annual snowfall of 402 inches (1,021 cm) for cover, enough to give good conditions every other day when averaged out over the whole season.

Snow King is Jackson's local ski area, entirely separate from the main slopes. There are 400 acres (162 ha) with 1,571 feet (479 m) of descent, some of which is floodlit for night skiing. It's mostly for advanced skiers with just a quarter for intermediates and 15 percent for beginners, so novices shouldn't mistake it for a nursery area.

Grand Targhee—just 90 minutes away—is famous for its powder. On average it gets 25 percent more snowfall over the season than Jackson, but is nearly deserted for much of the time. It has recently expanded its lift-served terrain to over 2,000 acres (809 ha) but still has a cat-skiing operation to access the best powder. It's ideal for keen intermediates to experience deep-snow skiing as the terrain is noticeably less steep than at Jackson, but bring your goggles: the frequent low cloud that shrouds the slopes earns the resort the name "Grand Foggee" from the locals.

SKI LIFTS

Jackson's lifts have a total capacity of 12,096 skiers per hour and run from 9:00 AM to 4:00 PM. The centerpiece of the system is still the old cable car, "the Tram;" there's also one gondola, eight chairlifts (two of which are high-speed quads) and one magic carpet.

The Tram carries a maximum of 63 people and, lift lines permitting, is the quickest way from base to the highest point on Rendezvous. It invariably attracts a lot of skiers right through the day, even when the rest of the resort seems empty. This is mainly because it's the only lift reaching the magnificent wide sweep of the Rendezvous Bowl—steep, but frequently in great condition and not as intimidating as its pitch might suggest—and the backcountry of Cody Bowl and beyond. With its height and exposure, the top is windy, which sometimes causes the lift to close.

The Bridger gondola, part of a recent lift-upgrading program, has helped relieve some of the pressure on the Tram. It bisects the ski area giving good access to much of the terrain including the

DAYCARE

JACKSON HOLE KIDS' RANCH
Infant & childcare: for ages 6 months to two years
Ski/snowboard programs for kids aged 3–14 years
307-739-2691

BABY-SITTING
Teton County Family Services
Certified independent childcare personnel
307-733-7757

▸ **THE TRAM**
The aerial tram and 63 people car, slow by modern standards, is still the quickest way up from base to the highest points on Rendezvous and the only lift to reach Rendezvous Bowl.

Casper Bowl backcountry area. The Sublette chair gives access to all of Rendezvous Mountain apart from the bowl.

The top of Après Vous Mountain is reached via Teewinot and Après Vous chairs.

LIFT PASSES

A daily pass costs US$61 for adults, US$31 for juniors/seniors (14 and under or 65 and over) and US$48 for those aged 15–21, but for beginners there is a restricted ticket allowing unlimited access to Teewinot and Eagle's Rest chair lifts at the base of Rendezvous Mountain for US$10 per day. Children aged five and under ski for free on these two lifts.

Ticketing is flexible, with passes allowing you to ski for three days within a four-day period and variations on this theme up to skiing 10 days within a two-week visit. A three-in-four pass costs US$174, with reductions for children and seniors.

Passes can be bought at the Bridger Center or at the Clock Tower in the base area. No photo I.D. is required for the passes. A Snow King day pass costs US$32. Night skiing, between 4:00–7:00 PM Tuesday through Saturday costs US$15 per session. Grand Targhee passes cost US$49. and the Targhee Express includes transport and lift pass for US$61 per day.

SKI SCHOOLS AND GUIDING

Jackson has one ski and snowboard school, which also teaches Nordic skiing. Normal hours are 9:00 AM until 4:00 PM, although some classes make use of the early tram at 8.30 AM. Group size is often from three to five people, but can reach over ten during peak times. And if you're considering a lesson for getting to know your way around, there is a free tour of the mountain starting from the Host building every day at 9.30 AM.

With the serious terrain on offer, Jackson also attracts specialist ski camps, including women only and steep and deep clinics. Guides can also be hired to take you into the backcountry in groups of up to five people.

There is a daycare facility at Jackson Hole Kids' Ranch for children aged from six months to three years, and kids' ski school for children aged 3–14. Supervision of young children during lunchtime is part of the package if they are enrolled for a full day.

BEGINNERS

Beginners have far fewer opportunities. Just 10 percent of Jackson's terrain is designated suitable for beginners, and the resort is not suitable for a party of novices. The terrain off Eagle's Rest and Teewinot chairlifts offers the best beginner skiing and it's all found on Après Vous Mountain's much gentler profile.

The beginner lift ticket does give access to the green terrain at very good value, but moving to blue trails gives a choice of tame link trails traversing the

SKI GUIDES

SKI & SNOWBOARD SCHOOL
Alpine guides for untracked powder, challenging trails, and backcountry skiing
307-739-2663
www.jacksonhole.com/skiing/gserve.html

GRAND TARGHEE GUIDES
Snowcat trips, alpine tours, mountain tours, backcountry, and X-C.
800-827-4433
www.grandtarghee.com

RENDEZVOUS SKI & SNOWBOARD
Guided tours in Grand Teton Park, Teton Pass, Targhee backcountry.
Nordic, alpine, snowboard & avalanche instruction.
877-754-4887
www.skithetetons.com

SNOW KING MOUNTAIN GUIDES
Guided tours off the back of Snow King and Teton Pass for both Nordic and alpine skiers 307-734-3030
www.snowking.com

mountain, or more serious intermediate terrain which doesn't really offer the stepping stone needed by progressing beginners. A further drawback is that all the easy terrain is at the lowest altitudes and is likely to suffer if there's a shortage of snow.

INTERMEDIATES

Although intermediates would be ill-advised to try skiing from the top of the Tram, they can still access enough of the resort—around 40 percent—from other lifts to give a taste of big mountain skiing and, therefore, a true taste of Jackson, although a willingness to explore (sensibly) the mountain rather than simply following the trail map will be helpful.

Après Vous Mountain provides much of the intermediate terrain; smooth groomers allow the skier to cruise through wide slopes. There are also opportunities for low-risk tree skiing and amazing views of the valley below.

From Bridger gondola more blues are accessible. The longest runs at this level—Gros Ventre and Sundance Gully—give 2,700 vertical feet (823 m) of descent. A total of 22 miles (35 km) of the resort is groomed; a grooming map explains the state of the trails each day, which is particularly relevant for skiers who are unable to cope with tough or deep conditions.

For upper intermediates, there's also the northern side of Laramie Bowl, probably the toughest skiing that could fall into this category. Bear in mind when venturing onto back terrain for the first time, that some guidance is useful—probably best attempted in the company of ski school—to help avoid getting caught out on steep, moguled terrain.

ADVANCED

Jackson has a well-deserved reputation for having much of North America's most advanced ski terrain. The shape of the mountains (steep), their size, and the fact that so much of the hillside is designated skiable, means that a lot of skiing is packed into the area. Around half the resort's trails are black or double black. There are crazy chutes, moguls, steeps, deeps, trees, and thousands of acres of backcountry.

Rendezvous Mountain via the Tram has to be the place to start, with the ultimate views. If you are feeling fit, there is 4,139 vertical feet (1,261 m) to ski down to base, almost entirely on black trails. Prevailing conditions will affect your day-to-day plans, with narrow gullies staying in shape long after powder bowls have been skied out. But when the powder's fresh, the hobacks are the place to go—a collection of bowls to the extreme (skier's) right of the resort. Part of the charm is their distance from lifts and their remote feel—you return to base via a low-level traverse.

Rendezvous Bowl is also unbeatable, if frequently windy and cold. It's steep, but wide and clear of obstacles, allowing skiers to let rip without fear of

▲ **TYPICAL TETON**
Mottled granite peaks and facades with powder bowls, spruce thickets below and wide open slopes form the patchwork that is Jackson Hole. This is an off-piste skier's dream—and the backcountry options in the Grand Teton National Park are limitless. Yet ironically for most Americans, Jackson Hole remains somewhere to stop off in summer en route to the nation's oldest, largest and best-known national park, Yellowstone, some two hour's drive north.

◄ **EXPERT REWARDS**
The skiing at Jackson Hole rates as one of the most exhilerating and challenging for experts —50% of the terrain is designated as advanced/expert.

EATING ON THE MOUNTAIN

CASPER RESTAURANT
At the base of the Casper Chairlift

THUNDER CAFÉ
At the base of the Thunder lift

CORBET'S CABIN
At the top of the Aerial Tram

NICK WILSON'S COWBOY CAFÉ
Mountain side of the Tram Tower building

BRIDGER BAGELS
Bridger Building at the base of the Gondola

BARS

- MANGY MOOSE
- NICK WILSON'S COWBOY CAFÉ
- OUT OF BOUNDS GRILL
- THE BAR AT THE ALPENHOF
- THE RANCHER
- CALICO
- VISTA GRANDE
- THE SHADY LADY
- THE MILLION DOLLAR COWBOY BAR
- SIDEWINDER'S SPORTS & CIGAR BAR
- THE STAGE COACH

collisions. From the Sublette quad, Laramie Bowl and the steep Alta Chutes are easy to find and can be skied without returning back to base each time. Likewise, for bump trails, Thunder (served by the Thunder quad) allows high-level skiing—ideal if it hasn't snowed for a while and the lower mountain becomes tough, bumpy, and has more natural hazards exposed.

In case of snowy weather, the Moran Woods between Headwall and Après Vous are the place for tree skiing. Also from the gondola are gates to Casper Bowl for more powder.

EXPERT

Jackson truly deserves this category, as distinct from "advanced." Along with much of the backcountry, there are plenty of real challenges, from Corbett's Couloir, near the top of Rendezvous, downward. Corbett's infamy stems from the view from the Tram as much as anything: seeing skiers from above making the ten- or twenty-foot leap (6-m) from the cornice into a 50-degree couloir is the closest many people get to this kind of skiing. But it's not the toughest trail on the mountain. The nearby Expert chutes from Thunder quad are part cliff, part steep chute and forgive very few mistakes.

▼ BEYOND THE BOUNDS
The most accessible back-country terrain is in Cody Bowl to the south of Rendezvous Bowl. A north-facing exposure and wide open bowl powder add up to superb serious skiing.

CODY PEAK
Pro riders love this spot on Cody Peak for arcing turns and getting fabulous views of the Teton Range. Access to Cody Bowl is through designated gates only.

Backcountry, accessed by several gates around the resort, is big. Rock Springs, Cody, and Casper Bowls are the main areas. All this terrain requires that groups are properly equipped and, ideally, accompanied by a guide.

Hiring a guide for backcountry trips is not just a safe option, but the way to find the best snow and terrain suited to the group's abilities. The terrain is not exclusively in the expert category, though it is peppered with natural hazards, requiring skiers to be able to operate in full control, whatever the conditions.

A backcountry yurt was built for the 2002/03 season. Just outside the resort boundary in lower Rock Springs Bowl, it gives skiers the opportunity to experience a backcountry hut-and-ski touring trip without venturing too far off the beaten path.

There is also heli-skiing available in the nearby Snake River Mountains with High Mountain Heli-skiing (307-733-3274).

BOARDING & FREESTYLE

Jackson is as much a mecca for expert boarders as it is for skiers.

There is a terrain park and halfpipe at the base of Après Vous mountain, but the real draw is the

natural terrain and the snow conditions. Some of the traverses are tough for boarders to maintain speed on.

EATING ON THE MOUNTAIN

There are snack food outlets at three points on the mountain, and Casper Restaurant—a cafeteria. Given the layout of the mountain, it's easy to return to base to eat where there is a greater choice and more capacity. Nick Wilson's at the Clock Tower has salads and an outdoor barbecue, while the Mangy Moose serves a wide range of food.

APRÈS SKI

In Teton Village most people head for the Mangy Moose at the end of the day. The party atmosphere is often boosted by live music, presided over by the stuffed moose hanging from the ceiling. There are micro brews to choose from as well as an extensive bar menu. One of the top bar-restaurant and entertainment complexes in North America, après ski at the Moose is legendary.

The quieter Village Café offers many beers on tap and the best pizza in Teton Village; it's a good spot to meet locals and hear about some extreme ski exploits. The Cascade Bar in the Teton Mountain Lodge has a fireside setting, an extensive beer and wine list, and avoids the noise and frenzy of more typical après-ski locations.

In Jackson the most famous watering holes are the western saloon bars such as the Million Dollar Cowboy Bar, and the Silver Dollar. In the Million Dollar, you can sit at the bar on a saddle, watching the pool players or just taking in the atmosphere. There's also dancing on some nights. The Silver Dollar is slightly quieter; it gets its name from the silver dollars that are inlaid into the bar.

The minimum age for consuming alcohol is 21, but children can accompany parents in bars.

There's no shortage of good eating in Jackson. The Vertical Restaurant, located in the Inn at Jackson Hole, offers comtemporary American cuisine in a modern setting and an extensive wine list. In town, the Kosho wine bar has an eclectic wine list and a menu to match.

OTHER ACTIVITIES

Saddlehorn Nordic Center at the base area offers 14 miles (22 km) of Nordic skating and touring lanes, in addition to snowshoeing and dog-sledding. Night skiing is available at Snow King resort. Jackson also has a recreation center and iceskating.

There are also snowmobile tours, sleigh rides and horse riding through the surrounding mountains. Yellowstone National Park, with wildlife and hot spring viewing, can be visited by snowcoach or snowmobile.

USEFUL PHONE NUMBERS

Tourist Information Center	307-733-2292
Central Reservations	800-443-6931
Doctor	307-739-2735
Ski Patrol & Rescue Service	307-739-2650
Teton Village Taxi	307-690-6676

USEFUL WEBSITES

Official Website	www.jacksonhole.com
Jackson Hole Dining Guide	www.focusproductions.com
Other Activities & Businesses	www.jacksonholenet.com
Avalanche Hazard & Weather Forecast	www.jhavalanche.org

RESTAURANTS

EXPENSIVE

GAMEFISH
At the Snake River Lodge & Spa
307-733-6040

CASCADE
In the Teton Mountain Lodge, Teton Village
307-734-7111

SNAKE RIVER GRILL
On the Square in Jackson, 84 E, Broadway, Jackson
307-733-0557

OFF BROADWAY GRILLE
30 S. King St., Jackson
307-733-9777

MODERATE

VISTA GRANDE (MEXICAN)
Teton Village Road
307-733-6964

THE ALPENROSE BISTRO
In the Alpenhof Lodge, Teton Village.
307-733-3462

SNAKE RIVER BREWERY & RESTAURANT
265 S. Millward, Jackson
307-739-2337

MODERATE

VILLAGE CAFÉ
Great a-la-carte, located slopeside next to the clock tower.

NICK WILSON COWBOY CAFÉ
Mountain side of the Tram Tower building.

BILLY'S BURGERS
On the town square at 55 N. Cache Drive

See www.focusproductions.com for Jackson Hole online dining guide and menus from over 60 restaurants.

▼ MOUNTAINSIDE SELF-SERVICE
Located mid-mountain, Casper's restaurant is a popular rest spot.

STRADDLING NEVADA AND CALIFORNIA, AND OVERLOOKING LAKE TAHOE, NORTHSTAR IS WITHOUT GLITZ OR ATTITUDE, A COMFORTABLE, LAID-BACK PLACE WITH BUCKETS OF SNOW—AND WHEN THERE ISN'T FRESH SNOW, STATE-OF-THE-ART MACHINES CREATE IT. THE SKI AREA IS COMPACT AND EASY TO GET AROUND, WITH ONE SIDE OF THE MOUNTAIN READILY ACCESSIBLE FROM THE OTHER. GOOD FOR FAMILIES BUT NOT EXPERTS.

NORTHSTAR AT TAHOE

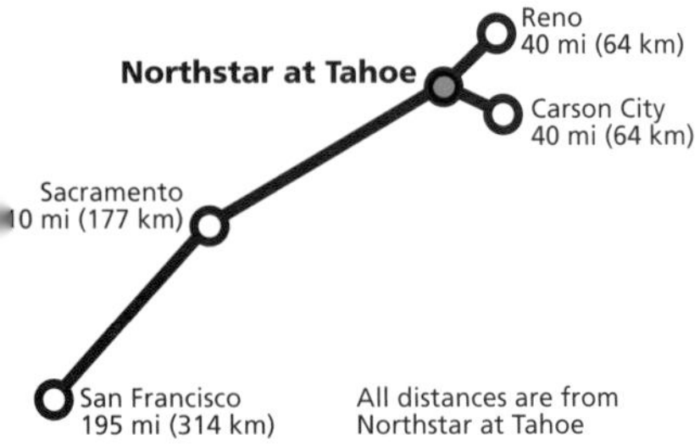

▼ LAKE TAHOE
The beautiful alpine Lake Tahoe is always visible from Northstar.

One of the Lake Tahoe ski resorts, Northstar has a reciprocal lift pass system with Alpine Meadows, Heavenly, Kirkwood, Sierra at Tahoe, and Squaw Valley. Between them they access over 17,000 acres (6,800 ha) of skiing. Northstar itself has 2,420 acres (968 ha) of skiable terrain and excellent snowmaking capabilities. With the ability to cover 24 football fields with a foot (30 cm) of snow in 24 hours, it can open early with a full mountain. The ski season runs from late November to mid-April. Peak season is December 20 to January 4, and February 14–22. There are 14 lifts serving the all-ability ski trails, two terrain parks, and facilities for cross-country skiing, snowmobiling and tubing.

GETTING THERE

Northstar is located halfway between Truckee and the north shore of Lake Tahoe. Truckee is 6 miles (9.6 km) away, on Highway 267. The nearest international airports are Reno/Tahoe, Sacramento, and San Francisco. Via Interstate 80, Reno is 40 miles (64 km) east (45 minutes), Sacramento is 110 miles

MOUNTAIN FACTS

Base	6,330 feet (1,899 m)
Summit	8,610 feet (2,583 m)
Elevation	2,280 feet (684 m)
Easy	25%
Intermediate	50%
Advanced/Expert	25%
Number of trails	70
Longest trail	3 miles (4.8 km)
Ski area	2,420 acres (968 ha)

SNOWFALL

Annual snowfall	350 inches (889 cm)
Snowmaking	50% of all runs

SKI LIFTS

Gondolas	1
High-Speed Quads	5
Triple Chairs	2
Double Chairs	1
T-bars	3
Magic Carpets	2
Total	14

SKI SEASON
Thanksgiving weekend to mid-April

(177 km) west (1 hour 45 minutes), and San Francisco is 195 miles (314 km) west (3 hours 30 minutes).

Amtrak (www.amtrak.com) has rail services and Greyhound (www.greyhound.com) has bus services to Truckee. Call 800-466-6784 24 hours in advance and you'll get a free shuttle to Northstar. To arrange transfer from Reno/Tahoe International Airport call Executive Limo (800-323-3958) or Tahoe Truckee Taxi (888-881-TAXI). Alternatively, you can rent a car, for although the complimentary on-site shuttle transportation eliminates the need to drive once you arrive at Northstar, a car will make it easier to explore the other Lake Tahoe resorts.

THE VILLAGE

At present, Northstar's small village includes three restaurants and a bar, winter apparel store, guest accommodations ranging from village lofts to studio condos and five-bedroom homes, and daycare for children. Over the next few years, Northstar plans to expand the resort and the village. As the initial step in the completion of the "Northstar vision," Northstar and East West Partners are enhancing the existing village by creating a warm, friendly, pedestrian-oriented village center with an outdoor ice-skating rink, adding more restaurants, sidewalk cafés, stores, and a world-class spa. There will be 200 new condominiums and townhomes located in the village area. At the time of writing we are unable to establish firm completion dates for some of these developments, so if they are important to you we advise you to check with the resort before booking.

ACCOMMODATIONS

There are 260 units on the mountain, ranging from hotel-style rooms through to five-bedroom homes. For reservations call 800-466-6784 or e-mail lodging.ns@boothcreek.com. There are lots of good deals available, including free lift passes and free lessons. Each unit is equipped with direct dial telephone, T.V. and V.C.R., all linens, and fully equipped kitchens.

The houses are scattered throughout the resort, with access to skiing and snowboarding, cross-country skiing and snowshoeing. All of the houses are located on beautiful wooded lots, and some boast

◄ WARM AND COZY
With 260 units Northstar can accommodate almost everyone, with options ranging from a cozy room in the Village to a spacious condominium or a custom mountain home.

▶ SUNSET
At the end of a day's fun exercise, kick your boots off, take a rest at one the two mountain restaurants and watch the sunset.

spectacular views of Martis Valley. Rooms and condos are not named, but on the website you can check out what you are getting. The houses are named, and range from three bedrooms with two bathrooms through to five bedrooms with three bathrooms.

All lodging guests can use Northstar's free on-site shuttle service and the Swim and Racquet Club. For further information on prices and availability refer to Northstar's website, www.skinorthstar.com. Alternatively, there are many hotels and motels in Truckee, about six miles (9.5 km) away.

NEARBY RESORTS

SKI AREA

Northstar's gladed ski area will appeal mostly to intermediates and beginners. Half the trails are for intermediates and although there is plenty of terrain for both beginners and advanced skiers and riders, experts are likely to be a little disappointed. The varied terrain includes long cruisers, moguls, tree skiing and a variety of freestyle terrain features for all levels of experience. The longest trail is 3 miles (4.7 km), and the most challenging trail—the black diamond Iron Horse—is a great challenge for intermediates. It's long and steep but groomed.

Lookout Mountain is a recent addition. It has 200 acres (80 ha) of advanced terrain accessed by a high-speed quad, Lookout Mountain Express. Lookout Mountain includes snowmaking, a vertical drop of 1,200 feet (360 m) and five black-diamond trails: Prosser, Stampede, Gooseneck, Boca, and Martis.

The ski area includes terrain parks for boarders and trick skiers, and for younger skiers and snowboarders, there are Paw Parks—terrain parks built just for kids where everything is their size. The parks are designed with bumps, jumps and secret hideouts as well as special snow play areas where kids can kick off their skis and snowboards and just have fun in the snow. And since the trails are built right off mainstream trails, parents are never far away. Paw Parks are patrolled by Northstar's ski patrol. There are Paw Parks at various locations—look for paw prints on the trail map to see where each park is located.

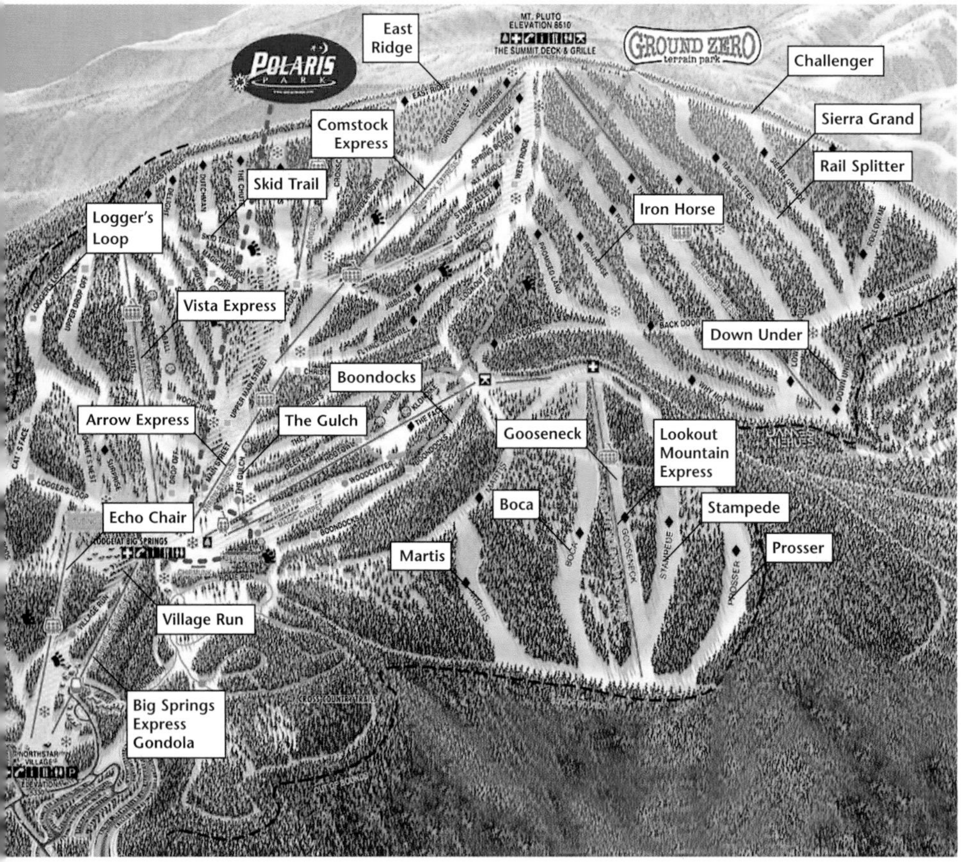

SKI LIFTS

Northstar has five high-speed quads, one triple chair that accesses the East Ridge, and a double chair that brings you to the freestyle terrain park. Out of the village, you can take either the Big Springs Express Gondola to mid-mountain or the Echo Chair triple chair to Vista Express. There are also four T-bars and one Magic Carpet. The lifts open 8:30 AM to 4:00 PM. Lift lines can be long on major holidays and busy weekends, but skiing on the Backside or Lookout Mountain can be surprisingly quiet even on busy days. There are plans to replace the Pioneer double chair with a high-speed quad and also to add a high-speed quad out of the village in 2003.

LIFT PASSES

There are lift passes to suit all ages and circumstances. Buy passes online at www.northstarattahoe.com, or in the village. Typically a day pass for a child (5–12 years) costs

US$19, a young adult (13–22 years) US$47, an adult (23–64 years) US$57, a senior (65–69 years) US$33, and for the over 70s it's just US$10. Half-day tickets start from 12:30 PM. Weekly passes cost US$102 for children, US$264 for young adults and US$318 for adults. There's also the useful "Parent Predicament" day ticket whereby for US$57 you get an interchangeable lift pass for both parents.

Vertical Plus is an innovative program that allows you to calculate the amount of vertical feet you ski or ride, while offering prizes, discounts and the convenience of electronic ticketing and members' only lift lines. Vertical Plus membership is interchangeable at one of Northstar's sister resorts, Sierra-at-Tahoe. Call 530-562-2267 or e-mail skinorthstar.com for more information.

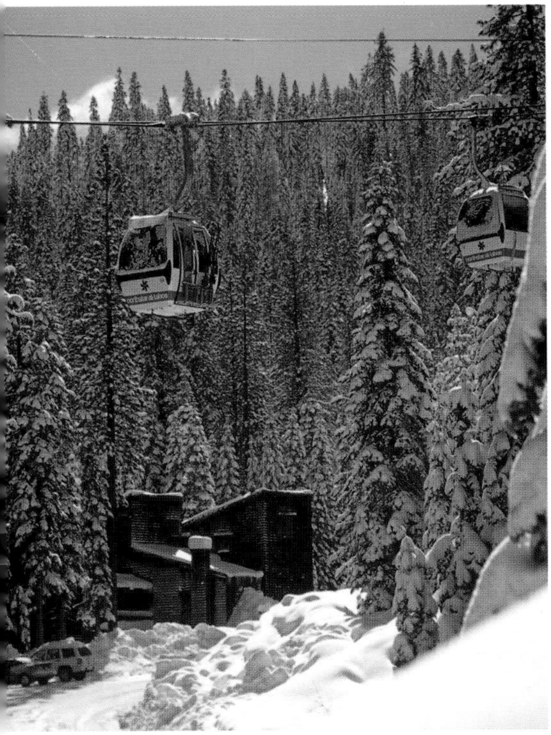

Daily lift passes are limited to avoid crowding. If a sellout occurs in the morning, afternoon tickets will not be sold. For a season pass, call 530-562-2267. If you aren't skiing, you can ride the Big Springs Express Gondola to the mid-mountain lodge for US$10.

SKI SCHOOLS AND GUIDING

There is one ski school, located at mid-mountain, which opens 9:00 AM to 3:30 PM. The maximum class size is 20 (too many!), but there are lots of different options for individual and smaller group lessons. Absolute beginners can opt for a special One-Day First Time package or a Three-Day Passport Package. Classes typically last two hours and include lessons, rental equipment, and lift passes.

Families of children aged 12 and under are well catered to with a range of options including Starkids (ages 6 to 12), Startykes (ages 4 to 6), and Tiny Tots (under 4).

During the low season, free two-hour lessons are offered daily to advanced intermediate and above skiers and riders (ages 13 and older), on a first-come, first-served basis. Instructors will be matched to your ability level. They'll show you the secret stashes only the locals know about. Meet at the top of the Comstock Express quad.

There are various freebies that go with private lessons: free demos, free hot wax and exclusive ski school lift lane access. Lessons last one to six hours. Reservations are recommended and remember to book early for peak season.

If you want to experience the peace of the mountain, away from the crowds, take a Nordic Ski Lesson. With just the sound of silence you can wind and dip through 30 miles (50 km) of groomed trails that lead via snow-filled forests to spectacular views of the Sierra Nevada and Lake Tahoe. Lessons in all styles of Nordic skiing are offered. Lesson packages include trail pass, equipment rental and lesson. The Nordic Ski & Snowshoe Center is at mid-mountain just past the Ski & Snowboard School.

BEGINNERS

The beginner area under the Bear Paw chair is ideal for first timers, with several trails all in one spot. Another option is to take the Vista Express quad and follow Skid Trail, then Lumberjack and into The Gulch, through the Bear Paw learning area and down Village Run to the base of the Big Springs Express gondola, where you started. Then you can do it all over again. Most beginners, once

▲ **PERFECTLY GROOMED**
State-of-the-art machinery creates both snow and groomed pistes in abundance.

SKI SCHOOL

ONE-DAY FIRST-TIME PACKAGE
Classes typically last 2 hours.
Includes lessons, rental equipment and lift pass.

THREE-DAY PASSPORT PACKAGE
Classes typically last 2 hours.
Includes lessons, rental equipment and lift pass.

STARKIDS FOR AGES 6–12
Kids' lessons for all ability levels.
Skiing, snowboarding, snow recreation, tubing.
Includes lessons, rental equipment and lift pass.
Lunch is included in the full-day option.

STARTYKES FOR AGES 4–6
Classes start indoors and then move out to the slopes for snow play.
Lunch is included in full-day lessons.

TEACH YOUR TOTS
For parents with smaller children.
Two-hour lesson for ages 4 and under.
Instructors help parents work with their children on developing their skills.

◄ **THE GONDOLA**
The Big Springs Express Gondola takes you out of the village to mid-mountain and plenty of adventures.

DAY CARE

Minors' Camp Day Care in the village offers childcare for ages two to six (must be toilet trained) from 8:30 AM to 4:30 PM daily. The day includes lunch, two snacks and the following activities: arts and crafts, science, language development, singing, lots of laughter, stories and storytelling. Learn-to-ski options are also available. Parents must remain on Northstar premises while their child is enrolled in Minors' Camp programs. Pagers are provided for parents of enrolled kids. Reservations recommended: 530-562-2278.

▼ LOOKOUT!
Lookout Mountain now has a dedicated expert area with steep moguls and tree trails.

comfortable on skis or a snowboard, can handle the blue trails off the Arrow Express chair.

INTERMEDIATES

With around 50 percent of the trails at Northstar designated suitable for intermediates, there are good long trails from the top of the mountain to the bottom. One choice might be to take the Arrow Express and then the Comstock Express quad to the summit. Then take the East Ridge trail to the top of the Vista Express quad, then Logger's Loop and The Woods to the base of the gondola. Alternatively you could take the West Ridge trail from the summit, then Lookout Road and Boondocks to join up with Home Run back to the base of the gondola. Between these two ridges are plenty of other single blues that join up easily with one another, making a day's skiing for intermediates full of variety.

ADVANCED & EXPERT

Advanced skiers have 25 percent of the mountain to entertain them. Take the Arrow Express and Comstock Express to the summit and head in the opposite direction from East Ridge along the black diamond Sierra Grande. There are several choices for descent (all black diamond trails): Rail Splitter or Challenger, or continue along Sierra Grande to join up with Challenger further down. Then either go for some backcountry skiing along Sawtooth Ridge (conditions permitting) or carry on along Down Under to the bottom of the Backside Express Chair and do it all over again. In 2000 a new black diamond area was opened on Lookout Mountain, with plenty of steep mogul and tree trails. It joins the rest of the mountain via the Pioneer chair. The Backside trees are best for powder. There are no double black diamond trails so experts may be disappointed. The only off-piste skiing area (conditions permitting) is at Sawtooth Ridge, off the black diamond trails below Mount Pluto.

BOARDING & FREESTYLE

Northstar is fairly easy for snowboarders to get around as most chairlifts have a continual fall line back to the bottom. For a shot of adrenaline, head to the SnowBomb Freestyle Parks and hit the bumps, jumps, jibs, tabletops, and halfpipes. The superpipe and halfpipe are located at mid-mountain, Northstar's biggest freestyle terrain park—nearly a mile (1.6 km) long. Other freestyle terrain parks and features are located on various runs on the front side of Northstar. All parks have snowmaking for solid cover. A professional grooming crew shapes and cuts the terrain features on a regular basis, providing fresh options for skiers and snowboarders. Look out for Epicenter, an on-mountain hangout with snacks, music and videos geared especially toward riders.

EATING ON THE MOUNTAIN

There are two mountain restaurants serving international, traditional, self-service, and fast food. All the restaurants have special kids' meals for those aged 12 years and under. On the mountain the best spot is the Summit Deck & Grille at the top of Mount Pluto, with great views of Lake Tahoe, but you must be able to ski/ride down on intermediate trails. The other choice is the Lodge at Big Springs. Open for breakfast and lunch daily, it has pizzas, burgers and salads, and for entertainment you can watch the boarders in the Superpipe below. Picnic tables are also available at the top of Vista, Pioneer and Comstock chairs.

APRÈS SKI

The two best places for après ski are the Alpine Bar in the village, and on the mountain the deck at the Lodge at Big Springs. All the bars are primarily après-ski places, so they are suitable for all and there

► BALANCING ON AIR
Boarders are kept entertained by a superpipe, halfpipe and several terrain parks.

RESTAURANTS & BARS

TIMBERCREEK RESTAURANT
CIPPOLINI'S PIZZERIA
THE VILLAGE FOOD COMPANY
ALPINE SPORTS BAR
MARTIS VALLEY GRILLE

◄ **RELAX ON HIGH**
With a wide variety of food on offer, Northstar's many restaurants and food halls caters to all tastes.

are no restrictions on children coming in. The Alpine Bar features major sporting events on multiple T.V.s, live music, games, pool tables and an arcade. Appetizers and full bar are available. The minimum legal age to be able to buy or drink alcohol is 21 years.

In the village, Timbercreek Restaurant has been voted one of Tahoe's best restaurants. Try out its California-American cuisine, with hints of Pacific Rim flair. The Ski Express breakfast buffet, lunch and dinner are served daily mid-December through April. There's also an après-ski bar with café and children's menu. Reservations recommended. At Cippolini's Pizzeria there's homemade pizza and calzones with soup and a salad bar. Use the on-mountain pizza phone at the top of the Big Springs Express Gondola to place your order. Takeout orders are welcome. Go to the Village Food Company for daily breakfast specials, sandwiches and sushi for lunch, and dinner specials.

A unique feature at Northstar is Polaris Park, across from the Lodge at Big Springs, an evening adventure park for skiing, boarding, tubing, snow toys, live entertainment and dancing. It's open most Fridays, Saturdays and peak season evenings until 7:00 PM. Tickets can be obtained from the Tubing Center at the top of the gondola.

OTHER ACTIVITIES

If you're tired of skiing and want to try something different, Northstar has 30 miles (50 km) of cross-country terrain, full work-out facilities at the Swim & Racquet Club, tubing, snowmobile tours and dogsled rides. The Swim & Racquet Club has a pool, three outdoor spas, a youth center with a full range of activities, and a fitness center.

Snowmobile tours are offered daily. Day tours are approximately two hours, and evening tours are one hour long. Call 530-562-2267 for reservations. Dogsled tours start at the front of Martis Valley Grille at the golf course. There are teams of eight or nine dogs and the maximum load for a sled is two adults plus two children, or four children. For reservations call Wilderness Adventures on 530-550-8133.

Snow toys are available from Tube Town at mid-mountain from noon to 4:00 PM. Head down the mountain on a snowbike or take to the half-pipe on a snowscoot. Or maybe try your hand at a skifox, which will carve short or long turns. All snow toys are for 12 years and older except for the K2 Juniorbike for ages 8 to 12. There's also a packed events calendar that takes shape every season—check out the website at www.northstarattahoe.com for full details.

USEFUL PHONE NUMBERS

Tourist Office	530-587-2757
Village Information Center	530-562-3555
Transportation Department	530-562-2257
Ski Rescue Service	530-562-2404
Taxi	888-881-8294
Central Reservations	800-466-6784
Lift Tickets	530-562-2267
Ski School	530-562-2470
Nordic Skiing	530-562-2475

USEFUL WEBSITES & E-MAIL ADDRESSES

Official Website	www.skinorthstar.com
Lodgings Reservations	lodging.ns@boothcreek.com

▼ **CROSS-COUNTRY**
There are 30 miles (50 km) of cross-country skiing at Northstar, with enough variety for beginners to advanced skiers.

SQUAW VALLEY—THE BIRTHPLACE OF AMERICAN EXTREME SKIING—IS A MECCA FOR FREERIDERS AND EXTREME SKIERS. BUT DON'T BE PUT OFF IF YOUR STYLE IS MORE SEDATE OR FAMILY ORIENTED, BECAUSE THIS RESORT ALSO BOASTS GENTLE MOUNTAIN TOP BEGINNER TERRAIN AS WELL AS MOUNTAIN TOP ICE SKATING AND SWIMMING.

SQUAW VALLEY

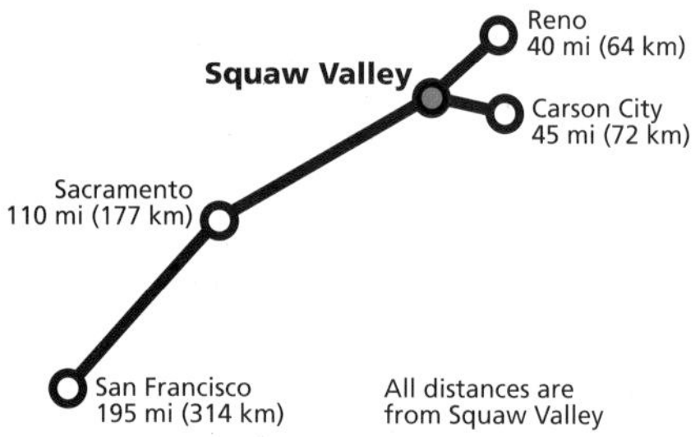

SKI SEASON
Mid November to late April

Located at the end of a stunning alpine valley, Squaw Valley lies cradled by six high Sierra peaks dominated by Squaw Peak at 8,900 feet (2,715 m). Squaw is historic: it famously played host to the 1960 Winter Olympic Games (the first to be televised), and Squaw Valley's Olympic heritage is still evident throughout the resort. The symbolic Tower of Nations and Olympic Flame still greet visitors at the entrance to the Valley, and Alexander Cushing, Squaw Valley's Chairman and Founder, still provides the vision and character by which Squaw Valley became, and continues to be, famous. Many wonder how he convinced the International Olympic Committee to select a town with no mayor, and a ski resort with just one chairlift, two rope tows, and a fifty-room lodge—but convince them he did, and the rest is history.

Since then Squaw has become one of the top destination resorts in the U.S. Ranked 4th Best Resort in North America by readers of *Skiing Magazine* and *Freeskier* magazine, it attracts those mad skiers who like to push the extreme envelope. Back in 1984, ski

► ADRENALINE AWAITS
There are ample proving grounds for extreme freeriders on Squaw's slopes—particularly after a hefty snowfall with plenty of fresh powder to cushion the impact.

filmmaker Warren Miller caught one Scot Schmidt jumping 100 feet (30 m) from the palisades (a cliff band at the top of Squaw Peak—the highest of six encompassing Squaw Valley) to give birth to "Schmidiots" and extreme skiing U.S.-style. No wonder top freeskiers and snowboarders like Shane McConkey, Brad Holmes, Darian Boyle, Aaron McGovern, Jeff McKitterick, Jenn Berg, and Tom Wayes can often be seen hurling themselves off Squaw's many cornices or trying new tricks in the park. Many agree too that the sheer depth and density of the snow here is another unique feature that gives some measure of control to even the wackiest stunts. If an ample 4,000 acres (1,620 ha) of bowl skiing doesn't turn you on, then how about mountain top ice skating and swimming which, at the Swimming Lagoon & Spa at High Camp (over 8,000 feet/2,450 m) overlooking Lake Tahoe, is free with all daily lift tickets.

GETTING THERE

It's an easy 42 miles (72 km) by car from the Reno/Tahoe International Airport Valley, along Interstate 80 (open in all weather) and it takes just one hour until you reach the single Squaw Valley Road that takes you into Olympic Valley. From Tahoe (5 miles/8 km away) or Truckee (8 miles/12 km) follow Highway 89. Sacramento lies 110 miles (177 km) away, and San Francisco 195 miles (314 km). There are daily shuttles from Reno (40 miles/64 km away) and Lake Tahoe, and rental cars and S.U.V.s (sports utility vehicles) are also available through Squaw Valley Central Reservations. The daily shuttle buses from Reno and South Lake Tahoe hotels cost only US$5 round trip per person!

THE VILLAGE

The village is small with around a dozen or so main buildings and has the close-knit feel of a quaint European village, but it is the ski area that draws visitors, not the village. The 2001/02 season marked the transformation of Squaw Valley into a true four-season recreation destination with major new developments by Intrawest. Highlighting the changes was the grand opening of Phase I (of 4) of the much-anticipated 13-acre village, estimated to cost around US$250 million.

Phase One, called First Ascent, brought new slopeside lodgings, shopping, and eateries to the resort's base area. It's dramatically changed the face of Squaw Valley by adding three buildings including 139 mountain side condominiums, 19 stores and restaurants, and approximately 250 underground parking spaces.

Phase Two of the project, named 22 Station, is scheduled for completion for the 2002/2003 winter season. At completion, the European-style village will include a total of 640 lodgings units and 80 boutique stores, restaurants, and galleries that will redefine the resort and meet the need for more accommodations within Squaw Valley.

ACCOMMODATIONS

There are over 50 properties in the area and in Reno, with seven hotels within the Valley (as well as condos, lakefront lodges, and bed and breakfast

NEARBY RESORTS

There are a dozen ski areas in the Lake Tahoe area. Squaw Valley and Heavenly are the main destination resorts but you can easily visit several others, such as Alpine Meadows, Kirkwood, and Sugar Bowl, spending a day or two at each.

MOUNTAIN FACTS

Base elevation	6,200 feet (1,889 m)
Summit	9,050 feet (2,758 m)
Elevation	2,850 feet (868 m)
Easy	25%
Intermediate	45%
Advanced/Expert	30%
Number of trails	100
Longest trail	3.2 miles (5.1 km)
Ski area	4,000 acres (1,619 ha)

SNOWFALL

'93-94	266 inches (675 cm)
'94–95	734 inches (1,864 cm)
'95–96	467 inches (1,186 cm)
'96–97	416 inches (1,056 cm)
'97–98	545 inches (1,384 cm)
'98–99	530 inches (1,346 cm)
'99–00	341 inches (866 cm)
'00–01	362 inches (919 cm)
'01–02	422 inches (1,071 cm)
9-year average	453 inches (1,150 cm)
Snowmaking	7 miles (11 km)

SKI LIFTS

Cable Car	1
Funitel	1
Gondolas	1
High-Speed Six-Pac	3
High-Speed Quads	4
Fixed Quad	1
Triple Chairlifts	8
Double Chairlifts	9
Surface Lifts	4
Magic Carpets	1
Total	33
Riders per hour	49,000

ACCOMMODATIONS

EXPENSIVE
RESORT AT SQUAW CREEK
PLUMPJACK SQUAW VALLEY INN
INTRAWEST SQUAW VALLEY INN

MODERATE
SQUAW VALLEY LODGE
OLYMPIC VILLAGE INN
RED WOLF LODGE

Squaw Valley Central Reservations
800-545-4350
www.squawvacations.com

inns). The PlumpJack Squaw Valley Inn is a luxury boutique hotel built in 1959 as a home for the 1960 Olympic delegation. Completely renovated in 1995 to create a special ambience of comfort and style, the tradition of entertaining guests as dignitaries continues. The Resort at Squaw Creek is a luxury resort hotel with its own chairlift connecting to the lifts system. The Intrawest Squaw Valley Inn has luxury condominiums, and the Squaw Valley Lodge offers moderately priced condominiums, likewise the Olympic Village Inn is a moderate hotel with condominiums. The Red Wolf Lodge and the Tavern Inn offer moderate condominiums. Squaw Valley Central Reservations represents most properties within Squaw Valley and nearby Tahoe City, Truckee, and also in Reno. Call Squaw Valley Central Reservations at 800-545-4350 or check out the website: www.squawvacations.com

SKI AREA

It's not unusual to hear a first-time skier at Squaw ask "Where are all the trails?" and it's true that Squaw is unique in the U.S. as it offers wide-open bowl skiing rather than traditional, named ski trails. The vast lift-served acreage is the fifth largest U.S. resort and you are actively encouraged to use the lifts as a reference. Lifts are rated beginner, intermediate and advanced, based on the type of terrain that they access. In that respect the area offers 25 percent beginner, 45 percent intermediate, and 30 percent expert terrain, encompassing 16 open bowls and well over 100 runs. The highest elevation is 9,050 feet (2,758 m) while the lowest elevation is 6,200 feet (1,889 m)—that's a vertical drop of 2,850 feet (868 m).

This ski area is famous for terrain ranging from the tamest to the toughest. The high peaks and bowls are treeless but lower down much of the terrain is lightly wooded. Skiers and snowboarders will delight in the variety. The steep chutes and dynamic descents of KT-22 (22 kick turns to make it down safely) beckon the wild freeskiers while miles of groomed trails, and wide open mountain bowls for cruising cradle the novice. And two beginner areas (one at peak level, one at base level) satisfy all other levels of skier. Mix in long intermediate cruisers, expanded terrain parks, halfpipes, and panoramic views of Lake Tahoe, and Squaw Valley is surely a must-visit ski destination.

The more advanced "expert only" skiing is not for adventurous intermediates nor for the foolhardy, who could easily find themselves in serious difficulty (or worse!) with cliffs and potentially fatal falls waiting for the unwary. Just about everything is

► NO WAITING IN LINE
"The most advanced lift network in the world" is a tough claim to make, but make it Squaw does...

visible from the lifts but newcomers wishing to venture into unfamiliar expert sections are well advised to join an Advanced Ski Clinic or find a guide. But there is no need for beginners and intermediates to be put off by Squaw's reputations for ski extreme: the ski area is well marked with a variety of safety markers including "slow" signs, ropes, bamboo poles, and markers that explain a range of characteristics of the terrain. In addition, members of the Ski Patrol regularly ski the mountain to ensure the safety of the guests and offer assistance if needed.

Lack of snow is not going to be a problem here, since Squaw has invested over US$8 million over the last decade in its state-of-the-art snowmaking system which enhances natural snow conditions and ensures consistent snow coverage. The artificial snow system includes over 500 snowmaking guns—some fixed, others portable, allowing the snowmaking crew to make snow in areas beyond the normal coverage zones—and it covers some seven miles (11 km) or 10 percent of the mountain's terrain. The season here is exceptionally long (November to end of May) and sometimes the resort is open for 4th of July weekend (two days only) but only when conditions permit.

Night skiing is an additional big draw, being available on the 3.2-mile (5-km) mountain run, and in the Riviera halfpipe and terrain park. Night operations are generally open mid-December through mid-March. Lift access is via the aerial cable car and the Riviera chairlift.

▲ SUPERLATIVES
Squaw Valley has the most skiable terrain in Lake Tahoe, and some of the deepest snow in the world.

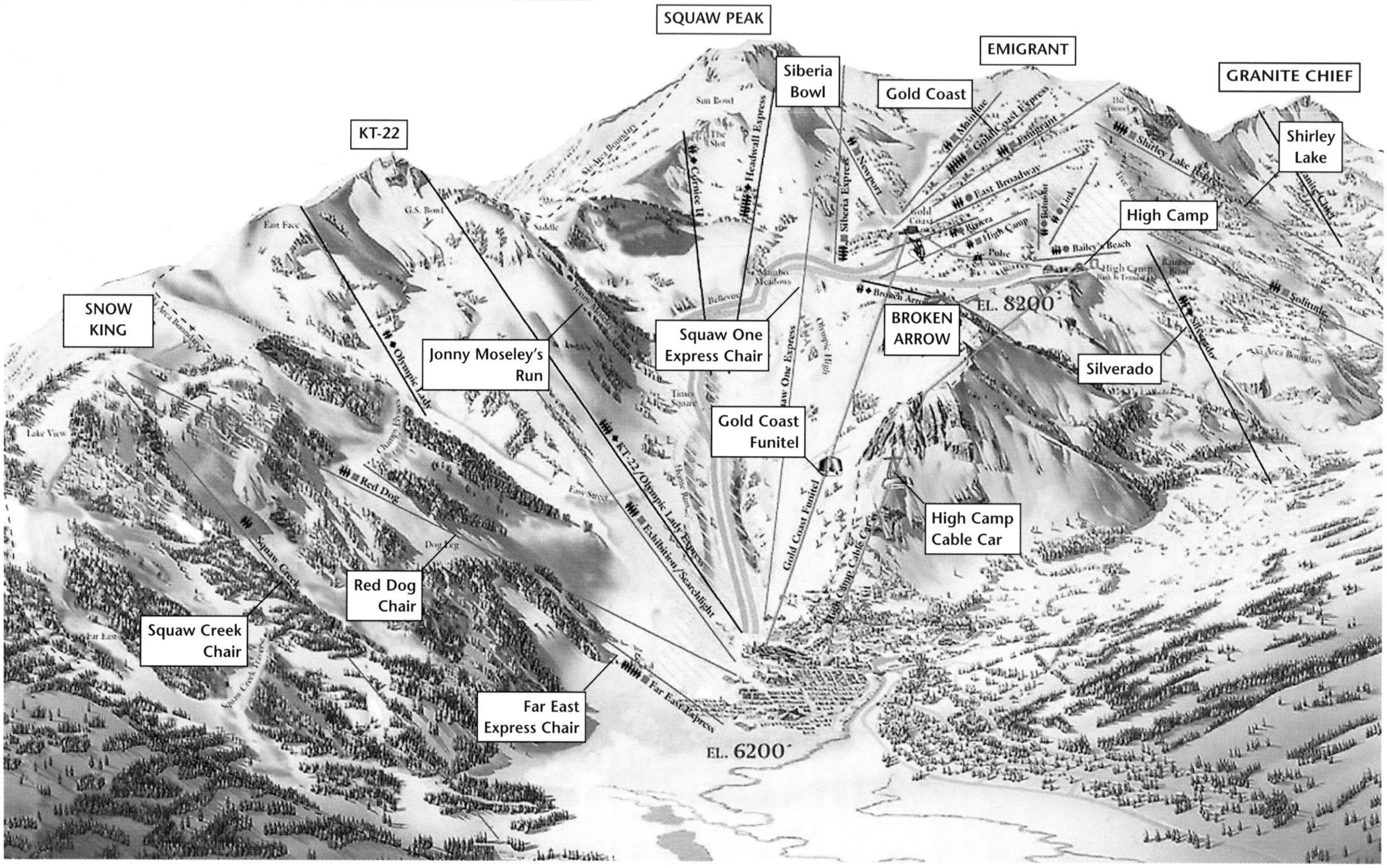

SKI LIFTS

With one of the most advanced lift networks in North America, the layout of Squaw Valley is carefully designed so that there are always two ways to access every area of terrain, cutting down the time that you might wait in line. Squaw has 33 lifts including a recently modernized 110-passenger cable car, and a powerful 28-passenger Funitel—only the fourth of its kind in the world and the only one in North America, replacing the Super Gondola. Squaw also has one Pulse Gondola, three new high-speed Six-pacs (six-passenger detachable lifts), four high-speed quads, one fixed quad, eight triples, nine doubles, four surface and one magic carpet. Put another way, that's a capacity of 49,000 people per hour. Start time is 8:30 AM on weekends and holidays, and 9:00 AM all other days. Lifts shut at 4:00 PM for regular lifts and at 9:00 PM for night operations.

LIFT PASSES

Lift pass prices include all-day tickets with free night skiing at US$58, afternoon from 1:00 PM at US$42, and night skiing (from 4:00–9:00 PM) at $20. If you're over 76 then you go free; 65–75s and 13–15 year-olds are US$29 and photo I.D. is generally required to prove age. Children aged 12 and under ski and ride for only US$5 a day. There is a beginner's lift ticket only available in conjunction with the First Time Beginner Package (available for both skiers and snowboarders), which includes rental equipment, a beginner (limited) lift ticket, and a two hour beginner lesson for $69. For deal-seekers there is the "Frequent Skier Club Plus," which gives you every fifth day free—you can join the club for US$5.

There are several ticket booths conveniently located at the base of the resort, and in the cable car lobby. Tickets are also available for purchase in all Ski Corp rental shops (Ski Rental, Alternative Edge Snowboard Rental, and the Far East Rental Center.) Day tickets can be purchased online at www.squawshop.com and they may also be purchased in conjunction with lodgings packages through Squaw Valley Central Reservations.

Busy holidays and some popular weekends are generally the only times noticeable lines can appear. To alleviate the waiting time for ticket purchasing, the Ski Corp will often have a cash-only line that moves significantly faster than lines where credit cards are being used.

On the mountain, to ensure that you have to wait as little as possible and in order to maximize your time on the slopes, Squaw Valley has cleverly designed the lift network in such a way that there are generally a variety of alternative ways to access each area of terrain. So when a line begins to form at one lift, you should look around because there is likely to be another lift close by that does not have a wait.

▼ HIGH CAMP
Ice skating, snowtubing, and skiing (with a ski school meeting area) as well as swimming and tennis await those taking the cable car to this year-round multi-activity center perched on a 8,200-foot (2,500-m) summit.

SKI SCHOOLS & GUIDING

Squaw Valley Ski & Snowboard School is the adult school, and it's located between the main ticket portals and the Squaw Valley Outfitters retail shop in the heart of the base area. The adult ski school also has an office at High Camp. This is also the meeting area for all group lessons. Adult group lessons begin every hour on the hour between 10:00 AM and 2:00 pm, and cost US$42. First-timers can get a special package including two-hour lesson and rental for US$69. Private lessons times can vary depending on availability and are double the class fee. For adults a variety of clinics such as carving clinics, expert skiing workshops, mogul workshops, and performance gate training, are on offer.

The Squaw Kids Children's Center welcomes children aged 2–12 and the kids are supervised at all times. Licensed toddler care is available for ages 2–4 with lessons for 3–4 year-olds. All-day sessions will set you back US$85, half-day US$62, depending on the season. It's conveniently located at the base of the resort adjacent to the preferred parking structure and the Member's Locker Room. The 12,000 square foot (1,114 sq m) facility has a special drop-off area and dedicated parking zone for participants in the program.

Saturday Morning Beginner Telemark Clinic is a first-time package designed to teach the fundamentals of basic telemark skiing. The package includes rental equipment, a lift ticket and two-hour lesson for US$69 and starts at 11:00 AM at the High Camp Sales Office.

BEGINNERS

The resort's easiest terrain is located on the resort's upper mountain and is accessed by the aerial cable car. This beginner area features five easy chairlifts in a wide open, gently sloping bowl overlooking Lake Tahoe. Being located on the upper mountain means beginners get the same exciting mountain experience as more advanced skiers and snowboarders—and they can enjoy the same spectacular panoramic views of Lake Tahoe and the surrounding Sierra as well as feel the freedom and serenity of being high up in the mountains.

The newest beginner area, the Papoose Learning Area is located on the lower mountain at a 6,200-foot (1,890-m) elevation. It offers beginners more terrain as well as a second option when inclement weather and wind affects visibility and operations on the upper mountain. This area features two new pony tows (surface lifts) and is conveniently located adjacent to the Far East Center, complete with a rental store, retail store, lockers, ticket sales, and rest rooms.

INTERMEDIATES

Intermediate skiers and snowboarders can continue to improve their skills on the 3.2-mile (5-km) Mountain Run, cruising from the upper mountain all the way down to the Base Village. They can test their skills on the upper mountain's Siberia Bowl, considered an advanced intermediate area of terrain. From the Base Area, ride Red Dog and Squaw

▲ **ALL YOU NEED IS SNOW**
Granite, trees, and a carpet of immaculate snow are a short step away from a chairlift.

SKI SCHOOL
SQUAW KIDS CHILDREN'S CENTER
Information: 530-581-7225
Reservations: 530-581-7166
Fax: 530-452-4563

SQUAW VALLEY SKI & SNOWBOARD SCHOOL
Info & sales: 530-581-7263
Fax: 530-581-7193

Address for both:
P.O. Box 2007
Olympic Valley, CA 96146
Website for both: www.squaw.com

▼ **IDEAL TEMPERATURES**
Average winter temperature is 30°F (-1°C) and three out of four days are full-on sunshine —hopefully the fourth adds fresh snow.

▲ **THEY CAME, THEY SAW...**
Extreme freeriders are drawn to this resort like golfers to St. Andrews —if you haven't been here you haven't skied.

▼ **BROKEN ARROW**
Proof that the resort is an experts' paradise is this vast bowl offering just one of a fleet of black diamond open bowls. Broken Arrow is one of Squaw's most sought-after pitches and powder stashes. The slightly higher-up KT-22 remains the flagship black diamond.

Creek for some warm-up cruisers. Then begin working your way up the mountain via the Funitel or Squaw One Express to the wide-open bowls of Gold Coast, and move on to the very popular Shirley Lake area.

ADVANCED & EXPERT

Look no further than famous pitches off the KT-22 peak and chairlift for steep terrain, tight chutes, and an excellent variety of off-piste skiing. This peak is often referred to as Squaw Valley's crown jewel, and virtually every inch of KT-22's terrain will thrill and challenge even the most seasoned skier and snowboarder. Other advanced terrain includes Headwall, Granite Chief, Broken Arrow, and the Silverado Bowl. The toughest skiing includes Moseley's Run, a land of monster bumps and jelly legs; it's the flagship of KT's fleet of double black diamond terrain. Bumps on the steep slope stay cold, hard, and gullied into massive mounds storm-to-storm. If you want to test endurance, this is it: skiers and snowboarders are confronted by a non-stop 2,000 feet (609 m) vertical descent down the slope's steep fall line that will get the adrenaline pumping. Originally called the West Face (strange, because it doesn't face west at all) it was renamed on February 27, 1998, in recognition of Jonny Moseley's life-long commitment to Squaw Valley, freestyle skiing, and his winning the gold at the Olympics in Nagano.

On a classic Californian, blue-bird powder day the line at KT-22 starts forming before the sun rises because the sensation of powering first tracks on the peak's bevy of perfect pitches is truly the experience of a lifetime. Those that don't want to climb into the powder circus KT-22 creates can veer left to the Red Dog chairlift to discover the often-overlooked glory found in Poulsen's Gully. Or ride the Funitel to the upper mountain where Headwall, Broken Arrow and Granite Chief await. The powder gets skied out fast at Squaw Valley so powder hounds should plan to get out early to make the most of the experience.

For a classic ski itinerary, start from the base area and head straight for KT-22. Considered one of the greatest chairlifts in North America it rises from the base directly to an expert skiers' paradise. After a few non-stop adventures in powder heaven, move further up the mountain to the bowls, chutes and gullies of Headwall and Cornice II. Then head over to the Broken Arrow peak where it is easy to drop in and discover some of Squaw's most sought-after and secret pitches and powder stashes.

Incidentally, the resort does not permit out of bounds skiing or riding. Nor does it offer "guides"; however, you can sign up for one of Squaw Valley's Advanced Ski Clinics where instructors offer helpful instruction for improving skills while exploring all the exciting advanced and expert terrain Squaw has to offer. Also, many skiers and snowboarders that want a personal tour opt for a private lesson where they get some tips and tricks and a personal guide all in one.

BOARDING & FREESTYLE

While all 4,000 acres (1,619 ha) of Squaw Valley's mountain might be considered one giant terrain fun park, Squaw Valley has two dedicated terrain parks with two halfpipes. Under the Riviera Lift is a terrain park with huge tabletop jumps, a quarterpipe, various rails and a 500-foot (152 m) long halfpipe with 12-inch (30 cm) walls. Between the Gold Coast and Siberia chairlifts is the Mainline Terrain Park and the 400-foot (122 m) Superpipe with 17-inch (43 cm) walls. This area also features tabletops, rails, fun boxes, volcanoes, and other features depending on conditions. The Riviera Park is open for both day and night boarding (night operations are 4:00–9:00 PM, weather permitting) and is loaded with a state-of-the-art sound system and a dedicated chairlift. It's all very easy for the boarder to get around, and the vast lift network means not much traversing is necessary.

EATING ON THE MOUNTAIN

Whatever your fancy—Mexican, Italian, pizza, sandwiches, salads, wraps, crêpes, soups, hamburgers, deli, full-service breakfast—Squaw's 31 restaurants (including delis) range from sit-down to self-service to fast food and vary in price and style from inexpensive and casual to fine dining. The most popular breakfast is at Mother Barclay's, most popular burger is at the Red Dog Bar & Grill, the best French fries are at the Gordon Biersch Sundeck Tavern, and the most popular Mexican food is at Salsa. The Resort at Squaw Creek has an excellent ski-up deck and outdoor BBQ, weather permitting.

APRÈS SKI

There are 22 bars in the Valley to choose from, most catering to the 25–35 crowd (and you have to be 21 or over to consume alcohol in California). Children are allowed in bars that also serve food. Bars close at 2:00 AM. The Loft Bar is the old-timer "local" hangout and the Red Dog Bar and Grill is a favorite with the Squaw Valley employees. Bar One has live music, dancing, and pool tables, while the Plaza Bar is the hang out for sports fans, with sporting events on the big-screen T.V. For a more intimate après ski experience, the bar at the PlumpJack Squaw Valley Inn has a cozy fireplace and an excellent selection of wine. The newest après-ski spot in the Squaw scene is the Balboa Café featuring tasty appetizers and a variety of beverage options. Look for it to become a hot spot next season. Nearby in Tahoe City guests enjoy Pete 'n' Peter's, the Naughty Dawg, and the Bridgetender. In Truckee, Casa Baeza, O.B.'s Pub & Restaurant, and the Tourist Club are popular. Of the many restaurants, if it's the wines you fancy, try the PlumpJack Café. Their selection of hard-to-find Californian wines and extensive wines by the glass program have garnered critical acclaim and a loyal following.

◄ FUNITEL
North America's only Funitel offers "No Waiting In Line or Your Money Back, guaranteed."

OTHER ACTIVITIES

Off the slopes, winter fun includes mountain top ice skating, snowtubing, shopping, and dining—all overlooking Lake Tahoe, and in the spring swimming at the High Camp Swimming Lagoon & Spa. Only at this resort can you ski or snowboard all morning and relax poolside over 8,000 feet (2,440 m) looking down over Lake Tahoe. On the lower mountain try the indoor climbing wall, cross-country skiing, snowshoeing, sleigh rides and dogsled tours in the Squaw Valley Meadow, or rejuvenate yourself at a number of relaxing health and fitness spa.

USEFUL PHONE NUMBERS

Squaw Valley Tourist Office	530-583-6985
Squaw Valley Central Reservation Service	800-545-4350
Squaw Valley Ski Patrol	530-583-6985
Alpine Skills Backcountry Guiding	530-426-9108
Doctor @ Tahoe Truckee Medical Group	530-581-8864
Tahoe Truckee Taxis	530-583-8294
Yellow Cab Taxis	530-546-9090
ZZ Cab Taxis	530-581-0222

USEFUL WEBSITES

Official Website	www.squaw.com
Central Reservations Service	www.squawvacations.com
Lift Passes	www.squawshop.com
Lake Tahoe Vacation Rentals	www.tahoeaccommodatons.com
Snow & Weather Report	www.wunderground.com

RESTAURANTS

EXPENSIVE
BALBOA CAFÉ
GLISSANDE
GRAHAM'S SQUAW VALLEY
MONTAGNA

MODERATE
CASCADES
CROSSROADS CAFE
RED DOG BAR & GRILL
MOTHER BARCLAY'S
POOLSIDE CAFÉ
SALSA

BUDGET
BURGER EXPRESS
CRÊPES DE DION
DAVE'S DELI

BARS

PLAZA BAR
BAR ONE
BAR SIX
SALSA
GORDON BIERSCH SUNDECK TAVERN
THE LE CHAMOIS LOFT BAR
THE BALBOA CAFE
PLUMP JACK SQUAW VALLEY INN
RED DOG BAR & GRILL
GRAHAM'S SQUAW VALLEY
ALEXANDER'S BAR
THE POOLSIDE BAR
TERRACE BAR
MERMAID BAR
BULLWHACKERS PUB

THE RELAXED PACE AND FAMILY-FRIENDLY ENVIRONMENT AT ALPINE MEADOWS MAKES IT A POPULAR RESORT. HERE YOU HAVE THE CHANCE TO ENJOY THE NATURAL LIFE WHILE SKIING SOME OF THE TOUGHEST TERRAIN IN NORTH AMERICA. LITTLE WONDER THAT *SKIING MAGAZINE* CALLED ALPINE MEADOWS "A MOUNTAIN WITH A DISTINCTLY SPLIT PERSONALITY: A MILD SIDE AND A WILD SIDE."

ALPINE MEADOWS

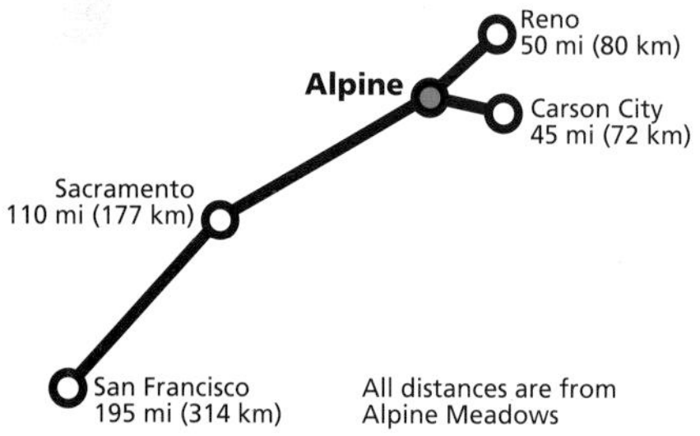

Alpine Meadows keeps a low profile compared with some other ski resorts around Lake Tahoe, and you'll be mingling with lots of locals if you choose this one for your ski vacation. Steep chutes, gentle glades and endless cruisers have made it a firm favorite with local skiers. It is less expensive than some of the Lake Tahoe resorts and offers a quieter atmosphere off the slopes, as well as some good off-piste skiing and riding. It shares an interchangeable lift pass with Heavenly, Kirkwood, Northstar at Tahoe, Sierra at Tahoe, and Squaw Valley. With 495 inches (1,257 cm) of snow per year, the snowmaking facilities, which operate on 12 of the 14 lifts, are required usually only during November. Then the natural snowfall takes over. The season is long, running from mid-November to the end of May or mid-June.

GETTING THERE

Alpine Meadows is located six miles (9.5 km) northwest of Tahoe City, California, off Highway 89, and 13 miles (21 km) south of Interstate 80 at Truckee, California. It is 195 miles (314 km) east of San Francisco, and 50 miles (80 km) west of Reno, Nevada. The nearest international airports are Reno/Tahoe, about an hour's drive along all-weather Highway 89, Sacramento (110 miles/177 km), about 90 minutes' drive along all-weather Interstate 80, and San Francisco or Oakland Airport, both about a three hours' drive (traffic permitting).

Amtrak trains run services to Reno. From the station in Reno take a taxi to Reno/Tahoe International Airport and then either hire a car or take public transportation to Tahoe City. Free shuttles operate from most north and west shore lodges. For convenience and on weekends, park at Sunnyside Resort and catch the Sherwood Shuttle (lift passes are available at the base of Sherwood Chair).

◄ **OFF PISTE**
Nothing compares to fresh, unmarked snow, blue skies and a stunning lake view.

MOUNTAIN FACTS

Base	6,835 feet (2,083 m)
Summit	8,637 feet (2,633 m)
Elevation	1,802 feet (549 m)
Easy	25%
Intermediate	40%
Advanced/Expert	35%
Number of trails	100
Number of bowls	6
Number of terrain parks	2
Longest trail	2.5 miles (4 km)
Ski area	2,000 acres (810 ha)

SNOWFALL

Annual snowfall	495 inches (1,257 cm)
Snowmaking	12 of the 14 lifts

SKI LIFTS

High-Speed Six-Seater	1
High-Speed Quads	1
Triple Chairs	4
Double Chairs	5
Surface Lifts	3
Total	14
Rider per hour	16,000

SKI SEASON

Mid-November to late May or June

◄ TAKE YOUR PICK

Ski the front or the back of the mountain, but if you're an expert go for the back where you will find challenging terrain like South Face.

Although the Lake Tahoe area is well known for its busy casinos, mostly to be found in South Lake Tahoe at the other end of the lake, guests who visit Alpine Meadows can enjoy fine dining, drinks at the locals' pub by the fire, live jazz or up-and-coming bands from San Francisco, sushi (brought in daily from San Francisco), and also get a good night's sleep for great skiing and snowboarding the next day.

The town of Tahoe City grew up as an historic crossroads where tourists disembarked from the train that connected Lake Tahoe and the main rail route through Truckee, then boarded ferry transports to other points around the lake. Today, most travelers arrive by road.

THE VILLAGE

Tahoe City is one of the main cities on the California side of Lake Tahoe. It has a community feel, with smaller restaurants than nearby cities.

ACCOMMODATIONS

There aren't any lodgings at the resort itself, but the many inns, hotels, condos and lodges in Tahoe City and around Lake Tahoe are easily accessible. Sunnyside, on the west shore of Lake Tahoe, is a good spot, close to the mountains and with great lake views. River Ranch, at the bottom of the Alpine Meadows road, is in a great location with beautiful river views, après-ski bar with a roaring fire, popular with the locals, and a fantastic dinner menu. For more information visit the Tahoe City visitor information website www.tahoe.com.

ACCOMMODATIONS

HOTEL/RESORTS
RESORT AT SQUAW CREEK
SUNNYSIDE
RIVER RANCH
BEST WESTERN TRUCKEE TAHOE INN
COTTAGE INN AT LAKE TAHOE

RESORT/CASINOS
HYATT REGENCY LAKE TAHOE
CAL NEVA LODGE, CRYSTAL BAY

CONDOMINIUMS
OLYMPIC VILLAGE INN
LAKE TAHOE ACCOMMODATIONS
CHINQUAPIN
COLDWELL BANKER VACATION RENTALS
BROCKWAY SPRINGS
ACCOMMODATIONS TAHOE

LODGES
SQUAW VALLEY LODGE

BED AND BREAKFAST
MAYFIELD HOUSE AT LAKE TAHOE

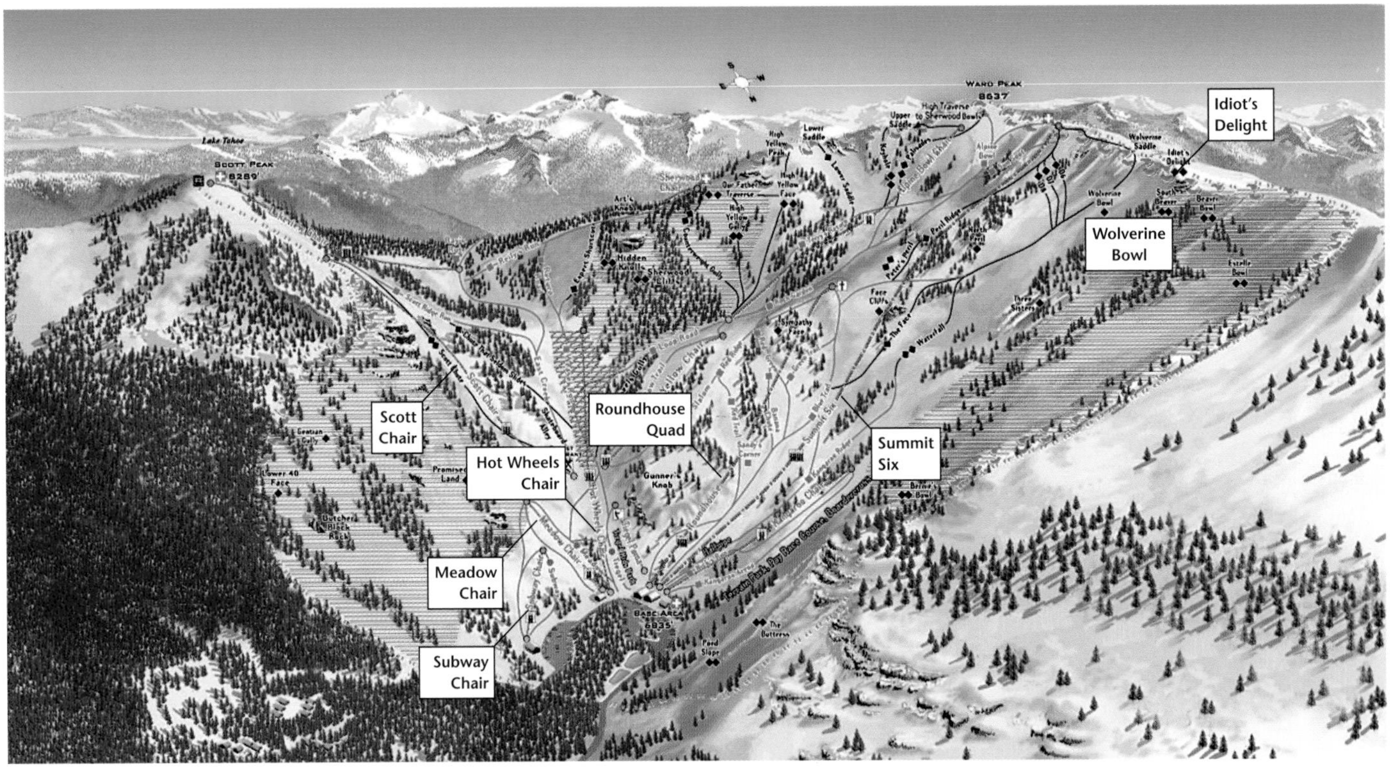

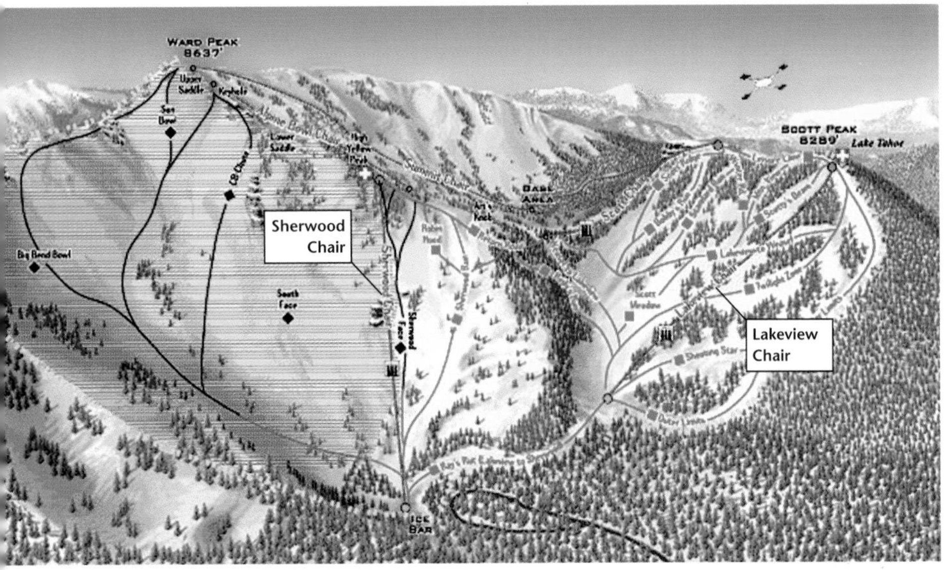

The interchangeable lift pass with Heavenly, Kirkwood, Northstar at Tahoe, Sierra at Tahoe, and Squaw Valley provides access to 17,520 acres (7,090 ha) of skiing and boarding.

SKI LIFTS

There are 14 chairlifts in total, including one high-speed six-passenger chair, one high-speed quad, four triple chairs, five double chairs and three surface lifts. The lifts are open from 9:00 AM TO 4.00 PM. The lift system is very efficient and waiting is not usually a problem.

LIFT PASSES

A full-day regular adult pass costs US$56 (interchangeable parents pass also US$56), US$10 for children aged 7–12, US$6 for children up to six years, US$30 for seniors aged 65–69, and US$42 for teenagers aged 13–18. Seniors 70 and over pay US$8, and the terrain park costs US$19. Half-day (from 12:15 PM) passes cost US$44 for adults, and there is no reduction for other categories from a full-day pass. A beginner package costs US$54 per day, including lift ticket (no access to advanced lifts), equipment, and a lesson. A three-day pass for adults costs US$156 and for children US$30. The Alpine 10-PAK gets you 10 days' skiing for US$450. The lift pass also allows you access to the other Lake Tahoe resorts mentioned above. You can buy passes at the lift ticket windows and most of the inns and lodges around Tahoe.

NEARBY RESORTS

SKI AREA

Alpine Meadows is backed by giant volcanic rock sculptures. There's over 2,000 acres (810 ha) of skiable terrain, with a summit, Ward Peak, reaching 8,637 feet (2,633 m). You can ski either the front or back of the mountain, although beginners won't find anything for them on the back. Famous for its off-piste terrain and "adventure zones," which are all around the mountain, Alpine Meadows draws advanced and expert skiers and snowboarders from around the world to try its bowls, chutes, trees, and backcountry hikes. But for families there's also a family ski zone off Hot Wheels Chair.

▶ SPEEDY ACCESS
The six-passenger chairlift whisks you quickly up the mountain in comfort.

GETTING TO THE BASE

The Alpine Meadows Shuttle transports skiers from the main road to the mountain base. Tahoe Area Regional Transit (TART) offers bus transportation on the north shore.

SKI SCHOOLS AND GUIDING

There's one ski school and one snowboard school with about 200 instructors. Alpine Meadows also has an Adaptive Ski School. Group lessons last two hours and run from 10:00 AM, 12:00 PM and 2:00 PM. The upper limit is six people. To register a child in a group lesson, the child must be at least five years of age, and parents may need to show I.D. as proof of their child's age. Young children are supervised at lunch. Private lessons are also available.

For beginners, Alpine's "Direct to Parallel" learn-to-ski program starts participants out on mini skis (approximately 40 inches/100 cm in length), which make negotiation easier. Beginners will be skiing down moderate trails by the end of the lesson. Intermediates can take a half-day or full-day refresher focusing on technique, and accomplished skiers can take a guided tour through the open powder fields. Guides can be booked through the private lesson ski school program. Specialty programs and camps run throughout the season, including a two-day race camp, three-day early season warm-up clinic, a 5-day high-performance clinic, and snowboard camps.

BEGINNERS

Around 25 percent of the ski area is graded "easy" for beginners, and the best areas are off Meadow Chair, Subway Chair, and Hot Wheels Chair, which are all easily accessible from the base area. There's a specially designated family ski area off Hot Wheels Chair, with green and blue trails.

INTERMEDIATES

Around 40 percent of the trails at Alpine are for intermediates. A good day's skiing would include the Roundhouse high-speed quad, and the many blue trails on the front of the mountain, or the Sherwood triple chair for the bowls on the back of the mountain. Also on the back of the mountain is Lakeview triple chair, for long, graceful and groomed trails.

ADVANCED & EXPERT

The best skiing for advanced skiers is off Summit Six high-speed six-passenger lift on the front of the mountain, and Scott triple chairlift on the back. The most challenging terrain is Wolverine Bowl—steep and a consistent, sustained distance, although groomed. If you're looking for moguls, steep and deep, and couloirs head off to Keyhole, Idiot's Delight, and Estelle Bowl, accessed via the Summit Six lift, or Promised Land off Scott Chair on the front of the mountain. Powder searchers are in heaven here—you can find powder anywhere on the mountain. Alpine Meadows is a telemark skiing hot spot, and provides lessons, high-performance equipment, and hosts many demo days. Because of its open boundary policy, ski touring is very popular and prevalent.

▼ SUNRISE
And another day dawns with plenty of untracked snow in the north facing bowls.

EATING ON THE MOUNTAIN

BASE AREA LODGE
CHALET RESTAURANT
ICE BAR

BARS

ALPINE MEADOWS
ICE BAR
COMPACTOR BAR
ALPINE BAR AND GRILL

TAHOE CITY
ROSIE'S CAFÉ

TRUCKEE
COTTONWOOD
CAL NEVA LODGE

NORTH LAKE TAHOE
HYATT REGENCY
INCLINE VILLAGE

RESTAURANTS

CHRISTY HILL, TAHOE CITY
WOLFDALE'S, TAHOE CITY
ROSIE'S CAFÉ, TAHOE CITY
ZA'S, TAHOE CITY
JAKE'S ON THE LAKE, TAHOE CITY
BIG WATER GRILLE, INCLINE VILLAGE

► **BRAVE BOARDING**
You'll need a few lessons to be able to emulate this talented boarder.

BOARDING & FREESTYLE

Skiers and boarders alike can use the terrain park and halfpipe off the Kangaroo double chair from the base area. For boarders it's easy to access non-hike terrain, but a little more effort is required to access hike-to destinations. The terrain park and halfpipe are sometimes open at night for special events. For the 2002/03 season a new 600-foot long (180 m) Superpipe is being installed, with walls that are 17 feet (5 m) high.

EATING ON THE MOUNTAIN

At the base lodge there's a full-service restaurant, cafeteria, deli, boulangerie, and large sundeck. The Chalet Restaurant on the front of the mountain has a full-service restaurant. At the base of Sherwood Chair in the back bowls, the Ice Bar offers a snack bar, music and a pleasantly laidback atmosphere in the cocktail lounge.

APRÈS SKI

There are three bars in the resort. The Ice Bar on the back of the mountain is the best bar, with reclining sunchairs, beautiful views, microbrews, BBQ, and music. The Compactor Bar, and the Alpine Bar and Grill are in the main base lodge. The minimum age for consuming alcohol is 21 and if children accompany their parents in bars and other places serving alcohol they cannot sit at a bar.

In Tahoe City there's plenty to entertain you. Jake's on the Lake is a waterfront grill, seafood bar and lakefront deck; Rosie's Café offers lots of charm and a friendly atmosphere, with live music and dancing on Tuesday. Za's has Italian cuisine that warms the soul. Big Water Grille in Incline Village has Californian cuisine in a beautiful mountain setting. Christy Hill (Californian cuisine and panoramic lakeside dining), and Wolfdale's (east/west fusion) are two good restaurants offering extensive wine lists.

If you can't find what you want in Tahoe City, there are over 160 restaurants in North Lake Tahoe and Truckee. Truckee also has plenty of bars, such as Bar of America, Moody's, Taps and the Squeeze Inn. Cottonwood has live jazz every Saturday. Bars close around 2:00 AM. And if you want to have a flutter, there are casinos at the Cal Neva Lodge in North Lake Tahoe, and at the Hyatt Regency in Incline Village.

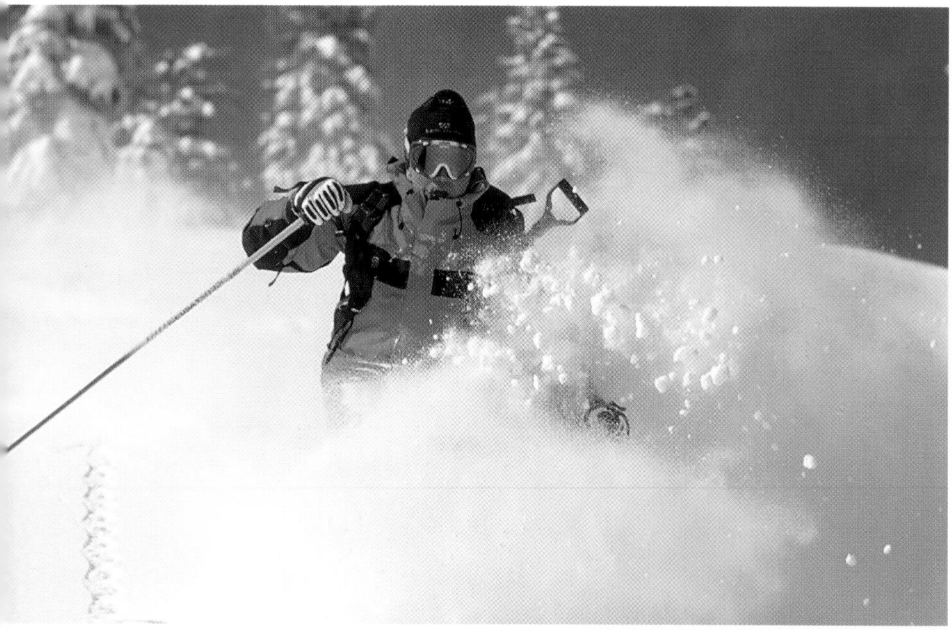

◄ **DIG IN**
Skiing in deep powder requires good rythmn —and a good pair of goggles.

◄ A GREAT DAY OUT
Take your lunch on your back and there's no need to sit down all day.

OTHER ACTIVITIES

In partnership with the Tahoe National Forest Service, Alpine Meadows offers marked snowshoe trails that begin near the base area lodge and meander through the forests around the base of the mountain. Snowshoe rentals are available on-site.

► DID YOU GET THAT?
Make sure your friends have the camera at the ready for the ultimate photo opportunity.

USEFUL PHONE NUMBERS

Central Reservations	530-583-4232
Resort Information	800-441-4423
Ski School Bookings	800-441-4423
Adaptive Ski School	530-581-4161
Ski Rescue Service	800-441-4423
Snow Phone	530-581-8374
Lodging Reservations	800-949-3296

USEFUL WEBSITES & E-MAIL ADDRESSES

Official Website	www.alpinemeadows.com
Official e-mail address	info@skialpine.com
Tourist Office Website	www.tahoevacationguide.com
Ski School bookings	www.skialpine.com
Visitor Information for Lake Tahoe	www.tahoe.com
Guide to Lake Tahoe	www.tahoevacationguide.com
Where to play and stay in Lake Tahoe	www.tahoefun.org
What's best in Lake Tahoe	www.tahoebest.com

INCREDIBLE VIEWS OF NORTH AMERICA'S LARGEST MOUNTAIN LAKE, 24-HOUR NIGHTLIFE, THE ABUNDANT SNOWFALL AND SUNSHINE: FEW SKI RESORTS MATCH HEAVENLY'S EXPANSIVE NETWORK OF LIFTS, TERRAIN, AND TRAILS. HEAVENLY SKI RESORT FEATURES LAKE TAHOE'S HIGHEST ELEVATION, LONGEST VERTICAL DROP AND LARGEST SNOWMAKING SYSTEM.

HEAVENLY

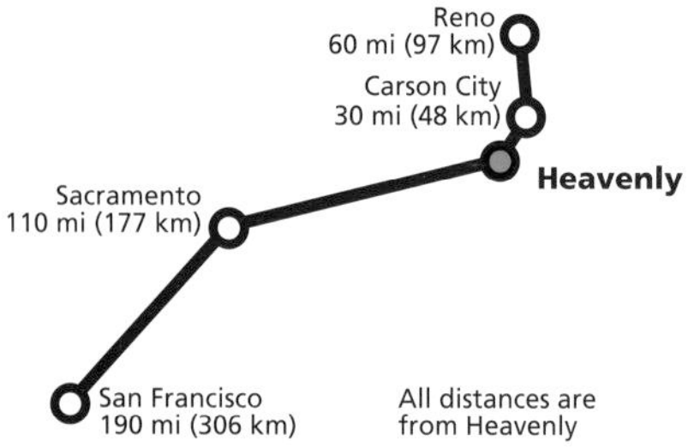

Nestling in the southeast corner of Lake Tahoe, on the border of Nevada and the sunshine state of California, Heavenly is appropriately named as it enjoys around 300 days of sun each year, not to mention 360 inches (914 cm) of snowfall. Heavenly is located in the heart of South Lake Tahoe in California and Stateline in Nevada.

Heavenly is the only major resort on the shore of Lake Tahoe itself. Lake Tahoe has an interchangeable pass system for Heavenly, Alpine Meadows, Kirkwood, Northstar at Tahoe, Sierra at Tahoe and Squaw Valley. Heavenly was bought by Vail Resorts in May 2002 and is also now a sister resort to Vail, Beaver Creek, Breckenridge and Keystone, all in Colorado. Over the next five years Vail Resorts plan to invest US$40 million in upgrading mountain facilities.

Heavenly is within walking distance of more than 5,000 lodging rooms and just minutes from star-studded nightlife, first-class restaurants and endless activities. If you don't like glitzy casinos, then it's probably not the place for you.

The ski season here starts in late October or early November and ends in early May. Peak seasons is from the end of December to mid-February, and low seasons November through mid-December and April.

GETTING THERE

The nearest international airports are Reno-Tahoe (55 miles/88 km) and Sacramento (110 miles/177 km). Transfer time by road is 75 minutes from Reno and two hours from Sacramento. If you are driving from elsewhere in the United States, Highway 50 provides direct, all-weather access and driving times are eight hours from Los Angeles, three hours from San Francisco and three hours from San José. Full directions for all of these routes are available on the official website, www.skiheavenly.com.

Amtrak trains connect to Reno. From the station in Reno take a taxi to Reno/Tahoe International Airport and then the Tahoe Casino Express to South

◄ ► LAKE TAHOE
You'll get fantastic views of Lake Tahoe, North America's largest alpine lake, from just about anywhere on the mountain at Heavenly.

MOUNTAIN FACTS	
Base	6,223 feet (1,866 m)
Summit	10,067 feet (3,020 m)
Elevation	3,844 feet (1,153 m)
Easy	20%
Intermediate	45%
Advanced/Expert	35%
Number of trails	85
Longest trail	5.5 miles (8.5 km)
Ski area	4,800 acres (1,920 ha)

SNOWFALL	
Annual snowfall	360 inches (914 cm)
Snowmaking	70% of skiable terrain

SKI LIFTS	
Gondolas	1
Aerial Tram	1
High-Speed Six-passenger	1
High-Speed Quads	5
Triple Chairs	8
Double Chairs	5
Surface Lifts	6
Magic Carpets	2
Total	29

SKI SEASON
Late October to early May

Lake Tahoe. There's a free shuttle service throughout South Lake Tahoe (California) and Stateline (Nevada), making stops at most major lodging properties and at the base facilities: the California Base Lodge, the base of the Heavenly Gondola in the new Village at Heavenly, and Stagecoach and Boulder Lodges in Nevada. Look for the colored "Shuttle Bus Stop" signs. An express shuttle runs from the Heavenly Gondola to California Base Lodge.

THE VILLAGE

Heavenly ski resort began in the 1950s and has changed ownership several times. Each new owner has had pioneering ideas that have made the resort grow from a couple of tow-ropes and a run of about 1,000 feet (300 m) to the present-day Heavenly. The developments on the mountain inevitably led to the boom in Stateline casinos and top celebrity shows.

A major redevelopment project, the Village at Heavenly, was unveiled in December 2002. With the Gondola as the centerpiece, the new pedestrian, alpine-themed village will include two Marriott properties with 793 luxury rooms and suites, retail space galore, an outdoor ice-skating rink and multiplex cinema. Just a few steps from the Village at Heavenly, you'll find star-studded nightlife, headline entertainment, and 24-hour fun at the Nevada casinos.

ACCOMMODATIONS

A wide variety of lodging options are available, from condos to large homes, all in the South Lake Tahoe area. Harrah's and Horizon Casino are two of the main casino hotels, famous for their 24-hour nightlife and Las Vegas-style headliners. Caesar's and Harvey's will also satisfy any desire for casino glamour. The Tahoe Seasons is near to the lifts at the California Base Lodge. The Lakeside Inn and Casino is a smaller establishment, still with a casino, but somewhere that you might see locals as well as tourists. American skiers and snowboarders can plan their entire vacation through Heavenly's own travel agency, Heavenly Tahoe Vacations, www.skiheavenly.com or call 800-243-2836. International skiers and snowboarders should contact a tour operator in their own country.

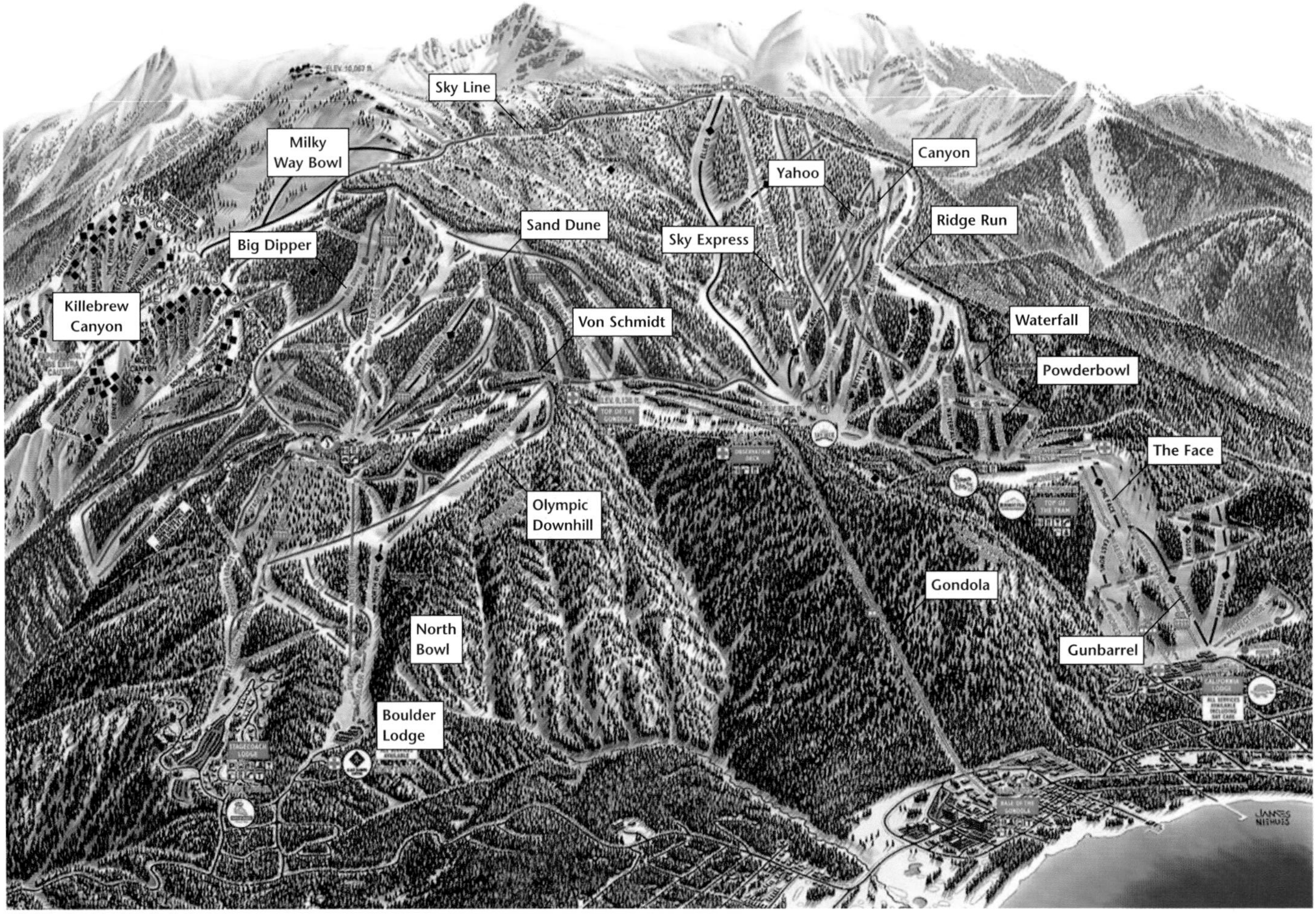

NEARBY RESORTS

SKI AREA

Discover the many sides of Heavenly, from the awe-inspiring scenic beauty and the heart-stopping Mott and Killebrew Canyons in Nevada to the gentle wide-open cruisers and beginners areas at California Base Lodge. With access to mid-mountain from mid-town in 12 minutes via the new high-speed Heavenly Gondola, skiing and riding the region's largest resort is easy. With 4,800 acres (1,920 ha) of skiable terrain, there's something for every level of skier or snowboarder. With an average 360 inches (914 cm) annual snowfall, boosted by the West Coast's largest artificial snowmaking system covering 70% of trails, there should be no concerns about lack of snow.

Beginners can enjoy the secluded beginner areas, intermediates the miles of wide open cruisers and famous corduroy, and experts can take to the gladed runs, the backcountry experience in the canyons, and the famous moguls of The Face and Gunbarrel. From the top of the Heavenly Gondola, skiers and snowboarders can ski or ride both the California and Nevada sides of the mountain or enjoy cross-country skiing, snowshoeing or snowtubing at the Heavenly's Adventure Peak. You need to return to the state from which you started out by 3:30 PM.

▶ THE GONDOLA
Connecting the new village development with the mountain, the gondola gets you slopeside in just 12 minutes.

◄ THE PERFECT COMBO
Wide open cruisers and breathtaking views make skiing simply heavenly at Heavenly.

SKI LIFTS

Heavenly has an extensive lift network with a large fleet of high-speed lifts spanning Nevada and California. The Gondola, opened in 2000, neatly connects the new Village at Heavenly to the mountain, whizzing skiers, riders and sightseers alike to an observation deck before finishing the 12-minute journey that takes you nearly 3,000 feet (900 m) above the sparkling waters of Lake Tahoe. From the observation decks are 360° views of Lake Tahoe, Desolation Wilderness, and Carson Valley.

In total there are 29 lifts, making Heavenly one of the United States' largest skiing areas. The lifts include the new high-speed Heavenly Gondola, an aerial tram, a high-speed six-passenger lift, five high-speed quads, eight triple chairs, five double chairs and eight surface lifts. Lifts operate from Monday to Friday 9:00 AM–4:00 PM, and Saturday and Sunday 8:30 AM–4:00 PM.

The Heavenly Gondola is one of five access points to the mountain. The other four are the aerial tramway and Gunbarrel in California and the Boulder lift and Stagecoach Express quad in Nevada. For the quickest way to the upper portions of the mountain, intermediate and advanced skiers and riders should take the Heavenly Gondola from the Village at Heavenly, or begin their day at the Stagecoach Lodge in Nevada. Beginners should start their day at the California Base Lodge.

LIFT PASSES

Lift passes can be purchased at any of Heavenly's four base facilities: the Heavenly Gondola, California Base Lodge, Stagecoach Lodge and Boulder Lodge.

Full-day passes cost US$59 for adults (19–64), US$29 for children (5–12), US$49 for teens (13–18), and US$35 for seniors (65+). A weekly pass costs US$270 for adults, US$125 for children, US$220 for teens and US$150 for seniors. Beginner passes are sold in conjunction with a beginner lesson package. Photo ID is not required for lift passes. If you just want to ride the Gondola and not ski, it will cost you US$20 for adults (13 and over), US$12 for children (5–12), US$18 for seniors (65+), with children under 4 riding free.

ACCOMMODATIONS

CAESAR'S TAHOE
Stateline, NV 89449
800-648-3353
www.caesars.com

HARRAH'S LAKE TAHOE
Stateline, NV 89449
800-427-7247
www.harrahstahoe.com

HARVEY'S RESORT HOTEL
Stateline, NV 89449
800-427-8397
www.harveys-tahoe.com

EMBASSY SUITES RESORT LAKE TAHOE
4130 Lake Tahoe Boulevard,
South Lake Tahoe, CA 96150
800-988-9895
www.embassytahoe.com

HORIZON CASINO RESORT
Stateline, NV 89449
800-648-3322
www.horizoncasino.com

TAHOE LAKESHORE LODGE AND SPA
930 Bal Bijou Road,
South Lake Tahoe, CA 96150
800-448-4577
www.tahoelakeshorelodge.com

TAHOE SEASONS RESORT
3901 Saddle Road,
South Lake Tahoe, CA 96150
800-540-4874
www.tahoeseasons.com

LAKESIDE INN AND CASINO
Stateline, NV 89449
800-624-7980
www.lakesideinn.com

SKI RENTAL
Heavenly's family of 11 sports stores, Heavenly Sports, on and off the mountain offer the region's largest selection of ski and snowboard equipment.

▲ POWDER STASHES
The powder on Heavenly's famous high trails are superb, with light dry snow creating perfect conditions.

SKI SCHOOLS AND GUIDING

The Heavenly Ski & Snowboard School is located at California Base Lodge, Boulder Lodge and at the top of Heavenly Gondola. For adults, there are several different packages. The Super Skier/Rider teaches you to walk, slide, turn, slow down, and stop in a "wedge," then learn to control your speed by linking your turns. Finally, you'll learn to turn both skis in the same direction and execute tighter turns, controlling your speed while skiing the trails. There are also Mountain Adventure/Rider clinics focusing on powder skiing, mogul skiing or carving. Children's group programs (4–13) are around five hours, and range from an introduction to skiing or snowboarding through advanced coaching. Children's snowboard clinics are for children aged 7–13.

SKI SCHOOLS AND GUIDING

SUPER SKIER/RIDER
Level 1 or full-day clinics (4-hours), equipment rentals and lift ticket. US$155

LEVELS 1 AND 2
First Timers (Level 1) includes limited lift access, 45-minute clinic, equipment rental. US$89
Novice Turners (Level 2) includes limited lift access, 45-minute clinic, equipment rentals. US$89

MOUNTAIN ADVENTURES & MOUNTAIN RIDER PACKAGES (LEVELS 3–9)
Clinics are geared toward improving skiing or riding skills and exploring the mountain with your coach. Mountain Adventure clinics depart daily at 10:00 AM and 1:00 PM from the California Base Lodge. US$129

Heavenly Ski Resort
PO Box 2180 Stateline, NV 89449
www.skiheavenly.com
775-586-7000 or 800-243-2836

BEGINNERS

Heavenly has the advantage that many of the beginner trails are on the upper portions of the mountain, so beginners can enjoy an incredible view of Lake Tahoe as well as the whole ski area experience. Beginners have an exclusive secluded area near California Base Lodge, the Perfect Ride as well as the Enchanted Forest. In Nevada there's another area near Boulder Lodge called Edgewood Bowl. On the upper portion of the mountain, beginners can ride the Waterfall or Powderbowl lifts and enjoy Mombo Meadows (complete with a view of Lake Tahoe) and Maggie's trails.

INTERMEDIATES

Heavenly is famous for wide-open cruisers and incredible corduroy, perfect for carving those early morning turns. Most of the blue trails are long cruisers, with stunning views of Lake Tahoe. Intermediates can access almost every trail on the mountain. Take the Heavenly Gondola from the Village at Heavenly, either take Von Schmidt blue trail to the Sky Express quad and ski Ridge Run, Canyon and Yahoo, famous for their spectacular views of Lake Tahoe and their gentle cruising slopes, or take Tamarak and ski in Nevada and enjoy many of the blue trails like Big Dipper, Sand Dunes, and Olympic Downhill to either Stagecoach Lodge or Boulder Lodge.

ADVANCED & EXPERT

In California, black diamond trails Gunbarrel and The Face are famous for 1,700 vertical feet (510 m) of moguls, while in Nevada, Mott and Killebrew canyons offer a true backcountry experience complete with double black diamond chutes, gladed runs and plenty of steeps! As Lake Tahoe's highest resort, Heavenly is famous for its light, dry snow and the gladed trails where powder stashes can generally be found days after a storm. The best powder can generally be found in Nevada on the Dipper Knob trees, and the trees off Stagecoach and North Bowl. In California it's to be found in Powderbowl trees, and Maggie's Canyon.

◄ EXTREME ADVENTURES
If steep skiing is what you're here for, head for Gunbarrel and The Face, two challending black diamond trails.

◄ THROUGH THE TREES
Enjoy paradise amid snow-laden trees in back country areas such as Echo Lake.

EATING ON THE MOUNTAIN

CALIFORNIA SIDE
CALIFORNIA CAFÉ
CALIFORNIA BAR
MONUMENT PEAK RESTAURANT
TOP OF THE TRAM
PATSY'S HUT
SKY DECK

NEVADA SIDE
BLACK DIAMOND CANTINA
EAST PEAK LODGE
SLICE OF HEAVEN

One of the favorite extreme adventures at Heavenly combines the best of pristine bowls, serene glade trails, and hair-raising chutes. From the top of Sky Express, skiers and riders venture east into Nevada via the blue Skyline trail into Milky Way Bowl. With wide-open northeastern exposure, the Milky Way Bowl offers some of the best and most consistent midwinter snow on the mountain. After several floating turns in the bowl, head east to the ridge line for some world-class tree skiing. Then it is off to Mott Canyon—enter through Gate 1 and veer slightly to the west to the top of Snakepit. Looking down the narrow chute, with a 38° pitch just barely wide enough to make a turn, this extreme terrain will make your heart flutter.

A few areas for backcountry skiing are Echo Lake and Echo Summit off Highway 50, and Taylor Creek on the west side of Highway 89. If you're going to go off-piste, contact the U.S. Forest Service on 530-573-2600 for maps, trail guides, safety guidelines and to check snow and weather conditions.

BOARDING & FREESTYLE

There's snowboarding on 100 percent of the mountain, with three snowboard parks and a superpipe, two terrain parks complete with bank turns, table tops, rollers, hits and rail slides, as well as a halfpipe. With the vast network of lifts, snowboarders can easily access everything.

EATING ON THE MOUNTAIN

There are nine mountain restaurants covering just about every palate.

On the California side, California Lodge has the California Café for daily lunch specials and a salad bar, and the California Bar for cocktails, beer and wine, main dishes and live music. Monument Peak Restaurant, at the top of the aerial tram, offers fine dining and fab views. Top of the Tram has burgers, hot dogs, sandwiches and salads. Patsy's Hut is useful for hot chocolate, cookies and snacks, and a

▼ JUMP TO IT
With snowboarding access to the whole mountain, boarders can soar through the area all over the place, enjoying the 300 days of sunshine that Heavenly gets every year.

► OBSERVE
Take the gondola to the observation decks, 3,000 ft (900 m) above Lake Tahoe, for panoramic views.

RESTAURANTS

EXPENSIVE
LLEWELLYN'S IN HARVEY'S CASINO
RIVA GRILL, SKI RUN MARINA
EVANS, SOUTH LAKE TAHOE
CHRISTIANA INN, SOUTH LAKE TAHOE
THE FOREST BUFFET AT HARRAH'S

MODERATE
CANTINA BAR & GRILL, SOUTH LAKE TAHOE
THE FOREST BUFFET AT HARRAH'S

BUDGET
MOTT CANYON TAVERN & GRILL
HARD ROCK CAFÉ IN HARVEY'S RESORT

snack store. More burgers and barbecued chicken can be consumed in the sunshine at the Sky Deck.

On the Nevada side there's Italian food at a Slice of Heaven at Stagecoach Lodge, Mexican favorites on an outdoor deck at Black Diamond Cantina at Boulder Lodge, and BBQ, sandwiches and a Cappuccino Bar at East Peak Lodge.

APRÈS SKI

On the mountain, the California Bar at California Lodge features live music from Wednesday to Saturday and plenty of drink and appetizer specials.

Spectacular casinos, jazz clubs, blues bars, and arcades fill the south shore of Lake Tahoe. The minimum age for consuming alcohol is 21, and children are not allowed to accompany parents in bars and other places serving alcohol. Bars are open 24 hours in Nevada, but they will close at around 1:00 AM in California.

There are more than 150 restaurants on the south side of Lake Tahoe. The Summit Restaurant at Harrah's has an extensive wine list. It's also rated as one of the top 100 restaurants in the United States.

Club Nero at Caesar's and Altitude at Harrah's feature dancing late into the night, or if you like a slower, quieter setting you can enjoy drinks by the fire at the Christiana Inn near the California Base Lodge, or at the Riva Grill at Ski Run Marina.

For guests in search of gaming and live entertainment, casino shuttles run virtually 24 hours

◄ FAMILY FUN
There's something for every member of the family in the 4,800 acres (1,920 ha) of skiable terrain—families can cruise together through the awe-inspiring scenery.

DAYCARE

The Daycare Center caters for children from six weeks to six years. They can come here for non-skiing activities as well as skiing programs. A full day non-skiing includes lunch and activities such as art, music and movement, circle time, storytelling, rest time and snow play. The Ski & Snow Play Program is for children aged 3–4 and introduces them to skiing through play. The Half and Half Ski Program is for 4- to 5-year-olds and is for those who aren't quite ready for a full day's skiing, with skiing in the morning, lunch, and play in the afternoon.
Call 775-586-7000.

◄ **TAKE IT TO THE LIMIT**
Glide through fresh powder first thing in the morning for an ultimate shot of adrenaline.

OTHER ACTIVITIES

SNOWMOBILING
Lake Tahoe Adventures
Tahoe Paradise
530-577-2940

Zephyr Cove Snowmobile Center
Zephyr Cove
775-588-3833

DOGSLED RIDES
Husky Express Dog-sled Rides
775-782-3047

HORSE-DRAWN SLEIGH RIDES
Borges Sleigh Rides, across from Caesar's
530-541-2953

NATURAL HOT SPRINGS
Grover Hot Springs, Markleeville
530-694-2248

Wally's Hot Springs, Genoa
775-782-8155

a day. For a morning shopping spree, a late-night show, or anything in between, taxis and limousines are available around the clock, as is the South Lake Tahoe public transportation.

OTHER ACTIVITIES

Although most visitors come to Heavenly to ski or ride, there are lots of other outdoor adventures to be enjoyed.

Adventure Peak at the top of the Heavenly Gondola has lift-accessed snowtubing, sledding, 2.5 miles (4 km) of cross-country skiing, and snowshoeing. The park is open daily, 10:00 AM–3:00 PM, and costs US$15 for two hours or US$25 for a full day, including rental of equipment.

See the wonders of the mountain from a dogsled, while teams of Huskies take you on an adventure. Alternatively, swap the dogs for a horse and take a one-hour horse-drawn sleigh ride.

To ease tired ski muscles you can relax in a natural hot spring. There's one in California and one in Nevada, Wally's Hot Springs, which is also the oldest Sierra resort.

For shopping you can try Emerald Bay Trading Company in the Crescent V Shopping Center in South Lake Tahoe for fashions, fine antiques, home furnishings, and gifts. Or try Heavenly Sports in California Lodge and Stateline, Nevada, for the latest in ski technology. The Boardinghouse, at Longs Drugs Shopping Center and in the Marriott Grand Residence Club next to the Heavenly Gondola, has the hottest snowboard selection. There are lots of other shopping centers around the south shore.

USEFUL PHONE NUMBERS

Tourist Office	530-541-5255
Ski Rescue Service	775-586-7000
Doctor @ Barton Memorial Hospital	530-541-3420
Taxi	530-577-4708
Snow Phone	775-586-7000
Ski Rental	775-586-7000
Lodgings Reservations	800-243-2836
Lift Tickets/Ski Schools	775-585-7000

USEFUL WEBSITES

Official Website	www.skiheavenly.com
Ski Rental	www.rentskis.com

▼ **FACE POWDER**
Keep your eyes open but with face powder flying into your mouth you may find yourself gasping for breath.

EVERYONE SHOULD EXPERIENCE THE MAGNIFICENT VIEWS OF LAKE TAHOE AND DESOLATION WILDERNESS FROM 8,852 FEET (2,655 M). AT SIERRA YOU CAN DO JUST THAT. BUT SIERRA IS ALSO KNOWN FOR ITS FINE TREE SKIING, GOOD VALUE, AND WEATHER-PROTECTED SEASON. WITH AN AVERAGE ANNUAL SNOWFALL OF 480 INCHES (1,219 CM) YOU'RE VIRTUALLY GUARANTEED A GOOD SEASON ANY YEAR.

SIERRA-AT-TAHOE

Sierra-at-Tahoe has been operating since 1947, when it was just a modest ski hill. Today it has matured into one of Lake Tahoe's best ski areas, sharing a lift pass with Alpine Meadows, Heavenly, Kirkwood, Northstar-at-Tahoe, and Squaw Valley. Most visitors to Sierra stay in South Lake Tahoe, 12 miles (19 km) by road, and other towns surrounding Lake Tahoe. There's no lodgings at the Base Lodge at Sierra, which is just a day lodge with restaurants and a daycare facility. In 2003 an additional access road improved the arrival and departure for cars and shuttle buses, and there's a new "Preferred Parking" area right next to the slopes, which will provide a much shorter walk to the car at the end of a day's hard work. Enhanced snowmaking capabilities have been added to the Superpipe, enabling Sierra to open its pipe earlier in the season than most other resorts.

GETTING THERE

Sierra-at-Tahoe is located 12 miles (19 km) from South Lake Tahoe, in California, off U.S. Highway 50. The nearest international airports are Reno, Sacramento, and San Francisco. Sacramento is 85

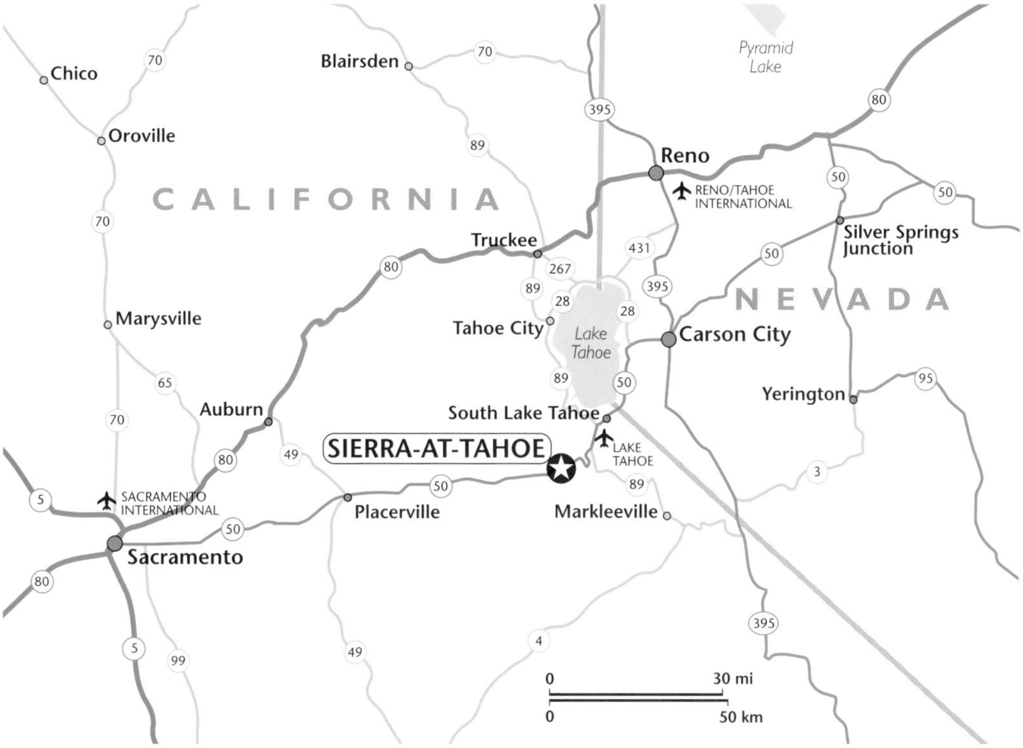

MOUNTAIN FACTS

Base	6,640 feet (2,024 m)
Summit	8,852 feet (2,698 m)
Elevation	2,212 feet (674 m)
Easy	25%
Intermediate	50%
Advanced/Expert	25%
Number of trails	46
Number of terrain parks	4
Longest trail	2.5 miles (4 km)
Ski area	2,000 acres (809 ha)

SNOWFALL

Annual snowfall	480 inches (1,219 cm)
Snowmaking	20%

SKI LIFTS

High-Speed Quads	3
Triple Chairs	1
Double Chairs	5
Magic Carpets	1
Total	10
Riders per hour	14,920

SKI SEASON
Mid-November to late April

◄ TREE SLALOM
You'll find plenty of opportunity to improve your off-piste skills on gladed slopes with great lake views, but watch out for those trees.

miles (137 km) away, around 1.5 hours' drive, Reno is 80 miles (129 km), which takes around two hours along Interstate 395 south through Carson City, Nevada, to U.S. Highway 50 West, and San Francisco is 170 miles (274 km), around three hours' drive along Interstate 80 east to U.S. Highway 50 and east through Placerville. An airport shuttle, the Tahoe Casino Express, takes you from Reno to your destination. There's also a free daily shuttle bus service from South Lake Tahoe to the mountain from 40 locations in the town.

THE VILLAGE

There is no real village atmosphere at Sierra. The Base Lodge has restaurants and a daycare center, but for accommodations and après ski you have to go to South Lake Tahoe or one of the other towns around Lake Tahoe.

ACCOMMODATIONS

In South Lake Tahoe, there are more than 20,000 rooms available, ranging in style from elegant to simple comfort. You can easily get from your accommodation to the slopes with the free shuttle bus service, the Tahoe Casino Express. Lodgings and lift packages are available through 800-288-2463.

◄ BREATHTAKING
Lake Tahoe view taken mid-May after the season ended but still plenty of snow on top. At left is Sierra-at-Tahoe taken from Mt. Rose, and Mt. Tallac center.

Some of Lake Tahoe's most famous casinos are on hand at South Lake Tahoe, such as Harrah's, Harvey's, Caesar's, and the Lakeside Inn. All offer luxury accommodations in elegant rooms with good views. For a less glitzy option there's Tahoe Valley Lodge in South Lake Tahoe, which offers ski

ACCOMMODATIONS

SOUTH LAKE TAHOE CASINOS
HARRAH'S
800-427-7247
www.harrahs.com

HARVEY'S
800-427-8397
www.harveys.com

CAESAR'S
888-829-7630
www.caesars.com

LAKESIDE INN
800-624-7980
www.lakesideinn.com

SOUTH LAKE TAHOE
TAHOE VALLEY LODGE
800-669-7544
www.tahoevalleylodge.com

RIDGEWOOD INN
530-541-8589
www.ridgewoodinn.com

AMERICAN RIVER
STRAWBERRY LODGE
www.strawberrylodge.com

NEARBY RESORTS

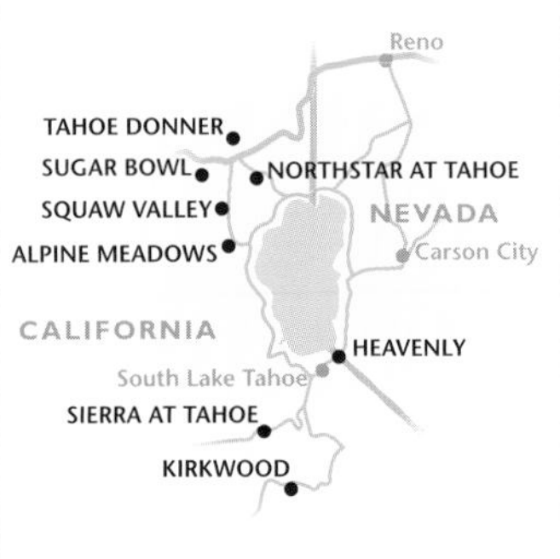

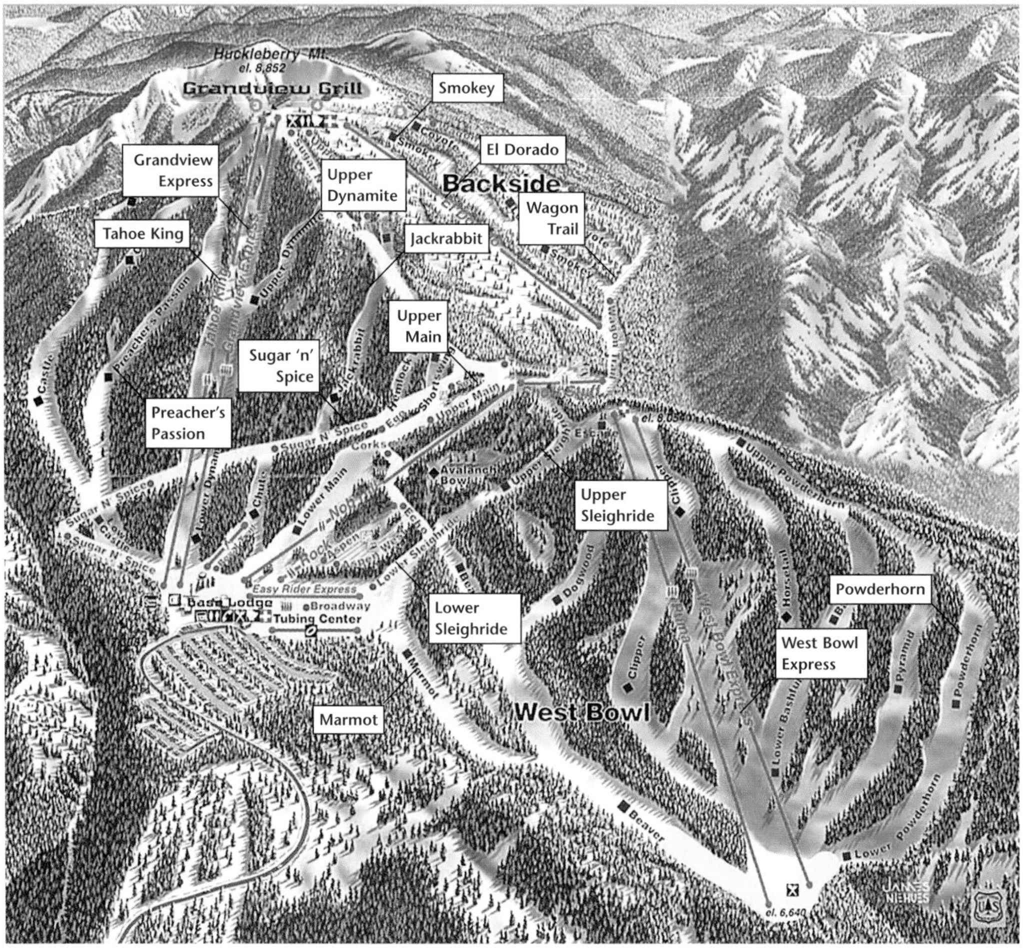

packages; the Ridgewood Inn in South Lake Tahoe, a small establishment with only 12 rooms set in two acres (0.8 ha) of forest; or Strawberry Lodge on the American River 20 minutes' drive west of Sierra, with rustic, charming rooms and views of the mountains.

SKI AREA

Sierra offers varied terrain for all levels of skiers and riders around its 2,000 acres (809 ha). In total there are 46 trails accessed by 10 lifts, with a 2.5-mile (4-km) beginner trail, Sugar 'n' Spice, from the summit. What's different about Sierra, though, is that there are also 600 acres (243 ha) of backcountry skiing and riding accessed via five backcountry gates and complete with free instruction for advanced skiers from a ski patrol guide.

SKI LIFTS

There are 10 lifts operating 8:30 AM to 4:00 PM on weekends and holidays, and from 9:00 AM until 4:00 PM on weekdays. The lifts consist of three Express quads, one triple chair, five double chairs, and a magic carpet for children.

LIFT PASSES

Remember that Sierra is affiliated to Alpine Meadows, Heavenly, Kirkwood, Northstar-at-Tahoe, and Squaw Valley, and shares a lift pass with all of them, giving masses of opportunity for skiing varied trails. A full-day pass costs US$53 for adults (23–64), US$43 for young adult (13–22), US$11 for children (5–12), US$32 for seniors (65–69) and US$12 for

▼ **MOUNTAIN BASE**
Base Lodge has restaurants and a day-care center, but there's no village and therefore no ambience at Sierra, so it's a 12-mile (19-km) drive to South Lake Tahoe for après-ski.

seniors 70+. Children aged four and under ski free. A 3- of 5-days pass costs US$134 for adults (23–64), US$112 for young adult (13–22), US$33 for children (5–12), US$81 for seniors (65–69) and US$36 for seniors 70+.

There are various special deals that can make life cheaper, including half-day passes at reduced rates, the Vertical Plus frequent skier and rider membership program that allows you to accumulate points for the number of feet you ride or ski, and the "After 2:00 PM, Tomorrow Too" lift pass, where you can buy the next day's full-day lift ticket after 2:00 PM and get a few free hours on the slopes at the time of purchase.

SKI SCHOOLS AND GUIDING

From private instruction and group lessons to multiday retreats and free clinics for intermediate and advanced skiers and riders, Sierra has a lesson plan for everyone. You can even learn freestyle mogul skiing. The following is just a selection.

The Get Good Quick Center is the learning hub at Sierra for skiers and boarders aged 13 and older. A variety of lesson packages are offered for first-time, beginner, and intermediate skiers and snowboarders.

A signature program at Sierra is free lessons for intermediate and advanced skiers and riders aged 13 or older. Offered daily at 11:30 AM and 1:00 PM, you'll receive 1.5 hours of instruction on the topic of the day. Lessons are available on a first-come, first-served basis and you'll need a lift pass.

The Burton Learn-to-Ride (L.T.R.) Method Center offers a program designed to accelerate the learning curve of snowboarding using two simple guidelines: small class sizes of no more than four students, and proper equipment. One- and two-day classes are taught by professionally trained Burton L.T.R. instructors. L.T.R. lessons are for snowboarders aged 13 and older.

For children aged 4–12, first-timers to advanced, the Wild Mountain Children's Center ski and snowboard camps focus on fun and sport. The program includes equipment rental, lift ticket, instruction, lunch, snacks, and a progress card. The early pick-up is an attractive option for families who want to brush up on their skills in the morning, and hit the slopes as a family in the afternoon. Reservations are strongly recommended.

BEGINNERS

Sierra is one of the few resorts with a beginner trail that leads from the summit to the base of the mountain. Sugar 'n' Spice is a 2.5-mile (4-km) cruiser off the Grandview Express quad chairlift. It's a truly fantastic way to cut your teeth on the art of skiing and allows beginners to really experience what it's like to stand on the top of a mountain without being terrified! As well as Sugar 'n' Spice there's Wagon Trail, another green trail reached from El Dorado

EQUIPMENT RENTAL

Legacy Lodge has the most recent, top-of-the-line ski and snowboard equipment.

▼ BETTER ACCESS

A new road allows better access and the new preferred parking area may not be pretty but it's right next to the slopes.

DAYCARE
Wild Mountain Ski/Snowboard Camp and Daycare has licensed daycare for children 18 months to five years. Call 530-659-7453 ext. 270.

double chairlift, which leads around the edge of the mountain and joins up with Sugar 'n' Spice to the base, or via Upper Main, Corks, Echo, and Lower Sleighride to the base.

INTERMEDIATES

Half the trails at Sierra are blues, for intermediate skiers and riders. For a good long trail take the Grandview Express quad to the summit and ski across to Smokey or Coyote beyond El Dorado double lift. Then join on with Wagon Trail green trail to the blue Upper Sleighride, then Marmot and drop into Beaver in the West Bowl. Take the West Bowl Express for some more blues: Upper Powderhorn, Bashful, Pyramid, and Lower Powderhorn.

ADVANCED AND EXPERT

With 25 percent of the mountain as black diamond trails, advanced skiers have a good choice of skiing and riding. Preacher's Passion off the Tahoe King double chair is probably the hardest trail—it's steep, long, and has the option of trees the whole way down. This trail is also really good for snowboarding as there are no flats. Avalanche Bowl is a powder playground, and Upper Dynamite and Jackrabbit are two of the expert's favorites on a powder day. If you want to escape the crowds you can ski off the trails, such as between Coyote and Smokey on the Backside, or find the less-crowded blues—Marmot is often quieter than other blues.

For advanced skiers and riders, backcountry tours explore Sierra's steepest terrain—considered locally as some of the region's best. Five backcountry gates provide access to forests and some of the steepest terrain found in the region. The cost for a 3.5-hour backcountry tour is US$25 in addition to a lift pass. Tours are led by professional ski patrol staff and include a briefing on safety procedures and proper use of avalanche transceivers. Reservations are required. Each registered person must participate in a skills assessment test to determine proficiency.

BOARDING & FREESTYLE

There are four terrain parks at Sierra, catering to all ability levels of skier and snowboarder, and each has a sound system, making them popular places to just hang out. Enhanced snowmaking was added in 2003 to the 17-foot (5-m) Superpipe. The Superpipe is groomed nightly.

EATING ON THE MOUNTAIN

Sierra is consistently recognized for having good food at reasonable prices. The Grandview Grill at the summit has breathtaking views over Lake Tahoe and Desolation Wilderness. Watch the colors of Lake Tahoe changing with the movement of the sun while filling up on burgers, tortilla wraps, East-meets-West entrées, and something from the bar. The summit of the West Bowl area has a new hospitality tent stocked with sandwiches, snacks, and drinks. At the Base Lodge there's a choice of eating establishments: the Aspen Café has entrées, fries, and Mexican selections; Cheeseburgers in Paradise does just what it says; the Sierra Pub has pizza, sandwiches, nachos, and alcohol; and the Front Porch does specialty coffee and snacks.

◄ **EARN YOUR TURNS**
5th Grade schoolteacher Matt Gold on Castle trail off Grandview chair kicks up the powder, but its May 15 and the resort is closed so he had to hike for it.

EATING ON THE MOUNTAIN

- GRANDVIEW GRILL
- WEST BOWL
- BASE LODGE
- ASPEN CAFÉ
- CHEESEBURGERS IN PARADISE
- SIERRA PUB
- FRONT PORCH
- BAKE SHOP

◄ STEEP 'N' DEEP
Matt Gold again, this time on Eastbowl run off the Grandview chair looking North over Lake Tahoe. Okay, so there's no village at Sierra, but what about the views and the skiing.

APRÈS SKI

There isn't any après ski at the Base Lodge, but in South Lake Tahoe there are around 90 restaurants, bars and, of course, casino nightlife in the main casinos, where there's usually a show or cabaret being performed, not to mention the slots. The restaurant choices in the town cover coffee shops through Chinese, Italian, Mexican, to sandwich shops. For further information on bars and restaurants, visit South Lake Tahoe's website, www.southlaketahoe.com.

OTHER ACTIVITIES

Tubing, snowshoeing, and snowtoys are all fun alternatives to skiing and snowboarding.

Tubing at Sierra is probably one of the highest thrill activities available. The lanes cover 425 feet (127 m) of high-banked turns and rollers, and a slick, quick surface. Tubing lanes are open daily, weather and conditions permitting. The cost is US$15 per person for two hours, which includes tube rental and access to the rope tow that carries the tube and its rider to the top of the hill.

Did you know that snowshoeing is recognized among fitness experts as one of the most effective cardiovascular activities, burning off a hefty 550–750 calories per hour! Sierra maintains three miles (5 km) of scenic, groomed snowshoe trails below the Base Lodge. Interpretive signs lining the trail system explain wildlife and other interesting facts about the Sierra Nevada mountains. Snowshoe rentals are available for US$15 per two hours.

For a new twist, hit the slopes on a snowbike, snowscoot, or skifox. Snowbikes are a high-thrill, low-skill activity. In place of tires are two mini skis that skim the surface of the snow. The rider grabs the handlebars and steers downhill. The snowscoot is a crazy adaptation of the foot-propelled scooter, and accomplished users even pull tricks in the halfpipe and terrain parks. The skifox is likened to a chair on a tripod. The rider is seated wearing a mini ski on each foot, while the skifox is mounted on its own ski. The tighter the traverse, the faster it goes.

USEFUL PHONE NUMBERS

General Information		530-659-7453
24-hour Snow Report		530-659-7475
Tahoe Casino Express		800-446-6128
Burton Learn to Ride	Ext. 290	530-659-7453
Wild Mountain Ski/Snowboard Camp	Ext. 270	530-659-7453
Daycare	Ext. 270	530-659-7453

USEFUL WEBSITES & E-MAIL ADDRESSES

Official Website	www.sierratahoe.com
Official E-mail	sierra@boothcreek.com
Road Conditions	www.sierratahoe.com/road.html
Tahoe Casino Express	www.TahoeCasinoExpress.com

▼ GOOD FRIENDS
Another friend of photographer Grant Barta—this time it's Hollywood scriptwriter Ben Bleichman sending the spring powder flying on Upper Dynamite off the Grandview chair.

PERHAPS THE MOST IMPRESSIVE THING ABOUT KIRKWOOD IS THE MOUNTAIN ITSELF—THE MASSIVE ROCK FACE OF THIMBLE PEAK AT 9,800 FEET (2,987 M) DOMINATES AND LEADS TO A FOREST OF GULLY TRAILS DROPPING DOWN TO ALLOW A MASSIVE VERTICAL FALL-LINE. HERE YOU'LL FIND THE DEEPEST AND BEST SNOW QUALITY IN THE LAKE TAHOE REGION.

KIRKWOOD

NEARBY RESORTS

SKI SEASON
Mid-November to late April

▶ LESS HUSTLE AND BUSTLE
On the southern side of Lake Tahoe, Kirkwood has a mainly northern aspect and a snowfall averaging 500 inches (1,270 cm). Add steepness to this cocktail and the recipe is for superb, chilled out riding.

Once a simple way-station for weary trans-Sierra travelers, then a humble ski resort founded in the early 1970s, the Kirkwood Mountain Resort is now a favorite for those who enjoy the best snow and some of the best skiing and riding in the western states.

Here's home to America's deepest snow sprinkled with luxurious accommodations, shopping and fine dining, all within the confines of a brand new mountain village. Kirkwood is famous for deep snow. In fact the resort has boasted the deepest snow in North America for seven of the past 10 seasons and measurements are verified against those taken by government agencies in the surrounding areas.

But forget the statistics, Kirkwood is all about powder—deep, dry, and a delight for boarders and free-skiers riding the horseshoe-shaped, cornice-lined mountains, filling in steep chutes and wide open bowls. Add to that a vast surround in every direction of endless miles of protected Wilderness and Forest Service Land, and you have a unique balance of a world-class mountain with all the creature comforts in a pristine sanctuary. No wonder the resort attracts a variety of enthusiasts, but unlike many other resorts with similar natural attributes, such as Jackson Hole, the atmosphere at Kirkwood is definitely low-key.

GETTING THERE

Kirkwood lies 35 miles (56 km) south of South Lake Tahoe, and 80 miles (128 km) west of the Reno Tahoe International Airport—approximately a 90-minute drive. It's three hours back to the greater San Francisco Bay Area depending on conditions. While the road to Kirkwood, Highway 88, is very well maintained, heavy snowfall can make the trip to the Kirkwood challenging at times during the course of the season.

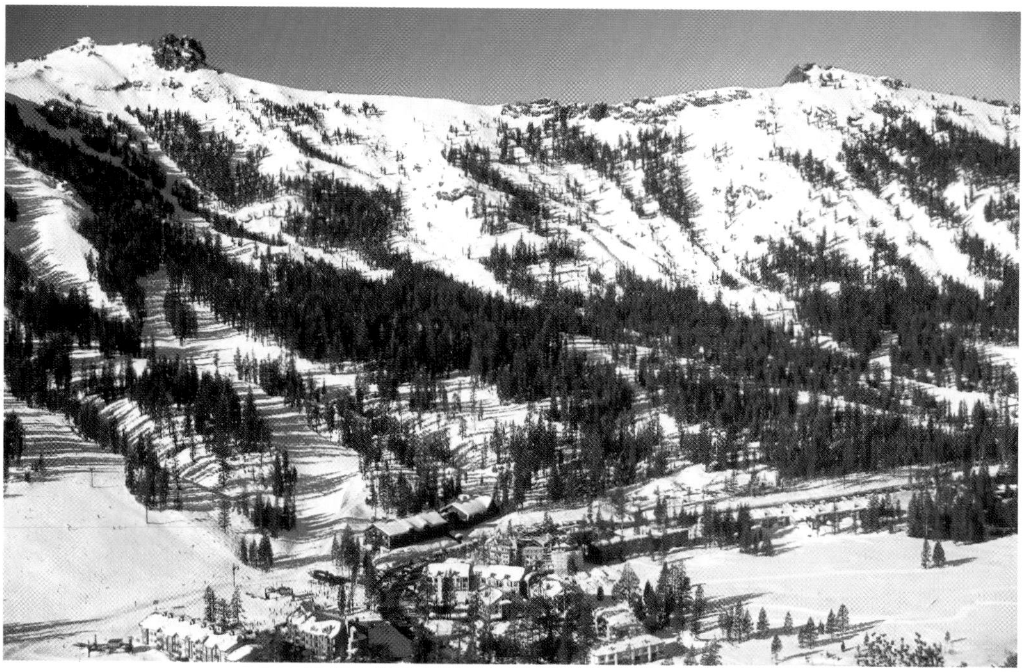

MOUNTAIN FACTS

Base	7,800 feet (2,377 m)
Summit	9,800 feet (2,987 m)
Elevation	2,000 feet (610 m)
Easy	15%
Intermediate	50%
Advanced & Expert	35%
Longest trail	2.5 miles (4 km)
Ski area	2,300 acres (932 ha)

SNOWFALL

Annual snowfall	500 inches (1,270 cm)
Snowmaking	55 acres (22 ha)

SKI LIFTS

Cable Cars	-
Gondolas	2
High-Speed Quads	1
Fixed Grip Quads	1
Triple Chairs	7
Double Chairs	1
Surface Lifts	2
Total	14
Riders per hour	17,905

THE VILLAGE

The small resort is currently undergoing a US$250 million metamorphosis from a day skier's mountain to a year-round destination resort. It's already showcasing a new ski-in, ski-out Mountain Village with numerous stores and restaurants and an ice rink at the plaza's edge, offering full amenities to serve both destination visitors and the local community, much like the famous Telluride Ski Resort in Colorado. Other new developments include Kirkwood's Cornice Café, remodeled and reopened as Bub's Sports Bar and Grill, and now a popular place for families. A swimming and fitness complex has also been completed for year-round operation.

ACCOMMODATIONS

Four new, luxury lodges opened in the village significantly increase overnight accommodations for visitors to the valley, and lodgings will be increased from the current overnight capacity of 2,000 to approximately 6,500. The village plaza will connect to the Red Cliffs Day Lodge with additional plaza-level stores and restaurants. So Kirkwood's overnight lodgings have increased substantially with the new village, but there are still no hotels within the resort.

Kirkwood Vacations rents privately owned slope-side accommodations including condominiums, lodges and cabins. Each unit is unique. All except singles feature a fully equipped kitchen with microwave, fireplace, color T.V., V.C.R. and telephone. All units are conveniently located within walking distance from the slopes.

SKI AREA

Because Kirkwood is at a much higher elevation than the rest of the South Shore resorts—its base elevation begins at 7,800 feet (2,377 m)—it consistently receives the most and the best snow. So its 2,300 acres (932 ha) of wide-open terrain promises something for everyone—from gentle groomed trails through hair-raising steeps and chutes, but most of the skiing is for intermediates and above with only 15 percent of the ski area suitable for beginners. Artificial snowmaking covers four major runs from top to bottom for a total of 55 acres (22 ha). From the base elevation of the village the highest point of 9,800 feet (2,987m) allows a maximum vertical descent of 2,000 feet (610 m).

▼ NEW MOUNTAIN VILLAGE
This is Tahoe's only true ski-in, ski-out village offering luxury slopeside lodgings, fine dining, a Performance Center, and Village Ice Rink. Nearby stores can outfit skiers and snowboarders with the newest equipment.

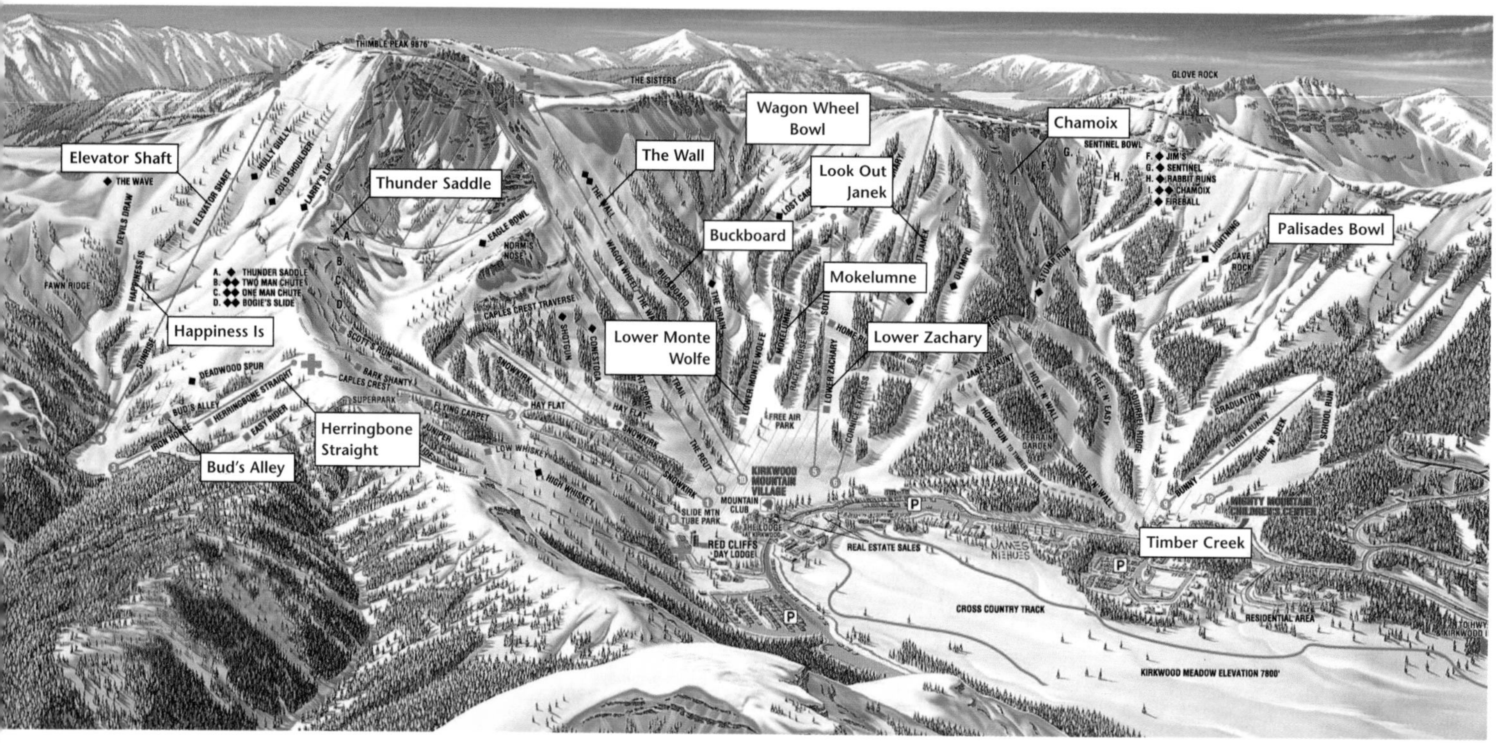

LIFT PASSES	
ADULT (19-64)	US$399
STUDENT (19-42)	US$319
JUNIOR (13-18)	US$319
SENIOR (65-69)	US$209
SENIOR PLUS (70+)	US$109
CHILD (6-12)	US$109
5 & UNDER	US$29

SKI PASSES
SKI & BOARD SCHOOL AND
MIGHTY MOUNTAIN
Post Office Box 1,
Kirkwood, CA 95646
www.kirkwood.com
209-258-7245

► UNCROWDED SLOPES
Big investment and big snow are transforming Kirkwood from locals' retreat to a ski resort worthy of a detour and a ski destination in its own name—with a growing reputation especially among freeriders.

SKI LIFTS

Kirkwood's ski area is served by two gondolas,10 chairlifts, and two handle tows, with a capacity for 17,905 skiers per hour. The lift system is graded to match level of difficulty of the terrain accessed from the top of each lift. The easiest, distinguished by the usual green circle, gives access to the beginners' trails off chairs #1 and #9, and off chair #7. The more difficult intermediate terrain is shown by a blue square and includes trails off chairs #2, #3, #4, #5,

#7, and #11. For advanced skiers and riders, a single black diamond is used which includes trails off chair lifts #4, #6, and #11. Finally the expert trails are denoted by two black diamonds and are reachable by chairlifts #4, #6, and #10. Lifts start from 8:30–9:00 AM and close at 4:00–4:30 PM.

The resort recently installed its first high-speed quad chair (the first of several planned detachable ones), which will transport skiers from the Mountain Village to the top of the mountain in just four minutes. Other new lifts and upgrades to three existing lifts will increase lift capacity from the Timber Creek area to the Mountain Village and incorporate an on-mountain restaurant at the top of Caples Crest. Kirkwood's new Mountain Master Development Plan (MMDP) will, over the next decade, provide lift access to hundreds of further acres of "hike-to" terrain and reduce travel time from the front side to the back side of the resort by more than 50 percent.

LIFT PASSES

Lift passes can be bought on the mountain, in South Lake Tahoe, at lodging properties and selected ski shops, and at Costco Stores throughout northern California and western Nevada. Lines, incidentally, are very rarely a problem. Over the most crowded weekends and holiday periods, advanced skiers can avoid lines by skiing chair #10 rather than #6; intermediates can avoid lines by heading to the backside chair #4 early in the morning. Beginners will find shorter lines on chair #1 than chair #9. Full adult lift passes cost US$399, with significant discounts for seniors, students and children. Special deals include a First Time Adventure pass and a Learn-to-ski package, both at discounted prices for limited access.

SKI SCHOOLS & GUIDING

Even with the emphasis on powder, the resort can still offer innovative First-Time Skier and Snowboarding programs on its wide, gentle slopes. Mighty Mountain Children's Center makes skiing more convenient for families and fun for kids, and is located at the Timber Creek Area. The other ski school is the Ski & Board School. The main office is located across from the Red Cliffs Day Lodge.

Lessons may also be purchased at the ski school meeting places on the mountain (at base of chairs #5 and #6 and at base of chairs #7 and #9) and at rental stores (Timber Creek Lodge, Red Cliffs Lodge). Schools start at 10:00 AM, Noon, and 2:00 PM for adult lessons, and 10:00 AM and 1:30 PM for Children's Ski School (arrive approximately one hour early for registration and for rental equipment.) Maximum class size is six to eight adults; minimum age for children is four for skiing and seven for snowboarding.

The Ski and Snowboard School act as guides either one-on-one, or in their Mountain Adventure package, and for the fifth consecutive season, the North American Ski Training Center (N.A.S.T.C.) will be based at Kirkwood. N.A.S.T.C. is a multi-day, total immersion, performance ski school for advanced intermediate, advanced, and expert skiers, with special clinics offered in backcountry skills and avalanche awareness. Camps include seminars, video analysis, meals, lift tickets, and instruction. Call 530-582-4772 for camp information and reservations

BEGINNERS

The Timber Creek base area is the best place to be if you are a beginner skier. Most of the green trails are located there, and because the area does not appeal to the advanced skier, it is a much more comfortable, less intimidating experience for the first-time skier. Beginners are not completely confined but cannot reach the top of the mountain.

INTERMEDIATES

Intermediates have 50 percent of the total terrain to carve up. Elevator Shaft is the steepest intermediate run. A classic ski itinerary might be to warm up on chair #7 for a couple runs then take it up and ski down Up 'n' Over to the front side of the mountain. Try the runs on chair #5 starting skiers right on Lower Monte Wolfe and moving skiers left to Mokelumne, and then Lower Zachary. Next head to chair #11 and take Buckboard, if with children, also try Snowsnake Gully. Good time for a lunch break at Bub's Sports Bar and Grill or Monte Wolfe. After lunch head to chair #2 and try Bark Shanty. After a couple runs on chair #2 head over to the backside, chair #4, via Herringbone Straight and Bud's Alley, and try Elevator Shaft and Happiness Is.

RESTAURANTS & BARS

OFF THE WALL BAR AND GRILL
Located in the Lodge at Kirkwood
Full service for fine dining
Cozy fireplace
Overstuffed chairs
Reservations are recommended..
209-258-7365

KIRKWOOD INN
Located on Highway 88
Built in 1864 by Zachary Kirkwood
Open daily for hearty meals anytime
Mouthwatering steaks and seafood.
209-258-7304

BUB'S SPORTS BAR AND GRILL
Located next to the General Store
Kirkwood's new sports bar restaurant
Great happy hour specials
Family-friendly atmosphere
All-American cuisine
209-258-7225

MONTE WOLFE'S COFFEE HOUSE
Located in the Village Plaza
Busy and bustling
Food on the move
Anytime of the day
Outdoor seating available
209-258-7246

RED CLIFF'S LODGE
Quick and affordable
Cafeteria-style breakfast or lunch
Outdoor BBQ at weekends
290-258-7426

ZAK'S BAR
Located in Red Cliffs Lodge
Full bar service
Three big-screen T.V.s
Imported and domestic beers on tap
290-258-7360

SUNRISE GRILL
Located near the base of Chair #4
A quick stop for avid skiers
BBQ ribs, burgers, chicken
Outdoor seating
290-258-7309

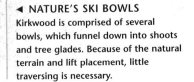

◄ **NATURE'S SKI BOWLS**
Kirkwood is comprised of several bowls, which funnel down into shoots and tree glades. Because of the natural terrain and lift placement, little traversing is necessary.

▲ **POWDER TRAILS**
Virtually everywhere is skiable in the "Wood," so even if the trail map shows a route or not this can be taken as a suggestion by the more advanced skier and boarder.

ADVANCED

The best area is accessed from chairs #6 and 10 and Thunder Saddle (off chair #4) while the toughest skiing is Look Out Janek; Steep and Deep Wagon Wheel Bowl and Thunder Saddle. For powder it has to be Palisades Bowl, Wagon Wheel Bowl, Thunder Saddle and Fawn Ridge. For advanced or expert skier the classic route really depends on the weather and conditions. Powder days are totally different than non-powder days and there are many powder days at Kirkwood.

On a non-powder day perhaps take a few warm-up runs on chair #11 (Wagon Trail and Conestoga). Next head to chair #6 and ski Sentinel Bowl, Olympic, and Monte Wolfe. When conditions are good off-piste, go for Lost Cabin and over to Rabbit Runs. After a few laps on each of these trails head to chair #10 and look for the best lines from the chair. The Wall, Eagle Bowl, and Norm's Nose are all popular trails. Finally make your way over to the backside and take a few trails off chair #4 before heading in via Thunder Saddle.

Boundaries are open at management's discretion and there is unlimited expert terrain accessible. Wagon Wheel Bowl from the top of the cornice (accessed by chair #6 or chair #10) offers steep terrain, which funnels into narrow chutes. Chamoix from chair #6 is a narrow, steep chute. If you continue to explore right of Chamoix, there is a series of great steep pitches with often some of the best snow (no sun exposure). There are numerous snow-filled steep chutes in the Thunder Saddle area, the toughest being Hell's Delight (right along the Cirque boundary line).

BOARDING & FREESTYLE

Kirkwood is a favorite among freestyle skiers and boarders. With the varied terrain, especially the number of steep shoots and gullies, the entire resort is a bit of a natural terrain park. In response to a growing demand by skiers and riders for a terrain park system that rivals Kirkwood's natural terrain, Kirkwood is committed to its terrain park program. The most recent addition is the Superpark, which contains the resort's most challenging manmade features. A special pass and liability release form is required (kids under the age of 18 must have parent/guardian's signature.)

In addition to the Superpark, Kirkwood's program includes a beginner park, a family park, and a halfpipe. Park riders can always find a variety of freestyle terrain suitable for their ability and interest. The parks offer hits, jumps, tables, spines, and handrails.

EATING ON AND OFF THE MOUNTAIN

There are eight restaurants on and (mostly) off the mountain offering cafeteria and deli-style refreshment as well as more upscale dining at the resort's main full-service restaurant, Off the Wall Bar & Grill. Located in the Lodge at Kirkwood, diners can appreciate spectacular views (along Kirkwood's ridge tops from Thimble Peak to Martin Point) in an intimate setting complete with a cozy fireplace and overstuffed chairs. Sunrise Grill near the base of chair #4 is a quick-stop place serving barbequed ribs, burgers, chicken, snacks, and beverages for avid skiers who want to keep their energy levels high without coming in off the slopes. Outdoor seating in

► **SNOWBOADERS' FAVORITE**
Of all the Lake Tahoe resorts Kirkwood is probably the snowboarders' favorite, not least because it is possibly the largest natural snowboard park in the U.S. The high ridge line arcs around to contain very steep chutes, long gullies, scary cliff drops, big wind lips, wide open bowls and enough extreme terrain to satisfy any freerider on a powder day. Below that, there's plenty of crisp corduroy trails to carve your boards.

beach-style chairs, and good music make it a great place to just relax in the sun. Bub's Sports Bar and Grill in the village is the place to go for a family-friendly atmosphere. Bub's specializes in all-American cuisine.

APRÈS SKI

Kirkwood has six bars and Bub's Sports Bar and Grill is the most popular bar and evening hangout for all age groups. Bub's boasts a full-service bar, big-screen T.V.s, pool tables, and a warm, inviting atmosphere. For a great spot to end the day, skiers head for Off the Wall Bar & Grill. Only 35 highway miles (56 km) away, South Lake Tahoe has over 100 dining establishments, 65 lodgings properties, shopping, dancing, live music, entertainment, and gaming action at the casinos where celebrities take the stage every night of the week.

OTHER ACTIVITIES

If you seek other snow thrills, sample some of the 50 miles (80 km) of scenic cross-country skiing, or try a horse-drawn sleigh ride. But you don't have to be skiing to enjoy your time at Kirkwood. Just outside Kirkwood there are several trails for snowmobiling. There are lakes for ice fishing, and Grover Hot Springs— a natural outdoor mineral pool —in Markleeville is just a 45-minute drive down the mountain. Slide Mountain Tubing Park opened two years ago.

USEFUL PHONE NUMBERS

Tourist Information Center	209-258-6000
Kirkwood Reservations	800-967-7500
Sleigh Rides	775-750-4054
Cross-Country & Snowshoeing	209-258-7248

USEFUL WEBSITES

Official Website	www.kirkwood.com
Weather Reports	www.wunderground.com

▲ DEEPLY IMPRESSIVE
Kirkwood's horseshoe-shaped, cornice-lined mountain is coated with the deepest, driest powder in the Sierra.

▼ POWDER PACKED
Powder is what Kirkwood is all about—as these carved tracks show on a typical sunny morning.

MAMMOTH HAS CONSISTENTLY BEEN VOTED ONE OF THE TOP SKI AND SNOWBOARD DESTINATIONS IN NORTH AMERICA. IT HAS ONE OF THE LONGEST SEASONS ANYWHERE IN THE WORLD, OPENING FROM EARLY NOVEMBER TO JUNE. IN THE MIDDLE OF THE INYO NATIONAL FOREST, ON THE EDGE OF WILDERNESS, MAMMOTH MIGHT BE A BIT ISOLATED, BUT WITH OVER 300 DAYS OF SUNSHINE PER YEAR AND 3,500 SKIABLE ACRES (1,400 HA), IT'S PRACTICALLY GUARANTEED THAT YOU'LL HAVE A GREAT VACATION HERE.

MAMMOTH MOUNTAIN

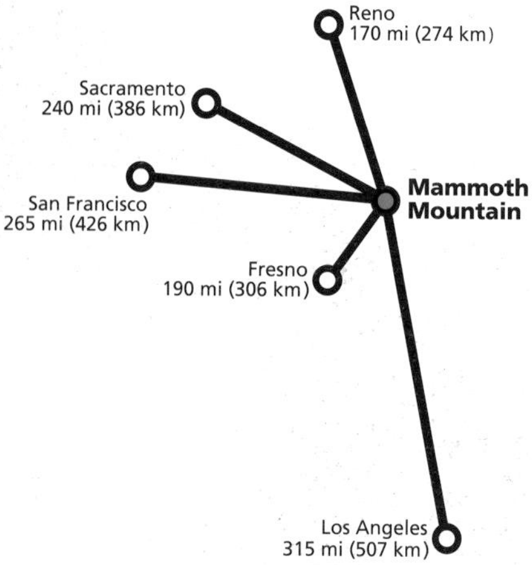

Mammoth enjoys an extremely reliable snow record, with an average 384 inches (975 cm) per year, and snowmaking exists on 46 of the 150 trails. With over US$100 million invested in the resort in the last four years, Mammoth is expanding. Specific improvements include the remodeled McCoy Station at mid-mountain, an ever-expanding lift system, and The Village at Mammoth, which opened in 2003. The Village provides a third lodge facility for the ski area, including gondola access, luxury accommodation, restaurants and stores. There are three other base lodges—Main Lodge, Canyon Lodge and Eagle Lodge. All have amenities that make it easy to get on the snow, with slopeside equipment rental and demonstrations, and free overnight equipment storage.

SKI SEASON
November through June

► A VAST LAND
Believe it or not, Mammoth is expanding! Apparently the 3,500 acres (1,400 ha) of skiable terrain just wasn't enough...

GETTING THERE

Mammoth dominates the eastern side of the Sierra Nevada mountain range in central California. It's quite remote compared to other resorts, and a long way from any international airports. The small airport at Mammoth Lakes is being developed for international flights and will be open during 2003. In the meantime the nearest international airports are Reno and Los Angeles. Reno is 170 miles (274 km) from Mammoth, and takes three hours by car along the scenic Highway 395. Two taxi companies offer transfers: Mammoth Shuttle and the Sierra Express. A free shuttle bus runs regularly from Reno to Mammoth. Los Angeles Airport is 323 miles (524 km) from Mammoth and takes five hours by car, via Yosemite National Park. There are no rail connections.

▲ NEW VILLAGE
The new village opened in 2003, and provides accommodation, restaurants and shops for hungry and tired skiers.

THE VILLAGE

The nearest town is Mammoth Lakes. Situated four miles (6.5 km) from the ski area, it offers accommodations, shops, over 50 restaurants and a free shuttle service. The new Village, opened in 2003, has created a skiing community linked to the main ski area by the Village Gondola and a return ski trail. Luxurious accommodations such as Lincoln House and White Mountain Lodge have direct access to the slopes as well as some luxury amenities, and there are stores and restaurants. For a virtual tour of the new Village, log on to their website at www.mammothmountain.com.

ACCOMMODATIONS

At the resort there are hotels at Main Lodge, Eagle Lodge and in the new Village, as well as countless hotels, motels, condos and inns in Mammoth Lakes town. Visit the website www.visitmammoth.com for a comprehensive list of all types of accommodation and prices.

Juniper Springs Lodge, Sunstone and Eagle Run, at Eagle Lodge, are Mammoth's finest hotel-condominium and townhouse-style, self-catering accommodation in an unparalleled slopeside location. The 213-room Mammoth Mountain Inn, at Main Lodge, offers the ultimate alpine experience.

MOUNTAIN FACTS

Base	7,953 feet (2,424 m)
Summit	11,053 feet (3,369 m)
Elevation	3,100 feet (945 m)
Easy	25%
Intermediate	40%
Advanced/Expert	35%
Number of trails	150
Number of terrain parks	3
Longest trail	3.4 miles (5.4 km)
Ski area	3,500 acres (1,400 ha)

SNOWFALL

Annual snowfall	384 inches (975 cm)
Snowmaking	33%

SKI LIFTS

Gondolas	2
Express Six-Passengers	1
High-Speed Quads	8
Quads	1
Triple Chairs	8
Double Chairs	6
Surface Lifts	4
Total	30
Riders per hour	56,000

ACCOMMODATIONS

JUNIPER SPRINGS, SUNSTONE AND EAGLE INN
800-MAMMOTH
760-924-1102
jsl@mammoth-mtn.com

MAMMOTH MOUNTAIN INN
760-934-2581
800-228-4947
the-inn@mammoth-mtn.com

TAMARACK LODGE RESORT
800-MAMMOTH
760-934-2442
info@tamaracklodge.com

The Panorama Gondola is just outside the door. There are hotel rooms and condominium-style units, many with forest and mountain views. Tamarack Lodge and Resort is on the shores of Twin Lakes, with rustic but refined cabins and rooms. It's part of the 27-mile (45-km) cross-country ski and snowshoe trail. The newly created Village has the Arts & Crafts Lincoln House, with one-, two-, and three-bedroom interiors and White Mountain Lodge, combining contemporary and traditional decor. Both are close to the Village Gondola.

SKI AREA

Mammoth Mountain ski area is indeed mammoth, although it was named not for this reason, but after the Mammoth Mining Company that operated during the Gold Rush. With 3,500 acres (1,400 ha) of terrain, 150 marked trails and 30 lifts, it's one of the biggest resorts in North America. The summit is a hefty 11,053 feet (3,369 m) and even the base lodges are at 7,953 feet (2,424 m), making sure that there's always plenty of snow. Naturally there's a wide variety of terrain to accommodate every level of skier, including large, open bowls above the treeline, steep couloirs and gullies and, on bad weather days, the bottom third of the mountain, which offers some top tree skiing/riding. You can also ski June Mountain, 20

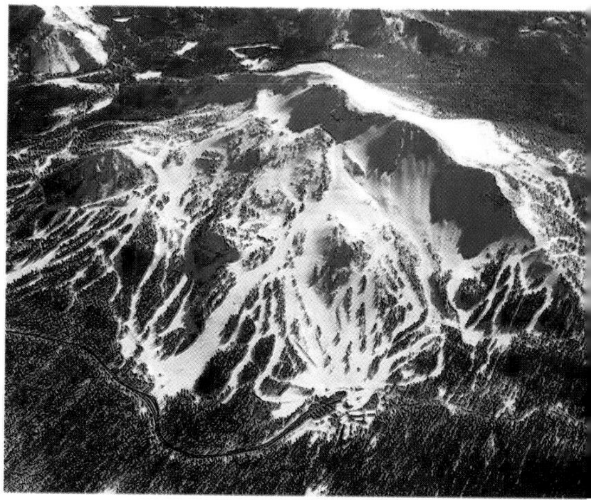

▲ **BIRD'S EYE VIEW**
From this angle you can see how the 150 trails spread out across the mountain, offering perfect skiing for anyone.

minutes' drive away, with the same lift ticket. Recent extensive terrain park and pipe development has put Mammoth at the forefront of boarding—over half the U.S. snowboard team live in Mammoth.

SKI LIFTS

With 30 lifts spread around the mountain, Mammoth's huge amount of terrain is easily accessible. There is one express six-passenger chair, eight express quads, one quad, eight triples, six

doubles and four surface lifts. There are also two gondolas: the Panorama, which leaves from the Main Lodge and stops first at McCoy Station and then the summit at Panorama Lookout; and the Village Gondola, which connects the Village with Canyon Lodge. The ski lifts operate from 8:30 AM to 4:00 PM. The large system of high-speed lifts means that lines are rarely a problem. Lines (always under 10 minutes) generally occur only at lifts leaving the main lodges on Saturdays and during vacation periods. If you really want to avoid any waiting in line at weekends, go to the smaller and more intimate sister resort of June Mountain, 20 miles (32 km) away. It shares Mammoth's lift pass and is very peaceful.

LIFT PASSES

Mammoth shares a lift pass with June Mountain, only 20 minutes' drive north. Lift passes are quite expensive on weekends compared with other resorts, but then there are 150 trails to entertain you. Full day passes for weekends and vacations cost US$60 for adults (19–64 years), around 25 percent less for teens (13–18), and 50 percent less for children (7–12), and Seniors (65+). Passes for six/eight days cost up to US$278 for adults (19–64 years), US$210 for teens (13–18), and US$141 for children (7–12) and seniors (65+). A beginner's chair pass is available, as are packages for beginners including lift, rental and lessons at a discount. Tickets are available at ticket windows all over the mountain, in town lodging areas, and by advance purchase, call 800-Mammoth.

▼ LOFTY TRANSPORT
There are two gondolas, one leaving from Main Lodge and the other connecting the new village development with Canyon Lodge.

▲ VIRGIN SNOWS
Get up early and be the first to make tracks.

SKI SCHOOLS AND GUIDING

SKI Magazine has voted Mammoth Sports School as one of the top 10 ski and snowboard schools in North America. Lessons are available from each of the service areas on the mountain, and from Main and Canyon Lodges. Group lessons are at 10:00 AM and 2:00 PM and the upper limit on ski group size is eight people. Children should be at least four years old for a group lesson, and they can be either supervised at lunchtime or collected by parents. The High Alpine Freeride Camp is for advanced skiers wanting to improve in challenging snow conditions. Skiing for people with disabilities is also available. Local volunteers undertake free tours of the ski area.

BEGINNERS

Eagle, Canyon and Main Lodges all have an area dedicated to beginners, and green runs surround these areas. From Main Lodge try Gus' Pasture, St. Moritz and Sesame Street. From chair 17 at Canyon Lodge there are several green trails, including Roundabout, Gingerbread and Hansel. Eagle Lodge's six-passenger Eagle Express chair accesses three good long greens: Holiday, Pumpkin and Sleepy Hollow. Once the green trails have been mastered, there are a lot of gentle blues to move on to, and with Road Runner, a blue trail running from the very top of the mountain, a strong beginner/early intermediate can ski or ride from the top of the mountain all the way back to the base area.

DAYCARE
Canyon Kids and the Woollywood Sports School offer daycare services. Morning and afternoon lessons for kids aged 4 to 14 years, plus daycare for non-skiers.

EQUIPMENT RENTAL

On the Edge Performance Center at Main and Canyon Lodges allows you to test the latest, greatest ski and snowboard equipment right on the slopes.

INTERMEDIATES

Around 4 percent of the mountain is good for intermediates. Gladed trees off the back of chair 22, and around chairs 12 and 13, offer good intermediate tree skiing with trails such as Surprise, Secret Spot and Bristlecone. Broadway, accessed by Broadway Express quad, and Stump Alley, off Stump Alley Express quad, are also recommended. The Gold Rush Express quad connects with several interesting blue trails, such as Solitude and some blue-black trails, which are basic blues graduating to intermediate /advanced terrain, including Relief, Quicksilver and Haven't the Foggiest. These trails are marked with a blue square within a black diamond.

ADVANCED AND EXPERT

Advanced and expert skiers have a fantastic choice of terrain and around 35 percent of the mountain to conquer. Few of the black trails are groomed. Best for moguls are the West Bowl off Face Lift Express, Viva off chair 22, and Roller Coaster from chair 21. These mogul fields are considered to be some of the most demanding in California. If steep and deep is more your thing, then head for Hangman's Hollow, Drop Out Chutes, Wipe Out Chutes, Climax Bowl and Paranoid Flats—a very steep and scary traverse to get in—all at the top of the mountain. Couloirs worth a try include Avalanche Chutes, Drop Out Chutes and Wipe Out Chutes. For the very brave, the entry to Phillipe's Couloir can be found halfway down Paranoid Flats. With nearly 400 inches (122 cm) of snow per year, just about anywhere is good for powder, but the best spots are probably the front side of chair 22 (Shaft, Grizzly) first thing, as this is always first to be cleared of avalanches, followed by the Avalanche Chutes, and then on to Face Lift Express chair for Christmas and China Bowls. By then the top of the mountain should be safe and open and the choices are endless—Huevos Grande, Climax, Drop Out Chutes, and Wipe Out Chutes.

There are endless backcountry possibilities off the back of both Mammoth and June Mountains, and untracked powder can often be found at the Dragon's Tail and Hemlock Ridge days after a storm. Backcountry skiing/riding is permitted, but at your own risk. Contact the Ski Patrol first to check out any avalanche danger. Sierra Mountain Center can provide backcountry guides and there are a number of "out of bounds" trails (e.g. Hole in

▲ **ON TOP OF THE WORLD**
At the summit there's always plenty of snow, and access to some of the best terrain in the Sierra Nevada.

▼ **STUNNING SCENERY**
Although maybe a bit isolated in the middle of the Inyo National Forest, Mammoth has stunning scenery hiding around every corner.

advanced riders, there's something for every type of boarder here, with three parks and three halfpipes, including a superpipe. The parks and pipes are groomed every evening and throughout the day.

Unbound Main is visible from Main Lodge, accessed by the Thunder Bound Express quad, and is suitable for advanced boarders, with a halfpipe, superpipe, tabletops and jumps. Unbound Canyon, a park and halfpipe at Canyon Lodge, is located on School Yard and caters to beginners. Unbound South, on The Roller Coaster express quad, is designed for intermediate riders and is a rail-lovers' paradise.

At June Mountain there's a superpipe and the JM2 Unbound Terrain Park. Many professional snowboarders live in and around Mammoth and June Mountains, which should tell you something...

It's very easy for boarders to get around the trails as Mammoth is largely a steep resort and therefore not much skating is required. In addition, most of the lifts are chairs, which are much easier to use than T-bars, and the parks also have their own dedicated chairlifts.

▼ TAKING THE PLUNGE
Experts will feel right at home on the chutes and bowls.

the Wall) which the ski school is allowed to access with its expert classes.

BOARDING & FREESTYLE

Mammoth Mountain is one of the top U.S. snowboarding destinations. The Vans Unbound Terrain Parks are known for their innovative design, style and unmatched grooming. From beginners to

EATING ON THE MOUNTAIN

There are 13 mountain restaurants offering a wide variety of food and beverages. At McCoy Station, Parallax is a full-service gourmet restaurant featuring Pacific Rim and Mediterranean food and fine wines. The food is reputed to be just as delicious as the view. Also at McCoy Station is the Marketplace, a self-service food court. There's a game room for children. At Steeps Bar there's cocktails and

◄ MAKING TRACKS
Mammoth has been voted one of the best snowboarding destinations in North America.

▲ POWDER PLUNGE
Steep trails and gullies make for an interesting challenge for intermediates.

coffee to be had, once you are finished or halfway through, as well as pastries and baked goods. Main Lodge has a variety of choices: The Broadway Bakery for sandwiches, pizza, beer and wine; the Cornice Café for steak sandwiches, hearty daily specials and salads; Roma's Mexican Cantina, a fast, good choice for lunch with a refreshing margarita; Main Lodge Sundeck BBQ and Bar for barbecues, chili, snacks, beer, wine and a full bar, as well as plenty of people- and park-watching opportunities. The Mill Café is a casual place featuring an outdoor bar and a variety of entrées. It's a favorite ski-in/ski-out spot and on snowy days the indoor fireplace is ideal for snuggling up with a hot chocolate. At the base of chairs 13 and 14 is Outpost 14, where you can enjoy inspiring mountain scenery and barbecues, chili, snacks, and a variety of beers and wines. At Canyon Lodge, the Canyon Beach Bar and BBQ has a tempting menu and a relaxing bar atmosphere. At Grizzly Square Food Court variety is the name of the game. At Eagle Lodge Talons Restaurant and Bar is located slopeside, right next to the six-passenger Eagle Express. Come here for breakfast, lunch and dinner, and a full bar.

APRÈS SKI

Mammoth Lakes can be pretty quiet during the week, but really gets going at weekends as Southern Californians drive in for the weekend to ski and party. Après-ski options include live music in bars and restaurants, or you can go and soak in a natural hot spring with panoramic view of the surrounding mountains. There are around 50 restaurants in Mammoth Lakes town, many of which have live music ranging from rock and reggae through folk, jazz and blues. By California State law, all venues must be licensed to sell either beer and wine, or all

► MAMMOTH BY NAME
With the sun setting on the slopes, Mammoth is a truly awesome experience.

alcohol. The minimum age for consuming alcohol is 21 years and children can only accompany their parents in restaurants, but not bars or clubs. Most bars close at 2:00 AM.

The new Village at Mammoth offers a variety of dining and drinking establishments. The Yodler Bar and Pub, across from Main Lodge, is a Swiss chalet with California atmosphere for après-ski cocktails, a casual dinner or snacks at lunchtime, but it shuts at 9:00 PM. Thunder Mountain Bar is a warm and cozy lounge upstairs at Main Lodge where you can get hot drinks, beer, a variety of delicious appetizers, plus a fantastic view of the Unbound Main terrain park and the blue Broadway trail.

There are around 20 bars at Mammoth Lakes, including the very popular Whiskey Creek, appealing to the 21–35 age group, with excellent live music on weekends, plus midweek disc jockey and dancing; the Clocktower Cellar at Alpenhof Lodge, a mellow pub atmosphere, popular with local residents; and La Sierra, lively and often crowded with 21–25 year olds.

If you want some retail therapy, there are plenty of sports stores and factory outlets for the big names, where you can get designer labels at a discount. In fact, the streets of Mammoth Lakes are lined with gift stores and galleries.

▲ TAKING A BREAK
Put your feet up at one of the 13 mountain restaurants and watch the skiers and boarders go by.

OTHER ACTIVITIES

If you're not interested in skiing on the mountain there are masses of other activities at Mammoth. It's one of the best places for non-skiing winter activities in the U.S. Cross-country skiing takes place at the Tamarack Cross Country Ski Center, where there is 27 miles (45 km) of freshly groomed track around the Lakes Basin on skis or snowshoes. You can ice skate at the outdoor ice rink in Mammoth Lakes, or try your hand at snowmobiling along hundreds of miles of forest-lined trails. Take a one-hour ride to Crater Flats or an all-day excursion through the Inyo National Forest. Contact Snowmobile Adventures at Main Lodge, (kid-sized sleds at Little Eagle). Dogsleds head up to Minaret Vista, and there is tubing and an athletics club with an indoor pool at Mammoth Lakes. You can find out information at any of the local shops as well as on the main reservations number for Mammoth. There are also music festivals, art shows and special events throughout the year. Contact 800-MAMMOTH for details.

USEFUL PHONE NUMBERS

Tourist Office	800-626-6684
Road conditions	800-427-7623
L.A. Excursions Taxi	310-937-9543
Mammoth Shuttle	760-934-6588
Sierra Express	760-924-8294
Mammoth Sports School	760-934-0685
24-hour Snow Report	760-934-6166
Mammoth Weather	760-934-7669
Tamarack Cross Country Ski Center	760-934-2442
Mammoth Dogsled Teams	760-934-6270
On the Edge Performance Center	760-934-2571
Mammoth Snowmobiling Adventures	760-934-9645

USEFUL WEB SITES

Official Website	www.mammothmountain.com
Useful Information	www.visitmammoth.com
Official E-mail	info@mammoth-mtn.com
June Mountain Terrain Park	www.JM2Unbound.com

RESTAURANTS

LAKEFRONT RESTAURANT
Tamarack Lodge, Twin Lakes
760-934-3534.
French and Californian cuisine

NEVADOS
Main Street and Minaret Road, Mammoth Lakes
760-934-4466
Good for a special night out

SHOGUN RESTAURANT
452 Old Mammoth Road, Mammoth Lakes
760-934-3970
Japanese cuisine

ROBERTO'S MEXICAN CAFÉ
271 Old Mammoth Road, Mammoth Lakes
760-934-3667
Mexican cuisine

BARS

YODLER BAR & PUB
THUNDER MOUNTAIN BAR
WHISKEY CREEK
CLOCKTOWER CELLAR
LA SIERRA

AT THE CANYONS YOU'LL EXPERIENCE BLUE SKIES, COOL, CRISP EVENINGS AND AWESOME POWDER DUMPS. SINCE THE RESORT OPENED IN 1997 THERE HAS BEEN GREAT PROGRESS AND EXPANSION, AND NOW WITH 8 MOUNTAINS, 18 LIFTS AND 3,500 ACRES (1,400 HA) OF TERRAIN, THE CANYONS IS THE LARGEST SINGLE SKI AND SNOWBOARD RESORT IN UTAH.

THE CANYONS

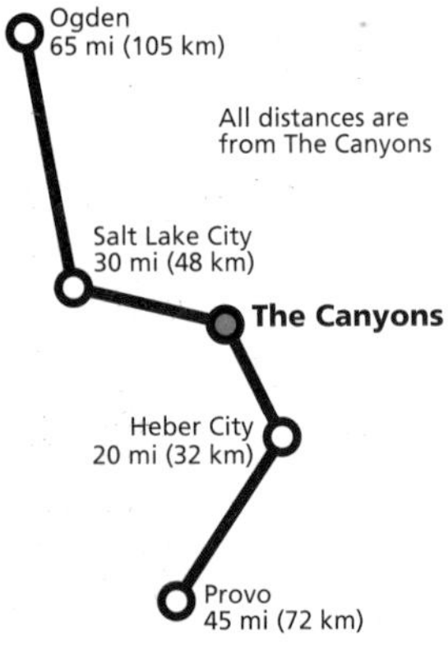

The Canyons is one of the largest ski and snowboard resorts in the United States. It is very close to Park City Mountain and Deer Valley and in fact you can ski from resort to resort. Note, however, that Deer Valley does not officially permit this, although Park City Mountain does. With recent changes and expansion The Canyons has grown from a small village into a bustling ski resort, although some say that it lacks character. The ski area covers eight mountains with 118 trails to suit all ability levels, but only 14 percent of the ski area is designated for beginners. The season runs from mid-November to early April, with the peak time February to March and low season early December and January. The snow record is impeccable with an almost guaranteed 355 inches (901 cm) of snow per year. Most visitors are from the U.S., but the dynamics are now changing with more visitors coming from elsewhere.

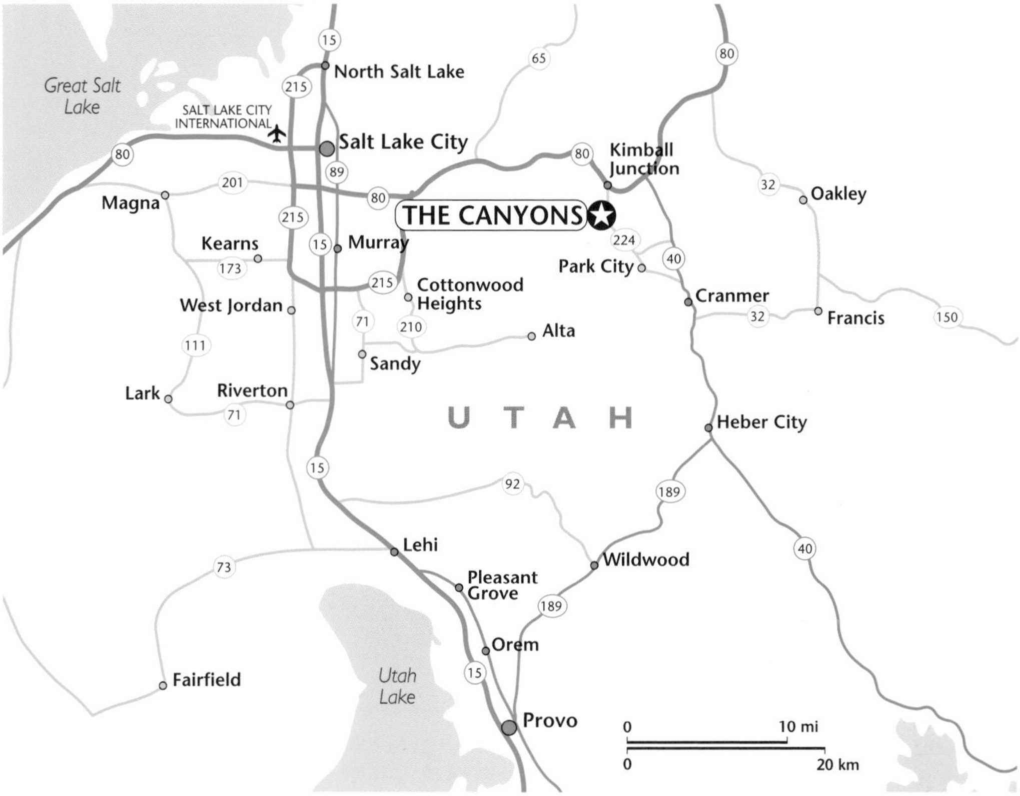

MOUNTAIN FACTS

Base	6,800 feet (2,040 m)
Summit	9,990 feet (2,997 m)
Elevation	3,190 feet (957 m)
Easy	14%
Intermediate	44%
Advanced/Expert	42%
Number of trails	118
Ski area	3,500 acres (1,400 ha)

SNOWFALL

Annual snowfall	355 inches (901 cm)
Snowmaking	160 acres (64 ha)

SKI LIFTS

Gondolas	2
High-Speed Quads	5
Quad Chairs	4
Triple Chairs	2
Double Chairs	1
Surface Lifts	3
Magic Carpets	1
Total	18
Riders per hour	25,700

SKI SEASON
Mid-November to early April

GETTING THERE

The Canyons is located four miles (6.5 km) from Park City and 30 miles (48 km) from Salt Lake City. The nearest international airport is Salt Lake City International, 35 minutes by road. There's a shuttle bus system from Park City to The Canyons Resort that runs every 20 minutes between 6:00 AM and 11:00 PM. There is no rail connection.

THE VILLAGE

The Canyons Resort Village has grown considerably over the past four years. The village grew from Utah's natural surroundings and a theme emerged using the natural elements: earth, wind, water and fire. Each neighborhood in the village promotes one of the four elements. In the amphitheater within the Village Forum stands the 30-foot (9-m) Tabegauche statue holding a flaming torch that remains lit throughout the year. The village includes retail stores, restaurants and cafes as well as the Sundial Lodge and Grand Summit Resort Hotel.

ACCOMMODATIONS

The impressive slopeside Grand Summit Resort Hotel has 365 rooms and a health club spa with full services and a salon. Condos ranging from studios to multi-room are at the 190-room Sundial Lodge, which has an exercise room and rooftop hot tub. At Park City, only four miles (6.5 km) away, there are many further options for accommodations. Visit www.thecanyons.com for information.

◀ CLEVER CANYONS
The sheer size of the Canyons means that all levels of ability will have a great experience.

▲ BACK TO NATURE
Most trails wind through natural terrain, so you really feel you're on a mountain.

ACCOMMODATIONS

GRAND SUMMIT	435-615-8040
SUNDIAL LODGE	435-649-7374

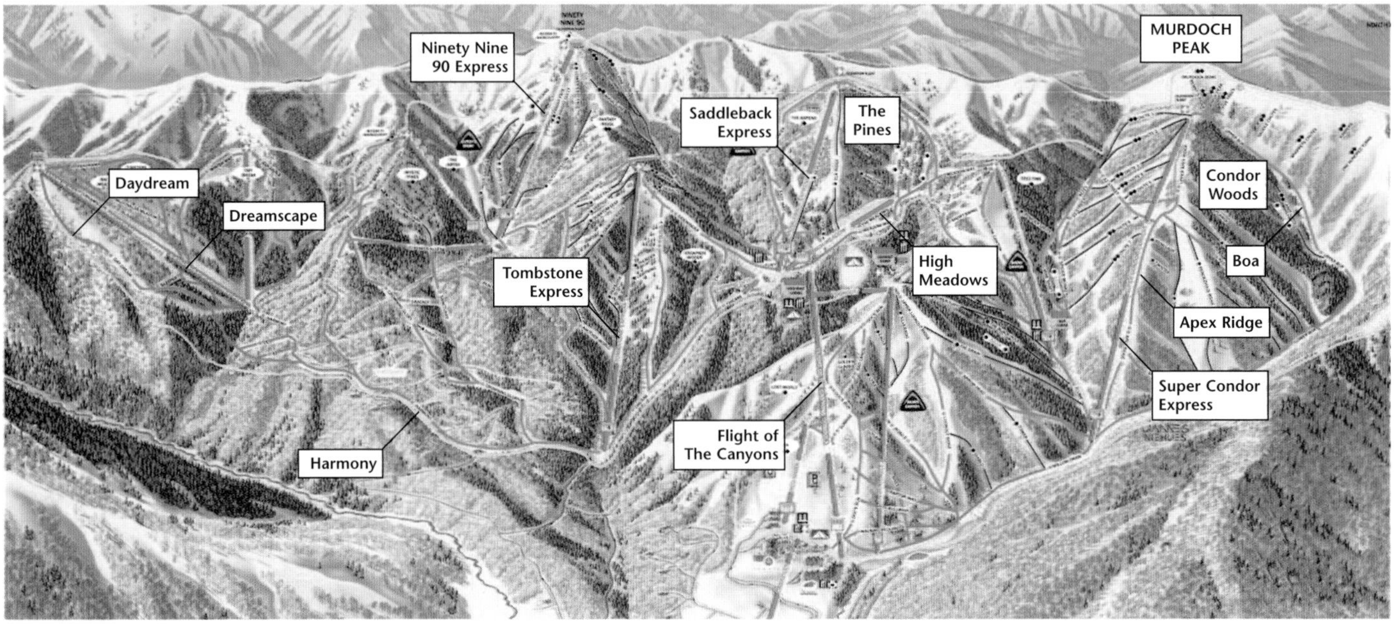

NEARBY RESORTS

THE CANYONS SHUTTLE

A free hotel shuttle bus runs from Grand Summit Resort Hotel to Park City Main Street, running 8:00 AM–11:00 PM daily, on the hour every hour.

SKI AREA

The Canyons is best suited for the skier who likes to ski the natural mountain. The trails are not so wide and void of trees that you forget that you are in the mountain, and there is a good variety of black and blue trails. The green trails are mostly located mid-mountain and provide a 7-acre (3 ha) learning area designated for first-time skiers and boarders. The Canyons also offers a backcountry feel, with several areas that are accessible by hiking only. No lifts are available to these areas and fresh powder is the payoff for the modest hike. In all there are 118 trails comprising 22 double black diamonds, 36 black diamonds, 9 double blues, 42 blues and 9 greens. The Canyons is acknowledged as a leader in the terrain park world, with six natural halfpipes and a dedicated terrain park.

SKI LIFTS

There are 18 lifts in total: two gondola-style lifts, five high-speed express chairs, four quads, two triples, one double chair, three surface lifts and one magic carpet, carrying around 25,700 people onto the mountain every hour. The lifts operate from 9:00 AM to 4:00 PM daily, and to 9:00 PM in the terrain park. The only queuing problem is on busy weekends and holidays. The gondola can have a line around 9:00 AM and the Tombstone Express quad can get a bit of a line, but the wait is usually not longer than 10 minutes.

LIFT PASSES

A full day pass for adults costs US$62, for children US$33 and for seniors US$33. Children six years and under are free. Weekly passes cost US$350 for adults, US$224 for children, and US$224 for seniors. You have to buy a pass that covers the whole eight-mountain area. No photo I.D. is required. You can buy passes online and at local distributors, and, of course, also in the Village. The Ski Utah Passport covers The Canyons, Park City, Deer Valley, Snowbird, Alta, Solitude and Sundance. It is not available in the resort and must be purchased via your tour operator or online before you travel.

SKI SCHOOLS AND GUIDING

Group and private lessons are available for adults and children at the Perfect Turn Ski and Snowboard School. Group levels are denoted by color from red (never skied before) to silver/black diamond

◄ BACKCOUNTRY HIKE
Several areas are only accessible by a hike, but you'll get great untracked powder for your efforts.

◄ **BLUE SKIES, GREAT SNOW**
What could be more perfect than a clear trail on a blue day, with lunch just half an hour away.

DAYCARE
Little Adventures Children's Center
Children aged six weeks to six years
435-615-8036

(advanced). The maximum number for a group lesson is five, and children's lessons are for ages two to 12 years. The all-day ski school program provides lunch for children. Adult group lessons cost US$95 for two hours and children's private two-hour lessons cost US$180 for up to two children. There are also free guided mountain tours that cruise the blue trails of all eight mountains. They leave at 10:30 AM and 1:30 PM daily.

BEGINNERS

Beginner skiers and snowboarders are lucky at The Canyons. They have a dedicated 7-acre (2.8-ha) area at the top of the Flight of The Canyons gondola. There are two beginner lifts, a magic carpet and surface lift that provide first-day beginners with a chance to work on improving skills. The High Meadow and Saddleback areas are best for beginners and the terrain offered here is varied enough to challenge most beginners. The other lift easily accessible from here is the Saddleback Express, which gives beginners a bit more choice, although these are all blue trails.

INTERMEDIATES

The Canyons has 44 percent of trails designated for intermediates. The best option for intermediates is to head for the Dreamscape quad where there's solitude, spectacular views and five blue and double blue trails to choose from. The longest intermediate trail is accessed from Dreamscape quad and combines Daydream trail and then Harmony to the base of Tombstone Express quad. Two other long trails are Apex Ridge and Boa, accessed from the Super Condor Express quad. The most challenging trail is Another World off the Tombstone Express quad. This is generally where moguls develop over the course of the day, and it also offers small sections that are steeper and will give the intermediate skier the opportunity to improve skills on all terrain.

ADVANCED & EXPERT

The advanced or expert skier will find 42 percent of the trails suitable for them. The black diamond trails offer tree runs and canyons, and the toughest skiing for those in search of moguls, steep and deep, and couloirs, are any of the double black diamond

▼ **BLACK DIAMONDS**
Experts have nearly half the mountain to explore, with black diamond trails created out of gladed slopes and canyons.

▲ **POWDER EIGHTS**
Check out the untracked powder and practice your short turns to leave your own Powder Eight signature.

trails down from Ninety Nine 90 Express quad, where you will be rewarded with spectacular views. The Devils' Friend off the Super Condor Express quad is particularly good for moguls. The Pines is good for powder, skiing through a charming grove of pine trees, near Saddleback Express quad, but the best trails for powder are those descending from Murdock Peak at 9,607 feet (2,882 m).

A good day's skiing for advanced or expert skiers on a big powder day would be to go up to Ninety Nine 90 early in the morning, then move over to Condor Woods below Murdock Peak, and then hike up to Murdock Peak before you get too tired. There's some magnificent backcountry skiing to be had here, but only expert skiers trained in avalanche safety and with the proper equipment should consider passing through the gates that access them (gates are subject to closure). Never go beyond a closed area boundary or a sign saying "Closed: Avalanche Danger." You are strictly on your own when leaving through the backcountry gates, so be sure to read the warning signs before leaving the resort.

BOARDING & FREESTYLE

The Canyons has a terrain park with its own lift, Red Hawk, and is not bothered by any other skiers or riders on the mountain. For the 2002/03 season terrain park improvements include: 25 new rails and box features, totaling 30 jibs, doubling the number of hits/jumps, a state-of-the-art sound system; two new halfpipes including a Superpipe and a beginner's pipe; a lighting system for night operation until 9:00 PM; and increased park size to 18 acres (7 ha). Smokie's Smokehouse is the prime viewing spot for the terrain park. On the rest of the mountain, boarders need to be aware of flat spots on green trails, but otherwise the entire mountain is a snowboarder's dream.

EATING ON THE MOUNTAIN

There are three lodges: Red Pine Lodge, Lookout Cabin and Sun Lodge. Red Pine Lodge, at the top of the gondola, offers grills, sandwiches, pizzas and soups inside or on the sun deck. Lookout Cabin is more upscale and open lunchtimes only, with high-quality service and panoramic views from 9,000 feet (2,700 m). It was voted Mountain Restaurant of the Year 2001 and 2002 by *Good Skiing and Snowboarding Guide* and reservations are preferred. Sun Lodge is a great place to bring your lunch and enjoy the deck. There are some food and beverages available here, but this is not a full-service lodge. Other possibilities are Dreamscape Grill at the base of Daybreak lift for

▲ **PRETTY PEAKS**
There are so many stunning peaks at the Canyons it's easy to get a bit blasé about their beauty.

◄ GRAND SUMMIT
Just a few steps away from the Flight of the Canyons Gondola, The Grand Summit Resort Hotel offers convience as well as great amenities.

burgers, hot dogs, and sandwiches, or Viking Yurt at the base of Saddleback Express lift for a gourmet dinner at 8,000 feet (2,400 m).

APRÈS SKI

Après ski is best at Doc's at the Gondola, just a few steps from the base of the Flight of The Canyons Gondola, where there's a full bar, tasty menu and great views. Relax and ponder what you're going to do for the rest of the evening. If you've really worked those muscles, have a soothing hot stone massage and then a soak in the hot tub at the Grand Summit Health Club and Spa in the Village. The Cabin Restaurant at the Grand Summit Resort Hotel tempts you with delicious Rocky Mountain cuisine. Kids eat free with a paying adult. Reservations recommended on 435-615-8060. Or go to the Cabin Lounge to relax with an aperitif or after-dinner drink. A light menu is also available and there's live piano music Thursday to Saturday at 8:30 PM.

In the Village try Smokie's Smokehouse and Tavern for casual dining with fun flavors. You can ski to the door and stop for lunch, drinks or dinner. There's a pool table, T.V.s and the best view of the terrain park. The Montaña Café and Bar is open for breakfast, lunch and après ski, with bagels, pastries, grills and beers. The Westgate Grill is in the center of the village and features a small bar, dining room and sunny deck.

A membership is required in all bars serving alcohol. The minimum age for consuming alcohol is 21 and children may not accompany parents in bars and other places serving alcohol. Bars must close by 2:00 am. At present there are no nightclubs in the Village, but Park City with its many bars and restaurants is only four miles (6.5 km) by car or free shuttle bus. For more information on nightlife in Park City, see Deer Valley.

OTHER ACTIVITIES

The Adventure Desk in the Grand Summit has information on snowshoeing, dogsled rides, cross-country skiing and snowmobiling. The White Pine Cross-Country Ski Area has 11 miles (18 km) of groomed track for all abilities. Lessons are available (435-615-5858). Or there are moonlit sleigh rides from Viking Yurt near Red Pine Lodge (435-615-9878). In Park City there are bobsled, rocket rides and aerial demos at Utah Olympic Park (435-658-4200).

For shopping try one of the factory outlet stores like Tommy Hilfiger, Levi and Banana Republic in Park City (435-645-7078). Check the website at www.thecanyons.com for details of annual events. The Sundance Film Festival takes place in Park City every January, and attracts the cream of the movie industry. Also annually is the "pond-skimming" and reggae show (early April). People sign up to try and glide across a pond of water on their skis or snowboard, usually wearing a crazy costume. The ones who make it across the pond are then judged upon their costume and win a prize.

USEFUL PHONE NUMBERS

Canyons Tourist Office	435-649-5400
Ski School	435-615-3449
Snow Reports	435-615-3456
Ski Patrol	435-615-3322

USEFUL WEBSITES

Official Website	www.thecanyons.com

EATING ON THE MOUNTAIN

- LOOKOUT CABIN
- SUN LODGE
- RED PINE LODGE
- DREAMSCAPE GRILL
- VIKING YURT

RESTAURANTS & BARS

- THE CABIN, GRAND SUMMIT RESORT HOTEL
- SMOKIE'S SMOKEHOUSE AND TAVERN
- MONTAÑA CAFÉ AND BAR
- WESTGATE GRILL
- DOC'S AT THE GONDOLA

▼ FRESH POWDER
Take one of the delightful blue trails for a long satisfying run that is easily accessed.

CARVE INTO UTAH'S FAMOUS POWDER AND EXPERIENCE THE MOST VARIED TERRAIN UTAH HAS TO OFFER AT PARK CITY MOUNTAIN RESORT. IT'S A LIVELY PLACE, WITH 100 TRAILS SUITABLE FOR ALL ABILITIES, FROM DOUBLE BLACK DIAMOND BOWLS TO A LONG, GENTLE GREEN TRAIL WINDING DOWN FROM THE SUMMIT TO THE BASE, PLUS THREE BRAND-NEW TERRAIN PARKS.

PARK CITY

Park City Mountain Resort is based in the town of Park City, Utah, which is also the base for several other ski resorts, including Deer Valley and The Canyons. The resort is generally considered an inexpensive place to stay, and represents good value for money. From the town you can access the main skiing and boarding area via two high-speed six-passenger lifts, which take all of 12 minutes from bottom to top. There are 3,300 acres (1,335 ha) of skiable terrain, including eight bowls, and skiers of all abilities will be able to find something for them anywhere on the mountain. There's floodlit night skiing from Christmas Day to the end of the season, and in January each year the Sundance Film Festival brings a different kind of visitor.

▼ **HAPPY HOLIDAYS**
Utah's blue skies and dry powder create some of the most perfect skiing conditions.

MOUNTAIN FACTS

Base	6,900 feet (2,103 m)
Summit	10,028 feet (3,056 m)
Elevation	3,128 feet (953 m)
Easy	18%
Intermediate	44%
Advanced/Expert	38%
Number of trails	100
Number of terrain parks	3
Number of bowls	8
Longest trail	3.5 miles (5.5 km)
Ski area	3,300 acres (1,335 ha)

SNOWFALL

Annual snowfall	350 inches (890 cm)
Snowmaking	500 acres (202 ha)

SKI LIFTS

Express Six-Passenger	4
High-Speed Quads	1
Triple Chairs	5
Double Chairs	4
Total	14
Riders per hour	27,200

SKI SEASON
Mid-November to mid-April

GETTING THERE

Park City Mountain Resort is located 35 miles (56 km) from Salt Lake City, Utah. Salt Lake International Airport is the nearest international airport, 45 minutes' drive via the all-weather Interstate 80 highway. The easiest way to get to the resort from the airport is by 10-person taxi vans—reservations are recommended, call 800-222-7275. There are no rail connections.

THE VILLAGE

Originally a mining town, founded in the mid-19th century, Park City is now a popular, busy tourist resort, and Park City Mountain Resort is located right in the heart it. Main Street, with restaurants, bars, boutiques, and art galleries, is a great spot for après ski or lunch on a day off. A new town bridge spanning Park Avenue means that skiers and snowboarders can now ski or ride directly from the mountain to Main Street. Park City's free skier-friendly shuttle bus system runs every 20 minutes and can take you from the hotels, restaurants and stores in Park City to the slopes and Deer Valley.

ACCOMMODATIONS

Most of the accommodations in Park City are condominiums. Good-value ski packages can be booked through Park City Mountain Reservations, and include your accommodation, continental breakfast and a daily lift pass. There are three hotels at the resort: the Lodge at Mountain Village, situated at the base on 1415 Lowell Avenue, with a variety of units from studios to four-bedroom condos; Shadow Ridge, a hotel/condo complex at the base of the resort with one and two-bedroom condos and a fitness center; and Snowflower, located slopeside near the Three Kings double chairlift, with a further selection of condos. In the town of Park City and around are many more hotels and condo complexes. The following is a selection—all are on the free shuttle route to the resort. Park Plaza, a modern condo complex, is 1.5 miles (2.4 km) from the resort; Edelweiss has more condos two blocks from the resort; Galleria on Main Street is a complex of condos within walking distance of the Town Lift triple chair; and the Yarrow Hotel, a moderately priced place with 180 rooms, is half a mile (0.8 km) from the resort.

◄ PARK CITY
A popular, busy town, Park City has everything you need to make your stay really memorable.

ACCOMMODATIONS

RESORT CONDOMINIUMS
THE LODGE AT MOUNTAIN VILLAGE
SHADOW RIDGE
SNOWFLOWER

PARK CITY CONDOMINIUMS
PARK PLAZA
EDELWEISS
GALLERIA
YARROW HOTEL

Central reservations at Park City Mountain Reservations 800-222-7275

NEARBY RESORTS

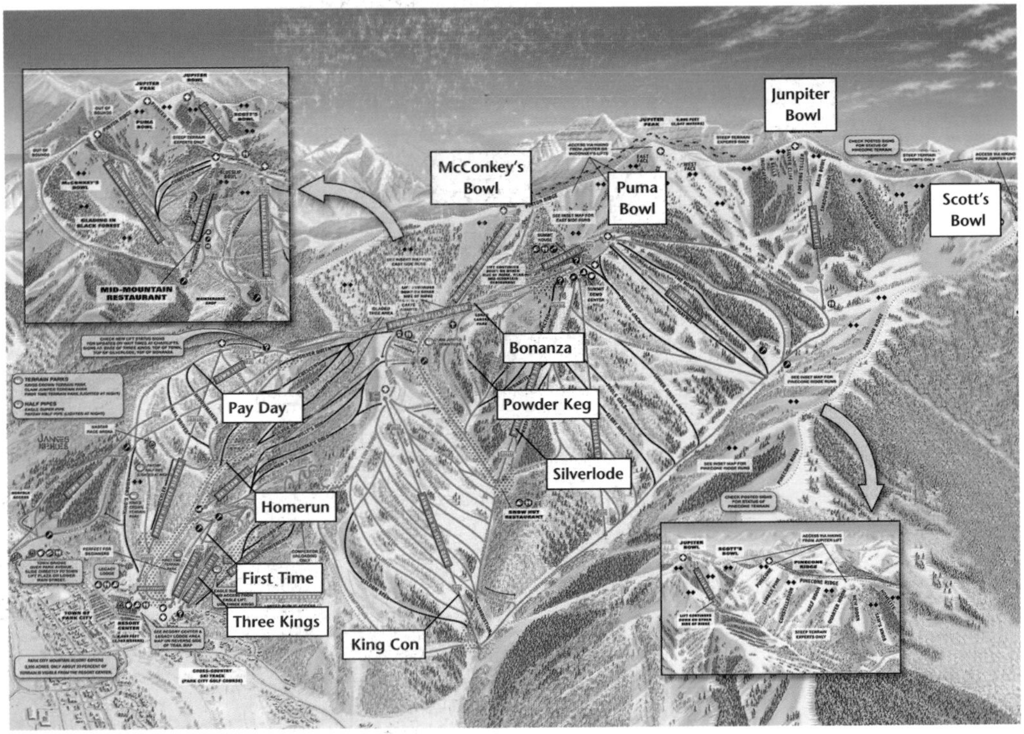

SKI AREA

With 100 trails winding over 3,300 acres (1,335 ha), Park City is a popular resort. Of these, 18 percent are beginner, 44 percent intermediate, and 38 percent advanced. The vertical rise takes you 3,128 feet (953 m) from base to summit, with 350 inches (890 cm) of snow guaranteed. There are also eight bowls—Jupiter, Scott's, Blueslip, McConkey's, Pinecone Ridge, West Face, East Face, and Puma—clustered mostly around the summit of the mountain, which between them total more than 750 acres (303 ha). The top of the mountain is reserved for black and double black diamond trails and bowls, accessed by the Jupiter Lift, but the rest of the mountain has a fair scattering of blue and green trails and other advanced trails.

▼ ENDLESS CHOICE
There are more than 100 trails here, so there's no excuse for staying in...

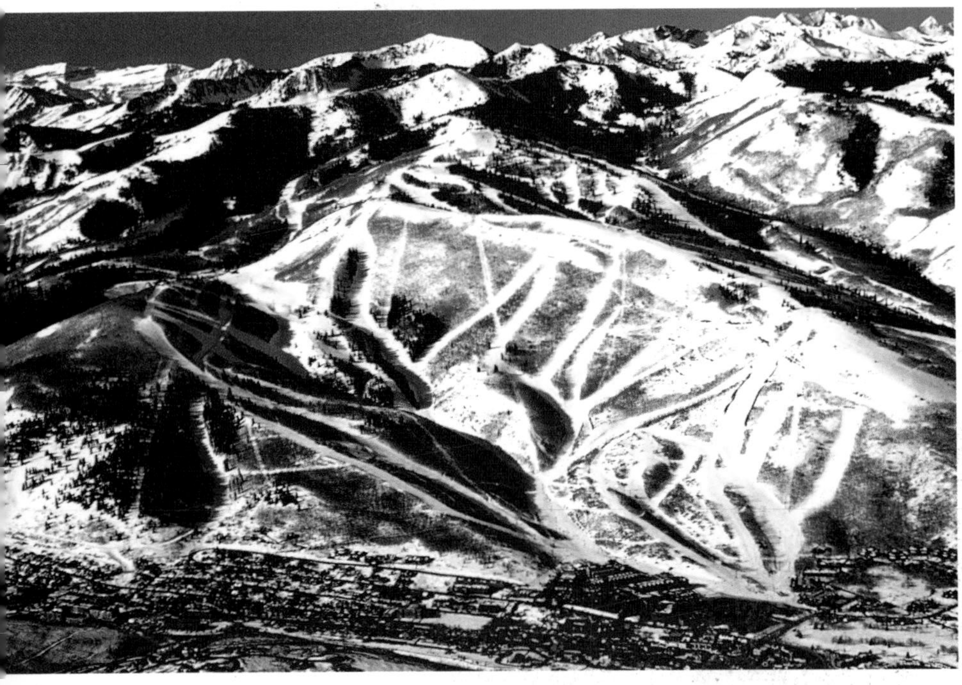

SKI LIFTS

Fourteen lifts access the 100 trails and eight bowls. The lift system includes four new high-speed six-passenger chairs, one high-speed quad, five triple chairs and four double chairs. There's also a children's Magic Carpet near the base. Lifts operate daily from 9:00 AM to 4:00 PM, and when night skiing begins (from December 25 until the end of the season,) the PayDay and First Time lifts close at 9:00 pm. Park City doesn't suffer from waiting line problems, and Jupiter Lift never has a line, even when the rest of the mountain is busy. The four high-speed six-passenger chairs transport around 27,000 people per hour on to and around the mountain.

LIFT PASSES

Lift passes are available for afternoon visits, night visits, full days and season visits. A full-day pass costs US$67 for adults, US$38 for youths (7–12 years) and US$36 for seniors (65–69.) Children aged six and under and seniors 70 and over ski free. A half-day ticket (12:30 to 4:00 PM) costs around 20–25 percent less than the full-day ticket and night tickets (4:00 PM to 9:00 PM) cost US$28 for adults and US$18 for youths (7–12 years.) Beginner passes (First Time and Three Kings lifts only) cost US$40 for adults and

US$24 for youths (7–12 years.) For Park City, Deer Valley, and The Canyons the pass costs US$336 for adults for six out of seven days.

The new Fast Tracks Pass allows adult full-season pass holders and multiday pass holders (four or more days) access to the mountain via special automated turnstiles in a separate lane on four of the most popular lifts: PayDay, Eagle, Bonanza, and Silverlode. At the time of writing this pass was free, and all you have to do is fill out a simple questionnaire, available at the ticket windows.

The Silver Passport allows access to Park City Mountain Resort, The Canyons and Deer Valley (note no snowboarding allowed at Deer Valley), but can only be bought in conjunction with accommodation. Call Park City Mountain Reservations for full details.

SKI SCHOOLS AND GUIDING

The Park City Ski and Snowboard School has a good reputation. It has a variety of programs and private lessons for skiers and boarders and is open from 9:30 AM to 7:30 PM. Private lessons for adults and children range from a six-hour Premier V.I.P. Lesson to a one-hour Kids Mountain School lesson. In a group lesson the different levels are clearly explained and you will be put with the group that best suits your ability. The Foundation Series covers levels 1–4 (green and green to blue trails) and the Performance Series covers levels 5 and above (blue to black and black trails.) At the Kids Mountain School the instructors are experts in creating a fun and safe learning environment. Group lessons include lunch and lift privileges, but your child must be three years old. The Burton Chopper Center allows 7–12-year-olds to practice their newly learned techniques on a trampoline. The Mountain Experience program takes intermediate and advanced skiers and boarders to the bowls on Jupiter Peak.

The National Ability Center has an extensive skiing program for individuals with disabilities, and works in cooperation with the Park City Ski and Snowboard School. All of the instructors are specially trained in the adaptive techniques of 3-track, 4-track, monoski, biski, and guiding blind skiers. Lessons are conducted on the main slopes of the ski resort. For more information visit the National Ability Center online www.nationalabilitycenter.org

BEGINNERS

Beginners are lucky at Park City as the longest trail on the mountain is the 3.5-mile (5.5-km) Homerun, a green trail. It is quite wide and flat and always well groomed. Up to now beginners have been advised to avoid the Homerun slow-skiing zone at the end of the day as all the other skiers came zooming through on their way home, but for 2003 the Homerun trail is being reconfigured and will be patrolled as a slow, family-oriented skiing and riding zone. There are two beginner areas, both designated slow-skiing zones and made up entirely of green trails. One is at the base of the mountain with three lifts (First Time triple chair, Three Kings double chair, and a Magic Carpet) and the other is from the Silverlode six-passenger express lift. Beginners can in fact go up to the top of the mountain and ski all the way to the bottom on green trails. Take the PayDay six-passenger express and then the Bonanza six-passenger express to the summit and ski down Homerun all the way to the base, or take

▼ CATCH ME IF YOU CAN
Take the long way down from the summit via blue, black or green trails that interconnect easily.

▲ **MINING HISTORY**
You can witness Park City's mining past as you ski past Thaynes Mine.

EQUIPMENT RENTAL
Legacy Lodge has the most recent, top-of-the-line ski and snowboard equipment.

DAYCARE
Park City Mountain Resort does not have on-site daycare, but daycare can be arranged via Guardian Angel, a licensed and insured babysitting service for the Park City area. Contact 435-783-2662 or gdangel@allwest.net.

► **WOODY ADVENTURE**
Shadow Ridge and Fortune Teller are ungroomed trails that take experts through wooded fields.

Claim Jumper to the base of the Silverload six-passenger express lift. There are more green trails on the east side of the mountain off the Bonanza six-passenger express chair.

INTERMEDIATES

Intermediates have almost half the mountain to play with, and are excluded only from Jupiter Bowl. Those trails to the west of the Bonanza six-passenger express—Hidden Splendor, Powder Keg, Assessment, and Mel's Alley—are easier blues than those to the east of it: Single Jack, Sunnyside, and Parley's Park. There are plenty of other blue trails, with 11 clustered below the King Con high-speed quad chair. You could do all these in one go, continually riding the King Con, or if you are looking for a longer route, try Jupiter Access, reached by the Bonanza six-passenger express chair and join on to Thaynes Canyon, which ends at the base of the King Con quad lift.

ADVANCED AND EXPERT

Jupiter Bowl and McConkey's Bowl are where the best advanced and expert skiing are to be found. Jupiter Bowl is the highest point on the mountain, accessed by Jupiter double chairlift. Up here there are black diamond and double black diamond trails and bowls to test even the most confident skiers and boarders. Jupiter Bowl is also the best place for powder and moguls. Utah is famous for its fantastic light powder, so if that's your favorite snow condition, you'll be glad to be here. If you're searching for some adventure, take Shadow Ridge and Fortune Teller from the Jupiter Bowl summit, to ride ungroomed trails that go through wooded fields. A 20-minute walk along the ridge to Jupiter Peak means you can go straight down the steep East Face into Puma Bowl. All skiing is in-bounds, and some trails are accessed through gates only, which are opened depending on weather and conditions. Backcountry skiing is not permitted.

BOARDING & FREESTYLE

In 2003 three new terrain parks opened—King's Crown near the base of the mountain, Claim Jumper off the Claim Jumper green trail, and Seldom Seen off the Seldom Seen black trail and Temptation blue trail. All are groomed daily and have extensive new snowmaking facilities. There's also a huge new superpipe off the Eagle quad chair at the base of the mountain (although it is accessed by the Three Kings double chair) and a halfpipe off the blue PayDay trail, that are floodlit at night. Park City hosted the World Superpipe Championships in 2003.

EATING ON THE MOUNTAIN

There are four mountain restaurants, as well as Legacy Lodge at the base. Legacy Lodge has some good après ski venues and an international food court, as well as Kristi's Coffee Café, the place to stop at the start of the day for coffee and pastries. On the mountain, Mid-Mountain Lodge, off the Pioneer triple chair at the summit, is an historic miner's lodge famous for high quality fast food and a large outdoor deck. The Summit Smoke House & Grill has sit-down full service and great views of Park City and beyond. The Snow Hut, at the bottom of the Siilverlode six-passenger express, is a lunchtime favorite, with café service and an outdoor deck. Café Amante is a European-style coffee house, considerately located halfway down Homerun, the green trail that leads

◄ DIGGING DEEP
Boarders have the whole mountain to explore, as well as three groomed terrain parks.

EATING ON THE MOUNTAIN

LEGACY LODGE
SUMMIT SMOKE HOUSE & GRILL
SNOW HUT
CAFÉ AMANTE
MID-MOUNTAIN RESTAURANT

down to the base. As well as the above there are "Skiosks" dotted around the mountain where you can stop for a drink and a snack.

APRÈS SKI

There's not a huge choice for après ski at the actual resort, but Park City itself is bursting with restaurants and bars. Legends Après Ski Bar in Legacy Lodge has a large fireplace, live music, a well-stocked bar and appetizers, and is as popular with locals as with visitors. The new Brewhouse, on the second floor of Legacy Lodge, is a sports bar where you can sit back and enjoy the views or watch the latest sports triumphs on the wide-screen T.V.

Utah's strict licensing laws eased a little around Park City when the 2002 Winter Olympics were staged, but restaurants must still serve food in order to sell alcohol and you must become a temporary member of a late-night club in order to drink alcohol. The minimum age for consuming alcohol is 21 years and children are not allowed in bars, although they can go to restaurants serving alcohol. Bars in Park City tend to close around 1:00 AM. Park City has around 100 restaurants with every flavor from Thai, Japanese, and Chinese through Italian.

For shopping, the Factory Stores at Kimball Junction, 4 miles (6.4 km) from Park City have designer seconds and end-of-the-line clothing. Take a taxi or shuttle service from Park City or rent a car.

OTHER ACTIVITIES

Park City has plenty of alternative mountain recreation even when you're not on your skis or your board. ZipRider™ offers a 60-second, 45 mph (70 kph) cable car ride featuring a 500 feet (150 m) vertical drop, suspending riders at 110 feet (33 m) off the ground at its highest point. Guided sled tours take you down the mountain on mountain sleds attached to four skis. Nightly guided tours start at the top of PayDay six-passenger express lift and follow the Homerun trail to the base. Reservations are recommended. Spectacular views can be had from the guided snowmobile tours, which use powerful, modern snowmobiles. Tours last 75 to 90 minutes. Minimum riding age is five years and the minimum driving age is 12 years.

Take a Snowed Inn Dinner & Sleigh Ride from the base to a mountain lodge where you'll have a gourmet meal awaiting you. The sleigh can take 12 people at one time. There's also ice skating at the resort. And if you've had enough of Park City, Gorgoza Park, just off Interstate 80, is a winter playground for everyone. Choose from snowtubing, snowmobiles, and a jib park.

USEFUL PHONE NUMBERS

General Information	800-222-7275
Tourist Office	435-649-6100
Park City Mountain Reservations	800-222-7275
Park City Ski and Snowboard School	801-649-8111
Sleigh Rides	866-647-3310
24-hour Snow Report	435-647-5449

USEFUL WEBSITES

Official Website	www.parkcitymountain.com
Official E-mail	pcinfo@pcski.com
Sleigh Rides	www.snowedinnsleigh.com
Transportation Information	www.parkcity.org
Useful information	www.parkcityinfo.com

BARS

LEGENDS APRÈS-SKI BAR
THE BREWHOUSE

▼ AFTER THE ADVENTURE
Once you've dominated the chutes and bowls, take a comparatively simple stroll through Park City for some retail therapy.

NESTLED IN UTAH'S PICTURESQUE ROCKY MOUNTAIN WASATCH RANGE, DEER VALLEY IS UNASHAMEDLY UPMARKET, OFFERING EXCEPTIONAL SERVICE AND FANTASTIC SKIING ON VARIED TERRAIN SPREAD OVER FOUR MOUNTAINS. THE RESORT APPEALS TO A MOSTLY UPSCALE CLIENTELE AND OFFERS SOMETHING FOR EVERY SKIER, BUT BOARDING IS NOT ALLOWED.

DEER VALLEY

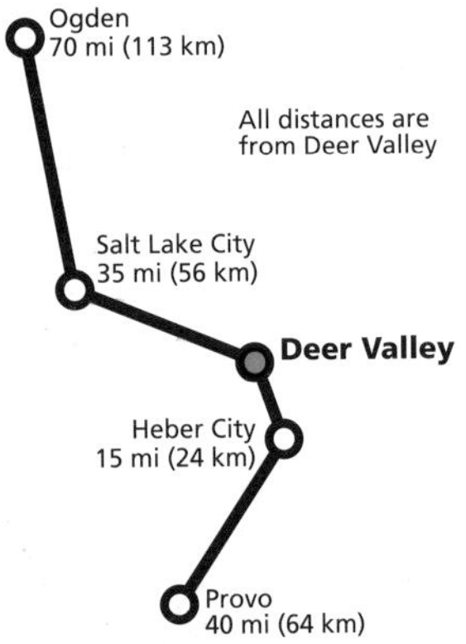

Once a beautiful mountain where silver miners enjoyed weekend diversion by sliding about on crudely-made wooden skis, today Deer Valley Resort offers the highest standards of service and amazing attention to detail both off and on the slopes. The varied terrain covers 1,750 acres (708 ha) and was home to the 2002 Olympic slalom, moguls and aerials events, and the 2003 freestyle F.I.S. world ski championships. The ski season runs from the first Saturday in December to the first Sunday in April (conditions permitting.) Peak season is December 26–January 1, and President's Day weekend in February. Low season is December 7–25, and from April 1 until the end of the season.

▼ BALD MOUNTAIN

Beginners and experts can find tracks just for them on Bald Mountain, one of the four mountains at Deer Valley.

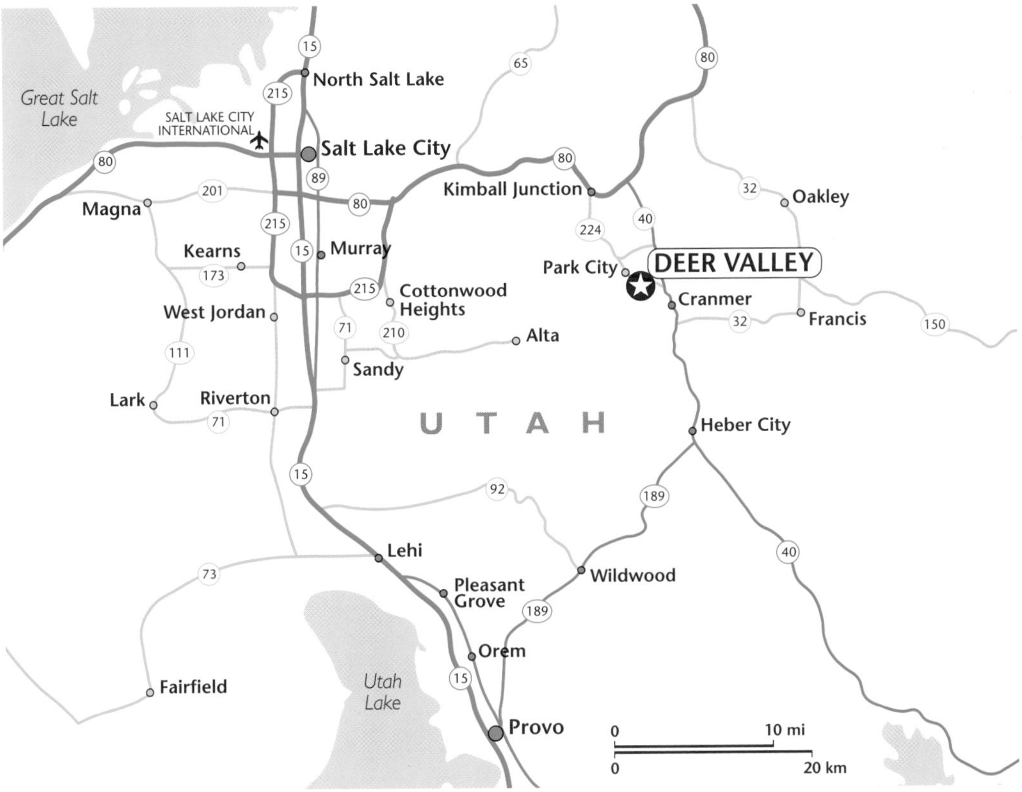

MOUNTAIN FACTS

Base	6,570 feet (2,002 m)
Summit	9.570 feet (2,916 m)
Elevation	3,000 feet (914 m)
Easy	25%
Intermediate	50%
Advanced/Expert	25%
Number of trails	88
Longest trail	2 miles (3.2 km)
Ski area	1,750 acres (708 ha)

SNOWFALL

Annual snowfall	300 inches (762 cm)
Snowmaking	Over 500 acres (200 ha)

SKI LIFTS

Gondolas	1
High-Speed Quads	9
Triple Chairs	7
Double Chairs	2
Total	19
Riders per hour	40,700

SKI SEASON
First Saturday in December to first Sunday in April

GETTING THERE

Deer Valley is located in the historic mining town of Park City, Utah, 36 miles (58 km) from Salt Lake International Airport. The transfer time by road (off the I-80, exit 145) is approximately 45 minutes. There is no rail connection.

THE VILLAGE

When developing Deer Valley Resort, its founder, Edgar Stern, fully utilized his hotel experience to create the most luxurious and service-oriented ski resort in North America. There is no village as such with most of the nightlife and shopping to be found on nearby Park City's historic Main Street.

The three day lodges: Snow Park Lodge (at the base), Silver Lake Lodge (mid-mountain) and the new Empire Canyon Lodge (at the bottom of Empire Canyon), are all styled after the grand old national park lodges built in the late 19th century—rustic elegance, with wooden beams, wide-planked wooden floors, and lots of windows to showcase the local beauty.

Park City, Utah—just one mile (1.6 km) away from the Deer Valley base area—is a blend of old and new, the older buildings reminiscent of the mining days in the mid-1800s. Sixty-four of Park City's buildings are listed on the National Register of Historic Places. Main Street is the hub of Park City, a bustling skiers' haven alive with more than 100 restaurants, 20 bars, clubs, interesting shops and galleries.

ACCOMMODATIONS

Deer Valley offers an enticing variety of upscale accommodations. Located in either the Snow Park base area or mid-mountain at Silver Lake Village, every room, suite, condo, or house is individually decorated and tastefully furnished. All Deer Valley accommodations are within minutes of a chairlift and some offer ski-in, ski-out access. The Central Reservations Department (435-645-6528 or online at www.deervalley.com) is the best option for booking accommodations.

Stein Eriksen Lodge (named after Norwegian ski

▼ SNOW PARK LODGE
One of three day lodges, Snow Park Lodge, great for après ski music and other entertainment.

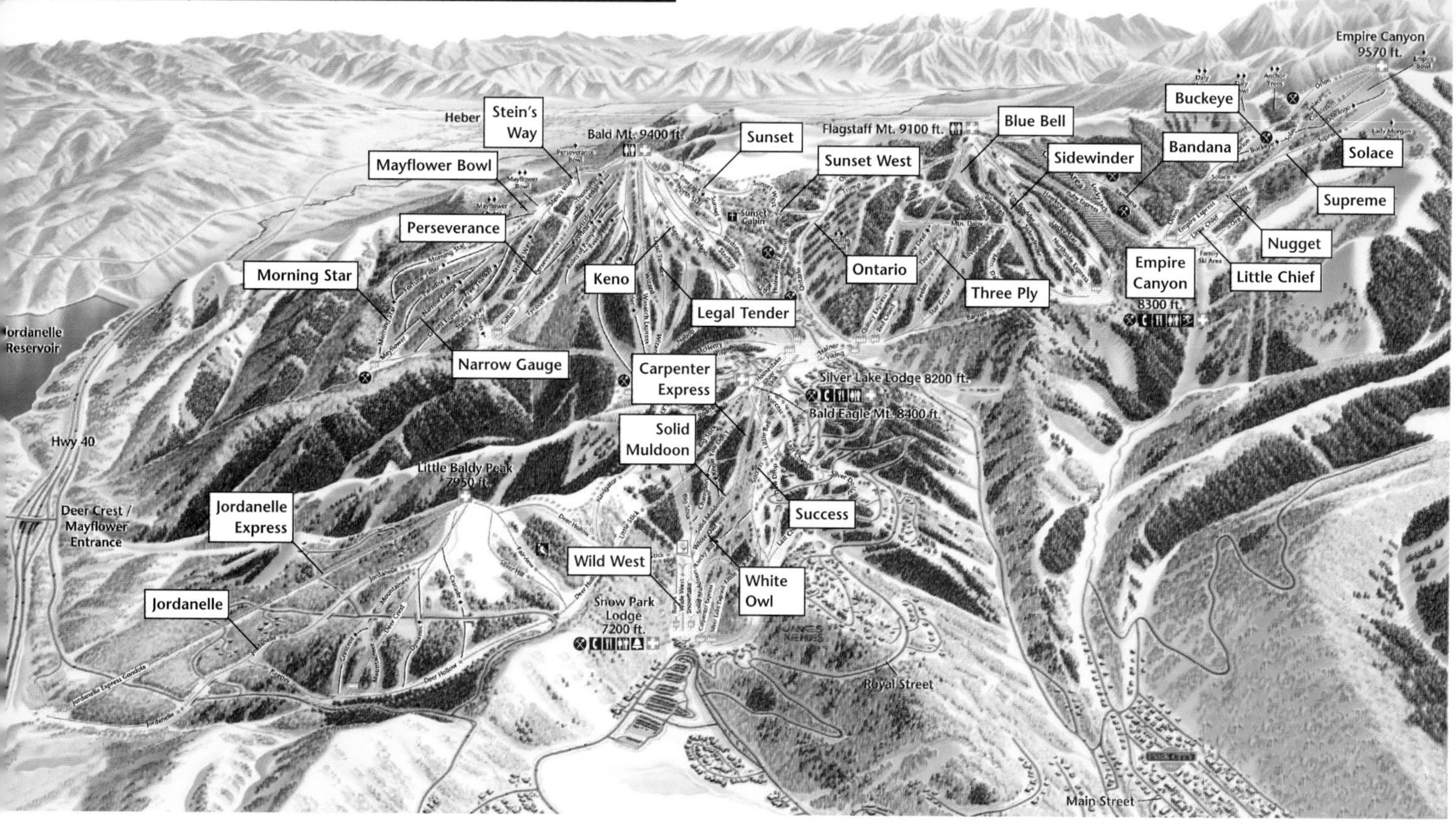

NEARBY RESORTS

Olympian Stein Eriksen) in the Silver Lake area, is top-of-the-line in luxury lodgings. It offers designer furnishings, unparalleled amenities, and the finest gourmet restaurants. Rooms cost from US$350 to US$910 per night (excluding taxes), depending on season and availability.

There are also numerous cheaper lodging options in Park City. Main Street is only one mile (1.6 km) from the slopes of Deer Valley and only a short shuttle ride away via Park City's complimentary bus service.

Private homes are available for a seven-night minimum stay. Most are decorated with cozy mountain charm. The homes range from four to six bedrooms and amenities include fireplaces, spacious living rooms and hot tubs. There are also condominiums available, ranging from one to five bedrooms. Most units offer hot tubs.

SKI AREA

All levels of skiers are catered to, but boarding is not allowed. Deer Valley's 1,750-acre (708-ha) ski area, offering 88 trails, is spread over four mountains: Bald Mountain (9,400 feet/2,865 m), Flagstaff Mountain (9,100 feet/2,774 m), Empire Canyon (9,570 feet/2,916 m) and Bald Eagle Mountain (8,400 feet/2,560 m.) Approximately half the trails at Deer Valley are blues and double blues, suitable for intermediate skiers, 15 percent green for beginners, 25 percent for advanced, and 10 percent for experts.

Beginners are able to ski each of the four mountains, while intermediate skiers can cruise to their heart's delight on Deer Valley's many famed, groomed trails. Advanced and expert skiers will find themselves skiing uncrowded black and double black diamond trails, and eight chutes, three bowls and extensive gladed areas covering 800 acres (324 ha).

Widely acknowledged as one of the ultimate full-body workouts, cross-country skiing in the Park City area is a unique opportunity. Nature lovers will enjoy a gliding cross-country stroll through the beautiful backwoods of the Wasatch Mountains.

In 2001 a new snowmaking pond holding 15 million gallons of water was created on Bald Mountain, and for the 2002/03 season another snowmaking pond was created in the Snow Park Lodge base area. This water storage facility will hold a further ten million gallons of water and will ensure snowmaking over 500 acres (200 ha).

SKI LIFTS

Deer Valley is one of the first ski resorts to implement a lift system that was engineered specifically by a mountain engineering firm, in 1981. This lift system was designed to allow for all-mountain accessibility, which translates into a consistent fall line and minimum traversing. Constant assessment makes the system work even better: for example, a lift tower or terminal may be moved to improve the flow of the lifts and to keep lift lines to a minimum. The lifts run from 9:00 AM to 4:15 PM. There are 18 chairlifts (seven high-speed quads, seven triples, two doubles, and two fixed-grip quads) and one gondola, carrying around 40,700 skiers per hour onto the mountain. To ensure a quality skiing experience, and avoid overcrowded trails, the number of skiers is limited, avoiding long lift lines as well as long lunch lines. Get there early to reserve a lift pass!

LIFT PASSES

As numbers are limited, during Christmas, New Year, and President's Day week capacity is nearly always reached. To avoid disappointment it is strongly advisable to reserve a lift pass, but this must be done by 9:00 AM on the day of skiing. You can also buy a next-day lift pass between 3:00 PM and 5:00 PM on the day prior to skiing, at the Snow Park Lodge Ticket Office or at the Main Street Signatures store between 3:00 PM and 9:00 PM. After 9:00 AM tickets are on a first-come, first-served basis. To reserve your lift pass prior to your ski day phone Deer Valley Central Reservations at 435-649-1000 or e-mail cenres@deervalley.com

Lift passes can be bought at Snow Park Lodge, Silver Lake Lodge, and the Jordanelle Express Gondola. Tickets can also be purchased through the Ski School Office, the rental store, and the Children's Center. You don't need photo I.D. for a lift pass.

Full-day lift passes cost US$67/69 for adults (13–64), US$36/38 for children aged 12 and under, and US$46/48 for seniors (65 and older). Half-day passes (12:30–4:15 PM) cost US$46 for adults, US$28 for children, and US$30 for seniors. Weekly passes cost around US$300 for adults, US$145 for children aged 4–12, and US$200 for seniors.

A Wide West only lift pass, giving access to the Wide West green runs only, costs US$20 for all ages. A foot passenger pass is available from Jordanelle Gondola or the Silver Lake Express lift for US$15 round trip.

Deer Valley is part of the Ski Utah Multi-Resort Passport lift ticket offer designed for international visitors. Information on this special program is available via pdenny@deervalley.com

SKI SCHOOLS AND GUIDING

The Ski School offers programs and activities for skiers of all ages and abilities. You can book lessons in the Ski School Office on the plaza level of the Snow Park Lodge 8:30 AM–5:00 PM, or call 435-645-6648. Lessons can run from half-day to full day, 9:00 AM–4:00 PM. The maximum number for group lessons is four people. For private corporate groups, anywhere from one to five people are allowed. The youngest age for lessons is three years old.

The Max 4 semi-private group lesson focuses on technique and skiing goals to help skiers to achieve the next zone of performance. Participants are closely grouped by ski ability, comfort level and lesson goals. A three-hour lesson costs US$100 and participants must be 18 years or older.

Innovative specialty programs for men and women plan the focus of the day, concentrating on stance, balance and alignment analysis, video analysis, and new equipment demo. The three-day weekend program costs US$385. For children aged

DAY CARE

Deer Valley offers a state-licensed Children's Center providing supervision and activities for non-skiing children. Located on the main level of the Snow Park Lodge, the center is open from 8:30 AM to 4:30 PM (888-754-8477 for reservations or 435-645-6648.) Children aged two months to 12 years are welcomed, as well as infants aged two to eight months on a 4:1 ratio. Full-day care is available, including lunch taken at the center. Diapers, change of clothing, and any special foods must be provided. Parents are welcome to join their children. Activities include story time, art projects, imagination activity, singing, and lots of play time and toys, along with some quiet time.

▼ **UTAH'S POWDER**
Steep, ungroomed trails with Utah's famous light powder are mostly on Bald Mountain, along with fabulous views.

► FLAGSTAFF
There are several wide blue cruisers on Flagstaff Mountain, as well as the most challenging run, ungroomed Three Ply.

SUPERIOR SERVICE

Guests of Deer Valley can ship their skis to and from the Resort via Federal Express two-day service for US$50 per pair, each way. To make arrangements to ship skis to the resort, phone Deer Valley Central Reservations 800-558-3337 or 435-649-1000 and collect your skis from the Snow Park Ski Storage upon arrival. Arrangements can be made to ship skis home the day of departure through the Snow Park Ticket Office.

Curbside attendants assist with equipment unloading and loading on arrival and departure at Snow Park Lodge. There is also complimentary day and overnight ski storage at Snow Park Lodge, Silver Lake Lodge, and at the Jordanelle Gondola. Day storage is also available at the Empire Canyon Lodge.

3–19, a wide variety of daily programs cost from US$120 including lift pass. A free video analysis is available for top-end beginners and above, and free hosted tours are also available for intermediate and advanced skiers.

Telemark lessons are available. For high-altitude ski touring, the Ski Utah Interconnect Adventure Tour takes skiers on a breathtaking ski tour of five peaks, and Wasatch Powderbird Guides offers heli-skiing from Snowbird.

BEGINNERS

One of the best areas for beginners is the separate, protected Wide West trail on Bald Eagle Mountain, reached by the Burns and Snowflake chairlifts. It's a very short trail on the lower half of Bald Eagle and void of any trees or other obstacles, making for a stress-free route. It's a very easy grade and ends at the back of Snow Park Lodge, so skiers can take off their skis and rest and relax. The ski area in the real estate development of Deer Crest is also accessible via the Little Stick or Navigator ski trails, or by catching the Jordanelle Express Gondola at the Mayflower/Deer Crest entrance on Highway 40.

Also for beginners on Bald Eagle Mountain is Success trail. This is a longer trail than Wide West, from the top of Bald Eagle Mountain all the way to the bottom, and is accessible from the Carpenter Express quad. It's an easy, wide slope for beginners who feel comfortable doing a full-length trail. On Bald Mountain, Sunset and Sunset West, trails wind around the mountain and join with Ontario to give the longest trail (2 miles/3.2 km). This is the highest beginner trail in terms of elevation—9,400 feet (2,865 m)—giving beginners the best views from any green trail on the mountain.

Once skiers make their way to Empire Canyon, via Bandana trail, they can ski the Nugget by riding the Little Chief chairlift. Empire Canyon is Deer Valley's furthest mountain so beginners can feel a little more adventurous but still ski on a green trail. In fact each of Deer Valley's four mountains has at least one green trail. The trails connect between the mountains, so a beginner skier can always be on trails they can ski confidently.

INTERMEDIATES

A classic ski itinerary for intermediate skiers is to begin on Bald Eagle Mountain to experience the blue trails such as Solid Muldoon, Big Stick, and White Owl, a double blue, which was the aerial venue for the 2002 Olympics. Then work your way to Bald Mountain for spectacular views. Single blues Keno and Legal Tender are popular, as is Stein's Way. Then try advancing to double blues such as Wizard and Perseverance. The longest trail is Jordanelle which runs 2 miles (3 km) from Little Baldy Peak to the bottom of the gondola.

On Flagstaff Mountain, Sidewinder and Blue Bell are single blue favorites due to their wide and moderately winding layout. Ski over to Empire Canyon to ski Supreme, a single blue, and then experience the Empire Canyon bowl area by skiing Orion, Solace, and Conviction, all double blues. The

▲ CREATIVE CARVING
With the Super Carve Clinic, run by Deer Valley's Ski School, you'll soon be doing the neatest parallels you've ever seen.

most challenging is Three Ply on Flagstaff Mountain, steep and seldom groomed.

ADVANCED & EXPERT

About 25 percent of the trails are black diamond suitable for advanced skiers and 10 percent are double diamond blacks for experts. A classic ski itinerary for advanced skiers would be to start on Bald Mountain to ski the single blacks in the Mayflower Bowl area: Rattler, Reward, Perseverance Bowl, Grizzly, Morning Star, Fortune Teller, Paradise, Narrow Gauge, and a few others. Next, head over to Empire Canyon to ski Domingo, Buckeye, and Lady Morgan Bowl. Finish the day by skiing the single blacks on Bald Eagle Mountain. To ski in the tracks of the Olympic athletes of 2002, try Know You Don't, which was the slalom venue, and Champion, the mogul venue.

Strong skiers in search of steeper, ungroomed trails and Utah's famous light powder will be rewarded with numerous trails in the Sultan and Mayflower areas of Bald Mountain. There are also spectacular views to be had up here. The chutes in Mayflower Bowl offer the challenges of steep, rocklined and narrow trails. Lady Morgan Bowl is a wide trail with bumps that eventually works its way into a glade-skiing section. Champion is a straight trail with bumps. Looked at from below it may not look much, but once you're standing at the top it's a different story!

Deer Valley has six bowls and many chutes, in addition to 800 acres (324 ha) of glade skiing. The Daly chutes offer eight very steep chutes (one of which is the steepest chute in Utah) and challenge even the most seasoned, expert skiers. Triangle Trees is one of Deer Valley's larger gladed areas, offering open shots and a variety of exposures. Glades and chutes are challenging because they may also have numerous unmarked obstacles and are not patrolled regularly. You can get a special experts-only trail map. There are plenty of opportunities for skiing off the beaten track but you should check conditions with the Ski Patrol or a mountain host prior to entering any off-piste area.

BOARDING

Deer Valley Resort does not allow snowboarding. Snowboarders are catered to at Park City Mountain Resort, or The Canyons ski resort, both nearby and easily accessible by shuttle bus.

EATING ON THE MOUNTAIN

There are three main areas for eating out on the mountain: Snow Park Lodge at the base, Silver Lake Lodge mid-mountain, and Empire Canyon Lodge at

▶ THROUGH THE TREES
With 800 acres (324 ha) of trails winding through the trees, you'll be able to get away from the crowds, and take a guide if you want.

▲ **THE DALY CHUTES**
Empire Canyon's Daly Chutes are eight very steep chutes that only experts should attempt.

EATING ON THE MOUNTAIN

SNOW PARK LODGE
Snow Park Lodge Restaurants

SILVER LAKE LODGE
The Silver Lake Restaurant
The Royal Café
Mariposa
Bald Mountain Pizza

EMPIRE CANYON LODGE
Empire Canyon Grill

BALD MOUNTAIN
Snowshoe Tommy's
Sunset Cabin

FLAGSTAFF MOUNTAIN
Cushing's Cabin

the bottom of Empire Canyon. The restaurants offer a good variety of dining options ranging from international, traditional, seafood, self-service, and fast food. There are 10 mountain restaurants: three open in the evening and seven during the day.

In Snow Park Lodge there's the Snow Park Lodge Restaurant, open for breakfast and lunch daily from 8:00 AM–2:00 PM. For evening dining, the Seafood Buffet offers a vast array of seafood appetizers and entrées, grilled fowl, pasta, prime rib—and some fabulous desserts. Fine wine and spirits are also available.

At Silver Lake Lodge there are several restaurants. The Silver Lake Restaurant has Continental-style breakfast and lunch daily. The Royal Street Café, new in 2003, replaces the former McHenry's Restaurant, and features award-winning cuisine in contemporary but rustic setting with sit-down waiter-service lunch, dinner and après ski daily. And the elegant Mariposa, the best restaurant on the mountains, offers a blend of classic and contemporary cuisine, as well as vegetarian and tasting menus and fine wines. Bald Mountain Pizza is open at lunchtimes only.

Empire Canyon Lodge gives breathtaking views of Daly Bowl and chutes, along with scenic deck dining. The Empire Canyon Grill is open for drinks only 9:15 AM–11:00 AM and lunch 11:00 AM–2:30 PM. Afternoon snacks are then available until 3:30 PM.

Also on the mountain, but not affiliated to any of the main lodges are Snowshoe Tommy's on Bald Mountain (open 9:30 AM–3:30 PM daily, conditions permitting) for chili, desserts, espressos, and cold drinks; and Cushing's Cabin on Flagstaff Mountain (9:30 AM–3:30 PM daily, conditions permitting) for snacks and hot and cold drinks.

APRÈS SKI

On the mountain, the Snow Park Lounge in Snow Park Lodge is a happening place for music, entertainment, videos, and televised sporting events. Hors d'oeuvres and cocktails are served seven days a week. It's popular with skiers of all ages due to its spaciousness and back deck, allowing skiers to view Bald Eagle Mountain while sipping cocktails and listening to live entertainment. Real open fires warm up cold limbs.

There are several choices on Main Street in Park City for après ski. The Wasatch Brew Pub, Utah's oldest existing brewery, has pool tables, games and big-screen televisions. The Broken Thumb also has a pool table, games, and a big-screen television that can be viewed from a comfortable couch and chairs. The No Name Saloon is a favorite of locals and visitors. Very often the numerous bars and restaurants in Park City offer a happy hour, in addition to live music.

Deer Valley is quiet at night but over at Park City there are about 20 bars and nightclubs in the Main Street area. For jazz lovers, Mother Urban's on lower Main Street has a cozy atmosphere with leather couches and candlelit tables. If you dislike smoke, Renee's on Heber Avenue is the place to go. Known for their wide selection of martinis, Renee's usually offers a pianist for entertainment, or a solo musical performer of some sort. For those who love to dance, Club Creation, Cisero's and Harry O's offer an eclectic array of bands, D.J.s and solo performers. These nightclubs draw the attention of locals, visitors, and many Salt Lake City residents who make the trip to Park City on weekends. Bars will close anywhere from 11:30 PM to 1:30 AM, and the minimum age for consuming alcohol is 21.

OTHER ACTIVITIES

Other sports activities in the area include snowmobile tours, sleigh rides, ski jumping, luge and bobsled rides at the Utah Olympic Park, hot-air balloon rides, snowshoeing, tubing, heliskiing, catskiing, cross-country skiing, ice skating, bowling and arcade.

USEFUL PHONE NUMBERS

Park City Tourist Office	435-649-6100
Ski Rescue Service	435-649-1000
Health Surgery, Park City	435-615-0240
Taxi: Ace Cab Company	435-649-8294
Ski School	888-754-8477
Lift Ticket Reservations	435-649-1000
Central Reservations Department	435-645-6528
Wasatch Powderbird Guides	435-649-9422
Signatures stores	800-833-2002
Snow Report	435-649-2000

USEFUL WEBSITES

Official Website	www.deervalley.com
Lift Ticket Reservations	cenres@deervalley.com
Ski Utah Interconnect Adventure Tours	skiinfo@skiutah.com
Lodgings	cenres@deervalley.com

▼ SILVER LAKE LODGE
There's a variety of eating spots at Silver Lake Lodge, including the best restaurant on the mountain, Mariposa.

RESTAURANTS & BARS

ON THE MOUNTAIN
SNOW PARK LOUNGE

IN PARK CITY
BARS
NO NAME SALOON
BROKEN THUMB
WASATCH BREW PUB

DANCE
CLUB CREATION
HARRY O'S
CISERO'S

JAZZ
MOTHER URBAN'S
VEGETARIAN/NON-SMOKING:
RENEE'S

A LOCALS' FAVORITE SINCE 1939, ALTA HAS MANAGED TO PRESERVE WHAT SOME CALL "THE SOUL OF SKIING." WITHOUT REAL ESTATE DEVELOPMENT ON THE MOUNTAIN AND VERY LITTLE CORPORATE CLUTTER, YOU CAN IMAGINE THE THRILLS FELT BY THE PIONEERS OF SKIING WHEN LITTLE GOT IN THE WAY OF THE NATURAL BEAUTY OF THE AREA.

ALTA

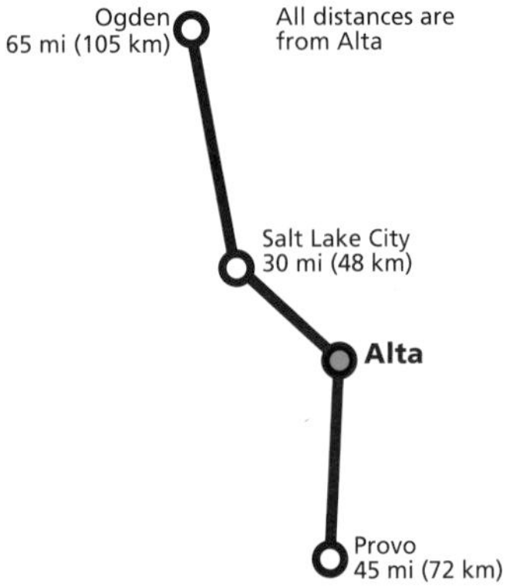

If you are looking for a ski vacation away from the bustle of everyday life, Alta just may be the place for you. Alta and Snowbird resorts now offer the Alta Snowbird Pass, enabling skiers to access both ski areas via the new high-speed quad in Mineral Basin that transports skiers to the saddle separating Alta's Albion Basin and Snowbird's Mineral Basin and connects the two resorts. The combined ski areas in Little Cottonwood Canyon are justifiably considered as having the best powder snow in the U.S., but if you're looking for loads of thrilling nightlife Alta may not be the right place for you. The lodges are traditional, cozy gathering places for family and friends, but not really good for people who are looking for dancing and drinking. The ski season at Alta runs for five months from the middle of November to mid-April. Note that Alta does not allow any snowboarding, while neighboring Snowbird does.

GETTING THERE

Alta is 30 miles (48 km) southeast of Salt Lake City at the top of Little Cottonwood Canyon, on State Highway 210. Salt Lake City International Airport is 33 miles (53 km) away, 45 minutes' drive. There are no rail connections.

THE VILLAGE

Skiing is the thing here. The village has five lodges, strung out in a linear-type arrangement and all offer accommodations and restaurants as well as bars and cafeterias. Created in 1939 with Alta Lodge, it's one of the longest-established ski villages in the U.S., and still very popular with well-heeled families who stay in the comfortable but not necessarily luxurious lodges. It's a quieter village than some, with not many après-ski opportunities apart from the lodges. But everything is within walking distance and the atmosphere is friendly and cozy.

◄► MOTHER NATURE

It's almost as if Nature favored skiiers and she wrote the blueprint for the ski area at Alta, generously carving out a playground for beginners, intermediates and experts.

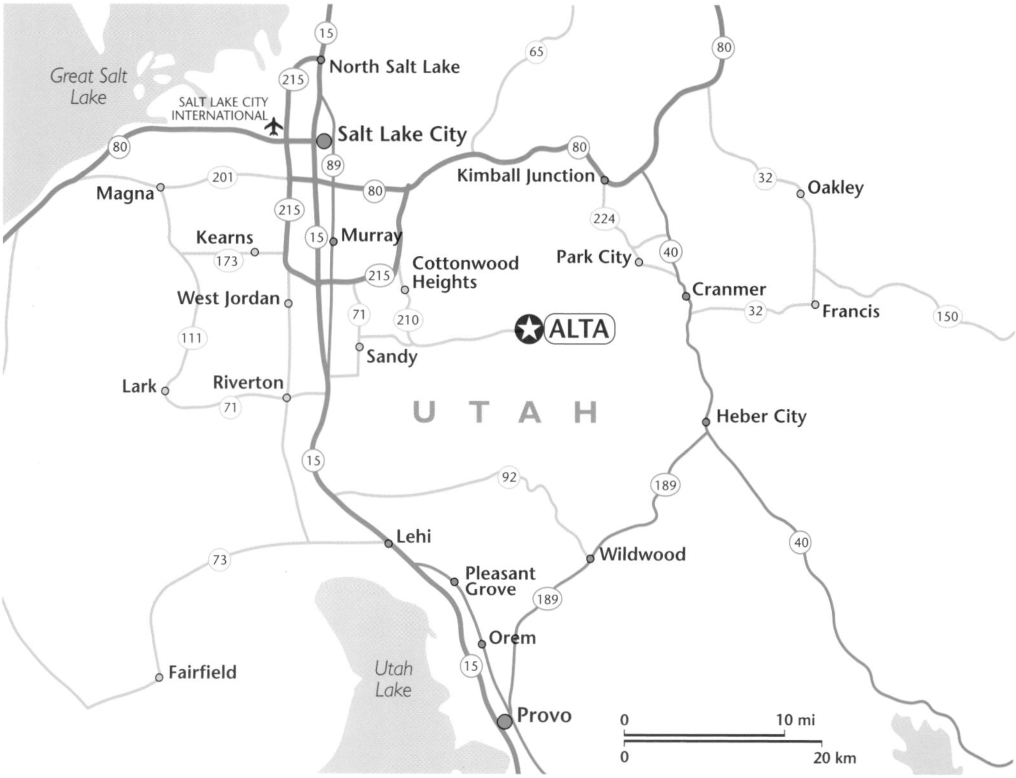

ACCOMMODATIONS

Some prefer to stay at the base of the lifts in one of Alta's unique lodgings or condominium properties, knowing they are just steps away from skiing the next morning. Others enjoy the ambience of Salt Lake City's much wider variety of lodging options and don't mind a short drive up the canyon as a trade-off for a "night on the town." Each of the five lodges at the base of the mountain has a unique history and a story to tell. They are Alta Lodge, Alta Peruvian Lodge, Goldminer's Daughter Lodge, Rustler Lodge, and Snowpine Lodge. As well as these there are condos within a mile (1.6 km) radius of the village that sleep another 1,137 guests. Blackjack and Hellgate are two choices. Private homes are also within walking distance of the village. The Alta Information Service 888-STAY-ALTA or Canyon Services 800-562-2888 provide all the information you may need on accommodations. The website www.alta.com has information on all lodging properties.

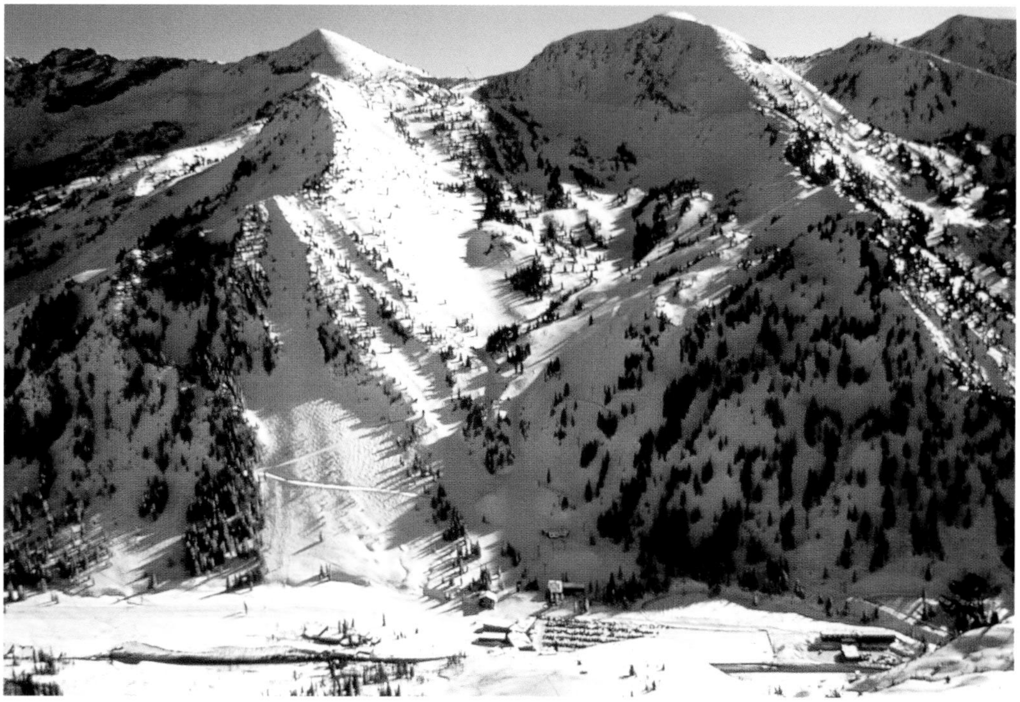

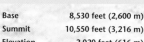

MOUNTAIN FACTS

Base	8,530 feet (2,600 m)
Summit	10,550 feet (3,216 m)
Elevation	2,020 feet (616 m)
Easy	25%
Intermediate	40%
Advanced/Expert	35%
Number of trails	23
Longest trail	1 mile (1.6 km)
Ski area	2,200 acres (890 ha)

SNOWFALL

Annual snowfall	500 inches (1,270 cm)
Snowmaking	50 acres (20 ha)

SKI LIFTS

High-Speed Quads	1
Triple Chairs	3
Double Chairs	4
Surface Lifts	5
Total	13
Riders per hour	11,200

SKI SEASON

Mid-November to mid-April

NEARBY RESORTS

ACCOMMODATIONS

LODGES
ALTA LODGE
ALTA PERUVIAN LODGE
GOLDMINER'S DAUGHTER LODGE
RUSTLER LODGE
SNOWPINE LODGE

CONDOMINIUMS
BLACKJACK
HELLGATE

PRIVATE HOMES
MILES
TRAVIS
PLOFCHANS

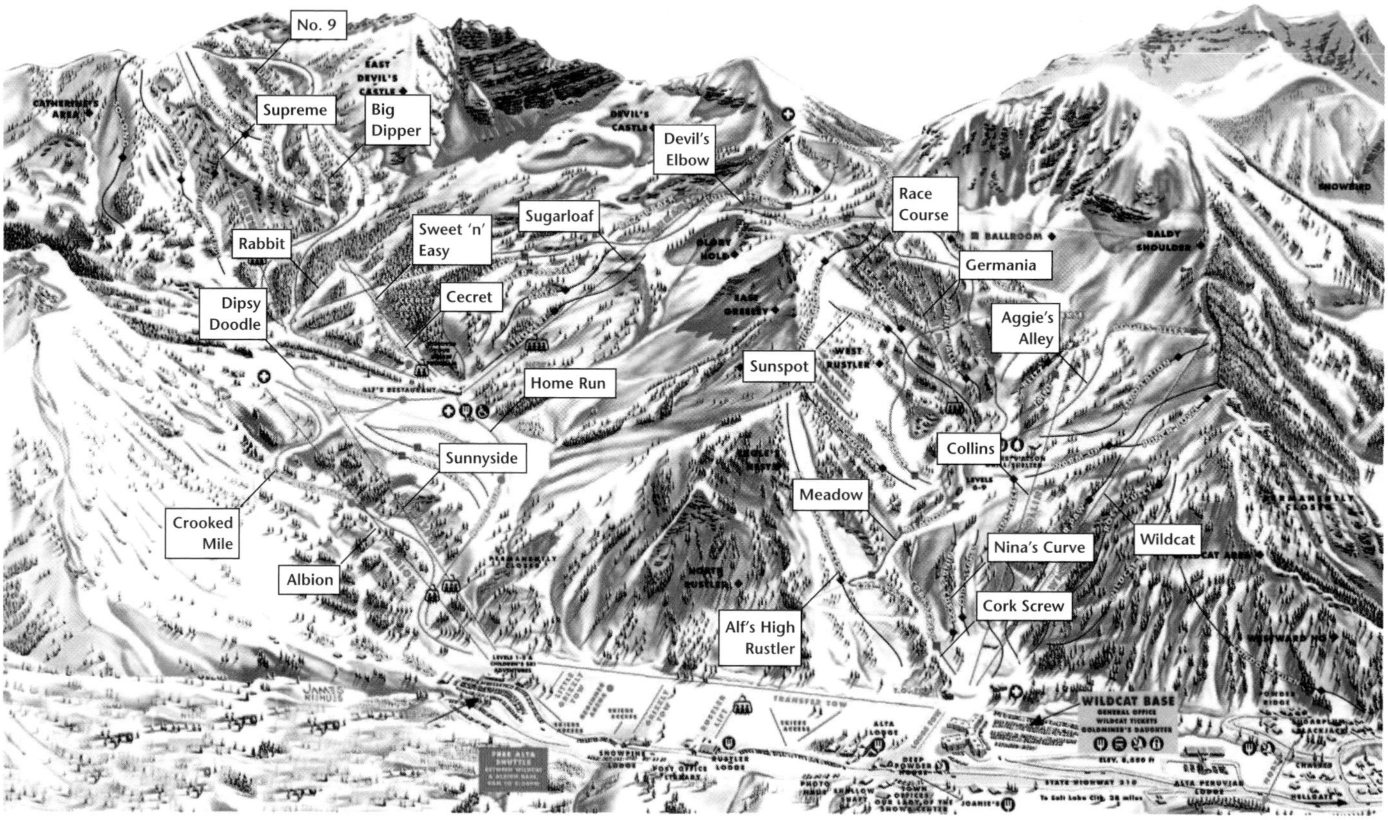

SKI AREA

Alta is recognized not only for its variety of terrain but also for stunning scenery and dry snow quality. There is plenty of beginner and lower-intermediate terrain, as well as some steep chutes and powder bowls that you will have to hike to.

▶ **ALTA PERUVIAN LODGE**
Stay at the Alta Peruvian, one of five lodges at the base of the mountain, with its rustic charm and outdoor heated pool and hot tub.

Most of the beginner trails are accessed from Albion Base, with intermediates scattered around the mountain and some great advanced black diamond bowls off the Sugarloaf quad lift.

SKI LIFTS

There are four double chairs, three triple chairs, one quad and five surface lifts. Lifts are open from 9.15 AM to 4.30 PM and they carry about 11,200 people per hour onto the mountain. At peak times there may be lines of 10–15 minutes. Come early or ski during the noon hour to avoid them. Some older lifts have been replaced in the past few years with faster ones, and further improvements are planned, pending United States Forest Service approval.

The Sunnyside lift is good for beginners and enables skiers to ride up the mountain and then gives them over a mile (1.6 km) of great learning terrain back to the bottom. In 2002, Sugarloaf lift, which leads to access to Snowbird resort, was upgraded to a detachable quad and offers good progression for the beginner who has conquered the Sunnyside terrain.

LIFT PASSES

A full-day pass costs US$40 for adults, US$32 for children aged 12 and under. There's a special price of US$22 for the three beginner lifts Albion, Sunnyside

and Cecret. Now Alta is connected with Snowbird the Alta Snowbird Pass is available, enabling skiers to access lifts in both resorts. This costs adults US$64 for a full day. A seven-day pass at just Alta is US$280, and for Alta Snowbird it costs US$364. You can buy passes at ticket windows at Alta and various ski stores in Salt Lake City.

SKI SCHOOLS AND GUIDING

The Alf Engen Ski School, named after Alta's founder and located at the Albion base, has 100 full-time certified instructors. There are adult and children's ski programs, and group classes are limited to eight people. The minimum age for group lessons is four years. Children under four must have private instruction. Instructors follow a nine-level skill progression that makes it easy to choose the right class. Levels 1–3 follow green trails, 4–6 blue trails, and 7–9 black trails. The ski school also teaches deep snow technique to a high standard.

BEGINNERS

Beginner skiers can access the mountain via the Albion, Sunnyside and Cecret lifts. The triple chair Sunnyside services a mile-long (1.6 km) beginner trail, originally named Never Sweat, now known as Crooked Mile, which gives beginners the chance to ski at altitude and enjoy the mountain views. A good day for a beginner would be to take the Albion double chair and ski down Crooked Mile to the base of Sunnyside triple chair, then take Sunnyside up and ski down Sunnyside green trail to Home Run, back to the base of Sunnyside lift. Then take Sunnyside up again, but this time cross over to Cecret double chair along Dipsy Doodle. Take Cecret lift and ski down Rabbit or Sweet 'n' Easy to join on with Home Run back to the base.

INTERMEDIATES

Intermediate skiers can ride the new Sugarloaf quad that accesses intermediate and advanced terrain. From Sugarloaf, you can ski the front of Alta by cutting back to the Supreme lift via Waldren's Way, Devil's Elbow and Razor Back, then take the Supreme triple chair for some good blue and black diamond trails. Or, if you have the right pass, drop into Snowbird's Mineral Basin from Sugarloaf. The ride up Supreme is an experience in itself. From the top you can enjoy a panoramic view of Alta and the beautiful Heber Valley. From here, challenging intermediate and advanced trails such as So Long, Big Dipper, and No 9 are favorites. On the front of Alta, the Wildcat, Collins, and Germania lifts provide more blue trails. From the top of Collins you can access the Germania lift, via Taint, as well as Aggie's Alley, the Meadow, and Corkscrew. Wildcat lift runs to the top of the Peruvian Ridge, accessing primarily advanced terrain. Aggie's Alley provides intermediate access off Peruvian Ridge to the Germania lift and additional intermediate terrain.

◄ **THE SOUL OF SKIING**
Alta's rugged mountainside has been largely tamed by its 13 lifts that take over 11,000 people onto its slopes every hour.

DAYCARE
Alta Children's Center:
801-742-3042
8.30 AM–5.00 PM

◄ **THE LONE PINE**
Just one of several advanced trails, Lone Pine is typical of the fantastic dry snow to be enjoyed at Alta.

▶ YELLOW TRAIL
Not yellow for cowardice, but for a great advanced trail—take Germania triple chair up and dive back down in style.

ADVANCED/EXPERT

With 35 percent of the mountain dedicated to black diamond trails, advanced and expert skiers have plenty to choose from. Germania triple chair loads midway up the mountain across from Watson Shelter. The lift provides access to a wide variety of advanced terrain. Race Course, Sunspot, Yellow Trail, Greeley Bowl, Lone Pine, and Alf's High Rustler, to name just a few, are for the expert skier. Advanced trails below Germania triple chair include Nina's Curve, Schuss Gully, and Collins Face. From the top of Wildcat, skiers can choose advanced trails down Peruvian Ridge, Punch Bowl, Rock Gully, Wildcat Face, and the Westward Ho Area (which connects with Snowbird resort). The toughest skiing in terms of moguls is Alf's High Rustler, the steepest slope is Gun Sight, and the best for powder are Greeley Bowl and Yellow Trail. Telemarking and high-altitude ski-touring is available through the Alf Engen Ski School, and heliskiing is available through Wasatch Powderbird Guides.

New for 2003 is guided backcountry skiing (and boarding) in Grizzly Gulch, located adjacent to the ski area. It's a unique skiing adventure of guided off-trail skiing. The day starts with check-in at the Albion base area, followed by an orientation and

continental breakfast at the Albion Grill. Then enjoy a heated snowcat ride to the top of Grizzly Gulch at 10,500 feet (3,200 m). The guided off-piste trails take skiers and boarders on pitches with an average of 1,500 feet (457 m) of vertical drop. The group may consist of any combination of up to 11 skiers and snowboarders and two guides. Snowcat skiing is only for advanced and expert skiers and riders with strong off-trail skiing skills and experience. Powder skis are recommended.

BOARDING & FREESTYLE

There's no within-bounds snowboarding at Alta.

EATING ON THE MOUNTAIN

There are three mid-mountain and six base area restaurants at the resort. Mid-mountain are the Collins Grill, on the second level of Watson Shelter, a traditional sit-down restaurant with waiter service; Watson Shelter, a cafeteria offering morning snacks, lunch and a shop; and Alf's Restaurant at the bottom of Cecret double chair, a cafeteria with lunch and snacks. At the base there are restaurants at Alta Peruvian Lodge, Alta Lodge, and Rustler Lodge, all offering waiter service. Goldminer's Daughter has a restaurant with sit-down lunch, breakfast and snacks, and the Goldminer's Bar serves Mexican food. The Albion Grill at Albion Base has a cafeteria where you can get breakfast, lunch and snacks and then there's Joanie's, above Deep Powder House, with made-to-order sandwiches and smoothies. The Shallow Shaft restaurant, opposite Deep Powder House, has a sophisticated menu and an extensive wine list.

◀ HIGH HIKING
Some steep chutes and powder bowls can only be accessed by a hike, but they're well worth it.

EATING ON THE MOUNTAIN

MID-MOUNTAIN
COLLINS GRILL
WATSON'S
ALF'S RESTAURANT

MOUNTAIN BASE
ALTA LODGE
ALTA PERUVIAN LODGE
RUSTLER LODGE
GOLDMINER'S DAUGHTER LODGE
THE ALBION GRILL
JOANIE'S
SHALLOW SHAFT

RESTAURANTS & BARS

GOLDMINER'S BAR
ALTA PERUVIAN BAR
SITZMARK CLUB
ALTA LODGE
EAGLE'S NEST BAR
RUSTLER LODGE

▲ MAIN CHUTE
Cut your teeth (hopefully not literally) on Alta's many long but not impossible chutes, a favorite with intermediates.

APRÈS SKI

The best places in the resort for après ski are Goldminer's Bar, the Alta Peruvian Bar, Sitzmark Club at Alta Lodge, and Eagle´s Nest Bar at Rustler Lodge. The minimum age for consuming alcohol is 21 and children cannot typically accompany parents in bars and other places serving alcohol. A few of the bars have a marked "zone" where children can hang out.

OTHER ACTIVITIES

The newest thing to do at Alta is cross-country or skate skiing on a three-mile (5-km) groomed track. Track tickets are only available at the Wildcat Base ticket office. There's a full range of classic skate, telemark, and snowshoe gear with sales of clothing, coffee, shakes and rentals. Lessons are available at the Alf Engen Ski School. Also available is snowcat skiing (see Advanced & Expert above).

There are four ski stores with rental and retail, but the shopping opportunities are not extensive at Alta—that's not the reason most people come here.

There are several massage therapists who will come to your ski accommodations to soothe away stressed muscles. Check out the Alta website, www.alta.com, for details.

USEFUL PHONE NUMBERS

General Resort Information	801-359-1078
Alta Visitor Information Service	888-782-9258
Ski Rescue Service	801-359-1078
Taxi	800-255-1841
Alf Engen Ski School	801-359-1078

USEFUL WEBSITES

Official Website	www.alta.com
Official E-mail address	info@alta.com

NESTLING AMID SPECTACULARLY RUGGED PEAKS IN THE WASATCH MOUNTAIN RANGE, SNOWBIRD'S EXCELLENT QUALITY OF SNOW AND SKIABLE TERRAIN HAS ATTRACTED SKIERS AND BOARDERS OF EVERY AGE AND ABILITY LEVEL. SO WHETHER YOU'RE SEARCHING FOR GENTLE, GROOMED TRAILS, INTERMEDIATE CRUISERS, UNTRACKED POWDER PITCHES OR BREATHTAKING PLUNGES, SNOWBIRD WILL NOT DISAPPOINT.

SNOWBIRD

At Snowbird you can expect a high level of service in a convenient pedestrian village with all amenities. There's a limited nightlife and bar scene, which may put some visitors off, as may limited shopping—as there's no "town" nearby. But if your main reason for coming is fantastic skiing, then look no further. Compared with other resorts Snowbird is not considered expensive, but compared with Salt Lake City hotels it is. About 30 percent of skiers come from the Salt Lake area.

Snowbird presents a more challenging mountain than more typical U.S. resorts. The ski season is nearly seven months, longer than any other Rocky Mountain resort, running from November to late May or early June. Peak season is December 20–31, and January 17 to April 5. The reliability of snowfall is the best in the U.S., dumping 500 inches (1,270 cm) in an average year. Utah's claim of having the "Greatest Snow on Earth" is really based only on snow in the Little Cottonwood Canyon where Snowbird is located. Friends and neighbors for 30 years, Snowbird and Alta began offering

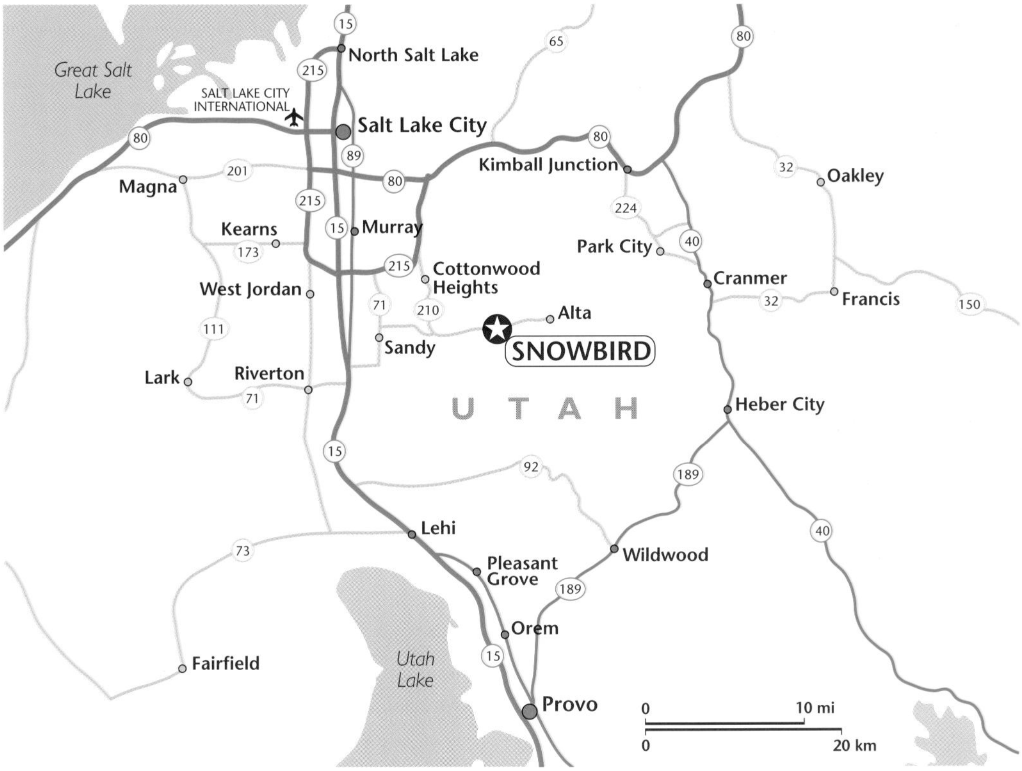

MOUNTAIN FACTS

Base	7,760 feet (2,365 m)
Summit	11,000 feet (3,352 m)
Elevation	3,240 feet (987 m)
Easy	27%
Intermediate	38%
Advanced/Expert	35%
Number of trails	85
Terrain parks	3
Longest trail	2.5 miles (4 km)
Longest descent	3.5 miles (5.5 km)
Ski area	2,500 acres (1,000 ha)

SNOWFALL

Annual snowfall	500 inches (1,270 cm)
Snowmaking	200 acres (80 ha)

SKI LIFTS

Aerial Tram	1
High-Speed Quads	3
Double Chairs	7
Surface Lifts	2
Total	13
Riders per hour	16,800

ACCOMMODATIONS

CLIFF LODGE AND SPA
LODGE AT SNOWBIRD
THE INN
IRON BLOSAM LODGE

interchangeable passes in 2001. The Alta Snowbird Pass provides 4,700 acres (1,880 ha) of great skiing in Little Cottonwood Canyon.

GETTING THERE

Snowbird, located 25 miles (40 km) southeast of Salt Lake City, is the closest ski resort to Salt Lake City, and one of the most accessible in the U.S. Salt Lake International Airport is 29 miles (46 km) away, 45 minutes by road. There are over 700 daily non-stop flights from and to most major U.S. cities. Flights from Los Angeles, San Francisco, and Dallas take around two hours, those from the East Coast around four hours.

THE VILLAGE

A pedestrian village with attractive, modern, avalanche-proof buildings offers all the skier services you will need, along with moderate and luxury accommodations, a range of restaurants, shopping, and other sporting activities.

ACCOMMODATIONS

There are four hotels in the village area, all sensitively designed to complement the natural surroundings and offering 882 rooms among them. Cliff Lodge is one of the U.S.'s best-known ski hotels. It's a ski-in, ski-out base with luxury full-service and all amenities as well as a spa. The Lodge at Snowbird, The Inn, and Iron Blosam Lodge all offer condos and hotel rooms at lower rates than Cliff Lodge. They are all very comfortable and friendly with easy access to lifts. Iron Blosam Lodge has its own health spa. Many skiers choose to stay in Salt Lake City and its suburbs. It's only a 20 minutes' drive away, and has every style of accommodations from youth hostels and motels to luxury mansions and five-star hotels.

▼ CLIFF LODGE
One of the best-known ski hotels in the United States, Cliff Lodge even has heated boot lockers in every room to make sure you start your day in comfort.

◄ WINTER VILLAGE
Snowbird encompasses four lodges and the Snowbird Center, as well as unforgettable skiing in the heart of the Wasatch Mountains.

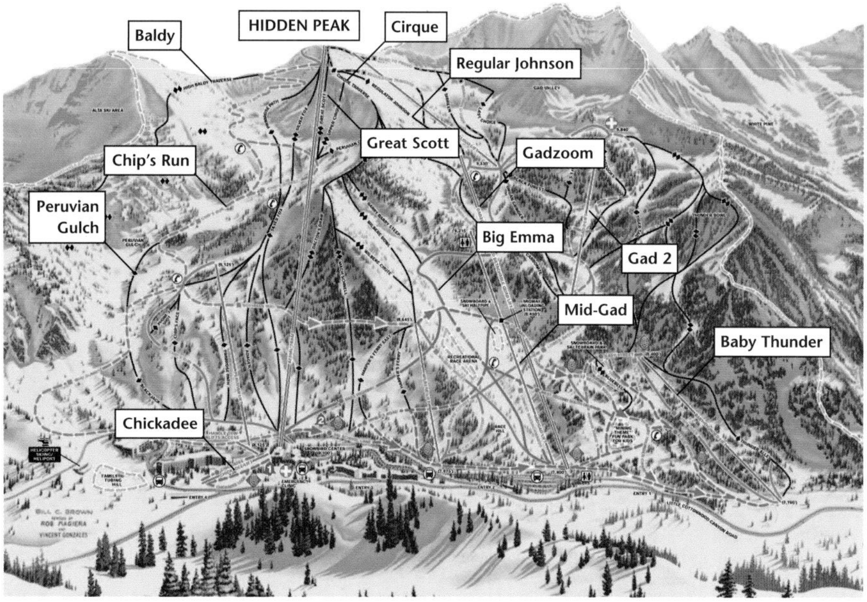

SKI LIFTS

The aerial tram carries 125 passengers at a time from the village up 2,900 feet (883 m) to Hidden Peak (11,000 ft/3,352 m) in seven minutes. Three high-speed quads and seven double chairs give access to additional terrain. Lifts open at 9.00 AM (except for the "Early Tracks" program, which allows guests to ski with a guide for an hour before the lifts open) and close at 4:30 PM. Chickadee is open until 8:30 PM for night skiing on Wednesdays and Fridays. The only line is for the aerial tram on Saturdays, holidays and powder days, but you can avoid this by using the chairlifts instead.

LIFT PASSES

Pass prices are split into chairlifts only, or aerial tram and chairlifts. An adult full-day pass costs US$47 for chairlifts only, or US$56 for tram and chairlifts. Up to two children aged 12 and under ski free on the chairlifts with any adult with a full-day pass. Half-day passes (9:00 AM–1:00 PM or 12.30 PM–4.30 PM) cost US$40 for chairlifts only, or US$48 for tram and chairlifts. Seniors 65 years and over pay US$36 for chairlifts only, or US$38 for tram and chairlifts. A weekly pass (five or more days) costs US$43 per day. The Chickadee (beginner lift) only costs US$11. Photo I.D. is required for season passes only. You can buy passes at the resort and at most hotels and ski stores in Salt Lake City. The Alta Snowbird Pass is great value. An adult pass costs US$64 per day, and US$52 per day for five-plus days and provides unlimited access to the top two powder playgrounds in the U.S.

NEARBY RESORTS

SKI SEASON

Mid November to late May

SKI AREA

Snowbird has 2,500 acres (1,000 ha) of skiable terrain that suits all levels of skier and snowboarder. Its particular appeal lies in the unparalleled powder snow that is the joy of upper ability skiers and boarders. Having said that, beginners are also well catered for, as are children, and families. In total there are 85 trails, ranging from green beginner trails through to a smattering of double black diamonds for those with a sense of adventure. Expansion into Mineral Basin in 2000 added 20 percent to the skiable area and opened up a huge back bowl skiing area. The second lift in Mineral Basin, opened in 2001, linked Snowbird to Alta via Sugarloaf Pass at 10,600 feet (3,230 m), thus creating one of the second largest skiable terrains in the U.S.—4,700 acres (1,902 ha).

▲ **AERIAL TRAM**
Rise up 2,900 ft (870 m) in under seven minutes to the fantastic views at Hidden Peak.

▲ LOOK MA, NO WAITING!
Join Early Tracks to beat the crowds, although Snowbird never really has any line-ups at chair lifts. Snowbird averages only 16,800 riders per hour, and with a total of 13 lifts it means you can move around with ease.

SKI SCHOOLS AND GUIDING

The Snowbird Mountain School at Snowbird Center and Cliff Lodge has been going for 30 years, so the 200 certified instructors have had plenty of experience. The upper limit on ski group size is eight persons and the minimum age for young children is three years. Supervised lunch is included with all full-day kids' lessons. The school runs a variety of camps throughout the season for men, women, adults and children from 4-day women's ski camps or 3-day boarding camps, through to ski steeps camps for advanced intermediates to experts.

For the more adventurous there are guided backcountry tours to a number of spectacular areas around Little Cottonwood Canyon. Experienced guides (members of the Snowbird Ski Patrol) will show you the joys of ski touring (including all equipment and lunch) but you'll need a certain level of fitness to enjoy them.

BEGINNERS

Beginners have around 27 percent of the mountain to test their nerves. You can enjoy much of the lower mountain and some upper trails if you use the aerial tram to return to base afterward. The most obvious place to start is the Chickadee area, very conveniently accessed from Cliff Lodge. Once you've found your ski legs you can venture over to Baby Thunder Lift and the green trails around it, and the Mid-Gad Lift, from where you can take the relatively long Big Emma green trails to the bottom of the lift. There are four beginner trails in the newly opened Mineral Basin area, the longest joining from the front of the mountain into Lupine Loop to the base of the Mineral Basin Express lift.

INTERMEDIATES

Thirty-eight percent of Snowbird is intermediate trails. The longest trail, Chip's Run (2.5 miles/4 km), is a blue trail providing a great workout with varying pitch from Hidden Peak summit to the base, via scenic Peruvian Gulch. A classic day's skiing for intermediates would be to take the aerial tram to Hidden Peak, follow Chip's Run, then ski over the back of the mountain to sample any of the four blue trails at Mineral Basin, then on to Alta via Mineral Basin and Alta's Sugarloaf area. There are also some excellent groomed blue trails from Gadzoom high-speed quad and Gad 2 lift, accessed from Gad Valley.

ADVANCED & EXPERT

Snowbird is particularly famous for its expert skiing terrain so it's no surprise that many professional skiers make their turns here. There are black diamond and double black diamond trails on both sides of the mountain, as well as access to Alta, of course.

From the aerial tram, experts can access the steep faces of Baldy and the Cirque, including Great Scott and Regulator Johnson, two of the steepest trails in the U.S. (Regulator Johnson is groomed). Great couloir skiing can be found in Gad Chutes, and there are steep moguls in Mineral Basin. For powder, Snowbird is one of the few places where 2–3 feet (60cm—1m) of light, unpacked snow is a common occurrence. Basically the whole mountain is good for powder, but the Cirque, Little Cloud Bowl, and Mineral Basin are outstanding.

Advanced or expert skiers have plenty of choice of trails all over the mountain. A good schedule would include starting at Hidden Peak to ski the

DAYCARE
Camp Snowbird Children's Center
Offering daycare services for children aged six weeks to 12 years.
Lunch included in a full day's care.
Skiing and boarding lessons available for children aged three and over.
Call 801-933-2256 or book online on campsnowbird@snowbird.com.

▼ MINERAL BASIN
The 2000 opening of Mineral Basin made Snowbird's skiing area a huge 2,500 acres (1,000 ha), and the new Baldy Express high-speed quad connects it to Alta.

Cirque Traverse and Gad Chutes on the front of the mountain, then Powder Paradise in Mineral Basin, and then linking to Alta for famous off-trail ski experiences there too. Snowbird has consistent, long steep pitches, often powder covered, and most of the upper mountain is bowl skiing where skiers find their own routes through the terrain.

Apart from signed "Permanent Closures" all in-bounds areas are available throughout the season. When conditions dictate, additional temporary closures are necessary. All out of bounds areas are roped off, and backcountry skiing must be accessed through designated gates. Having said that, the backcountry opportunities are fabulous. From the Cirque Traverse at Hidden Peak skiers can go down either side of the mountain to discover chutes and gullies. Below Twin Peaks in Gad Valley there's also good backcountry skiing.

EATING ON THE MOUNTAIN

MID-GAD RESTAURANT
MID-GAD ESPRESSO BAR

BOARDING & FREESTYLE

Boarders and skiers can ski together on the whole mountain, from Chickadee green trail to expert off-piste flights. It's very easy for boarders to get around the mountain as there are few flat spots. The incredible natural terrain features and sculpted halfpipe provide just about every kind of hit a diehard rider could want. The new terrain park opened in 2001 has been a big success. There are now three parks. For beginners there's Witch's Ditch with a beginner halfpipe, banked turns and rollers, then graduate to the intermediate halfpipe on Big Emma, and finally get your snowboard medals at Baby Thunder, where there are thrilling rails, hips, spines, jumps, tabletops, and quarterpipes.

▼ PUSHING POWDER Snowboarders can access the whole mountain easily, and the steep terrain and famous powder conditions will give you a great day.

HELISKIING

Wasatch Powderbird Guides tailor their heliskiing tours to the weather conditions and abilities of the group. The thrill of the chopper ride is nothing compared to the chance of making virgin tracks in some of Wasatch's most remote backcountry powder bowls. Call 801-742-2800 or visit www.heliskiwasatch.com.

EATING ON THE MOUNTAIN

Most of the refueling opportunities at Snowbird are at the base of the aerial tramway. Up the mountain is Mid-Gad Lodge, at 9,215 feet (2,808 m), with its Mid-Gad Restaurant offering burgers, pizza, salad and chili in a self-service atmosphere. Also here is the Mid-Gad Espresso Bar, open for specialty coffee, hot chocolate and tea, as well as cookies, fudge and ice cream.

In the village, Cliff Lodge and Spa, the Snowbird Center, the Lodge at Snowbird, and Iron Blosam Lodge have a variety of dining options among them. In Cliff Lodge there's the Aerie Restaurant, with a creative New American menu and award-winning wine list; the Aerie Sushi Bar; The Atrium, an enlightening spot for pastries and coffee, a sunny buffet lunch or a warming après-ski snack; Keyhole Junction for ribs, enchiladas and moles as well as plenty of choice for the kids; and Superior Snacks by the family pool, serving pizza, hot dogs, soups, sandwiches, draft beer, smoothies and soft drinks.

At the Snowbird Center, indulge in diner-style breakfasts and hearty lunches in Forklift, or head to the legendary Steak Pit, Snowbird's original steakhouse, for flame-broiled beef, king crab, lobster, chicken and bottomless salads. Rendezvous is a convenient spot for a fast lunch—natural salad bar, burgers, sandwiches pasta, etc. Birdfeeder is good for a quick bite or beverage between tram rides—coffee, cookies, sandwiches, hot dogs, soup, chili and microbrews. Pier 49 specializes in gourmet sourdough pizzas, by the slice or whole, and also does deliveries. General Gritts is Snowbird's general store, stocked with an ample selection of groceries and other items.

The Lodge at Snowbird offers the Lodge Bistro, with elegantly prepared main meals, and the Lounge, famous for fondues and deluxe burgers. And finally, in Iron Blosam Lodge there's the Wildflower Restaurant, with a menu influenced by Italian, Spanish, Provencal and Middle Eastern flavors. Enjoy it all and the incredible mountain views.

APRÈS SKI

There are four bars and 15 restaurants in the village area of Snowbird. The Wildflower Lounge in Iron Blosam Lodge is a locals' favorite for après ski,

◄ TORVILL & DEAN
When you've got your skiing and boarding medals sorted, try the Cliff Lodge ice rink for a different experience.

with a pool table and big-screen T.V. Otherwise there's the Keyhole Cantina for relaxing après-ski, in Cliff Lodge. The Aerie Lounge, also at Cliff Lodge, has regular live jazz and the Tram Club in the Snowbird Center is a sports bar and nightclub with live dance music or a D.J.

The minimum age for drinking is 21 and membership is required for entering the lounges, although this is automatically included for guests at Snowbird hotels. Children can only accompany parents in bars and other places serving alcohol if they are eating. The good news is that there's no set time for bars to close, so you can party on into the small hours if you want.

USEFUL PHONE NUMBERS

Tourist Office	801-933-2222
Central Reservations	801-947-8220
General Information	801-933-2298
Accommodations Reservations	801-742-2222
Ski Rescue Service	801-933 2134
Doctor	801-933-2222
Taxi	800-255-1841
Snowbird Activity Center	801-933-2147
Snowbird Mountain Ski School	801-933-2170
Cliff Spa	801-933-2225

USEFUL WEBSITES & E-MAIL ADDRESSES

Official Website	www.snowbird.com
Wasatch Powderbird Guides	www.heliskiwasatch.com
Cliff Spa	www.cliffspa.com
Official E-mail Address	cres@snowbird.com
Snowbird Mountain School	mountainschool@snowbird.com
Snowbird Daycare Center	campsnowbird@snowbird.com

OTHER ACTIVITIES

New for 2002/03, snowmobile guided tours provide an exciting adventure beginning in Mineral Basin and taking you deep into the Wasatch Mountains. Or take a snowshoe tour or go ice-skating on the slopeside rink at Cliff Lodge. There's a family tubing hill adjacent to Cliff Lodge.

For alternatives to winter sports activity, the Snowbird Canyon Racquet and Fitness Club features 10 indoor tennis courts, racquetball, squash, spinning classes and more. The Cliff Spa offers 24 treatment areas to rejuvenate your entire body after a hard day on the mountain. Services offered range from specialty massages to herbal wraps. There are also yoga, aerobics and meditation classes.

As far as shopping goes, Snowbird is not as extensive as some resorts, but there's a variety of specialty stores and boutiques, featuring ski gear and fashions, jewelry, home decorations and gifts. There's also a pharmacy, general store and sundries shop.

RESTAURANTS & BARS

RESTAURANTS
CLIFF LODGE
AERIE RESTAURANT
AERIE SUSHI BAR
THE ATRIUM
KEYHOLE JUNCTION
SUPERIOR SNACKS
SNOWBIRD CENTER
FORKLIFT
STEAK PIT
RENDEZVOUS
BIRDFEEDER
PIER 49
LODGE AT SNOWBIRD
LODGE BISTRO
IRON BLOSAM LODGE
WILDFLOWER RESTAURANT

BARS
CLIFF LODGE
KEYHOLE CANTINA
AERIE LOUNGE
IRON BLOSAM LODGE
WILDFLOWER LOUNGE
SNOWBIRD CENTER
TRAM CLUB

▼ SPA STYLE
The Cliff Spa has 24 treatment rooms to help you relax after a hard day's skiing. It also has a 49-foot (15-meter) rooftop lap pool with amazing views.

SUNDANCE HAS MOUNTAIN TERRAIN THAT IS UNMATCHED IN ITS NATURAL BEAUTY. THE SPECTACULAR SCENERY IS ALPS-LIKE, WITH THE TOWERING PEAKS OF 12,000-FOOT (3,600-M) MOUNT TIMPANOGOS. THE RESORT IS THE RESULT OF ACTOR ROBERT REDFORD'S VISION TO PROTECT THOUSANDS OF ACRES OF WILDERNESS AND OFFER A PEACEFUL SKI SANCTUARY WITH UNHURRIED SKIING AND UNSPOILED SOLITUDE. SUNDANCE IS FOR THOSE SEEKING A PEACEFUL, LOW-KEY VILLAGE COMMUNITY. IT OFFERS A NOSTALGIC STEP BACK IN TIME TO THE WAY SKI AREAS ONCE WERE.

SUNDANCE

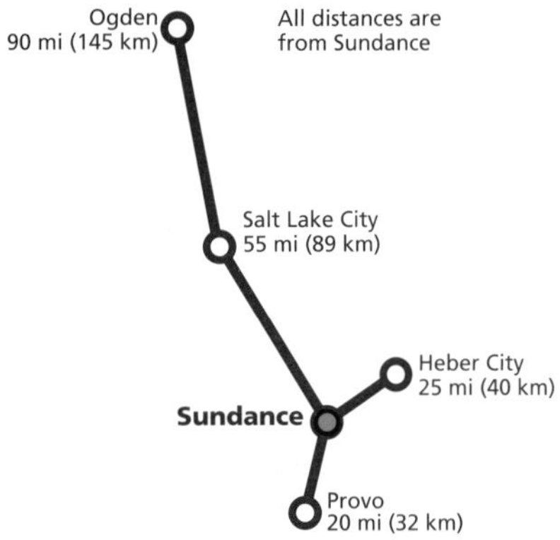

SKI SEASON
Late November to first Saturday in April or Easter (weather permitting)

Sundance exists in harmony with the surrounding natural environment, and is tiny compared with other U.S. ski resorts. There are just four lifts serving 41 trails, a fraction of the numbers found elsewhere. Robert Redford founded the resort in 1969 to rescue the area from over-development. It takes its name from his famed role in the movie Butch Cassidy and the Sundance Kid. The season runs from the last week in November (Thanksgiving) to the first Saturday in April or Easter (weather permitting). Peak season is December 20 to January 2, and January 15 to March 15. Since the installation of snowmaking facilities, there's now seamless coverage from the bottom of the front mountain to the top of the back mountain.

GETTING THERE

Sundance is located in peaceful Provo Canyon in the state of Utah. The nearest international airport is Salt Lake City, 55 miles (89 km) away, and around an hour by road. Park City is the closest major town, 40 minutes' drive away through the scenic Heber Valley.

► UNSPOILT
Stand at 8,250 ft (2,514 m) and survey the beauty of Sundance.

MOUNTAIN FACTS

Base	6,100 feet (1,859 m)
Summit	8,250 feet (2,514 m)
Elevation	2,150 feet (655 m)
Easy	20%
Intermediate	40%
Advanced/Expert	40%
Total number of trails	41
Longest trail	2.5 miles (4 km)
Ski area	450 acres (182 ha)

SNOWFALL

Annual snowfall	300 inches (762 cm)
Snowmaking	90%

SKI LIFTS

High-Speed Quads	1
Triple Chairs	2
Surface Lifts	1
Total	4
Riders per hour	5,000

ACCOMMODATIONS

GRAND SUMMIT RESORT HOTEL
SUGARLOAF INN
CONDOMINIUMS

There are car rental companies in the airport terminals and you can get a taxi to Sundance from Salt Lake City. There are no rail connections.

THE VILLAGE

Robert Redford's vision was to create a village where recreation, the arts, and the environment could all live happily alongside one another. He has succeeded with this intimate, western-style village, set in 6,000 acres (2,400 ha), with old-fashioned boardwalks that retain the friendly atmosphere of a past age. Within the village are accommodations, restaurants, bars, a general store, an artisan center, a 150-seat private movie theater, and the recently added Native American Spa.

ACCOMMODATIONS

Sundance has 95 stylish guest cottages and 11 spacious mountain homes ranging from two to five bedrooms. The Sundance Cottages are characteristically trimmed with pine walls and have balconies or picturesque decks. They have been designed to echo the simplicity of the wild and natural setting surrounding them, with handmade wooden posts, rough-sawn beams, and the rich colors of the land. The rooms have the cozy comfort of stone fireplaces or wood stoves, handcrafted furnishings, Native American art, and comfortable bedding. A collection of 11 mountain homes is located on the mountainside around the village. They range in size from intimate one-bedroom cottages through five-bedroom homes, and so are suitable for families, couples, or groups of friends. Prices are not cheap, but the quality of Sundance's accommodations is worth that bit extra.

SKI AREA

At Sundance you'll find just 450 acres (182 ha) of alpine skiing and snowboarding, 14 miles (22 km) of cross-country trails and six miles (10 km) of dedicated snowshoeing trails. If you're looking for tons of variety this might not be the best place to

▼ **NICE 'N EASY**
Sundance has many gentle cruises lower down, with more challenging skiing higher up on the back mountain.

NEARBY RESORTS

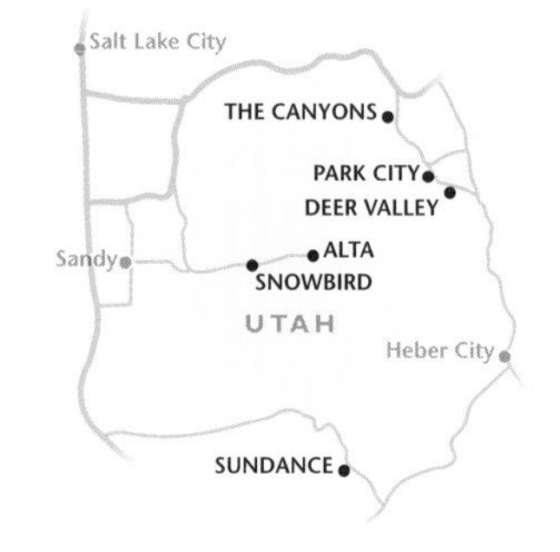

come, as the skiing acreage is far smaller than many U.S. ski resorts, many of which have over 2,000 acres of skiable terrain. Having said that, Sundance does cater to skiers and snowboarders of all levels and it is particularly good for familes, as one lift accesses beginner, intermediate and advanced/expert terrain. Intermediate and advanced skiers could probably satisfy themselves in one day so Sundance is not ideal for mileage-hungry intermediates or advanced skiers.

Other notable resorts nearby are those forming the Park City Resorts: Park City Mountain Resort, Deer Valley, and The Canyons, about 40 minutes' scenic drive from Sundance through the Heber Valley.

SKI LIFTS

There are only four chairlifts to choose from here, so you probably won't get lost. The quad lift takes visitors from the village to access the other lifts and all the terrain. Also down near the village is the handle tow lift for beginners. Two triple chairs serve the back mountain, which is where the highest terrain can be found. The lifts are open from 9:00 AM to 4:30 PM. Waiting lines are rarely a problem anywhere on the mountain.

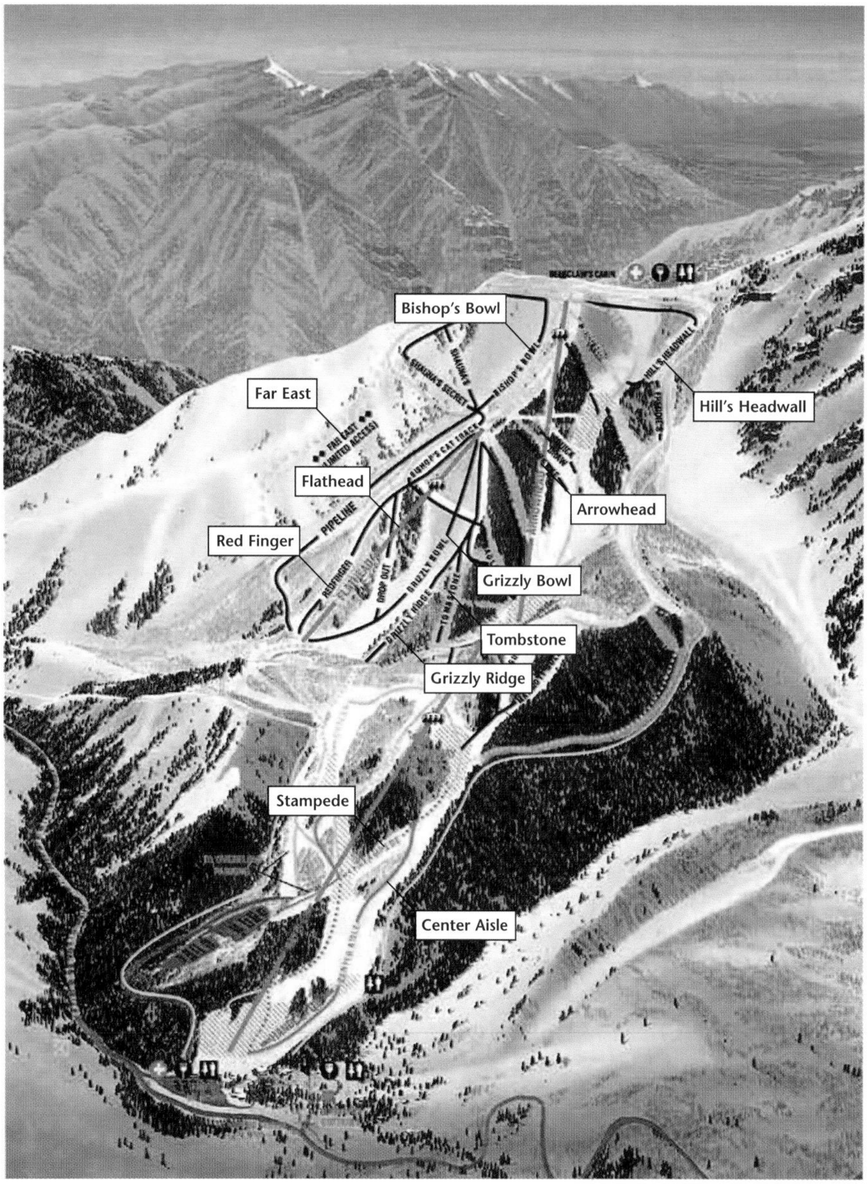

LIFT PASSES

There are lift passes for all abilities, ages and times of day. As you might expect, the passes are much cheaper than at other resorts, as there are fewer trails and lifts. A full-day pass costs US$29 for adults Monday to Friday (US$36 on weekends), US$16 for children (6–12), US$10 for seniors 65 and over, and children five years and under ski for free. Half-day passes run from 12:30 PM and cost US$22 for adults Monday–Friday and US$29 on weekends. No photo I.D. is required for passes. You can buy passes at the resort as part of the Ski Utah Passport multi-area lift program. The handle tow is complimentary for beginners.

SKI SCHOOLS AND GUIDING

The ski school is located at the base of the mountain. Group lessons, for which the upper limit is eight people, run from 10:00 AM to 12:30 PM, or from 1:30 PM to 4:00 PM. The minimum age for children taking part in group lessons is four years. Supervised lunch is included for children's lessons.

Sundance Kids is for children aged 4–12 and includes ski instruction and lift pass. This costs US$45 for a half-day (same times as adult group lessons) or US$80 for a full day, which includes lunch. Snowboard lessons for ages 7–12 years costs the same as the Sundance Kids lessons. Private lessons cost US$60 for one hour, US$100 for two hours, and US$140 for three hours.

A complimentary ski-guide service heads out each day, remaining within the ski area boundaries. The ski school also offers all types of instruction, from racing, moguls, powder, steeps, telemarking, and cross-country skiing to special coaching seminars for those who need them.

BEGINNERS

Beginners have around 20 percent of the mountain to cut their teeth on. The best area for beginners is to take the Theater handle tow near the village, then Center Aisle, a green trail. Once this has been mastered, take Stampede from midway up Ray's Lift—another green trail—and then venture onto some of the blue trails from the summit of Ray's Lift, such as Long Nose running into Flatnose, which then joins up with Center Aisle again.

◄ A WEALTH OF OPPORTUNITY
Sundance is close to the Park City Resorts and is small by comparison—but perfecty formed.

FILM FESTIVAL
The world-renowned Sundance Film Festival takes place in mid-January every year at the Sundance Summer Theater. If you are visiting around this time, you can expect to see some famous movie faces.

INTERMEDIATES

Of the 40 percent of intermediate trails, the most challenging is a black, Red Finger, a steep trail that gets narrower as you get further down. For a good day out, take Ray's Lift to the summit and ski Ray's Ridge to Lone Pine and the base of Flathead lift. Get off Flathead and take Cassidy to Bear Claw and ski to the base of Arrowhead lift. Ride Arrowhead lift, get a warm drink or snack at Bear Claw's Cabin at its summit, and take blue and black trails from the summit down to the base.

ADVANCED & EXPERT

The best skiing for advanced and expert skiers is on the back mountain. Forty percent of the trails are for advanced and expert skiers. Take Arrowhead and Flathead lifts to Bishop's Bowl and the Far East (which has limited access). The best terrain for moguls is Jamie's, for steep trails it's Red Finger and Far East, for deep snow it's Far East, Bishop's Bowl, and Drop Out, and for powder it's Far East. For a classic day, warm up on Bear Claw, then head for Bishop's Bowl and Grizzly Bowl. The best trails for

► A RUSH OF BLOOD TO THE HEAD
... is what you'll get when you see what you can do with a snowboard here at Sundance.

▼ CROSS-COUNTRY
Over 14 miles (22 km) of daily groomed trails for all levels keep cross-country enthusiasts happy.

experts are Far East, Red Finger, Drop Out, Upper Grizzly Bowl, and Snow Stake. You don't have to traverse all day to get to any of these trails, the powder lasts a long time, and the steepness causes even the best to take a deep breath. Skiing outside the ski area boundaries is not permitted, but there are some areas that you can hike to within the area boundaries that offer challenging terrain for the expert skier.

BOARDERS & FREESTYLE

There are no dedicated areas for boarders. The terrain makes it easy for boarders to access the whole mountain. Only a very few areas require a cat track for access.

EATING ON THE MOUNTAIN

There are six mountain restaurants: one at the top, Bear Claw's Cabin, and four in the village. Bear Claw's Cabin offers a rustic and comfortable mountaintop experience with soup, sandwiches and hot drinks, and—from the sundeck—fantastic views of the Utah Valley, Wasatch Peaks, and the Uinta Mountains. The Foundry Grill, at the base, offers a casual, western-style atmosphere with waiter service, and full menu and wine list. Creekside has soups, sandwiches, snacks and drinks, and an outdoor BBQ (weather permitting) plus a great deck for soaking up the rays. The Owl Bar is a great après-ski meeting place with a bar menu and full bar. The Tree Room is an award-winning fine dining restaurant open nightly for dinner. It features an extensive wine selection, preserving some of the finest wines available, and is decorated with Robert Redford's personal collection of Native American crafts and artifacts. It also has a tree growing out of the middle of it! The Sundance Deli, for those in a rush, dishes out sandwiches, soup, coffee, smoothies, ice-cream,

gourmet packaged goods, room delivery, and organic products from the Sundance farms.

APRÈS SKI

Sundance is inevitably quieter than some other ski resorts when it comes to après ski. The Owl Bar is the perfect spot for après ski, featuring the original rosewood bar, complete with bullet holes, which was frequented by Butch Cassidy's Hole in the Wall Gang in the 1890s. Great drinks, full grill menu, and weekend live entertainment. There are two restaurants in the village, The Tree Room and the Foundry Grill (see Eating on the Mountain above). The Library next to the Tree Room offers fireside cocktails. The minimum age for consuming alcohol in Utah is 21 years old. Children can accompany parents in all restaurants and in The Owl Bar until 9:00 PM. Bars close at 1:00 AM Monday to Saturday, and at midnight on Sunday.

OTHER ACTIVITIES

A recent addition to Sundance is the Native American-inspired Spa—a sacred environment where the restorative powers of nature are summoned for healing the body and restoring the spirit. It's a peaceful space with six quiet treatment rooms: five dedicated to massage and bodywork and one for esthetics. Therapies inspired by Native American ceremony, culture and ritual are designed to reconnect the body and the mind. In addition there are yoga classes to strengthen overworked muscles.

Cross-country enthusiasts will discover 14 miles (22 km) of daily groomed, scenic trails for skating and traditional cross-country skiing, plus six miles (10 km) of separate snowshoe trails. There are lantern-lit trails for cross-country skiing at night. Snowmobile tours are available daily.

The Artisan Center is committed to developing the creative potential in everyone and features pottery, jewelry making, photography, glassblowing, sculpture, and painting—for all ages—with a backdrop of unparalleled views of the surrounding mountain ranges. The General Store (home of the Sundance catalogue) offers clothing, jewelry, handcrafted items, artwork and signature Sundance merchandise.

USEFUL PHONE NUMBERS

General Information		801-225-4100
Sundance Ski Patrol	ext. 4150	801-225-4107
Doctor	ext. 4045	801-225-4100
Sundance Cottages Reservations		801-225-4107
Taxi (Executive Charter)		801-434-8945
Snow Line		801-223-4510
Cross-country Snow Line		801-223-4170

USEFUL WEBSITES

Official Website	www.sundanceresort.com
Official E-mail address	info@sundanceresort.com

EATING ON THE MOUNTAIN

BEAR CLAW'S CABIN

BARS

THE OWL BAR
THE TREE ROOM
THE FOUNDRY GRILL
THE LIBRARY

RESTAURANTS

THE TREE ROOM
THE FOUNDRY GRILL
CREEKSIDE
THE OWL BAR

▼ RELAX
Plenty of sunshine hours every season makes relaxing as enjoyable as the action.

CHAMPAGNE POWDER SPRINKLED OVER HIGH-SPEED, TREE-LINED TRAILS. FOR A COLORADO RESORT, STEAMBOAT IS RELATIVELY REMOTE, BUT THAT MEANS IT DOESN'T GET THE DAY TRIPPERS. IT IS ALSO RELATIVELY LOW COMPARED TO ITS NEIGHBORING SKI RESORTS—YET IT CONSISTENTLY MANAGES A BETTER SNOWFALL RECORD.

STEAMBOAT

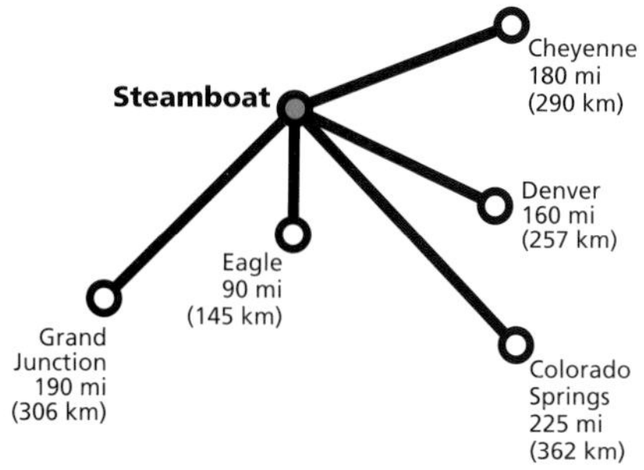

Now in its 40th season, Steamboat continues to lure with its authentic western atmosphere and friendly locals—Stetson hats and cowboy boots mingle with the latest ski gear—and not one but six peaks with varied terrain. Top that with "champagne powder" and it's clear to see that this resort is up there with the best. As if to prove it, the resort was busy last season unveiling Mavericks, the longest superpipe in the Rocky Mountains.

GETTING THERE

The resort at Steamboat Springs, Colorado, lies 160 miles (257 km) northwest of Denver—a three-hour drive from Denver International Airport. The Yampa Valley Regional Airport, known as Hayden (H.D.N.), is just 22 miles (35 km) from the resort, and Eagle Airport is 95 miles (158 km) away. There are scheduled shuttle transfers to and from the airports and around town there is a free local bus

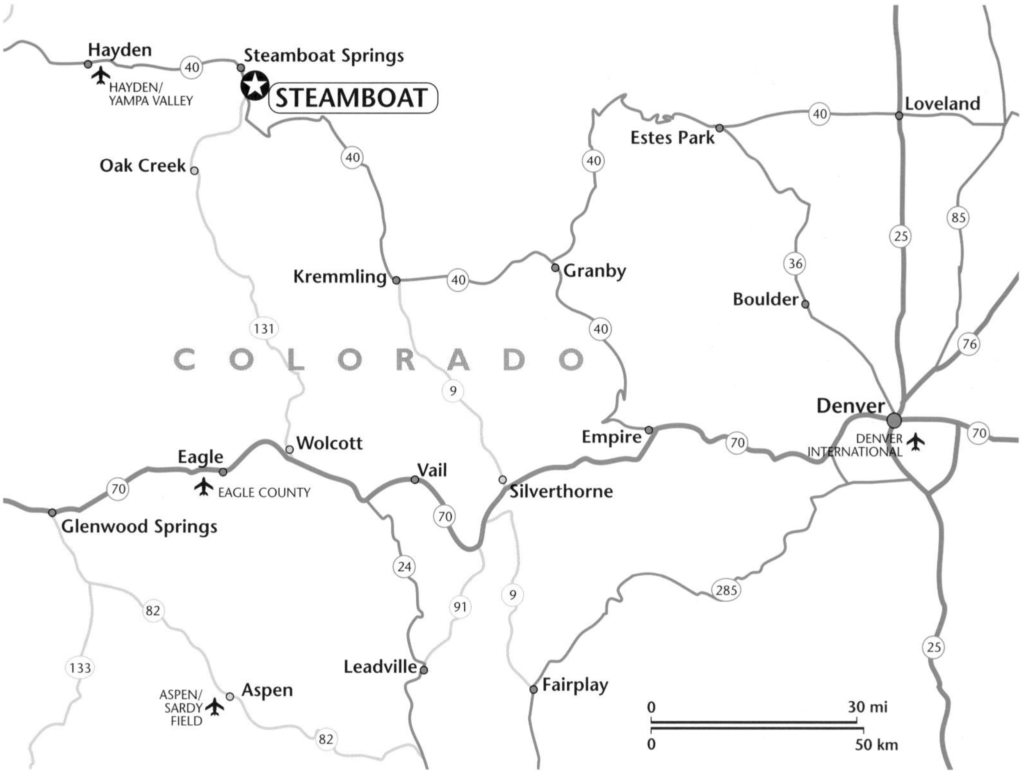

MOUNTAIN FACTS

Base	6,899 feet (2,103 m)
Summit	10,568 feet (3,221 m)
Elevation	3,668 feet (1,118 m)
Easy	13%
Intermediate	27%
Advanced	56%
Expert	4%
Number of trails	142
Longest trail	3 miles (4.8 km)
Ski area	2,939 acres (1,189 ha)

SNOWFALL

Annual snowfall	360 inches (915 cm)
Snowmaking	438 acres (174 ha)

SKI LIFTS

Gondolas	1
High Speed Quads	4
Fixed Grip Quads	1
Triple Chairs	6
Double Chairs	6
Surface Lifts	2
Total	20
Riders per hour	32,158

SKI SEASON
Late November to mid-April

between the resort base area and the town (about five minutes' drive). Many lodging properties provide shuttle services too.

THE VILLAGE

Seven thousand feet (2,134 m)up in the Colorado Rockies, nestled at the foot of Rabbit Ears Pass below one of the largest ski mountains in North America, sits a small ranching community that sits happily side-by-side with a thriving ski resort. Never far from its ranching roots, Steamboat remains firmly linked to a Western tradition that sets it apart from other ski resorts. Cattle are still reared in this genuine cow town and Steamboat remains firmly linked to a Western tradition that sets it apart from other ski resorts. Steamboat Springs lies three miles (5 km) from the purpose-built ski base area, and has both the look and feel of an old Western town: its long main street (dominated now by Dodges and S.U.V.s rather than horses and stagecoaches) is lined with frontier and Victorian architecture. It's a bustling, small town that 9,000 people call home. In fact, long before people strapped on skis for fun, Steamboat residents in the late 1800s were using skis and snowshoes in their daily lives. The base area "Mountain Village" is a typically purpose-built development, dominated by the Steamboat Grand Resort & Conference Center and also the site for condo-style lodgings, the ski school meeting area, ski rental and sports accessories stores, and the Bear River Bar & Grill and Gondola base complex.

ACCOMMODATIONS

Steamboat has more than 18,300 beds including 25 hotels, like the new, luxurious 328-room Steamboat Grand Resort Hotel located in the heart of the Mountain Village, just 120 yards (120 m) from the slopes (though it's not ski-in/ski-out). This

▼ WESTERN HERITAGE
Pubs, boutiques, restaurants and plenty of friendly locals—some in Stetson hats and cowboy boots—make Steamboat a relaxed but busy town.

◄ HIGH HOME
Nestled 7,000 feet (2,134 m) up in the Colorado Rockies, Steamboat is one of North America's largest mountains. Some 9,000 people live here year-round.

US$80 million complex has an outdoor heated pool and hot tub. The Sheraton and Best Western also offer top of the range hotel, motel and lodging options.

Most lodgings in fact are in the form of condominiums. Condos start at ski-in/ski-out distance and move away from the ski area back to Steamboat Springs. There are also a number of houses in town that can be rented, as well as B&Bs and catered chalets. Steamboat Central Reservations has all the lodging options and a rating system from 1 to 4 (from limited amenities to the highest level), plus a quality rating from EX (excellent) to NR (not rated) and a price guide showing fluctuations in costs depending on season.

Basically, the choice is wide and nightly rates can vary from US$49 for an economy motel room to US$2000 for a premium house or duplex. Don't forget local taxes are added on top. Your best bet is to go for one of several Snowsaver Value Packages on offer, combining competitively priced skiing and lodgings. You can book your entire vacation online, from air travel, lodgings, and lift ticket through to equipment rental and ski school, with Steamboat Central Reservations (www.steamboat.com).

ACCOMMODATIONS

EXPENSIVE

STEAMBOAT GRAND RESORT HOTEL
2300 Mt. Werner Circle
970-871-5500
www.steamboatgrand.com

STEAMBOAT SHERATON
2200 Village Inn Court
970-879-2200
www.steamboat-sheraton.com

SKY VALLEY LODGE
PO Box 773132
970-879-7749

MODERATE

STEAMBOAT BED & BREAKFAST
442 Pine Street
970-879-5724

PTARMIGAN INN
2304 Après Ski Way
970-879-1730
www.steamboat-lodging.com

BUDGET

RABBIT EARS MOTEL
201 Lincoln Ave
970-879-1150
www.rabbitearsmotel.com

ALPINER LODGE
970-879-1730
www.steamboat-lodging.com

▲ SUNSHINE AND STORM
Standing at 10,384 feet (3,167 m) and 10,372 feet (3,163 m), respectively, Sunshine and Storm Peaks offer plenty of difficult and more difficult cruisers, bumps and legendary tree skiing.

► TREE LINED
Located in the Routt National Forest, the slopes running off Steamboat's six peaks have plenty of trees and gladed trails.

▶ **PLENTY OF SLOPE-SIDE LODGING**
From condos to bed & breakfast's, lodgings are either at the purpose-built Steamboat base or in the town four miles (6 km) away.

SKI AREA

For those who think Colorado skiing is all Aspen and Vail, think again. Steamboat, the next largest ski area, nestled in the Routt National Forest, is a complete mountain range with six peaks: Mount Werner, Sunshine Peak, Storm Peak, Thunderhead Peak, Christie Peak, and Pioneer Ridge. Mount Werner is named after local boy Buddy Werner, who conquered the Hahenkamm at Kitzbühel in 1957 (the first American man to win a major European downhill title). At 10,600 feet (3,223 m) it's the highest peak of the six, and the main access to plenty of backcountry stashes with double black diamond chutes at East Face and North St. Pat's, plus lots of other challenging runs. Pioneer Ridge opened in 1998 with the Pony Express—a high-speed quad chairlift allowing skiers and riders to easily explore 260 acres (105 ha) of gladed terrain that Steamboat locals have loved for years. Steamboat is large: there's 2,939 acres (1,189 ha) of permitted terrain with a diversity of 65 miles (105 km) of trails. That translates into 142 trails and 3,668 vertical feet (1,118 m) for all ability levels—18 green, 80 blue, 38 black and six double black. Ropes, signs, placards, gates and access points are used throughout the area to mark closures, ski area boundaries and access points for the backcounty terrain.

Take your pick: from late November through to mid-April you can ski beautiful gladed areas or groomed cruisers, or go for the bumps, steeps and open meadows with champagne powder in the trees for the most avid powder hounds. In fact, the term champagne powder was coined here and there's plenty of it, with an average snowfall of 30 feet (915 cm) every season. Steamboat's snowmaking systems cover 438 acres (174 ha) of terrain, from the base area through mid-mountain, to the top of Storm Peak. A total of 35 runs are serviced by snowmaking, accessed by 13 lifts.

Night skiing is available at historic Howelsen Hill, located in downtown Steamboat Springs. This ski area dates back to the early 1900s and is the oldest continuous operating ski area in Colorado. Night tubing is also available at the Steamboat ski area. There are snowcat-drawn sleigh-ride dinners in the evenings and the gondola is open at night for dinner atop the mountain.

SKI LIFTS

The Steamboat Ski Area is serviced by 20 lifts including an eight-passenger gondola and four high-speed quad chairlifts. Thunderhead Express, a high-speed quad chairlift enables skiers and riders to access more than 720 acres (290 ha) of terrain for all ability levels on Thunderhead Mountain. In 1998, Pony Express, a high-speed quad, was installed providing access to 260 acres (105 ha) of gladed terrain in Pioneer Ridge. Approval has been given for the installation of a high-speed detachable quad and trails for a second phase of development there that

▼ **HIGH RISE**
Steamboat's gondola rises vertically 2,200 feet (671 m) in 9 minutes giving access to beginner intermediate and expert slopes. It opens at 8:30 AM.

SKI SCHOOL
Ski Services
2305 Mt. Werner Circle
Steamboat Springs, CO 80487
http://www.steamboat.com/skischool.html
skischool@steamboat.com;
Phone: 970-871-5375; Fax: 970-871-5380

will open up a further 510 acres (206 ha). Lift capacity is 32,158 skiers per hour and opening times are 8:30 AM to 4:00 PM. The only time that waiting in line can become a real problem is on big powder days. During busy times (Christmas and President's Day) there may be a slight wait at the gondola when it first opens, but there are other options beside the gondola to get to mid-mountain, including a high-speed quad.

SKI PASS

There are a number of specially priced "lift-with-lodgings" options offered by Steamboat Central Reservations, such as the White Sale Snowsaver offering six nights' condo accommodation with a five-day lift ticket for US$471. Individual or multi-day tickets vary from US$46 to US$64, depending on season and number of days. Steamboat has an excellent Kids Ski Free deal which enables children 12 years of age and younger to ski free when their parents or grandparents purchase a five-or-more-day lift ticket. Proof of age is required and it's only one child per ticket. A lower mountain ticket is available at reduced rates and allows skiers and riders access to nearly all of the resort's beginner terrain on three chairlifts. Certain tickets and lift passes require photo I.D. and/or proof of age. Lift tickets can be bought at the ski area, or purchased before arrival by Internet, phone, fax or mail.

SKI SCHOOL AND GUIDING

Steamboat prides itself on its ski classes—from simple half-day kids' programs to some serious technique refinement—and the ski school offers one of the best family programs in the West. There are 400 trained instructors offering a full range of clinics to suit all ages and ability levels. The Steamboat Ski & Snowboard School claims it has more Olympians and Olympic coaches on staff than any other resort in the nation, and it is located at the base of the ski area. In fact, no other town in North America has produced more winter Olympians than this resort—a record 54 and counting.

Adult intermediate and advanced classes are limited to a maximum of seven persons. All other programs have no upper limit but typically average seven individuals per group. There is also instruction available for telemarking. For young children, the minimum age is three for normal programs, and two for 1-hour privates combined with daycare. Lunch is

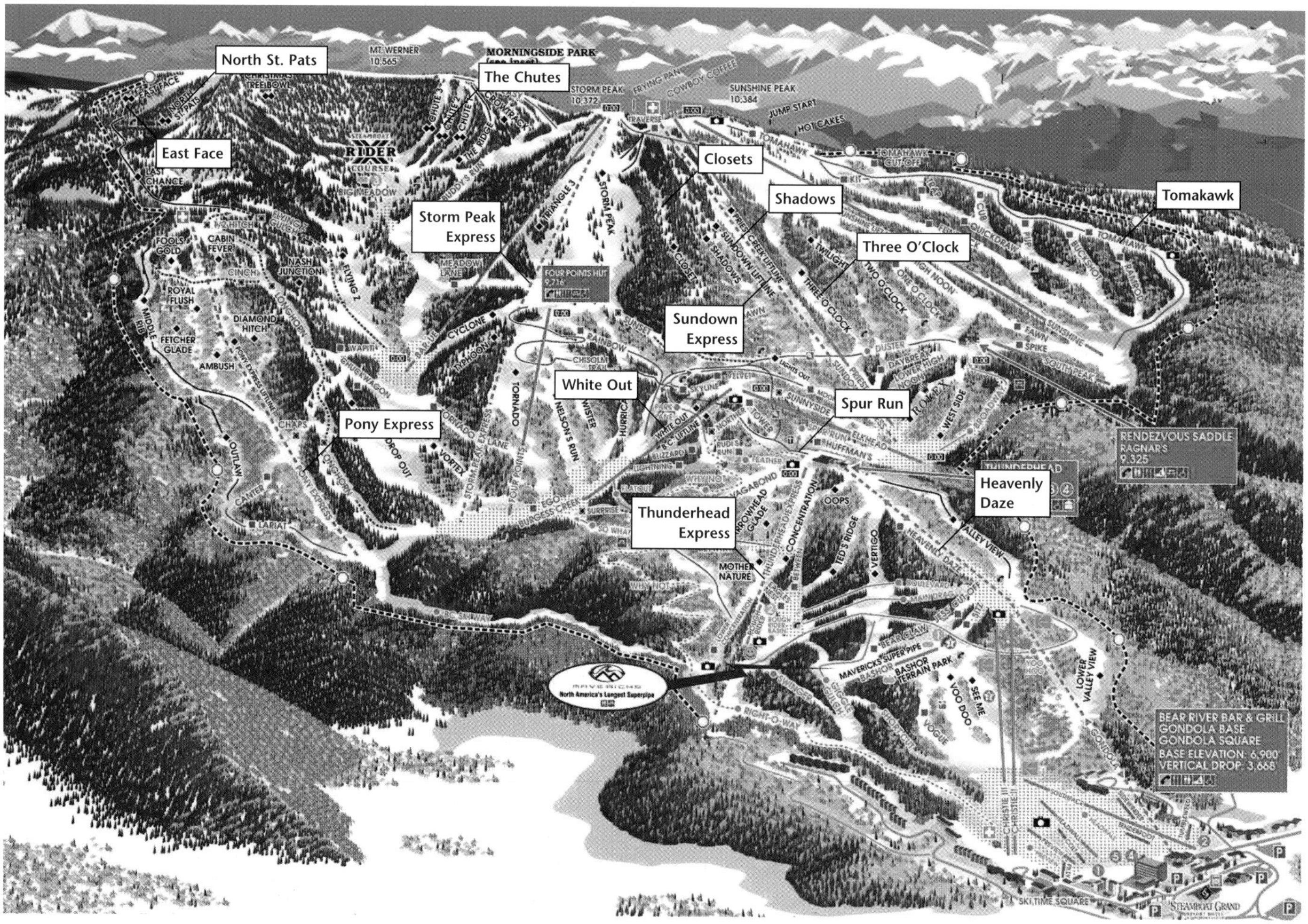

included with children's programs. Parents do not need to pick up children until the end of the day.

BEGINNERS

Steamboat recently re-shaped its beginner terrain, improving the grade of the slope and fall line. This beginner terrain, located at the base of the mountain, allows beginner skiers and riders to gain confidence before taking the gondola to enjoy Why Not, the resort's longest beginner trail—over three miles (4.8 km) in length on Thunderhead. Spur Run, also on Thunderhead, is a great beginner run off the top of the gondola. The Sunshine lift area is groomed for beginners and low intermediate skiers and riders.

INTERMEDIATES

Fifty-six percent of the trails are given over to intermediate skiers and boarders, and the longest trail is Tomahawk at two miles (3.2 km). Heavenly Daze (the Women's World Cup downhill run) is one of the most challenging intermediate trails in the ski area. It is a steep trail—descending nearly 1,000 ft (300 m)—that winds under the gondola and provides views of the entire Yampa Valley. Intermediate skiers and riders will also enjoy skiing the trails accessed by Storm Peak Express or Sundown Express lifts on the upper mountain.

ADVANCED & EXPERT

For the most experienced skiers the chutes, bowls and double blacks at the top of Mount Werner provide the best skiing and riding. In addition, the gladed areas of Priest Creek, including the resort's legendary Shadows and Closets trails, are a favorite among experts. The toughest skiing comes courtesy of The Chutes, East Face, St. Pat's, The Ridge, White Out, Three O'Clock, Nelson's, Shadows, Closets, Twilight, Priest Creek Lift Line, Triangle 3, and areas within Pioneer Ridge with moguls and steep, deep couloirs.

For powder, the gladed areas of Pioneer Ridge, Sunshine, and Storm Peak are Steamboat's particular claims to fame, with Champagne Powder in the trees for the most avid powder hounds. To test your skiing, ride up the gondola then down White Out to the Storm Peak lift and then up to the top of Storm Peak. Drop down the backside of the mountain into Morningside Park, head down the Ridge, Chutes or East Face to Pony Express. Then, ride up Pony Express and ski the gladed areas of Pioneer Ridge. There's a multitude of bumps, trees and steeps for even the most advanced skiers/riders.

Skiers and riders are only allowed to enter backcountry areas from the ski area through designated access points. Again, The Chutes and terrain such as East Face and North St. Pat's will keep expert skiers pumping adrenaline. In addition, the

▲ FRESH POWDERED TREES
Many of the 142 trails are tree-lined and the tough terrain in forest glades is a real attraction for experts at Steamboat.

◄ CHAMPAGNE POWDER
Steamboat coined this bubbly phrase for its powder, which is claimed to have 70% less moisture content than average snow. It is certainly pretty dry and fluffy by any standards.

EATING ON THE MOUNTAIN

HAZIE'S
RAGNARS
FOUR POINTS HUT
EXPRESS OH!

▲ **BOARDERS' DELIGHT**
Steamboat lures experienced riders to the bumps and grinds of Bashor Bowl Terrain Park.

▼ **MAVERICKS**
One of North America's longest competition superpipes resides at Steamboat.

mogul trails of White Out, Nelson's and Three O'Clock are favorites with expert skiers.

BOARDING & FREESTYLE

For boarders, the Mavericks Superpipe is claimed to be the longest in the Rocky Mountains—it has 15-foot walls, is 600 feet (915 m) long and 50 feet (915 m) wide. The terrain park also contains rails, jumps, mini-pipe and quarter pipe. Bee Hive, not far away on Thunderhead, is the other terrain park.

Away from the parks, the well-groomed open pistes at Mount Werner down to Sunshine Peak have a variety of trails to tempt carvers. Start with the Morningside Lift to the Morningside Bowl and head off from there—there are several demanding black diamond and intermediate trails. This is also the exit point via an access gate to backcountry options with steep north-facing slopes and quite open terrain. Steamboat has plenty of north-facing slopes that provide good high-speed tree-lined trails. With limited catwalks and one base area, Steamboat ski area is easy for snowboarders to get around.

EATING ON THE MOUNTAIN

There are a handful of restaurants on the mountain including a coffee and snack bar, cafeteria, Western-style buffet, and two fine dining restaurants that open for dinner as well as lunch.

The latter includes Hazie's, named for Hazie

Werner, mother of three Olympians; this alpine bistro at Thunderbird mid-station offers the perfect setting to enjoy a special Continental dinner while enjoying the sparkling lights of the Yampa Valley below. There's à la carte dining Thursday through Saturday nights and additional holidays.

Another mid-mountain venue, via the Steamboat gondola and then on a waiting sleigh that draws you underneath starry skies, is Ragnar's at Rendezvous Saddle. Enjoy a five-course Continental dinner with a Scandinavian flavor and excellent live acoustic entertainment. Ragnar's Sleigh-Ride Dinners are offered on Thursday, Friday, and Saturday nights, and additional holidays only.

Moving downscale, at both the Thunderbird and Rendezvous Saddle mid-mountain stations, you will also find self-service with sundecks and BBQs, while at the base area the Express OH! is convenient for breakfast or lunch snacks. While the Four Points Hut at the top of the Four Points lift keeps you warm with chili, hot dogs, soups and capuccino.

APRÈS SKI

With over 70 restaurants and bars to choose from, Steamboat's après-ski and nighttime scene has something for everyone. The Bear River Bar & Grill is always busy after a great day on the slopes. It is located at the base of the ski area, as close to the slopes as you can be. Live daily entertainment happens on the outdoor deck, with comedy shows on the weekends. The Comedy Club attracts nationally renowned stand-up comedians.

There are around 20 lively bars in the resort: Slopeside is a big hit, featuring afternoon specials and a location where you can ski right up to have a drink. Tugboat is a good bar to listen to live music and dance the night away. Levelz is Steamboat's Premier Night Club for the younger crowd. Steamboat Brewery & Tavern offers microbrews and food specials, with a non-smoking happy hour, while the Old Tub Pub (non-smoking) bar and restaurant has live music and a Western atmosphere.

There are plenty of more down-to-earth steakhouses in downtown Steamboat Springs, as well as restaurants and bars. The minimum age for consuming alcohol is 21; proof of age required. Children can accompany parents in bars and other places serving alcohol unless the establishment has a minimum entry age, but this is not usually the case until later in the evening. Bars close at 2:00 AM.

OTHER ACTIVITIES

Steamboat "Ski Town U.S.A." has lots to offer aside from great alpine skiing and riding. You can cross-country ski over 18 miles (30 km) of groomed trails, or explore the backcountry on guided snowshoe tours. Snowmobiling tours are also available, and Blue Sky West offers powdercat guided tours on Buffalo Pass. Other outdoor options include fly-fishing, horseback riding, hot-air ballooning, and rock and ice climbing.

Alternatively, after a hard day's skiing you can relax in the local natural hot springs at Strawberry Park or in downtown Steamboat—the waters are said to help ease rheumatism and skin complaints. Indoor activities include ice skating at an Olympic-sized rink, indoor tennis, heated pools, and a water slide, as well as a fully-equipped fitness center and an indoor climbing gym. More leisurely pursuits on offer are movies and museums, art galleries and a wide variety of stores.

USEFUL PHONE NUMBERS

Steamboat Central Reservations	970-879-0740
Ski Rescue Service	970-871-5911
Doctor	970-879-1322
Taxi	970-879-8294

USEFUL WEBSITES

Official Website	www.steamboat.com
Snow Report & Web Cams	www.rsn.com/cams
Weather Reports	www.wunderground.com
Vacation Planner	www.summitnet.com

RESTAURANTS & BARS

RESTAURANTS

EXPENSIVE
- L'APOGEE
- GIOVANNI'S
- CAFÉ DIVA
- COTTONWOOD GRILL
- RAGNAR'S

MODERATE
- CUGINO'S
- CREEKSIDE CAFÉ & GRILL
- HAZIE'S
- THE CABIN
- STEAMBOAT SMOKEHOUSE

BUDGET
- PISAS
- STEAMBOAT BREWERY TAVERN
- JOHNNY B GOODS

BARS
- SLOPESIDE
- TUGBOAT
- LEVELZ
- STEAMBOAT BREWERY
- OLD TOWN PUB

► NO IT'S NOT A COWBOY
Director of Skiing, Olympic Medallist and World Champion Billy Kidd runs a performance center and does wear a Stetson when skiing!

WINTER PARK MAY BE AN EASY WEEKEND COMMUTE FOR DENVER CITY SKIERS, BUT IT ISN'T A "PARK"—IT'S A HUGE SKI AREA COMPRISING FIVE INTERCONNECTED BUT HIGHLY VARIED MOUNTAIN TERRAINS WITH OVER 64.5 MILES (104 KM) OF TRAILS. THERE IS AN EASYGOING MIX OF OLD RURAL WEST AND MODERN RESORT CHIC, WITH THE ADDED VALUE OF MORE SNOWFALL THAN ANY OTHER COLORADO DESTINATION.

WINTER PARK

▼ SOMETHING FOR EVERYONE
Winter Park's five mountains offer a huge variety of ski area—from cruisers to the toughest bumps in Colorado.

Winter Park Resort is the closest major resort to Denver and gets incredible snow—the most recorded for any Colorado resort. Add the deepest powder in the state to long, wide trails, tons of bumps, and plenty of affordable lodgings, and you have a heady mixture. Good value and Winter Park go hand in hand, but what really scores here is just how vast the ski area is and the abundance of snow.

GETTING THERE

Just 65 miles (105 km) west of Denver, Winter Park is Colorado's commutable resort, and as it's reachable by car, bus, and railroad, it can get very busy at weekends. It's tucked away at the base of the Continental Divide in the Arapahoe National Forest, below Berthoud Pass. From Denver International Airport (D.I.A.) it's roughly a one- to two-hour drive to cover the 85 miles (136 km). Alternatively you

can travel by rail on Amtrak's Californian Zephyr with services from Chicago, Omaha, Los Angeles, San Francisco, and Salt Lake City. On-board sleeping accommodations are also available.

Winter Park is the only U.S. resort with direct rail access downtown. From Denver's Union Station the Ski Train, that runs every weekend from mid-December to March, takes approximately two hours directly to the base of the slopes.

THE VILLAGE

It wasn't so long ago that the resort of Winter Park comprised a couple of ski services buildings and the lift terminal, but that has changed with the development of Zephyr Mountain Lodge, right at the base of the resort. The resort now has its first ski-in, ski-out accommodations, with 230 luxury units at the base of the slopes, as well as a restaurant and shops. The town of Winter Park lies two miles (3 km) north of the resort, and is concentrated along a half-mile (0.8 km) stretch of road with most stores, restaurants, bars, and lodgings along Highway 40. There are restaurants to satisfy any palate and a large selection of lodging properties from bed & breakfasts to luxury slopeside accommodations. Intrawest, owners of Copper Mountain, Whistler Blackcomb and seven other ski resorts, took over management in December of 2002, so expect things to happen on the mountain as well as the base.

ACCOMMODATIONS

The various lodges around the village offer over 630 rooms within walking distance of the slopes—or their private shuttles will take you to the base of the mountain. The already mentioned Zephyr Mountain Lodge is located in the center of the village just steps away from the Zephyr Express lift, so you can ski in and ski out. The Iron Horse Resort offers ski out lodging and the Vintage Hotel and Winter Park Mountain Lodge are a two-minute shuttle ride away.

MOUNTAIN FACTS

Base	9,000 feet (2,743 m)
Summit	12,060 feet (3,675 m)
Elevation	3,060 feet (932 m)
Easy	9%
Intermediate	21%
Advanced	13%
Expert	57%
Number of trails	134
Longest trail	5.1 miles (8.2 km)
Ski area	2,886 acres (1,168 ha)

SNOWFALL

Annual snowfall	367 inches (914 cm)
Snowmaking	294 acres (119 ha)

SKI LIFTS

Gondolas	-
High-Speed Quads	8
Fixed Grip Quads	-
Triple Chairs	4
Double Chairs	7
Coneyor Lifts	3
Surface Lifts	1
Total	23
Riders per hour	36,230

NEARBY RESORTS

ACCOMMODATIONS

EXPENSIVE
ZEPHYR MOUNTAIN LODGE
IRON HORSE RESORT RETREAT
WILD HORSE INN BED & BREAKFAST
DESTINATIONS WEST, INC.

MODERATE
OLYMPIA LODGE
SUNDOWNER
BEAVER VILLAGE/THM
SNOWBLAZE

BUDGET
VIKING LODGE
BEAVER VILLAGE LODGE

Winter Park Central Reservations
P. O. Box 36
Winter Park, CO 80482
www.skiwinterpark.com
970-726-5587 (Phone)
970-726-5993 (Fax)

▲ **TREES FROM THE WOODS**
Mary Jane is a heady mix of hard-bump skiing and tree-level trails for those who like tight turns.

SKI SEASON
Mid-November to mid-April

A popular site is the Timberhouse Ski Lodge, nestled so close to Winter Park Resort guests can ski to it at the end of the day. The lodge is a home away from home for guests; very family oriented as it still serves breakfast and dinner, and it's been around since the resort first opened.

Within the Winter Park/Fraser Valley, the choice of accommodation is varied from youth hostel to fully serviced hotels with on-site restaurants, gift stores, and swimming pools. Virtually all can be booked via Winter Park Central Reservations who also offer a selection of packages that are worth checking out. Other types of lodgings include bed & breakfast inns ranging from small and rustic through to luxurious. There are several chalets and mountain inns that include breakfast and dinner daily. There are modest motels, luxury hotels, and thousands of condominium/apartment units. Accommodation can be arranged via www.skiwinterpark.com.

SKI AREA

Winter Park's vast terrain is spread over five summits—Winter Park, Mary Jane, Parsenn Bowl, Vasquez Cirque, and Vasquez Ridge—and the new Rail Yard Terrain Park. Winter Park Mountain is the largest and most versatile hub, offering well-manicured terrain for beginner, intermediate and advanced skiers from its summit, Sunspot, at 10,700 feet (3,261 m) down to its base at 9,000 feet (2,743 m.) On its slopes you'll find Discovery Park, an award-winning enclosed learning area open to all sliders with its own lifts and gentle slopes. More experienced skiers head for the wilder Mary Jane Mountain, at 11,200 feet (3,414 m), rising behind Winter Park summit and named after a legendary local prostitute who laid claim to the land.

The above-treeline Parsenn Bowl is the highest point on the mountain at 12,060 feet (3,675 m), offering a maximum vertical descent of 3,060 ft (932 m) and fabulous views of the Rockies: you're actually looking down onto the Continental Divide. Here you will find ungroomed trails with moguls and extensive off-piste and gladed terrain of varying density, and an untouched blanket of irresistible powder. The wide-sweeping Vasquez Ridge is the westernmost part of the resort with wide-open cruisers, exciting bump trails, plenty of fresh snow, and afternoon sun, while Vasquez Cirque at 11,900 feet (3,627 m) is for black and double-black diamond experts seeking steep cornices and 687 acres (278 ha) of extreme backcountry terrain.

In all there are 134 trails and 2,886 acres (1,168 ha) of ski area or 64 miles (104 km.) The resort also receives more than 360 inches (914 cm) snowfall a year, more than any other major Colorado resort.

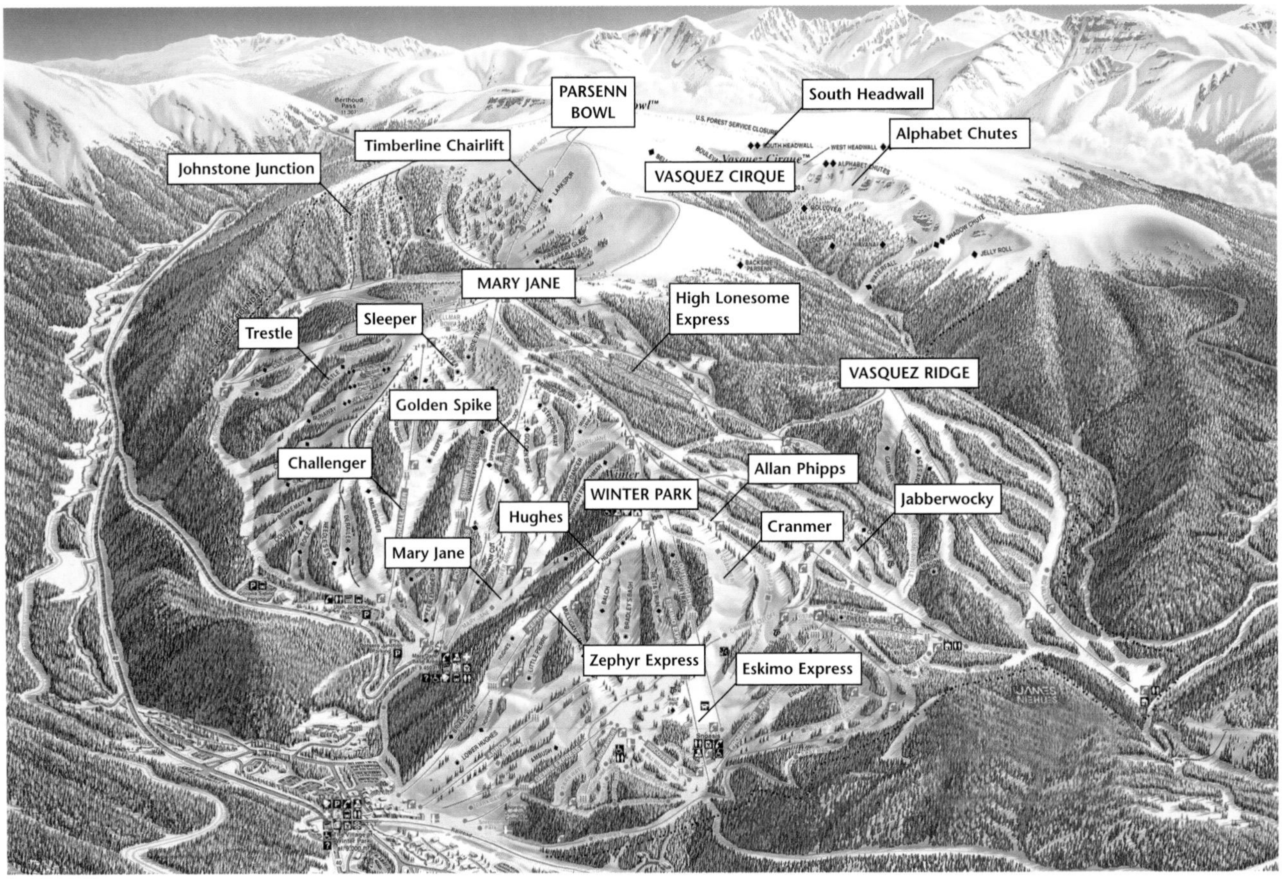

LIFT SYSTEM

Winter Park Resort has 23 lifts, including eight high-speed quads, and capacity to carry 36,230 people per hour. A new addition is a T-bar added from the top of Allan Phipps trail to the Lodge at Sunspot, eliminating a 100-yard (91-m) hike uphill to the restaurant. Lines are an issue in holiday periods and on Saturday mornings. Most lines are less than 20 minutes, even at Christmas, and they are at the main base lift. The best way to avoid lines is to spread out over the mountain and use mid-mountain lifts where the wait is even less, usually five minutes. Weekdays waits are never a problem at Winter Park. Lifts are open 8:30 AM weekends, 9:00 AM weekdays until 4:00 PM.

LIFT PASSES

Adult lift pass prices for a two out of three day pass is US$36 per day in early and late season, and US$57 per day during the regular season which runs from just before Christmas to end March. The per-day price decreases as more days are added—US$41 per day or US$246 for a six-day pass. Children aged five and under are free, and ages 6–13 receive discounted rates: US$15 per day in early and late season and US$21 per day in regular season. Beginners, and anyone else, can buy an all-day lift ticket for the Galloping Goose for US$5. Lift passes can be bought as part of any lodging package through Winter Park Central Reservations via reservations@mail.skiwinterpark.com and at ticket window locations, as well as at the ski school desk, and rental shop center at the base of the resort.

SKI SCHOOL AND GUIDING

From a "Quick Tips Learning Lane" (on the lower Cranmer trail) complete with video analysis for just 15 minutes and US$5 (one run), through to a full Guest-Centered Teaching system, Winter Park has a highly flexible ski school program. There are two schools. The Ski and Snowboard School lesson desk is located in Balcony House at the base of Winter Park Resort (970-726-1551) and offers lessons to everyone aged 15 and older. Adult beginner lessons are offered at 9:30 AM and 12:45 PM daily, and adult mogul lessons are offered at 12:45 PM daily. Private lessons (one or two people) can be scheduled for 9:30 AM, 11:00 AM and 1:00 PM daily. Ski group size is limited to eight for adult lessons. An adult day lesson costs US$30-40, and an adult private lesson US$120–375.

The Children's Center caters to kids aged two months to 14 years and is located next to West Portal at the base of Winter Park Resort (970-726-1551.) Children's Center lessons begin at 9:30 AM and continue until 3:00 PM but children can utilize the facilities from at 8:00 AM through 4:00 PM. A non-ski program for children from two months to five years, with structured activities and lunch, is available on site. Reservations are required and ski group size is restricted to six for kids' lessons. The minimum age for childcare is two months. Children's Center lessons are for kids aged three and older if potty trained and willing. All-day lessons are US$80 without equipment rental, US$90 including equipment rental. All-day childcare will cost you US$75.

For disabled skiers—children and adults alike—The National Sports Center for the Disabled has, for 33 years, been offering outdoor therapeutic recreation programs on the ski slopes with specially trained instructors. For details visit www.nscd.org. Reservations are required.

In "big" snow years, Parsenn Bowl offers summer training camps for alpine and freestyle skiers that are open to the public. Snow Mountain Ranch offers cross-country skiing at night. The Fraser Tubing Hill offers tubing during the day on weekends and at night.

BEGINNERS

Discovery Park is an award-winning area that is fenced off from the rest of the mountain and is designated for children and adults who are learning to ski or snowboard. It is served by three chairlifts—a double, triple and quad—to help novices learn lift riding skills on different configurations. There are wide-open meadows for learning to turn and several fun trails through the adjacent wooded areas. These trails feature small bumps to allow novices to practice balancing and weight shift skills. The area also has its own restroom facilities, sparing beginners the inconvenience of having to return to the base or

▲ **GROOMING**
The slopes are well maintained with snowmaking on 26 trails covering 294 acres (119 ha) and a fleet of snowcats to get that perfect corduroy.

▶ **NO PAIN, NO JANE**
Mary Jane has been voted number 1 in North America for mogul skiing. The bumpy trails are also relentlessly long, so beware – your knees could turn to rubber.

RESTAURANTS

TOP END

RANCH HOUSE AT DEVIL'S THUMB
3530 County Road 83, Tabernash, CO 80478
970-726-5633

WILDCREEK RESTAURANT
78491 Highway 40, Winter Park, CO 80482
970-726-1111

THE SHED
78672 Highway 40, Winter Park, CO 80482
970-726-9912

MODERATE

SMOKIN' MOE'S RIBHOUSE
Cooper Creek Sq., Winter Park, CO 80482
970-726-4600

CARLOS AND MARIA'S
Cooper Creek Sq., Winter Park, CO 80482
970-726-9674

DENO'S MOUNTAIN BISTRO
78911 Highway 40, Winter Park, CO 80482
970-726-5332

BUDGET

RANDI'S IRISH SALOON
78521 Highway 40, Winter Park, CO 80482
970-726-1172

CROOKED CREEK SALOON
401 Zerex, Fraser, CO 80442
970-726-9250

DE ANTONIO'S
551 Zerex, Fraser, CO 80442
970-726-9999

a lodge when nature calls.

Winter Park mountain offers many green trails for beginners. Some of the best green trails—found at the top of the High Lonesome Express at an 11,220-foot elevation (3,420 m)—gently wind back down to the bottom through tree-lined trails and more open gentle runs.

INTERMEDIATES

For intermediates, Hughes and Mary Jane trails are challenging. Hughes is a blue-black and is fairly steep but groomed. Mary Jane is long with several steep areas. Take the Zephyr Express to the top of Winter Park mountain, take Cranmer (blue) down to the Eskimo Express. At the top, follow blue square trail signs to Jabberwocky. Take the Olympia Express up to the Mary Jane trail. At the base of Mary Jane, take Summit Express back up to the top, and then head over to the Timberline chairlift to ski anything in the more exposed Parsenn Bowl. This bowl offers several blue and blue-black trails, some of which are gladed for a new experience. The longest trail at this level is Primrose at 7,250 ft (2,293 m.)

ADVANCED & EXPERT

Over half the ski area is dedicated to serious skiers with Mary Jane mountain offering very challenging mogul terrain. For bumps, try Trestle and Golden Spike; for trees and steeps, Johnstone Junction; for couloirs head higher up to Vasquez Cirque, Winter Park's most extreme terrain. The South Headwall and the Alphabet Chutes offer several extreme routes down the mountain. Aside from vertigo-causing steeps, Vasquez Cirque and anywhere in the trees on the Jane is best for powder. Vasquez Cirque is undoubtedly very steep, ungroomed, and is a terrific example of extreme backcountry terrain. Little wonder expert skiers flock to Winter Park because of this.

An ideal ski day would be to start at the base of Mary Jane by heading up the Summit Express. Warm up on Sleeper, then take the Challenger lift up to Derailer. Ride the Challenger to access additional black mogul trails including Boiler, Runaway, Cannonball, and Brakeman. Head up to the Parsenn Bowl for trees on the right. Ride Timberline back up to access Vasquez Cirque, via Parsenn Bowl and head for Boulevard, or the South or West Headwall.

No skier may enter onto a trail that is marked "closed." In-bounds closures may occur on any trail at any time for myriad reasons. In addition, a significant amount of the boundary is closed by the U.S. Forest Service because of hazard immediately outside the boundary. If you should choose to leave the ski area at a point not marked as "closed," you may do so, but the ski area no longer has responsibility. Rescue, if available, may turn out to be a prolonged and expensive business, and is the responsibility of the Sheriff's Office.

◄ FEISTY LADY
Mary Jane is where you'll find super-steeps as well as bumps galore. Real tough tests include the double black diamond chutes such as Hole in the Wall, and Jeff's Chute—all reached by the Express chairlifts.

BOARDING & FREESTYLE

Aside from avoiding the massive bumps on Mary Jane, most of the mountain is very user friendly for boarders except for Wagon Train and Big Valley trails. These are both relatively flat trails with long runouts and snowboarders should avoid them or contrive to have some speed going before moving onto these trails. The new Rail Yard Terrain Park is the masterpiece and handywork of top local riders and freeskiers. Offering something for everyone, the park runs the length of one of the longest trails, the Alan Phipps, and crosses over to Lower Cranmer.

The Park starts out with a bunch of rails, hits and tables followed by a roller coaster of lifts and dips. And to make sure you get the full exposure you deserve, the new Vertigo halfpipe has been built right in plain view of the lift riders as well as the beach crowd at Snoasis. At 3,450 feet (1,052 m) Rail Yard takes up 15-acres (6-ha) and you can access the park from express lifts mountain-wide.

EATING ON THE MOUNTAIN

Winter Park has 12 on-mountain eateries ranging from casual cafeterias to full-service restaurants. The

best is The Dining Room at The Lodge at Sunspot, offering fine dining at the summit of Winter Park mountain. The Provisioner, adjacent to the Dining Room, is a food marketplace with grilled sandwiches, soups, salads, baked-potato bar, pasta and an assortment of freshly baked goodies. During the day the restaurant has breathtaking views of the Continental Divide and the surrounding mountains. At night, there's no better place to stargaze. Ride the Zephyr Express gondola to Sunspot for two dining options, an elegant four-course dinner in The Dining Room or The Provisioner buffet. A close second is The Club Car, located at the Mary Jane Center, also offering sit-down dining with a wide variety of home made seafood chowder, soup-with-sandwiches, salads, and daily specials. The mud pie dessert (mocha ice cream, chocolate cookie crust, fudge topping) is not to be missed. For more of a pit stop, fuel-filler, the lower level at Snoasis has Mamma Mia's Pizzerias and other food court options, while West Portal Station's food court has something for every taste. Boxcar Deli offers cafeteria-style breakfasts and lunches. Pepperoni's and the food court at the Mary Jane base and Lunch Rock Café at its summit are all good lunchtime venues.

APRÈS SKI

Nightlife is informal and friendly. For après ski, the Derailer Bar at the base of Winter Park has a sun deck, and The Kickapoo Tavern located in the adjacent Zephyr Mountain Lodge offers two levels of outdoor decks for après ski. In total there are over 50 restaurants and bars to choose from and there is even an après-ski trail taking in 19 of the 50 or so bars, kicking off at the The Club Car and ending at The Crooked Creek Saloon in nearby Fraser. At the resort itself check out Higher Grounds, The Pub, and Deno's Mountain Bistro. Wildcreek Restaurant offers live music and is popular on weekends with both locals and visitors or check out the Crooked Creek Saloon, but it's very difficult to find a place to dance. So, if you're seeking more hustle and bustle with funky live music in authentic Western bars, head for Fraser. Colorado's liquor laws apply and bars for the most part do not allow children under 21 although restaurants with lounge areas do. Closing time is 2:00 AM.

OTHER ACTIVITIES

Winter Park is first and foremost a ski area and there is not a great deal for non-skiers apart from other winter sports activities. The Tour Center offers guided backcountry snowshoeing and snowcat tours. You can also take a snowcat up to The Lodge at Sunspot or Snoasis for lunch. Snowcat tours are one of the most popular options for non-skiers. A few stores are located at the base of the resort but a wider selection of options is available in town, including jewelry, sporting goods, gifts, and art.

◄ STRUNG-OUT TOWNS
The mountainside towns of Winter Park and Fraser are 2 and 4 miles (3 and 6 km), away respectively from the base area, strung out along the main highway—so it's a bus ride to the slopes for most.

BARS

HIGHER GROUNDS MARTINI BAR
78941 Highway 40
Winter Park, CO 80482
970-726-0447

THE PUB
78260 Highway 40
Winter Park, CO 80482
970-726-4929

DENO'S MOUNTAIN BISTRO
78911 Highway 40
Winter Park, CO 80482
970-726-5332

▲ APRÈS-SKI TOURS
The Crooked Creek Saloon is a popular après ski hang-out with the locals. It's one of the spots on Winter Park's après-ski 'trail maps.' The resort has over 50 restaurants and bars.

USEFUL PHONE NUMBERS

Tourist Information Centre	970-726-4221
Winter Park Central Reservations	970-726-5587
Medical Centre	970-726-8066
Ski Patrol Search & Rescue	970-726-1490
Taxi	970-726-5060

USEFUL WEBSITES

Official Website	www.skiwinterpark.com
Vacation Planner	www.skiwinterpark.com
Snow Report & Web Cams	www.rsn.com/cams
Weather Reports	www.wunderground.com

VAIL RANKS AS ONE OF THE WORLD'S GREAT SKI RESORTS. IF YOU HAVE SKIED EVERYWHERE ELSE BUT NOT SKIED VAIL, FRANKLY, YOU SHOULD GRAB THE NEXT FLIGHT TO DENVER AND EXPERIENCE THE LARGEST SINGLE SKI MOUNTAIN IN NORTH AMERICA.

VAIL

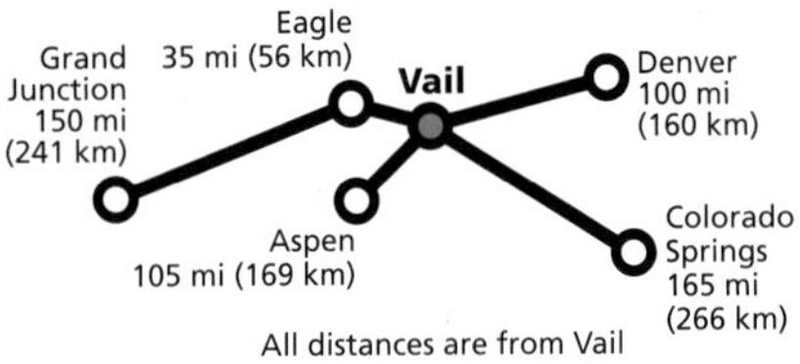

All distances are from Vail

In the ranking of U.S. ski resorts, Vail is the tops, and for a variety of reasons. Years of investment in ski facilities have provided an unrivalled range of lifts and runs. Constant attention to the slopes throughout the season keeps them in pristine condition and when you move off the slopes Vail has that essential sense of style—mock Austrian-Tyrolean in parts, certainly—but style nevertheless. To sum up, Vail has fabulous skiing, glitz, a lively crowd, great skiing, and good nightlife. But sometimes it is crowded, suffers lift lines that are long by American standards, and prices both in the resort and on the mountain are relatively expensive.

GETTING THERE

Vail, Colorado, is located in the heart of the Rocky Mountains, 100 miles (160 km) west of Denver via Interstate 70. Some people are surprised to find that this Interstate, a major highway, runs right through Vail. However, once in the village and on the mountain, skiers do not even realize that it's there. The nearest international airport is Denver International Airport 120 miles (190 km) east of Vail; that's a two hours' drive. Vail/Eagle County Airport is a handy hub roughly 35 miles (56 km) west of Vail on U.S. Highway 6 and Interstate 70. Colorado Mountain Express provides a shuttle service on a frequent schedule to and from both airports—around US$60 one-way from Denver—or take a High Mountain Taxi (up to six passengers) for around US$125 one-way.

While parking in the resort is available, it is limited and visitors are encouraged to leave their cars at home and use the town's convenient public transportation system. The town of Vail offers the country's largest free intra-city bus service: one service includes Beaver Creek, Keystone, Breckenridge, Silverthorne, Frisco, Dillon, and of course Vail. Vail lies some 39 miles (59 km) west of Keystone and 37 miles (58 km) west of Breckenridge over Vail Pass.

MOUNTAIN FACTS

Base	8,120 feet (2,475 m)
Summit	11,570 feet (3,527 m)
Elevation	3,450 feet (1,052 m)
Easy	18%
Intermediate	29%
Advanced/Expert	53%
Number of trails	193
Longest trail	3 miles (4.8 km)
Ski area	5,289 acres (2,140 ha)

SNOWFALL

Annual snowfall	346 inches (866 cm)
Snowmaking	380 acres (154 ha)

SKI LIFTS

Gondolas	1
High-Speed Quads	14
Fixed Grip Quads	1
Triple Chairs	3
Double Chairs	5
Surface Lifts	9
Total	33
Riders per hour	53,381

SKI SEASON
Mid November to mid April

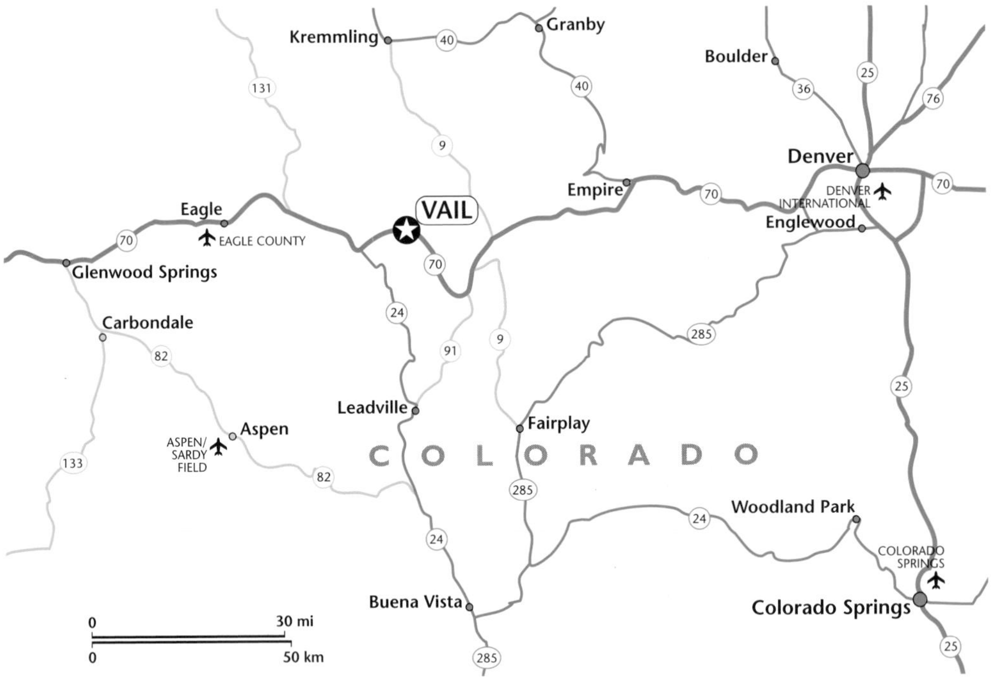

There also are numerous outlying routes, so no matter where visitors stay in the Vail Valley, it's easy and convenient to hop on the bus. The Vail Resorts Express shuttle is the fastest, easiest way to travel between resorts. Winter bus schedules run 5:00 AM to 2:30 AM daily. Within Vail another route runs from Lionshead on the west end of Vail to Golden Peak on the eastern edge of town.

THE VILLAGE

The village is pedestrian-only with three base areas centered around a mock-Tyrolean theme. The three base areas include Vail Village, Lionshead, and Golden Peak. Vail Village—originally built in the 1950s but now part of a vast resort complex—is the main base area. This is the most expensive area to stay, convenient for the lifts and the many restaurants, stores, and hotels. The Vista Bahn lift allows easy ski-in, ski out access from the village. Lionshead is the western base area and also features shopping and dining.

New developments planned for Vail Village include enhancing the skier entrance to Vail Village and upgrading skier services, a new park, additional parking and more. The Lionshead Development project includes a new skier services portal; a five-star, luxury hotel; riverfront town homes; and over 400 additional beds; 50,000 square feet (4,645 sq. m) of retail space; a small number of single family home sites; and improved auto and pedestrian access. Complementing the historical architecture of Vail, classic European architecture will be featured throughout the Lionshead area.

ACCOMMODATIONS

Vail is glitzy. There is the usual wide range of accommodations, the kind available in every major ski resort but, essentially, Vail caters to the carriage trade. The top hotels are the Lodge at Vail and the Sonnenalp Resort—note that touch of Austria—but the Vail Village Inn and the Chateau Vail are very good, and the Roost and the West Vail Lodge a little cheaper. The Lionshead Inn is popular and close to the Eagle Bahn gondola, while the Vail Cascades Hotel & Club is great fun with lots of sports facilities.

Where to stay is a matter of personal choice and depth of pocket but if you are splashing out—and why not, it's a vacation—then either the Sonnenalp Resort or the Chateau Vail would be recommended. On the condo front, the East Vail Condominiums are well equipped but 15 minutes by shuttle bus from the main action. Shop around, for the choice is wide—whether your pocket is Economy (at US$150–300) or premium hotel (up to US$500). Vail Valley provides guests with spacious hotels, quaint bed and breakfast inns, and comfortable homes and condominiums for every taste and budget. And the quality of lodging continues to improve as properties upgrade and enhance what they currently offer to provide guests with more value for their vacation dollar. The list of lodgings properties goes on and on.

◄ TIROLEAN-STYLE
Neither an Old West cowboy town or Victorian mining settlement, Vail has settled for a mock-Tirolean-style architecture.

▲ ROMANCE IN THE AIR
With fairy lights and wreaths decorating the town, there is a romantic feel to Vail town. It's big by ski resort standards—13 square miles (33 sq. km)—but much of that is condo country.

ACCOMMODATIONS

EXCLUSIVE PRIVATE RETREAT
GAME CREEK MOUNTAIN CHALET

PLATINUM
SONNENALP
GASTOF GRAMSHAMMER
COLORADO VACATION HOMES

GOLD
LODGE AT VAIL
VAIL CASCADE RESORT & SPA
CHRISTIANIA
LIONSHEAD INN
LODGE TOWER
MANOR VAIL

SILVER
EVERGREEN
ANTLERS AT VAIL
VAIL INTERNATIONAL
VAIL RACQUET CLUB

Reservations and information available at www.vail.com and www.visitvailvalley.com

or Vail–Beaver Creek Central Reservations system at 800 427-8308, and Vail Valley Chamber & Tourism Bureau Central Reservations at 800 525-3875 or 970-949-5189.

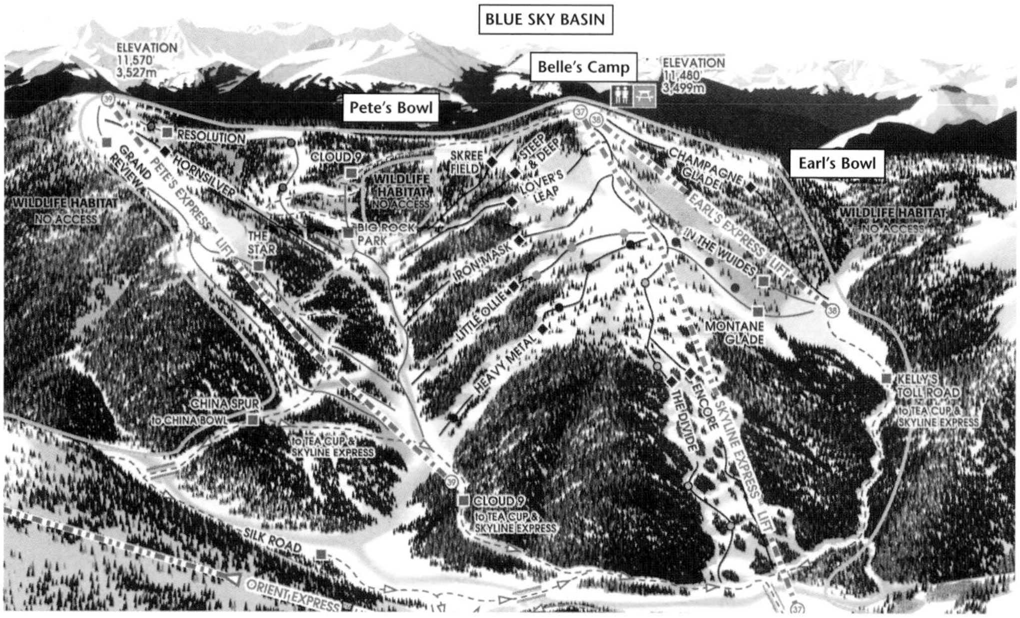

SKI AREA

The ski and snowboard experience at Vail is enveloping, and keeps ahead of its rivals by investment in facilities—lifts, runs, ski school, and instruction. There are plenty of runs, very short lines and should you tire of the local slopes, there is easy access, some of it linked, to other good resorts in the valley. Base elevation is 8,120 feet (2,475 m) while the summit reaches 11,570 feet (3,527 m) giving a vertical descent of 3,450 feet (1,052 m).

With 193 trails and 5,289 acres (2,140 ha) of skiing, Vail is basically a vast and varied mountain. The front side of Vail Mountain—mostly north facing—offers a conventional trail design cut through the trees, featuring terrain for every ability level. Vail's seven legendary Back Bowls offer 2,724 acres (1,102 ha) of wide-open expansive terrain that is a must-ski on a powder day.

Blue Sky Basin, the new jewel in Vail's terrain crown, is a must for intermediate to advanced skiers

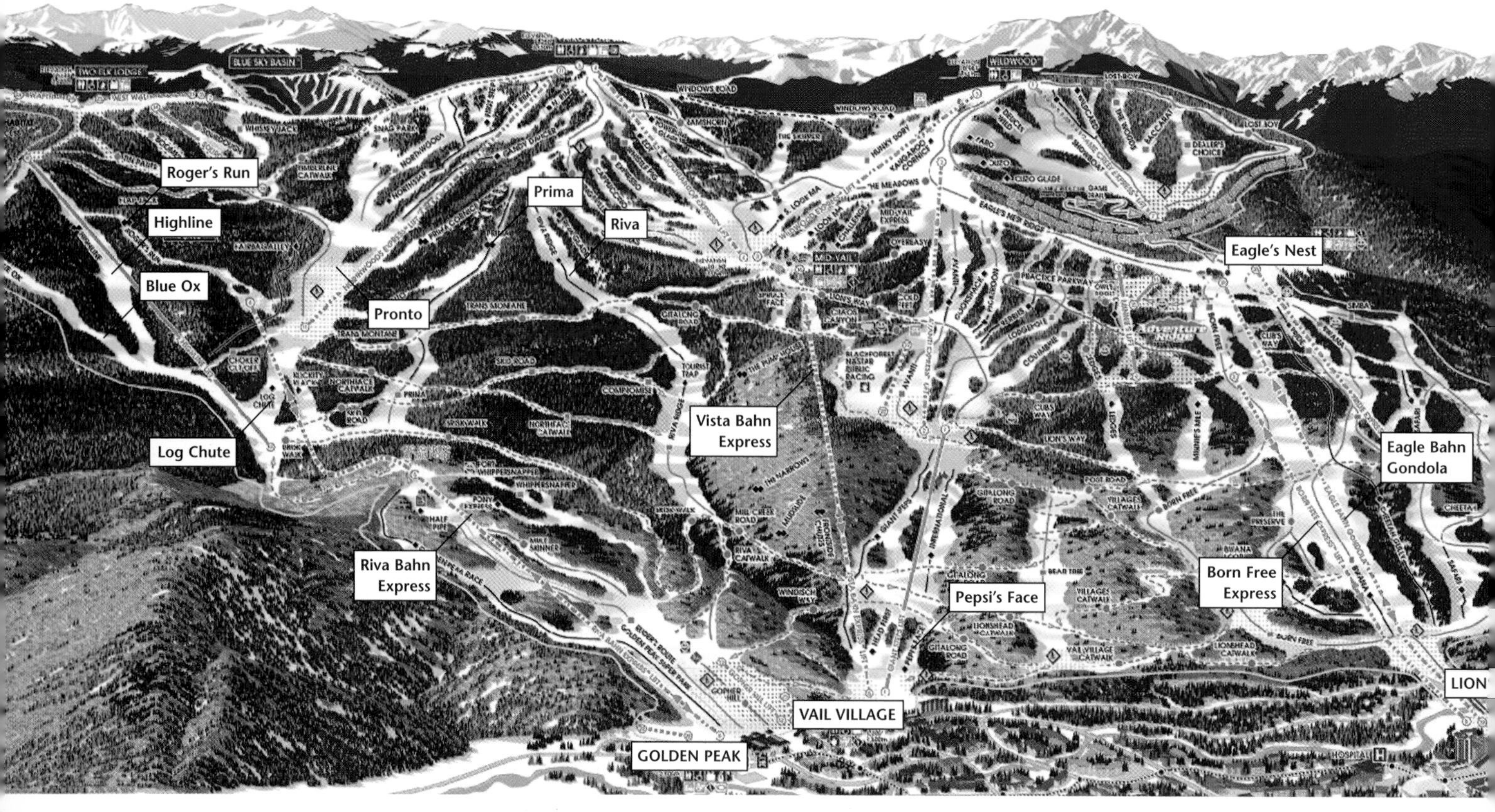

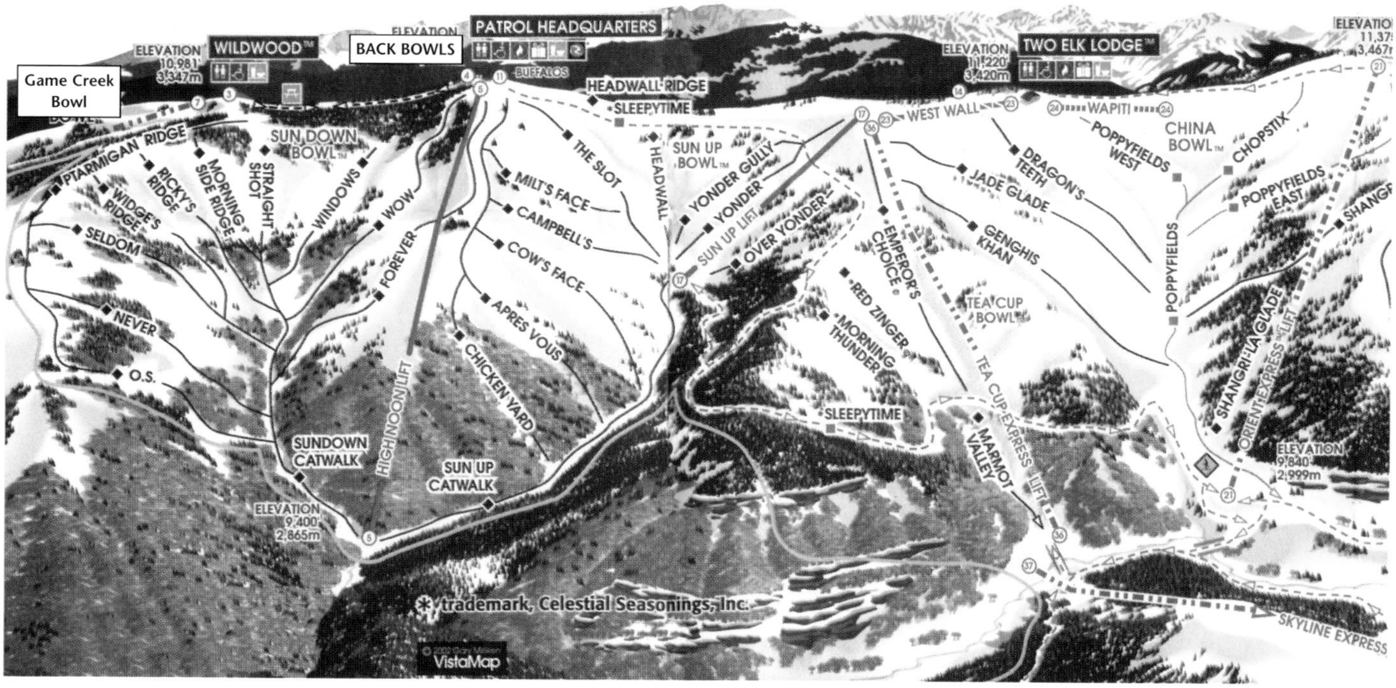

and boarders. Fully completed in 2001, it provides a genuine backcountry ski experience and is different from any other area on Vail Mountain, Blue Sky Basin features 645 acres (261 ha) of intermediate to advanced terrain in Pete and Earl's Bowls. There are some easy groomed (blue) trails but most of the terrain is ungroomed, and because it is mostly not very steep it allows intermediates the opportunity to experience the thrill of exploration and adventure as they find their own way on in-bounds ungroomed terrain. It also provides a means of escaping the crowds on other parts of the mountain.

Ski trails are graded green for beginner, blue for intermediate, black for advanced/expert, and double black for experts only. With 18 percent beginner, 29 percent intermediate and 53 percent advanced /expert, the emphasis is less on cozy, more on challenging. Having said that, Vail is good for beginners and, for the past three years, Vail has been recognized as having an exemplary skier-safety program for both education and enforcement. The program includes a stand-alone safety group tasked with monitoring, education, enforcing, and providing positive reinforcement of "Your Responsibility Code." Skiers and snowboarders are taught about Your Responsibility Code through increased signage on the mountain, in on-mountain restaurants, and elsewhere.

In comparison to some other resorts—especially the more challenging European resorts—there is a tendency to over-classify some black runs, and some visitors may occasionally find the yellow-jacketed ski patrollers a little overzealous.

Snow reliability on north-facing slopes is excellent with an exceptional natural snow record supplemented by extensive snowmaking facilities. Snow quality is not always so good in the Back Bowls as these are mostly south-facing slopes, except Blue Sky Basin—largely north-facing and sheltered from the sun by trees—which holds good powder for several days after the last snowfall.

SKI LIFTS

Vail's lift system is a combination of 33 lifts, including one gondola, making it one of the top lift networks in the world. With 14 high-speed quads, the lifts move people up and around the mountain in a most efficient manner with a capacity for 53,381 people per hour, up from 51,781 with the addition of new chairs on the existing lifts in Blue Sky Basin. Lifts open at 8:30 AM and close at 3:30 PM. Vail has added four new high-speed quad lifts in the last three years, enabling visitors access to the new Blue Sky Basin's in-bounds backcountry skiing.

The Eagle Bahn Gondola leaves from Lionshead, taking visitors to Eagle's Nest, home to Adventure Ridge, Vail's mountaintop activity center. Golden Peak is the eastern base area and features the Golden Peak, Superpipe and Terrain Park, the Nordic Center, daycare, and much more. The Riva Bahn takes skiers and riders up to the middle of the mountain, allowing for easy access to the legendary back bowls and Blue Sky Basin.

With high-speed lifts transporting skiers around the mountain in the most efficient, timely manner, Vail's lift system is world class, but with the influx of day-skiers from nearby Denver, the lines for some

▼ BLUE SKY BASIN
Reachable via the Back Bowls, Blue Sky Basin is nestled more than 2 miles (3 km) into the wlderness and is mostly ungroomed and wooded. On a fresh powder day this ski area gives a great sense of adventure for the serious skier or boarder.

▲ **BIG COUNTRY**
Vail is vast, with over 5,000 skiable acres (2,025 ha) and with many other resorts linked by the interchangeable Colorado Ticket.

SKI SCHOOL

VAIL ADULT SKI & SNOWBOARD SCHOOL
Offers a variety of programs to improve technique and mountain education.
Information: www.vailresorts.com

LEARN FROM A VAIL INSTRUCTOR
Learn from one of 850 knowledgeable and certified alpine, snowboard, telemark, and Nordic instructors. Instruction available in 30 languages. Private and group lessons can focus on particular techniques, terrain, or tours of local "hot spots."

GENERAL SKI SCHOOL INFORMATION
Locations: Base area locations at Golden Peak, Vail Village, and Lionshead; also on-mountain at Mid-Vail and Eagle's Nest.
Packages: Prices vary and some packages may include lift tickets and rentals.
Information: 970-476-3239 or fax 970-479-4377

PRIVATE INSTRUCTION
Availability: Full-day and half-day (morning or afternoon) private lessons are available.
Two-hour and one-hour private lessons offered depending upon availability.
Locations: Base area locations at Golden Peak, Vail Village, and Lionshead; on-mountain at Mid-Vail and Eagle's Nest.
Information: (800) 475-4543

lifts can be bad (15 minutes and more) especially at weekends. The base area lifts, the Vista Bahn and the Eagle Bahn Gondola, tend to have the worst problem with lines. However, it's easy to avoid them by taking the Riva Bahn Express out of Golden Peak, or the Born Free Express up out of the Lionshead base area. These two lifts provide easy access to the entire mountain with no lines.

LIFT PASSES

The Colorado Ticket is a fully interchangeable lift pass valid at Vail, Beaver Creek, Breckenridge, Keystone, and Arapahoe Basin. If you book a 10-day package you get four days extra for free. Check out www.snow.com for ticket prices. Adult tickets range from US$245 to US$270 depending on low or high season for six or nine days. Peak season is the week between Christmas and New Year's, and mid-February through the end of March, while low season is November through mid-December, and April. Junior and senior tickets cost less than adult ones. The cheapest day pass is US$32.50 from opening to December 21.

If you're a beginner and would like a lesson, there is a special beginner ticket included with the ski lesson. There are several ways to purchase lift passes. They can be bought through the website or, once in the resort, every base area has a lift ticket window where lift passes can be purchased. Note that the Colorado Ticket is only available to international visitors booking via a recognized tour operator, it cannot be bought in the resort.

SKI SCHOOLS AND GUIDING

The Vail Ski & Snowboard School enjoys an excellent reputation and offers instruction in every kind of skiing—bumps, carving, powder, extreme skiing, teenager programs, beginners—plus special snowboarding classes for those who want to try it.

The Vail school is distinctly cool—it's consistently rated one of the top 10 ski schools in North America and one thing about Vail instructors is that they understand that it's not just about learning, it's also about having fun. And Vail isn't short on instructors —at the last count there were 850 knowledgeable and certified alpine, snowboard, and telemark instructors giving the lowdown in 30 languages including Spanish, German, Italian, French, Japanese, Korean, Portuguese, and even Croatian. In fact a number of top instructors here train other instructors for different ski resorts in North America and throughout the world.

Class sizes are small and another benefit of joining a class is the quick access to the slopes via exclusive ski school lift lines. The Vail Ski & Snowboard school operates out of all three base areas (Golden Peak, Vail Village, and Lionshead) as well as at Mid-Vail for a total of four locations where visitors can sign up for lessons. Prices vary and some packages may include lift tickets and rentals.

Group lesson and lift packages are available for select ski and snowboard school programs that will

▲ **FREESTYLING FUN**
The TAG Heuer Terrain Park is spread over a dozen trails and combines natural and man made features for freestylers. Vail hosts top freeskiing and snowboarding events each winter. The spectator -friendly U.S. Freeskiing Open also puts on great parties and live music.

save you money against purchasing elements separately. All adult group lessons are for guests aged 15 and older. You could start with the First Time Series: participants get three adult ski or snowboard lessons for the price of one, but days must be used consecutively. In addition, graduates will be given a coupon good for an additional three consecutive days of class lessons for the price of one. The package includes three days of lessons, beginner lift tickets, and rentals.

Telemark skiing has gained great popularity at Vail and The Nordic Center offers world-class instruction with top of the range equipment for every type of telemark skier from the beginner to the expert. Cross-country skiing is available at The Nordic Center and at the base of Golden Peak.

At the other end of the spectrum you could hire a private guide to tour the mountain to uncover the secret stashes only the locals know. This can be a full day or half-day (morning or afternoon), with private lessons. Two-hour and one-hour private lessons are offered depending upon availability. In between are all the variable ski school group lessons you would expect from a premier resort operating a full-day session from 9:45 AM to 3:30 PM.

BEGINNERS

At Vail, beginners get to start at the top—at the top of the mountain that is. The beginner area is located at the top of the Eagle Bahn Gondola at Eagle's Nest. Nursery slopes at altitude and lower down at resort level are excellent but they can be overcrowded. While Vail's legendary Back Bowls and Blue Sky Basin are meant for more experienced skiers, beginners can ski in places all over the front side of Vail Mountain from Golden Peak to Lionshead.

INTERMEDIATES

The bulk of the Vail's front face is intermediate level with plenty of easy cruising trails—and that means it is well suited to the bulk of the skiers—but intermediates wanting something more challenging can check out the easier black diamond trails on the front face before moving on to the Back Bowls where you can find easy, groomed blue trails as well as ungroomed slopes which—snow conditions permitting—offer good opportunities to learn to ski powder.

Get to know the more than 5,200 acres (2,106 ha) of skiing with a free "Meet the Mountain" tour, starting at 9:15 AM from the Eagle Bahn Gondola. A guide takes intermediate skiers and snowboarders to the best spots on the mountain. Stop for lunch at the best restaurant on the mountain, Two Elk. Featuring gourmet pizza, pasta and wraps, Two Elk provides one of the best views of the Gore Range. In the afternoon, ski the legendary Back Bowls until 3:00 PM and then finish the day on the front of the mountain. Ski down Pepsi's face, the old World Cup downhill course, into the Vail Village.

The longest trail, Riva, is three miles (5 km) and is also the most challenging for a number of reasons. It has an interesting fall line in places and tends to have steeper sections as well as bumps.

◄ **NORTH-FACING SLOPES**
The groomed slopes are mainly north-facing, cut through the trees and and accessible from three vantage points: the Vista Bahn in Vail Village, the Riva Bahn Express at Golden Peak, and the Eagle Bahn from Lionshead. Ski patrols are conspicuous in their yellow jackets checking for speeding and other safety breaches.

Intermediates can ski much of the same terrain as advanced skiers It's a matter of choosing different trails in the same areas, like the Back Bowls and Blue Sky Basin, and selecting trails with gradients that suit your ability and confidence level.

ADVANCED & EXPERT

Although just over half the ski area is designated advanced (some of it over-classified) and expert, the best skiing is to be found on the Back Bowls: Game Creek Bowl on the front of the mountain, and Blue Sky Basin. The back bowls, Blue Sky Basin and the infamous bumps trails on the east side of the mountain including double black diamond trails Highline, Blue Ox and Roger's Run, are all challenging for this level skier. Skiers can also try the locals' favorite, nicknamed the P.P.L., a combination of the Prima, Pronto and Logchute runs.

There is no place to be on a powder day except the Back Bowls—that's what's made them famous. More than 6 miles (10 km) of glades skiing offer skiers everything from trees, cliff drops, expansive stretches and more, and when snow conditions are good try the mile-long trail into Minturn—a good spot for lunch.

Blue Sky Basin has redefined the adventure ski experience with open glades, cornices, trees, and

▲ UNGROOMED BLISS
The Back Bowls can get crusty when warmer weather arrives (in February) and sometimes they can have a porridge-like consistency, but more often than not they are powder heaven.

▼ SETTING THE STANDARD
The unpisted Back Bowls are renowned for powder skiing. Altogether they add an impressive 6 miles (10 km) of off-piste terrain. Such huge expanses have helped Vail become the showcase resort that others try to emulate.

steep pitches— accessed by a high-speed quad. Belle's Camp, at the top of Blue Sky Basin, is the perfect place for a picnic lunch. From Belle's Camp, you can see the Ten Mile Range and Mount of the Holy Cross—one of Colorado's "fourteeners." First-time visitors may wish to hire explore Blue Sky Basin with an "adventure guide" from the ski school.

Expert skiers can access backcountry skiing in the White River National Forest through four access gates on the mountain. These gates are the only places where skiers are allowed to access this terrain. If skiers do not use the permitted gates, they have broken the law and if caught will be punished. On powder days, expert skiers should head for the Back Bowls. For those looking for bumps, Vail has the famous Highline, Blue Ox, and Roger's Run trio.

BOARDING & FREESTYLE

Freeriders can spend the day at the Golden Peak Superpipe and Terrain Park which features an award-winning Superpipe and more than 30 rails. Vail's lift system makes it easy for riders to avoid catwalks and flat areas so they can spend the day accumulating vertical trails instead of going across the mountain. Vail hosts top freeskiing and snowboarding events each winter, including the spectator-friendly U.S. Freestyle Open in early February—complete with great parties and live music.

EATING ON THE MOUNTAIN

Before you hit the slopes try The Daily Grind for great coffee and specialty drinks or DJ's for any breakfast craving, be it omelets or French toast.

There are more than 15 restaurants to choose from on Vail Mountain, such as Two Elk Restaurant, Vail Mountain's flagship restaurant at the top of China Bowl. It's open for lunch only and has expanded outdoor picnic seating to enjoy Southwestern menu items including wraps, gourmet pizza, pasta and more. Many self-service restaurants are pricey and can be crowded at lunchtimes, and in this respect there is a need for some improvement in mountain restaurant facilities.

If rustic indoor or outdoor barbecueing of smoked chicken, soups and grilled sandwiches are your preference you'll want to get to Wildwood Smokehouse at the top of Wildwood Express and Game Creek Express. Sample the spectacular views of the Sawatch Range from here. Mid-Vail Food Courts has a New York-style deli, fajita bar, grill and pasta bar on the Terrace Level. There you'll also find an American diner, and the Gore Range Grill on the Look Ma level, with spectacular views of the Gore Range. There's a "Great Lunch for less" option with pasta, salad, and drink for less than $8. Skiers and snowboarders can take advantage of great lunch options at Larkspur, which features chef Thomas Salamunovich's mix of American and rustic French cuisine at the base of Golden Peak. It's been listed as a "Don't Miss while in Vail" in *U.S.A. Today*.

Undoubtedly Vail's finest on-mountain restaurant is Game Creek, overlooking Game Creek Bowl at the top of Vail Mountain. Ride the Eagle Bahn Gondola to the top for a snowcat ride to the restaurant. Guests are treated to a multi-course menu of Colorado cuisine by chef David Wiehler. It's a private club at lunch and open to the public for dinner.

APRÈS SKI

It's late afternoon and Vail is known for a great après-ski scene. After the lifts close check out the Red Lion or Los Amigos in the village, or for great margaritas, Garfinkel's in Lionshead, which sports a large outside deck overlooking the base area and features live acoustic music.

The Red Lion in Vail Village has earned the reputation as "the place to be after you ski." Get there early on a nice day to claim a prize spot on the front deck. Live music nightly. Or there's Los Amigos in Vail Village offering one of the best views of the base area—you sit on the outside deck and watch skiers and snowboarders make their final runs down Pepsi's Face. Or you might spot one of the many Vail celebrities who either have a place here or are "passin' thru"—and there are quite a few. If we mention in passing Joe Montana, Oprah, John Glenn, Buzz Aldrin, Arnold Schwarzenegger, Clint

EATING ON THE MOUNTAIN

QUICK EATS
TWO ELK RESTAURANT
BUFFALO'S
EAGLE'S NEST
THE MARKETPLACE
GOLDEN PEAK GRILL
MID-VAIL
WILDWOOD SMOKEHOUSE

FULL SERVICE
GAME CREEK
BLUE MOON
LARKSPUR
CUSINA RUSTICA

▲ JUMPING SKILLS
If you like taking laps on high-speed, lift-accessed enormously long parks then Vail is the place. Just get in those high-speed, motocross-style park runs and test out your sliding, jumping and twisting skills.

RESTAURANTS & BARS

BLUE MOON BAR AT EAGLE'S NEST
GARFINKEL'S
GRAVITY
LOS AMIGOS
KALTENBURG
PEPSI'S
THE CLUB
THE RED LION
THE TAP ROOM
VENDETTA'S
LIVE MUSIC
8150
POWDER HOUNDS
DANCE CLUBS
THE BRIDGE
CLUB CHELSEA
SANCTUARY

▲ **LIFE IS A HALF-PIPE**
Vail is a mecca for boarders and not just for freestylers in the terrain park – though the two halfpipes at Adventure Ridge are impressive enough.

Eastwood, Roger Daltrey, Jean-Claude Van Damme, Mimi Rogers, Phil and Steve Mahre, Kelsey Grammer, and Cameron Diaz, you'll get the drift.

The Tap Room at the top of Bridge Street is the place to try one of several types of martinis, while Sanctuary in Vail Village, above the Tap Room, boasts Vail's best sound system and dancefloor. In Vail Village, try Vendetta's, a popular locals' place, or head to Kalentenberg Castle for steins of German beer.

If eating out is your (other) favorite activity Vail is the perfect choice. Vail caters to wide-ranging palates and budgets with 73 restaurants and 16 bars, and apart from Whistler no resort in North America has such a range of cafés and restaurants offering every kind of cuisine, from Chinese and Mexican through to native Californian, for which the Terra Bistro or the Vail Athletic Club are the tops. The Tyrolean Inn is, well, Tyrolean, and Vendetta's is Italian and very very good—and who doesn't like Italian? Colorado is a long way from the sea but the fish at Montauk in Lionshead is always fresh and excellent, while for something a little lively the Half Moon Saloon in West Vail is the place to stop by. But restaurants rise and fall, and chefs move about, so ask around among your fellow guests and find out where the good food is really at this season.

The Wildflower is the only Mobile four-star rated restaurant in Vail. It boasts one of the best wine lists in Vail. Sumptuous breakfasts and skiers' lunch buffets are on offer slope-side for quick dining breaks at Cucina Rustica. It transforms into an authentic Tuscan grill for dinner. Established in 1977, Sweet Basil in the heart of Vail Village is renowned as one of Vail's finest restaurants. The wine list continually receives the Award of Excellence from *Wine Spectator* magazine and the food features imaginative American entrées with Mediterranean and Asian influences from chef Bruce Yim.

For the family, the Red Lion is great for every member, with a children's menu, great beer selection, and live entertainment, while Bully Ranch is a locals' favorite serving true Colorado Western and barbecue, featuring everything from hand-cut prime beef to veggie wraps. On the budget side Bart & Yeti's in Lionshead offers a variety of burger and sandwich options from US$5 to US$10, while Flying Burrito in Lionshead serves tasty burritos for less than US$6. They're a meal in themselves.

It is strongly recommended that you make table reservations in advance, but beware that in this well-heeled resort standards are high and in the better restaurants (on and off the mountain) New York prices (expensive) are not uncommon.

After dinner, it's time to check out Vail at night and find out why *SKI Magazine* rates Vail's nightlife tops. There's great entertainment with live music, offering everything from piano jazz and 80s music through hip-hop and reggae at places like 8150, Club Chelsea, and Mickey's Piano Bar. The George has sofas you can sink into, pool tables, and foos-ball, and the Tap Room specializes in great martinis.

Vail's streets come to life every Wednesday night during the Budweiser Street Beat. This free series features nationally and locally recognized acts including the Young Dubliners, the Hazel Miller Band, and William Topley. After the concert, stop by the local's favorite and ski patrol hangout, Vendetta's, for a beer and a slice of pizza. Then hit the Club Chelsea to sing along with Scott Ma.

OTHER ACTIVITIES

The skiing in Vail may be legendary but the excitement and fun in Vail run deeper than the powder. Given that Vail is the tops, it follows that the alternative activities are all outstanding. You want it, Vail has it—tennis, swimming, dogsledding, hot air ballooning, (very popular, somewhat chilly)—

RESTAURANTS

AMERICAN RESTAURANTS
BARTS & YETI'S
BULLY RANCH
TERRA BISTRO

INTERNATIONAL
CAMPO DE FIORI
CHAP'S GRILL & CHOPHOUSE
CHINA GARDEN TOO
FLYING BURRITO
MONTAUK SEAFOOD GRILL
SWISS CHALET
TYROLEAN

indoor climbing, ice-climbing (very chilly, somewhat dangerous)—sleigh rides (very chilly, very romantic) —tubing, thrill sledding, (good for screaming), skating...you name it—and of course, shopping.

Visitors of all ages will find endless activities off the slopes from Adventure Ridge to Vail's world-class spas. Adventure Ridge is Vail's headquarters for non-skiing fun. This on-mountain activity center located at the top of the Eagle Bahn Gondola at Eagle's Nest caters to kids of all ages. Here they can try out sledding head-first down the mountain at night to the bottom of the Eagle Bahn gondola (headlamps and clear goggles provided). Or travel from peak to peak with a guide through alpine meadows and mountain roadways on a snowmobile, or have a go on the unique, multi-lane tubing hill with some lanes that are steep and fast, and others that are shorter and milder for tame tubers.

Ski-biking is another option with nighttime tours from Adventure Ridge to the bottom of the gondola. Instructors provide an introduction to ski-biking techniques, before leading tour groups down the mountain.

For something way more relaxing there are more than a handful of day spas in Vail offering specialty services to reinvigorate and rejuvenate tired muscles and bodies after hours on the slopes. Not least in this category is the Aria Spa & Club at the Vail Cascade Resort, undergoing a US$4 million renovation and expansion to incorporate the creation of a grand luxury spa called Aria within the existing massive spa and club facility. The spa will include massage, plus body, facial, and hydrotherapy treatments.

Back on the streets, Vail offers more than 145 stores and boutiques, nearly 50 art galleries and museums including the Colorado Ski Museum (check out the old skis and other artifacts), casual apparel, gift and home furnishing boutiques, ski and snowboard stores, a wine shop and florist, and handcrafted jewelry. Finally, why not feast your eyes on flowers as they break through the snow at Betty Ford Alpine Gardens, the highest public garden in the United States. For those into self-catering there are a dozen liquor and grocery stores. Just remember that Vail is big; it doesn't do things by half, and with 1.5 million visitors flowing through a town seven miles long by two miles wide (11 km x 3 km) you'd expect non-skiing activities to be varied and attractive.

MAGIC NUMBER
Vail claims 346 inches (866 cm) of snowfall annually and over 300 days of sunshine each year – math that makes the resort very appealing.

▼ BACK BOWLS BLAST
The Back Bowls are awesome especially after a dump. Ungroomed chutes, bowls, cliffs and not too many trees help stoke up the adrenaline.

USEFUL PHONE NUMBERS

Vail Resorts	970-476-5601
Vail Central Reservation Center	970-949 5189
Vail Valley Medical Center	970-476-2451
Colorado Mountain Express	970-926-9800
High Mountain Taxis	970-524-5555
Snow Line	970-476-4888
The Activities Desk	970-476-9090
Family Adventure Line	970-479-4090
Ski and Snowboard School	970-476-3229

USEFUL WEBSITES & E-MAIL

Official Website	www.vail.com
Consumer Website	www.snow.com
Colorado Mountain Express	www.cmex.com
High Mountain Taxis	www.hmtaxi.com
Snow Report & Web Cams	www.rsn.com/cams/vail
Weather Reports	www.wunderground.com
Vacation Planner	www.summitnet.com/vail
Consumer E-mail	vailinfo@vailresorts.com

OTHER ACTIVITIES

THRILL SLEDDING
Sled head-first down the mountain at night from Adventure Ridge to the bottom of the Eagle Bahn gondola. Sleds have a hand-activated brake system and four independently suspended skis. Headlamps and clear goggles provided. Helmets available. Must be at least 14 years old. Reservations required.

SNOWMOBILE TOURS
Travel from peak to peak with a guide through alpine meadows and mountain roadways.
See the mountain by the setting sun or by the light of the moon.
Must be 4 years old to be a passenger and 16 years old with a valid driver's license to drive, and children must be accompanied by a parent or guardian on the tour. Reservations required.

TUBING
Unique, multi-lane tubing hill offers some lanes that are steep and fast, and others that are shorter and milder for tame tubers. Lift-served tubing hill. Nearby warming hut and bathrooms. Minimum height of 36 inches (91 cm) required.

SKI-BIKING
Nighttime tours from Adventure Ridge to the bottom of the gondola. Instructors provide an introduction to ski-biking techniques, before leading tour groups down the mountain. Clear goggles and headlamps provided. Guests should wear or bring ski boots to participate. Snow skates are provided as an alternative. Must be at least 12 years old and 4 feet 6 inches (137 cm) tall. Must be at least an intermediate skier or rider. Reservations required.

A MERE 20-MINUTE DRIVE FROM THE RAZZLE AND DAZZLE OF VAIL SITS THE SECLUDED, UPSCALE FAMILY RESORT OF BEAVER CREEK. RENOWNED FOR ITS EXCELLENT SERVICE AND EMPHASIS ON LUXURY, THIS IS THE PLACE TO HEAD FOR IF YOU LIKE YOUR SKIING STYLISH AND ON WELL-GROOMED SLOPES.

BEAVER CREEK

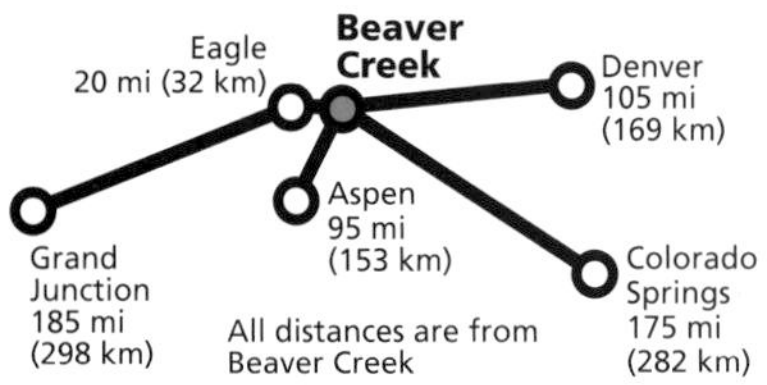

SKI SEASON
Mid-November to mid-April

We asked a bunch of experienced skiers to sum up Beaver Creek in one word and they came up with half-a-dozen; classy, expensive, sophisticated, elegant, intimate, upscale. Well now, ask yourself, is this your kind of town? Do you really need a "ski-valet" to carry the planks or have someone warm your boots and ease you into them every morning? Maybe yes, maybe no, but you get the picture. The upside of this frankly-pretentious mix is that the ski facilities are first class, the runs well groomed, the ski teachers and hotel staff professional, the accommodations five-star and, a real bonus, the crowds much reduced. All in all, go for it.

GETTING THERE

Beaver Creek is approximately 105 miles (169 km) west of Denver. The nearest airport, Eagle County Airport, is about 25 minutes west of Beaver Creek by car. Denver International Airport, with more than 700 daily flights from across the globe, is 126 miles (201 km) from Beaver Creek, around a two-hour drive by car. Van shuttle companies operate from both airports and can drop visitors off at the front door of their lodge or condominium—or you can rent a car at the airport.

Getting around the resort is easy, with most lodging properties located within walking distance

► **EXCLUSIVE EMPHASIS**
Beaver Creek is the grander cousin of its brasher neighbor Vail, just 20 minutes down the road. Quiet, attractive, and good for families, the resort also has a pricey reputation.

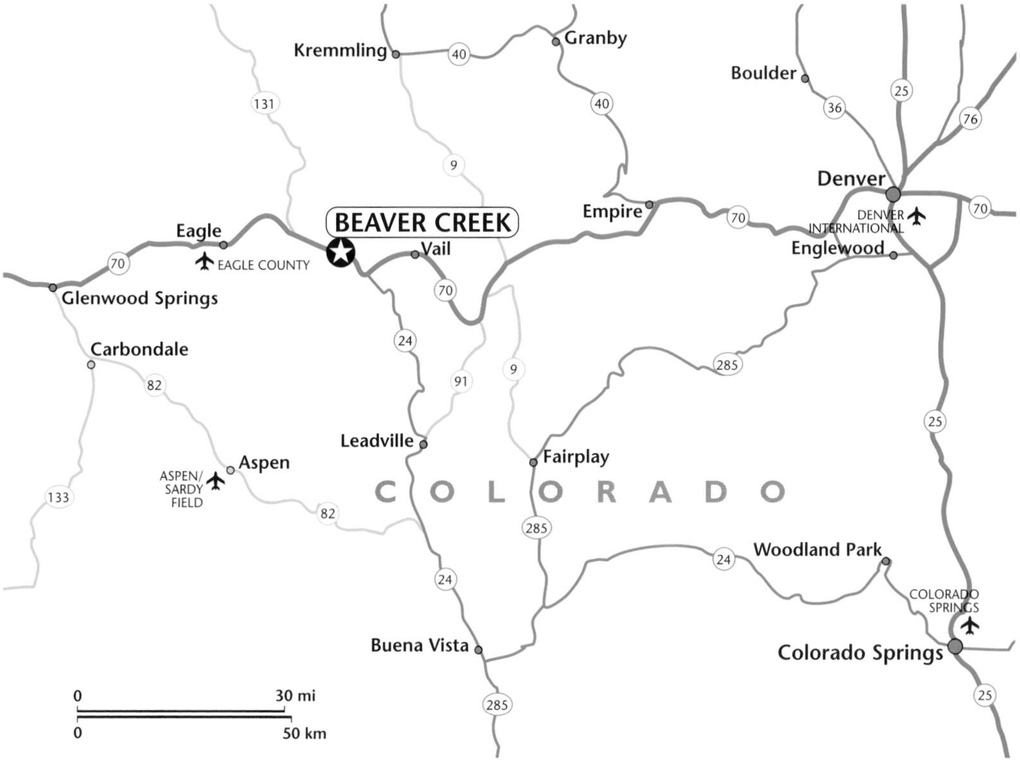

of the lifts and core village. There is an excellent complimentary shuttle service in the village, transporting guests to any location within the resort from 6:00 AM to 2:00 AM daily. Guests can call or make arrangements through their concierge and within minutes the shuttle arrives.

Shuttles between Beaver Creek and Arrowhead run from 8:00 AM to 11:00 PM daily. The much larger resort of Vail is easily accessible via the Avon Beaver Creek Transit bus, which operates every half-hour throughout the day from 6:00 AM until 2.00 AM daily to Beaver Creek. Cost is US$2 one way.

THE VILLAGE

Beaver Creek skiing is now linked to two new hamlets, Arrowhead, with its own chairlift, and Bachelor Gulch, which offers good skiing. Beaver Creek itself is an exclusive pedestrian village with European-style architecture, an alpine ambience and a covered escalator service from the village directly to the slopes. A year-round outdoor ice rink, exclusive stores and art galleries, and top-quality restaurants attract guests of all ages to the heart of the village.

The Vilar Center for Performing Arts, in the heart of the village, hosts an all-star lineup of world-class performances. Complimentary family programs, including BMW Thursday Night Lights—a glow-stick ski-down for the whole family—take place throughout the winter.

ACCOMMODATIONS

The accommodations emphasis is on upscale hotels and condos, and prices reflect that. Beaver Creek has three hotels, while nearby Avon (accessible by free shuttle bus) has seven. For cheaper places to rent try Edwards and Avon within six miles (10 km) of Beaver, or even consider Vail, 10 miles (16 km) away. Of the hotels, The Pines Lodge, The Inn at Beaver Creek, and The Park Hyatt are top notch—the latter was recently rated the best hotel in a ski town by *Powder* magazine. The Ritz-Carlton at Bachelor Gulch further down the valley is another promising addition with 237 guest rooms and a state-of-the-art spa and fitness center.

SKI AREA

The base elevation of Beaver Creek and Bachelor Gulch is 8,100 feet (2,469 m) rising to the summit of

MOUNTAIN FACTS

Base	8,100 feet. (2,469m)
Summit	11,440 feet. (3,487 m)
Elevation	4,040 feet. (1,231 m)
Easy	34%
Intermediate	39%
Advanced/Expert	27%
Bowls	2
Number of trails	146
Longest trail	3 miles (4.8km)
Ski area	1,625 acres (658 ha)

SNOWFALL

Annual snowfall	310 inches (787 cm)
Snowmaking	605 acres (245 ha)

SKI LIFTS

Gondolas	-
High-Speed Quads	6
Fixed Grip Quads	-
Triple Chairs	3
Double Chairs	4
Surface Lifts	-
Total	13
Riders per hour	24,739

ACCOMODATIONS

THE PINES LODGE
www.beavercreek.com
970-845-7900

THE INN AT BEAVER CREEK
www.beavercreek.com
970-845-7800

PARK HYATT BEAVER CREEK RESORT AND SPA
www.hyatt.com
970-949-1234

THE RITZ CARLTON BACHELOR GULCH
www.bachelorgulchvillage.com/ritz.cfm
970-845-2300

▼ PLEASANT STAY
Beaver Creek accommodations are typically upscale with prices to match.

▶ LINKED VILLAGES Beaver Creek is linked to Bachelor Gulch and Arrowhead Village and offers a smaller version of the type of village you find in European resorts.

NEARBY RESORTS

Beaver Creek Mountain at 11,440 feet (3,487 m). The adjacent Grouse Mountain is marginally higher, with a steep forested gully between the two. Beaver Creek has its beginner terrain positioned at the summit. Though higher, it is flatter and more open than Grouse Mountain, which is the resort's expert-only area and offers long, steep, thigh-burning bump runs and amazing gladed terrain, also the "Birds of Prey" World Cup trail.

The skiing also has village-to-village possibilities—you can ski or snowboard to and from Beaver Creek, Bachelor Gulch, and Arrowhead. Steeps and endless trees are the key to skiing here, and with a northerly orientation the snow tends to be light and dry. The resort's strong commitment to grooming means you can cruise fresh corduroy on over 30 percent of the mountain's terrain daily.

One of the resort's best-kept secrets is the Beaver Creek Snowshoe and Cross-Country Ski Track at McCoy Park—a vast plateau at 9,840 feet (2,999 m) elevation offering 20 miles (32 km) of snowshoeing and cross-country ski terrain, and some fantastic outlooks.

Beaver creek is hot on safety, which is not surprising given the strong emphasis on beginner, intermediate and family skiing. Therefore designated "speeder control" staff are positioned in high-traffic areas at specific times to monitor speed and

behavior. Any skier or snowboarder who speeds or demonstrates dangerous or reckless behavior on the mountain is liable to receive a warning or have their lift ticket revoked.

SKI LIFTS

Beaver Creek is highly regarded for its virtually non-existent lift lines and uncrowded slopes. There are 13 chairlifts offering access to 1,625 acres (658 ha) of skiing and snowboarding terrain in Beaver Creek, Bachelor Gulch, and Arrowhead. If the

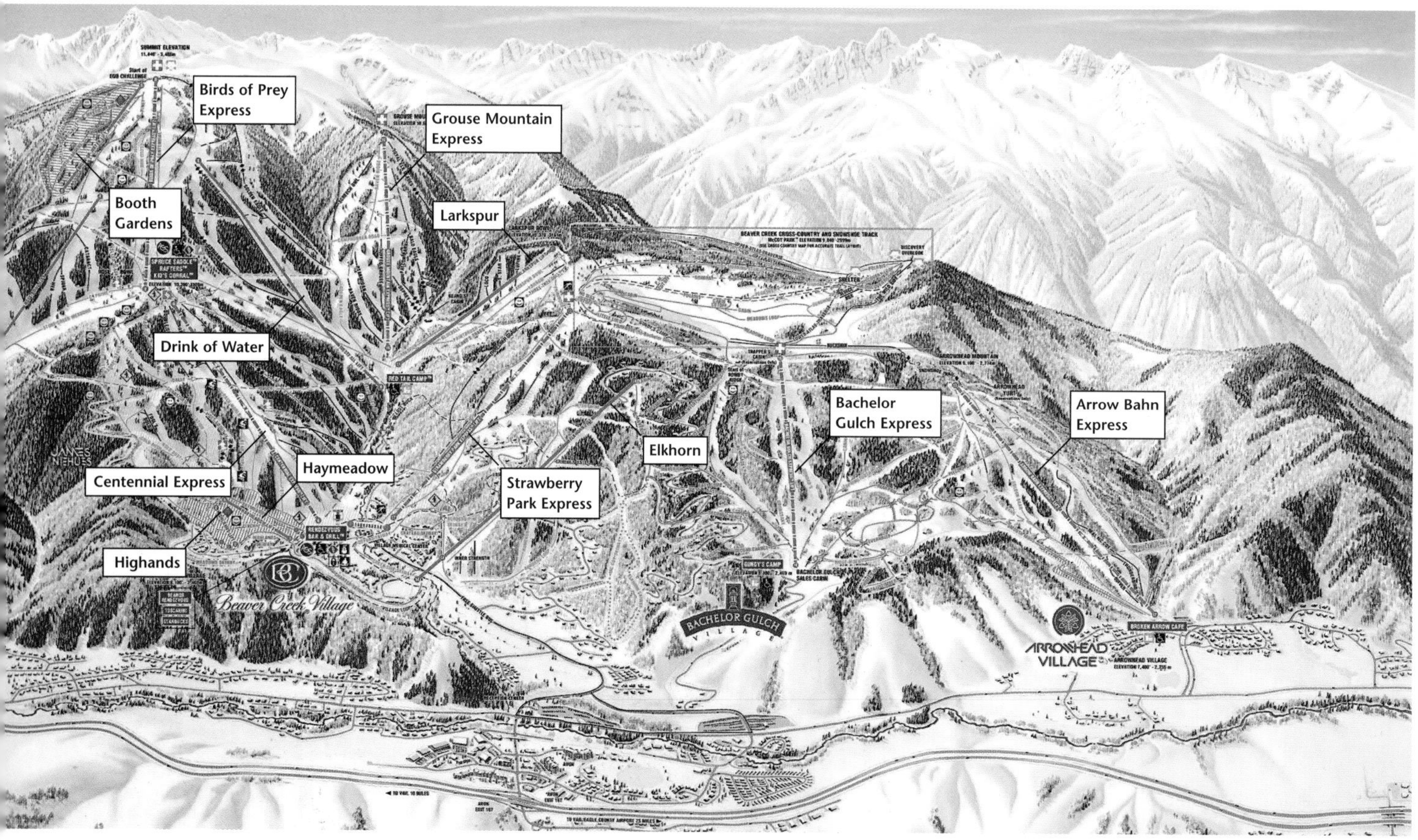

Centennial Express Lift (carrying six) should get busy, ride the adjacent Strawberry Park Express Lift (12) to access the main mountain. On select busy days, you might even get to sample homemade chocolate chip cookies in the lift lines.

LIFT PASSES

The "Perfect 10" Ticket allows you to ski 10 days at Vail, Beaver Creek, Breckenridge, Keystone, and Heavenly, as well as Arapahoe Basin, for less than US$33 a day throughout the season. This multi-day lift ticket program rewards those who ski early and often. Early, because it must be used at least once before January 31, and often, because it includes up to 10 days of skiing and snowboarding which can be used consecutively or non-consecutively throughout the season. It's valid all season with the exception of Christmas and New Year and costs US$329 for adults and US$159 for children (ages 5–12). The Perfect 10 is on sale at any season pass office in Beaver Creek, Vail, Breckenridge, or Keystone, or online at www.vailresorts.com

SKI SCHOOL

There are two ski schools in the resort: one for adults, the Beaver Creek Adult Ski and Snowboard School, while the Beaver Creek Children's Ski and Snowboard School teaches the kids. Children are supervised at lunchtime too. Both are located slopeside at the top of the escalators in Beaver Creek village, 9:30 AM– 3:30 PM for full day. Children enrolled in ski school are not required to purchase additional lift tickets. There are also women-only, children-only, and co-ed telemark ski workshops on offer, and group lessons are available for snowshoeing. If you can walk, you can snowshoe. It's easy and fun.

BEGINNERS

Beaver dedicates a significant portion of its terrain to teaching beginner skiers and snowboarders. In fact, Beaver Creek Mountain is virtually laid out upside down with most of the prime beginner trails located at the top. This layout gives beginner skiers a true "ski-down-the-mountain" experience, not to mention spectacular views of the nearby Gore Range. The Beginner's Center is a living room environment at the base of the beginner area, in which students preview their ski or snowboard experience, watch video presentations on aspects such as loading and unloading a chairlift, and ask questions before they move onto the snow. A surface lift transports students up to the bottom of the Highlands lift (No.2), so there's no need to struggle with new equipment at altitude. A second beginner chairlift is located nearby.

A good beginner itinerary might be to begin by exploring trails like Red Buffalo and Booth Gardens off The Birds of Prey Express (No.8) or begin at Arrowhead Village on the lower part of Little Brave (No.17). The Haymeadow Lift (No.1) services all beginner terrain. The Buckaroo Bowl introductory terrain park in the beginner area is used by instructors to enhance and quicken the learning process, helping skiers and riders learn to use their edges. A snow-made "spine" allows students to practice shifting weight from edge to edge before they tackle the slopes.

INTERMEDIATES

With 39 percent of the slopes groomed for intermediates there is plenty of scope for this level of skier and rider. The longest trail is Centennial (though it's part-intermediate, part-advanced) and runs for 2.75 miles (4.5 km). Sticking to the intermediate level, try Raven Ridge that often gets moguls and is the most challenging trail. It's part of Grouse Mountain, the expert-only area.

SKI SCHOOL

ADULT SKI AND SNOWBOARD SCHOOL

Prices: US$115–158 per day, depending on season.

970-845-5300

CHILDREN'S SKI AND SNOWBOARD SCHOOL

Prices: US$95–120 per day, depending on season.

Includes all-day lesson, lift access, and lunch.

970-845-5464

www.beavercreek.com

▼ SPRUCE SADDLE
Spruce and other conifers abound in this resort—especially around Spruce Saddle, the mid-mountain point at 10,200 foot (3,109 m) elevation—so for hardcore tree riding it's hard to beat. The gladed trails, especially off Grouse Mountain, are legendary.

RESTAURANTS

BEANO'S CABIN
ZACH'S CABIN
ALLIE'S CABIN
BROKEN ARROW CAFÉ
REDTAIL CAMP
GRUNDY'S CAMP
SADDLE LODGE
DUSTY BOOT SALOON
COYOTE CAFÉ
THE BLUE MOOSE
BEAVER CREEK CHOPHOUSE
TOSCANINI
GROUSE MOUNTAIN GRILL
SPLENDIDO
MIRABELLE

BARS

THE COYOTE CAFÉ
DUSTY BOOT SALOON
RENDEZVOUS BAR & GRILL
ICE BAR @ HYATT REGENCY
INN AT BEAVER CREEK
McCOY'S CAFE AND BAR

▼ **TREE-SHELTERED**
Wall to wall trees keep the powder pristine at Beaver Creek—until, that is, a powder hound susses it out.

Alternatively, take the Strawberry Park Lift (No.12), then ski or snowboard over to Bachelor Gulch and Arrowhead for fun, groomed cruisers and not many people. Check out Stone Creek Meadows in Rose Bowl, off the Centennial Express Lift (No.6). Or try Village-to-Village skiing in Bachelor Gulch on trails like Grubstake and Gunders off the Bachelor Gulch Express (No.16), or in Arrowhead on Golden Bear trail off Arrow Bahn Express Lift (No.17).

ADVANCED & EXPERT

Grouse Mountain has moguls, super steep bumps, and gladed terrain. The trails are very long and serviced by a very fast chair. The Golden Eagle trail is part of the prestigious Birds of Prey Downhill Course and offers extreme steeps and bumps in the late season. It was specifically designed for the 1999 World Cup Men's Downhill and Super G races. Take the Birds of Prey Chair (No.8) down to Red Tail Camp.

Royal Elk Glades, off the Grouse Mountain via Express Lift (carrying 10) will give you the best powder. To get the most of Beaver at this level, take the Centennial Lift (No.6), then Birds of Prey Express Lift (No.8) to the summit. Ski or snowboard down Golden Eagle. Take the Grouse Mountain Lift (No.10) for several expert mogul trails, trees, and powder stashes.

Out-of-bounds terrain can be accessed by hiking or skiing past the boundary ropes. Be warned though, if you ski outside of boundary ropes you are on your own; no ski patrol or rescue service is provided. Advanced and expert skiers are encouraged to go with a guide to find some of the mountain's best powder stashes and discover where the locals ski and ride.

BOARDING & FREESTYLE

Frankly, if snowboarding is really your scene, get on the shuttle bus and head for Vail. Beaver Creek has seven dedicated snowboard trails with all the usual joys, a fun park and tuition at the Children's Ski and Snowboard School, but the razzmatazz that goes with snowboarding is not really available in Beaver Creek. Having said that, the resort does boast one of Colorado's largest superpipes attracting both beginner and pro boarders.

Several terrain parks provide exciting places for boarders and trick skiers. Zoom Room is an intermediate park while Moonshine offers excitement for expert and pro-level riders. Getting around the ski area is easy for boarders as there is a lot of steep expert terrain and very few catwalks.

▲ **TREES FROM THE WOODS**
Nearly 150 tree-lined trails undulate on highly attactive terrain at Beaver Creek.

EATING ON THE MOUNTAIN

Here's the snag. Some of the Beaver Creek mountain restaurants are private clubs, while others seem to cater to an exclusive clientele who book their tables a year in advance. Beano's Cabin is now open to the public in the evening but not at lunchtime, and Zach's Cabin and Allie's Cabin are also out-of-bounds at midday—so where can you go for lunch?

Broken Arrow Café in Arrowhead Village is fine, with its outdoor deck seating and a full-service bar serving traditional American fare from its popular outdoor grill. Redtail Camp at the finish of men's downhill course has an indoor-outdoor barbecue and an expansive deck, and Grundy's Camp in Bachelor's Gulch also has an outdoor BBQ. Of the five mountain restaurants, Spruce Saddle is located at the top of the Centennial Express lift (chair No.6) and offers spectacular views of the Gore Range and surrounding White River National Forest.

For dinner high upon the mountain, try the aforementioned Beano's Cabin. This rustic log-style restaurant is open to the public for dinner only, with a fixed-price menu. Guests are transported to this unique getaway via snowcat-drawn sleigh. Allie's Cabin is also a sophisticated dining option beginning with a snowcat-drawn sleighride and finishing with after-dinner drinks nestled in overstuffed chairs by the fire. With its cathedral ceilings and cozy river rock fireplace, the cabin boasts views of the entire village. In the winter,

Allie's is open to the public for dinner only and has a fixed-price menu.

APRÈS SKI

Beaver Creek does not have the kind of nightlife found in Vail. The bars close by 12:30 AM and anyone seeking a late night out head should head to Avon (2 miles/3.2 km) or Vail (10 miles/16 km). But there are 24 restaurants and 10 bars in Beaver Creek village itself. Dusty Boot Saloon serves tequilas and microbrews as well as top-notch steaks, burgers, and seafood. Coyote Café, the locals' stomping ground and most popular local bar, includes Mexican dishes and salads for lunch and dinner.

The Blue Moose is for casual, budget dining with great pizzas, subs and fries. For a mid-priced to upscale dinner, Beaver Creek Chophouse has live piano entertainment, an extensive martini and wine menu, and a cigar bar. Also, for fine dining check out Toscanini, with upbeat and casual Italian dinners with fine views of Beaver Creek plaza, excellent wine menu, and a kids' menu. Grouse Mountain Grill, Splendido, and Mirabelle are also good après-ski options.

OTHER ACTIVITIES

There's plenty to do on and off the snow. There is snowshoeing, cross-country skiing, telemark skiing, hot air ballooning, dogsled rides, ice skating, spa treatments, fitness centers, and hot tubbing to complete your winter sports vacation. For shoppers there are various stores and boutiques that provide upscale shopping options.

▲ LIMITED CUISINE
Prices for food can veer on the high side because this is a resort that caters to the wealthy wallet. In fact, most of the mountain restaurants are private clubs not open to the public.

USEFUL PHONE NUMBERS

Beaver Creek Information Center	970-845-9090
Accommodation Reservation Center	800-355-3452
Beaver Creek Medical Center	970-959-0800
Bus Service	970-949-1938
Vail Valley Taxi	970-476-8294
Beaver Creek Ski Patrol & Rescue	970-845-6610

USEFUL WEBSITES

Beaver Creek Website	www.beavercreek.com
Bachelor Gulch Website	www.bachelorgulchvillage.com
Resorts Accommodations	http://reservations.snow.com
Snow Report	http://beavercreek.snow.com
Weather Reports	www.wunderground.com
Snow Report & Web Cams	www.rsn.com/cams/conditions

OTHER ACTIVITIES

Beaver Creek Nature Tours
970-845-531

Ultimate Snowshoe Tours
970-845-531.

Cross-Country & Snow Shoeing
970-479-3210

◄ OUT OF THE TREES
Thigh-deep light, dry snow awaits the powder skier and boarder—even days after a dump.

PURPOSE-BUILT AND BIG, KEYSTONE IS AN INTERMEDIATE'S DREAM. BUT THERE'S PLENTY TO CHALLENGE THE NOVICE AND EXPERT TOO, AS THE THREE LINKED MOUNTAINS NESTLED IN THE WHITE RIVER NATIONAL FOREST EXPAND INTO DEEPER AND STEEPER TERRAIN. KEYSTONE HAS SEVERAL UNIQUE FEATURES, NOT LEAST A SKI TRAINING CENTER RUN BY U.S. OLYMPIC MEDALISTS PHIL AND STEVE MAHRE.

KEYSTONE

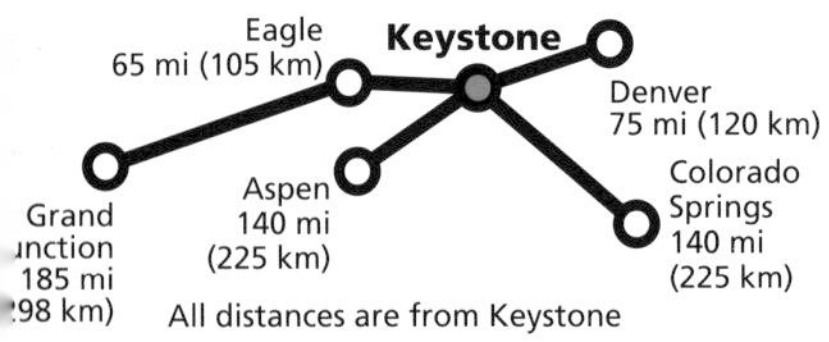

Try to arrive after dark and your first impression of Keystone will be a good one. Keystone offers the best night skiing in North America and the surrounding slopes sparkle in the star-dusted sky. Keystone has been improved in recent years and is now a complex of villages linked by the Keystone shuttle and collectively rated as a great resort for families. As a bonus, Keystone has some of the best restaurants of all the U.S. ski resorts, and is close to Denver so the transfer time is short.

GETTING THERE

Lying in the heart of the White River National Forest, Keystone Resort is located 90 miles (144 km) west of Denver International Airport, just off Interstate 70 in beautiful Summit County, Colorado. Complimentary shuttle buses run every 10 minutes within the resort, and there is a free shuttle service between Keystone and neighboring Breckenridge. Transfer time from Denver is around one to two hours by road.

THE VILLAGE

Keystone is an attractive, purpose-built development comprising three pedestrian-only villages: Keystone Village, River Run, and Mountain House Base Area. Each of the village areas is located along the base of Keystone Mountain and closed to vehicular traffic. They are modern Colorado-timber in style and feature stores, restaurants, ski schools, and cafés. Keystone Village also has a large lake that becomes the nation's largest outdoor ice-skating venue in the winter. Very family-friendly, Keystone also caters to business parties with the expansion of the large Conference Center—now the largest and most sophisticated facility in the Colorado Rockies.

◄ AFTER-HOURS ACTION

Keystone's floodlit night skiing has 3 miles (4.8 km) of trails with 40% "easiest" and 55% "more difficult" . Lifts run till 8 PM. The entire terrain park is fully-lit.

The River Run village has developed significantly during the past several years with many condos, restaurants and stores making up the new, biggest hub of the resort.

ACCOMMODATIONS

The resort has more than 1,600 lodging options in seven side-by-side "neighborhoods." There are deluxe hotels and ski-in, ski-out condominiums (from studios through to four bedrooms, and in all price ranges), in bustling villages or quaint units tucked away in the forest. Popular accommodations are in the River Run area at the base of the gondola, and in the more economical Forest Area. Wherever you choose, you are not more than several minutes from the slopes.

Keystone Lodge is top rated, with loft suites as well as hotel rooms all with mountain views. It's in the US$325 to US$450 price bracket and is located on Keystone Lake, where winter ice skating is a must. Balconies are available, so ask at check-in. The Inn at Keystone is a less expensive six-story hotel with views of the mountain and valley, and is about five minutes' walk from the base of the mountain. There are 3 outdoor hot tubs, and Razzberrys Restaurant is also located here. Both hotels are owned by Keystone Resort and can be booked online at www.keystoneresort.com or by calling 800-427-8308.

Also at the top end of the scale, the Ski Tip Bed and Breakfast was a stagecoach stop in the 1800s and the rooms come with massive stone fireplaces, antique furniture and many rustic charms, including one of Summit County's finest restaurants.

MOUNTAIN FACTS

Base	9,300 feet (2,835 m)
Summit	12,200 feet (3,719 m)
Elevation	2,900 feet (884 m)
Easy	16%
Intermediate	37%
Advanced	47%
Number of trails	116
Longest trail	3 miles (4.8 km)
Ski area	1,861 acres (754 ha)

SNOWFALL

Annual snowfall	230 inches (584 cm)
Snowmaking	859 acres (348 ha)

SKI LIFTS

Gondolas	2
High-Speed Six-Passenger	1
High-Speed Quads	5
Fixed Grip Quads	1
Triple Chairs	1
Double Chairs	4
Surface Lifts	2
Magic Carpets	5
Total	21
Riders per hour	35,175

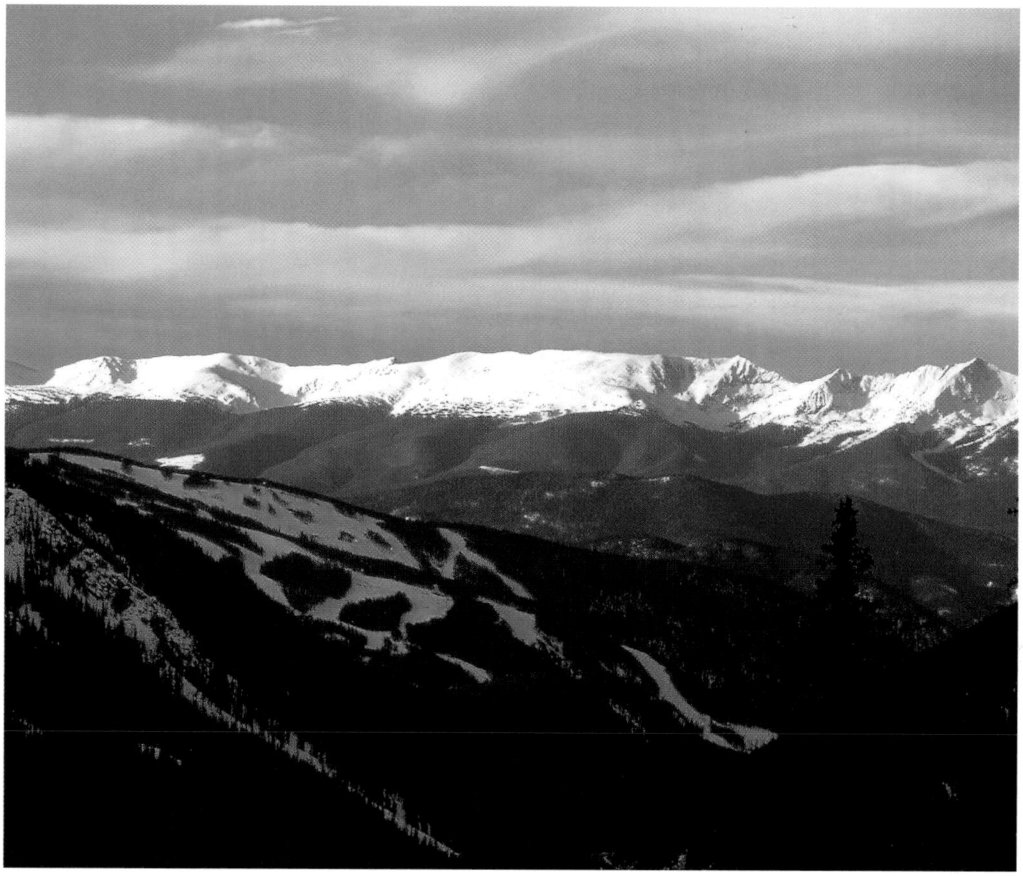

◄ **WELL GROOMED** Surrounded by peaks of the Continental Divide and the Ten Mile Range, Keystone has many great treelined trails.

NEARBY RESORTS

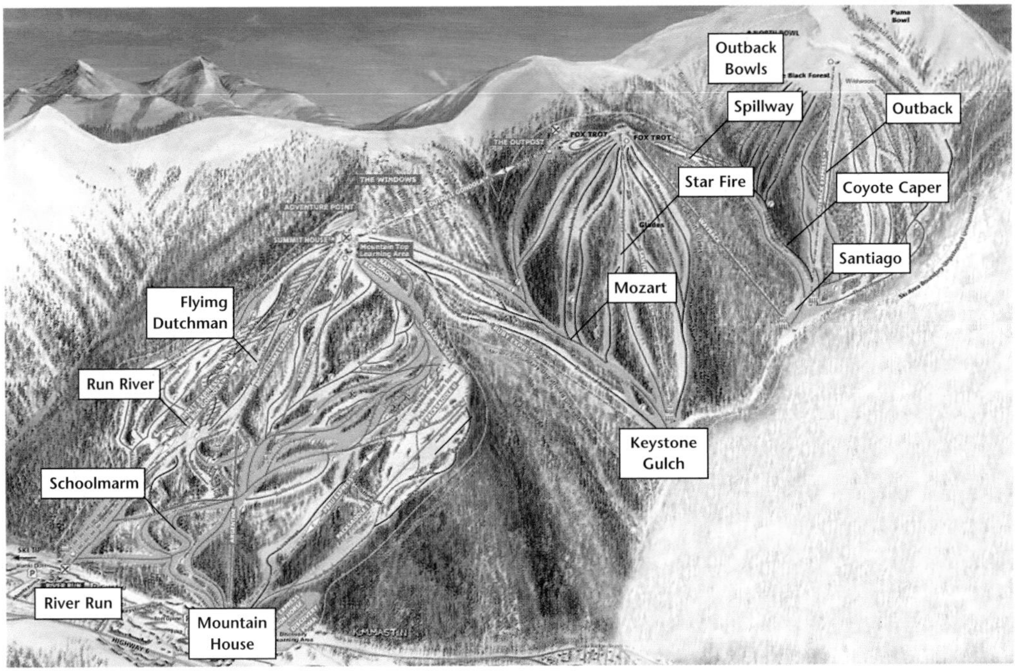

SKI SEASON
Late November to mid-April

SKI AREA

Keystone is surrounded by the high peaks of the Continental Divide and the Ten Mile Range. To the west is scenic Lake Dillon and to the east is Loveland Pass. The resort nestles below three big mountains: Keystone Mountain at 11,640 feet (3,548 m), behind which is the 20 feet (6 m) higher North Peak, and behind that is the highest and largest summit, The Outback, at 12,200 feet (3,719 m). This gives a vertical rise of 2,900 feet (884 m) and you are not just skiing across the front of a mountain at Keystone but skiing and riding deep into the mountains—truly exploratory. The three back-to-back-to-back mountains offer just about anything the skier or rider cares to tackle, but with only 16 percent of the trails designated as easy, the emphasis is on advanced and intermediate skiing. So it's the more demanding trails on North Peak and The Outback that beckon, with plenty of terrain to explore and the hikeable bowls catering to expert skiers and riders. The front side of Keystone Mountain attracts skiers for its superbly groomed cruising trails that overlook a vast expanse of pristine National Forest, two of the villages, and the beautiful Snake River Valley below. Night skiing and boarding is also available with lighted terrain, including a park and halfpipe, well into evening hours—something not on offer at many other Colorado resorts. It adds up to 235 acres (95 ha) of skiable terrain, 17 trails with the longest trail of three miles (4.8 km) and a vertical drop of 2,340 feet (713 m).

SKI LIFTS

Keystone has everything from T-bar lifts through enclosed gondolas and six-person high-speed lifts. Beginners use the T-bars and carpets at the base of the mountain and also at Keystone Mountain's summit, while more experienced skiers can take two enclosed gondolas to North Peak and the Outback. Keystone has added a high-speed quad, as well as improved gondola systems for the River Run and Outpost gondolas. Keystone has also added a magic carpet to the Discovery Learning Area to supplement the lift and T-bar there. The efficient six-seater high-speed chairs mean the lifts are very rarely crowded except at the base of the mountain. You can avoid lines by going to Keystone's North Peak and Outback areas (in other words, getting off Keystone Mountain and exploring the other peaks.) Because there is night skiing here, lifts can stay open from 8:30 AM—8:00 PM.

◄ **STAR FIRE**
A beautiful long straight 'more difficult' trail from below North Peak to LaBonte's Cabin, Star Fire is reached via the Santiago Express Lift.

◄ **IMPRESSIVE INTERMEDIATES**
Keystone's north-facing slopes are mostly linked intermediate and curving trails cut into a series of forested ridges. Freeriding boarders and skiers are naturally drawn here.

LIFT PASS

There are two ski tickets available for the Vail Resorts area: the Colorado Ticket and the Keystone Mountain Passport. The pre-booked Colorado Ticket offers discounted skiing. Buy a ten-day pass and get days 11–14 free. Buy a five-day pass get and days 6–7 are free. This offers a one-pass access to Vail, Beaver Creek, Breckenridge, Keystone, and Araphoe Basin—more than 11,000 acres (4,451 ha) of skiing. It will cost you US$245 to US$270 depending on high or low season. Expect to pay around US$60 a day for a lift pass, and US$27 a day for children aged 5–12. Lift passes can be purchased at the River Run and Mountain House Base Areas, or they can be bought at off-site outlets in Denver such as selected grocery and sports stores in the area. The Mountain Passport applies to Keystone. Every guest visiting the resort gets a passport offering US$300 worth of off-piste activities and a 25 percent shopping discount.

SKI SCHOOL AND GUIDING

The adult and child ski schools at River Run, and at the Mountain House, are very accessible to the villages and to the mountains. Ski school hours are 8:00 AM to 5:00 PM. The minimum age for young children joining a class is three years, and children are fully supervised in ski school if a full-day lesson is booked. Half-day lessons are available (but these don't include lunch). Youngsters aged two months to 12 years can be looked after at the Children's Daycare Center.

Keystone is also home to the Mahre Training Center—three- and five-day ski camps with one of the Olympic-medalist Mahre brothers—as well as special women's workshops. Some advanced ski school classes take groups to the outermost edges of the resort. There they practice tree and powder skiing, jumps and more. The Keystone Resort Cross Country Center offers telemark clinics daily for all ages and abilities, as well as rental equipment for that discipline. Classic and skate Nordic ski instruction and equipment are available as well. Full Moon Tours takes skiers to high points around the resort to view the full moon—part of Keystone's unique night-time ambience.

BEGINNERS

Keystone has three distinct ski areas spread over three mountains. Beginners are advised to head for Keystone Mountain, which caters especially to first-time skiers with a range of easy green and slightly more testing blue trails—and a reduced chance of being intimidated by more experienced skiers and riders. The front side of Keystone Mountain is best for beginners, including the Discovery Learning Area by the Mountain House Base Area, and the learning area at the top of Keystone Mountain. Beginners start on the Discovery slope but progress is swift from there onto the long and narrow Schoolmarm, or onto the next stage—the Flying Dutchman blue down the side of the mountain. The green (beginner) trails, on Keystone Mountain and North Peak, allow

LIFT TICKETS

US$32.50 per day Colorado Ticket interchangeable lift pass

Also valid for skiing at Vail, Beaver Creek, Arapahoe Basin, and Breckenridge.

Regular adult 6 to 9 days US$270

Value (junior & senior) and seasonal tickets available

RESTAURANTS

TOP END
KEYSTONE RANCH
ALPENGLOW STUBE
SKI TIP LODGE
THE GARDEN ROOM

CASUAL & FAMILY DINING
KEY STONE VILLAGE
BIG HORN STEAK HOUSE
PIZZA ON THE PLAZA
EDGEWATER CAFÉ & EXPRESS
IDA BELLE'S
THE INN AT KEYSTONE
RAZZBERRYS
RIVER RUN
GREAT NORTHERN TAVERN
INXPOT
KICKAPOO TAVERN
PAISANO'S
PIZZA ON THE RUN
STARBUCKS
FRITZ ALPINE BISTRO
MOUNTAIN HOUSE
ERNIE'S PIZZERIA
GASSY THOMPSON'S
J.B.'S JAVA HUT
MOUNTAIN HOUSE FOOD COURT

ON THE MOUNTAIN
LABONTE'S CABIN
KILLIAN'S PUB
SUMMIT HOUSE HIGH NOON CAFÉ
TIMBER RIDGE FOOD COURT
MILE HIGH PIZZA COMPANY
Call 970-496-4386 for reservations

▼ **BIG HORN**
Below South Bowls the long Big Horn trail offers a rush down to The Willows flattening out to the Outback Express lift.

beginners to enjoy the views from the River Run and Outpost gondolas and ski in different areas. Keystone's longest trail is three miles (5 km) and it is a beginner trail. Remember that this is high-altitude terrain and you could be susceptible both to chilly winds and headaches because of the thin air, which can make the learning experience uncomfortable.

INTERMEDIATES

Intermediates make up the majority of skiers in every resort and so it is here too. Improving skiers can test their legs and last year's skills on Keystone Mountain and then find good trails all around the area, notably on the North Peak which has five blue trails of varying character, with the Star Fire trail being the most demanding. It's pretty steep and right below the lift, so you need to look good! Another good trail is to take the River Run Gondola up Keystone Mountain and drop back to North Peak on Mozart trail. Then take the Santiago Express to the summit of North Peak and follow Spillway to Coyote Caper in The Outback. The Outback is even more challenging terrain with plenty of tree trails and steep groomers without the crowds. Lunch at the summit of North Peak is a must, so try the Outpost or the Alpenglow Stube for much more than a lunchtime pit stop.

ADVANCED & EXPERT

All three Keystone mountains have some challenging trails—there are six double black diamonds on the generally intermediate North Peak for example. However, the hardest skiing around

Keystone is on Outback Mountain, where the Black Forest has a number of steep, moguled trails, made yet harder by snowboarders. So make your way three mountains back to The Outback and play around in the Black Forest and the Outer Limits. Nothing beats the hiking terrain atop the Outback. The Outback Bowls (North and South) beckon with the toughest skiing—especially The Windows and The Black Forest. From the top of the Outback lift, off-piste skiers can ski across to these open, steep-sided bowls, well above the treeline, and just great after fresh snow. The South Bowls is best for powder.

BOARDING & FREESTYLE

Boarders first came here in '96–97. Freeriders head for the Outback Bowls and hike beyond to find good start-off points. Keystone has three terrain parks featuring more than 12 tables, 15 rails, and a halfpipe—reputed to be the best in Summit County. Keystone doesn't have long "catwalks" so it's relatively easy getting around the slopes. Keystone currently lacks an intermediate-level terrain park. However, as a family resort, Keystone has made a special effort to cater to teenage snowboarders with a 20-acre (8-ha) fun park in Area 51 with plenty of pipes and nighttime illumination. Otherwise snowboarders head for the Black Forest trails on Outback, or cruise happily down the steeper trails on Keystone Mountains or North Peak.

EATING ON THE MOUNTAIN

Fine dining and a family atmosphere do not always sit easily together but Keystone manages to cater to both. To go upscale, take the gondola to the Alpenglow Stube mountain restaurant, which claims to have the best haute cuisine of any ski resort in North America—it stands at 11,444 feet (3,488 m) so

one hopes the "haute" is not a pun. The Wild Boar is recommended and the wine list extensive. Another restaurant requiring transport is the Soda Creek Homestead, reached by horse-drawn sleigh, but for a really reliable gourmet evening try the Ski Tip Lodge or the Keystone Ranch—both highly rated by regular customers. You can eat very well indeed in and around Keystone—and, as a final tip, try the steaks at the Keystone Lodge. Keystone has four mountain restaurants: two cafeterias, one gourmet dining, and one BBQ. At night, one of the cafeterias converts to the Der Fondue Chessel, a Bavarian-style fondue restaurant complete with raclette, live music, dancing, and lots of food.

APRÈS SKI

The Vail area offers a wide variety of nightlife from the upscale to the downhome and Keystone, to be perfectly frank, does not cater to ravers. This is really a resort for families and that tones down the wilder spirits. On the other hand, look at the facilities. Night skiing until 9:00 PM, sleigh rides, ice skating, snowmobiling and tennis. Of the 20 bars in the resort, the Goat is the locals' hangout for all ages; Kickapoo Tavern attracts the 25–35 group, as it's close to the slopes and is a good place to see and be seen; Ski Tip has high-end cocktails in a cozy, romantic setting, for mostly 35+. Out of Bounds is the "sports bar" at Keystone and twentysomethings go there to catch their favorite games. LaBonte's Cabin is another place to seek Keystone's après-ski vibe. Liquor and licensing laws are strict in Colorado with no open containers except at restaurants and in designated events/locations, and a minimum age for consuming alcohol of 21. However, children can accompany parents in bars and other places serving alcohol and there are no closing time restrictions.

There are 35 restaurants in the resort catering mainly to families. They range from Out of Bounds, a sports bar with appetizers and burgers, and Gassy Thompson's with BBQs for the budget-minded, through to Garden Room, serving fresh seafood and steaks, Bighorn for mid-wallet spenders looking for prime rib and salad bar, and the aforementioned Ski Tip, Keystone Ranch, and Alpenglow Stube for more pricey meals. The Ranch has been voted Colorado's Number One restaurant in a recent Denver/Salt Lake City Zagat Survey.

There are three nightclubs: Out of Bounds, Snake River Saloon, and RazzBerrys, all with live music of different kinds, drink specials, and a cool night scene.

OTHER ACTIVITIES

Keystone's non-skiing key ingredient is its Mountain Passport (free with your stay), which is good for more than a dozen free activities at Keystone Resort and is worth up to US$300. During the ski season you can try the outdoor ice skating and hockey rink, Cross Country Center (including skate, classic, and snowshoe trails,) Discovery Tubing Hill, fitness center and pool, indoor tennis courts, sledding hill, and jogging trail. For non-skiers there's ice skating, tubing, gym workouts, sledding, tennis, swimming, horse-drawn sleigh rides, wine tasting, yoga, snowshoeing, Nordic skiing, spa services, shopping, fly fishing, hockey clinics, Living in Wellness lecture series, and a wine appreciation seminar. Many, but not all, of these activities are free with the Keystone Mountain Passport. Most of the stores are in River Run Plaza or Keystone Village and offer everything from handmade jewelry to luxury coffees and fine wines. To rent or buy ski equipment check out Specialty Sports in River Run, and the Mountain House.

USEFUL PHONE NUMBERS

Tourist Information Center	800-427-8308
Accommodation Reservation Center	970-496-4242
Restaurant Bookings	970-496-4386
Children's Center Reservations	970-496-4181
Medical Center	970-496-4000
Bus Service	970-496-4000
Ski Rescue Service	970-496-4000
Snow Report	970-496-4111

USEFUL WEBSITES

Official Website	www.keystoneresort.com
Vacation Planner	www.summitnet.com
Interactive Resort Map	http://keystone.snow.com/info/rst.map.asp
Snow Report & Web Cams	http://keystone.snow.com/sr.report.asp

◄ **BOARDER POSSIBILITIES**
Banned until 1996-97, boarders are now a big part of the Keystone scene—not least with the Jackwhaker terrain park and one of best half-pipes in Summit County and no long "catwalks" so it's easy to get around.

BARS

- THE GOAT SOUP & WHISKY
- GREAT NORTHERN TAVERN
- IDA BELLE'S
- KICKAPOO TAVERN
- LAST LIFT BAR
- MI CASA
- OUT OF BOUNDS
- RAZZBERRYS
- SNAKE RIVER SALOON
- TENDERFOOT LOUNGE
- SKI TIP

▲ **RIVER RUN**
The River Base Area and Day Lodge has lockers, seating, vending machines and snacks and is open from 8 AM to 8.30 PM.

COPPER HAS AN INCREDIBLE MOUNTAIN LAYOUT, IN WHICH ALL THE BEGINNER, INTERMEDIATE AND EXPERT SKIING TRAILS ARE SEPARATED NATURALLY INTO THREE DISTINCT ON-SLOPE SKI AREAS. ABOVE THE TREE-LINE, THERE'S EXCELLENT SKIING INCLUDING SOME OF THE BEST OFF-PISTE IN COLORADO, AND A MUCH-IMPROVED NEW VILLAGE.

COPPER MOUNTAIN

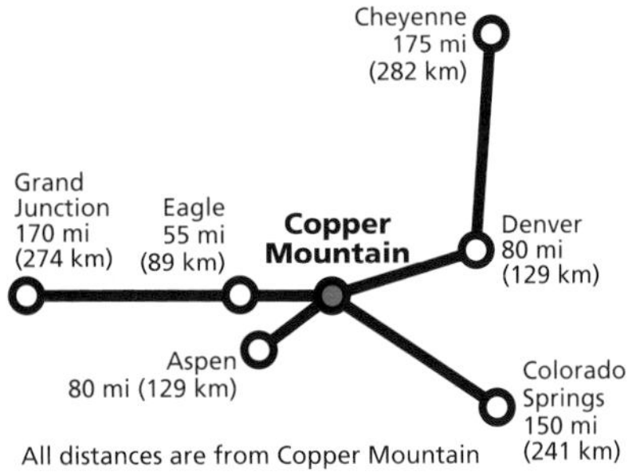

All distances are from Copper Mountain

Copper Mountain, Summit County's largest and least crowded ski resort, is located in the heart of Summit County, Colorado. Consistently ranking in the top five for "accessibility" in the yearly polls, Copper Mountain boasts the convenience of a simple 90-mile (144-km) drive from Denver International Airport and right off Interstate-70 at exit 195. Copper also enjoys the strategic location of being just west of the 10 Mile Range, as storms tend to roll in and get stopped by the ensuing range, dropping ample amounts of the legendary Colorado White. Copper boasts 280 inches (710 cm) annual snowfall, and a base elevation of 9,712 feet (2,960 m) allows for superior snowmaking. It also allows some of the best early and late season snow in any North American ski area.

GETTING THERE

Copper somehow manages to combine that desired "getting away from it all" location with an "easy to reach" destination. Denver International Airport is located virtually due east, by road about one to two hours away. Frisco is the nearest town, located five miles (8 km) away, and there is a free shuttle service—the Summit Stage—connecting Copper Mountain by a short drive to the nearby resorts, like Keystone, Arapahoe Basin, and Breckenridge, as well as a free local shuttle bus

► **VIBRANT VILLAGE**
True to the Intrawest way, Copper Mountain Village is a high-energy gathering place at the base of Summit Mountain's largest but least crowded resort.

MOUNTAIN FACTS

Base	9,712 feet (2,960 m)
Summit	12,313 feet (3,753 m)
Elevation	2,601 feet (793 m)
Easy	21%
Intermediate	25%
Advanced	36%
Expert	18%
Longest trail	2.8 miles (4.5 km)
Ski area	2,433 acres (985 ha)

SNOWFALL

Annual snowfall	280 inches (710 cm)
Snowmaking	380 acres (153 ha)

SKI LIFTS

Gondolas	-
High -Speed Chairs	1
Quad Chairs	4
Triple Chairs	5
Double Chairs	5
Surface Lifts	6
Total	21
Riders per hour	30,630

SKI SEASON
Early November to late April

within the resort. The ski resorts of Vail, Steamboat and Winter Park are within one to two hours' drive.

THE VILLAGE

While Copper certainly stands today on its own as a world-class ski resort, it would be fair to say that Copper Mountain used to sit somewhat in the shadow of its more illustrious Summit County cousins, like Breckenridge; but that changed when Intrawest Corporation (owners of Whistler-Blackcomb, among other A-list resorts) pumped money into on-slope improvements, but above all Intrawest was quick to fix upon one badly-needed element in the resort—a village.

When Intrawest acquired Copper in 1997, some of the first improvements were on-mountain, although the mountain itself was nearly perfect to begin with. The Super Bee, Colorado's first high-speed six-passenger chairlift, was installed in the East village, and Copper expanded its expert bowl skiing to the limits of Tucker Mountain. The pedestrian-only village at Copper, however, truly represents the renaissance of Copper Mountain. US$400 million later, Copper boasts the finest in mountain villages complete with heated walkways connecting dining, shopping, nightlife, après ski, activities, and events.

Parking is all underground with easily accessed lifts to the buildings and units—a neat and aesthetic touch to keep the cars out of sight and the village free for strolling in. Every attention to detail, such as the movement of the sun and "gathering places," has been taken into consideration, and it truly makes for a world-class village just steps away from the lifts.

A short bus ride, ski, or walk away is the East Village, sporting Copper Springs Lodge as its majestic flagship lodge. Located on the expert side of the mountain, the East Village also plays host to après-ski legend Moe Dixon at JJ's Rocky Mountain Tavern, just a few steps from the Super Bee lift.

The last stage of the village involves the Lake Buildings, which will feature shops, restaurants and bars surrounding the West Lake ice skating/boating area. New après ski venues will include Pravda (a Russian vodka bar) and Larkin's Cross Irish pub.

An expanded beginner learning area will debut on the west side of the mountain adjacent to Union Creek, and the expert skier can look for new expansions to the back bowl area of Copper's Tucker Mountain area—adding expert terrain to the already challenging area. No confirmed details are available as yet.

ACCOMMODATIONS

All of the lodgings are slopeside or just steps to the free transportation system to take you right to any of the three base areas. Copper Mountain operates the entire bed base at the foot of the mountain, and there are accommodations for every need and every budget. Throughout Copper, there are over 880 units to rent from the rental pool.

NEARBY RESORTS

ACCOMMODATIONS

Reservations:
509 Copper Road,
Copper Mountain,
CO 80443
www.coppercolorado.com
866-837-2994
cmwholesale@coppercolorado.com

Copper Mountain resort operates the entire bed base at the foot of the mountain, with a good range of accommodations.

Copper's rental pool features hotel rooms, studios, one-, two-, and three-bedroom condominiums as well as four-, five-, and six-bedroom houses. You can chose from two villages, The East Village and The Village at Copper—each with two levels of lodgings—Premium lodging units represent the finest in accommodations, and are strategically located throughout the Village allowing convenient access to the Resort's activities. Included are a private fitness room, outdoor spa, a game room and heated underground parking in the buildings. The rooms offer a large soaker tub, gas fireplaces, cable T.V., V.C.R., and full kitchens in condo units. Deluxe units are well designed for comfort, and aim to meet every lodger's need. Located mountainside or within yards of the complimentary shuttle system, they remain some of the most requested and valued guest units.

SKI AREA

The mountain's wooded slopes are neatly "zoned" with all the beginner trails located on the west side of the mountain (right on the piste map), all the intermediate trails in the center, and the advanced and expert skiing on the East side and up and over to the backside bowls. This creates many positive scenarios. Beginner skiers have their own area and don't have to worry about taking a wrong turn onto a difficult trail, while the expert skier doesn't need to worry about a beginner traversing across an advanced trail. In short, you have your level and you go to the part of the mountain groomed for your ability.

The trails are graded green for beginner, blue for intermediate, black-diamond for advanced, double black diamond for expert and break down to 21 percent beginner, 25 percent intermediate, 36 percent advanced, and 18 percent expert ski trails. The longest trail is 2.8 miles (4.5 km). The highest lift- serviced point is 12,313 feet (3,753 m), but you can hike up to 12,337 feet (3,760 m), and the maximum vertical descent is 2,625 feet (800 m).

Copper has over 380 acres (153 ha) of snow-making capacity, and at a base elevation of 9,712 feet (2,960 m) the quality is superb. So, while Copper has a season spanning from early November to late April, the higher elevation and impressive snowmaking capabilities ensure quality snow from

▼ COZY CONDOS
At the foot of the mountain there is a full range of non-budget accommodations including steam-baths, saunas, and pool.

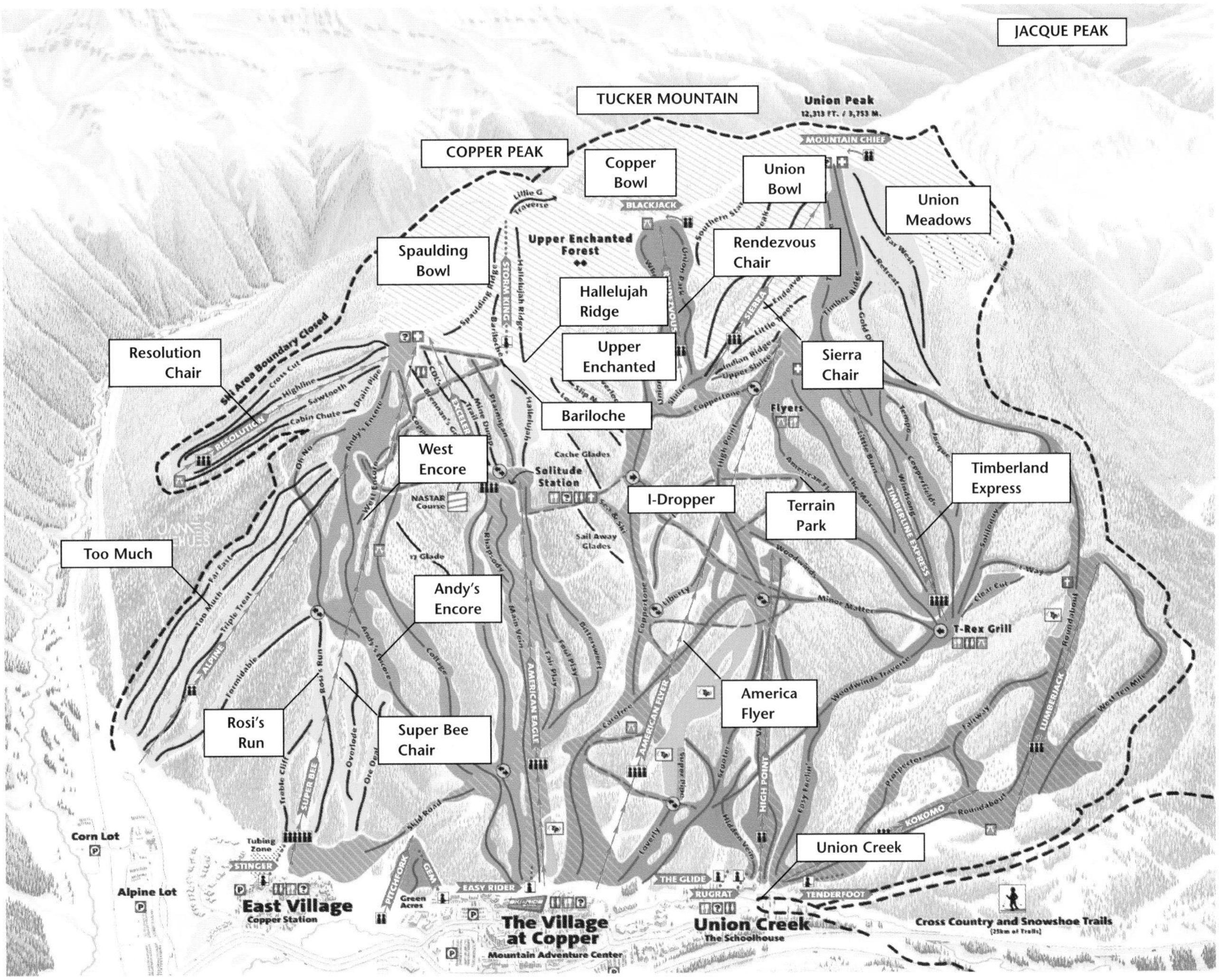

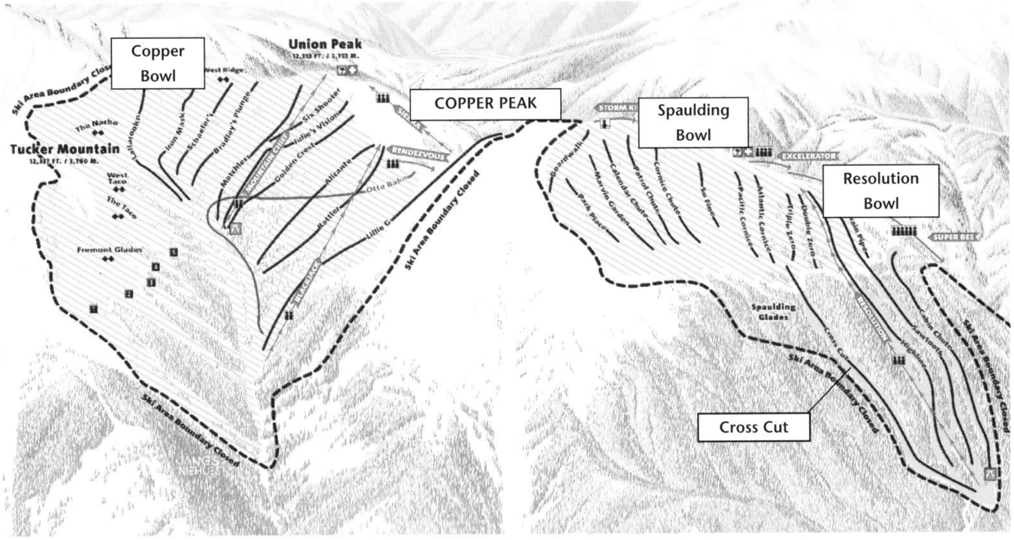

start to finish. For skiing lasting into the summer, neighboring Arapahoe Basin has received extended snowmaking privileges, and is considering year-round skiing.

With 2,433 acres (984 ha) to play around in, Copper is a family oriented resort that's growing to accommodate even the most diehard skier and party-goer. Therefore, given the mix of skiers on the hill, safety is taken seriously. Copper has "slow skiing zones" for areas of high traffic, and "family skiing zones" dedicated to wide open cruising. "Speed Control" volunteers are in place on heavily skied trails, and Copper Ski Patrol does an exceptional job of marking natural hazards on the mountain.

EQUIPMENT RENTAL

Eleven of Copper's stores offer gear for skiing, boarding and/or telemarking. In The Village at Copper, try The Mountain Adventure Center for all ski gear needs, or The Fall Line for telemark gear, SureFoot for ski gear, Polar Revolution for all gear and 9,600 Feet also for all gear needs. In The East Village, Wheeler General store has gear for all, and in Union Creek, Union Creek Rentals & The Schoolhouse offer equipment for all.

▲ RENTALS
Friendly staff, great snowboard choice and some insiders' tips are available at Dr Stone's Tune Shop at Copper Station.

SKI SCHOOL

Copper Ski & Snowboard School
www.coppercolorado.com
1-888-229-9475 or within Copper x4info.

SKI LIFTS

Copper's lift system moves skiers in a very efficient manner. The naturally divided terrain and the general layout of the mountain create a perfect situation to move about the ski trails. Families can actually take the same lift in the middle of the mountain, choose from greens, blues, or blacks, and meet at the bottom of the same lift to take it up once again. Experts can escape to the east side of the mountain and ski the lifts with experts, while beginners can start on the west side of the mountain and ride the extensive system to entirely beginner terrain.

All in all you'll find six surface lifts, 15 chairlifts, and Colorado's first high-speed six-passenger chairlift, the Super Bee, carrying 30,630 people per hour. The Super Bee reduced a 22-minute, two-lift ride from bottom to top to the current eight minutes. The first lift opens at 8:30 AM on weekends and 9:00 AM on weekdays. However, if lift tickets are booked in conjunction with lodgings, prior to arrival, the BeeLine Advantage Lift Ticket will allow skiers access to the mountain 15 minutes before the general public. Lifts shut at 3:30 PM on the upper slopes and 4:00 PM on the lower. Lift lines are not a problem during the week; on the weekends during high season, waiting time can be up to 12 minutes.

SKI PASSES

For the 2002/03 ski season, standard adult (ages 14–59) day ticket rates are US$39 up to November 28, rising to US$61 between November 29 and March 30, and falling back to US$34 from March 31 until the season ends around April 20.

Children aged five and under, and adults 70 and over ski free at Copper every day. Advanced purchase is not necessary for these groups. You simply come to the Copper ticket window (and present I.D. if 70 or over) to get your free lift ticket. There are special four-day deals that involve 14-day advanced Internet bookings for US$109–US$119 depending on the season (US$49 for a child). The four days of skiing must be used within a seven-day period. Beginners should be aware that they can ski free on the Kokomo and Lumberjack lifts— no photo I.D. required.

The BeeLine Advantage Lift Ticket surpasses the latest hi-tech chip technology. A dedicated lift line allows BeeLine lift pass holders the opportunity to bypass the regular line and enter a subway-style gate, without even taking out their pass, and load the chair through their own lift lane. It's available when you are a lodgings guest of Copper, and is quite a perk, allowing access to the mountain 15 minutes early, as well as express lines for equipment rentals.

You can buy lift tickets in many places: at the time of booking through Copper's Central Reservations, through a wholesale/tour operator, on-site at time of skiing, off-site at many stores throughout Summit County, or in Denver at partnered establishments.

SKI SCHOOLS AND GUIDING

Copper has one major Ski & Snowboard School that can accommodate all skier and boarder types. The schools are located at each base area, The East Village, The Village at Copper, and Union Creek.

Classes begin at 9:00 AM and go on until 3:30 PM, with variable start times depending on the type of class. The largest group lesson is eight skiers. If you have young children remember that three years old is the minimum age for junior ski school, but the Belly Button childcare facility offers kindergarten for children from two months to three years. All children's classes include lunch, and are of course supervised.

The Copper Ski & Snowboard School caters to freeriders and offers snowboarding sessions, women's clinics, telemark clinics, and race clinics. For more information search the Copper Mountain website www.coppercolorado.com or call 888-229-9475. Mountain tours with a guide are available daily.

BEGINNERS

Copper's naturally divided terrain lends the west side of the mountain to beginners of all sorts and the best areas for beginners is the west village, Union Creek learning center. Gentle, uncrowded slopes make a perfect unintimidating learning scene. There are family ski zones, wide trails for cruising, and slow skiing zones, patrolled for speeders, and quite often an intermediate trail is only a turn away—perfect for groups of varying abilities. The 9,712-foot (2,960-m) base elevation ensures optimal conditions throughout the winter season. While Copper extends an entire beginner area within the Union Creek section, beginners can also head to the top of the mountain, on Rendezvous lift, to experience the breathtaking views from atop the 10 Mile Range, while still enjoying very gentle slopes.

INTERMEDIATES

With 25 percent of the trails, intermediates are spoiled for choice. Copper's most challenging trail for the intermediate skier is undoubtedly Andy's Encore, off the Super Bee lift, with a finish onto Rosi's Run, also under the Super Bee Lift. For a classic Copper ski experience, ride up the American Flyer and drop into the trails under the Timberline Express lift where you'll find groomers and

ALL THAT GLISTENS IS NOT COPPER
There's plenty of sunshine at Copper Mountain but as many of the slopes are north-facing, the snow lingers for longer. For backcountry skiers and boarders there are some serious full-day options.

RESTAURANTS

T-REX GRILL
SOLITUDE STATION
THE MILL CAFÉ

BARS

THE FOGGY GOOGLE
ADRENALINE CAFÉ
THE SWIVEL
INDIAN MOTORCYCLE
JJ'S ROCKY MOUNTAIN

intermediate bump trails. Or check out I-Dropper, bumps that'll make you feel like a pro. If you ready to take the next step to black, head east to test out your skills on West Encore.

ADVANCED & EXPERT

Above the treeline, Copper Mountain's east side boasts some of the best off-piste skiing in Colorado. Up top on Resolution and Spaulding Bowl, in back for Copper Bowl and Tucker Mountain, and Sierra lift and Union Bowl in the middle, up top. If you want tougher skiing, for moguls try Resolution Bowl; for steep and deep go to Spaulding Bowl or Tucker Mountain, or Union Bowl; and for couloirs it's Spaulding Bowl. For those seeking the best powder, head off to Tucker Mountain or Graveline Gulch. The upper mountain and east side are home to much of Copper's expert terrain. Hallelujah Ridge, Bariloche, and Cross Cut are great trails for that transition from blue to black. If you seek marathon bumps, ride the Alpine chair and find out how "Too Much" got its name.

Check out 17 Glade of Upper Enchanted for trees, then head to Spaulding Bowl for steeps and cornice drops. Resolution Bowl is great for endless bumps. Excellent hiking terrain can be found in Union Bowl and on Tucker Mountain accessed from Copper Bowl, which has classic bowl terrain. Go west to Union Meadows for a different type of on-mountain adventure. The ski patrol runs free—and heated—snowcats up a gulch to the ridge of Tucker Mountain.

Experts can ski tour or snowshoe to Janet's Cabin for the day or an overnight trip. Janet's Cabin is a 10th mountain division backcountry hut. Copper takes its skiing very seriously, and the free snowcat ride up to Tucker Mountain for an "inbounds/ backcountry" experience is not to be missed. Other challenging possibilities might be the knee-pounding bumps of Resolution Bowl, the Steeps of Patrol, and Cornice Chutes, or even the new-school spins in the Terrain Park. With 18 percent of the mountain labeled as expert, there are no shortages of trails to stretch your skills.

▶ GRAVELINE GULCH
An out-of-bounds bowl with tree skiing—what more could the expert skier want? And there's a patrolled entry gate and free van pickup.

Under Colorado law, skiing or entering any trail or area marked by a closed sign is not allowed, nor is entering land adjacent to the well-marked ski area. Graveline Gulch, described below, is the one legal exception to this rule for expert skiers. Graveline Gulch is out of the ski area boundary but has a patrolled entry gate where expert skiers can enter and ski a steep bowl into wide glades. A ski patrol will check you out and you ski a backcountry trail all the way down to a free shuttle on Highway 91, that will be waiting to give you a short ride back to the lifts at the East Village.

BOARDING & FREESTYLE

Snowboarders can head west to Loverly for Copper's newly redesigned Terrain Park and Super Pipe. There are three lanes in the Terrain Park ranging from beginner to intermediate to expert with jumps to suit all levels. In addition there is a hip jump in each lane and a variety of new rails—including the new roller coaster S and the famous 100-footer—and the 400-foot (122-m) long Super Pipe with 15-foot (4.5-m) walls. Or check out the halfpipe on lower Carefree.

Copper Bowl, Resolution Bowl, and Spaulding Bowl beckon freeriders and Copper has bigger, wider trails to suit carvers. However, one drawback is the lack of serious steeps, which can bog the rider down on deep powder days.

EATING ON THE MOUNTAIN

There is a limited choice available. The main place to eat on the mountain is Solitude Station's fast-food eatery serving breakfast and lunch with the best views around. Solitude offers panini sandwiches, homemade pizzas, fresh sandwiches, burgers, soups, chili, salads and delicious vegetarian food. Quick and easy refreshment is on tap with a combination of outdoor grills and decks, and self-serve pizza, wraps, and sandwich stations. Coffee shops serve espresso, hot chocolate, bagels and pastries. T-Rex Grill, located on prime intermediate terrain, has a deck that soaks up the sun and serves up Brontosaurus burgers, Dino fries, snacks, beer and wine. The Mill Café is a perfect family stop, located in Union Creek, and it features great soups, chili, salads, BBQ pork, burgers, beer and wine.

APRÈS SKI

Jack's Slopeside Grill features The Foggy Goggle for après ski on a great deck where you can watch

weary skiers come down from the mountain. Endo's Adrenaline Café is a high-energy, high-alpine restaurant and bar for the younger crowd, with outdoor seating, right in the middle of the village at Copper.

The Swivel serves up beer and margaritas right at the base of the American Eagle lift. Sharing the same centrality is the Indian Motorcycle Café & Lounge boasting 21 beers on tap and fantastic lounging opportunities both outside—seated on the deck—or inside on leather loungers near the pool tables. It's a little higher end and the bar is accompanied by tasty American-style cuisine.

In The East Village, the only place to be for après ski is JJ's Rocky Mountain Tavern. JJ's offers comfortable mountain cuisine, and features Colorado's longest bar with acoustic guitarist Moe Dixon to keep you dancing and singing as he jams along. There's an open and lively atmosphere here appealing to all ages, with live music most days for après ski. The appetizers are great. And that's not all: Copper has an excellent tubing facility that goes well into the evening, with ample lighting, and the end of the tubing run conveniently finishes right at JJ's Rocky Mountain Tavern.

Licensing laws mean a minimum age of 21 for consuming alcohol, though children may accompany parents in bars and other places serving alcohol. Bars close at 2:00 AM. There are 21 restaurants in the resort. Indian Motorcycle Café offers fine dining in a cosmopolitan atmosphere; Endo's Adrenaline Café, as its name suggests, is for the high-energy crowd; Maui Taco for the boarder crowd, Columbine Café for homestyle breakfasts and lunches.

OTHER ACTIVITIES

Aside from skiing and boarding, there is also ice skating, tubing, snowshoeing, 15 miles (25 km) of cross-country skiing in the White River Forest, snowmobiling and sleigh rides. Copper boasts 22 retail stores, selling varied goods from fly fishing gear through to chocolate. The Copper Mountain Racquet & Athletic Club has excellent facilities including an indoor pool, indoor tennis and racquetball courts.

USEFUL PHONE NUMBERS

Tourist Information Center	970-968-6477
Accommodations Reservation Center	970-968-6227
Copper Mountain Medical Center	970-968-2330
Summit County Bus Service	970-668-0999

USEFUL WEBSITES

Official Website	www.coppercolorado.com
Snow Report & Web Cams	www.rsn.com/cams/copper
Weather Reports	www.wunderground.com
Vacation Planner	www.summitnet.com/copper

▲ **SCENIC DELIGHT**
For freeriders Copper Bowl is a prime spot on a powder day. You may need to hike for 15 to 30 minutes, but after that the lure—and the vistas — are irresistible. Spaulding Bowl and Resolution Bowl also have great hike skiing possibilities if you should ever get bored.

BRECKENRIDGE HAS A MORE CASUAL ATMOSPHERE THAN ITS LIVELIER SISTER RESORT, VAIL, BUT IT BOASTS AN EQUALLY STUNNING LANDSCAPE: A BACKDROP OF FOUR PEAKS—CRISSCROSSED BY BEAUTIFULLY GROOMED TRAILS. THE AREA IS STEEPED IN GOLD-MINING LORE, BUT DON'T BE FOOLED BY THE QUAINT ATMOSPHERE.

BRECKENRIDGE

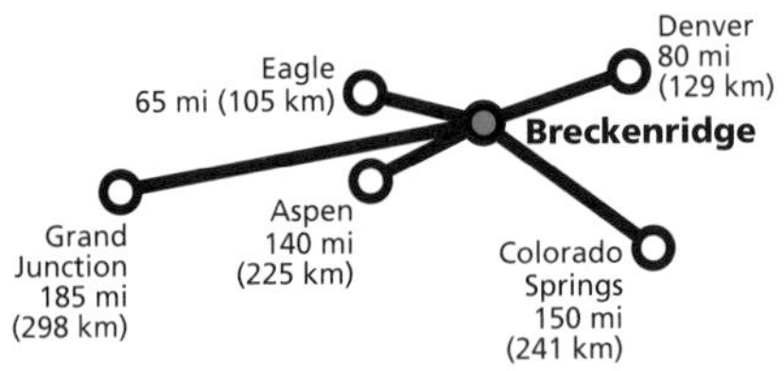

Long before the ski industry came, Breckenridge and Summit County pulsed with mining labor. Gold was discovered in August 1859 and prospector Tom Groves, who claimed the largest single gold nugget ever found in Colorado, now has a trail—Tom's Baby—named after him and his precious find. Years of mining did more than build the county's character; time and the miners changed the face of the land. Summit County is still pockmarked with mines and remains rich in frontier history and folklore. Breckenridge has some claims in skiing history too, as it was the first resort in Colorado to permit snowboarders and the first in the world to install a high-speed detachable quad chair lift. It also witnessed the first wave of overseas skiers, notably the Brits in the 1980s, and some 10 percent of visitors still arrive from overseas. But the largest influx is caused by the weekenders from Denver.

GETTING THERE

Breckenridge is located in north central Colorado in the heart of the Rocky Mountains, 80 miles (129 km) west of Denver, on Colorado State Highway 9. Breckenridge is less than 20 miles (32 km) from Summit County's other ski resorts—Beaver Creek, Keystone, and Arapahoe Basin—and 34 miles (55 km) from Vail to the west. Together, all of these "Vail Resorts" as they are termed are linked by an interchangeable lift ticket. Denver International Airport is 104 miles (166 km) west, or about two hours by road. As with other Colorado resorts there are no rail links.

THE VILLAGE

The town has real Wild West roots and is 100 years older than Vail—the town's pastel-painted weatherboard buildings reflect this. It was formally created in the 1860s as miners flocked to the area in search of gold. World War II officially ended the mining era but in December of 1961 the

◄ AMERICAN ALPINE
Breckenridge's skiing is pretty high by Alpine standard, with plenty of scope above 12,000 feet (3,660 m). Be wary of possible altitude sickness.

Breckenridge Ski Area opened for business. Today, the Town serves as the county seat and in 1981, the Secretary of the Interior designated the greatest concentration of the Town's historic structures a National Register Historic District in Colorado. But it is the people rather than the public buildings that make Breckenridge such a welcoming place. There is a thriving local community and you'll feel the welcome as you are strolling along the streets or sampling the cafés and coffee houses.

ACCOMMODATIONS

Breckenridge has many types of lodgings available including bed and breakfasts, hotels and condos, private homes and chalet homes. Nearly a third of the area's 20,000 beds are ski-in, ski-out. The best way to enquire or book is online with the Breckenridge Resort Chambers (B.R.C.) Central Reservations at www.gobreck.com. The B.R.C. system holds more than 90 percent of the lodging beds in town. Phone 800-221-1091 in North America or 800-89-7491 if calling from the U.K.

For upscale accommodations in the US$200 to US$375 per night bracket, try The Village at Breckenridge (800-800-7829; 453-2000) with its on-site health club facilities, indoor/outdoor pools, hot tubs, racquetball, steam, sauna and exercise room. It surrounds the Peak 9 base area and is located next to the Quicksilver Super-Six chair. Also at the top end is The Great Divide Lodge (800-321-8444; 453-4500). New owners Vail Resorts poured $4 million into remodeling the guestrooms, lobby and pool area, and it's only 50 yards (45 m) from the slopes.

For those on a tighter budget the Breckenridge Mountain Lodge offers a rough, log cabin exterior with warm, Wild West hospitality inside from US$100 a night. Located at the south end of Main Street, it's just a couple of minutes from the ski lifts and rentals. There are also budget accommodations options, and other good-value deals to be had at www.skivillagelodging.com for as many as six people squeezing into a two-bedroom condo.

MOUNTAIN FACTS

Base	9,600 feet (2,926 m)
Summit	12,998 feet (3,963 m)
Elevation	3,398 feet (1,036 m)
Easy	13%
Intermediate	32%
Advanced/Expert	55%
Number of trails	146
Longest trail	3.5 miles (5.6 km)
Ski area	2,208 acres (894 ha)

SNOWFALL

Annual snowfall	300 inches (761 cm)
Snowmaking	560 acres (227 ha)

SKI LIFTS

Gondolas	-
High Speed Six-Passenger	2
High Speed Quads	6
Fixed Grip Quads	-
Triple Chairs	1
Double Chairs	6
Surface Lifts	5
Magic Carpets	7
Total	27
Riders per hour	36,880

SKI SEASON
Mid November to mid April

▼ THRILLS 'N' SPILLS
There are ample chutes above tree line offering steep and deep thrills for skiers and boarders alike.

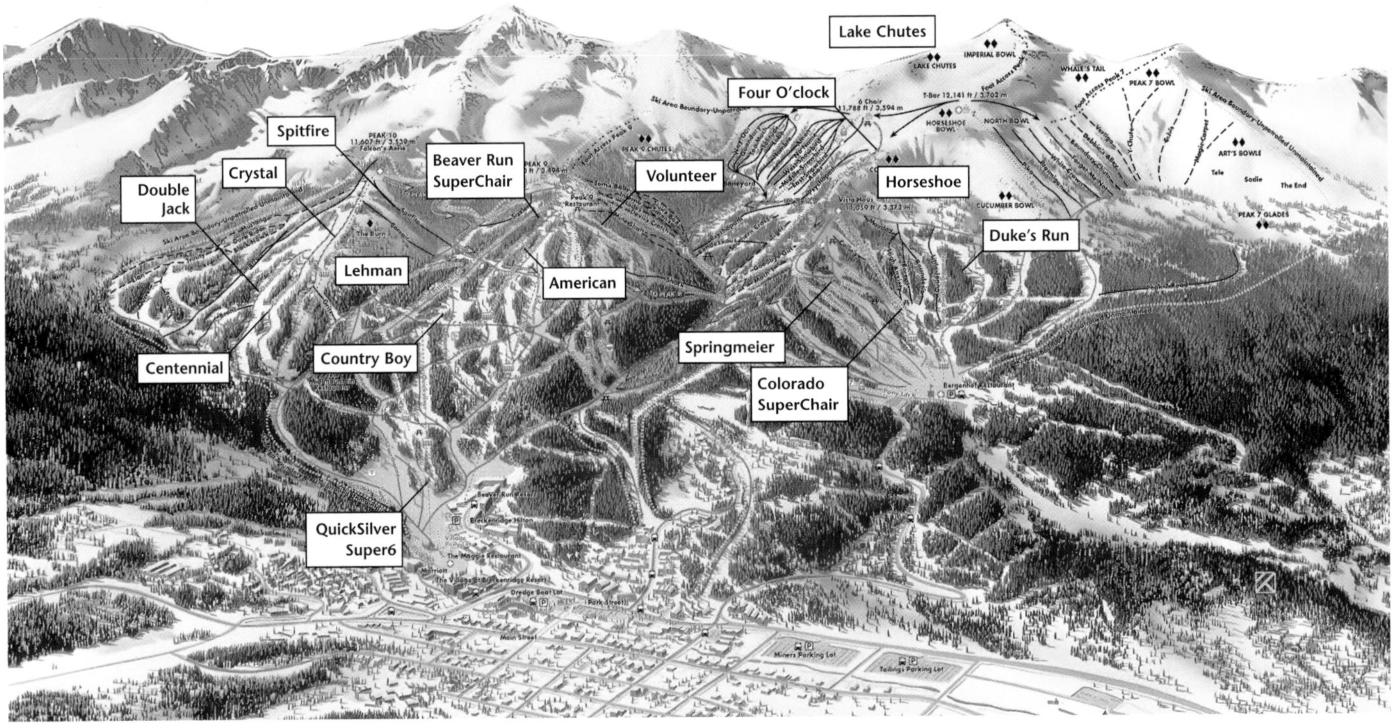

NEARBY RESORTS

▼ LAKE CHUTES
When conditions allow, the Lake Chutes area offers 20 acres (8 ha) of near vertical off-piste pitches.

SKI AREA

With 2,208 acres (894 ha) of skiing spread across four interconnected mountains (Peaks 7, 8, 9, and 10), the skiing at Breckenridge is exceptional and exciting for every level of skier and boarder. Artificial snowmaking includes 380 snowmaking guns covering 560 acres (227 ha)—27 percent of the mountain.

Peak 7 made its debut for the 2002/03 season, opening up 165 acres (66 ha) of intermediate terrain and seven new trails, and although it has been "tamed" there are still the ungroomed areas of Peak 7 to attract hardcore skiers. Peak 10 is by consensus the toughest, and Peak 9 the easiest of the other mountains, while Peak 8 is a bit of everything. The town and the ski area base are both at 9,600 feet (2,926 m) above sea level. The highest lift-serviced point is at 12,142 feet (3,703 m).

There are 24 green beginner trails, 38 blue intermediate trails, and 74 black and double black diamond trails for advanced and experts. If you're concerned about safety, you can be assured of a safe skiing and riding experience at this resort: Breckenridge Ski Patrol monitors each run every morning to check for safety hazards that may exist. All manmade objects are padded to specification and/or marked with bamboo, rope and flagging for visibility.

The ski area also includes world-renowned terrain parks and halfpipes, and to accommodate new trails and a new terrain park, the Breckenridge grooming fleet got three additional snowcats and new pipe-grooming implements.

SKI LIFTS

Breckenridge offers two base areas with interconnecting lifts. Peak 8 has two high-speed quads, accessible from the base, that connect with other lifts servicing higher terrain. These are the Colorado SuperChair and the Rocky Mountain SuperChair. Beginner lifts are chair 7 and chair 5 starting from the base area on Peak 8. These are double chairs. Peak 9 has the Beaver Run Super Chair at the base of Beaver Run, which accesses intermediate terrain. The QuickSilver Super6 passenger chair leaves from The Village area at the base of Peak 9 and serves beginner terrain. It also accesses several other on-mountain lifts including the more advanced Peak 10 Falcon Lift.

Simplifying the transfer between mountains is the new Peak 8 SuperConnect high-speed quad that replaces the old Chair 4. While skiers and riders will not be able to access the chair from the base area of Peak 9, a quick ride up the Beaver Run SuperChair or QuickSilver Super6 accesses the new lift and whisks riders to Peak 8, terminating near the (recently renovated) Vista Haus restaurant. The two-lift ride now takes 13 minutes instead of the former 30-minute, three-lift ride. The SnowFlake Lift also takes skiers and riders from Four O'Clock road on Peak 9 to Peak 8. Additionally, the new high-speed six-passenger Independence SuperChair on Peak 7 will take skiers from bottom to top in seven minutes and opens up 165 acres (66 ha) of intermediate terrain (that is to say, 30 percent more) including seven new trails and the famous Peak 7 glades.

The QuickSilver SuperChair on Peak 9 was upgraded to a six-passenger chair for the 2000/01 ski season and it accesses beginner terrain. There will also be a new gondola, whose base area begins in the town and whisks skiers and riders to the base of Peak 7, and continues to the base of Peak 8 for easier access to the mountain.

LIFT PASSES

Lift tickets are interchangeable between Keystone and Arapahoe Basin, and one day out of a three-day pass is good at Vail. Expect to pay around US$60 a day for a lift pass, and US$27 a day for children aged 5–12. There are no special ski pass deals. Lift passes can be bought at all lift ticket windows located at the base of Peaks 8 and 9, as well as online at www.breckenridge.com.

Rush hour on the lift lines is usually 10:30 AM and 1:30 PM but you can beat the lines by starting first thing in the morning at 8:30 AM, and at lunch time, at around 12:00 noon. Intermediates can use the Beaver Run Chair on Peak 9 and the Rocky Mountain Chair on Peak 8, which are usually less crowded.

SKI SCHOOL AND GUIDING

The Breckenridge Ski and Ride School has offices at the base of Peak 8, at the Village at Peak 9, and the Beaver Run Ticket office at the base of Beaver Run on Peak 9. Average group class size is seven. For kids, the minimum age is three. The free two-hour Mountain Orientation tours depart daily at 9:30 AM from the base of the Colorado SuperChair on Peak 8, and from the base of the Beaver Run SuperChair on Peak 9. Tours are open to skiers and riders with intermediate ability and above. Breckenridge Ski and Ride School also offers telemark on Saturdays.

BEGINNERS

Remember that Breckenridge is high—even the bottom station stands at 9,600 feet (2,926 m) and the top soars to 12,998 feet (3,963 m), so beware of breathlessness and don't attempt too much until you are acclimatized. You may pant a bit at first but you will live.

Breckenridge offers several trails designed for those who prefer to ski at a slower speed. Bonanza is the designated slow skiing trail on Peak 9, with Springmeier on Peak 8. These runs are patrolled and monitored by Ski Patrol and Guest Service staff. The resort's reputation as one of the best in the country for beginners was enhanced two seasons ago with the addition of the high-speed QuickSilver Super6, the country's highest-capacity chairlift. This lift serves hundreds of acres of exclusively beginner terrain and its double-loading configuration allows beginners ample time to load comfortably. The wide-open, gentle beginner terrain aims to instill confidence and increase enjoyment for all novice skiers and riders.

INTERMEDIATES

To begin with, try starting off with Peak 9 which offers open cruising all the way from the 11,460-foot (3,725 m) top, right down to the bottom. After a few runs up there you can move on to other slopes—there are plenty to choose from—and the new intermediate runs and glades on Peak 7. Two favorites for the permanent intermediate are both off Peaks 8 and 9: Peak 8 terrain varies from intermediate to advanced, but if you stick to the open, swoopy Four O'clock—the longest run—you can have some great downhill skiing and not get too stressed. Also check out Spruce, and Frosty's, and Dukes, all of which runs are groomed nightly and have a slightly steeper pitch.

From Peak 9, a favorite way down is via the Lehman run, which offers plenty of space and some deep moguls. Peak 9 also has Volunteer, American, and Peerless, while Peak 10 challenges intermediates with Doublejack, Centennial, and Crystal, which are groomed and designated "blue/black." So a good day's skiing might include a warmup on Peak 9 with Cashier, Bonanza, or Country Boy, or on Peak 8 with Springmeier or Four O'Clock, gradually easing into the more difficult "blue/black" runs.

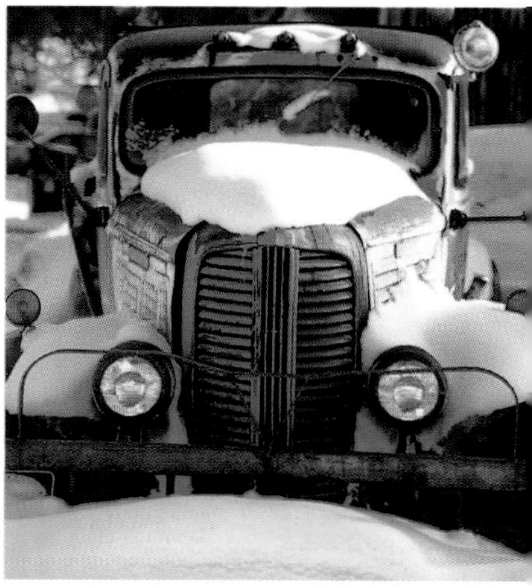

▲ OLD WORLD, NEW WORLD
Breckenridge brims with North American history—the original mining town dates back 140 years to Victorian times; skiing started here in the 1960s, and the first boarding world championships were held here in 1985.

▼ EXPERT TERRAIN
Breckenridge gets better for experts each year and real experts will head for Peak 10 which offers the toughest terrain. Currently 55% of the terrain here is designated 'advanced/expert.'

▲ GLADED RUNS
Peak 10 has a network of steep, bumpy trails linked to the main downhill course. One area to the left of the chairlift, called The Burn, offers excellent lightly wooded off-piste skiing.

ADVANCED & EXPERT

If one word sums up the challenge of Breckenridge skiing, that word is—moguls. Big ones, deep ones, curvy ones, you name it; here they are. Peak 10 offers the toughest terrain. It has steep, groomed runs on the face of the mountain with tree skiing on the north side, called The Burn, along with the difficult and challenging bump trails of Corsair and Spitfire.

The south side of Peak 10 is a hidden paradise for bump-skiers with spectacular views of the valley. Try that out before moving onto the even steeper and tougher Lake Chutes—the best challenges for experts with pitches of up to 51 degrees and some areas accessible only from cornices or by going off-piste or into one of the bowls. Also try Horseshoe, Cucumber or Contest—all three are worthy double black diamond trails.

Breckenridge offers many in-bound bowls for expert skiers. Most are accessible by short hikes. However, if you want to go beyond the ski area boundary and access the backcountry, use the designated gates only. Areas beyond the ski area boundary are not patrolled or maintained. Avalanche slopes, unmarked obstacles and other natural hazards exist. Rescue in the backcountry, if available, is the responsibility of the Summit County Sheriff, and your wallet. The backcountry avalanche hazard may be extreme. It will be costly and may take time. Also there's no sponsored guiding available for off-piste adventures.

Hiking is allowed above the highest lift to access bowl skiing with a summit elevation of 12,998 feet (3,963 m) and a total vertical rise of 3,398 feet (1,036 m). With over half the ski area given over to experienced skiers, advanced terrain is to be found on each mountain. Peak 9 offers many diverse trails, from the steep, groomed American run to the more difficult face of Volunteer.

For those wishing to try the expert terrain, the north side of Peak 9 drops off into trails that offer no escape to easier slopes. With runs named Inferno, Devil's Crotch and Hades, you can imagine what the topography is like. Advanced skiers can warm up on Peak 8 with the groomed blue-black trail of Spruce, then progress to Dukes or Rounders.

For those wanting more, Breckenridge's Chair 6 has plenty of back bowl skiing. If wide-open bowl skiing with plenty of snow is what you desire, then you should head to Horseshoe Bowl, which is accessed by Chair 6 and the T-bar lifts. As for the best powder, that's definitely to be found on the bowls of Peak 8, but this means you must be willing to hike above the tree line.

EATING ON THE MOUNTAIN

- TEN MILE STATION
- VISTA HAUS
- BORDER BURRITOS
- THE MAGGIE
- PEAK 9 RESTAURANT

BOARDING & FREESTYLE

"Breck" was the first major Colorado resort to encourage boarders and it hosted the world's first freestyle snowboarding event in 1985. Today Breckenridge boasts three first-class Terrain Parks for snowboarding and freestyle skiers, and hosts various World Cup Events.

The Peak 8 Freeway Terrain Park is renowned for its award-winning SuperPipe, a 300-foot (90 m) half-pipe, and it was voted one of the four best in North America by *American Snowboarder* magazine. The resort's adjacent snowboard park was rated the second-best facility in the country in the same readers' poll. The park's impressive series of large tabletops and spines, with slopes of up to 15 degrees, makes it a popular site for the advanced and expert boarder. Peak 9's Gold King Terrain Park is a less daunting facility. Its hits and features are more subdued for the budding freerider and skier. Additionally, the new Swinger Terrain Park on Peak 8 is designed specifically for beginner freestyle riders. It has smaller features and an introductory halfpipe.

Overall, Breckenridge's network of lifts between mountains allows for easy access for boarders but you may want to stay away from Lower Sawmill, as its extremely gentle slope is not conducive to snowboard gliding.

EATING ON THE MOUNTAIN

Breckenridge's mountain restaurants are mostly food-court style and some serve breakfast as well. The TenMile Station is Breckenridge's latest—it's at the top of the QuickSilver Lift on Peak 9, and is a mining-themed restaurant and Coffee Depot with a spacious heated deck. The Vista Haus Restaurant on Peak 8, at the top of the Colorado and Peak 8 SuperConnect chairs, is a recently renovated facility

► CONTINENTAL COOL
The ambience at Breckenridge is much more international than with other U.S. resorts—reflecting the long association with European vacationers since the 1980s.

◀ HISTORIC CHARMS
Breckenridge now attracts over 1 million visits a year thanks to its its middle-of-the-road charms—that is, the resort is neither too racy nor too sleepy. The downtown Victorian center, houses hundreds of boutiques, scores of pubs and dozens of restaurants and this brightly colored, restored 19th-century area represents Colorado's largest historic district. Around the base area is an array of more modern architecture.

with fantastic views, serving breakfast and lunch with an open seating area. Border Burritos is a hot spot for healthy and affordable lunches and is located at the base of Peak 8, downstairs in the Bergenhof. The Maggie, at the base of Peak 9, serves breakfast and coffee in the morning and a variety of American favorites for lunch. Also on Peak 9, at the top of the Beaver Run Chair, is the Peak 9 Restaurant.

APRÈS SKI

Breckenridge is a lively, sophisticated resort with an international clientele. The town has over 50 restaurants to satisfy all appetites and pockets. The choice runs from American through Chinese, Cajun, Italian, French, Tex-Mex and Japanese, but the main snag with Breckenridge restaurants is pretension—what you see is often less than what you get. This being so, personal recommendations count a lot and will vary from year to year. Places that have stood the test of several visits are the Café Alpine, the River Walk Café, and the pricey (but just worth it) Top of the World at the Lodge and Spa. That apart, talk to last week's guests and see what they suggest.

The Maggie Restaurant located at the base of Peak 9 is a lively après-ski hangout. The Silver Bullet Saloon in the Bergenhof Restaurant at the base of Peak 8 serves specialty drinks for après ski.

Breckenridge's nightlife is consistently rated among the best in the reader polls conducted by skiing magazines and a whole spectrum of nightspots await. Alligator Lounge, Cecilia's, Sherpa and Yeti's, Tiffany's, the Liquid Lounge, and Clancy's Irish Pub are a just a few of the hot spots around Breckenridge. The Underworld Club is a popular hangout for snowboarders.

OTHER ACTIVITIES

There is a wide variety of annual winter events including Ski and Snowboard Competitions. In addition to Alpine skiing, there are numerous other winter recreational activities including Nordic skiing, snowshoeing, snowmobiling, sleigh rides and dogsled tours. Off the snow you could visit a fully functioning gold mine, go fishing, or browse the many quaint stores on Main Street. Other sporting activities to be found at The Breckenridge Recreation Center include indoor tennis, swimming, an indoor rock-climbing wall, a gym, saunas and spa, and you can ice skate either outdoors or indoors at The Breckenridge Ice. In addition to all that, there is a skateboard park featuring a nine-foot (2.7 m) deep bowl.

USEFUL PHONE NUMBERS

Tourist Information Center	970-453-2913
Breckenridge Reservation Center	877-234-3989
Breckenridge Medical Center	970-453-1010
Resort Express Taxi	970-468-7600
453 Taxi	970-453-8294
Breckenridge Ski Patrol	970-496-7393

USEFUL WEBSITES

Official Website	www.gobreck.com
Snow Report & Web Cams	www.rsn.com/cams/breckenridge
Weather Reports	www.wunderground.com
Vacation Planner	www.summitnet.com

RESTAURANTS & BARS

BLUE RIVER BISTRO
BRECKENRIDGE BBQ
BRECKENRIDGE BREWERY
THE BIG EASY LOUNGE
CLANCY'S IRISH PUB & RESTAURANT
DOWNSTAIRS AT ERIC'S
THE DREDGE
GOLD PAN BAR
BROWN HOTEL RESTAURANT
HORSESHOE II
JULIUS CAESAR LOUNGE
MI CASA MEXICAN RESTAURANT
PARK AVENUE PUB
SALT CREEK RESTAURANT & SALOON
TIFFANY'S
THE OVERLOOK TAVERN AND GRILL
ULLR'S SPORTS GRILL

FOUR SEPARATE MOUNTAINS WITH FOUR DISTINCT MOODS, ASPEN IS BIG ON SUPERLATIVES: ITS MOUNTAINS OFFER SOME OF THE STEEPEST OFF-PISTE EXPERIENCE OF ANY U.S. SKI RESORT AS WELL AS OUTRAGEOUS BUMPS, STEEPS, PIPES, AND CHUTES FOR BOARDERS. AND THEN THERE'S THE APRÈS-SKI, FOR WHICH ASPEN IS RATED THE NUMBER ONE RESORT IN AMERICA.

ASPEN SNOWMASS

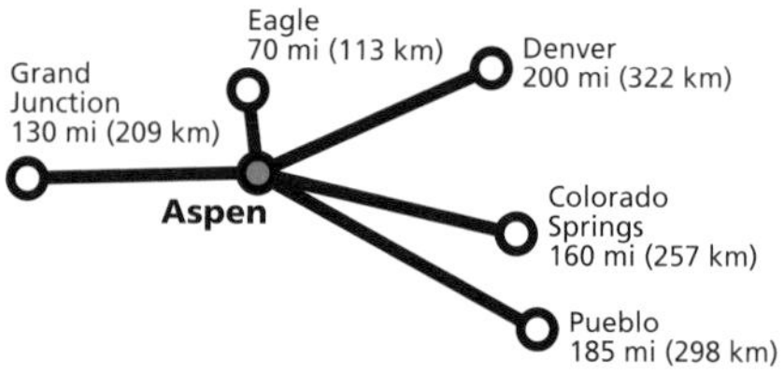

▼ HIGH TECH
The Silver Queen Gondola zooms you up a vertical rise of 3,267 feet (996 m) to the top of Aspen Mountain at 11,212 feet (3,147 m) in just 14 minutes.

Nestled within The White River National Forest in the Rocky Mountain region of Colorado, the U.S. ski resort of Aspen is rightly one of the premier destinations in the world. Aspen is actually part of a four-resort complex including Buttermilk, Snowmass, and Highland that makes up the Four Mountain ski resort area.

Aspen skiing is not for the faint-hearted nor the absolute beginner who would be better off aiming for Snowmass, which is nine miles (15 km) away from downtown Aspen and more tuned-in for families. Buttermilk and Highlands are nearer—just three miles (5 km) away as the crow flies—and cater to a broader spectrum of skiing ability.

GETTING THERE

Two regional airports and one international airport service Aspen. Visitors can fly into Denver International Airport (D.I.A.) and connect into Aspen/Sardy Field, which is located only three miles (5 km) or about eight minutes away from Aspen and six miles (10 km) from Snowmass. Many of the lodges provide complimentary airport transfers and taxis meet every flight. If you're traveling the 200 miles (322 km) by car or coach from Denver, the resort lies roughly 4-hours' drive away. Another option is Eagle County Regional Airport, located 70 miles (112 km) away, about a 90-minute drive from Aspen Snowmass.

◄ **HELL'S BELLS**
The double black diamond trail Ridge of Bell takes skiers down along the central ridge of Aspen Mountain back to town (visible in the distance) via various short, sharp and steep black offshoots called Face of Bell, Shoulder of Bell and Back of Bell.

THE VILLAGE

Aspen is chic and cozy with lodges and condominiums nestled right on the slopes. With the average home costing over four million U.S. dollars, Aspen is one of the most upscale ski resorts on the planet and a playground for the wealthy. Aspen is certainly not your run-of-the-mill destination and if you want it ritzy you can have it—rubbing shoulders with showbiz and sport celebrities, many of whom have homes here—but it is also a great ski area. Some come to Aspen just to see and be seen, but skiers and ski-bums in the know are coming here in increasing numbers to test themselves on Highlands, which boasts some incredibly challenging terrain, including spectacular backcountry access.

Aspen can be very expensive (if you go 5-Star) but it can also be affordable. If you're on a tight budget it is cheaper to stay in Snowmass or Highlands or commute from one of three more modest towns up to half an hour away. And there are the occasional freebies such as complimentary mountain tours, free shuttles between the four mountains, and free coffee and cookies at the base of the mountains.

Famous for its diverse terrain, spectacular dining, shopping and celebrated nightlife, Aspen Snowmass is one of the premier destinations in the world. The historic Victorian-era town of Aspen sits at the base of Aspen Mountain and offers a wide variety of hotels, condos, B&Bs, and chalets. The town of Aspen features incredible restaurants, art galleries, stores and boutiques, along with an opera house, two movie theaters, an ice rink, skateboard park and more.

ACCOMMODATIONS

Aspen is a destination (not a day-skier) resort. The town offers accommodations for around 8,000 destination guests with a further 6,000 beds at Snowmass, where 95 percent of the accommodations are conveniently located right on the slopes.

The Little Nell and The St. Regis are famous for star spotting. The Hotel Jerome is a famous historic property. Renowned for its tradition of quiet elegance, gracious hospitality and unobtrusive pampering, the Hotel Jerome in Aspen, Colorado offers all the amenities and services of a luxury hotel. Built in 1889 at the height of Colorado's silver boom, and restored in 1985 to its original Victorian splendor, the Jerome has been an Aspen landmark for over a century.

Whether star-spotting or on a budget, there are over 50 hotels in the Aspen area. This does not include other lodging options including condominiums, private homes, chalets, and bed & breakfasts.

The Virtual Hostel, accessed through Aspen's website www.aspensnowmass.com, offers last-minute accommodations listings in Aspen Snowmass Village. Good deals can be found here but bear in mind that the prices offered depend on the time of year and occupancy. Updated bargains are posted weekly. For more information on lodgings in Aspen visit www.stayaspensnowmass.com

ACCOMMODATIONS

THE LITTLE NELL
970-920-4600 www.thelittlenell.com

HOTEL JEROME
970-920-1000 www.hoteljerome.com

THE ST. REGIS
970-920-3300 www.stregis.com

SARDY HOUSE
970-920-2525 www.sardyhouse.com

SKY HOTEL
970-925-6760 www.theskyhotel.com

HOTEL LENADO
970-925-6246 www.hotellenado.com

ST. MORITZ LODGE
970-925-3220 www.stmoritzlodge.com

SNOWFLAKE INN
970-925-3221 www.snowflakeinn.com

SKI LIFTS

Gondolas	1
High-Speed Quads	12
Fixed Grip Quads	2
Triple Chairs	4
Double Chairs	14
Surface Lifts	4
Magic Carpets	3
Total	40
Riders per hour	51,623

SKI SEASON
Late November to mid-April

MOUNTAIN FACTS & SNOWFALL

	ASPEN	BUTTERMILK	HIGHLANDS	SNOWMASS
Base	7,945 feet (2,442 m)	7,870 feet (2,399 m)	8,040 feet (2,451 m)	8,104 feet (2,473 m)
Summit	11,212 feet (3,147 m)	9,900 feet (3,018 m)	11,675 feet (3,559 m)	12,510 feet (3,813 m)
Elevation	3,267 feet (996 m)	2,030 feet (619 m)	3,635 feet (1,108 m)	4,406 feet (1,343 m)
Number of trails	76	40	115	84
Beginner	-	35%	20%	7%
Intermediate	35%	39%	33%	55%
Advanced	35%	26%	17%	18%
Expert	30%	-	30%	20%
Longest trail	3 miles (4.8 km)	3 miles (4.8 km)	3.5 miles (5.6 km)	5 miles (6.7 km)
Snowfall *	300 inches (762 cm)	200 inches (508 cm)	300 inches (762 cm)	300 inches (762 cm)
Snowmaking	210 acres (84 ha)	108 acres (43 ha)	110 acres (44 ha)	180 acres (73 ha)

* Average snowfall over a 10-year period

► FRESH TRACKS
You can have an early-morning bonus ski or ride down empty, freshly groomed slopes with the Aspen ski school pros if you are one of the first to sign up to the "Free First Tracks" the morning before. It's on offer every day at Aspen Mountain.

NEARBY RESORTS

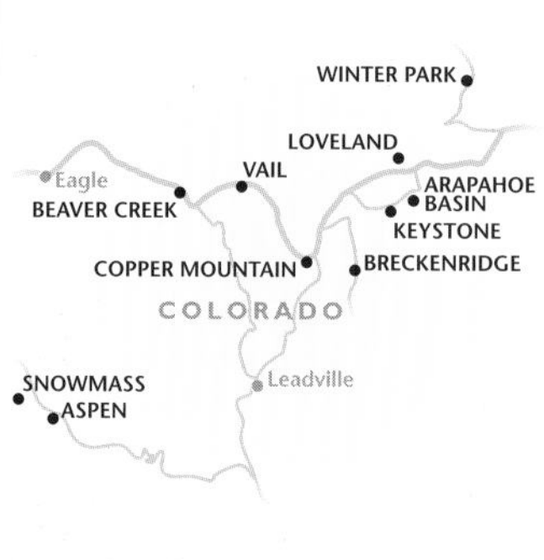

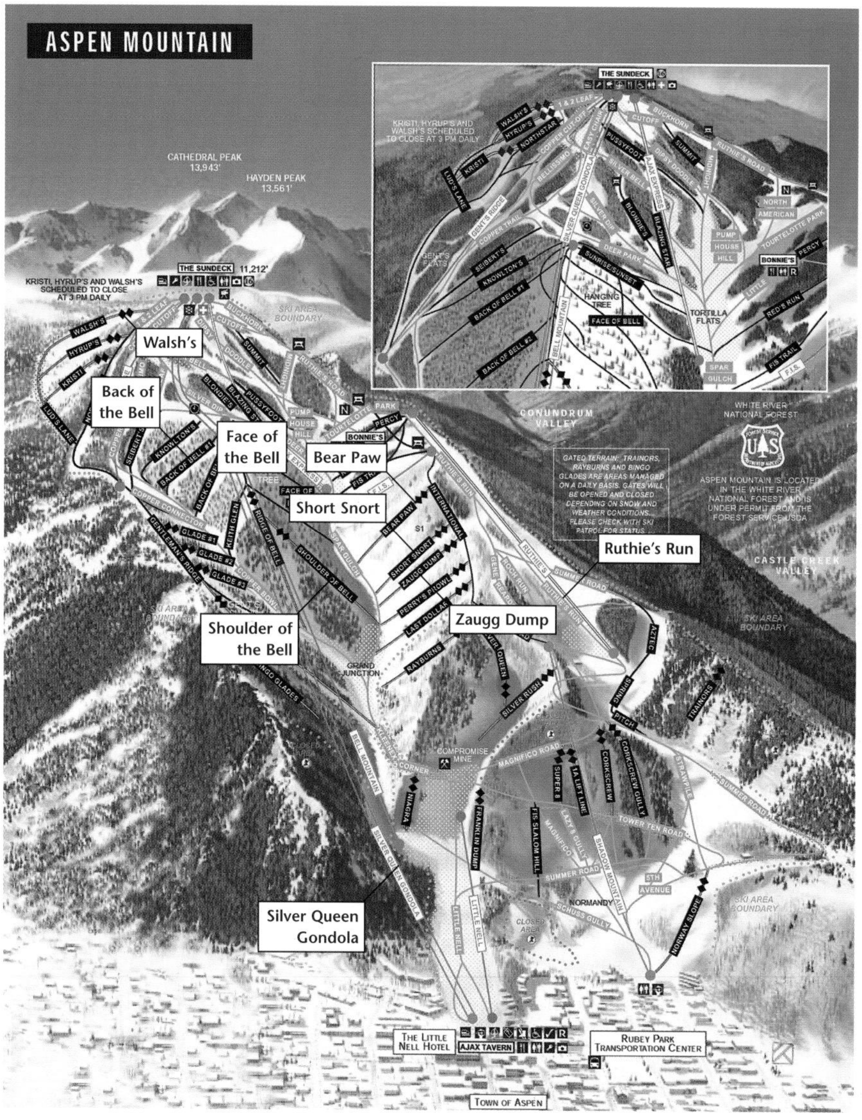

SKI AREA

At Aspen, one ticket allows you to experience four mountains—Snowmass, Aspen Mountain, Aspen Highlands, and Buttermilk—each with its own personality. That's 4,805 acres (1,945 ha) of terrain, 37 lifts, 315 trails, thousands of feet of vertical drop, hundreds of inches of fresh snow and endless blue skies—all within a 12-mile (20 km) radius and accessible by free shuttle. And the sky really is blue: if you ski powder you really need brilliant sunshine and this resort has plenty of both: temperatures average 30°F (-1°C) during the day and around 18°F (-7°C) at night, while spring temperatures can reach an enjoyable 50°F (10°C) and higher during the day.

The slopes are graded—easiest to hardest—green, blue, black diamond and double black diamond. Around 10 percent are graded beginner, 48 percent intermediate, 21 percent advanced, and 21 percent "strictly for the experts." Buttermilk is the best place to learn, indeed there is no expert terrain there. Conversely, Aspen Mountain has no beginner terrain. Know your limits and take your choice.

Suing and being sued in the U.S. is an occupational hazard so it is not surprising that safety is paramount in the area, with a ski patrol on each mountain, and a surfeit of ropes, signs, poles, avalanche safety measures and speed controls.

ASPEN MOUNTAIN

The flagship Aspen Mountain rises imposingly out of the heart of downtown Aspen to 11,212 feet (3,147 m) and covers 673 acres (272 ha). Now open to snowboarding, the mountain is known for steeps and bumps and is a favorite among many upper-intermediate and advanced skiers and snowboarders. Intermediate cruising is a delight on the wide open Ruthie's Run, accessing the world's only high-speed double chair. The Silver Queen Gondola transports skiers to the summit in only 14 minutes, providing access to a number of activities, including world-class skiing, guided snowshoe tours and paragliding.

BUTTERMILK

Buttermilk is located just three miles (5 km) outside Aspen, and most of the mountain is groomed each night. It is virtually impossible to define. First it's the quintessential beginner's mountain known for smooth, rolling trails. But if that's Buttermilk, then why do all the locals pound down "Tiehack Parkway" when there's a foot (30 cm) of fresh snow? Well, the Tiehack trail has steep left-handed funnels and glades that make it anything but beginner's country, even if the main fall lines are

easy (and what is wrong with that?) And how about the freeriders' Buttermilk? It's home to a superpipe and one of the world's longest terrain parks from the top of the mountain to the base, Crazy T'rain, nearly two miles (3 km) long and features dozens of hits and over 30 rails. The Crazy T'rain Park has also been home to the 2002 and 2003 ESPN Winter X Games. The Park has a newly dedicated trail allowing for more hits and jumps. Also, a sound system has been installed near the superpipe and the X Games Slopestyle Course constructed for all to ride.

▲ BACK COUNTRY

Rising over the Aspen Highlands in the White River National Forest, Pyramid Peak reaches 14,018 feet (4,275 m) while to the right stands the double-peaked summit of Maroon Bells at 14,156 feet (4,318 m).

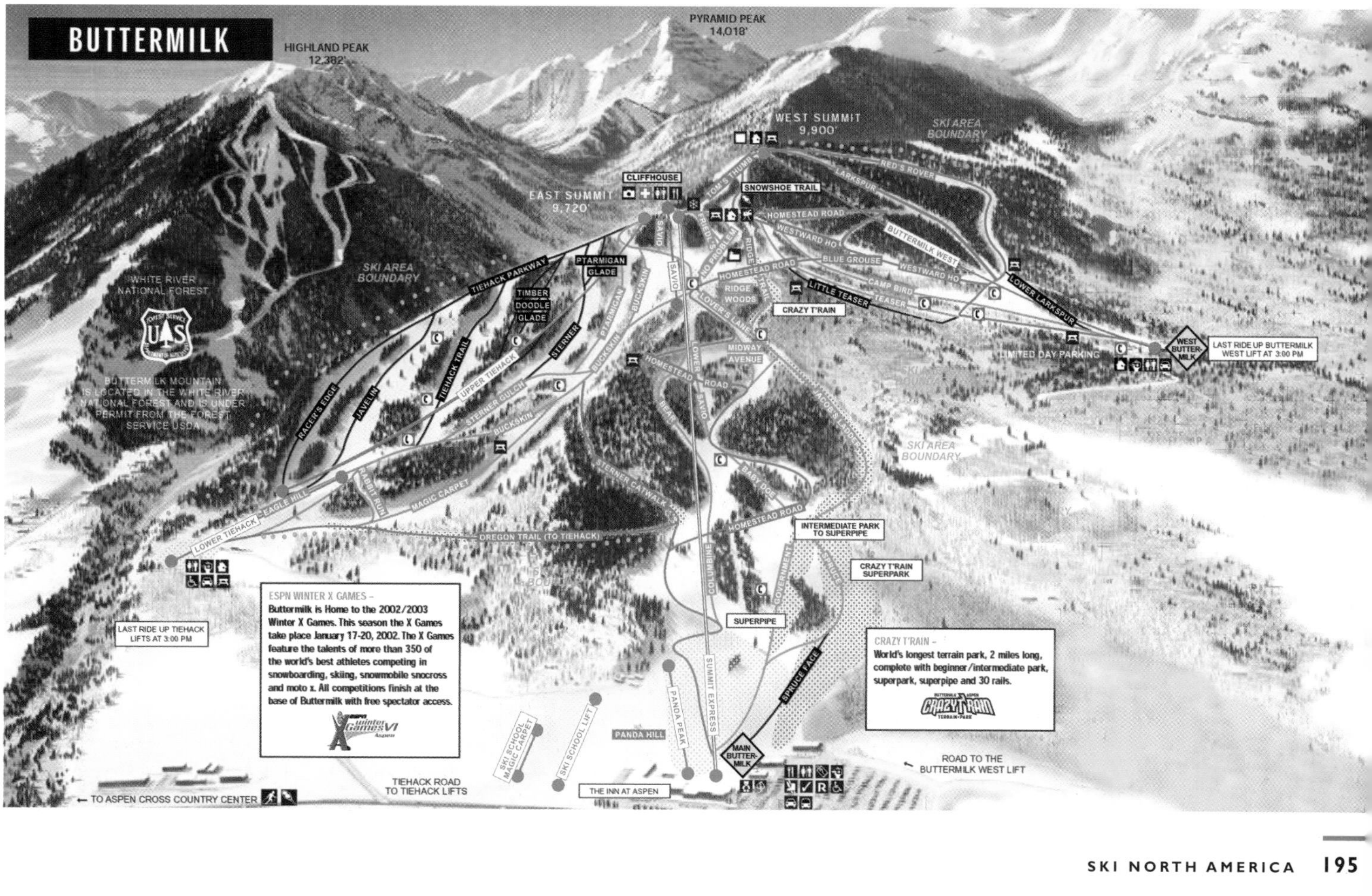

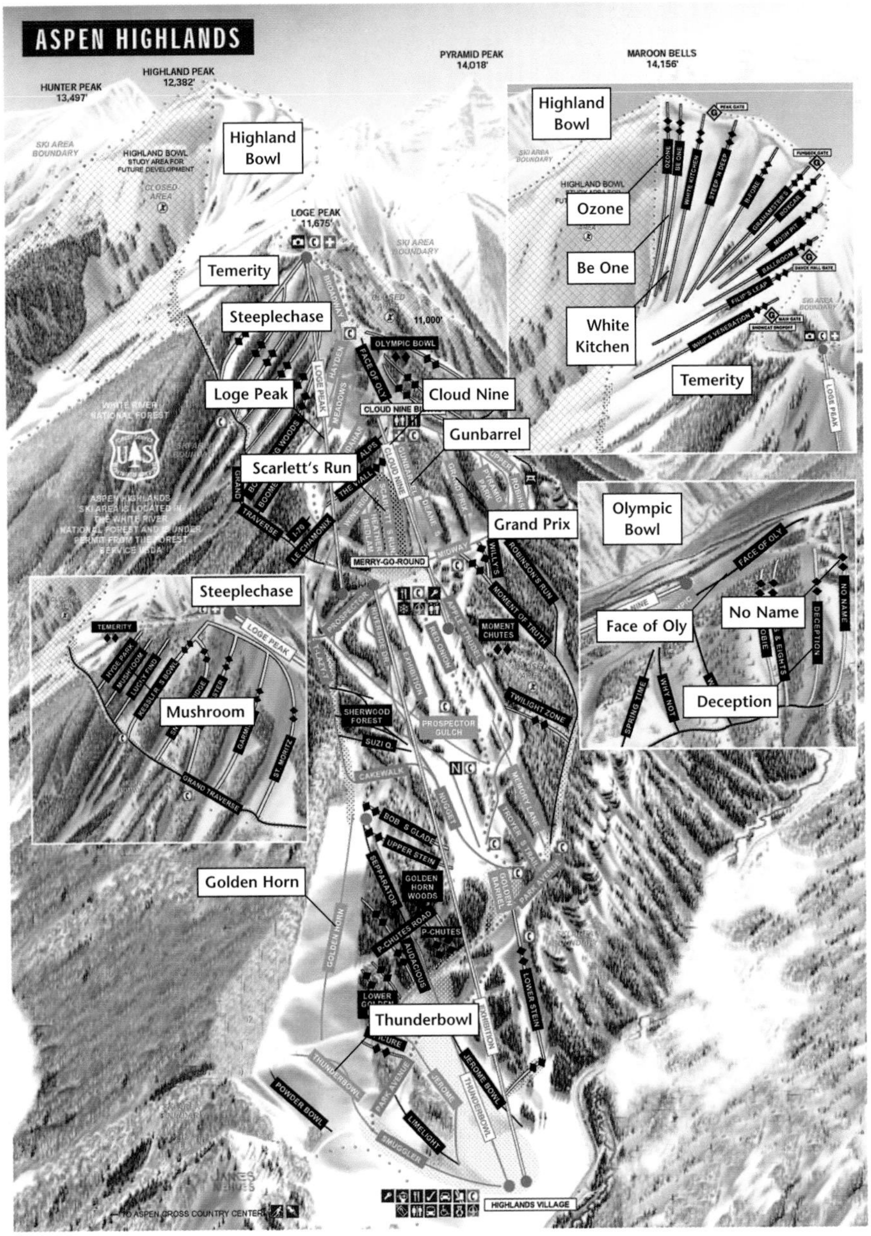

HIGHLANDS

Located just three miles (5 km) from downtown Aspen and accessible by free shuttle, Highlands' 720 acres (290 ha) feature stunning views of the world-famous Maroon Bells, and the new Highlands Village offers affordable lodgings, dining and shopping.

Highlands is where the locals go to get humble. At Highlands, there are wide-open trails and killer views—enough to keep an intermediate happy for a month, even greens you could send your mother down. But experience its hike-accessible terrain just once, and you'll be amazed. Beyond the lift network and a short hike from the top of the Loge Peak lift, Highland Bowl features some of the steepest terrain in the United States.

For years Highland Bowl stood grand and empty, an enticing, snowy siren, inviting, but off limits. The bowl is divided into four zones; the south-facing R(ed) zone which receives the greatest amount of sun exposure, with Y(ellow) zone following, then B(lue) zone and finally, the coolest north-facing G(reen) zone.

The bowl has a rich history. In 1981 the Aspen Highlands Ski Patrol was allowed to open the bowl for guided hiking tours and for the next three years backcountry skiers gained access to the bowl, but this all ended when three ski patrollers were killed in 1984. For the next 13 years the bowl remained closed except for the gladed trails in the Temerity area off the lower ridge.

The R-zone remains closed but the lower Y-zone was reopened in 1997 and gradually since then the patrol has opened the B-zone (allowing descents from the 12,392 foot/3,777 m peak) and a small part of the G-zone in 2001. From the peak the fall line has pitches of up to 48 degrees and is prime avalanche terrain. To safely open the area the ski patrol and local volunteers descend into the bowl (sometimes clipped into a belay!) and compress the snow step by step as they walk down and back up the mountain. The patrol does this with each new snowfall for the first few months of the winter to ensure that the weak Colorado snowpack forms a firm base. In the absence of these safety measures the bowl would be far too dangerous.

▶ KILLER SLOPES
Kiffor Berg, one of Aspen's elite Freeride Team, who call this resort home, kicks it down on big Snowmass like a maniac. Snowmass is five miles (8 km) across and has everything from easy, long blue trails to disappearing steep; chutes and access to high —and dangerous—Alpine backcountry.

▶ SPLENDID ISOLATION
Highland Bowl is 70 acres' (28 ha) worth of north-facing, mostly stark and steep high-alpine terrain. The area in the shade is closed but in the sun lie the double black diamond trails of Ozone, White Kitchen, Steep'n'Deep, B-Fore, and Boxcar to name a few. You take the Loge Peak lift to 11,675 feet (3,559 m) then you hike the rest.

SNOWMASS

Snowmass has had its problems in the past, not least of which were having a mess of a base area, and a slightly soulless feel. Now Snowmass is getting back on top and offering the whole gamut of downhill experiences from gentle cruisers to scary steeps. In fact you'll find the greatest diversity of terrain among the four mountains here on Snowmass, with hundreds of acres of beginner trails, steep and deeps, wide open cruisers, endless moguls, terrain parks, half-pipes and more.

Snowmass is the second largest mountain resort in Colorado and with 3,010 acres (1,218 ha), including glades, cruisers and bumps as well as three terrain parks and a halfpipe, it would be hard not find a perfect trail. And for getting up the slopes Snowmass has the longest lift-served vertical rise in the United States.

Snowmass is family-friendly skiing and more improvements are being made to the Family Zone on Snowmass. New interactive kids' trails will be added to the current kids' facilities that include a picnic shelter, training gates and sculpted moguls. The Trenchtown terrain park at Snowmass will also double in size, running from top to bottom of the Coney Glade lift. Tube Town at Snowmass offers tubing seven days a week, and tubing on Snowmass is open until 8:00 PM.

Accessible by free shuttle from anywhere in the Aspen/Snowmass area, Snowmass is located just nine miles (15 km) from downtown Aspen and 95 percent of Snowmass's accommodations are ski-in, ski-out.

The whole ski area and the award-winning Ski & Snowboard Schools of Aspen are operated by the Aspen Skiing Company. Contact 800-525-6200 or

▶ **PURE POWDER**
Hard to tell but this local resident and two-times World Ski Champion is Chris Davenport. He's part of the Aspen Freeride team drawn here by the pristine powder mornings and the easily accessible but serious ski territory beyond the ski barriers.

970-925-1220, or you can visit the websites at www.skiaspen.com and www.aspensnowmass.com

SKI LIFTS

If you're keen you can catch the first lift at 8:30 AM and hop on the last lift at 3:45 PM. Lines are not a problem: even if lodgings were at full capacity, and every single guest were to be on the slopes at the same time—an unlikely scenario—the mountains would still average only three people per acre. The results for visitors are no long lift lines to wait in, and lots of open space in which to experience the wonderful exhilaration of skiing and riding. Aspen has eight chairlifts (including a gondola), Buttermilk has seven; Highlands four, and Snowmass eighteen.

LIFT PASSES

There are no reduced price schemes so everyone must buy a regular lift ticket (which requires an I.D. photo) except that there is free skiing and boarding for children six years and under.

Lift tickets are available at some lodges, at the base of each mountain, or through the offical website at www.aspensnowmass.com

The lift pass covers all four mountain areas and guests may have their equipment transferred at the end of the day to any of the four mountains in Aspen/Snowmass for only US$5. The equipment will be waiting at the base of the mountain the next morning. Guests may also store their equipment overnight at any mountain.

To rent or buy ski equipment D&E Snowboard Shop & Ski Rental, and Pro Mountain Sports have a complete selection of adult and children's ski and snowboard packages available with convenient locations at the base of each mountain, plus free inter-mountain equipment transfers. For a complete listing of equipment and pricing go to www.aspensnowmass.com

SKI SCHOOLS AND GUIDING

Adult or child, skier or snowboarder, beginner or expert, there is a ski school or tutor to suit you and your needs, including women-only tutorials. Every program offered by Ski & Snowboard Schools of Aspen is 100 percent guaranteed in two ways. First, all lesson tickets purchased but not used are fully refundable. Second, if you are not completely satisfied with your ski instructor, you will be enrolled in a new lesson or provided a full refund. Group lessons cost around US$105 (US$70 for kids) for one day, and about US$460 (US$320 for kids) for five days. Private lessons in Aspen are expensive: US$460 for one day or US$2,150 for five days!

SKI LIFTS

	ASPEN	BUTTERMILK	HIGHLANDS	SNOWMASS
Gondolas	1	-	-	-
High-Speed Quads	1	1	3	7
Quad Chairs	2	-	-	-
Triple Chairs	-	-	1	3
Double Chairs	4	5	-	5
Surface Lifts	-	1	-	3
Magic Carpets	-	-	-	3
Total	8	7	4	21
Riders per hour	10,755	7,500	5,400	27,968

For those wanting guiding, off-piste adventures for skiers and boarders are offered at Snowmass (Wednesdays) and Highlands (Fridays). Off-Piste Adventures are designed to give advanced and expert skiers and riders a chance to discover some of the area's famous terrain. Explore Steeplechase and Highland Bowl at Aspen Highlands, or the Cirque and Hanging Valley areas at Snowmass with experienced guides. Programs depend on snow and weather conditions. Adventures begin at 10:00 AM and end at 3:00 PM. You should arrive at the meeting place at 9:45 AM with your lift ticket and Off-Piste Adventure ticket (price US$105).

Heliskiing is not on offer at Aspen but cat-skiing is. Luxury snowcats take guests to prime, untracked stashes on the backside of Aspen Mountain. Fresh tracks are guaranteed, and lunch is served at a wood-stove heated cabin set in the Elk Mountains. Snacks and drinks are provided on board the cat throughout the day. Cost is around US$275 per day and you can expect around 10 runs.

BEGINNERS

Buttermilk is the best place for beginners: it's located three miles (5 km) from the center of Aspen and is the quintessential learner's mountain known for smooth, rolling terrain. The mountain consists of three sections—Main Buttermilk, Tiehack, and West Buttermilk. Main Buttermilk is its central part and has a selection of green and blue trails. Tiehack is located off the east ridge and is considered an advanced area where intermediates head to master steeper slopes, bumps and powder. West Buttermilk's rolling terrain comprises mostly easy green trails and is a favorite among first-timers. It's also a favorite among hikers, snowshoers and other uphillers for a great workout at any time of day or night. Spectacular views of Pyramid Peak, Highlands, Snowmass, Capitol Peak, Mt. Daly and Mt. Sopris await guests at its summit. Kids love Max the Moose, Buttermilk's friendly purple mascot, and Fort Frog, an adventure center that features a Western-style fort and Native American Village where they can explore specially

SKI SCHOOL

SKIING, SNOWBOARDING OR TELEMARK, ALL LEVELS
877-282-7736

SKIING OR SNOWBOARDING, LEVELS 7–9
Adrenaline sessions
970-923-1227

WOMEN'S EDGE (SKIING, LEVELS 4–9)
877-282-7736

SPECIALIZED PROGRAMS
1-800-525-6200.

THE MAGIC OF SKIING
970-925-7099
www.aikiworks.com

JOHN CLENDENIN'S SKI & SNOWBOARD DOCTORS
970-925-8900
John@SkiDoctors.com

JOHN CLENDENIN'S ALL-MOUNTAIN SKI CAMP
970-925-890
www.CampWithTheChamps.com.

SKIING FOR THE DISABLED AND VISUALLY IMPAIRED
970-923-0578
possibilities@challengeaspen.com

▲ **NO LIMITS**
Local freeriders Frank Shine and Chris Davenport hit the powder on Aspen Mountain. Chris has also been World Extreme Skiing Champion while "Fast" Frank, as he's known around town, taints the townies with stylized skiing and tenacious turns, but that's before he hits huge cliffs in a single bound. If you are the adventurous type then this resort has no physical bounds—only imaginary ones.

designated trails. Panda Peak, the learning hill at the base of Buttermilk, is another kid magnet because it's where beginners make their first turns in the children's ski school. Beginners are encouraged to enjoy a complete ski experience. Often they begin their day in specific beginner-friendly areas and as their confidence and ability increase, they move to more challenging areas of the mountain.

INTERMEDIATES

Virtually half the terrain over all four mountain ski areas is suitable for intermediates so there is plenty of strong intermediate skiing with top-to-bottom cruising to be found on Aspen Mountain. The best area for intermediate skiers at Aspen Highlands is near the top of the mountain, where the Cloud Nine lift accesses trails such as Scarlett's, Grand Prix and Gunbarrel. Golden Horn and Thunderbowl offer enjoyable cruising. The longest intermediate trail is just over five miles (8.5 km) and is located in Snowmass, which is also the location for one other unique offering: the 10-minute hike to Burnt Mountain, with its backcountry style experience for intermediates on Long Shot, a trail that winds three miles (5 km) through forests. Long groomed intermediate trails such as the "mile-wide" Big Burn offer excellent cruising.

ADVANCED

With the exception of Buttermilk, some 42 percent of the Four Mountain area is suitable for advanced skiers. For those in search of moguls and steep deep, couloirs Aspen Mountain has short, sharp and quite steep double black diamond (and very difficult) chutes, including the famous "dump trails" such as Bear Paw, Short Snort and Zaugg Dump which were created by miners throwing out spoil as they tunneled their way into the mountain. Walsh's is considered to be the most challenging trail on Aspen Mountain. Bell Mountain, part of Aspen Mountain, provides first-rate opportunities for mogul skiers with its variety of individual faces, including Face of Bell, Shoulder of Bell, and Back of Bell. Skiers also relish the breathtaking views of downtown Aspen as they descend Ajax.

Highlands has exhilarating steeps, trees, and powder bowls that challenge and delight advanced skiers and riders. Temerity, between Steeplechase and the Y-Zones, is the ultimate in tree riding. Mushroom Chutes, Thermals, and South Castle Chute in Temerity are not for the faint of heart and are sure to produce glory stories for even the most hardcore skiers and riders. The Oly side of the mountain has the aptly named Deception and the No Name Chutes for challenging gladed skiing and riding. Highlands is the spot for big mountain freeskiing and freeriding.

Each year, new terrain in Highlands Bowl is opening—the steepest off-piste experience of any U.S. ski resort—and skiers and snowboarders have been flocking to Highlands to try out the new terrain. In 2001/02, Ozone, White Kitchen, and Be One opened, making it possible for the first time to lay down tracks from the 12,392-foot (3,782 m) summit of the bowl on 40 to 45 degree slopes. For 2002/03, the Bowl was expanded by nearly 50% to include the steep, north-facing, heavily treed parts of the G-zone.

The bowl offers deep-powder skiing after a snowstorm and is accessible via a 20 to 60 minute hike from the top of the Loge Peak chair. The hike can be shortened by 15 to 20 minutes by catching the free snowcat from Loge Meadow to the first access gate. The snowcat runs from 11:00 AM to 1:00 PM, conditions permitting. Check the board at the top of the Loge lift for more information.

Dropping in from the summit is just one of the choices. One thousand vertical feet (300 m) lower, some of the steepest terrain can be found in the Lower Y Zones. Between the Y Zones and the summit there are dozens of other choices. You can drop in anywhere along the ridge to the left via four access gates but you MUST observe closures at these gates. Be aware that the steep and narrow chutes of Maroon Bowl—to the right of the ridge—are uncontrolled, and that avalanches in this area have claimed many lives over the years.

Snowmass's Hanging Valley has been called the closest thing to the backcountry without actually going out of bounds. Steeps, glades, cornices, cliffs, and deep snow all await those seeking thrills and spills. On a powder day, skiers and riders wait anxiously for ski patrol to drop the ropes and open the area. Because Snowmass is so big, powder stashes can be found on the mountain days after a major snowstorm. The off-piste experiences in the Hanging Valley, Burnt Mountain, and the Cirque are also ideal for advanced skiers and boarders.

The Cirque at Snowmass—a world of steeps, cornices, chutes and cliffs—is legendary among advanced skiers and boarders. Some say Snowmass is the most underestimated adventure mountain in the world. At 12,510 feet (3,815 m) above sea level, the Cirque provides a breathtaking experience. Skiers can explore the huge Cirque Headwall or come all the way around and take the steep shots down the East Wall. When the snow is deep, hop into Rock Island where you can link turns on or between the giant snow-covered boulders that look like huge marshmallows. Cliff jumpers can get hang time on Hanging Valley Wall, Baby Ruth—and Gowdy's: with a huge cornice, narrow choke in the center and a wide open powder field at the bottom, this trail has it all. Don't forget AMF (some say it stands for "adios, my friend"), Garrett Gulch, and Bearclaw, and the locals' secret powder stash—Reidars' trees.

BOARDING & FREESTYLE

Aspen, one of the last U.S. resort to open to snowboarders, is now extremely boarder-friendly and makes every effort to welcome snowboarders and make their experience hassle-free. Benches and repair tools can be found on all of the mountains. The gondola and all the buses are equipped to handle

▲ KIDS' CAMP
Snowmass has doubled the length of the Trenchtown terrain park adding more rails, jumps and new interactive kids ski and snowboard trails.

SNOWBOARDERS

Buttermilk is ideal for beginner, intermediate and advanced boarders. Bombardier cutters and snowcats pipe cut twice a week. There are no halfpipes but Buttermilk has one superpipe that's 350 feet (107 m) long, with walls 15 feet high, creating a 17- foot (5-m) transition with a 15-degree pitch slope. Trenchtown, the intermediate and advanced park at Snowmass, were doubled in length for the 2002/03 season. This means more jumps, rails and hits. This park can be accessed off the Coney Glade lift. The lower half of the park and the halfpipe can be accessed from the Burlingame lift as well. Riders will experience hits, jumps and rails. A handle tow hugs the halfpipe back to the top for easy access. A beginner terrain park runs down Funnel and is accessible from the Funnel lift. There is also a mini terrain park in the children's area off Scooper. Snowmass has one halfpipe 300 feet (91 m) long on a 17-degree pitch slope. Bombardier cutters and snowcats-pipe are cut twice a week.

◄ BUTTERMILK BACKSIDE
World Boards and U.S. Olympic team boarder Adam Longnecker rips it up on Buttermilk's north-facing, high-altitude slopes.

EATING ON THE MOUNTAIN

ASPEN
SUNDECK
ASPEN MOUNTAIN CLUB
BONNIE'S
MONTAGNA
AJAX TAVERN

BUTTERMILK
THE CLIFFHOUSE
BUMP'S

HIGHLANDS
CLOUD NINE CAFÉ
MERRY-GO-ROUND
WILLOW CREEK
THUNDERBOWL MARKET-CAFÉ
WORLD LINK CAFÉ

SNOWMASS
GORDON'S HIGH ALPINE
SAM'S KNOB
LYNN BRITT CABIN
TWO CREEKS
UP 4 PIZZA
ASSAY HILL YURT
CAFÉ SUZANNE
KRABLOONIK
ULLRHOF
CIRQUE CAFE

RESTAURANTS & BARS

RESTAURANTS

EXPENSIVE
THE LITTLE NELL
PINONS
RENAISSANCE
OLIVES

MODERATE
AJAX TAVERN
L'HOSTERIA
JIMMY'S
MIRABELLA

BUDGET
J-BAR
LA COCINA
BOOGIES
SU CASA

BARS
ASPEN BILLIARDS
39 DEGREES
THE CIGAR BAR
CLUB CHELSEA
BARERIC'S BAR
THE GROTTOS
THE J-BAR
MCSTORLIE'S PUB
THE RED ONION
BENTLEY'S

snowboards. New terrain has been cleared on the two miles (3.2 km) long Crazy T'rain park through Uncle Bob's Glades, giving the Crazy T'rain its own dedicated trail. The park features over 30 rails and 25 jumps of different sizes with table tops, hips and spines on the advanced side, and easier versions for intermediates.

EATING ON THE MOUNTAIN

There are 22 restaurants including some of the best mountain restaurants in North America serving international, traditional, self-service and fast food. The Sundeck, at the top of Aspen Mountain, offers a good self-service menu but the neighboring Aspen Mountain Club—one of the world's most exclusive clubs—is open only to members. At upper mid-mountain Bonnie's restaurant, with its famous two-tiered outdoor deck is a popular hangout, and Ajax Tavern, at the base of the Silver Queen Gondola, is a favorite après-ski venue. Buttermilk's Cliffhouse does an excellent stir-fry and the outdoor deck has renowned views of the Maroon Creek Valley. On Highlands, the Cloud Nine Café, at the top of the high-speed quad, is a quaint Alpine-style chalet featuring excellent European food with table service and magnificent views.

Mid-mountain the Merry-Go-Round has the largest outdoor deck in the valley. Over at Snowmass, Gordon's High Alpine includes an elegant European-style restaurant and cafeteria-style self-service for guests on the move while Sam's Knob has both self-service and an Italian full-service restaurant with beautiful views down the Brush Creek Valley.

▲ ELEGANCE REVISITED
Restored to its original Victorian splendor, with rooms decked out in period antiques, the Hotel Jerome lies in the heart of downtown Aspen on Main Street.

APRÈS SKI

In Aspen après ski has been around since the beginning. Skiers came off the mountain, skied right through town and parked on a barstool at the 100-year old Red Onion. Today the tradition continues with over 100 bars and restaurants offering après ski across town, in every price category and for every lifestyle.

Rated tops for après ski by *Ski magazine*, *Powder magazine* and *Playboy*, whatever kind of nightlife, Aspen's got it—from laid back to high glam—and heaps of it. From wings and a pitcher of beer, or fondue with a mulled wine, through to a bottle of champagne and caviar, at Aspen there's an après for everyone. The place is chock full of restaurants, bars and nightlife from romantic dinners to social get-togethers, quiet tête-à-têtes or non-stop partying. Put on blue jeans, or designer gear—it doesn't matter as "wear whatever, anywhere" is what goes here.

On the legal side, you must be 21 years old to drink alcohol, and you cannot walk the street with an open container of alcohol. Children can accompany their parents in restaurants but not in bars or clubs which, by the way, shut at 2:00 AM.

Aspen enjoys an international reputation for both its restaurants and its chefs, and many of the restaurants are also bars. In Aspen, options range from upscale and elegant (The Little Nell, Piñons, Renaissance, Olives in The St. Regis, and Syzygy) through to casual spots with lots of local flavor (the

J-Bar, La Cocina, Boogie's and Su Casa). In between, Ajax Tavern, L'Hostaria, Mezzaluna, Jimmy's, and Mirabella will satisfy culinary cravings with ease. In Snowmass, top spots include Krabloonik, Sage, Village Steakhouse and La Boheme. Restaurants that add a little adventure to the dining experience include the ever-popular Pine Creek Cookhouse up Castle Creek Road.

OTHER ACTIVITIES

With such an enormous variety of galleries and stores—including Chanel's highest-grossing store—there is something for every taste and pocket. The town is fun for window shopping or just walking around, and there are plenty of activities for non-skiers including daily snowshoe tours—led by naturalist guides—on Aspen Mountain, and in Snowmass at Two Creeks. Tours include easy walks along 11,000-foot (3,353-m) Richmond Ridge on the backside of Aspen Mountain, and follow a secluded, off-trail loop through the woods at Two Creeks. Along the way, mountain ecology, flora and fauna are explored and explained. Tours depart twice daily at 10:00 AM and 1:00 PM.

OTHER ACTIVITIES

Snowshoeing	800-525-6200
Snow Cycles	970-920-0987
Tube Town	970-925-1220
Snowmass Nordic Touring Center	800-525-6200
The Aspen Cross Country Center	970-544-9246
Dogsled Rides	970-923-4342
Aspen by Air	970-925-7625
Ice Skating	970-925-6360
Cooking School of Aspen	970-920-1879

USEFUL PHONE NUMBERS

General Information	970-925-1220
Tourist Office & Lodgings Information	970-925-9000
Doctor Aspen Valley Hospital	970-925-1120
High Mountain Taxis	970-925-8294
Aspen Expeditions	970-925-7625

USEFUL WEBSITES

Aspen Official Website	www.aspensnowmass.com
Accommodations online	www.stayaspensnowmass.com
List of hotel websites	www.gowesttours.com/hotels-est.htm
Weather Report	www.wunderground.com
UIAGM Backcountry Guides	www.aspenexpeditions.com
Jon Barnes's multi-media taxi	www.ultimatetaxi.com

▲ **FROM SILVER TO SKIS**
Hyman Avenue is just north of Main Street in downtown Aspen, close to the free skier shuttle. The avenue has upmarket stores, a mall and, in The Snowflake Inn and St Moritz Lodge, two excellent economy lodgings.

PRONOUNCED "BEAUT" THIS RESORT IS A REAL ONE – NO PRETENSIONS, NO ASPIRATIONS TO ASPEN, IN FACT IT PLAYS UP TO ITS ANTI-GLITZY, "DOWNHOME" IMAGE. THIS IS WHERE YOU GRAB AN EARLY LIFT, SAVOR THE UNTRACKED POWDER, AND GO BIG. WHICH IS WHY THE NORTH FACE OF THE MOUNTAIN HAS HOSTED MANY CHAMPIONSHIPS.

CRESTED BUTTE

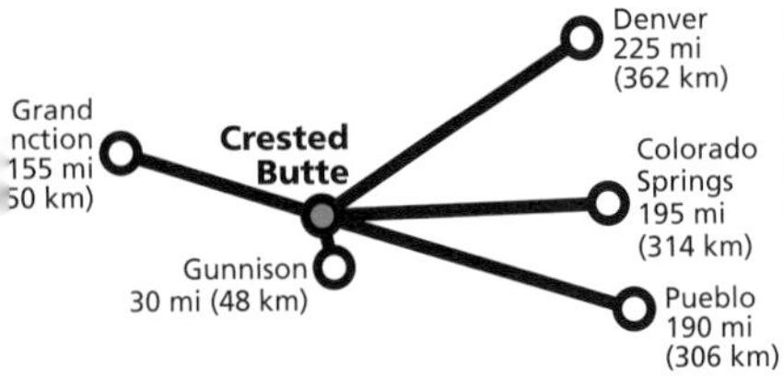

Whatever their Colorado allegiances, skiers in the know regard Crested Butte as unique. In a state with some of the world's best powder and several very high-profile resorts, the Butte claims to be more real on every level, from its old mining village center to its gnarly mountain terrain. The result is a mountain community first, ski resort second. Local skiers certainly reflect this—the town has more than its fair share of telemarkers and backcountry skiers who revel in an average of nearly 298 inches (745 cm) of snow each season. The closest they come to chic is during the annual Crested Butte-to-Aspen overnight ski race across the mountains, which must rate as much culture shock as mountain marathon for the participants, who arrive at dawn into the glitz of Aspen. The connection between the two resorts is as tenuous as this crazy trek implies—it might be just a few miles as the crow flies, but it's hours by the most direct winter road link and even further in spirit.

For Europeans and many Americans, that's the appeal: Wild West of the genuine variety. It's also far enough from Denver and the Interstate that crowds are almost unknown. The one lift that regularly has a line is the North Face poma, where you might have to wait long enough to read the instructions on how to ride it. Only when you try to put them into words do the actions seem complicated, yet this style of lift is such a rare challenge in the U.S. that if you make it to the top first time you're considered good enough for the expert terrain that it accesses: the ungroomed bowls and steeps interspersed with bands of rock that are home to the U.S. Extreme Freeskiing Championships each year.

GETTING THERE

Crested Butte lies at 8,885 feet (2,708 m) in the Elk Mountain Range of Southwest Colorado's Rocky Mountains, surrounded by over a million acres (404,700 ha) of National Forest, and within a few miles of the Black Canyon of the Gunnison, the newest National Park in the U.S. The town is 225 miles (362 km) southwest of Denver, the state capital and location of the nearest international airport.

From Denver International Airport (D.I.A) there

◄ WHAT YOU SEE IS WHAT YOU GET
Nightfall on the northwestern face of Crested Butte Mountain revealing over 50 percent of the skiable trails and terrain.

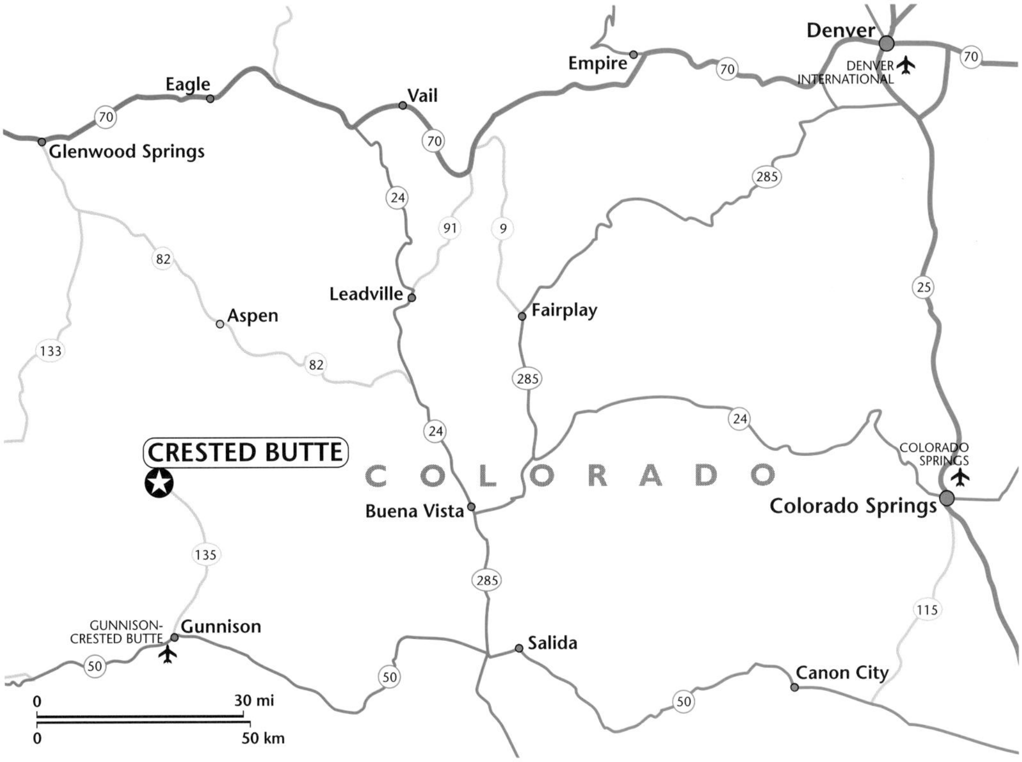

MOUNTAIN FACTS

Base	9,375 feet	2,858 m
Summit	12,162 feet	3,707 m
Highest Lift	11,875 feet	3,620 m
Lowest Lift	9,100 feet	2,774 m
Elevation	3,062 feet	933 m

Easy	14%
Intermediate	32%
Advanced	12%
Expert	42%
Number of trails	85
Longest trail	2.6 miles (4.2 km)
Ski area	1,058 acres (428 ha)

SNOWFALL

Annual snowfall	298 inches (745 cm)
Snowmaking	300 acres (121 ha)

SKI LIFTS

Gondolas	-
High-Speed Quads	3
Fixed Grip Quads	-
Triple Chairs	3
Double Chairs	3
Surface Lifts	3
Magic Carpets	2
Total	14
Riders per hour	18,160

SKI SEASON
Mid-December to early April

ACCOMMODATIONS

HOTELS AT BASE AREA
THE SHERATON
CLUB MED
THE NORDIC INN
MANOR LODGE
BED & BREAKFAST
CLAIM JUMPER
ELIZABETH ANNE
PURPLE MOUNTAIN LODGE
THE GREAT ESCAPE

are short connecting flights to Gunnison on United Express year-round. During the winter months, there are also daily direct jet flights from Houston on Continental Airlines. From Gunnison to Crested Butte is a 30-minute drive, by Alpine Express Shuttle or rental car. By road from Denver is about 4 to 4.5 hours' drive—a tiring option if you've flown direct from Europe. There is no rail connection to the resort.

THE VILLAGE

There are two distinct parts to Crested Butte: the original town and, three miles (4.8 km) up the valley, the resort's base area known as Mount Crested Butte, where most skiers stay. The free shuttle between the two is your chance to ride a real American school bus, like in the movies. Americans hate them—they are reminded of school—and everyone else loves them, though once the novelty has worn off, having to commute for a night out is an undeniable drawback.

Crested Butte started as a mining town back in the late 1800s. The historic Victorian district is home to the resort's best dining, shopping, and nightlife, where every quaint wooden building looks as though it's off the set of a western. As with every other old Colorado mountain town, Butch Cassidy and the Sundance Kid are alleged to have hidden out here but in this case you can believe it.

Mount Crested Butte has the resort's main hotels, condominiums, and some restaurants and bars. The cluster of buildings is right on the base area, making most accommodations virtually ski-in, ski-out.

ACCOMMODATIONS

The resort's hotels (at Mount Crested Butte) are the Sheraton, Club Med, the Nordic Inn and Manor Lodge. Club Med Crested Butte claims to be the only family "ski village" in North America offering an all-inclusive ski vacation. The Sheraton is the ritziest of the lot, with all the amenities you would expect and a large outdoor hot tub, as has the Nordic Inn. Other options, in town and at Mount Crested Butte, include condominiums, bed and breakfasts, and lodges. Budget lodgings are available in Gunnison, half an hour away.

▶ MAIN STREET
Crested Butte Town is based on a gridiron pattern and Elk Avenue is a main drag. With its angular buildings and pastel trims and Rocky Mountain backdrop it's certainly eyecatching.

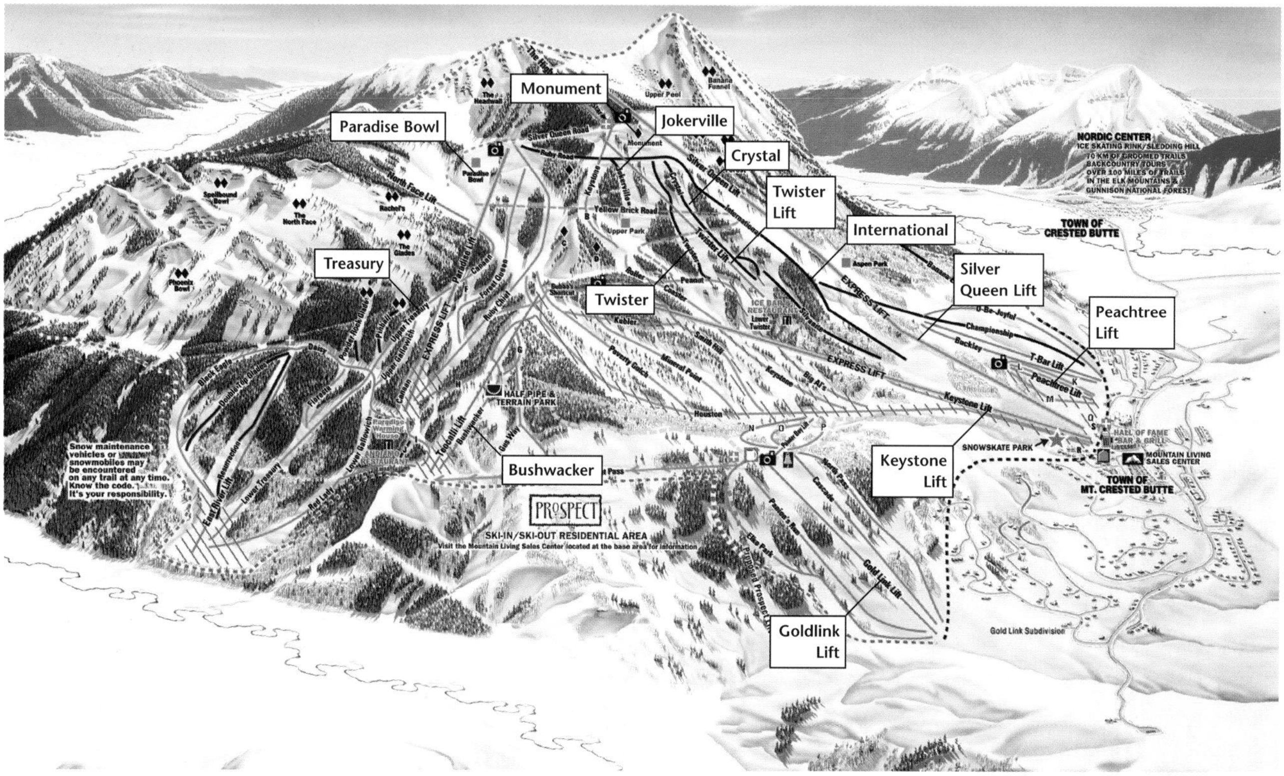

SKI AREA

As with many other high-altitude North American resorts, beware that base level is high (not just the peaks); the elevation may be good for snow conditions, but sea level-dwelling vacationers will need to acclimatize to the altitude. Base is at 9,375 feet (2,858 m) and the highest lift-served point is at 11,875 feet (3,620 m), giving a vertical drop of 2,775 feet (846 m) to the lowest chairlift at 9,100 feet (2,774 m); or with a hike to the peak, it's 3,062 feet (933 m.)

Though the resort is now promoting itself as a family destination and offers some quality skiing for beginners, it is best known as host to the U.S. Extreme ski and snowboard championships held on the "steepest lift-served terrain in North America." It's not only steep but, thanks to a mainly northerly aspect and high altitude, by mid-season it is usually well covered with the snow it needs to make the rockiest sections skiable. None of this terrain is groomed, much of it involves a hike to get to, and it's only patrolled at the end of the day. The intention is to make you feel that you're really out there, and you are: cautiously following tracks is as likely to lead you to a cliff jump as to the easiest route down the forty-degree plus terrain. The ungroomed Extreme Limits terrain covers 448 acres (181 ha) and is covered in detail by a photo-based map—entirely separate from the standard trail map, available in local stores. It provides a useful guide to the area which, compared to the marked trails, has very little signposting.

The rest of the skiing is a mix of easy, well-groomed terrain with beginner-friendly slow-skiing zones clearly marked and enforced, and plenty of flattering intermediate slopes, but there is not really enough terrain suitable to satisfy keen intermediates. The 85 trails total just 8.2 miles (13 km) in length, of which the longest trail is 2.6 miles (4.2 km). Three hundred acres (121 ha or 29 percent) of the ski area are covered by snowmaking facilities.

A new area, Prospect at Mt. Crested Butte, is being developed to provide ski-in, ski-out homes, hotel, and retail space. This will culminate in the expansion of ski facilities on to a second mountain to provide more intermediate terrain. Eleven lifts and 35 trails over 417 acres (169 ha) will be connected by gondola

▼ FROM EXPERT TO BEGINNER
"Beaut" isn't really an intermediates' resort and the options are limited. Ironically for a resort hailed for its expert terrain, there's still plenty of scope for beginners and early intermediates with good nursery slopes near the base, well-focused beginners' and childrens' ski instruction, and some of the best easy skiing around.

to the main mountain, but no date is yet confirmed for completion.

SKI LIFTS

The Crested Butte lift system has a capacity of 18,160 skiers per hour, with three high-speed quads, three triple chair lifts, three doubles, three surface lifts, and two magic carpets for children. Lifts run from 9:00 AM to 4:00 PM.

The resort is known for its lack of lift lines but not for waiting. During peak holiday times chairs are filled by an efficient loading system, with "singles" lines allowing people skiing alone to slot into spare spaces. The North Face lift, leading to the Extreme Limits, is the one exception to the no-waiting rule, particularly on powder days.

LIFT PASSES

An adult day pass costs US$55. Children aged 16 and under "pay their age" per day to ski, so a six-year-old child (or its parents) pays US$6 per day to ski. Photo I.D. is required for discounted passes. Complete beginners can buy a pass at a reduced rate with a "Never-Ever" lesson.

Lift passes can be bought at the lift ticket window, at Crested Butte Mountain Supply, and with lodging packages at Crested Butte Vacations. The ticketing system uses lift operator scanning—it's not hands-free, but you don't have to grapple with a turnstile.

SKI SCHOOLS AND GUIDING

The ski and snowboard school is divided into Adults' and Kids' Ski and Snowboard World, located in the Gothic Building for adults and the Whetstone Building for kids, both slopeside. The drop-off point for children is the parking lot behind the school. Details are available on www.CrestedButteResort.com. For reservations and information call 970-349-2252 or email skischool@cbmr.com.

Thanks to the terrain on offer, the ski school is well regarded not just for beginners, but also to help strong skiers learn advanced skills. A cost-effective "workshop," with at most four participants, in the Extreme Limits terrain is a unique opportunity to learn to ski exceptionally challenging trails, rather than merely survive them. Crested Butte is also the venue chosen by a number of specialist ski clinics, including two time World Extreme Skiing champion, Kim Reichhelm's women-only ski adventures.

Adult group lessons start at 9:45 AM and workshops (maximum of four) at 9:45 AM and 1:15 PM. Private lessons are from 9:00 AM until 4:00 PM. In Kids' World, all-day lessons start at 8:30 AM, half-day lessons at 9:30 AM or 1:00 PM. The minimum age for children is three years. Daycare and non-skiing activities are available for kids aged 6 months to three years, and there is lunchtime supervision, allowing parents a full day's skiing.

Group sizes are dependent on the season—they are bigger in busy periods, but ski school will never turn anyone away. Prices for adults—private lessons: 2 hours, 1 person US$180; 3 hours, 1 person, US$245; 6 hours (all day) 1–5 people US$435; 2.5-hour workshop US$75; group lessons US$60 (additional lessons US$55); complete beginner lessons, 3 hours and lift ticket, US$75. Daycare costs US$12 per hour or US$70 all day, 8:30 AM–4:30 PM.

BEGINNERS

Despite the resort's "extreme" tag, beginners are well served at Crested Butte—in fact the amount of well-groomed, easy terrain that's simple and safe to access is one of the resort's great strengths. In addition to piste patrollers enforcing slow skiing areas, skier numbers tend to be so low that beginners can turn and stop as they please, or as their skis dictate, without fear of being mowed down. The main area for beginners is off the Peachtree lift; the Keystone lift is also surrounded by gentle terrain. From there you can also access the Painter Boy lift and Goldlink to find more green trails.

▲ MAKE YOUR OWN TRACKS
There aren't classic tree-lined trails as much as open slopes with widely dispersed spruce and the like as well as jutting rocks and cliff lines. You carve out your own territory. Crested Butte gives Jackson Hole a good run for its money when it comes to extreme double black diamond adventures.

◄ SNOWFALL SECURITY
You're never very far from rocky outgrowths when skiing extreme at Crested Butte, so a fair amount of snow cover is a must before skiing any tricky terrain. Powder days are also therefore even more welcome at this resort to cushion potentially painful falls! It also means skiing can be limited at the start and end of the season here if the dumps have not been heavy.

▲ **NIGHT-TIME GIGS**
Like the old cowboy movies but with added psychedelia and pastels, the saloon atmosphere can be boisterous with hard-hitting après-ski. Live bands, DJs and night-life generally happen along Elk Avenue.

EATING ON THE MOUNTAIN

BUBBA'S @ PARADISE
PARADISE WARMING HOUSE
LAST TRACKS FONDUE

INTERMEDIATES

One third of Crested Butte's terrain is suitable for intermediates, though it's mostly at the easy end of the scale. For the more adventurous much of it is undemanding, while the gap between the blue trails and the advanced and ungroomed areas is too large for skiers at this level to bridge. Nevertheless, for a relatively modest-sized ski area, it packs in plenty of variety. Newcomers to Crested Butte feel they are constantly discovering new areas, thanks to the shape of the mountain and the effective interweaving of the trails.

The resort's longest trail—2.6 miles (4.2 km), from Peak to Treasury—is ideal for intermediates. The Bushwacker is more challenging than most blue terrain, with one particular short, steep pitch; Paradise Bowl offers plenty of wide, cruising trails, along with a few small mogul fields which are ideal for learning to ski bumps. The high-speed quad and a restaurant at the bottom make this a good area for groups to ski laps.

ADVANCED & EXPERT

Just 12 percent of the terrain is rated advanced, but this makes a clear distinction between advanced and expert, for whom there is a huge amount of skiing (42 percent). Moguls and steeps can be found from the Twister Lift on Upper Keystone, Jokerville, Crystal, Twister, and International; Resurrection provides big bumps; additionally, Horseshoe, Horseshoe Springs, and Monument should all be tried before heading to the Extreme Limits territory. For powder, International is the place to go. It's a long run from the Silver Queen Lift, with a steep start followed by bumps before the runout into the base area. There are great views along the way, if you bother to stop.

The ungroomed Extreme Limits terrain, accessed by one Poma drag lift at the top of the resort, is the focus for expert skiers. It's also the venue for the SAAB U.S. Extreme Freeskiing Championships and the Subaru U.S. Extreme Boarderfest. There are 448 acres (181 ha) to play in and no skiing beyond these limits is permitted. Though it is (minimally) patrolled, you should obey instructions, and especially the restriction on the third bowl, which may not be hiked to after 2:30 PM—offenders lose their ski pass. Across the whole area there is no grooming, signposting is limited, and obstacles are unmarked, although warnings at the bottom and top of the final lift leave you in no doubt about what's in store. There are steep, narrow chutes, bowls, trees, and cliff bands to ski and jump. Some trails, such as Rambo, are in excess of 50 degrees. Others, like Body Bag, tell you all you need to know before you get there.

As well as the single drag access (followed by a hike, for much of the area), getting out from this side of the mountain is also less than ideal, with a traverse followed by a series of lifts back to the top. That aspect, and the amount of snow needed to make

► **BUTTE FOR BOARDERS**
Expert boarders are lured to Crested Butte by the Extreme Snowboarding Championships and by the extreme freeriding possibilities. From steep, wooded glades to more laid back terrain with lots of ungroomed carving, the resort is radical enough for different style riders.

the area skiable—it won't necessarily be open early season, or even in January—are the only drawbacks to what is rightly acknowledged as some of the U.S.'s best resort-based extreme skiing. Though you could spend all your time here, there are also serious challenges on the Headwall and down the funnel from the Peak, though it too needs plenty of snowcover.

Finding your way around is made easier with the aid of a guide from Guest Services (970-349-2211) or one of the excellent (small) group ski school lessons, some of which are specifically designed for skiers heading for the Extreme Limits. Other "workshops" include telemark skiing, bumps, and powder.

Powder hounds should head for the backcountry at Irwin Lodge, North America's largest snowcat operation, just 12 miles (19.3 km) from Crested Butte. With 2,200 acres (890 ha) and vertical trails of 2,100 feet (640 m), it's a powder heaven, with accommodations and guided snowcat skiing for intermediates to experts.

▲ A TALE OF TWO TOWNS

While Crested Butte Town is historic and naturally attractive, the base area of Mount Crested Butte is rather more severe—more like a French purpose-built resort: functional and serving all skiing and après-ski needs with upscale condos, hotels, bars and eating places.

BOARDING & FREESTYLE

Boarders and freeriders have full access to the mountain. The compact layout means big traverses and flats are infrequent. There's a terrain park and halfpipe accessible from the Teocali lift. The park includes three tables and five rails, and is home to the U.S. Extreme Boarderfest competition's Triple Air Event every year.

EATING ON THE MOUNTAIN

Many skiers head back to base for lunch. A quick-snack option is the burrito stall near Tom's Coffee Cart (best in town) by the main bus stop. On the hill is the Paradise Warming House at the foot of the Paradise lift with a good range of self-service food, a barbecue, and Bubba's table-service restaurant. Much smaller and more basic is the Twister Warming House—good for hot drinks and snacks and the "Last Tracks Fondue" followed by a ski or snowshoe torchlight parade back to the base area. Bubba's also features "Dinner at 10,000 Feet" where you ride to dinner in an open sleigh pulled by...a snowcat.

APRÈS SKI

Rafters is central to Mount Crested Butte's après ski, which runs for a couple of hours before people head for town. Live music and wet T-shirt contests are among the highlights, the later not being to everyone's taste. The Avalanche and a handful of other bars are quieter options. Several bars in town feature live music, including Talk of the Town, the Eldo, the Idle Spur, The Black Whale, and Kochevar's.

There are ten restaurants in Mount Crested Butte and many more in town; several double as bars and music venues. The minimum age for drinking alcohol is 21 but children may accompany their parents in bars and restaurants serving alcohol. The best restaurants are in town, where you can find something to suit most tastes. Le Bosquet, and Soupçon for French food, Italian at the Bacchanale, and excellent game at the Buffalo Grille. Just wander down Elk Avenue to pick from a dozen more—in Crested Butte you'll probably run out of skiing before you run out of eating options.

OTHER ACTIVITIES

Sledding, tubing, cross-country skiing with 37 miles (60 km) of groomed trails, snowshoeing and ice-skating take place at the Nordic Center in town.

USEFUL PHONE NUMBERS

Guest Services	970-349-2211
Crested Butte Vacation Reservations	888-463-6714
Alpine Express Shuttle Transfer	800-822-4844
Crested Butte Mountain Guides	970-349-5430
Snow Report	970-349-2323

USEFUL WEBSITES

Official Website	www.crestedbutteresort.com
Crested Butte Resort	www.crestedbutte.org
Crested Butte Mountain Guides	www.crestedbutteguides.com
Weather Reports	www.wunderground.com
Snow Report & Web Cams	www.rsn.com/cams

RESTAURANTS & BARS

THE WOODSTONE GRILLE
THE WOODSTONE DELI
RAFTERS EATERY & BAR
GOTHIC CAFETERIA
CASEY'S RESTAURANT & BAR
BROWN LABRADOR PUB

There are around 30 or more restaurants in town; many of them double as bars and music venues.

DRAMATIC MOUNTAIN BACKDROPS, SPECTACULAR VIEWS, AND THE SIGNIFICANT ADDITION OF PROSPECT BOWL IN 2002 MAKE THIS ATTRACTIVE HISTORIC MINING TOWN AN INCREASINGLY POPULAR DESTINATION RESORT. UNPRETENTIOUS AND REMOTE, THE RESORT AND THE SKI AREA OFFERS SOMETHING FOR ALL—FROM BEGINNER THROUGH EXPERT AND NON-SKIERS ALIKE.

TELLURIDE

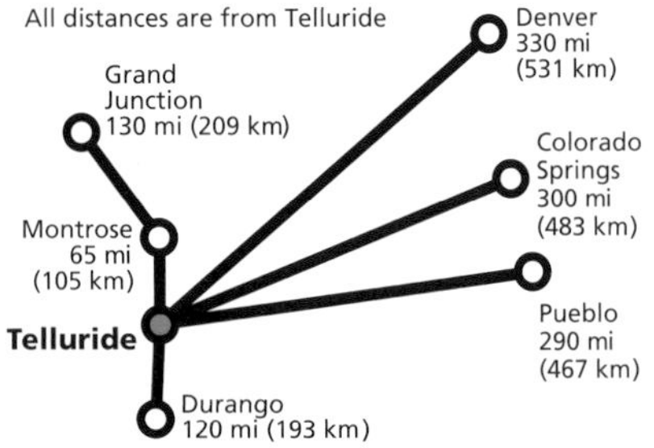

After the Gold Rush this gold and silver mining camp once boasted more millionaires per capita than New York City, and its wealth attracted Butch Cassidy who made his first bank heist here in 1889, but Telluride eventually replaced its picks, shovels and hammers with skis, sticks and boots in 1972. Thirty years later it is a gem of a ski resort, with Victorian architecture cradled under majestic peaks. Telluride is remarkable in that it has continued to stay true to its historic mining roots. The opening of Prospect Bowl in January 2002 almost doubled the size of the spirited and unpretentious ski area, and it has transformed this tiny canyon town from what was once generally viewed as a weekend resort into a full-fledged destination resort.

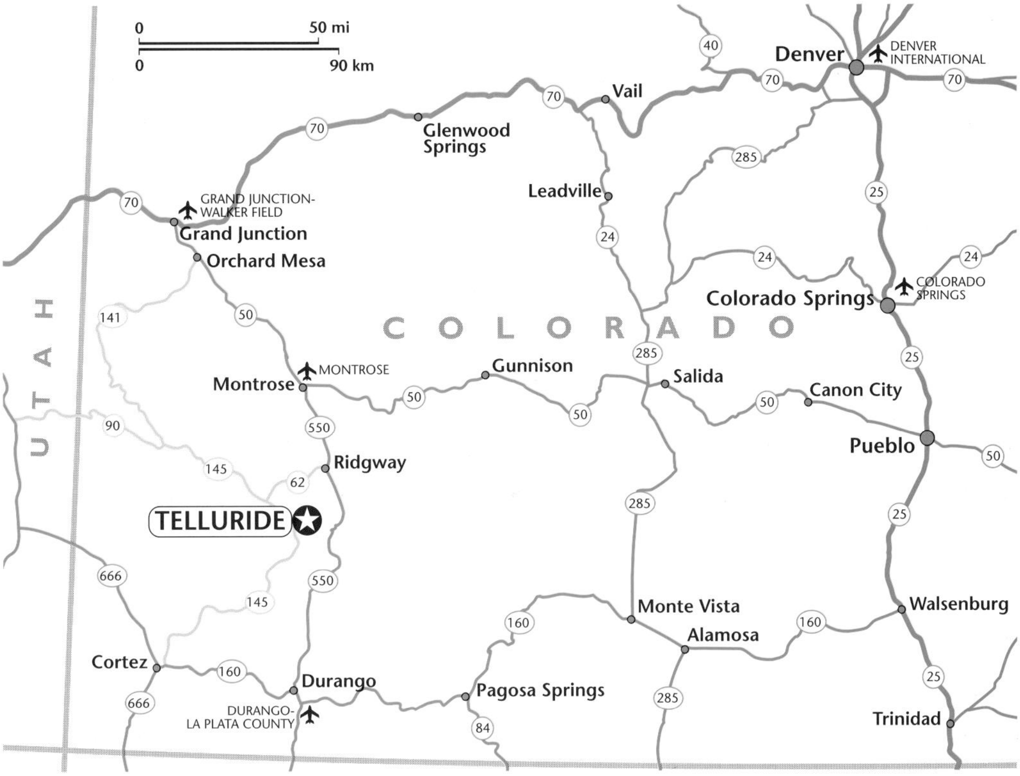

MOUNTAIN FACTS

Base	8,725 feet (2,660 m)
Summit	12,260 feet (3,738 m)
Elevation	3,530 feet (1,978 m)
Easy	24%
Intermediate	38%
Advanced & Expert	38%
Number of trails	84
Longest trail	4.6 miles (7.4 km)
Ski area	1,700 acres (680 ha)

SNOWFALL

Annual snowfall	309 inches (789 cm)
Snowmaking	204 acres (82 ha)

SKI LIFTS

High-Speed Gondolas	2
High-Speed Quads	7
Fixed Grip Quads	-
Triple Chairs	2
Double Chairs	2
Surface Lifts	3
Total	16
Riders per hour	21,186

SKI SEASON

Late November until early April

Peak season:

Christmas and late Feb to end March

GETTING THERE

Telluride's biggest asset is also its biggest challenge—its remote location: the closest traffic lights are a good 45 miles (72 km) away so it requires a bit more of an effort to get to, but the trip is well worth it. Located in the scenic San Juan Skyway in southwest Colorado, Telluride is far removed from any major cities. Nearby towns include Montrose 65 miles (105 km) south, Grand Junction 130 miles (209 km) south, and Durango 120 miles (193 km) northwest. The resort is approximately 330 miles (530 km) or seven hours from Denver, nine hours from Phoenix, and five hours from Albuquerque. The nearest international airport to Telluride is Denver International Airport, but you can fly closer to the Telluride Resort via Telluride Regional Airport, just six miles (10 km) away, or via Montrose Regional Airport, a scenic 65 miles (105 km) from Telluride.

THE VILLAGE

Just eight blocks wide and twelve blocks long, and at a base elevation of 8,750 feet (2,668 m), Telluride offers visitors small stores and galleries, historic charm, and mountain spirit. Just over the ridge—via Station St. Sophia at 10,535 feet (4,027 m)—lies the Mountain Village at 9,540 feet (2,910 m), which is a 92-acre (37-ha) purpose-built condo-dominated alpine enclave with luxury hotels, stylish boutiques and a few, select eateries. You won't find fast-food outlets, strip malls and chain stores in either Telluride or Mountain Village, and there is no need for a car as everything is within walking distance.

The main town and the resort are connected by a free gondola—roughly a 13-minute up-and-over-ride — and it's open from 7:00 AM to midnight. As well as fine restaurants, Mountain Resort also has a bank, post office, a market, antiques, galleries, jewelry, and gift stores. Telluride's bed base is not large enough to

▼ TRADITIONAL TASTES
Built in 1891, the 32-room New Sheridan is one of the town's oldest hotels and is located on Telluride's Main Street.

◄ THERE'S GOLD IN THEM HILLS
Set in a picturesque box-canyon in the San Juan Mountains, Telluride is an isolated but charmingly restored Victorian gold- and silver-mining town.

▼ LINKED VILLAGE
The modern Mountain Village has a sprinkling of upscale hotels and condos and is linked to Telluride by gondola and road.

create lift lines, and because Telluride is a destination resort, it is not bombarded by day traffic. Wide-open slopes and no lift lines are the norm in Telluride.

ACCOMMODATIONS

Telluride Ski Resort is pretty upscale, with the emphasis on luxurious lodgings, but there are also basic hotels for the budget-conscious traveler and a wide variety of condos and bed & breakfasts. Between the Town of Telluride and the Mountain Village there are approximately 16 hotels and a bed base of 5,200 pillows, so plenty to choose from. But one primary question you must ask before coming here is whether you prefer being in the middle of all the action or whether you crave solitude, because the houses, rustic lodges, and guest ranches are more off the beaten path (one is reachable only by snowmobile), forcing individuals to travel some distance.

If there is one premium hotel to single out it would have to be The Golden Door Spa at Wyndham Peak Resort at Mountain Village, which has become a favorite among locals and visitors. This elegant hotel features an extensive health spa, outdoor pool and an indoor climbing wall. The Franklin Manor Bed & Breakfast specializes in

romantic getaways and houses an impressive art collection. The five bedrooms have a Victorian flavor. The San Sophia Inn is right in the heart of the historic district, one block from the gondola. Full gourmet breakfast and afternoon cocktail hour with free drinks come as part of the service for the 16 guest rooms. For all lodgings enquiries check out www.telluridelodging.com

▼ PROSPECT BOWL
This newly opened area is mostly intermediate cruises among thickets of trees.

SKI AREA

Located in the Uncompahgre National Forest, under the massive Palmyra Peak at 13,320 feet (405 m), Telluride Ski Resort virtually doubled its size to 1,700 acres (680 ha) in 2002 with the grand opening of Prospect Bowl. This added 733 acres (297 ha) of new terrain and now provides the highest point on the mountain with the Gold Hill Lift standing at 12,260 feet (3,738 m). So skiers and boarders really have ample space to enjoy themselves on the mountain and its corduroy, bowls, glades, trees and chutes, and world-class views. Prospect Bowl links two sides of the mountain and bridges the gap between experts and novices. From serene to extreme, this inviting stash of intimate glades, open slopes and no lift lines has enhanced Telluride's charm as an "off the beaten path" destination. Of the 84 trails, 33 are for advanced and expert, 32 intermediate, and 19 beginner; and the mountain is naturally laid out, forcing runs to be segregated and preventing beginners from crossing over into expert terrain. The Telluride Ski Resort has 204 snowmaking acres (82 ha) located on most major lifts, with partial snowmaking on the other remaining lifts.

SKI LIFTS

There are a total of 16 lifts which are capable of transporting 21,186 people per hour. There are two high-speed gondolas, seven high-speed quads, two triples, two doubles, one platter, one magic carpet, and one surface lift, plus a couple of T-bars. The lift system on the Telluride Ski Mountain has drastically changed within the last couple of years. Lifts 4 and 5, which used to be triple and double lifts, have been transformed into high-speed quads, and now three new high-speed detachable quad lifts operate on the open bowls and trails of Prospect Bowl. In the

▲ SCENIC SETTING
The dramatic, craggy mountain backdrop is unusual for Colorado but is a bonus for beginners and intermediates heading down to Prospect Bowl and the Mountain Village.

▼ STEEP AND CRAGGY
A gondola and 2 chairlifts serve the steep wooded slopes above Telluride as well as giving access to the Mountain Village.

▲ **SEE FOREVER**
Open slopes and no lift lines add to Telluride's charms as an off-the-beaten-track ski destination. 'See Forever' is the resort's most popular trail keeping the panorama open from Mountain Village all the way to the La Sal Mountains of Utah.

coming years it is hoped to add two more lifts in Prospect Bowl, plus an additional on-mountain restaurant. The lift system uses the latest hi-tech chip technology and operates from 8:45 AM to 4:00 PM.

LIFT PASSES

Regular season day rates are US$65 for adults, US$36 for children (6–12 years) while children aged five and under ski free. Seniors (65-69) pay US$46, and seniors (70+) US$31. Adaptive passes (for physically and mentally challenged skiers) are US$31, and Nordic passes allowing two rides on Lift 10 cost US$20. Multi-day tickets are offered at reduced daily rates and can be purchased in advance at the two ticket offices in Telluride, one at the base of Coonskin Lift 7, another at the base of the gondola, and there are also two ticket offices in the Mountain Village, one in the Activity Center and the other in The Golden Door Spa at Wyndham Peaks Resort.

DAILY LIFT PASSES

Adults:	US$65.00
Senior (65-69):	US$46.00
Senior (70+):	US$31.00
Adaptive:	US$31.00
Nordic:	US$20.00
Children (6-12 years):	US$36.00
Children (5 & Under):	Free

SKI SCHOOL & GUIDING

The Telluride Ski & Snowboard School offers alpine, telemark, and snowboard lessons for novice to expert abilities. It is located in the Mountain Village Plaza near the base of the gondola and operates from 10:00 AM to 3:00 PM. Ski groups should be no more than ten people, and three years old is the minimum age for young children. Children are supervised during lunch and the cost of lunch is included in the cost of the lessons. There are some good deals for beginners taking ski lessons at Telluride that allow you to pay one rate, which includes ski lessons, ski pass and lunch, for a cost of about US$70 (compare this to a regular adult ski ticket of US$65). Also, not associated with the ski resort are a variety of companies that offer special instruction for snowshoeing, Nordic skiing, snowmobiling, and ice climbing.

SKI SCHOOL
565 Mountain Village Boulevard
Telluride, CO 81435
(800) 801-4832
www.tellurideskiresort.com
970-728-7496

BEGINNERS

The mountain has 24 percent of trails and four areas ideal for beginners. The main area for beginners is Meadows and Lift 1, with gentle green trails that will boost the confidence of any new skier. Also, Lift 1 is an enclosed gondola, which first-time skiers and young children will find much easier than chairlifts or T-bars. Once you've mastered Meadow's, progress to Lift 10 with its long, rolling trails. There are double green trails, long in distance, allowing for more skiing and less lift riding. The Enchanted Forest also provides beginners and intermediates with the chance to test their skills in beginner tree skiing. Gorrono Basin, accessible from Lifts 7, 4 and 5, is primarily laced with friendly blue trails and a couple of greens too, and is very family-friendly, especially as it's in close proximity to Mountain Village's amenities and the Gorrono Ranch restaurant. The new Prospect Bowl terrain with its dramatic mountain backdrops and

▼ **TAKING THE PLUNGE**
One of the most popular runs in the U.S. is the Plunge, a jaw-dropping black-diamond bump trail descending 3,140 vertical feet (958 m) into Telluride.

◀ SIMPLE, SMOOTH AND SUNNY
Prospect Bowl was opened on January 12, 2002, and offers ample opportunities for freshies and face shots in its 733 acres (297 ha).

spectacular views is accessible for beginners via Ute Park—a beginner's and low intermediate's dream, with meandering green and blue trails nearly two miles (3.2 km) long.

INTERMEDIATES

The mountain has plenty of intermediate trails (38 percent of the terrain) and lift 5 is the perfect hideaway offering a variety of rolling terrain, wide chutes with moderate pitches, and a handful of open tree runs. The longest and most challenging trail for intermediates is See Forever, which is three miles (5 km) long. It starts at the top of Gold Hill Mountain and stretches all the way down to the base of lift 4, allowing intermediates to view all the wonderful scenery of the mountain by staying on the same trail from top to bottom. For the intermediate skier or boarder there is a lot of terrain to cover in order to get the true Telluride skiing experience. For instance, all the Lift 4 and 5 trails are spectacular areas to hit. These two lifts primarily consist of double and single blues, but provide a variety of terrain. Misty Maiden on Lift 4 is known for its fabulous corduroy and speed, and Palmyra on Lift 5 is good for moguls. Also, the new Prospect Bowl has plenty of tailor-made trails—check out Magnolia and Sandia.

ADVANCED & EXPERT

For those wanting to enjoy Telluride's renowned steeps and bumps, Lifts 9 and 6 provide the advanced skier with plenty of thrills. These two lifts are an advanced skier's paradise on powder days. The Plunge, located on Lift 9, is the must-hit trail. This black diamond bump trail descending 3,140 vertical feet (958 m) from the top of the Mountain into Telluride is like an "upside-down egg carton turned vertical", but the trail is made less formidable by split-grooming, which leaves one side of the trail bumped up, and the other half groomed. Bushwacker, Mammoth, Joint Point, and the testing Kant-Mak-M and Spiral Stairs, also located on Lift 9, provide a variety of steep trails and moguls. Also, the thrills of the bumps and trees can easily be found on Lift 6, which is an advanced skier's paradise on powder days. Apex—located on Lift 6—is a great place to do some tree skiing while the aforementioned Plunge, located on Lift 9, is a great combination of bumps and corduroy.

For powder hounds in search of the "sweetest powder shots," Gold Hill is the place to go and find Colorado's renowned "Champagne Powder," and the terrain under the new Gold Hill Lift provides experts

▼ UPPING THE EXPERT ANTE
The emphasis on skiing at Telluride is cruising and beginner slopes, but experts are not left out. They head for the double-black diamond Spiral Stairs trails above the town with steep gladed trails along the ridge from Giuseppe's to Gold Hill with a summit of 12,260 feet (3,738 m). The Gold Hill Lift accesses former hike-only terrain filled with chutes, above-treeline bowls and heart-stopping steeps. The views of the San Juan Mountains are dramatic.

▲ **POWDER SEEKERS**
Gold Hill Lift has the deepest of fresh powder with an abundance of open bowls and chutes. Late in the day powder stashes can still be found in the trees off Lifts 6, 9 and 12 (Prospect Lift).

with steep chutes, open bowls and leg-burning bumps. Telluride also offers a variety of inbound hikes to expert terrain off Bald Mountain in Prospect Bowl. In addition, experts have access to a back-country gate at the top of the Gold Hill Lift, and in good snow conditions this provides some amazing powder stashes. The terrain out of the gate is out of bounds and is not patrolled. It is only recommended for expert skiers with a broad knowledge of the backcountry and avalanches. It is an extremely dangerous area and involves intricate route-finding and challenging skiing through a variety of risky conditions.

For the ultimate backcountry experience, the San Juan Hut System beckons. It's a 45-mile (73-km) expanse of trails from Telluride to Ouray with intermediate and expert trails up and over the Sneffles Range. Guided trips are available for day-trips and longer. The huts provide shelter and overnight accommodation (padded bunks, wood-burning stoves, chopped wood and a kitchen) and are spaced every 6–9 miles (10–15 km). And if that isn't enough to challenge you, Heliskiing is also an option here. Helitrax—the only helicopter skiing in Colorado—will whisk you from Mountain Village to the secret stashes of the San Juan Mountains.

BOARDING & FREESTYLE

For snowboard and trick skier enthusiasts Telluride provides some of the best riding in Colorado. The Air Garden Terrain Park, the largest in the southwest United States, has more than 8 acres (3 ha) of terrain and 23 hits of berms, banks, tabletops and pyramids as well as new sliding rails. And there's Ute Park with its freestyle terrain with halfpipes and other features. For free riders—Telluride's slopes are freeriding par excellence—check out the steeps, cliffs, and chutes on Gold Hill. A no-nonsense way up is to take Lifts 8 and 9 rather than the gondola, and then hike up to find your preferred chute, glade or open meadow. East and West Drain are two natural pipes with great tree riding. All in all Telluride is snowboard friendly, making it easy for snowboarders to cruise around and with only a few cat tracks, boarders do not usually have to worry about navigating long, flat areas. However, due to Prospect Bowl's natural, rolling terrain snowboarders may find it difficult to maintain speed in certain areas.

EATING ON THE MOUNTAIN

Telluride offers a variety of on-mountain restaurants and cuisine. Gorrono restaurant, located mid-mountain on Misty Maiden, is an historic ranch-style building that offers American favorites and barbecues on a huge, sunny deck with great

▶ **BRIGHT LIGHTS SMALL TOWN**
In a town just eight blocks wide and 12 blocks long everything is walkable in Telluride. Come nightfall that means seeking the après ski as well as the shops.

RESTAURANTS & BARS

SMUGGLER'S GRILL
FLORADORA
EXCELSIOR CAFÉ
EAGLE'S BAR GRILL
FINE DINING
HARMON'S
LA CAMPAGNA
ALLRED'S
WILDFLOWER
LEIMGRUBER'S
SWEDE FINN HALL
NEW SHERIDAN BAR
GREAT ROOM
NOIR BAR

views. Whether it is spending just a few minutes here to grab a quick bite or staying hours to soak up some sun on the deck, Gorrono is a big hit with locals and visitors alike. Big Billie's at the base of Lifts 1 and 10 also has American favorites, barbecues, and Southwestern fare. The Pizza Chalet offers pizza, salad, sandwiches, espresso drinks, and ice cream. Guiseppe's, located way up at 11, on the top of Lift 9, features quick Italian fare in a cozy setting. Finally, the newest restaurant addition to the mountain is Allred's, very haute cuisine and spectacular views to boot. At night, it becomes a glittering après-ski gem.

APRÈS SKI

There are around 20 bars and many more restaurants, and after a day on the slopes, locals and visitors can be found enjoying a late afternoon drink in many of Telluride's favorite après spots such as The Wildflower or Leimgruber's for beer, or sipping a margarita at Swede Finn Hall.

After hours the resort veers more to quiet sophistication and family-friendly restaurants. Cocktail hour at the historic New Sheridan Bar, with a turn-of-the-century hand-carved wood bar and a billiards room, has a great social atmosphere and is located on Main Street. A new cool venue is Blue Point's Noir Bar, the swank and hip martini bar, replete with leather sofas, faux fur bench seats, and leopard-print spotted carpets. For those who prefer a drink in a quiet and cozy place, Allred's and the New Sheridan Bar are also great hangouts for drink.

Between them, the town of Telluride and the Mountain Village have approximately 60 restaurants and several of them including The Cosmopolitan, Harmon's, Rustico Ristorante (for Italian wines), Campagna, and Allred's are noted for their wine lists. Nestled on top of the mountain and accessible only by the gondola, Allred's gives diners spectacular views of the massive peaks that frame Telluride. For the late-night younger set there's live music at Fly Me to the Moon Saloon, the only nightclub in town. The bars in Telluride and the Mountain Village close at 1:30 AM.

OTHER ACTIVITIES

The new Station Recreation offers nighttime tubing in the Mountain Village or you can take a spin around the ice or even join in a hockey or broomball game at the ice skating rink. Ice climbing, indoor climbing, Nordic skiing, and sleigh rides are available and there are snowmobiling, snowshoeing and dogsled tours too. If none of that appeals, or you need to soothe those aches and pains, the resort has plenty of spas offering relaxing massage, saunas, and steam rooms—Condé Nast's *Traveler* magazine put Telluride in its Top Five for pampering. For shopaholics, the variety of the stores is amazing for such a tucked-away resort and includes boutiques, clothing stores, sports stores, art galleries, and bookstores with coffee shops.

The best place to rent or buy ski equipment is Telluride Sport, with six locations between town and Mountain Village each providing ski and snowboard equipment. Easy Rider Sports and Slopestyle are must-stop shops for board enthusiasts, and Jagged Edge Mountain Gear, Paragon Ski & Sport and the Telluride Mountaineer all offer a variety of outdoor gear and equipment. Also, Boot Doctors is a great place for custom boot fitting, and rental ski equipment.

▲ **ALPINE CHARM**
Gorrono's Ranch is located mid-mountain on Misty Maiden and is an historic ranch-style building offering refreshment and outdoor barbecue on the sunny deck with stunnig views.

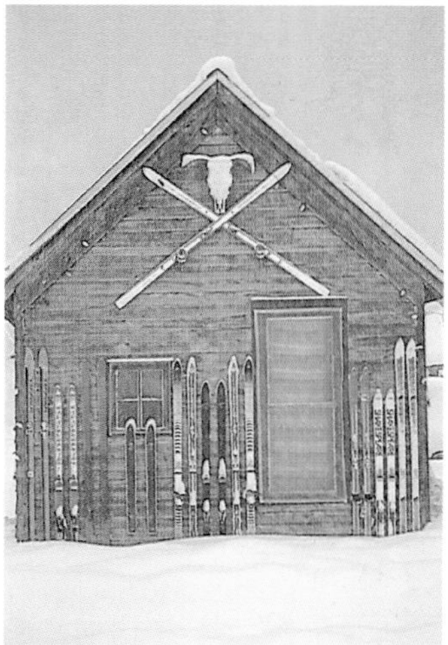

▼ **HUT SYSTEM**
The San Juan Hut System beckons backcountry skiers and boarders to brave a 45-mile (73-km) expanse of trails from Telluride to Ouray.

USEFUL PHONE NUMBERS

Visitor Information Center	970-728-4431
Telluride Central Reservations	866-287-5016
Daily Grooming Report	970-728-7425
Telluride Ski Patrol & Rescue Service	970-728-7587
Telluride Medical Centre	970-728-3848
Telluride Express Shuttle & Taxis	970-728-6000
Alpine Luxury Limo	877-728-8750
Mountain Limo	970-728-9606

USEFUL WEBSITES

Official Website	www.tellurideskiresort.com
Vacation Planner	www.summitnet.com
Weather Reports	www.wunderground.com
Snow Report & Web Cams	www.rsn.com/cams
Images of Telluride	www.telluridepress.com

IF YOU FANCY YOUR SKIING STEEP AND DEEP IN AN UNCROWDED RESORT WITH VIEWS OF THE NEW MEXICAN DESERT, THEN TAOS VALLEY IS YOUR VALHALLA. UNLESS, THAT IS, YOU ARE A SNOWBOARDER—IN WHICH CASE FORGET IT, BOARDERS ARE NOT ALLOWED. THERE ARE FEW SKI AREAS LEFT THAT ARE STILL RUN BY THE FOUNDING FAMILY WITH A PASSION FOR SKIING, AND WITH SUCH A WELCOMING FEEL, BUT TAOS IS ONE OF THEM.

TAOS

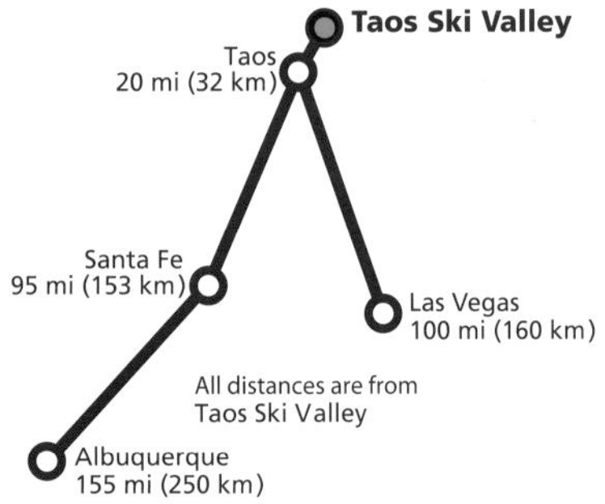

The cacti and sagebush of the arid New Mexican desert might not seem an obvious location for a ski resort, but the big mountain that overshadows Taos Ski Valley offers some of the most legendary double black diamond skiing to be found in the United States. And intermediates and beginners won't feel left out either, with plenty of varied runs and an excellent ski school that all levels are encouraged to join. Taos is about as far south as you can get for big skiing in the Rockies, and it is very Alpine, very welcoming, very secluded, and very much still family-run. You'll not find a big development with lots of razzamatazz, just good, honest, challenging skiing in unique and breathtaking surroundings.

GETTING THERE

Taos, in northern New Mexico, is not really near anywhere. It lies as it always has, somewhat hidden from the glare of the better-known Colorado resorts (Vail is one of the nearest at 276 miles/444 km). Albuquerque International Sunport, the nearest international airport, is about 135 miles (217 km)

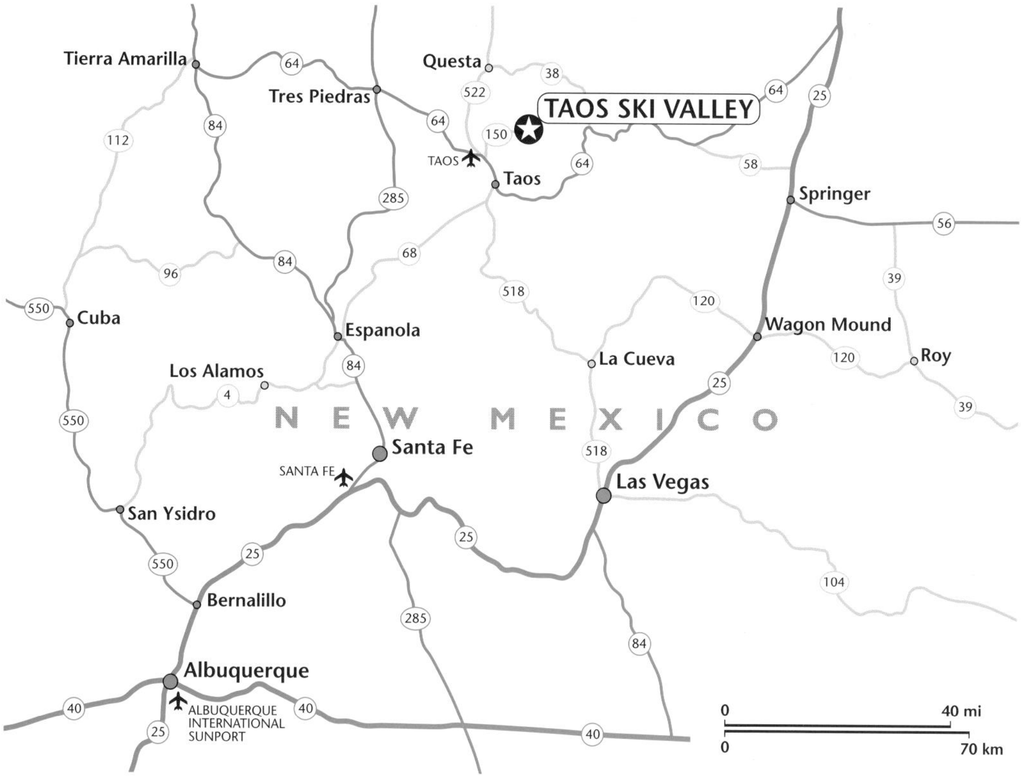

MOUNTAIN FACTS

Base	9,207 feet (2,806 m)
Summit	12,481 feet (3,804 m)
Elevation	3,274 feet (998 m)
Easy	24%
Intermediate	25%
Advanced & Expert	51%
Number of trails	72
Longest trail	2.5 miles (4 km)
Ski area	1,294 acres (524 ha)

SNOWFALL

Annual snowfall	312 inches (792 cm)
Snowmaking	100% on beginner & intermediate slopes

SKI LIFTS

Gondolas	-
High Speed Quads	-
Fixed Grip Quads	4
Triple Chairs	1
Double Chairs	5
Surface Lifts	2
Total	12
Riders per hour	15,500

SKI SEASON
Late November to first Sunday in April

away, which translate into a 2 hours 15 minutes' journey by road (Highways 64 or 68).
The town of Taos, 20 miles away (32 km), sits on a branch of the Rio Grande in the Sangre de Cristo Mountains, near Wheeler Mountain (the highest point in New Mexico) and 55 miles (86 km) from Santa Fe.

THE VILLAGE

The resort grew out of one man's vision: Ernie Blake spotted from his Cessna 170 what seemed to be a vast natural snow basin and he moved to Taos valley lock, stock, and camper van in 1955. The Hondo Lodge (now the Inn at Snakedance) was his first building and the first lift was installed with the help of 16 locals and a mule. The resort is still run by Ernie's family and this "hands-on" heritage gives the village a compact, cozy, welcoming feel. But don't just take our word for it—editors at *Ski magazine* have given the resort their "Top Choice" accolade too.

Nearby Taos town has plenty of accommodations and attractions. It is a former Spanish settlement featuring picturesque adobe architecture typical of the local Native American culture. (Adobe is earth mixed with water and straw, then either poured into forms or made into sun-dried bricks.) The climate and architecture made Taos an artists' and writers' colony—D.H. Lawrence lived here during the 1920s (his ranch is maintained by the University of New Mexico) and famous frontiersman Kit Carson lived here too. The local Indian (Pueblo) culture goes back over 1,000 years. Today Taos is well known as a haven for artists and it boasts many varied galleries. Taos is also the home of the oldest inhabited Native American Pueblo (village) in the U.S.

▼ ROMANTIC AND SCARY
With a scenic backdrop like this it's not surprising that the ski press vote Taos a favorite spot to ski, eat and party. And while the vertical may not be in the records, the skiing is good.

◄ TOTALLY TAOS
Taos has long been a magnet for seekers of the steep and deep as well as offering some gently novice slopes from the rather indeterminate ridge.

► STAYING CLOSE
Lodging at the resort is fairly limited—from the St Bernard to the more modern Inn at Snake Dance which is less than 10 yards from the chairlfit. Warm hospitality, good food and great ski packages make the latter the village's most convenient, comfortable lodging. Hot tub, sauna, spa, massages are all on tap.

ACCOMMODATIONS

THUNDERBIRD LODGE & CHALET
THE INN AT SNAKEDANCE
CHALET MONTESANO
ST. BERNARD HOTEL

Central Reservations Center
www.taosskicentral.com
central@taos.newmex.com

ACCOMMODATIONS

For somewhere in the American Southwest, the Taos Valley has a strangely Austrian feel. This may be partly due to the chalet-style Valley architecture and partly to the fact that German Luftwaffe pilots training near El Paso, tend to come up here with their families—you can hear quite a lot of German on the slopes. Once inside though, the atmosphere turns Western, especially at the Thunderbird Lodge & Chalet, which has live music in the Twining bar and the best food in the valley. This European-style ski lodge is within a short walk form the lifts. There are 30 units with private bathrooms and aside from the whirlpool and saunas there is haute cuisine dining with an extensive wine cellar. The Inn at Snakedance pre-dates the ski boom, so you have to go there. It's less than 10 yards (9 m) from the chairlift and offers good ski packages. Hot tub, sauna, spa, and massages all add to the comfortable setting. For a little peace and quiet try the Chalet Montesano—somewhat precious but no kids under 14. Hot tubs, lap pools, fitness centers and saunas are common, and most of these places are close to the lifts and trails.

So all in all there is a fair selection of hotels, lodges, condos and B&Bs in the resort and a far greater choice for all budgets in Taos Town, from cozy adobes to cottages in the mountains. In the resort, the St. Bernard Hotel is famous for having been there forever, also because owner, Jean Mayer, is an amazing character who welcomes every guest into his lodge and serves every family-style gourmet meal himself. There are also condos as part of this complex. Also in the Village there are vacation homes to rent. For information check Central Reservations website or you can email skicentral@taosskicentral.com, central@taos.newmex.com or res@VisitNewMexico.com.

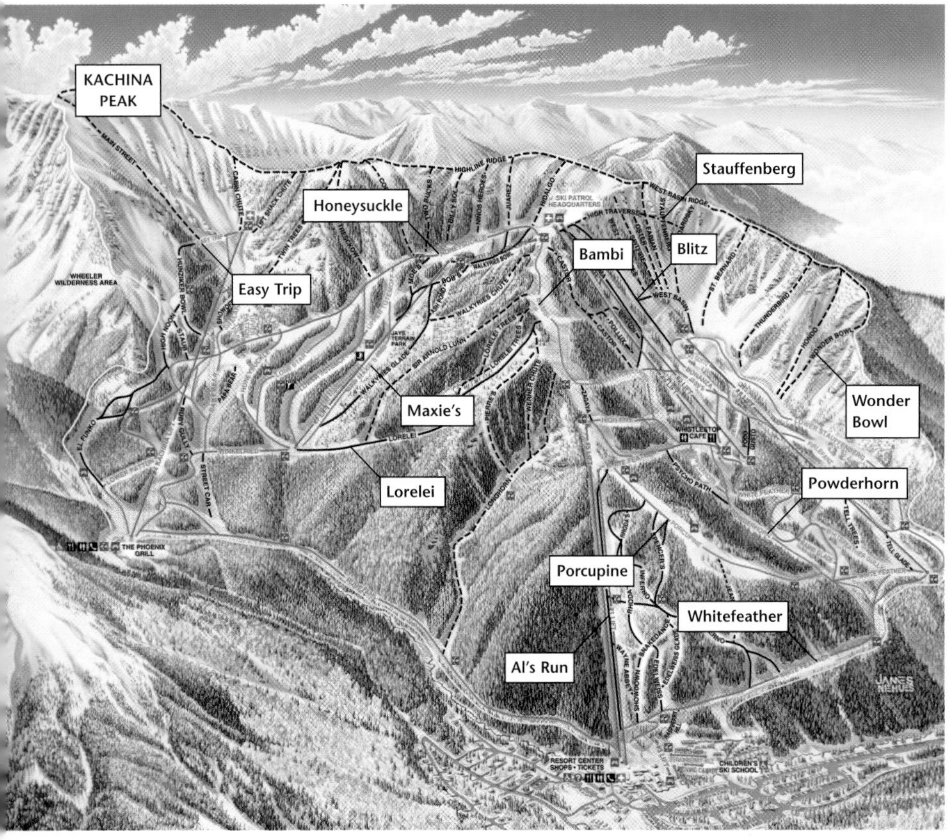

SKI AREA

Taos Valley is set in a north-facing bowl in the Carson National Forest and is known for its expert terrain. "You don't have to be an expert to ski Taos, but there is no better place to become one," is how the resort pitches its appeal—and the steep powder snow certainly favors advanced skiers. However, there are some nice novice slopes and the ski school, located at a base elevation of 9,207 feet (2,806 m), has been rated Number One several times by various ski magazines, so there is scope for beginners.

The highest point is Kachina Peak at 12,481 feet (3,804 m), abutting the Wheeler Wilderness Area, and the highest lift served is No.2 at 11,819 feet (3,408 m) below the West Basin Ridge, giving a vertical drop of 2,612 feet (796 m). If you add on the extra hike up to Kachina Peak that's 3,274 feet (998 m). But the skiing is not about vertical feet to be skied, rather it's all about demanding black trails and testing yourself, possibly on an extreme trail down from the elongated ridge summit. Indeed, the ski valley is dominated by a line of ridges from Kachina Peak along Highline Ridge onto West Basin Ridge and curving out into Wonder Bowl. The ski area encompasses 1,294 acres (524 ha) with 72 trails

◄ ONE MAN'S VISION
When Ernie Blake flew over this mountain in the 1950s he knew classic ski ground when he saw it. All this founder, planner and mastermind did was to logically extend what was available and imbue a sense of the small European resort.

—17 beginner, 18 intermediate, and 37 expert. Jay's Terrain Park is a new addition, located on Maxie's trail under lift No.7, offering two huge airs, a hip, a quarter pipe, and rails. The park is groomed nightly.

One thing you have to be aware of: snowfall is not reliable especially early season (the resort opens November 28th and closes the first Sunday in April). To say the snowfall varies here would be fair because while Taos can achieve an average annual snowfall of 312 inches (792 cm), a recent season's snowfall was only 140 inches (355 cm), although that year was considered a total fluke. Having said that, artificial snowmaking facilities cover 100 percent of the beginner and intermediate trails. The weather does fluctuate with the coldest month always being January, while March temperatures nudge over 50 ˚F (-4˚C).

SKI LIFTS

There are 12 lifts in total, which is double what it used to be: 4 quads, 1 triple, 5 doubles, and 2 surface lifts. This is small stuff but perfectly adequate for the demands of Kachina Basin and other trails. There's a total capacity 15,500 riders per hour and the lifts run from 9:00 AM to 4:00 PM. There are also night skiing opportunities with tubing three nights a week from 5:00 PM to 7:00 PM.

LIFT PASS

Taos has several ski pass-with-lodgings deals, such as US$299 for three nights' lodging in the Village with a three-day lift ticket. Day-tickets are reasonably priced: as little as US$33 for low-season adult; children aged six and under ski free with the purchase of an adult ticket; special tickets for novice skiers cost US$20; seniors over 70 ski free, with special rates on hand for the 65–69 age bracket. Lift passes can be bought at the Ski Valley or by calling 800-347-7414.

SKI SCHOOL

Taos has excellent ski schools and its instructors are second to none —indeed, *Ski Magazine* named Olympic Gold Medallist and Taos Valley Ski Instructor Deb Armstrong one of three "Instructors of the Year". There are two different ski schools in the resort. The Ernie Blake Ski School and Taos Ski Valley Children's Ski School are located in the main base area (the children's ski school is about five minutes' walk from the base in its own building). Lessons are at 9:45 AM or 1:45 PM for two hours, and children's daycare is at 8:00 AM every day. Eight is the upper limit on ski group size and the minimum age for daycare is six weeks. So long as they are potty trained, any child can attend ski classes. Children are supervised all day.

BEGINNERS

Although Taos was built as a ski resort for advanced and expert skiers, the current management is very insistent that it is an equally good place for first-time skiers. Frankly, seen from the valley floor, the Taos slopes are somewhat steep but the Yellowbird Program, crafted for beginners, is well balanced and, as always in the U.S., the instructors

▼ AL'S RUN
Running directly under the chairlift, this tough mogul trail is bound to make a big impact on those skiing it and those watching from below.

▲ **EXCELLENT POWDER**
The top of the highest lift served is 11,819 feet (3,408 m) while Kachina Peak is 12,481 feet (3,804 m). The vertical drop (lift served) works out to 2,612 feet (797 m) and with Kachina Peak that becomes 3,244 feet (999 feet). So if you don't mind hiking to terrain you'll find some super challenging trails above the chairlift range.

► **STICK TO SCHOOL**
Still European in feel (it was started by a German-born Swiss) Taos promotes the ski school ethos even for American skiers who think they know it all. The emphasis on skiing here may be major moguls, off-piste powder and double black diamond trails galore, but the essential ski school training is excellent here and highly reccommended.

are patient and encouraging—and there are no snowboarders, a real boon for novice skiers! As is often the case with steep ski areas, you have to go high to find the more gentle slopes but the curving, swoopy Honeysuckle Run is a good place to make progress and brace yourself for the faster trails. At the start of the new millennium the beginners' hill area was redesigned and a warming hut facility built there. Head for the beginners' hill or Whitefeather on the main mountain, and tackle a gentle trail through the trees from the Whistlestop Café. Easy Trip in Kachina Bowl, and Honeysuckle from ski lift No.7 are also among the best novice-friendly trails with plenty of other interconnecting green trails. As already mentioned, lessons are strongly encouraged, and discounted, because Taos tends to be a more difficult mountain than other ski areas.

INTERMEDIATES

The intermediate class is the broad church of skiing and intermediate skiers in Taos will enjoy it more if they are not at the lower end of the performance curve. Take the advice of a permanent intermediate and stick initially to the trails off Lift 7 and content yourself with a little fast cruising on Porcupine and Powderhorn, not too narrow if sometimes steep, and great preparation for the harder trails off the ridge. A day in one of the Race Clinics or a short "Mogul Mastery" course might also come in handy. For moderate skiers there are a quarter of the marked trails to try out, but you feel sandwiched between novice and expert, especially if the snow is deep. Nevertheless, Bambi is a good long trail from the top of the No.7 lift. It links up with Powderhorn and then Whitefeathers to the bottom of the mountain. If you're feeling adventurous you can also link up from here with several other black trails. Upper Tottemoff links with Maxie's below No.7 lift to give a challenging trail connecting with the long black Lorelei.

ADVANCED & EXPERT

Taos lives up to its reputation as the resort for hard, fast skiers. The moguls on Al's Run look awesome from the lift and are not to be taken lightly in the early morning before the sun softens the snow somewhat. The real challenges lie off the ridge, on the Blitz, Oster and Stauffenberg trails—but with more than half the trails graded expert, a really good skier will be totally spoiled for choice here. The super-difficult skiing is not physically tortuous, just a logical progression of what founder and developer of Taos Ski Valley, Ernie Blake, wished to exploit. Fifty-one percent of the trails are advanced and expert. Basically you hike to any part of the Ridge to take advantage of nature's extreme chutes. There are over 20 trails to sample off the Ridge, either from Highline or West Basin, and plenty of off-piste scope. It's a hike, but worth every turn. Probably the best skiing for experts is West Basin Ridge. Begin on lift No.2 and spend the entire day there (or as long as you can handle), hiking the ridge and end with Longhorn. The route through Lorelei Trees onto Lorelei is another long challenging trail and again you can finish off on Al's Run with its mogul fields heading straight down the mountain under the ski lift back to base.

EATING ON THE MOUNTAIN

Taos features an amazing array of intimate restaurants for such a compact resort. The emphasis is romantic, whatever your fancy food-wise—from enchiladas or wienerchnitzel. To make your trip even more romantic, plan lunch on the deck at the Hotel St. Bernard. According to U.S. snowsports journalists it is the second best deck in the West. Lambert's in Town, and the Inn at Snakedance's Hondo Restaurant in the Valley area are also must-visit eateries.

There are a handful of lunchtime rendezvous eateries in the pizza and cafeteria mold. Rhoda's Restaurant, located slopeside in the Resort Center, open from 11:00 AM to 9:00 PM, has a quiet sit-down atmosphere and on the outside deck you can watch skiers coming down Al's Run. Elsewhere in the base

◄ TOUGH TAOS
Taos' mountain ranks in the U.S. top 10 for challenge and terrain. it also has one of the highest rated ski schools to give you the skills to ski it.

area you can find all types of food from casual through to fine dining, and from New Mexican through to French cuisine. Tenderfoot Katie's is the place for a quick, economical breakfast or lunch.

The Bavarian, on the mountain, is a beautiful setting for lunch or a leisurely German-style dinner, while the St. Bernard deck is perfect for sunny days and meeting locals. The Whistlestop Café is located at the base of No.6 lift, close to the No.2 quad chair, and is the best place to meet friends, get a coffee, a slice of pizza, or a bowl of soup. Over at the quad chair for Kachina Bowl is The Phoenix Grill, a handy spot for enjoying lunch—and the outdoor deck is a good place to soak up the sun.

APRÈS SKI

There are some half dozen bars including Martini Tree Bar (upstairs from Tenderfoot Katie's) which is one of the hot spots for après-ski action with live music, pool tables, a sushi selection, and wall hangings displaying Taos's history. Tim's Stray Dog, also at Taos Ski Valley, is a must for margaritas, while the Old Blinking Light in town is another watering hole with good food. The Thunderbird Lodge has a popular bar for the 35+ set where they play lots of jazz and the atmosphere is old ski lodge style with fireplaces. In town, for the young crowd, the Alley Cantina hosts a continuous party and has pool tables and live music. However, Taos is not nightclub friendly and those looking to bop till they drop will be disappointed.

OTHER ACTIVITIES

Taos Ski Valley is not Colorado so don't go there expecting non-stop glitz and entertainment. But it is one of the most romantic spots in the West and just soaking up the sunshine (over 300 days of it) on one of the restaurant decks can pass as a consummate "activity." If you are feeling energetic then you can try the tubing hill, ice skating, snowmobiling, and snowshoeing. There are several ski and boot rental, repair and retail stores. For convenience and price, renting in the Valley as opposed to the Town of Taos is best. Both Taos and Taos Ski Valley have shops selling everything from T-shirts to Southwestern jewelry. The big event here each year is the Taos Winter Wine Festival, featuring tastings, wine dinners and seminars from January 23rd to February 2.

In Taos Town a visit to the artists of Taos Pueblo is a must. They produce beautiful handcrafted wares using techniques passed down through generations. Tanned buckskin moccasins and drums are characterized by simplicity and enduring quality. Sculpture, painting and jewelry are contemporary expressions of traditional art forms. Check out the micaceous clay pottery, which has been the utilitarian cookware through the ages. Today, Taos Pueblo potters are challenged to produce high quality pottery by putting a high polish on vessels. When you visit Taos Pueblo, you will have an opportunity to learn about the history and culture, as well as to purchase fine arts and crafts.

USEFUL PHONE NUMBERS

Tourist Information Centre		800-732-8267
Central Reservations		505-776-9550
Medical Centre	Ext. 1213	505-776-2291
Ski Patrol & Rescue Service	Ext. 1209	505-776-2291
The Ernie Blake Ski School	Ext. 1355	505-776-2291

USEFUL WEBSITES

Official Website	www.skitaos.org
Taos Village Site	www.taosskivalley.com
Visitors Guide	www.taoswebb.com
Central Reservations	www.taosskicentral.com
Accommodations	www.visitnewmexico.com
Weather Reports	www.wunderground.com
Snow Report & Web Cams	www.rsn.com/cams/

RESTAURANTS & BARS

RESTAURANTS
THE BAVARIAN
THE WHISTLESTOP CAFÉ
THE PHOENIX GRILL
HOTEL ST. BERNARD
RHODA'S RESTAURANT
TENDERFOOT KATIE'S
THE INN AT SNAKEDANCE HONDO
LAMBERT'S

BARS
MARTINI TREE BAR
TIM'S STRAY DOG
THUNDERBIRD LODGE
OLD BLINKING LIGHT
ALLEY CANTINA

IF THE IDEA OF SKIING WITH MOGUL MOUSE AND HIS FRIENDS STICKS IN YOUR THROAT, YOU MIGHT EASILY GIVE FAMILY-FRIENDLY SMUGGLERS' NOTCH—SMUGGS, TO ITS MANY YOUNG PALS—A MISS. BUT TO DO SO WOULD BE TO PASS UP ON SOME OF VERMONT'S MOST EXTENSIVE SKIING AND SOME STEEP TERRAIN.

SMUGGLERS' NOTCH

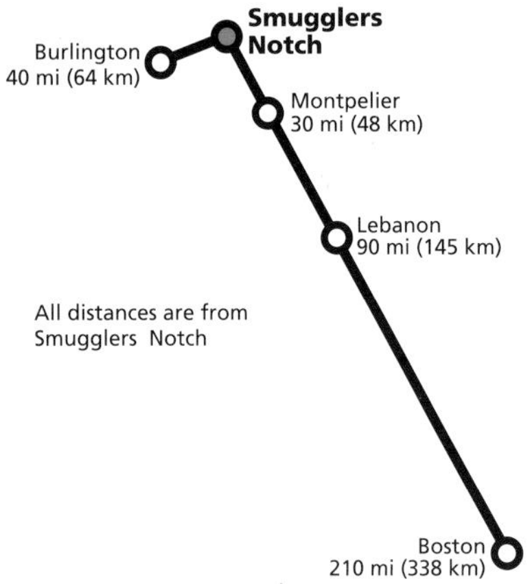

On the far side of historic Stowe's mountains, Smugglers' Notch has enthusiastically sought the family market with great success, providing excellent New England skiing for everyone, from toddlers to octogenarians.

The purpose-built village, with its ski-in, ski-out accommodations and an average of 284 inches (721cm) of snow per year with 62 percent snowmaking coverage are all good reasons to go there. The most obvious drawback (other than, for some, an excess of

► GREEN GLADES
270 acres (109 ha) of designated trails, that's over 1,000 acres (400 ha) of pure Vermont Green Mountain gladed slopes—Smugglers' Notch has great views and great skiing.

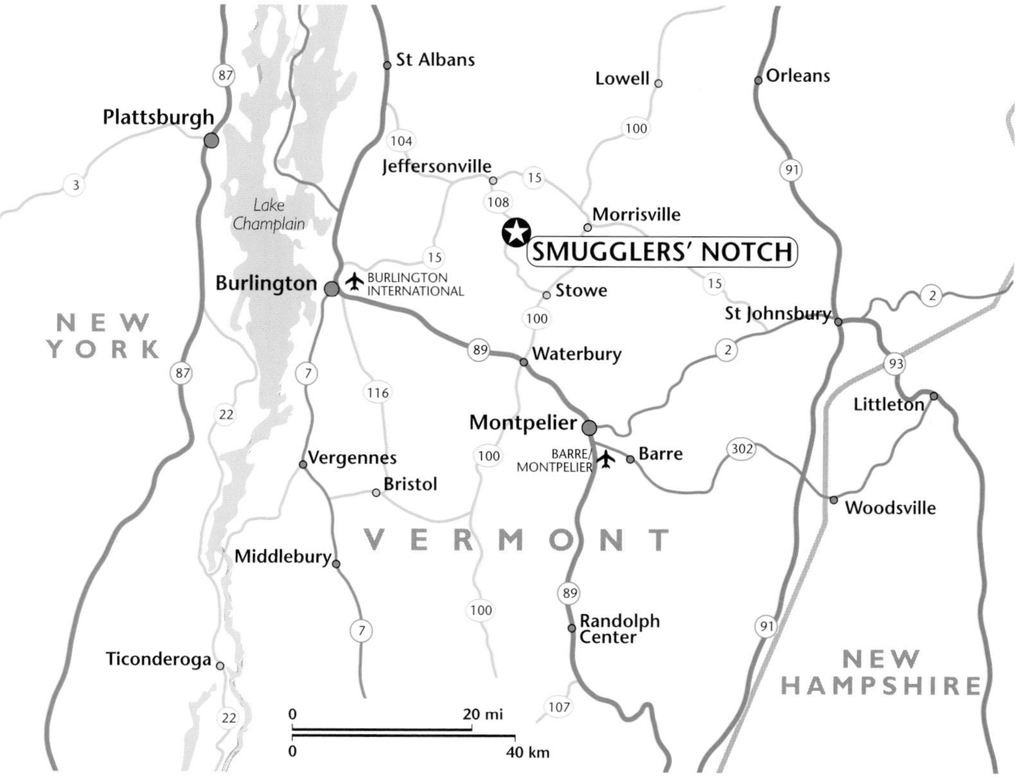

MOUNTAIN FACTS

Base	930 feet (283 m)
Summit	3,640 feet (1,110 m)
Elevation	2,610 feet (796 m)
Easy	22%
Intermediate	53%
Advanced/Expert	25%
Number of trails	72
Longest trail	3 miles (4.8 km)
Ski area	1,000 acres (405 ha)

SNOWFALL

Annual snowfall	284 inches (721 cm)
Snowmaking	141 acres (57 ha)

SKI LIFTS

Gondolas	-
High Speed Quads	-
Fixed Grip Quads	-
Triple Chairs	-
Double Chairs	6
Surface Lifts	2
Total	8
Riders per hour	7,053

SKI SEASON
Early December to mid-April

children) is the elderly lift system, consisting mainly of slow double chairs that give you ample time to pause and reflect on your busy lifestyle.

GETTING THERE

Smugglers' Notch lies in the northern half of Vermont's Green Mountains, about 45 minutes' drive from the Canadian border and 40 miles (64 km) from Burlington, Vermont. Transfer time from Burlington International Airport is 45–50 minutes. If traveling from Europe, Montreal and Boston are the closest major airports. Driving time from Montreal is around two hours; from Boston it's about four. When planning your journey, note that Route 108 through Smugglers' Notch Pass is closed from mid-October to mid-May.

THE VILLAGE

The resort is a purpose-built mountain village designed for families. It is self-contained, with the majority of condominium lodgings slopeside. All activities and facilities are within an easy walk or free shuttle ride, and the two upper mountain ski areas are also connected by ski trail. If you plan not to venture beyond the village in the evenings, a car is not essential. The village center has a sports store, grocery, equipment rental store, several restaurants, ice skating, tubing, a Nordic center, an indoor pool and hot tub, and the FunZone—an indoor sports and game center for all ages. New this season is a state-of-the-art daycare center that aims to maintain the resort's leading status within the U.S. as a family destination. The nearest town is Jeffersonville, 6 miles (9.6 km) away at the base of the mountain, which has more restaurants, antique stores, and art galleries.

ACCOMMODATIONS

There are no hotels in the resort. All accommodations are based in condos of various sizes, with fully-equipped kitchens; most are slopeside with decks and fireplaces. Over the last two seasons Smugglers' has constructed the West

▼ **APPALACHIAN APPEAL**
With views like this it's not hard to believe there's over 750 acres (303 ha) of woods available between trails for off-piste skiing.

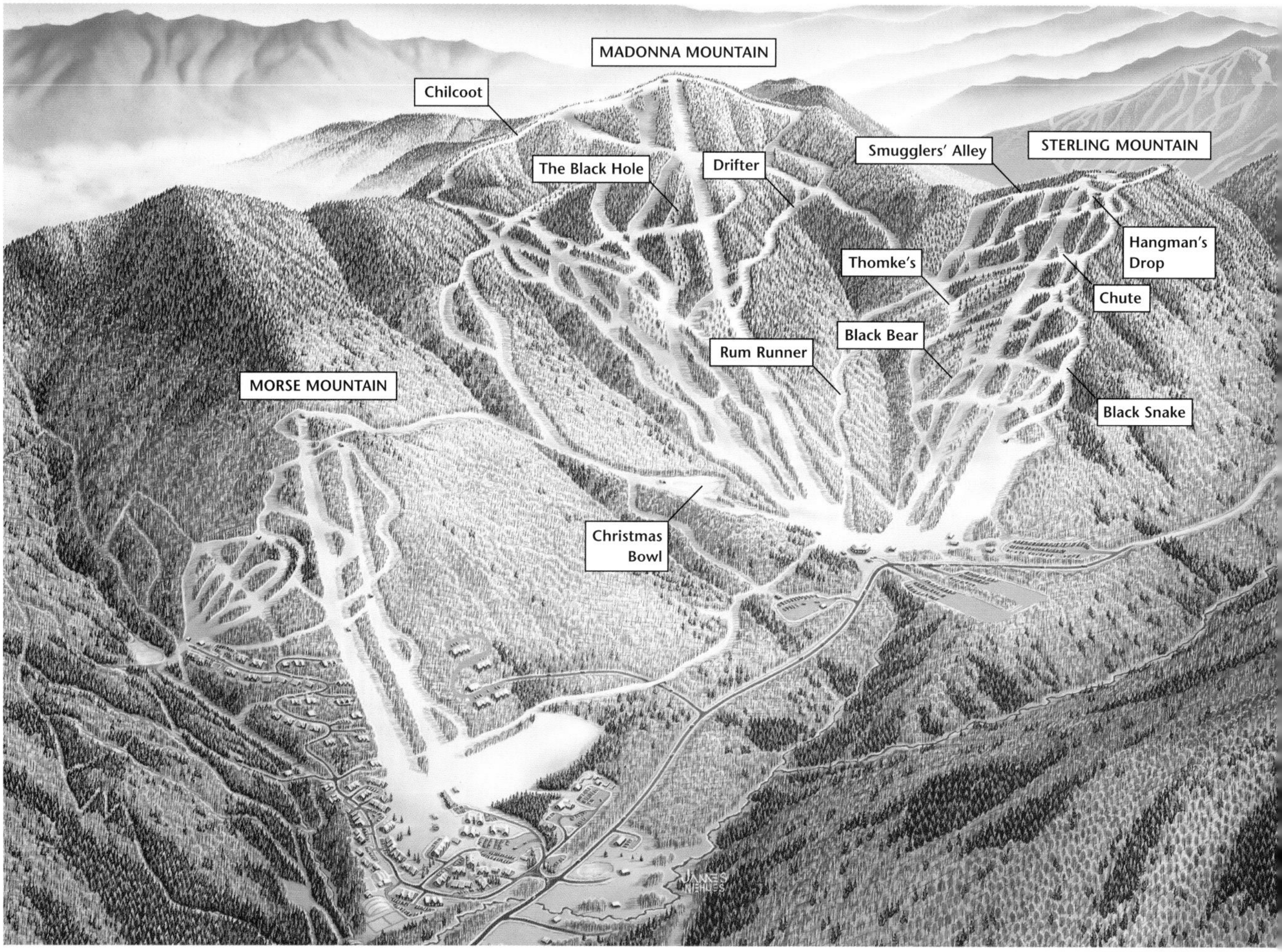

Hill development, a grouping of luxury slopeside condominiums bringing total bed numbers to 2,000. Information on all accommodations and packages is available on www.smuggs.com. Six miles (9.6 km) north of the resort is the Deer Run Motel, a couple of B & Bs, and The Smugglers' Notch Inn (802-644-5848, www.smugglers-notch-inn.com) in Jeffersonville.

SKI AREA

The ski area is spread over three hills. Madonna, the highest, rises to 3,640 feet (1,110 m) at the end of the valley, with Sterling to its right and Morse to its left. All the mountains are trail linked. A total of 27 miles (43 km) of trails are graded green for beginner, blue for intermediate, black for expert, and double and triple black for extreme expert.

Morse Mountain, directly above the village, is the center of the beginner slopes and children's areas. Madonna has some double black diamond trails and the East Coast's only triple black diamond. Between the trails there is plenty of tree skiing; some local knowledge on where best to go is helpful. The woods are not patrolled but there is an open trail policy, allowing you to go anywhere within the resort boundary.

▶ TRAILS GALORE Madonna Mountain (the main face) makes up the bulk of the three skiable mountains at Smugglers' Notch and is interconnected by lifts and trails to Sterling Mountain (lower right) . The visible trails are predominantly intermediate (53%) and expert (19%). Morse Mountain (foreground) and Morse Highlands (not visible), are also linked and have the beginner trails (22%). All in all there are 72 trails totaling 27 miles (43 km) not to mention 17 miles (27 km) of cross-country trials and 12 miles (20 km) of snowshoe trails.

LIFT SYSTEM

Smugglers' has eight lifts: six double chairs and two surface lifts, with a total uphill capacity of 7,053 people per hour. Lines are rare, although the main beginner lifts on Morse Mountain can become congested on busy weekends. There is an alternative lift to use on the nearby Morse Highlands beginner/ intermediate area.

The lift system is undeniably slow—reminiscent of skiing twenty years ago—but the base to summit Madonna I double chair lift has recently been reconditioned to reduce the chances of wind closure, which had been a frequent problem on this ridgeline route.

The Village Lift, Madonna I, and the Sterling Lift open at 8:00 AM on the weekend; all other lifts open at 9:00 AM. On weekdays, the Village Lift and Sterling Lift open at 8:30 AM and all other lifts open at 9:00 AM. All lifts close at 4:00 PM, except for the handle tow, which closes at 3:30 PM.

LIFT PASSES

Smugglers' package holidays come with daily lift tickets, which are issued at check-in. An adult day pass (ages 19–64) costs US$54; senior (ages 65–69) US$38; youth (ages 7–18) US$38; children six and under ski free. Beginners can buy a Morse Mountain lift ticket for US$36 (adult) or US$28 (children), or a Morse Mountain season pass for US$199, which covers all the beginner terrain. Photo I.D. is required for season passes only.

SKI SCHOOLS AND GUIDING

There is one ski school, the Snow Sport University (S.S.U.), with offices by the Three Mountain Equipment rental area in the resort village. Guests can arrange lessons at the Guest Services Desk. The S.S.U. has been voted the best ski school in North America on more than one occasion, reflecting the resort's focus on children and beginner skiers. A wide range of lessons are available, including all-day ski lessons for 3–14 year olds, and all-day snowboard lessons for 4–14 year olds, amongst others. Lunchtime supervision allows parents the whole day for themselves.

All day "camps" cost US$95 per child, but only US$69 per child per day with paid "Club Smugglers" packages. Ninety-minute group lessons for kids aged six and older, and for adults, cost US$36. Lessons start at 10:00 AM and noon. Children's ski and snowboard camps run from 9:00 AM until 4:00 PM daily. Group sizes vary, with a maximum of ten. The S.S.U. can also arrange guiding and teach telemark skiing.

▲ **BEGINNER'S DELIGHT**
Gentle and groomed green and blue trails carved between acres of pine and spruce make Smuggs a beginner's dream.

BEGINNERS

About one fifth of Smugglers' trails are suitable for beginners. All the relevant terrain is within easy reach of the village, so you're never far from home. The Village Lift, Mogul Mouse's Magic Lift, and the Morse Highlands Lift all service beginner trails and even the lift speeds calm nervous novices—one of them goes at half speed which in this context means that it could be very hard to tell, at a glance, if it's actually running. There are no green trails on Sterling and Madonna Mountains.

INTERMEDIATES

Over half the area is made up of intermediate terrain. The longest single trail is the three-mile (4.8 km) Thomke's Trail, a narrow, challenging switchback trail. Both Madonna and Sterling Mountains have a variety of blue trails. Rum Runner and Black Snake trail top to bottom on Sterling, while two scenic trails start from the Madonna summit: the Chilcoot and the Drifter. The Chilcoot winds over the backside of the mountain before returning to the main face. The Drifter hugs the saddle of the mountain for views across the chain of the Green Mountains, before opening to wide meadows and gently gladed areas. All of this is ideal intermediate skiing but despite the high proportion of this type of trail, there will still be a lack of mileage for keen piste-bashers intent upon skiing more than a couple of days at the resort.

▼ **SNOWBOARD-FRIENDLY**
On Madonna lies the 425-foot (130-m) Olympic-size Superpipe with a 16.5-foot (5-m) radius to test your freestyle. Birch Run Terrain Park on Sterling Mountain is designed for entry and intermediate level riders with modified table-tops, rolls, and spines.

TOUGH TERRAIN
Despite its family-friendly image, Smuggler's Notch has some hidden gems of accessible tree-skiing and riding terrain that is anything but friendly. Boulders, granite slabs and lots of mini-leaps of faith into well-powdered wooded steeps.

ADVANCED & EXPERT

There is advanced terrain on both Madonna and Sterling Mountains making up 19 percent of the total area. The toughest is on Madonna and in the 750 acres (303 ha) of woods between the trails, where the best powder is usually found. Six percent of the resort is rated for experts only, including the triple black diamond Black Hole that starts with a pitch of more than 50 degrees. There are also short, narrow, steep trails on Sterling, such as Smugglers' Alley, Hangman's Drop, Chute, and Black Bear, and two expert glades: Powder Keg and Pirate's Plank. Skiing is allowed anywhere within the resort area boundary marked on the trail map, but the between-trail terrain is recommended to be skied in groups of three or more for safety—it comes with a full complement of natural hazards and is not patrolled.

BOARDING & FREESTYLE

Each of the three mountains has a terrain park for boarders and riders corresponding to the level of the surrounding terrain. Morse Mountain and Highlands have gentle terrain features; the 450-foot (137 m) Superpipe and 3,500-foot (1,066-m) long Prohibition terrain park are on Madonna Mountain, aimed at intermediates to experts; the 1,000-foot (304-m) long Birch Run terrain park, for entry and intermediate level terrain park riders, is on Sterling Mountain; the SnowZone, for expert trick air demonstrations only, is also on Sterling. The rest of the resort is fully open to boarders.

EATING ON THE MOUNTAIN

The real options are back at base, with a choice of cafeteria or table service in several restaurants in the base lodge and village. At the top of Sterling Mountain is the Top-of-the-Notch warming hut for drinks, soups, stews and views. There's also Snow's Bistro, a ski-in outdoor snackbar that offers grilled sandwiches, snacks, and beverages, weather permitting.

APRÈS SKI

With the family emphasis and a large proportion of self-catering accommodations, après ski is about as quiet as it gets. The base area and village have several options for eating and drinking: the Black Bear Tavern and Morse Mountain Grille; the Bootlegger's Lounge, and the Rhino Tavern—both full service bars. The Hearth & Candle has three dining rooms of which one is adults-only. Banditos Mexican Restaurant and the Brewski are two other popular venues near the resort. Also nearby are the Three Mountain Lodge Restaurant, serving Vermont specialties, and the Hungry Lion at the Smugglers' Notch Inn, a typical old Vermont building that was once an inn on the stagecoach route. Both are in Jeffersonville.

In all Smugglers' Notch bars you must be over 21 to drink alcohol but children can accompany parents in bars. Smoking is allowed in the bars, but not in other public places including restaurants.

▲ WOODED PARADISE
Stumps, boulders and trees lie in waiting for more adventurous freeriders. The trees also provide shelter when the winds get up.

OTHER ACTIVITES

Family orientated: tubing, snowboarding night school twice weekly, skating, 16 miles (27 km) of cross-country and snowshoe tours.

USEFUL PHONE NUMBERS

Tourist Office	802-644-8851
Central Reservations	802-644-8851

USEFUL WEBSITES

Official Website	www.smuggs.com
Tourist Office	smuggs@smuggs.com
Weather Reports	www.wunderground.com
Snow Report & Web Cams	www.rsn.com/cams

RESTAURANTS & BARS

TOP-OF-THE-NOTCH
SNOW'S BISTRO
BLACK BEAR TAVERN
MORSE MOUNTAIN GRILLE
BOOTLEGGER'S LOUNGE
THE RHINO TAVERN
THE HEARTH & CANDLE BANDITOS
BREWSKI
THREE MOUNTAIN LODGE RESTAURANT
THE HUNGRY LION
SMUGGLERS' NOTCH INN

AN AMERICAN ORIGINAL AND FULL OF TRADITION AND CHARACTER, FROM THE CHARMING NEW ENGLAND VILLAGE TO THE CHALLENGING TRAILS CARVED INTO THE FACE OF MT. MANSFIELD, STOWE HAS THE LONGEST AVERAGE TRAIL LENGTH AND THE MOST CHALLENGING FALL LINE IN NEW ENGLAND.

STOWE

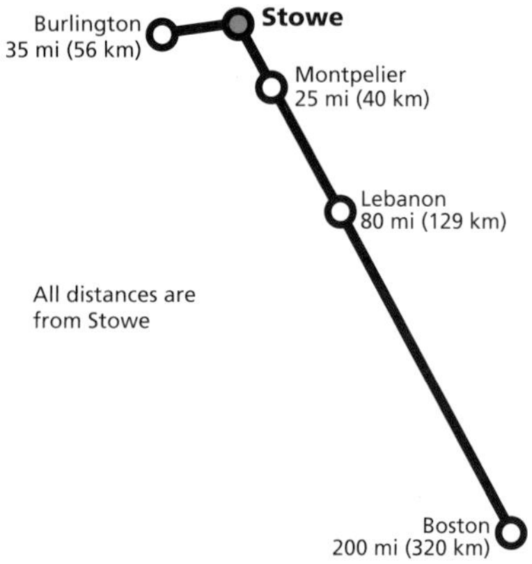

▼ THREE SECTORS
Skiing at Stowe stretches over 3 faces: Mt. Mansfield (center, in the sun) and Octagon (left), and Spruce Peak (in the shadows to the right).

Of all the Vermont resorts, Stowe takes quaint New England to the extreme. If you're looking for some good skiing and the charm of wooden clapboard buildings surrounded by snowy forest, this is the one to go for. It's further north than Killington and other Vermont resorts such as Stratton and Okemo, making it less susceptible to weekend commuter crowds from Boston and beyond, while the skiing—on Vermont's highest peak, Mount Mansfield—is in the East Coast's top league.

Stowe doesn't just seem old: it really is, and so too is its skiing. It was first developed as a resort in the first half of the last century, but its infrastructure is considerably newer and includes a quad and a gondola that are bang up to date. The town itself—which probably does more summer than winter business—is six miles (9.6 km) from the skiing and is sufficiently charming to make Stowe one of the few North American snowsport resorts that non-skiers can enjoy as much as skiers.

GETTING THERE

Stowe is in north central Vermont, most easily reached from Montreal (140 miles/224 km), and Boston (200 miles/320 km) away. For European visitors, Boston International Airport is the normal gateway, followed by a four-hour drive; drive time from Montreal is under three hours. The city of Burlington, with its international airport, is just 45 miles (50 minutes) by road, and 15 minutes from

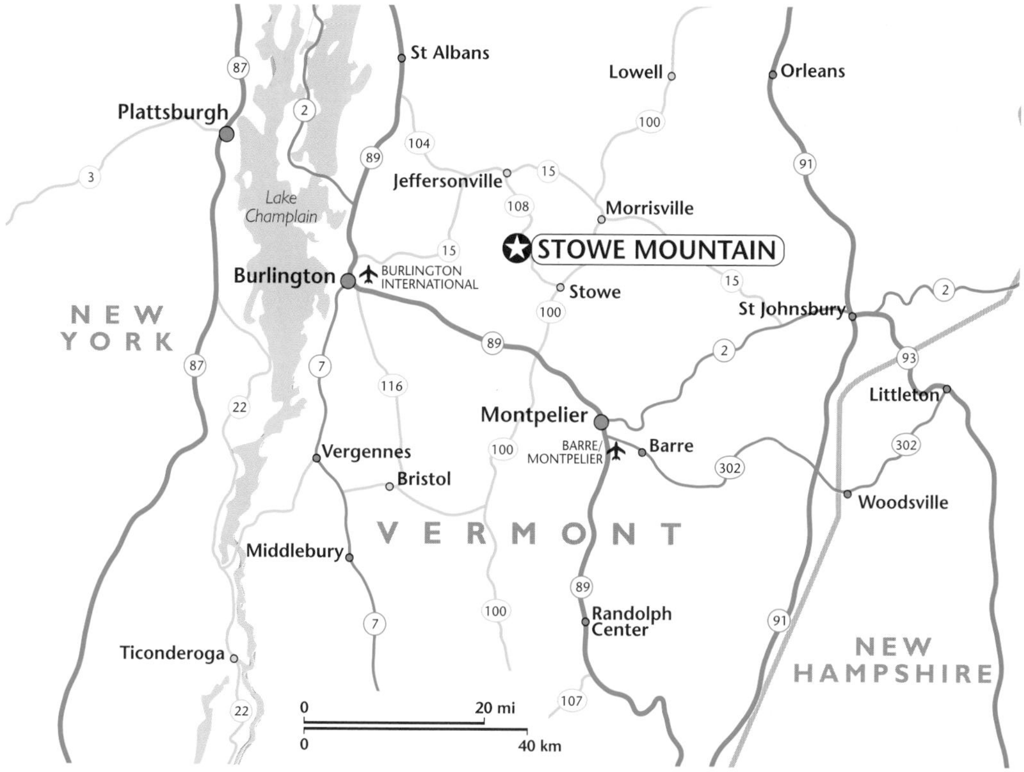

Interstate 89. The nearest rail connection is at Waterbury, which is 15 minutes from Stowe; daily rail connections run from Washington and New York.

THE VILLAGE

Stowe is a picture postcard New England village, with a white church steeple marking its center, general stores, galleries and a wide range of options for eating out. There are plenty of lodging choices from four-star resorts to 150-year-old, B&Bs. Dating back to the early 1800s as an old stagecoach town, Stowe is one of America's oldest tourist destinations. Skiing came early to Stowe—it's one of America's first ski resorts and, as with many of the resorts that followed, the skiing is quite separate from the village. In Stowe's case, the foot of the mountain is 6 miles distant (9.6 km). There is a regular shuttle bus service that takes people from the village to the mountain with regular stops along Mountain Road.

ACCOMMODATIONS

At the mountain base there's just one slopeside hotel: the Inn at the Mountain, which also has condos, near the Toll House lift. All other accommodations—around 60 options, including hotels, houses and apartments—are spread along Mountain Road that connects the town and the resort road, or are found in Stowe itself. The most famous hotel is the Trapp Family Lodge (www.trappfamily.com), about 2 miles (3.2 km) out of town on Trapp Hill Road and home to the "Sound of Music" family. For maximum Stowe atmosphere and the easiest access to nightlife, stay in town; unless you're right at the foot of the mountain at the Inn, you'll have to travel to the slopes each day anyway. There are around a dozen options in Stowe village including the attractive Green Mountain Inn (www.greenmountaininn.com) on Main Street. For information and reservations call 800-253-4754 or visit www.stowe.com.

MOUNTAIN FACTS

Base	1,280 feet (390 m)
Summit	4,395 feet (1,340 m)
Highest skiing	3,640 feet (1,109 m)
Elevation	2,360 feet (719 m)
Easy	16%
Intermediate	59%
Advanced & Expert	25%
Number of trails	48
Longest trail	3.7 miles (5.9 km)
Ski area	480 acres (194 ha)

SNOWFALL

Annual snowfall	260 inches (660 cm)
Snowmaking	350 acres (142 ha)

SKI LIFTS

Gondolas	1
High-Speed Quads	1
Fixed Grip Quads	-
Triple Chairs	1
Double Chairs	6
Surface Lifts	3
Total	12
Riders per hour	12,326

SKI SEASON
Mid-November to late April

▼ QUAINT HISTORY
One of the America's oldest tourist destinations, Stowe has history dating back 200 years when its was used as a stagecoach stop.

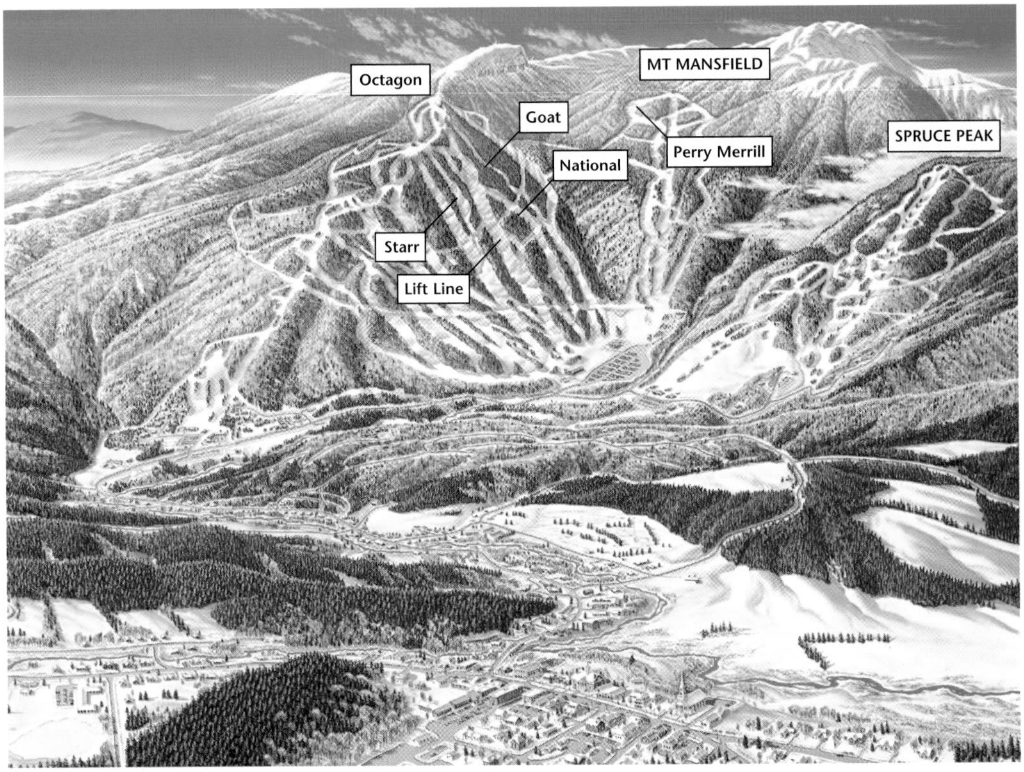

▼ **LOG ON, CHILL OUT**
At the top of Octagon which, at over 3,600 feet (1,100 m), has the bulk of the demanding trails (and is reachable on the Quad Lift) you can send and receive emails from its mountaintop Web Café and Gallery.

SKI AREA

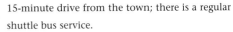

Set on Vermont's highest peak, Mount Mansfield, Stowe resort has a good snow record, averaging 260 inches (660 cm) per year, backed up by snowmaking on 73 percent of its trails. It also has an impressive vertical drop (by New England standards) of 2,360 feet (719 m) from the highest lift elevation at 3,640 feet (1,109 m) to base. From the top of Mt. Mansfield you have views of the Green Mountains of Vermont, the White Mountains of New Hampshire, and the Adirondack Mountains of New York. The resort is a 15-minute drive from the town; there is a regular shuttle bus service.

Stowe's 48 trails ("The Great 48") cover a distance of 39 miles (62 km) and include the longest average trail length and the most challenging fall line in New England. Best known are the imposing double black diamond "Front Four" trails—Starr, Goat, National, and Lift Line—but as a whole the resort is perfect for typical recreational skiers, with a wide range of intermediate terrain and plenty of variety from top-to-bottom trails with groomed cruisers, bump trails, and some truly fine glade skiing. There is also good beginner skiing, mainly on Spruce Peak.

There are free daily mountain tours led by a mountain host to introduce skiers to the area. Despite the resort's popularity, midweek skiing, outside peak holiday times, is uncrowded. Night skiing is laid on from Thursday to Saturday from mid-January to mid-March.

SKI LIFTS

Most of Stowe's twelve lifts run from bottom to top of the mountain, so that on most trails you ski the full vertical drop of the peak. There are eight chairlifts including a high-speed quad, one eight-seater gondola that carries skiers from bottom to top in just seven and a half minutes, and three surface tows. The high-speed quad chair and the gondola are state of the art and the fastest way up the mountain.

Normal operating times are generous: 8:00 AM to 4:00 PM, although the quad opens at 7:30 AM on

weekends and holidays. Lift lines can be expected, according to the resort, principally between 10:00 AM and 2:00 PM on Saturdays, at Christmas, and during President's Week, but you can take it for granted that weekends will be busy.

More lifts, trails, and snowmaking may be installed as part of a major five- to ten-year investment plan, scheduled to start in 2004 but currently unconfirmed.

LIFT PASSES

Stowe Vacation Program lift tickets can be pre-purchased via a participating Stowe Area Inn or Lodge, or by calling 888-253-4849. Day tickets cost US$62 per day for adults (13–64), and US$42 per day for juniors (6–12) and seniors (65+), with a six-day pass costing US$341 and US$208 respectively. Mid-week and weekend ticket prices outside main holiday periods are cheaper. Children under five ski free when accompanied by a paying adult, and novices are eligible for discounted passes. For beginners, the Spruce Peak pass gives access to the main nursery area. No photo I.D. is required for lift passes.

SKI SCHOOLS AND GUIDING

Stowe has one ski and snowboarding school based at Spruce Peak. It has over 200 instructors offering tuition from beginner basics to advanced skills. There are a variety of different classes for adults (Levels 1–9) offering up to two 90-minute lessons per day from 10:00 AM and 1:00 PM including the benefit of extra attention and feedback for smaller groups of up to three adults.

There are full-day programs (including lunch and lift pass) from 9:30 AM until 3:30 PM for children aged 4–6 and 7–12, teaching skiing and snowboarding for all levels. In holiday periods, advanced skiers and riders aged 11–14 can explore the terrain with Holiday Adventure Camp and receive coaching in bumps, glades, steeps, and freestyle terrain.

The minimum age for ski school lessons is three. Cubs Day Care offers a licensed child care facility for kids aged six weeks to six years, from 8:00 AM until 4:30 PM, including a nutritious lunch and ski lesson option for children aged three and over. For reservations call 802-253-3000

Also in response to the growing interest in telemarking the resort has introduced Tele Tuesdays, a successful clinic aimed at aspiring telemark skiers.

BEGINNERS

Novices will have a good time in Stowe. Spruce Peak is the main beginner area, where ski school is located. But novices and early intermediates can access the whole mountain via the Toll Road green trail on Mt. Mansfield, which stretches for 3.7 gentle miles (5.9 km) from the top of the Lift Line quad back to the resort base at Toll House. Even though only 16 percent of the terrain is graded suitable for beginners, there is plenty of chance to progress from easy greens to gentle blue intermediate trails.

▲ SUN-SEEKERS
Despite the sunshine it can get really chilly in this part of the U.S., especially when exposed on the chairlifts. To get the best of the solar warmth ski the Mansfield trails in the morning followed later by Spruce which enjoys the afternoon sun. For on-mountain photo-ops, the best sites are atop the Forerunner Quad and Gondola Lifts.

▲ PLENTY OF PRECIPICES
Stowe is demanding with many steep gladed areas and sometimes icy conditions and gusty winds to further unsettle the unwary freeskier.

▲ DIVERSITY
Waterfall cliffs and tree riding make up the most demanding freeskiing on the north-facing slopes.

INTERMEDIATES

The majority of the mountain—59 percent of the terrain—is aimed at intermediates. The longest trail in this category is Perry Merrill from the top of the gondola; at the upper limit, Lord has a few pitches that would qualify it as a black diamond trail at some resorts. That apart, there's not much between normal intermediate terrain and the more seriously demanding advanced trails for confident top-end intermediates to try.

ADVANCED & EXPERT

The "Front Four": Goat, Starr, National, and Lift Line are renowned double black diamond trails—practically New England benchmarks for tough skiing and all easily accessed by two lifts from the Mansfield base area. They account for most of the 25 percent of Stowe's terrain that is suitable for advanced skiers. Goat has a double fall line and big moguls; Starr is the place for steeps. The best powder is usually found at Lookout.

Stowe gets its fair share of powder, so if you want fresh tracks, it is best to arrive early. The high-speed quad opens at 7:30 AM and the gondola fires up at 8:30 AM. It's not uncommon to find a dozen people ahead of you waiting for the first lift to open, and on powder days there can be many more skiers eager to grab the best snow conditions of the day in the stunning early morning light on Mansfield. For the first couple of hours the pace is quick and the average standard of skier and rider out on the slopes is noticeably higher than later in the day.

Almost all the out of bounds terrain is for expert skiers only, and visitors are recommended to go with someone who knows the area. Several gladed areas are skiable, but if you ski or ride in the woods outside the designated ski area you must be aware that it is not patrolled and there are no first aid or rescue services. There is no organized guiding for off-piste groups.

BOARDING & FREESTYLE

Snowboards are definitely welcome in Stowe, which is home to Burton snowboards, the brand that started the whole thing. The Burton Method Center is a popular place to take up boarding, with its combination of special techniques and learning equipment to get you over the painful early stages. The success rate for newcomers to snowboarding (in terms of them continuing to board) is far higher here than elsewhere.

► JUMP AND TWIST
For freestylers, Tyro Terrain Park has all the necessary ingredients.

▲ CLASSIC AMERICAN
Stowe wears its classical New England architecture well. Quaint tree-lined streets, red-and-white weather-boarded buildings, church steeples and a ski heritage dating back to 1937 (then the only real ski resort in the East) give Stowe an authentic edge over some other ski "villages"—though it's still six miles (10 km) from the actual slopes.

Carvers and freeriders have plenty of options and there are few flat spots on the mountain. There are several terrain parks, of which Jungle, on Lower Standard, is the toughest, with rail slides and barrels. There's a halfpipe on North Slope and there's even a separate website dedicated to boarders and freestylers at www.ridestowe.com.

EATING ON THE MOUNTAIN

There are eight restaurants at the resort, mostly near lift bases, such as the cafeterias at Mansfield, Spruce, and Midway base lodges. The Cliff House at the top of the gondola is an upmarket restaurant with quality wines and great views; it is also open for dinner. Also on-mountain is the Octagon Web Café at the top of the quad. For mid-range eating, try the Fireside Tavern at the base of the Toll House lift.

APRÈS SKI

Some après ski takes place at the mountain, but in town there are more options for eating and drinking. Nightlife is generally quiet. Most popular venue is The Matterhorn—it has a very lively atmosphere when full at the weekends. The Rusty Nail has dancing and live music; The Shed also has music and brews its own beer. You need to be over 21 to drink alcohol in the bars, although children can accompany their parents.

There are plenty of restaurants serving American, European, Italian, Mexican, and Japanese cuisine but they are not all to be found in the village itself, so be prepared to travel a few miles along Mountain Road and Route 108 to experience the best of them.

Charlie B's Pub & Restaurant at 1746 Mountain Road offers a diverse menu and award-winning wine list with over 50 wines by the glass and 10 beers on tap; Winfield's Bistro at the same address also has an award-winning wine list. For more information on restaurants check out the websites www.stowe.com and www.gostowe.com

OTHER ACTIVITIES

Stowe offers a good variety of winter activities. Skating at the Jackson Ice Arena, snowmobile rental, snowshoeing and cross-country skiing with Stowe's interconnected cross-country centers covering more than 90 miles (150 km) of groomed and 60 miles (100 km) of backcountry trails, much of it very scenic.

USEFUL PHONE NUMBERS

Stowe Tourist Information	802-253-7321
Lodging Reservations	800-253-4754
Medical Center: Copley Hospital	802-888-4231
Mt. Mansfield Ski Patrol & Rescue	802-253-3619
Taxi: Peg's Pick-Up	802-253-9490
Cubs Day Care	802-253-3000

USEFUL WEBSITES

Official Winter Website	www.stowe.com
Official Main Website	www.gostowe.com
Weather Reports	www.wunderground.com
Snow Report & Web Cams	www.rsn.com/cams

RESTAURANTS & BARS

EXPENSIVE
EDSON HILL MANOR RESTAURANT
EMILY'S AT THE STOWEHOF
TRATTORIA LA FESTA
WINFIELD'S BISTRO
TRAPP FAMILY LODGE
BLUE MOON CAFE

MODERATE
THE MATTERHORN
CHARLIE B'S PUB & RESTAURANT
SHED RESTAURANT & BREWERY
WHIP BAR & GRILL
SWISSPOT
DUTCH PANCAKE CAFÉ & BISTRO
MR PICKWICK'S
MICHAEL'S ON THE HILL
FOXFIRE INN
PARTRIDGE INN
GREEN MOUNTAIN INN
SUNSET GRILLE & TAP ROOM
RUSTY NAIL

BUDGET
PIE IN THE SKY
PIECASSO N.Y. PIZZA
DEPOT STREET MALT SHOPPE

EATING ON THE MOUNTAIN

THE FIRESIDE TAVERN
CLIFF HOUSE
MANSFIELD CAFÉ
MANSFIELD DEN
MIDWAY CAFÉ & BAKERY
JOSE'S CANTINA
EASY STREET CAFÉ
OCTAGON WEB CAFÉ

SEVEN MOUNTAINS MAKE UP THE RESORT OF KILLINGTON, GATHERING IN MORE TERRAIN, MORE SNOW, AND MORE LIFTS THAN ANYWHERE ELSE IN EASTERN NORTH AMERICA. KILLINGTON PEAK, AT 4,241 FEET (1,292 M), IS THE HIGHEST POINT AND CAN BE REACHED IN A MERE SIX MINUTES ON THE WORLD'S FASTEST—AND FIRST HEATED—EIGHT-PASSENGER LIFT.

KILLINGTON

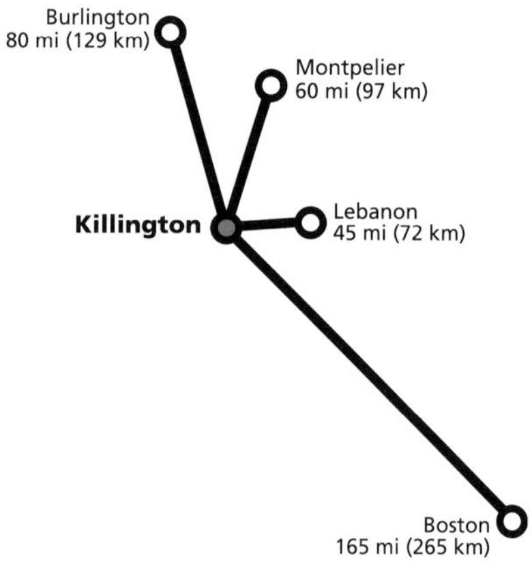

SKI SEASON
Mid-October to last weekend in May

MOUNTAIN FACTS

Base	1,091 feet (332 m)
Summit	4,241 feet (1,292 m)
Elevation	3,150 feet (960 m)
Easy	30%
Intermediate	39%
Advanced/Expert	31%
Number of trails	200
Longest trail	6.2 miles (9.9 km)
Ski area	1,182 acres (478 ha)

Killington—The Big K—is a big ski area catering to all standards of skier with the biggest mountain of all the East Coast resorts, an excellent lift system, and excellent nursery slopes for beginners. It considers itself a place to rival some of the top domestic and international resorts but it is not a village resort in the European sense, and in spite of some very strong plus points there are a few drawbacks, most notably that there is no real focal point and you really need a car to get around.

Killington enjoys an exceptionally long ski season kicking off in mid-October until Memorial Day Weekend (last weekend in May) and sometimes running into June. During the season the area receives 250 inches (625 cm) of natural snowfall per year; and if that isn't sufficient, Killington is home to the largest snowmaking system in North America. In spite of a good snow record and a long season, the New England climate is changeable and inconsistent from one year to the next. Also, it can be bitterly cold.

Killington is big on après ski with plenty of action late into the night, but it is a resort devoted to skiing and partying, catering mainly to day and weekend visitors from the East Coast cities and with very little to interest or amuse non-skiers.

GETTING THERE

Killington lies 15 miles (24 km) from Rutland, Vermont, and approximately 25 miles (40 km) from Rutland Airport, which has flights daily to and from Boston. Also nearby is West Lebanon airport, which is 39 miles (62 km) and about a one-hour drive. There is no regular shuttle bus service from either of these airports, so renting a car is the best option.

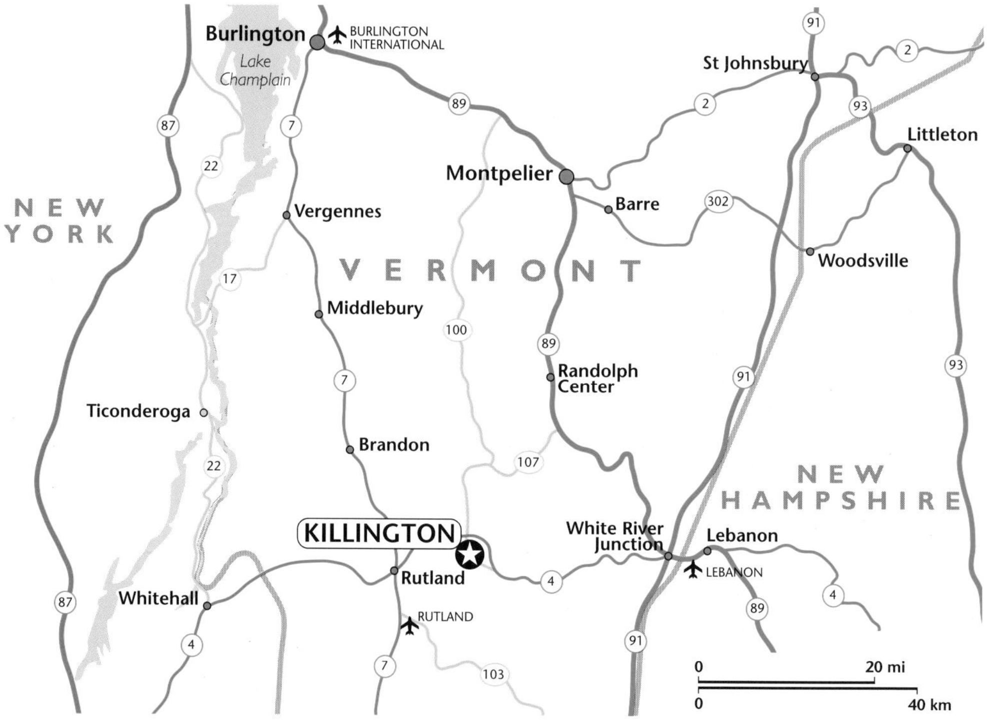

▲ **VAST SKI AREA**
Skye Peak and Killington Peak in the distance—the highest point reached by aerial lift in Vermont—offers by far the largest skiable area on the Eastern Seaboard.

Flying times to Rutland take around one hour from Boston, two to three hours from New York and three to four hours from Washington DC. London, England, to Boston is around seven hours by plane.

Boston is 158 miles (252 km) and around two hours away by car; New York City lies 250 miles (400 km) to the south—around five hours by road; and from Montreal to Killington is about a three-hour drive. You can also reach Killington by bus from New York and Boston, or by rail to Rutland on a line that runs between New York and Montreal. Amtrak's Ultimate Ski Train—the Ethan Allen Express—runs every afternoon (c.2:45 PM) from New York City's Penn Station to Rutland in just over five hours. Train times and rail fares can be found on www.amtrak.com

THE VILLAGE

The fact that there is no village as such is one of Killington's drawbacks. The main ski area lies at the end of Killington Road in the heart of the Green Mountains of central Vermont, surrounded by beautiful vistas and mountain terrain. Most of the 100 or so places to stay, and a similar number of bars and restaurants are built up along the five-mile (8 km) Killington Road, which explains the lack of any focal point. There is a good shuttle bus service between the many lodges, stores and restaurants on the Killington Road, but in spite of this most people would consider it essential to have a car for getting around. There is car rental in the resort with reduced New England package rates.

◄ **ALL-AMERICAN**
There is little evidence of mock-Tirolean or pseudo-Swiss-chalet styles here. Just good old fashioned and modern American lodgings.

ACCOMMODATIONS

As the largest and highest ski resort in the East drawing day visitors and weekenders from the big East Coast cities, Killington has plenty of varied accommodations ranging from the aptly named Killington Grand Resort Hotel (the only on-mountain hotel) with its steaming outdoor pool, cocktail bars and restaurants, through to charming New England inns built around the 1840s and offering high-standard accommodations. Most lodgings options—hotels, condos, motels, B&Bs, and country inns—are situated a drive or shuttle bus-ride away from the slopes down Killington Road or on Route 4.

The many 19th century inns vary in price and not all accept young children. Red Clover Inn is an upmarket inn but does not accept children under 12, the Vermont Inn accepts children aged six and over, while children aged 14 and under stay free at the popular Cortina Inn. The inns offer day rates and

SKI LIFTS

Gondolas	3
High-Speed Quads	6
Fixed Grip Quads	6
Triple Chairs	6
Double Chairs	4
Surface Lifts	6
Total	31
Riders per hour	52,361

SNOWFALL

Annual snowfall	250 inches (625 cm)
Snowmaking	70%

ACCOMMODATIONS

RED CLOVER INN
Woodward Road
Mendon, Vt 05701
802-775-2290 or Toll-free 800-752-0571
FAX: 802 773-0594
E-Mail: redclover@vermontel.net
www.redcloverinn.com

THE VERMONT INN
H.C. 34 Box 37K
Route 4
Killington, VT 05751
802-775-0708 or Toll-free 800-541-7795 cf
E-Mail: relax@vermontinn.com
www.vermontinn.com

THE INN OF THE SIX MOUNTAINS
2617 Killington Road,
Killington, VT 05751
800-228-4676 or Toll-free 802-422-4302
E-Mail: iosm@vermontel.net
www.sixmountains.com

CORTINA INN
Zola's Grille Restaurant
Theodore's Tavern Burger Bar
802-773-3333 or Toll-free 800-451-6108
E-Mail: cortina1@aol.com
www.cortinainn.com
German, French and Spanish spoken

MOUNTAIN MEADOWS LODGE
285 Thundering Brook Road
Killington, Vermont, 05751
802-775-1010 or Toll-free 800-370-4567
E-Mail: havefun@mtmeadowslodge.com
www.mtmeadowslodge.com

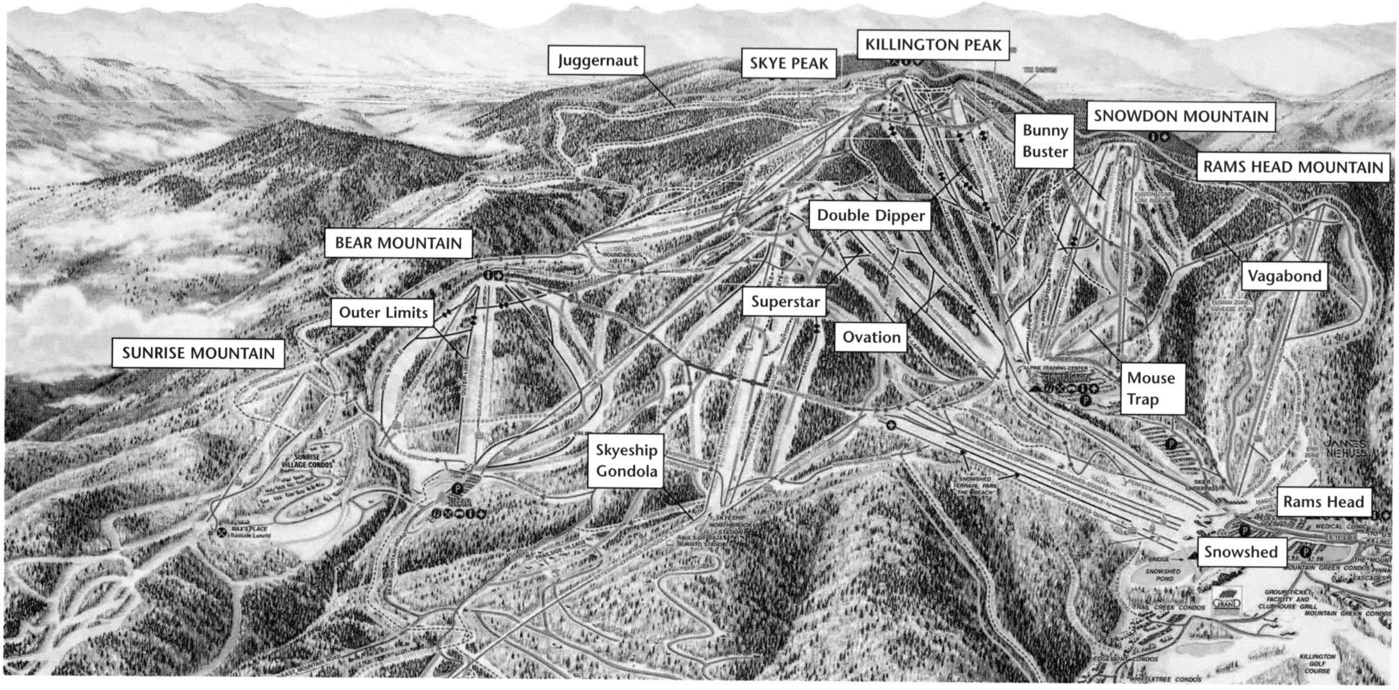

▼ RECREATIONAL SETTING
From left to right: Sunrise Mountain, Bear Mountain, Skye Peak, Killington Peak, Snowdon Mountain, and Ram's Head Mountain—plenty of good skiing, something for everyone.

packages including half-board options with gourmet dinners. The Inn of the Six Mountains and Mountain Meadows Lodge offer good accommodation in well-appointed condos and being larger than most inns they have better facilities for families and larger ski parties.

There are around 18,000 beds within a 30-mile (50-km) radius of the resort. Guests can book through www.killington.com, or call the Central Reservations number at 800-621-MTNS. It's open from 8:00 AM to 9:00 PM. There are numerous 2–7 day packages on offer, together with ski lessons or more advanced ski clinics if required. Prices range from under US$70 a night to US$100 or more, but check whether the Vermont state tax (9%) is in the quoted price—and remember to allow for gratuities.

SKI AREA

The ski area extends across seven heavily wooded mountains—Sunrise, Bear, Skye Peak, Killington, Snowdon, Rams Head, and nearby Pico—and because Killington has such a vast trail network, there is something for everyone. The base area is at 1,091 feet (332 m). Killington Peak, the second highest peak in Vermont, is 4,241 feet (1,292 m) and overall the maximum vertical drop is 3,150 feet (960 m).

Thirty percent of the 200 trails are graded "easier" (59 beginner trails), 39 percent "more difficult" (78 intermediate trails), and 31 percent "most difficult' (63 trails). But the ski trails are tightly packed into 1,182 acres (478 ha) so the ski area is quite complex —averaging only 5.9 acres (2.3 ha) and 0.4 miles (0.7km) per trail. All together the ski trails add up to 87 miles (140 km) with the longest trail (Juggernaut) at 6.2 miles (10 km).

Killington is also home to the largest learning complex in eastern North America—this area is called Snowshed—and Rams Head is an ideal mountain area for families. Outer Limits, the steepest mogul slope in the East, covers 1,200 feet (365 m) of vertical in half a mile (0.8 km).

Of the seven mountains, nearby Pico is altogether much more low-key and deserves a detour for a few quiet trails and the quaint intimacy of old-time New

England skiing on less-crowded slopes over 14 miles (22 km) of diverse terrain. This includes a 1,967-foot (600-m) vertical and 48 trails, plus a central base village and lodge complete with roaring log fire. Or, for a little of that 1960s-style, drop in at Suicide Six close to Woodstock.

Killington's 19-vehicle Stealth Grooming fleet—one of the best around—is state-of-the-art and busy each night. Some trails are half-groomed, allowing bumps and terrain features to develop on the other side of the trail. Killington has thinned out some forest areas to create so-called "Fusion Zones" (the resort's official glades) and although they get tracked quickly, they offer great rides for intermediates and above when covered in fresh powder.

▼ BIG LIFT CAPACITY
Killington has a comprehensive ski lift system with some 31 lifts ranging from the world's fastest and first heated 8-passenger gondola lift to quads, triples, pomas and handle tows – all designed to get you up the seven mountain areas as speedily as possible.

SKI LIFTS

Killington's lift system is the most extensive in eastern North America. It has 31 lifts, including two eight-passenger heated express gondolas. The K1 Express gondola takes just six minutes to reach Killington Peak—one of the highest lift-serviced peaks in New England—and at 2.5 miles (4 km) the Skyeship Gondola is the longest continuous gondola in the east. There are also six high-speed quads—each accessing a different mountain area—six fixed grip quads, six triple chairs, four double chairs and six surface lifts. The powerful lift system has an uphill capacity of 52,361 rides per hour which means that very rarely will you find lift lines, although the trails can get crowded on Saturdays and busy holiday periods. Lifts operate from 9:00 AM to 4:00 PM Monday–Friday, and from 8:00 AM to 4:00 PM at weekends and on Public Holidays.

LIFT PASSES

The mEticket system gives access to seven mountains for as little as US$42 a day with junior and senior tickets at just over half the price. The best deal going is the five-day Killington Ski Week, including Mon–Fri lift ticket and Sun–Thur lodgings from around US$240 to US$320 depending on season.

Tickets cover weekends and holidays and are available at any ticket window or online at the resort's website, www.killington.com. Children aged five and under ski free when accompanied by an adult, and children 12 and under ski free when accompanied by an adult purchasing a five-day or more lift pass. If you're a beginner taking a Learn to Ski clinic, included in that clinic is a limited access lift ticket to Snowshed and Rams Head; you cannot buy this pass by itself. Photo I.D. is not needed for day lift tickets, but they are for season passes.

SKI SCHOOLS

"Give us a week and we'll give you a lifetime" is how Killington's Perfect Turn Ski and Snowboard School sums up its ethos. And it's taught more people to ski than any other ski resort in North America, so it knows what it's talking about. From the right gear to the perfect turn by way of video and the pros' personal attention and tons of beginner trails, this is progressive "can-do" coaching at its best. All clinics are out of the Snowshed and Rams Head areas; all learn to ski/ride clinics are at the Sprint Perfect Turn Discovery Center, also located at Snowshed. Coaching is available for the youngest recruits at 2–3 years for on-snow; and at six weeks for daycare. Children are supervised at lunchtime if your child is in a full-day program.

▲ SERVICING THE SLOPES
There are so many snow-makers and piste-bashers that lack of snow is not an option. Killington also has one of the longest ski seasons running from mid-October to the last weekend in May.

SKI SCHOOL
PERFECT TURN
SKI AND SNOWBOARD SCHOOL
802-422-6200 or 800-621-6867
www.killington.com

▲ **COOL KILLINGTON**
Ask anyone to describe New England skiing and the first word they come up with is 'cold.' There is some truth in this and the mountains of Vermont, New Hampshire, Maine and even New York are no place for skiing in jeans and a sweat shirt. Wear the full number, do up those zips, carry a scarf and keep the ears covered.

BEGINNERS

Roughly a third of the area is designated novice but beginners can go anywhere they wish at Killington. There are easier "green" routes from the top of six of Killington's seven mountains. Great Northern and Great Eastern in particular offer long green circle trails with panoramic views along the way. You can start on the 0.75-mile (1.2-km) long Snowshed Learning Slope. Serviced by three lifts, it provides a gentle way to begin skiing or boarding.

INTERMEDIATES

Start off perhaps at Snowdon Mountain and warm up on more difficult trails such as Bunny Buster, Mouse Trap or Vagabond, then head over to Rams Head Mountain later in the morning for some more enjoyable cruising. Look out for Juggernaut, a 6.2 mile (10 km) trail that is tailor-made for confident skiers, while Skyeburst on Bear Mountain offers upper intermediates a taste of challenges that lie ahead.

ADVANCED & EXPERT

The best skiing for advanced or expert is in the Canyon area off Killington Peak or at Bear Mountain, with the toughest skiing on Outer Limits—the steepest mogul slope in the East, covering 1,200 feet (365 m) of vertical in half a mile (0.8 km). The Canyon area offers steep terrain on Double Dipper, and Ovation, on Skye Peak, is the steepest trail on the mountain with more than a 50-degree pitch. Machine-made bumps can be found on trails like Outer Limits, Superstar, and Needles' Eye.

Officially there is no off-piste skiing at Killington and powder hounds will normally opt for the designated tree skiing in the Fusion Zones, or for Pico where you can find long-lasting powder without having to venture off-piste. But the Big K has been home to many great off-piste skiers and riders, and members of the original Tasmanian Telemarkers club have long been skiing off-piste in the backwoods. Local knowledge is essential! The difficulty of navigating off-piste in the woods should not be underestimated otherwise you are likely to find yourself stuck overnight in the forest. If you have the necessary skills, knowledge, and equipment to venture into the backwoods be sure to travel in groups of three or more or —better still, you may like to try and team up with the Tasmanians who allegedly meet at the Skyeship Gondola every Wednesday (November through May) at 10:00 AM.

BOARDING & FREESTYLE

For boarders there is a superpipe and a terrain park called The Beach, located on the Snowshed Trail. The lineup at The Beach includes a hip jump

► **NOT FOR POWDER OR OFF-PISTE**
Powder can be hard to come by in New England resorts and Killington is no exception. Much of the skiing is on-piste or on long winding trails needing plenty of edge on a frosty morning but there is a wide variety of skiing and lots of places to cruise about on the open tops.

at the top, then a tall table (with two take-offs), the CKY jump, which is followed by yet another two take-off table, and the one love jump (single poppy take-off). You then have a three-option table leading to a tall table with a nice hip landing before finishing with the grinder-shaped 15-foot (4.5-m) quarterpipe at the bottom.

The rails are off to the side of the jumps and include four main rail features of between 20 feet (6 m) and 30 feet (9 m) in length. Boarders can get around the ski area without running into too many flat-outs, except some green "traversing" trails that tend to be somewhat flat.

EATING ON THE MOUNTAIN

The smart set tends to get in early and grab a table for lunch at the Bear Lodge and catch a few rays on the sun deck. It's the place to be in the spring for deck parties, live music, barbecues and loads of sun and snow. Or you can try a little Tex-Mex at Raul's Burrito Stand on the Skyeship trail. If you want a real sweeping view of the mountains head up to the Killington Peak Restaurant where on a good day you can see five states. That done, don't forget to drop in at either the Mahogany Ridge Bar or Max's Place, good watering holes for thirsty skiers. Better make it both.

Off the mountain Hemingway's Restaurant (the only four-diamond restaurant in Vermont) is housed in a traditional 1860s homestead off Route 4 and has been cited in the Top 25 restaurants in all of North America, as voted by *Food & Wine magazine*. Zola's Grille at The Cortina Inn is also recommended for its food and extensive, quality wine list. The Long Trail Pub at Snowshed is a rustic pub that pours fresh the local brew of the Long Trail Brewing Company, made just 15 minutes down the road from Killington. The Bakery at Snowshed offers freshly baked bread daily and mile-high sandwiches made to order, plus cakes, pastries, and other goodies. Roadhouses and diners offer traditional hamburgers, hot dogs and chicken to salads, sushi, Mexican, pizza, and Italian.

APRÈS SKI

Killington is lively and commercial. There are bars and cabarets and discos and plenty of good restaurants. Killington is therefore known among the Alpine cognoscenti as a Party-ers' Paradise. Strong men (and women) have been carried home from the Lookout Bar and Grill after a great night out, and there is live music at the Pickle Bar, the Wobbly Barn, and other points around town. You might try Bear Lodge— as described above, it really is great in spring for eating, drinking, parties, and fun in the sun and snow. Killington ranks number one in après ski in ski country and has hundreds of bars on and off the mountain, including Mahogany Ridge in the Killington Base Lodge, The Lookout Bar and Grill, Casey's Caboose, and the Grist Mill. Unlike the Rocky Mountain states, Vermont allows older teenagers into bars (but not clubs) provided they don't drink alcohol.

OTHER ACTIVITIES

If skiing or riding isn't your bag, Killington has ice skating, backcountry snowmobiling, rock and ice climbing, snowshoeing, cross-country skiing, and dog-sledding, as well as spas, saunas and hot tubs to soothe away all your aches and pains. Apart from the usual places selling equipment for skiers and boarders, the shopping opportunities are limited. You can catch a movie, read a book, or go bowling—but compared to many other resorts there is little else to do and non-skiers will soon get bored.

USEFUL PHONE NUMBERS

Central Reservation Center	802-422-6200
Doctor	802-422-6125
Taxi	802-422-9718

USEFUL WEBSITES

Official Website	www.killington.com
Snow Report & Web Cams	www.rsn.com/cams
Weather Reports	www.wunderground.com
Ethan Allen Express	www.amtrak.com
Good Inn with helpful travel pages	www.cortinainn.com

RESTAURANTS

HEMMINGWAYS
ZOLA'S GRILLE
LONG TRAIL PUB

BARS

BEAR LODGE
MAHOGANY RIDGE LOOKOUT BAR AND GRILL
THE WOBBLY BARN
PICKLE BARREL
CASEY'S CABOOSE
GRIST MILL
..... and lots more!

▼ **CHILL OUT AFTER SKIING**
Killington has no 'village' as such but there is a varied choice of lodging options a drive or shuttle bus ride away from the slopes.

SUGARLOAF IS MAINE'S LARGEST SKI RESORT. IT HAS THE ONLY ABOVE-TREE-LINE SKIING IN THE EAST, AND ALTHOUGH IT IS FOUR HOURS FROM THE NEAREST MAJOR AIRPORT, MOST AGREE THAT IT IS WORTH THE TRIP.

SUGARLOAF

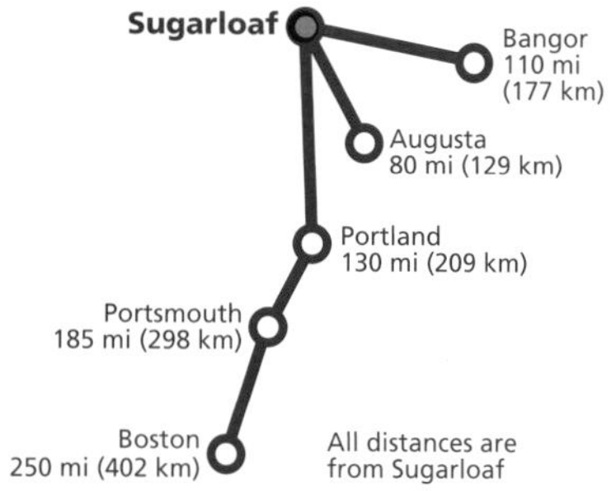

SKI SEASON
Early November to April

The "Sugarloaf Experience" begins a few miles before reaching the mountain when Route 27 rounds a bend and affords the first full view of the mountain. The season here lasts from early November to April. Peak season is mid-February. to mid-March, and low season November to December 24 and mid-March to the end of the season. The snow record is based on a 10-year average that includes significant swings from 154 inches (391 cm) to 396 inches (1.5 m), but with a snowmaking system covering 92 percent of the skiable area including 10 new state-of-the-art tower guns and revamped pipe system on the eastern side, the resort is able to ensure sufficient high-quality snow on a consistent basis.

GETTING THERE

Sugarloaf is located in the Carrabassett Valley, Maine, off Route 27 North. Boston Logan International Airport is the nearest international

▼ MAJESTIC MOUNTAIN
Ride your chosen trail all the way from the summit of this whopping mountain to the cozy village at the base.

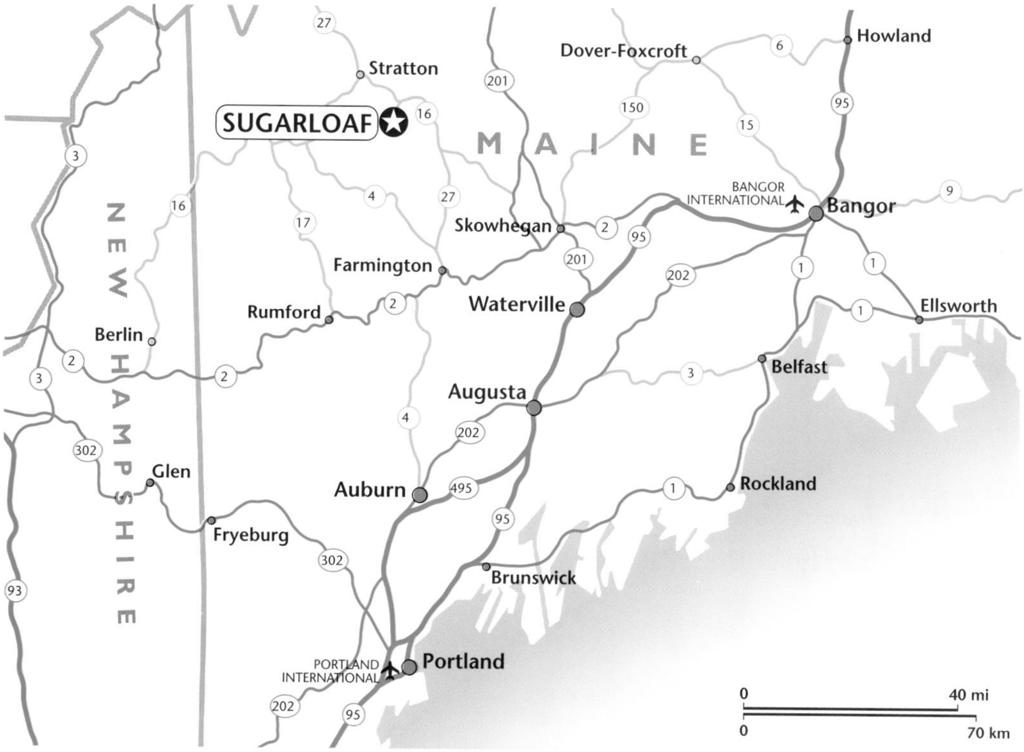

MOUNTAIN FACTS

Base	1,417 feet (425 m)
Summit	4,237 feet (1,271 m)
Elevation	2,820 feet (846 m)
Easy	27%
Intermediate	30%
Advanced	27%
Expert	16%
Number of trails	129
Longest trail	3.5 miles (5.5 km)
Cross-country trails	62 miles (99 km)
Ski area	1,400 acres (560 ha)

SNOWFALL

Annual snowfall	216 inches (548 cm)
Snowmaking	490 acres (196 ha)

SKI LIFTS

High-Speed Quads	4
Triple Chairs	1
Double Chairs	8
Surface Lifts	2
Total	15
Riders per hour	21,805

ACCOMMODATIONS

GRAND SUMMIT RESORT HOTEL
SUGARLOAF INN
CONDOMINIUMS

airport, 350 miles (563 km) from Sugarloaf, four hours by road. Transfer services and car rentals are available at the airport. For full directions by road go to the website www.sugarloaf.com. There are no rail connections.

THE VILLAGE

The village at Sugarloaf was created in the 1970s and has more than 40 restaurants and stores. Centrally located at the base of the mountain, it offers the only true slopeside village in the East. Visitors return year after year because of the welcoming community setting. Trails all lead back to the base area, providing convenient meeting points for families and friends. With the shuttle services available you can leave your car parked from arrival to departure if you wish.

ACCOMMODATIONS

On-mountain lodging at Sugarloaf comes in many distinct styles, from a luxury hotel through to one-bedroom condos. Guests in any of the locations receive full membership at the Sugarloaf Sports and Fitness Club during their stay. The Grand Summit Resort Hotel has 120 rooms offering luxury accommodations, while Sugarloaf Inn, at the base of the Birches trail, is a quaint, country-style inn with comfortable rooms and great views of the mountain. In addition to these examples, there are 900 mountainside condominiums ranging from studios to five bedrooms. All of the accommodations are located on mountain, most of them with ski-in, ski-out access.

SKI AREA

Sugarloaf is one big mountain that includes some challenging terrain. The resort is most famous for its black diamond Snowfields, but below them is a huge assortment of terrain for all ability levels. The learning area for beginners allows them to ski or ride below the lodge before attempting to board the chairlift. Intermediates enjoy the long, winding cruisers of Tote Road and Timberline, and experts are thrilled by the boundary-to-boundary policy that

▼ A GREAT WELCOME
The friendly village at Sugarloaf has more than 40 restaurants and shops and is the only true slopeside village in the East.

allows skiers and riders to go anywhere within the boundaries of the resort's 1,400 acres (560 ha) of terrain. Sugarloaf has recently added 13 new trails and glades, which are now groomed nightly with 12 grooming machines, and they are working on upgrading the mountain trail signs.

SKI LIFTS

There are 15 lifts in total, including four high-speed quads, one triple, eight doubles and two surface lifts, taking 21,805 skiers per hour onto the mountain. The lifts operate from 8:00 AM to 3:45 PM.

LIFT PASSES

A full-day pass for adults (19–64) costs US$53, teens (13–18) US$48, juniors (6–12) and seniors (65+) pay US$36, while children aged five and under ski free. There's a "Mid Mountain" pass, also an "Amosland" pass which provides limited lift access. You can purchase lift passes in the lower level of the base lodge, and at any of the check-in locations. The mEticket, only available online, must be bought at least 14 days in advance and can save you 10 percent on all lift pass costs. The mEticket can be used at Sugarloaf and at eight other American Ski Company resorts (Attitash Bear Park in New Hampshire, Killington, Pico, Mount Snow, Haystack in Vermont, Sunday River in Maine, The Canyons in Utah and Steamboat in Colorado). Adult regular passes for five days or more cost US$47 per day, and if you ski or ride for six days the seventh day is free.

Having to wait in line is generally not a problem at Sugarloaf. During peak periods, use of the SuperQuad may require waits of about 10 minutes, but with a ride time of six minutes, guests don't

▲ **RIDING HIGH**
This is one of eight double chairlifts that contribute to Sugarloaf's 15 lifts.

DAY CARE
Gondola Village Daycare Center
Children aged 10 weeks to five years.
Full-day and half-day care available, plus evenings.
Organised non-ski activities for ages 10 weeks to three years.
Moosketeers ski program for children aged 3–5 years.
Call 207-237-6804 for details.

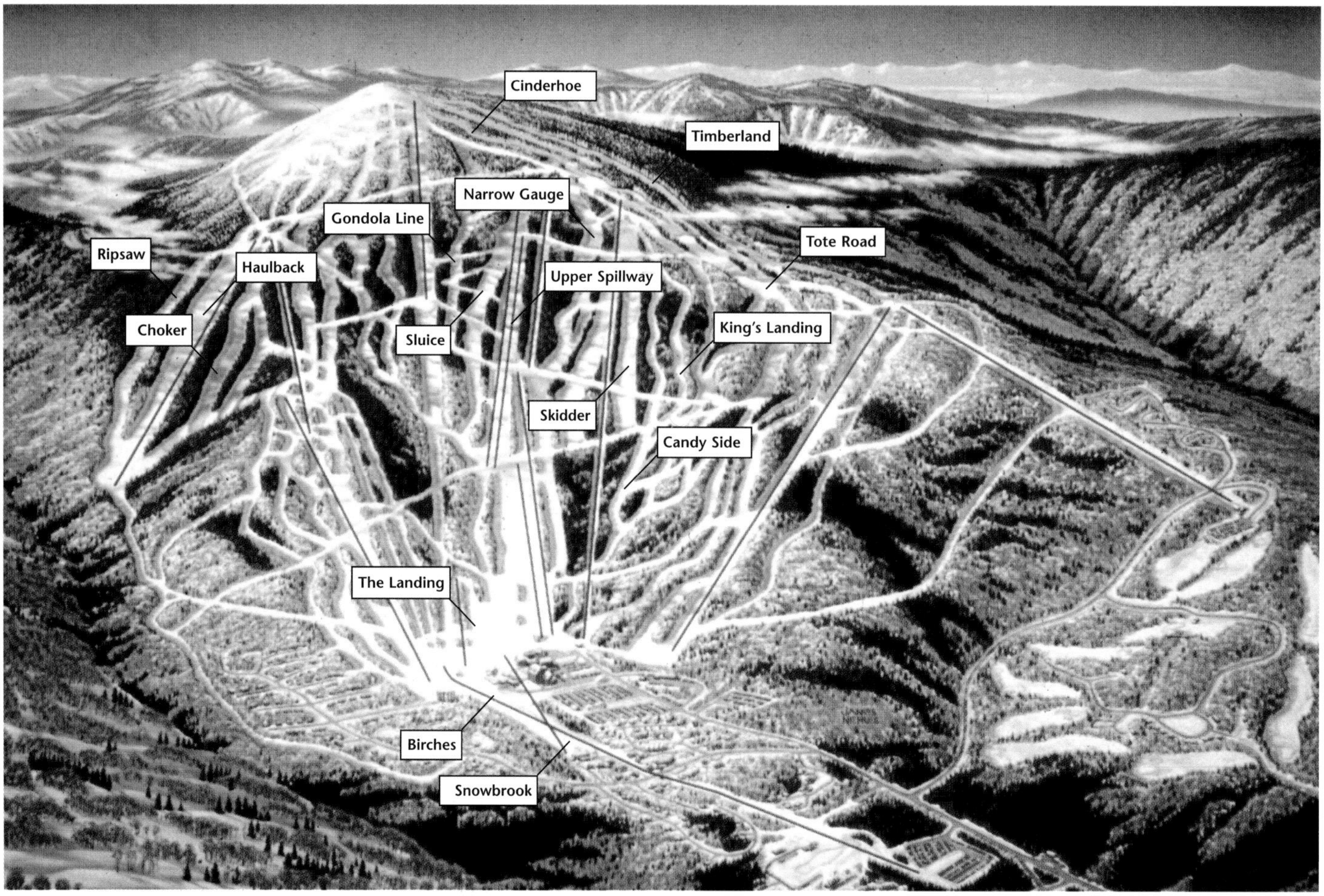

usually view this as a problem. Locals generally avoid the SuperQuad at peak times and use alternate lifts that have short to no lines.

SKI SCHOOLS AND GUIDING

The Perfect Turn Ski School is located in the lower level of the Base Lodge in the heart of the village. The office operates from 8:30 AM to 3:30 PM. The upper limit on ski group size is eight (for one instructor) and the minimum age for group lessons is three years. All young children are supervised if they are enrolled in a children's program. There are a variety of children's programs, such as Moosketeers (3 years old), Mountain Magic (3–6 years), and Mountain Adventure (7–14 years). Adult, teenager, group clinics, and private clinics are also available.

BEGINNERS

The best areas for beginners to ski or snowboard are The Birches, The Landing and Snowbrook trails. A key and unique benefit is that these slopes are located below the base lodge, thus beginners can get their bearings on these gentle slopes before attempting to ride a lift for the first time. After that, beginners can enjoy top to bottom terrain on all green trails. Whiffletree is a superb family area with blues and greens that everyone can enjoy together. The Whiffletree SuperQuad whisks you to the top of the trails in under six minutes.

INTERMEDIATES

The most challenging trail for intermediates, a blue trail, is Sluice Headwall, with the steepest pitch of the blue trails. Intermediates can then head down Upper Spillway, which starts as a black trail but levels out somewhat in the middle section. This steep, wide trail is a favorite with those who enjoy making big arcing turns. A suggested itinerary for intermediates would be to take Cinderhoe or Tote Road from the top of the Timberline quad, or from the Superquad take King's Landing down to Candyside.

ADVANCED & EXPERT

The best places for advanced skiing and riding would be Mid-mountain and East Mountain, including the snowfields. For steep trails, the Gondola Line is a classic trail that goes straight down the center of the mountain. Narrow Gauge, Sugarloaf's most famous trail, has been the venue for

▲ PERFECT PARALLELS
Bend your knees, like the instructor told you, and you'll soon be carving your own way down any trail.

◄ STEEP AND DEEP
Sugarloaf's most famous trail is Narrow Gauge, a long, steep trail.

▲ **BE THE BEST**
Snowboarders are not excluded from any part of the mountain, just don't touch the ground on your perfect turns.

EATING ON THE MOUNTAIN

GRAND SUMMIT RESORT HOTEL
SUGARLOAF INN
CONDOMINIUMS

many racing competitions through the years and offers a long, steep trail. For moguls try Ripsaw and Choker in the King Pine Bowl. These two trails remain ungroomed for most of the season, and as they are on the farthest east side of the mountain, they tend to collect snow that drifts from the prevailing west to easterly winds. For constructed mogul lines, Skidder is the training and competition trail for freestyle mogul skiers at Sugarloaf. Ripsaw, Back Side Snowfields, and the Glades are best for powder snow.

A suggested itinerary for advanced skiing and riding would be to ski or ride in the King Pine Bowl with the morning sun: Haulback, Widowmaker, Ripsaw. Then head west and enjoy Gondola Line and Narrow Gauge from the Spillway Chair in the Central Mountain area, then proceed further west in the afternoon to enjoy Competition Hill, Skidder, Hayburner or Double Bitter. The best trail for experts would be White Nitro, which has one of the steepest pitches in the East. Ripsaw, Bubblecuffer, Winters Way, Choker, Misery Whip and Skidder for moguls, and the Glades for fresh, steep powder. Head to the summit from the top of the Timberline quad for the only above-tree-line skiing in the East and a panoramic view into New Hampshire to Mount Washington, or across to Mount Katahdin, Maine's highest mountain. The Perfect Turn Ski School offers Level 8 ski instruction.

BOARDING & FREESTYLE

Sugarloaf boasts a 7-acre (2.8-ha) terrain park, perfect for introducing someone to tricks—"It's small on air, but big on flow." The park is good for both skiers and riders wanting to try out table jumps and washboard bumps. The first Superpipe built in New England is 400 feet (120 m) long and offers an abundance of freestyling opportunities. There's also a Quarantine Zone for skiers and riders learning the basics of jumps and tricks. Boarders are not excluded from any part of the mountain.

EATING ON THE MOUNTAIN

There is only one on-mountain restaurant, the ski-in, ski-out Bullwinkle's, although in the village are 16 further restaurants offering a choice of fast food or a multicourse, elegant meal. In 2003 the seating capacity of Bullwinkle's was doubled. In the

► **TURBO TUBING**
Four chutes off Lower Whiffletree offer fun for everyone, even at night when it's all lit up.

village, Season's at Sugarloaf Inn, the Bag and Kettle Restaurant and Pub, and Gepetto's Restaurant are among the favorites with locals and visitors alike.

APRÈS SKI

There are seven bars in the resort that appeal to most ages. The Widowmaker Lounge in the Base Lodge is the best place for après ski, with live entertainment every Friday and Saturday night. The Bag and Kettle Restaurant and Pub offers "Blues Night" on Mondays. The Shipyard Brewhaus in Sugarloaf Inn has "Open Mic Night" on Wednesdays; the Double Diamond Restaurant and Pub, in the Grand Summit Hotel, offers live entertainment nightly; and Theo's Sugarloaf Brewery has "Margarita Night" on Wednesdays. Season's Restaurant in Sugarloaf Inn, Double Diamond Restaurant and Pub, and Bullwinkle's all have an extensive list of quality wines. Sugarloaf liquor laws allow alcohol to be served to adults aged 21 years or over. Children can accompany parents in bars and other places serving alcohol only until they stop serving food. Bars generally close at 1:00 AM.

OTHER ACTIVITIES

The Turbo Tubing Park, with four 1,000-foot (304-m) chutes off Lower Whiffletree, has its own lift and lighting system for night tubing. The Sugarloaf Sports and Fitness Center and the Antigravity Recreational Complex (A.G.C.) are located near the resort entrance. The Fitness Center has a pool, weight room, hot tubs, tanning beds and racquetball courts. The A.G.C. offers a wide variety of indoor activities including Maine's largest climbing wall, plus a skate park and skate bowl. Cross-country skiing at the Outdoor Center offers 65 miles (105 km) of trails weaving through the Longfellows between Sugarloaf, Crocker and Bigelow mountains. The Outdoor Center also has an Olympic-sized outdoor ice skating rink with music and lights, and snowshoeing, with guided snowshoe safaris and moonlight snowshoeing. The village has several stores but apart from the usual logoed merchandise, Maine-made gifts, skiing and snowboarding gear and clothing, there's not that much in the way of shopping.

USEFUL PHONE NUMBERS

General Information	207-237-2000
Central Reservations	800-843-5623
Guest Services	207-237-6939
Ski Patrol	207-237-6862
First Aid	207-237-6994
Snow Phone	207-237-6808
Outdoor Center	207-237-6830
Antigravity Recreational Complex	207-237-5566
Ski Rentals	207-237-6951
Snowboard Rentals	207-237-6970
Perfect Turn Ski & Snowboard School	207-237-6924

USEFUL WEBSITES

Official Website	www.sugarloaf.com
Official email	info@sugarloaf.com
On-mountain lodgings reservations	lodging@sugarloaf.com
Off-mountain lodgings reservations	arealodging@sugarloaf.com

▲ **CLASSIC COMFORT** The Grand Summit Resort Hotel can offer world-class service, style, comfort, and it's a snowball's throw away from the lifts.

BARS

WIDOWMAKER LOUNGE
BAG AND KETTLE AND PUB
SHIPYARD BREWHAUS
THEO'S SUGARLOAF BREWERY
DOUBLE DIAMOND

RESTAURANTS

SEASON'S RESTAURANT
DOUBLE DIAMOND
JAVA JOE'S
NARROW GAUGE
KLISTER KITCHEN CAFÉ
HUG'S
ONE STANLEY AVENUE
PORTER HOUSE RESTAURANT
THE BAG AND KETTLE
WIDOWMAKER LOUNGE
SHIPYARD BREWHAUS
THEO'S
GEPETTO'S
TUFULIO'S
D'ELLIE'S DELICATESSEN
WHISTLESTOP CAFÉ

ARCTIC OCEAN
Ellesmere Island
Axel Heiberg Island
GREENLAND
Prince Patrick Island
Queen Elizabeth Islands
Melville Island
Bathurst Island
Devon Island
Baffin Bay
Resolute
Parry Channel
BEAUFORT SEA
Banks Island
ALASKA
Prince of Wales Island
Amundsen Gulf
Inuvik
Victoria Island
Boothia Peninsula
Baffin Island
Davis Strait
Melville Peninsula
Mackenzie
Mackenzie Mountains
Selwyn Mountains
Franklin Mts.
Yukon
Foxe Basin
Iqaluit
Great Bear Lake
Back
Mt. Logan
19,525 ft (5,951 m)
Whitehorse
ROCKY MOUNTAINS
COAST MOUNTAINS
Southampton Island
Hudson Strait
Thelon
Yellowknife
Dubawnt Lake
Ungava Bay
Ungava Peninsula
Great Slave Lake
Hay River
CANADIAN SHIELD
Slave
GREAT PLAINS
Hudson Bay
Churchill
Lake Athabasca
Peace
Athabasca
Prince Rupert
Queen Charlotte Islands
Reindeer Lake
Belcher Islands
Dawson Creek
Churchill
Laurent
Nelson
Prince George
Thompson
James Bay
Mt. Waddington
13,104 ft (3,994 m)
Fraser
Columbia Mountains
Flin Flon
Edmonton
Prince Albert
Saskatchewan
Fort Albany
Lake Winnipegosis
Lake Winnipeg
Vancouver Island
Kamloops
Saskatoon
Calgary
Vancouver
Columbia
CANADA
Alma
Lake Manitoba
Lake Nipigon
Québec C
Lethbridge
Regina
Brandon
Winnipeg
Timmins
Rouyn-Noranda
Thunder Bay
Montréal
Lake Superior
Sudbury
Ottawa
Sault Ste. Marie
Lake Huron
Toronto
Hamilton
Lake Ontario
Lake Michigan
Lake Erie
UNITED STATES

CANADA

CANADA'S SKIING REFLECTS THE COUNTRY: BIG AND EMPTY. THANKS TO A UNIQUE COMBINATION OF NORTHERLY LATITUDE AND LARGE MOUNTAINS, MANY OF WHICH ARE PERFECTLY PLACED TO CATCH PACIFIC STORMS, CANADA HAS DEVELOPED A REPUTATION FOR GREAT SNOW WITHOUT TOO MANY SKIERS TO SPOIL THE VIEW, OR MORE IMPORTANTLY, YOUR FRESH TRACKS.

Most of the skiing in Cananda shares the same Rocky Mountains that stretch north to south through the continent of North America. Though the peaks are not as lofty as in the U.S., the skiing starts at lower altitudes, so they still offer as many if not more vertical feet to be skied.

Whistler Blackcomb is a case in point, topping the North American league table with 5,280 vertical feet (1,609 m). Only Mike Wiegele's helicopter skiing operation claims more vertical and that too is in British Columbia, Canada. Meanwhile, Banff Lake Louise comes out top for ski acreage with 7,358 acres (2,977 ha). That's around 40 percent bigger than Vail. There's strength in depth too, meaning more to choose from and also more to have to leave until next time around—there was no room in the book, sadly, for resorts such as Kicking Horse, Panorama and Red Mountain in this edition of Ski North America but they and others will be in the next one.

Though the country might be huge, the population is small and most of it is centered in Ontario and Québec, far from the best skiing. Even allowing for visitors from abroad, it all adds up to good news for skiers who like their snow untrammeled. A simple calculation of lift capacity divided by size of ski area suggests a lower skier density than the U.S. In Canada you can expect to clash poles with no more than eight skiers per acre in most resorts, though Tremblant is the exception that proves the rule.

There has been heavy investment in technology and infrastructure in many resorts to provide more high-speed lifts and improve mountain bases. Though some of the smaller resorts have further lift improvements to make, ski area management in Canada is driven by the same competitive instincts as in the U.S., with a focus on service and efficiency. It's leading to improvements for skiers year on year, with the distinct advantage that Canadian resorts are in less danger of killing the goose that laid the golden egg - driving skiers away through overcrowding—than resorts in many other parts of the world.

The type of terrain and the range of skiing, from groomed cruisers to untouched deeps, is as varied as in the U.S. The top forty resorts in North America average around 20 percent beginner, 40 percent intermediate and 40 percent advanced. Beyond that broad statistic, only closer study of individual resorts will determine which one is for you. As in the U.S., key advantages for skiers make a refreshing change for Europeans. Some seem prosaic, but can make all the difference on vacation: orderly lift lines and generally responsible skiers (or at least, better policing). Others are more fundamental, and also affect skiers at every level: high-quality tuition (with no language barrier for English speakers); immaculate grooming; and, particularly for advanced skiers, an abundance of in-bounds terrain to allow skiing that in the European Alps would be classified "off-piste" and might require a guide to experience. At this level, both B.C. and Alberta offer plenty of deep powder and steeps, not to mention the biggest heliskiing operations in the world.

Canada's strong multicultural base is reflected by the amazing choice of international cuisine, and—in a laid-back kind of way—it's very friendly. Québec City and Montréal offer a more European flavour while the British Columbia resorts, led by Whistler Blackcomb - which rivals any resort worldwide—are more international. But Canada is also special for its wonderfully preserved mountain environments. The Rocky Mountains of Alberta are the jewel in the crown, with breathtaking scenery and wildlife in Jasper and Banff National Parks attracting millions of visitors annually. Most come in the summer months, so the towns of Jasper, Lake Louise and Banff are off-season in winter, making them even better value. The same may be true of Jackson Hole and neighboring Yellowstone Park in the U.S., but visitors to Canada also benefit from a favorable exchange rate.

WHISTLER–BLACKCOMB IS ONE OF THE WORLD'S TOP SKI RESORTS AND AN ABSOLUTE MUST DESTINATION FOR SKIERS OF ALL LEVELS. THE SKIING AND RIDING ARE SECOND TO NONE WITH THE TWO GREATEST VERTICAL RISE MOUNTAINS IN NORTH AMERICA, LONG TRAILS, GLACIERS, EXTENSIVE SNOW BOWLS, AND A RELIABLE 360 INCHES (914 CM) SNOW RECORD.

WHISTLER-BLACKCOMB

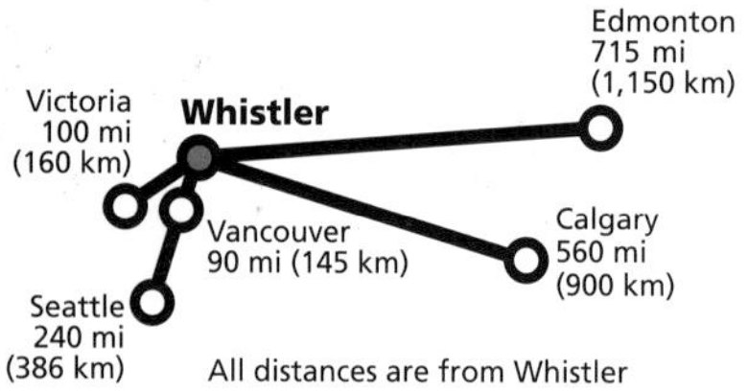

▼ BIG COUNTRY
Whistler and Blackcomb may be massive mountains, but they are mere markers in the mass of rock and snow that makes up the Coast Range heading 200 miles (320 km) northward.

Whistler–Blackcomb ranks high among the world's top ski resorts in any guide you care to open—and we agree. This is not simply because of the fantastic skiing, varied and splendid though this is, but because Whistler-Blackcomb is a truly efficient and complete resort with superb facilities for skiers and non-skiers alike.

No wonder then that it is consistently voted one of North America's top ski resort. And it's not just U.S. and Canadian skiers that are lured here. Whistler-Blackcomb takes a lion's share of all the skiing holidays taken in North America by overseas visitors. Better ski schools, safer family slopes, top-quality accommodations and service, fantastic skiing, and good facilities for non-skiers are the reasons.

The season in Whistler runs from late November until early June and snowfall averages 360 inches (30 feet/9.1 m) per season, supplemented by extensive state-of-the-art snowmaking facilities over 565 acres (229 ha). If the weather is ever an issue it

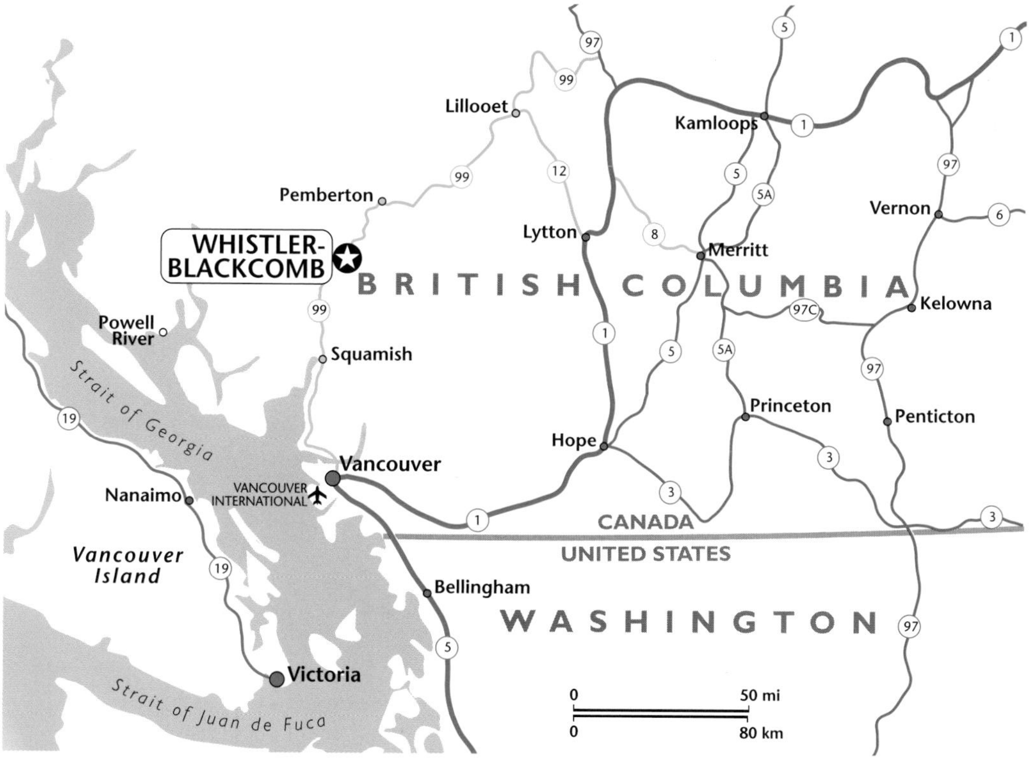

▲ **SLICK CITY** Whistler Village is an attractively designed cobblestoned area which melds into Village North, with courtyards linked by walking paths housing plenty of shops, and places to meet and chill out.

is likely to be because of too much snow rather than too little, and because the village is at low altitude (2,140 feet/653 m) and given its coastal proximity and mild climate, when snow falls on the mountain it often rains in the village.

GETTING THERE

Whistler-Blackcomb is located in the Coast Mountain Range of Whistler, British Columbia, on Canada's west coast just 90 miles (145 km) north of Vancouver, with a transfer time of around two hours by road from Vancouver International Airport (YVR). The route follows Highway 99 North—known as the "Sea to Sky Highway" for its panoramic views of Howe Sound and the Coast Mountains—as it curves northward from Horseshoe Bay to Whistler.

There is no rail connection but Perimeter's Whistler Express regular scheduled bus service takes you directly from the airport to Whistler village for around Cdn$60 one-way (Cdn$40 for children 11 and under) or at greater cost you can hire a limo to take you there in luxury.

Flying times from overseas to Vancouver are just under 10 hours from Europe (London, Amsterdam, and Frankfurt) and 8–12 hours from the Far East (Hong Kong and Japan.)

THE VILLAGE

There are four main areas: Whistler Village, Upper Village (Blackcomb), Village North, and Whistler Creek. Whistler Village and Upper Village (Blackcomb) centers—about 10 minutes' walk apart —are most convenient for the slopes with easy access to both Whistler and Blackcomb Mountain lift systems. Whistler Village extends northward for around 0.6 miles (1 km) to Village North, and Whistler Creek (the original Whistler base station) is some 1.8 miles (3 km) away from the main center. In Whistler Village you can stroll through cobblestoned streets in the pedestrian-only village center with its

MOUNTAIN FACTS

	WHISTLER	BLACKCOMB
Base	2,140 feet (653 m)	2,214 feet (675 m)
Summit	7,160 feet (2,182 m)	7,494 feet (2,284 m)
Elevation	5,020 feet (1,529 m)	5,280 feet (1,609 m)
Easy	20%	15%
Intermediate	55%	55%
Advanced	25%	30%
Number of trails	100+	100+
Longest trail	7 miles (11 km)	(7 miles 11 km)
Ski area	3,657 acres (1,480 ha)	3,414 acres (1,382 ha)

SKI LIFTS

	WHISTLER	BLACKCOMB
Gondolas	2	1
High Speed Quads	6	6
Fixed Grip Quads	-	-
Triple Chairs	2	3
Double Chairs	1	-
Surface Lifts	5	7
Total	16	17
Riders per hour	29,895	29,112

SNOWFALL

Annual snowfall	360 inches (914 cm)
Snowmaking	565 acres (229 ha)

SKI SEASON

Late November to late April

ACCOMMODATIONS

UPPER VILLAGE
FAIRMONT CHATEAU WHISTLER
CLUB INTRAWEST
LE CHAMOIS
LOST LAKE LODGE
MARRIOTT RESIDENCE INN
THE ASPENS
WILDWOOD LODGE
GLACIER LODGE

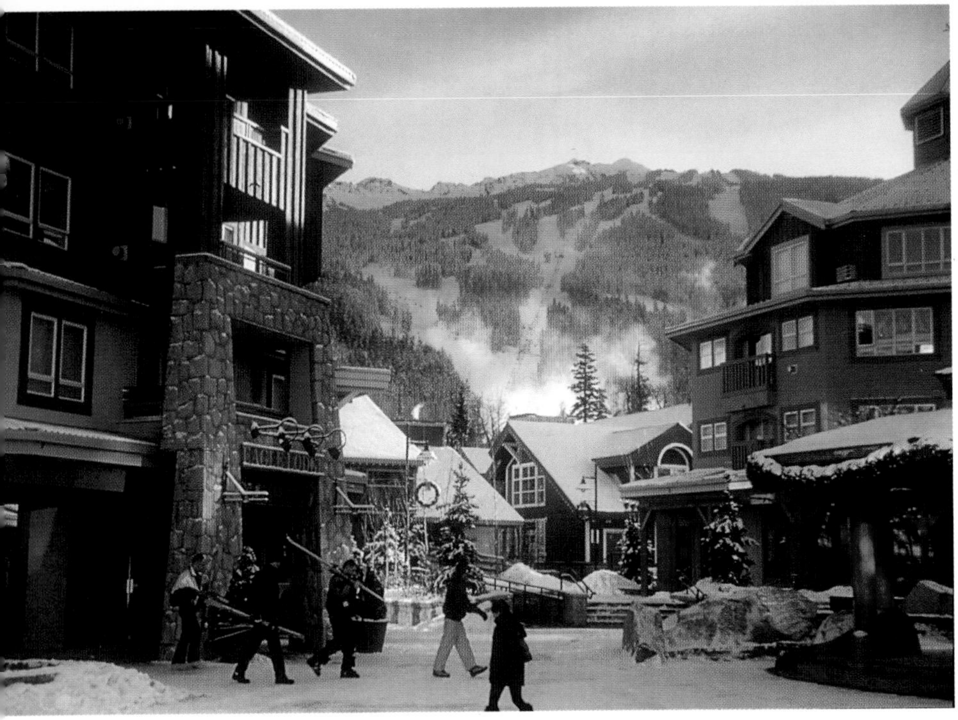

◄ SHOP TILL YOU DROP
Whistler resort actually comprises some 10 shopping, après-ski, and accommodations bases—and the shopping here is world class. From familiar retailers through showcase stores, to local boutiques and art galleries.

covered walkways creating a cozy atmosphere, and more than 200 shops, including a selection of well-known North American retail chain favorites.

ACCOMMODATIONS

Whistler-Blackcomb offers a wide range of accommodations at an equally wide range of prices. Most of the accommodations are in Whistler Village and that is where you should stay if you want to be nearest to the main shopping area and the nightlife.

If you come here privately, in a group or with a family, shop around before you book. The easiest way to book is via Whistler Central Reservations (604-664-5625 or 1-800-WHISTLER in Canada and the U.S.) or www.mywhistler.com. Finding a room is not a problem with over 60 hotels and

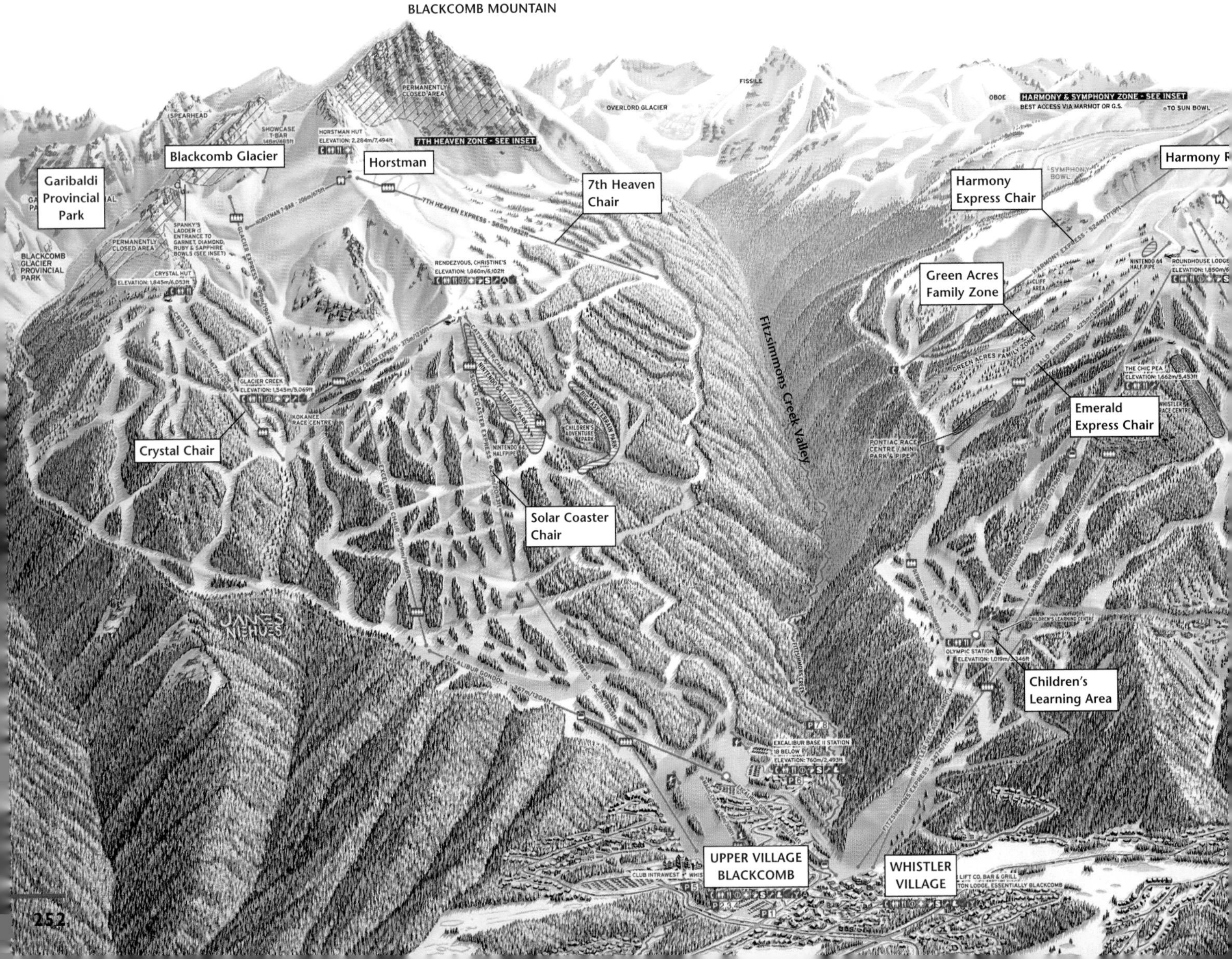

condominiums providing over 2,700 rooms. "Slopeside" properties are defined as those with less than a five-minute walk to the lifts or ski areas, but there are many more options if you wish to stay outside the village.

The choice runs from self-catering suites and condos, to bed and breakfasts, two- and three-bedroom townhouses, and a good selection of hotels. For those on a budget and wanting to self cater, the standard of accommodations is still very high and a one-bedroom den unit will sleep three, but those seeking higher levels of luxury will find plenty of places to splash out in.

Some hotels are large and expensive, like the Westin Resort & Spa at the foot of Whistler Mountain, and the Fairmont Chateau Whistler over at Blackcomb, but there are cheaper well-situated hotels like Crystal Lodge and Listel Whistler Hotel, as well as smaller alternatives like the charming Chalet Louise in Village North, with just eight bedrooms.

Beware that there's a local 7 percent sales tax not included in quoted prices, but overseas visitors can claim back the 7 percent G.S.T. on accommodations.

SKI AREA

Whistler-Blackcomb has the greatest vertical rise —5,280 feet (1,609 m)—of any ski area on the North American continent. It also has the largest ski area—double the size of Snowmass, for example. Imagine the ski area as two hands spread across the

▲ ACROSS THE GREAT DIVIDE

In any head-to-head, Whistler-Blackcomb vies tightly with any premier European resort, and in many respects can claim to offer better powder, safer ski slopes for families, and superior hospitality, accommodations, and service. It's really down to the choice between Old World or New World culture.

ACCOMMODATIONS

WHISTLER VILLAGE
WESTIN RESORT & SPA
DELTA WHISTLER RESORT
PAN PACIFIC WHISTLER
CRYSTAL LODGE
EXECUTIVE INN
HOLIDAY INN AT SUNSPREE
LISTEL WHISTLER
MOUNTAINSIDE LODGE
THE COAST WHISTLER HOTEL
TIMBERLINE LODGE
WHISTLER VILLAGE INN
BLACKCOMB LODGE
HEARTHSTONE LODGE
TANTALUS LODGE
WESTBROOK HOTEL

ACCOMMODATIONS

For details of more hotels, condominiums, chalets and other accommodations options go online at www.whistler-blackcomb.com or contact your tour operator.

SKI SCHOOL FOR ADULTS

PRIVATE LESSONS
Private lesson with an instructor for skiers and boarders of any level.

LEARN TO SKI/RIDE
Beginner's program for adults.

SKI AND RIDE ESPRIT
3 or 4 days of mountain guiding with instruction.

WOMEN ONLY SKI CLINICS
Developed by former World Champion Stephanie Sloan, this 3-day program features top coaches for women only.

EXTREMELY CANADIAN FREESKIING CLINICS
Confident intermediates to advanced skiers can refine their off-piste techniques with top guides.

ATOMIC DAVE MURRAY SKI CAMP
This legendary program combines gate training with all-mountain skiing and top coaching.

WHISTLER ADAPTIVE SKI PROGRAM
For all levels of skier, this program is designed to provide people with disabilities access to the mountains.

SKI SCHOOL FOR CHILDREN

INFANTS
An infant childcare program is available for children aged 3-18 months.

TODDLERS
The toddler program for 18 months to 3 years of age includes both indoor and outdoor playtime in a special childcare facility.

WHISTLER KIDS
Offers various skiing and boarding programs to children of all ability levels ages 3 to 17 years.

All children's programs include lunch.

Advance registration (604 932 3434) is strongly recommended.

Blackcomb and Whistler mountains separated by the deep Fitzsimmons Creek Valley with the resort villages side-by-side at the wrists.

But it's not the just the extent of these two massive side-by-side mountains—encompassing over 7,000 acres (2,800 ha) of ski terrain, with 200 marked trails and lots of unmarked ones—it's the sheer diversity. Steep powder chutes, challenging mogul fields, secluded tree skiing and miles of pistes groomed every night attract skiers and snowboarders of all levels.

The keynote of Whistler-Blackcomb skiing is its variety—bowls and glaciers, piste and powder—there truly is skiing here for every standard and every mood, and the many high-speed ski lifts make it quite feasible to choose to ski one mountain in the morning, take in some lunch, and ski the other in the afternoon.

Whistler-Blackcomb also has more than 17 miles (27 km) of cross-country trails set throughout the village, including the Lost Lake area, the Chateau Whistler Golf Course, and Nicklaus North Golf Course. Rental equipment and trail maps for cross-country skiing are available at Lost Lake Hut. Contact the Whistler Information Center 604-932-2394 for further information.

SKI LIFTS

Whistler-Blackcomb has North America's largest high-speed lift system rising from five different base stations, and a capacity of 59,007 riders per hour which almost invariably avoids long lift lines. In total there are 33 lifts, half of them high speed—only Vail comes close to this. Lifts on each mountain are also accessible for people with disabilities.

The lifts run from 8:30 AM to 3:30 pm during the peak season, and the last lift closes between 3:30 PM and 4:00 PM, although this hour is subject to change. Keen skiers can buy a "Fresh Tracks" ticket giving them access to Whistler Mountain from 7:15 AM, a cooked breakfast at Roundhouse Lodge, and then first choice of the freshly groomed trails or, after a dump of new snow, fresh powder!

The most recent improvement was the addition of the Fitzsimmons Express, which rests at the base of Whistler Mountain. This lift connects with the Garbanzo Express and provides access to the north-facing slopes historically known as the Garbanzo Basin.

Whistler-Blackcomb plans to expand its lift system to open up another area of Whistler Mountain. The Flute area is a favorite among backcountry enthusiasts, and the new lift system—when it opens—will make this area safe and accessible to less experienced skiers and boarders. It will also take the pressure off other parts of the lift system and further decrease lift lines. We are told that the decision to open the Flute has now been made but it is not yet known when construction work for the new lift system will be started and completed.

LIFT PASSES

There are lift passes to suit most people and circumstances depending on your age, and on how long and when you plan to ski. Reduced prices apply to veterans in the 65–74 and 75+ age groups, and to younger skiers where lift passes are progressively cheaper for those aged 13–18, 7–12, and six or under. There are also parent passes (for those accompanying young children,) a midweek pass, and a single mountain pass which is unlimited on the mountain of your choice. Five-day full lift passes cost Cdn$315 and Cdn$158 for adults and children (aged 7–12) respectively in the main season. Children aged six years and under ski free. Lift passes can be bought at all mountain base stations, via the www.whistler-blackcomb.com website and at 7/11 stores.

SKI SCHOOLS AND GUIDING

There is one ski and snowboard school offering excellent tuition in a range of well-defined programs designed for adults, children, women-only groups, and people with disabilities.

The Ski Esprit ski school has an excellent grading system. Levels 1–8 range from beginner to expert, each of which is described sufficiently clearly in writing to help prevent people from overstating or understating their abilities. Three-day and four-day group lessons cost Cdn$299 and Cdn$319 respectively.

There is a comprehensive program available for children, starting with an infant childcare program for babies aged 3–18 months, and the toddler program for 18 months to three years includes both indoor and outdoor play time in a special childcare facility. Whistler Kids offers various skiing and snowboarding programs to children of all ability levels, ages 3–17 years. All programs include lunch. Advance registration (604-932-3434) is strongly recommended.

Free guided tours are offered daily for intermediates and experts at 11:30 AM. Whistler Mountain Tour runs from the Guest Satisfaction Center under the lightboard at the top of the Whistler Village Gondola, and Blackcomb Mountain Tour starts from the top of the Solar Coaster Express. The Blackcomb Glacier Tour starts from the same place, weather permitting.

BEGINNERS

If you are a beginner it is likely that you will join one of the many classes available but you will still have plenty of time available to explore the ski area outside class.

For those not joining a class, take the Whistler Village Gondola or Fitzsimmons Express to Olympic Station at 3,346 feet (1,019 m) where you'll find the Children's Learning Area and the best area for beginners on either mountain. Return to the gondola at Olympic Station and progress higher up the mountain to Roundhouse Lodge at 6,069 feet (1,850m) from where you can access the Green Acres Family Zone off the Emerald Express, or take the "easiest way down" trail and ski all the way back down to the village.

On Blackcomb, you can get started low down at the Magic Chair, but Whistler Mountain is by far the better mountain for beginners and children.

Two vast mountains may seem rather daunting but do not be put off by the fact that only 15–20 percent of the mountain area is graded for beginners. One of the great things about Whistler is that beginners are not restricted to the lower slopes. You can learn fast here and confident beginners can quickly progress to enjoy some of the high altitude beginner trails like Burnt Stew Trail off Harmony Express chair (6,939 feet/2,115 m)—a perfect area for groups of mixed ability with some breathtaking 360-degree views and easy trails running down to the village. This gives beginners a "whole mountain" experience and a strong sense of achievement as they ski well-groomed green trails from high altitude all the way down to the village.

The Trail Map is clearly marked to show slow-skiing zones on both mountains. Highlighted

▲ COURAGE TESTER
Hidden chutes, secret spots, and a vast array of fresh backcountry tracks beckon extreme skiers and boarders alike on Whistler Mountain. With the biggest vertical drop on the continent, respect is the name of the game.

▲ **BACKCOUNTRY ROAMIN'**
Fantastic bowls and lots of steep couloirs at the top of Whistler and Blackcomb mountains are even more alluring after a fresh fill of glorious powder, which happens often.

yellow on the Trail Map, they are well patrolled by the Mountain Safety Team—recognizable by their bright yellow jackets—who are quick to seize upon would-be-racers skiing too fast in beginner areas or at intersections where skiers of mixed abilities meet.

INTERMEDIATES

With so much terrain available it's difficult to know where to begin. Both mountains offer excellent skiing and boarding and there is more than enough to keep you busy and tested if you return here year after year. Improve your technique on mile after mile of well-groomed marked trails, or test your off-piste skills in the high alpine terrain.

About half the trails you'll find are graded for intermediates and many are quite long. Blackcomb has some great skiing and riding in the areas off Solar Coaster, Crystal Chairs, and 7th Heaven chairs. Ridge Runner from the top of Crystal, and Panorama off 7th Heaven are not to be missed. On Whistler Mountain try Emerald Express area for tree skiing, or from the top of the Peak check out Highway 86, then Franz's trail all the way down to Whistler Creek.

It is wrong to assume that heliskiing is only for experts. Heliskiing certainly means backcountry and powder—but it doesn't have to be neck-deep and steep. Fat skis are available and a day's guided heliskiing is within the capabilities of most confident and aspiring intermediates. It very much depends on the prevailing weather conditions and having the local heliski operator select terrain that is appropriate to your group's abilities.

ADVANCED

It is in the high alpine areas that Whistler-Blackcomb stands above most other resorts with wide-open alpine bowls, steep chutes, and almost limitless choices. Whistler has more bowls and Blackcomb has more couloirs. Whistler also has the Horstman and Blackcomb glaciers.

On Whistler Mountain take the Peak Chair up to Frontier Pass/The Peak Zone. Whistler's bowls offer plenty of fun. There are some relatively easy descents like The Saddle—an exhilarating trail when freshly groomed—but for those in search of more adventure, the steep and deep can be found on many a powder day in Whistler Bowl and Shale Slope. Do laps on the Peak Chair and work your way out to Bagel Bowl. West Bowl keeps the powder longer and offers some of the toughest skiing with double black diamond trails like Cockalorum and Stefan's Chute.

Or take the Harmony Express and check out the couloirs to the left of Harmony Ridge where there are plenty of single black diamond descents including Little Whistler, Harmony Horseshoes, McConkeys, and Boomer Bowl.

For a classic ski outing on Blackcomb Mountain get up early and be first in line. Warm up with a few laps on 7th Heaven and head for the high alpine. Drop into the Horstman Glacier, check-out the T-bars, then decide if you want to hike a little and ski the Blackcomb Glacier, or drop into the Couloir Extreme. Ride back up on the Glacier Express or Jersey Cream Express and scout your route among an amazing collection of chutes and gullies—The Bite, Staircase, and Blowdown. On a powder day the entire mountain is a playground but those in the know head for the trees on 7th Heaven.

Expert skiers on Blackcomb can also make the short hike up Spanky's Ladder which allows access to four magnificent bowls—Garnet, Diamond, Ruby, and Sapphire—but these double black diamond steep powder pitches are not for the fainthearted.

BACKCOUNTRY

Whistler-Blackcomb borders Garibaldi Provincial Park—480,000 acres (195,000 ha) of rugged wilderness. Access to the backcountry is available to experienced skiers and boarders but anyone entering this area must be prepared with proper survival and self-rescue equipment.

Approximately 80 percent of the world's heliskiing is in British Columbia, and weather conditions permitting, Whistler Heli-Skiing will take you into the backcountry to ski or board four or more drops per day, with each drop giving you access to around 2,500–5,000 vertical feet (762–1,524 m) of untracked powder. Contact Whistler Heli-Skiing on 604-932-4105, toll free on 888-HELISKI or via the website www.whistlerheliskiing.com. For backcountry tours with professional guides contact the Whistler Alpine Guides Bureau or log on to www.whistlerguides.com

BOARDING & FREESTYLE

What's good for skis is good for boards at Whistler-Blackcomb, and with snowboard heliskiing also on offer, the backcountry options especially are mind-boggling. Freeriders have plenty of bowls to snake their first tracks, while freestylers have well-groomed pipes to choose from, and carvers are just spoiled for choice whether beginner, intermediate or advanced.

Both mountains have snowboarding lessons and clinics, and there are specialized camps offering

▼ **STEEP POWDER**
With a huge 7,071 acres (2,862 ha) of area to ski Whistler-Blackcomb has something thing for all, including steeps that will blow the mind.

▲ **LEAP OF FAITH**
Extreme freestylers have no shortage of amazing steep skiing and powder on both Blackcomb and Whistler mountains. On Blackcomb, if you go down the spine toward the back side, keep left and you can peer over the cornice into the double black diamond chutes. Just viewing the abyss (or someone hurtling into it) is not for the faint hearted. The best known of these severe, narrow chutes is the aptly named Couloir Extreme. The entry requires a leap of faith and not a little skill.

EATING ON THE MOUNTAIN

WHISTLER
STEEPS GRILL
ROUNDHOUSE LODGE
DUSTY'S BAR & BBQ
THE CHIC PEA
RAVEN'S NEST MOUNTAIN DELI

BLACKCOMB
CHRISTINE'S
CRYSTAL HUT
RENDEZVOUS
GLACIER CREEK
HORSTMAN HUT
18° BELOW

accommodations, instruction, and fun activities. Each mountain has its own (Nintendo Gamecube) terrain park and halfpipe facilities. Whistler is entry level and up, while Blackcomb is for experts, and guests need a Highest Level I.D. to access its park. The World Cup Halfpipe is located at the bottom of the Blackcomb terrain park and is considered one of the best in North America. It is cut every night with a 17-foot (5-m) radius and 15-foot (4.5-m) walls, and has a permanent groundshape with a 17-degree pitch. Snowmaking keeps it in shape all day.

EATING ON THE MOUNTAIN

Whistler and Blackcomb have between them a dozen on-mountain restaurants serving breakfast as well as lunch, and the standard and choice of food is generally very good.

Step off the Whistler Village gondola into Roundhouse Lodge's market-style eateries with West Coast specialties plus enchiladas and fajitas, salads, soups, main-course sandwiches, and full-service dining at Steeps Grill. The Chic Pea—a cabin-style hut and patio on Whistler is popular, while Raven's Nest Mountain Deli has a fabulous valley-view deck and a menu featuring sandwiches, soup, chili and an outdoor grill.

Blackcomb's original mountain restaurant is Rendezvous, offering Mexican food, salads, BBQ, and full-service dining at Christine's. Also on Blackcomb Mountain is Glacier Creek, a spectacular lodge with two restaurants, and Crystal Hut—a cozy log cabin with hearty home-style food, while Horstman Hut serving café cuisine is perched high up on Blackcomb at 7,494 feet (2,285 m.)

The main mountain restaurants are big and busy. They offer an excellent choice of food but do not expect the same eating experience as a long lunch with wine in a quality Swiss or Austrian mountain restaurant. Eating on the mountain is pleasant enough, cheaper than Europe and excellent value for money, but the self-service arrangement in many restaurants means people linger less over lunch and consequently spend more time on the slopes.

APRÈS SKI

Nestled into the base of Whistler Creekside, and Whistler's original après ski bar, Dusty's was established in 1965 and is home to Whistler's sunniest patio. Rebuilt in 2000 and a favorite among locals, Dusty's looks like a classic Western ski lodge with wood-beamed ceilings and a cozy fireside, but it has a distinctly contemporary atmosphere with the excellent sound and video system turned on.

Garibaldi Lift Co.—G.L.C. for short—overlooks the base of Whistler mountain and is a popular haunt for those ending the ski day in Whistler. A sophisticated synthesis of lounge, restaurant, bar, and club, the G.L.C. has a signature tapas and martini menu, plays the latest ski and snowboard videos, and reggae and ambient house music most evenings.

Merlin's Bar & Grill in the Upper Village, with the resort's largest outdoor patio and plenty of live entertainment, is the favorite among mountain employees and local stars, and the place to party after a day on Blackcomb.

All of the above have outdoor patios, play live music, and serve both classic and creative après-ski food and beverages. Naturally, they all boast a lively fun atmosphere, but for those wanting a quieter end to the ski day there are plenty of tamer bars to choose from and plenty of late night shopping.

Visitors to British Columbia, those from outside North America especially, will need to get acquainted with the local liquor laws. In Whistler-Blackcomb you have to be 19 to consume alcohol, and young children cannot accompany their parents in most bars. This one of the few downsides to a family skiing holiday in Whistler-Blackcomb, but the nature of the restrictions vary according to the exact nature of the establishment's license.

Whistler's reputation as an international resort is

▼ **TEST OF THE BEST...**
Whistler has tested the best of the world's skiers, and today attracts high-caliber, adrenaline-seeking skiers and riders who are lured by the vast skiing terrain potential.

◄ WINTER WONDERLAND
When the shops have long closed, the bars, bistros, clubs and restaurants are still going strong. Romance is in the air—locals and Japanese tourists alike marry here.

reflected in the variety of cuisine on offer at over 90 restaurants catering to all tastes and budgets. There are well-stocked supermarkets for the self-caterers, but the eating out is superb with a choice of sushi, Chinese, Italian, Greek, French, and North American restaurants, plus plenty of cafés and coffee shops.

For late night revelers there is plenty of action with a number of fashionable bars, discos, and nightclubs playing a variety of good music, such as Garfinkel's, Maxx Fish, Moe Joe's, Savage Beagle, and Tommy Africa's.

OTHER ACTIVITIES

Whistler–Blackcomb is a year-round resort. Intrawest Corporation (the resort owners), the staff and residents are dedicated to pleasing visitors and there is a lot on offer. Besides skiing and boarding, other snow-related activities include snowshoeing, an alternative and peaceful way to explore some of those hard-to-access backcountry areas, snowmobiling through dense forests up into the alpine bowls, or for a really traditional North American alternative, try dogsledding. If you are interested in climbing—whether you are completely new to the sport or an experienced climber—there is an indoor climbing wall available, and ice climbing tours are also possible.

Elsewhere in the neighborhood you can enjoy the pool or kids' pool, hot tub, sauna, steamroom, indoor ice skating, ice hockey, squash courts, and fitness center at the Meadows Park Sports Center. For something a little more cerebral, the Whistler Museum and Archive Society offers exhibits, information on the region, natural history and skiing. The museum also has research facilities and a gift store: www.whistlermuseum.org

Whistler-Blackcomb is the largest resort-based retailer in North America and shopping facilities are very good. With over 200 shops there is plenty to interest non-skiers, and for skiers and riders keen on adding to their equipment there are 28 sports stores in Whistler resort.

USEFUL PHONE NUMBERS

Whistler Activity & Information Center	604-932-2394
Whistler Alpine Guides Bureau	604-938-3228
Whistler Blackcomb Snow Report	604-932-4211
Whistler General Enquiries	604-932-3434
Whistler Heli-Skiing	604-932-4105
Whistler Medical Clinic	604-932-3977
Whistler Perimeter Express Buses	604-266-5386
Whistler Reservation Center	604-664-5625

USEFUL WEBSITES

Official Whistler Website	www.mywhistler.com
Vacation Planner	www.whistlerblackcomb.com
Whistler Alpine Guides	www.whistlerguides.com
Whistler Heli-Skiing	www.whistlerheliskiing.com
Interactive Resort Map	www.findwhistler.com
Airport Bus Service	www.perimeterbus.com

RESTAURANTS

EXPENSIVE
ARAXI
BEARFOOT BISTRO
CAMINETTO DI UMBERTO
RIMROCK
TEPPAN VILLAGE

MODERATE
LA BOCCA
MILESTONE'S
PORTOBELLO
SUSHI VILLAGE
TRATTORIA DI UMBERTO

BUDGET
LA BRASSERIE DES ARTISTE
CASA TAPAS AND WINE BAR
CRAB SHACK
OLD SPAGHETTI FACTORY
WHISTLER NOODLE HOUSE

BARS & CLUBS

BARS
AMSTERDAM CAFE
BBK'S
BLACK'S PUB
BRANDY'S AT THE KEG
BUFFALO BILL'S BAR & GRILL
CINNAMON BEAR BAR
CRYSTAL LOUNGE
DUBH LINN GATE IRISH PUB
DUSTY'S
FIREROCK LOUNGE
HAVANA LOUNGE
GARIBALDI LIFT CO
LONGHORN SALOON
MALLARD LOUNGE
MERLIN'S BAR & GRILL
TAPLEY'S

NIGHTCLUBS
GARFINKEL'S
MAXX FISH
MOE JOE'S
SAVAGE BEAGLE
TOMMY AFRICA'S

REPRESENTING EXCELLENT VALUE FOR MONEY, FERNIE ENJOYS SOME OF THE BEST POWDER IN THE ROCKIES. AN AMAZING 348 INCHES (884 CM) OF NATURAL SNOW BLANKETS THE FIVE ALPINE BOWLS NESTLED IN THE MAJESTIC LIMESTONE CLIFFS OF THE LIZARD RANGE. THERE ARE EXTENSIVE BACKCOUNTRY POSSIBILITIES AND MUCH OF THE MOUNTAIN IS GIVEN OVER TO ADVANCED SKIER BOWLS AND DOUBLE BLACK DIAMONDS.

FERNIE

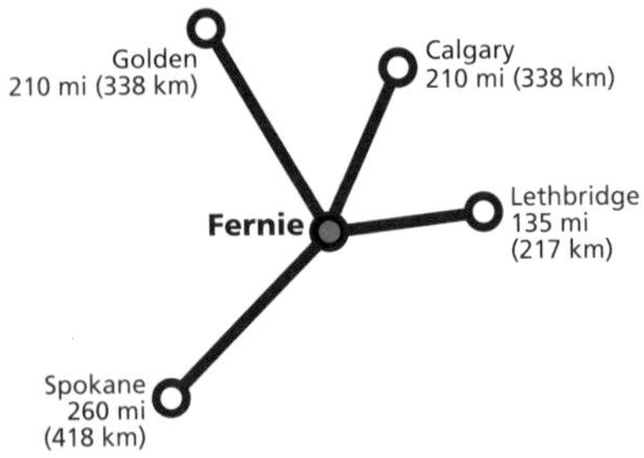

SKI SEASON
Early December to late April
Peak season Christmas and Easter

Fernie is the fastest-growing resort in Canada, and was awarded the Most Improved Resort of the Year 2003. The snow conditions and friendly Canadian welcome ensure that the resort is likely to win more awards in the future. Over 100 uncrowded trails and extensive piste grooming are two of the reasons Fernie has become so popular in recent years—get here soon if you want to experience it before commercial success takes over.

Day road trips or overnight trips to other ski areas include Kimberley (85 minutes), Schweitzer (3 hours), Panorama (2 hours), Banff (4 hours), Big Mountain (2 hours), and Red Mountain (4 hours). There's a shuttle service from Fernie to Kimberley every Thursday, and the Canadian Rockies Connector Service operates on Saturdays between Fernie, Kimberley, Panorama and Banff/Lake Louise Resorts.

GETTING THERE

Fernie is located in the Lizard Range of the British Columbia Rockies in Canada, on Highway 3 about 40 miles (60 km) from the Alberta—U.S. border. The two nearest international airports are Calgary International Airport, 3.5 hours' drive away, a distance that has until now kept foreign visitors at bay, and Glacier International Airport in Kalispell, Montana, a two-hour drive. The road to Fernie leads through some of the most spectacular mountain scenery in the world. The drive is easy with no major mountain passes and the roads are well maintained. There are no nearby rail connections, but Fernie is serviced twice daily by Greyhound Bus Lines (800-661-8747 or 250-423-6871, www.greyhound.com).

There are several airport transfer companies, offering shuttles, taxis, and even a helicopter, but transfers must be prearranged. The Rocky Mountain Sky Shuttle offers two return trips daily between Calgary Airport and Fernie, or try the ultimate in airport and inter-resort transport, Bighorn Heli-Taxi Ski Resort Service. Kootenay Taxi offers a taxi and van service from Calgary Airport to Fernie. CSI Tours run a taxi service from Glacier National Airport. Rocky Mountains Transportation Inc. have car rental, van and bus services to and from Glacier National Airport. Contact Guest Services at Fernie for more information.

◄ **THE VILLAGE**
The alpine resort rises up behind the village, which is quiet and residential.

MOUNTAIN FACTS

Base	3,500 feet (1,067 m)
Summit	6,316 feet (1,9254 m)
Elevation	2,816 feet (858 m)
Easy	30%
Intermediate	40%
Advanced/Expert	30%
Number of trails	107
Number of terrain parks	1
Number of bowls	5
Longest trail	3 miles (4.8 km)
Ski area	2,504 acres (1,013 ha)

SNOWFALL

Annual snowfall	348 inches (884 cm)
Snowmaking	1%

SKI LIFTS

High-Speed Quads	2
Express Quads	2
Triple Chairs	2
Handle Tows	3
Surface Lifts	1
Total	10
Riders per hour	13,716

ACCOMMODATIONS

LIZARD CREEK LODGE
SNOW CREEK LODGE
TIMBERLINE LODGE
BEAR PAW LODGE
POLAR PEAK LODGE
FERNIE LODGING COMPANY
WOLF'S DEN MOUNTAIN LODGE
GRIZ INN
THUNDER RIDGE CHALETS
CORNERSTONE LODGE
STONE CREEK

THE VILLAGE

The mining community that emerged in 1897 was named after prospector William Fernie, whose discovery of coal here led to a mining boom and the establishment of the industrial town at Fernie.

Although it is identifiably Victorian, the town is not yet what you would call charming or pretty, but it is improving and as each year passes, more of the old buildings are renovated and new restaurants, bars, and stores are opened. But if you are coming here for the skiing—and there are good reasons why you should—then you'd be better off staying at Fernie Alpine Resort, a quiet, mainly residential village located at the base of the mountain.

The village has ski in, ski out accommodations, eight restaurants, one après ski bar, shopping, and daycare. The resort is three miles (4.8 km) from the town of Fernie, which has accommodations, bars, restaurants, shopping, and services. New hotels at the base village and in the town have increased the number of rooms available in recent years and more development is planned. A shuttle run by Kootenay Taxi is available from the town to the resort 14 times daily, and on an on-call basis in the evenings. A taxi service between the two is also available.

ACCOMMODATIONS

Many new, tastefully appointed hotels and lodges with year-round services are now available at the resort base village, with more improvements and accommodations development to come over the next few years. At present there are around a dozen or so hotels in the resort including the award-winning Lizard Creek Lodge which is a ski-in, ski-out luxury condominium/hotel featuring fine dining, spa, pool and all amenities. The Fernie Lodging Company owns Snow Creek Lodge and Chalets, Timberline Lodges, Bear Paw Lodges, and Polar Peak Lodges and has a central reservations line. Snow Creek Lodge and Chalets is one of the best sites on the mountain, offering luxury condominiums with underground parking. Timberline Lodges are tastefully decorated one- and two-bedroom condos

► TIME OUT
The base area at Fernie Alpine Resort is a great place to congregate and meet up with family and friends. The area is mainly residential but it has access to the lift system, as well as places to chill out.

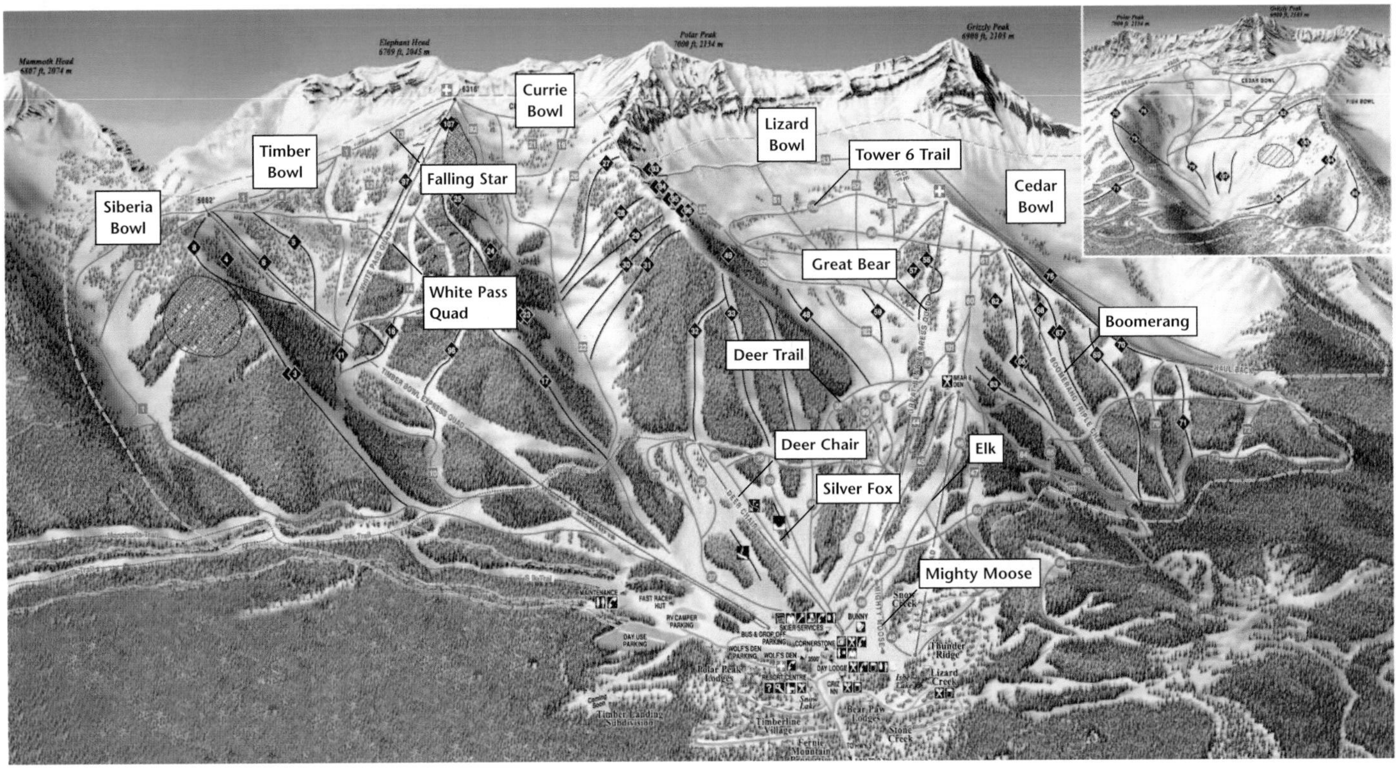

DAYCARE
Resort Kids' Daycare is a safe, licensed facility for children newborn to six years. The center is open daily from 8:30 AM to 4:30 PM throughout the season, and children will be given supervised activities, quiet time, and outdoor play. Reservations are required for infants, with all other spaces available on a first come, first served basis. You can also arrange ski lessons for three- to four-year-olds. Lunch is available by request. Snacks are provided free of charge.

with great views, balconies, equipment lockers, fully equipped kitchens, and a free shuttle service to the lifts. Also at the base resort, Wolf's Den Mountain Lodge has 42 rooms, ski-in, ski-out convenience, two indoor hot tubs, and a games room. You can ski to your door if you stay at the Griz Inn at the bottom of the Elk quad chairlift as well as enjoy fabulous views from the Powder Horn restaurant or from the panoramic deck. There are also hot tubs, a sauna, and an indoor pool. Thunder Ridge Chalets are ski-in, ski-out luxury townhouse suites and studios located on Highline Drive, while Cornerstone Lodge, a new addition to the village, has luxury one- and two-bedroom condominium/hotel units.

In Fernie there is a wide selection of hotels, motels, hostels, and bed & breakfast places, as well as chalets (fully catered or self catered, on and off the mountain), and houses to rent.

▶ **TELEMARK TRAIL**
Fernie's famous backcountry bowls, such as Cedar Bowl, are all great for telemarking after a big snowfall.

SKI AREA

Fernie is 2,504 acres (1,013 ha) of skiable terrain with 10 lifts accessing 107 trails and five alpine bowls. It has an extensive beginner area at the base of the mountain and increasingly more difficult terrain on the upper mountain. The vertical drop of 2,816 feet (858 m) means that it is a great place for snowboarders of all levels, and learning to board here is comparatively easy as there isn't too much traversing to be done. The majority of the trails are for intermediate to advanced skiers, with higher altitude powder skiing for experts, for which it is famous.

SKI LIFTS

Ten lifts serve the mountain, including two high-speed quads, two express quads, two triple chairs, three handle tows, and one surface lift. Lifts operate from 9:00 AM to 4:00 PM. Waiting lines (as at most resorts in Canada) are generally non-existent, except during peak periods, and lines for purchasing lift

◄ ELK VALLEY
The valley spreads out at the base of the mountain, offering accommodation and lots of places to eat out.

EQUIPMENT RENTAL
The Mountain Edge Rental shop at the base of the resort underwent a major renovation, increasing rental fleet and service efficiency. Excellent range of equipment to choose from including high-performance demos.

MOUNTAIN TOURS
Need to get your bearings? Meet at the base area for a complimentary Mountain Host Tour departing at 9:30 AM and 1:00 PM daily.

passes can be avoided by buying them the evening before from Guest Services (open 8:00 AM–7:30 PM) or the ticket office. More investment is needed to create lift access to some of the best steep terrain, and to enable the lift system to operate efficiently during and after periods of heavy snowfall, but in spite of the obvious limitations of the lift system there is some great skiing to be had.

LIFT PASSES

A full-day pass costs Cdn$56 for adults, Cdn$45 for teenagers (13-17), students (18-24) and seniors (65+), and Cdn$14 for children (6–12). Half-day passes (from 12:00 PM) are available at reduced rates, and a beginner lift pass is available—providing access on the lower mountain only, via Mighty Moose Lift—and costs Cdn$14 for everyone. A six-day pass costs Cdn$318 for adults, Cdn$258 for youths, students and seniors, and Cdn$84 for children. Rates do not include G.S.T. (7%).

SKI SCHOOLS AND GUIDING

The Fernie Alpine Resort Winter Sports School is located at the base of the resort. The offices are open from 9:00 AM to 4:00 PM. For all ages and abilities there are lessons from certified instructors offering professional instruction in alpine skiing, boarding, telemarking ,and cross-country, from group lessons to specialty clinics and one-hour to full-day private lessons. The ski school also offers special adult programs, men's clinics, women's clinics, kids' weekend clubs, and camps in both skiing and snowboarding.

Group lessons are limited to 10 people and children must be five years old and above for the ski school groups (supervised lunch included). The Resort Kids' Daycare operates lessons for three- and four-year-olds.

Mountain Pursuits is a fully certified company that offers backcountry tours, for which Fernie is recommended. Professionally guided day trips or overnight camps discover the best-kept secret powder stashes in the region. Tours start at Cdn$125 per person (minimum two people) and group rates cost around Cdn$65 per person (minimum six people). The First Tracks Program lets you access fantastic powder before anyone else. It costs Cdn$60 per person (minimum two people, lift pass not included). For more information and reservations contact Guest Services.

BEGINNERS

Green trails cover 30 percent of the mountain, and are mainly clustered around the resort base off the Mighty Moose Platter and Deer Chair, although there are two below Lizard Bowl and three in Cedar Bowl. Start with the Mini Moose and Mighty Moose lifts, taking the Elk trail to get your legs warmed up. Then take Deer Chair for a choice of green trails either side: Deer and Meadow one way and Silver Fox and Deer to the other, joining on to Bambi and Incline, both of which lead back to the base of the resort. These trails are all wide-open, daily groomed rolling

► MOUNTAIN PURSUITS
Mountain Pursuits is a tour company running backcountry thrills through deep powder.

◀ **POLAR PEAK**
At 7,000 feet (2,133 m), treat Polar Park with respect as you charge down trails with names like Concussion and Surprize.

slopes perfect for all ages of beginner skiers/riders. Once you've mastered these, take the Great Bear express quad and ski from top to base along Lizard Traverse or Tower 6 Trail, both long green trails that join up with the lower green trails back to base.

INTERMEDIATES

Intermediates have 40 percent of the mountain to zoom down. Falling Star, the longest trail at three miles (5 km) is a blue intermediate running from the summit of White Pass quad back to the base of the resort. The blue trails off the Elk chairlift are some of the best warm-up trails; then try the Boomerang triple chair for the easiest access to the fabulous Cedar Bowl terrain. Most of the trails in Lizard and Cedar Bowls are blue. The high-speed Timber Bowl express quad and White Pass quad take you to Falling Star and six other long blue trails.

ADVANCED AND EXPERT

Fernie is particularly famous for its deep powder and backcountry options, so advanced and expert skiers will be spoiled for choice. Twelve double black diamond trails, mostly between Currie and Lizard Bowl, and in Cedar Bowl, are just part of the 30 percent of the mountain designated for advanced and expert skiers. Most of the most difficult trails are on the upper mountain, with the best moguls, steep and deep, and couloirs in Bootleg Glades. After a snowfall all five bowls—Cedar, Currie, Lizard, Timber, and Siberia—are great for powder skiing. Backcountry skiing is permitted, but at your own risk.

The nearest heliskiing is RK Heli-Ski (two hours away), but closer to Fernie there are a number of cat-skiing operators offering all-inclusive packages (with accommodations) to confident intermediates and advanced skiers wanting to ski deep powder in the backcountry. The best known is Island Lake Lodge nearly six miles (9 km) away in the mountains and reached by a 45-minute snowcat ride from the Snowcat pickup point off Highway 3, 1.5 miles (2 km) west of Fernie. The lodge is at an elevation of 4,600 feet (1,402 m) and the skiing starts from as high as 7,000 feet (2,133 m) with breathtaking bowls, exciting tree runs, and gentle rolling slopes with a variety of aspects and pitches. A day from 9:00 AM–4:00 PM normally consists of 8–12 runs and around 12,000 to 15,000 vertical feet, depending on the level of each group. There is a minimum age requirement of 19 years, and you are required to sign a waiver of claims agreement. Each of the three snowcats operates with groups of 12 guests and two guides. Island Lake Lodge operates from mid-December to first week of April. Rates at Island Lake

▼ **DEEP POWDER**
Island Lake Lodge, a cat-skiing operation, runs some great backcountry packages. You can access deep powder, breathtaking bowls, and exciting tree runs in just 45-minutes.

EATING ON THE MOUNTAIN

BEAR'S DEN

RESTAURANTS

MOUNTAIN BASE
DAYLODGE
DAYLODGE CAFETERIA
GRIZZLY BAR

RESORT CENTER
GABRIELLA'S LITTLE ITALY PASTA PLACE
GRIZ INN
POWDERHORN RESTAURANT
CORNERSTONE LODGE
KELSEY'S RESTAURANT
THE MEAN BEAN
LIZARD CREEK LODGE
SNOW CREEK LODGE

DOWNTOWN FERNIE
THE WOOD RESTAURANT
THE CURRY BOWL

BARS

GRIZZLY BAR IN DAYLODGE
EL DORADO IN FERNIE

Lodge for three- or four-day tours are from Cdn$695 to Cdn$850 per day depending on which of the three lodges you choose (Bear, Red Eagle, or Cedar). Island Lake has acquired its former rival—Powder Cowboy—thereby allowing an additional 12 guests. It is open from December 27 to March 31. Rates for three- or four-day tours are available from Cdn$575 per day. Avalanche transceivers are provided and a range of powder skis and snowboards is available. Island Lake Lodge has very limited space each season so book early to avoid disappointment. Contact Island Lake on 888-422-8754 or visit the www.islandlakelodge.com website for more information.

BOARDING & FREESTYLE

Fernie has one terrain park, off the Deer Chair, and a halfpipe off Bambi trail. Both are on the lower mountain and open only when snow conditions permit. But boarders can also get their kicks from the natural gullies and hits that are to be found all across the mountain. It's a good place for boarding, although for advanced snowboarders some of the terrain requires long traverses.

EATING ON THE MOUNTAIN

Nine resort eateries will keep you energized. Everything from sit-down dining to grab-and-go is available. There's only one mid-mountain place, though, Bear's Den at the top of Elk quad, for snacks and drinks. Otherwise you have to go to the base of the mountain. The Daylodge has a cafeteria open daily for burgers, sandwiches, and drinks, and the Grizzly Bar is upstairs. In the Resort Center is Gabriella's Little Italy Pasta Place. The Griz Inn houses the Powderhorn Restaurant and Lounge, a family spot for buffets and grills. At the Cornerstone Lodge are Kelsey's Restaurant, for a great atmosphere and good food at lunch or après ski, and The Mean Bean, serving coffee and snacks. Lizard Creek Lodge has its own restaurant with a gourmet menu and great views, and the Snow Creek Lodge has a café for breakfast and snacks, and lunchtime refuels.

APRÈS SKI

At the resort there's only one après ski bar, the Grizzly Bar in the Daylodge, with live music at weekends. The minimum age for consuming alcohol is 19 and children cannot accompany parents in bars and other places serving alcohol.

You can also choose from over 20 restaurants and numerous bars in downtown Fernie, five minutes' drive away. Several new restaurants have opened, including The Curry Bowl and the award-winning The Wood Restaurant, which was awarded the 2003 Resort Restaurant of the Year.

Bars tend to close at around 2:00 AM. El Dorado, the only dance bar in the town, is located below The Wood Restaurant.

OTHER ACTIVITIES

The Mountain Adventure Center offers a variety of day or evening activities to supplement skiing and riding. You can take moonlight snowmobile tours, go dogsledding, take a sleigh ride with a cowboy dinner option, go cross-country skiing or snow-shoeing, and/or ski by torchlight. In Fernie there's an ice-skating rink, a curling rink, an aquatic center, a fitness center, and a bowling alley.

USEFUL PHONE NUMBERS

Tourist Information	250-423-4655
Guest Services	250-423-2435
Accommodations Reservations	403-209-3321
Rocky Mountain Sky Shuttle	403-762-5200
Kootenay Taxi	250-423-4408
CSI Tours	406-756-0333
Rocky Mountains Transportation	406-863-1200
Fernie Resort Winter Sports School	250-423-4655
Island Lake Cat-Skiing	888-422-8754

USEFUL WEBSITES & E-MAIL ADDRESSES

Official Website	www.skifernie.com
Official E-mail	info@skifernie.com
Transportation Information	www.greyhound.com
Rocky Mountain Sky Shuttle	www.rockymountainskyshuttle.com
Kootenay Taxi	www.elkvalley.net/koottaxi.com
CSI Tours	www.csitours.com
Rocky Mountains Transportation	www.rockymountaintrans.com
Fernie Resort Winter Sports School	www.skifernie.com
Island Lake Cat-Skiing	www.islandlakelodge.com

▲ **DELUXE VIEWS**
The Cedar Lodge, the newest edition to Island Lake Lodge, offers deluxe accommodation plus some stunning views.

▼ **HIGH TRAILS**
Tua Time trail is just one of many trails accessible by snowcat. The skiing starts at 7,000 feet (2,133 m) and you can be sure of some excitement.

MIKE WIEGELE HELICOPTER SKIING AT BLUE RIVER, B.C., OFFERS THE PERFECT COMBINATION OF WEATHER AND TERRAIN. HERE THE BEST POWDER FOR SKIING IS GUARANTEED. RISE OVER THOUSANDS OF ACRES (400HA) OF PINE FORESTS AND TREMENDOUS GLACIAL EXPANSES, THEN LAND AMID THE SNOW-SPIRED RIDGELINES OF THE CARIBOO AND MONASHEE MOUNTAIN RANGES. AND ALL OF IT ACCESSED ONLY BY HELICOPTER.

MIKE WIEGELE
HELICOPTER SKIING

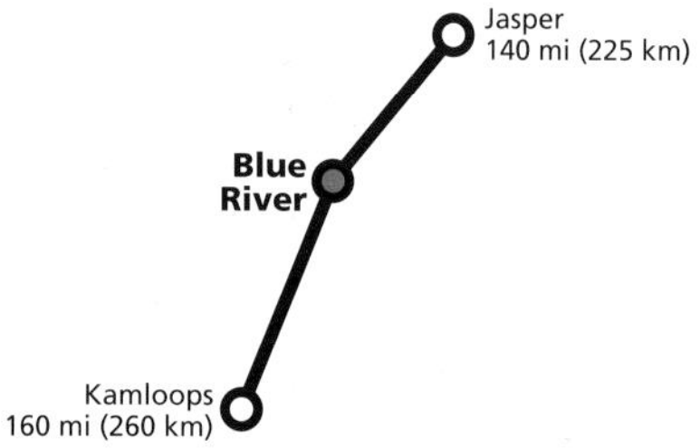

SNOWFALL

Annual snowfall 360 inches (914 cm)

SKI SEASON

Year-round skiing.

Winter skiing from late November until mid-May. The months of April and May are a special time. Favored by Mike Wiegele for a generally more stable snow-pack, also the glacier crevasses are covered, allowing groups to set forth deeper and deeper into the mountains for steeper runs. Summer skiing on the glaciers starts June and ends October.

Founded in 1970 and located in a beautiful part of British Columbia, Canada, in the heart of the magnificent Monashee and Cariboo mountain ranges, "Wiegele's World" covers 3,000 square miles (8,300 sq km) and over 1,000 peaks in one of the most reliable snow belts in the world for high-quality, reliable powder snow. Consistent accumulations of 30 feet (914 cm) or more are normal.

GETTING THERE

Blue River is three hours' drive north of Kamloops, B.C., via Highway 5, making it easily accessible by car or bus. The nearest international airports to the resort are Vancouver and Calgary with daily flights to Kamloops. Vancouver to Kamloops is 232 miles (373 km) and Kamloops to Blue River is 160 miles (260 km). Calgary to Blue River is 394 miles (634 km).

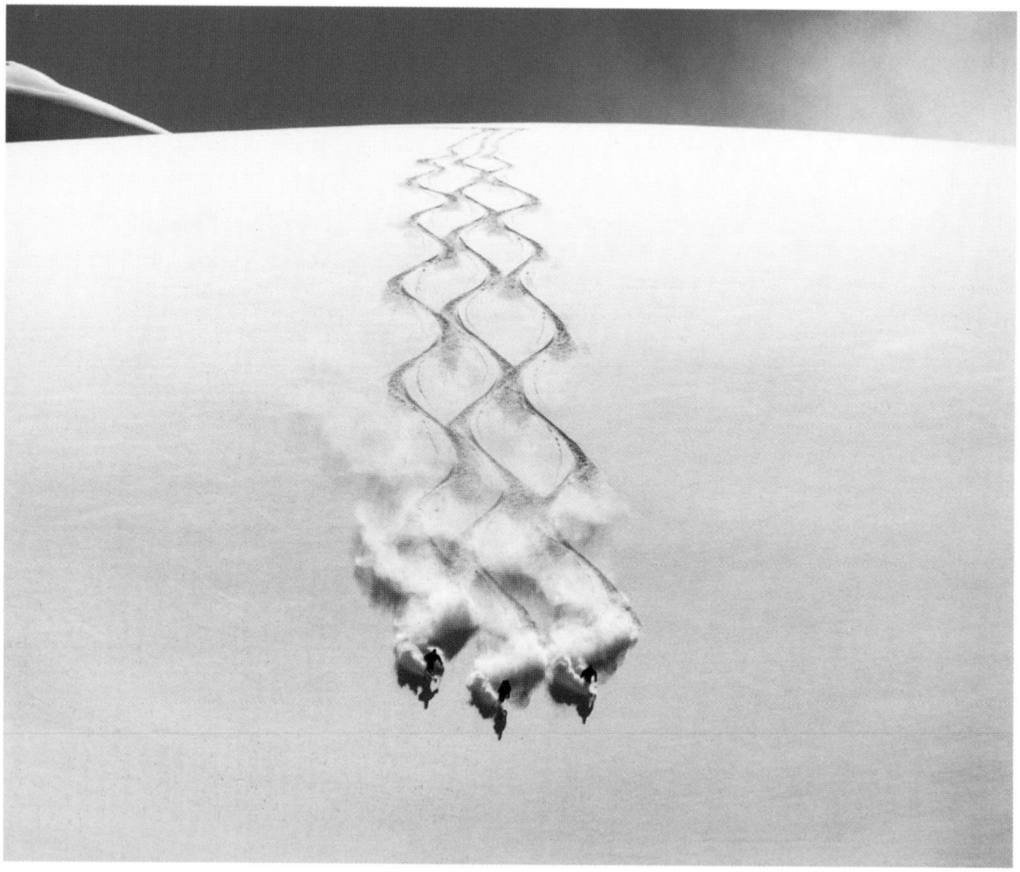

► MAN ON A MISSION
Mike Wiegele has long been encouraging clients to use "fat boy" skis which have a wider girth than conventional skis and enable the skier to stay close to the snow surface in deep powder.

Edmonton to Blue River is 366 miles (590 km). You can even fly in with your own private aircraft on the 5,600 feet (1,706 m) long and 80 feet (24 m) wide private airstrip (weather permitting).

THE VILLAGE

The resort features 24 guest chalets, Lodge, Administration Building/Guest Lobby, Sports Store, Laundry, and Guides Haus. Local services include two grocery stores, two service stations, post office, Red Cross Outpost, ambulance service, library, and motels. There is also an elementary school should you decide to relocate and live here permanently with your family!

ACCOMMODATIONS

The accommodations range from standard rooms and private chalets to luxury chalets. All rooms are located in individual chalets ranging in size from two to six bedrooms, each with private bath and telephone. All chalets have a living room with large stone fireplace and a fully equipped kitchen. At the top end you also find satellite T.V., video, sundeck, jacuzzi tub, and steam shower.

The ultimate in luxury is The Bavarian House Estate. Across Lake Eleanor and ten minutes' walk from the main lodge, this property boasts the 9,000 sq feet (836 sq m) five-bedroom Bavarian House and the 6,000 sq feet (557 sq m) three-bedroom Cabana.

▲ REMOTE ACCESS
Helicopters drop skiers off at elevations from 11,600 feet (3,536 m) down to 3,400 feet (1,036 m)—well within the comfort zone for day long skiing.

SKI AREA

It is the largest single helicopter skiing area in the world and heliskiing and boarding packages are available in three, five and seven-day deluxe and private options. For such a huge ski area you also get

MOUNTAIN FACTS

Base	2,400 feet (731 m)
Highest Peak	11,600 feet (3,536 m)
Longest vertical	6,000 feet (1,829 m)
Number of named runs	258
Ski area	3,000 sq miles (7,770 sq km)

▼ REMOTE ACCESS
Meanwhile back at base, luxurious facilities such as Guides Haus await.

HELICOPTER TRANSPORTATION

Bell 212 twin engine	5
A-Star	5
Total	10

a huge map—40 x 28 inches (100 x 71 cm)—to chart your progress. The ski area, measuring around 80 miles (128 km) from north to south and some 40 miles (64 km) from east to west, is divided into 24 named territories (15 Monashee and nine Cariboo) and there are 258 named trails. Your ski map includes a Run Log so you can record the date, trail name, and number of vertical feet skied each day.

THE ULTIMATE LIFT SYSTEM

The only way to the top is by helicopter. Mike Wiegele's has five Bell 212 twin engine helicopters and five of the smaller but powerful A-Stars. Each Bell 212 helicopter can accommodate three groups of 10 skiers plus leading and trailing guides, and the A-Star option carries one guide and four skiers per group and can have up to four groups. The pilots have extensive mountain flying experience and undertake special mountain training as well as Wiegele's own comprehensive training program. To ensure an improved and reliable service, Mike Wiegele's Helicopter Skiing has invested in a heated hangar in which all helicopters are thoroughly and regularly serviced.

SPRING STEEP CAMP
Improve your ability to ski steep slopes and chutes with top guides and video analysis. This camp is for expert skiers who want to go beyond, with a focus on steep skiing technique and crevasse rescue practice. A helmet is required for all sessions.

▶ SKY LIFTS
Mike Wiegele's squad of Bell 212 helicopters are heated inside, and hold up to 10 skiers, 2 guides and the pilot. The helicopters are specially configured for the requirements of helicopter skiing.

◀ **VIRGIN TRACKS**
In the Bugaboo and Cariboo ranges of British Columbia, average accumulations of 30 feet (9 m) of powder snow are typical—and this from November onward. Every named run is through untracked, virgin snow.

GUIDING AND SAFETY

Guides are carefully chosen for their ability to find the best conditions, and their understanding of the clients needs. The professionally trained guides, certified by the Canadian Ski Guides Association (C.S.G.A.) or equivalent organization, are also certified ski instructors and chosen for their ability to provide guests with an exciting and memorable vacation while caring for their safety and comfort at all times. Most senior guides have been involved at Mike Wiegele's for more than ten years.

Going beyond the industry standard ratio of 11:1, guests to guide, the Deluxe Tour has groups of ten skiers with two professional guides, bringing the ratio down to 5:1, and the Private Tours operate on a 4:1 ratio. Mike Wiegele Helicopter Skiing is one of the few operators with a dedicated infrastructure including three weather stations, three radio repeater stations, advance guides training, and an avalanche research program.

Every ski week involves instruction. Whether you are a first-time heliskier or an expert the guides will assist you in attaining a higher level of skiing, and if you are a first timer or an intermediate you can expect to be offered tips and techniques to help you ski with greater confidence and enjoyment.

Skiers must be, at minimum, strong intermediates capable of dealing with the challenges presented by deep snow, helicopter transportation, and backcountry skiing. If you are unable to satisfy these criteria you would be restricted from skiing and no refund would be given. Guests are required to sign a liability waiver that recognizes the dangers of backcountry helicopter skiing and gives up the right to sue in the event of an accident.

Guides meet each morning and night to analyze snow conditions based on snow pit data and information received from remote weather stations. Guides and pilots do their best to get you out on the mountains but safety is paramount so you must respect their decision should they choose not to fly. When snow stability is good it is possible to select steeper slopes, but if the rating is poor to fair the guides will recommend more moderate slopes that are less prone to avalanche.

THE SKIING

The number of drops is determined by weather conditions and the ability of the skiers, but you can expect to average 8–10 trails per day and as many as 15 trails per day is possible. The skiing is done at

PRIVATE TOURS
A-STAR from Cdn$54,362 to Cdn$64,512 for four people. 10 hours flying time (6 hours skiing guaranteed). Extra hours Cdn$2,360 per hour.
Bell 212 Private from Cdn$114,345 to Cdn$125,610 for 10 people. 8 hours flying time (6 hours guaranteed). Extra hours Cdn$3,795 per hour.

WORLD CHAMPIONSHIPS
2003 marks the 23rd season for the ultimate test in powder skiing, the POWDER 8 WORLD CHAMPIONSHIPS. The competition is the culmination of a series of events held around the world. Powder 8 skiing is a team competition where pairs of skiers, one skiing behind the other, match their turns to leave a long, sinuous figure-eight track in the deep powder snow. The competition is open to anyone with a partner, plus the skill and the stamina to beat the best in the world. For information contact Carla Knollenburg 800-661-9170 or carla@wiegele.com

▶ **HELI-GOOD BYE**
Once the beat of the twin-engine machine has vanished you are left in the deafening silence of unexplored and untracked mountains and glaciers.

◄ **KEEPING FIT**
It has been reckoned heli-skiers will cover the equivalent of 8 to 10 per day, carving verticals of about 20,000 feet (6,096 m) per day.

elevations between 3,400–11,600 feet (1,036–3,535 m) and the average landing is at around 8,000 feet (2,438 m). Wide Atomic powder skis make skiing deep snow much easier and a broad range of skis is available for guests.

Guides make every effort to select skiing routes that suit your ability and comfort level. Weather conditions permitting, your group will start on open, moderate glacier trails or gentle runs through trees, and as the week progresses so will you, advancing to steeper slopes and faster skiing. After the third day of powder skiing it's common to feel slightly tired, but this feeling usually passes quite quickly as you rise to the challenge of the fourth day. After that your confidence is increasing and you'll find yourself on nonstop runs linking 50 to 100 consecutive turns.

For many, high alpine glaciers provide the most exciting skiing experience as you carve your way down a blanket of powder surrounded by snow-covered peaks. The higher the elevation, the longer the run and 300 to 600 consecutive turns is common here so you also need to be fit.

For many élite skiers the trees are the ultimate experience and because the loose powder is protected from the wind and sun the very highest quality of powder is found in the trees. You will ski trails like Steinbock, Mike's Warm Up, Lempriere, Lower Most Magnificent, Redmond, Screwball, Freefall, and Jimmy's Preserve, all in the Cariboos. In the Monashees you have trails like Saddle Mountain, Ptarmigan, Finn Creek, Rusty Nail, Salmon Lake, Erich Ridge, and Elk Run. These are legendary trails and unmatched anywhere.

Snowboarders, monoskiers and telemarkers are welcome but you should have a strong and confident technique and may need to traverse or climb uphill to reach some destinations. April is a great time for snowboarding. At this time of year, the deep slab stability is good and it should be possible to ride the higher peaks.

Professional photographers are on hand to record your progress and proofs are usually available for viewing and purchase each evening.

APRÈS SKI

After a massive day's powder skiing you can relax in the Health Center with its stretch and fitness room (50 Nautilus machines), massage, and Jacuzzi, then take an aperitif in the Silver Buckle Lounge

BARS & RESTAURANTS

SLIVER BUCKLE LOUNGE
POWDER MAX DINING ROOM

2003–04 SCHEDULE & RATES

DELUXE RATES
3 days from Cdn$3,361 to Cdn$3,915
5 days from Cdn$5,050 to Cdn$5,810
7 days from Cdn$6,545 to Cdn$8,463
Prices are subject to tax at 7% G.S.T.

50% of G.S.T. on ski packages is refundable to foreign guests.

15% single supplement, subject to availability.

All packages start Saturday and include all meals and bus transfers from and to Kamloops.

30,000 feet (9,144 m), 50,000 feet (15,240 m) and 80,000 feet (24,384 m) of heli-lift guaranteed for 3-day, 5-day and 7-day packages.

Non-skiing packages available at a cost of Cdn$300 per day, double occupancy including meals.

► **BLUE RIVER**
A collection of spruce and pine log chalets line the shores of Eleanor Lake, B.C., some 160 miles (260 km) north of Kamloops in pristine wilderness. This is base camp.

before enjoying a sumptuous dinner in the Powder Max Dining Room. Dinner is served at 7:00 PM each evening and the Silver Buckle Lounge is open until 11:30 PM—and if by that time you are not ready for bed, you've probably not been skiing hard enough!

OTHER ACTIVITIES

If you are not wanting to ski, or are looking for other activities then Blue River is really not the place for you. Cross-country skiing is available, but guests at Wiegele's come here in search of deep powder and once hooked they rarely have time or energy for very much else.

USEFUL PHONE NUMBERS

Reservations	250-673-8381
Guest Fax Number	250-673-2442
First Class Limo Transfer	250-314-7733
B.C. Highway Department	250-673-8229
Weather Station	250-673-8448
Red Cross Outpost	250-673-8311
Doctor Helmcken Memorial Hospital	250-674-2244
Royal Inland Hospital Kamloops	250-374-5111
Don Harvey Photos	250-673-8400

USEFUL WEBSITES & E-MAIL ADDRESSES

Official Website	www.wiegele.com
Reservations	reservations@wiegele.com
Photography	www.dcharvey.com
First Class Limo Transfer	firstclasslimo@telus.net

▲ GLACIER GLIDES
Endless glacier trails, as with Kermit Glacier of more than 5,000 vertical feet (1,525 m), await the heli-skier. Fantastic carves on massive fields of gentle powder are followed futher down by widely spaced tree trails.

▼ BAVARIA IN B.C.
Wiegele's base camp also features the Bavarian House Estate for more private gatherings. Other amenities include a boutique, a games room, and health club. This is guest pampering as far as you can take it.

HOTELS

EXECUTIVE INN
PLAZA HERITAGE HOTEL
COAST CANADIAN INN

You are recommended to arrive in Kamloops on Friday and stay over Friday night before taking the courtesy bus transfer to Blue River early Saturday morning.

WITH 830,000 ACRES (336,150 HA) OF UNTRACKED TERRAIN AND AN AVERAGE BASE OF 10–12 FEET (3-3.6 M) OF SNOW—FOR 75 PERCENT OF THE SEASON—TLH HELISKIING IN THE SOUTHERN CHILCOTIN MOUNTAINS, B.C., OPERATES "SEMI" PRIVATE DELUXE TOURS OF ONLY TWO GROUPS OF 11 SKIERS, ALLOWING YOU TO EXPLOIT THIS AWESOME TERRAIN TO THE MAX, WITH VIRTUALLY NO WAITING.

TLH HELISKIING

In 1991 Georges Rosset realized his dream of combining a passion for heliskiing and pleasure in doing business, by operating his first heliskiing season at Tyax Mountain Lake Resort on the shores of remote Tyaughton Lake, British Columbia. Blessed with heavy coastal snowfalls and terrain ranging from high Alpine glaciers to endless snowfields through forest glades, helicopters allow seasoned skiers and boarders to ride endlessly through perfect powder.

GETTING THERE

TLH Heliskiing is 215 miles (345 km) north of Vancouver and 127 miles (205 km) from Whistler-Blackcomb. A six-hour bus transfer from Vancouver via Whistler is included in the Deluxe package but more attractive options include direct heli-transfers from Vancouver and Whistler heliports, or, in very good weather, flying in and out by floatplane. Or take a limo to Whistler-Blackcomb where you can warm up, lose any jetlag and then travel onward by helicopter. TLH retains a concierge in Whistler to help with arrangements and accommodations.

Heli-transfers add Cdn$450 from Vancouver, and Cdn$215 from Whistler, each way, for a minimum of five guests. The floatplane charter costs Cdn$1,500 one-way from Vancouver, seating up to six people

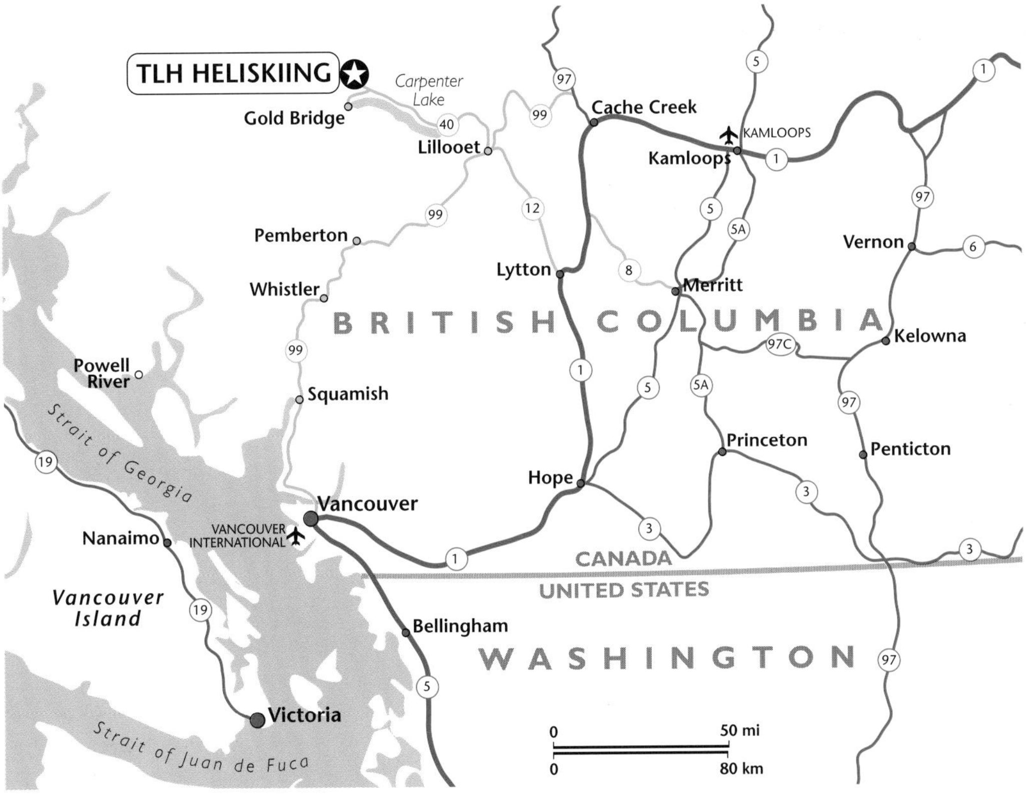

MOUNTAIN FACTS

Base	3,000 feet (914 m)
Summit	9,200 feet (2803 m)
Elevation	6,200 feet (1889 m)
Average run	2,300 feet (701 m)
Number of named runs	300
Ski area	830,000 acres (336,150 ha)

SNOWFALL

Annual snowfall	540 inches (1,372 cm)

SKI SEASON

Skiing runs from mid-December until late April—it's not possible to recommend any particular week, but mid-February to mid-March are typically the most popular. Late season is great for snowboarders, when the skiing tends to be higher and more on the glaciers, while in January you can expect a little more tree skiing.

with a 1,100 lb (498 kg) maximum weight limit for each passenger plus luggage.

TLH packages begin on arrival in Vancouver and end with your departure, and you are definitely recommended to arrive a day before you are due at the lodge in case of air delays. Individual helicopter transfers are extremely expensive, if not impossible, as a late-running guest may arrive when all the helicopters are occupied with the heliskiing. TLH can arrange all transfers and transfer hotels.

THE VILLAGE

Tyax Lodge, originally designed as a summer fishing resort, is the largest traditionally built log structure in Canada. Overlooking the head of Tyaughton Lake in the southern Chilcotins, the local area is stunningly beautiful and popular with wealthy Vancouverites in summer. With the nearest neighbor the gold mining ghost town of Bralorne, it's rich in prospecting history while offering little to do in winter when you aren't skiing.

◀ **OPEN SPACES**
TLH Heliskiing has access to over 830,000 acres (336,150 ha) of terrain. That's an area one hundred times bigger than Whistler or Vail.

▶ **THE SKY'S THE LIMIT**
The A-Star B2 helicopter services TLH's Private Tours with 4 skiers/snowboarders per group—the ultimate in luxury.

▲ **PLATINUM COMFORT**
Tyax Mountain Lake Resort, the base for TLH Heliskiiing, is located on the shores of Tyaughton Lake.

ACCOMMODATIONS

The impressive main lodge, Tyax Lodge, houses the restaurant, bar, lounge, sports center, mini gym, massage rooms, sauna, hot tub, meeting rooms, and ski store. It can accommodate up to 44 guests in 22 comfortable rooms—all with en-suite showers and two large beds. Single occupancy is possible, subject to availability and a nightly supplement. Package prices for a Deluxe seven-day tour include a 100,000 vertical feet (30,480 m) guarantee, and, as a clear indication of the quality of the usual conditions, high season (and high-end prices) runs from mid-January until early April.

Adjacent to the main lodge on the lakeshore are chalets for the private Platinum parties. These take skiing to epicurean levels with dedicated physiotherapists, massage therapists, and chefs, and offer unsurpassed privacy and discretion—to the extent that European royalty are frequent guests.

SKI AREA

With over 830,000 acres (336,150 ha) of terrain—an area one hundred times bigger than Whistler or Vail—and 300 "controlled" runs at their disposal, the guides have immense scope to deliver an unforgettable experience. The terrain varies from huge, glaciated descents to long runs through gladed woods, and it is usual to ski many different but exciting conditions every day.

A good day offers up to 12 runs and around 25,000 vertical feet (7,620 m) with it not uncommon to ski over 35,000 feet (10,668 m) on a long, spring day. The record for a Deluxe party is just over 39,000 vertical feet (11,887 m). Average days rack up between 20,000 to 25,000 feet (6,096–7,620 m)—but you should remember that notching up vertical isn't a competition, honest. That said, the average vertical skied on a Deluxe package is 130,000 feet (39,624 m) and you should bear in mind that extra vertical makes for extremely cost-effective heliskiing.

In good weather it's usual to ski the glaciers, keeping the lower and treelined runs for poorer weather days. Glacier skiing is immensely dramatic—huge runs sweeping down open bowls—and typically the runs are longer than those into the trees. For safety reasons, however, you will ski less extreme gradients.

In snowy or cloudy conditions skiing will normally be through the trees, bounding down through gladed areas with plenty of natural obstacles

ACCOMMODATIONS

VANCOUVER
PAN PACIFIC
RADISSON PRESIDENT HOTEL & SUITES

WHISTLER
PAN PACIFIC LODGE
THE COAST WHISTLER HOTEL
CRYSTAL LODGE
FAIRMONT CHATEAU WHISTLER

► **ICE POWDER**
The Ochre Zone at TLH offers some of the most spectacular glacier skiing/snowboarding anywhere in the world.

to avoid. Bark munching, as it's known, is made a lot easier by TLH managing the trees to open up areas where the forest density would otherwise make skiing tricky. You can often ski steeper slopes through the trees, as they tend to hold snowpack better. Perhaps surprisingly, many veteran heliskiers consider tree skiing to be the best you can get.

The area typically gets 50–60 feet (15–20 m) of snow in the winter, which gives an average base of 10–13 feet (3–4 m).

THE ULTIMATE LIFT SYSTEM

Forget chairlifts. It is an exceptional experience to have a hugely expensive aircraft waiting for you at the end of every run. For deluxe guests TLH operate a pair of specially adapted Bell 212s (maybe familiar as the direct descendant of the Vietnam "Huey") in which they cunningly fit 11 guests. Unusually in a standard package, TLH fly only two groups per helicopter, which hugely increases your skiing and almost entirely removes any waiting.

Private packages fly Bell A-Stars with only four skiers plus guide, giving more flexibility in terms of terrain that you can ski and areas you can visit. It makes a big difference to have your own helicopter at your beck and call.

This does allow optimization of parties. The guides try to keep groups together but will adjust groups for major differences in ability. Arriving with a full helicopter of like-minded friends of similar ability allows you to get close to the advantages of a private group at rather less cost.

With such a large area to exploit, TLH strategically locate radio repeaters, fuel dumps, and emergency caches throughout the terrain, allowing you to stay out all day, even in the more distant ski zones. This also means that you are rarely aware of any other helicopters in your area.

As usual, safety is the top priority. Guests are comprehensively briefed before setting out and the pilots are incredibly skilled and experienced. Amazingly, they seem to be able to land these rather large flying machines on exactly the same spot they landed on previously—truly precision flying.

GUIDING AND SAFETY

Part of heliskiing's total exhilaration is skiing fresh tracks in untouched wilderness, but it's very reassuring to watch the guides at work. Fully qualified to C.S.G.A. (Canadian Ski Guide Association) or U.I.A.G.M. (Union International de l'Asscociation de Guide de Montagne) standards, they are all extremely experienced in backcountry mountain safety—especially assessing snowpack

▲ SNOW PROPULSION
The location for TLH, in the South Chilcotin Mountains, offers weather and snow conditions ideal for heliskiing.

2003/2004 SCHEDULE & RATES

DELUXE RATES

2 days from Cdn$1,932 to Cdn$2,316
3 days from Cdn$2,431 to Cdn$3,507
4 days from Cdn$3,241 to Cdn$4,675
5 days from Cdn$4,828 to Cdn$5,790
7 days from Cdn$6,545 to Cdn$8,463

Low to high season prices are subject to a tax of 7 percent GST. TLH charges foreign residents net of GST.
Cdn$85 single supplement, subject to availability
All packages start Friday and include all meals and bus transfers from and to Vancouver—supplemental charges apply to alternate transfers.

29,000 feet, 43,000 feet, 57,500 feet, 72,000 feet and 100,000 feet of heli-lift guaranteed for 2-day, 3-day, 4-day, 5-day, and 7-day packages.
Not all day combinations are available at all times.

PRIVATE TOURS

7 days A-Star:
Cdn$51,750 for four people, with eight hours of flying time.
Extra hours at Cdn$1,950 per hour.

7 days A-Star:
Cdn$91,200 for eight people, with 14 hours of flying time.
Extra hours at Cdn$1,800 per hour.

HELICOPTER TRANSPORTATION

Bell 212 twin engine	2
A-Star	2
Total	4

RESTAURANTS

TYAX LODGE DINING ROOM

BARS

TYAX LODGE

▼ **TIGHT TURNS**
Where else can you link hundreds of turns in virgin powder snow?

▶ **ANOTHER DREAMY RUN**
Vayu Zone, one of the many fanastic areas to ski. If the snow isn't perfect, then no problem, the guides have a gift for finding what you want.

stability and ensuring that you only ski safe terrain.

To make sure you ski in both the safest and most enjoyable conditions, guides spend considerable time sharing information about what they see as you ski and fly through the ranges. A constant radio chat relays information from thermal transitions seen in snow pit data through to the best aspects to ski at any given time—each guide hears what the other groups are seeing.

In addition, there is a Snow Safety Guide nominated each day, dedicated to testing snow conditions, assessing the snowpack, and ensuring that all groups are aware of where best to ski.

Adequate insurance is essential and you are advised to opt for the additional helivac insurance offered by TLH, which not only ensures that you are covered for emergency transfer out, but also covers you if you develop a less serious skiing injury which causes you to return to the lodge and stop skiing—but which doesn't require medical attention.

Safety is not limited to the guides: each group skis with two emergency backpacks—one with the guide and one with the "packman" who also carries a radio. The backpacks contain spare kit such as gloves, hats, an avalanche probe, and a snow shovel. You'll spend the first hour of every trip being trained in avalanche rescue using transceivers, probes, and shovels, and in the safety protocol for helicopters and the rules you must follow when skiing with a guide. The helicopters carry additional equipment, spare skis, and sticks, but be warned: there are no spare boots—so if you have boot failure you are likely to be grounded for the remainder of your week.

THE SKIING

The beat of the rotors fades and the whipped-up spindrift settles in your collar. You're crouching at the top of a range of outstanding beauty with a gang of like-minded skiers, as everything turns wonderfully quiet. A few clicks of bindings and you're whooshing through feather-light powder, punctuated only by the whoops and whistles of your companions. A thousand feet later and you're running a natural slalom through pine glades, bouncing down small cliffs—and having the experience of a lifetime.

If it were not so perfect it could get tedious. Skiing in any "normal" resort you might be lucky to get one powder day and two or three runs through fresh snow, while heliskiing can easily get you an

entire week of skiing fresh tracks in perfect snow—which may well change your perception of the economics involved.

A surprise might be that you will ski in "runs," descents well known to the guides and marked as "open" or "closed" depending on conditions or whether anyone has skied them since the last fall of snow. "No, someone's skied that run, we'll find another mountain!" is what you're likely to hear.

It's normal to ski a huge variety of terrain unified only by an abundance of fantastically light, fluffy powder. Every foot of snow on every run isn't always perfect, but the guides are preternaturally gifted at finding great stuff to ski, even on "bad" days. The terrain may not be as steep as you might expect but it's rare for it not to be totally absorbing.

The guides will assign you to groups based on whether you arrived together and how well you are skiing upon arrival; groups may include mixed disciplines of skiers, boarders, and—occasionally—telemarkers. The guides will endeavor to keep traveling groups together where possible.

Whether skier or boarder, you need to be competent and comfortable riding on the average blue trail, in powder, and in more difficult conditions. You should consider yourself a competent skier or boarder, at least comfortably capable of blue trails and happy to attempt any off-piste conditions—including challenging, unpisted snow.

Boarders need to bring their own equipment, but for skiers TLH maintain a range of powder skis from the popular mid-fat Volant Chubbs and Machetes through full-fat Volkl Explorers and Guides, which make off-piste nearly as easy as skiing groomed corduroy. Most skiers now use mid-fats, but if a guest is struggling the guides will tactfully advise moving to fatter and easier skis. If the guides consider, however, that a guest's lack of ability poses a risk to the group's safety or enjoyment, then they reserve the right to change groups or refuse to allow them to ski. Because there are no boots available, you are advised to bring them in carry-on luggage, having made sure that they are comfortable and robust enough for the task!

Most guests are good advanced skiers, and many are skilled and experienced heliskiers and boarders. It is worth noting that you will be expected to ski in courteous, tight lines—neither hogging a whole slope nor poaching first tracks every time!

With such a large area TLH can tailor skiing to fit almost any weather conditions or, indeed, level of skier ability. In adverse conditions, the Taylor ski zone nearest the lodge is mostly below the treeline and has lower landing sites, making it possible to ski in weather that would ground other operators.

APRÈS SKI

Given that you are in a single building in the middle of nowhere, there's a surprising range of things to do in the evening—after a big day, sleep is an attractive option. Before dinner, recovery in the hot tub is a good idea; two qualified physios do massage (booking essential); and there's a small gym, table tennis, video games, pool, and a football table.

With the restaurant now directly managed by TLH, dinner itself is a treat. Served buffet style, the chef, Ty, reveals his Vietnamese origins with subtle Asian influences to the menus; notably fresh sushi a couple of times a week, good fresh fish every night, and occasional spicier dishes.

After dinner the bar is lively, although—unless there's a definite "down" day the next morning—most people retire early. It is not a good idea to take a hangover into a helicopter or on the slopes.

OTHER ACTIVITIES

It has to snow sometime and it doesn't always dump overnight between blue-sky days. TLH reckon on average that you will have one "down" day a week. Most weeks, that's no big issue as you are likely to have exceeded your vertical anyway, and 100,000 feet (30,480 m) is a lot of fresh tracks, so you'll be glad of the rest. No one likes "down" days though: typically, they mean sitting out the morning in the lodge, with hourly updates on conditions before the day is officially declared "down." The guides also want to ski and will not declare the day "down" until they're really sure that you won't get skiing safely. If all else fails they'll organize ice hockey on the lake, or tower climbing in the lodge. In winter, Tyax is really intended for serious skiing only, but it is pretty fine at achieving that. There are also snowmobiles, cross-country skis, ice-fishing gear, and snowshoes available for hire—although it's sensible to bring a good book.

▲ BLUE SKY
TLH's terrain is ideal for the advanced intermediate skier right through to the expert. Even if the weather's bad there are areas to ski, including the low-level Taylor ski zone below the treeline.

▼ YELLOW LIFT
The Bell 212 carries groups of 11 guests and their guide. At TLH you ski with only two groups per helicopter.

USEFUL PHONE NUMBERS

Reservations	250-558-5379
Guest Fax Number	250-238-2528

USEFUL WEBSITE & E-MAIL ADDRESS

Official Website	www.tlhheliskiing.com
Reservations	sales@tlhheliskiing.com

YOU STAY AT JASPER—YOU SKI AT MARMOT BASIN (A 25-MINUTE DRIVE AWAY). THAT'S THE DEAL BECAUSE THERE ARE NO ON-MOUNTAIN ACCOMMODATIONS IN THIS RAW, BEAUTIFUL, AND HIGHLY CONSERVED WILDLIFE HABITAT. RUBBING SHOULDERS, OR AT LEAST VIEWS, WITH DEER AND ELK AND TAKING IN JUST HOW REMOTE, UNCROWDED AND POWDER-COVERED THIS NATURAL BASIN IS, YOU REALLY GET THE FEELING OF SKIING A FINAL FRONTIER.

JASPER

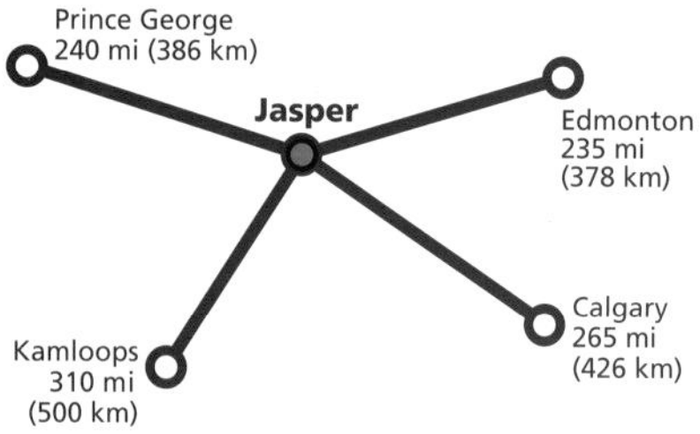

▼ SIZE MATTERS
Jasper is located in the heart of Jasper National Park—the largest preserved wilderness area in the Canadian Rockies.

The small town of Jasper with its clapboard and stone lodgings, restaurants and shops is complemented by the 4,200 square miles (10,878 sq km) of Jasper National Park wilderness, and the recreational mountains of Marmot Basin lying within. One unique feature of the resort is that when you arrive at Marmot Basin you simply park and ski straight off to the nearest chairlift—and at the end of the day you can ski directly back to your vehicle too. But it's the sheer beauty of this back-to-nature ski area that will impress you most, especially in winter, which is off-season. Summer may draw the crowds to see the natural beauty and wide open spaces, but the scenery is most spectacular in the winter—elk move through the lowlands and waterfalls are suspended, frozen in time.

GETTING THERE

Marmot Basin is located in the heart of Jasper National Park—the country's largest Rocky Mountain National Park, and bordered by Banff National Park to the south, in western Alberta, Canada. This means

it's a long way from anywhere including the larger cities of Calgary and Edmonton. Jasper lies 265 miles (426 km) northwest of Calgary and 235 miles (378 km) west of Edmonton. It's a five-hour drive from Calgary, or three hours from Edmonton on the all-weather four-lane Trans-Canada highway and Yellowhead Trail Highway 16. The ski area is also 190 miles (330 km) west and north of the Banff resorts, and is connected via Highway 1 and one of the most spectacular mountain highways anywhere —the Icefields Parkway—a two-hour drive past ancient glaciers and towering peaks. You can also get to Jasper by rail. It's a five-hour trip from Edmonton, or 17 hours (overnight) from Vancouver on board "The Canadian" and this is a recommended trip in itself. Those on a budget can also access Jasper via Greyhound buses.

THE VILLAGE

Here is a real Rocky Mountain town—Canada-style. Its roots go back to 1811 when explorer-mapmaker David Thompson got his men to build a base here while searching for a fur-trading route through the Rockies. Today it's a relaxed mix of rustic lodges, cappuccino bars, eateries, a cinema, contemporary and historic Canadian art galleries and museums, excellent indoor sports and swimming center, and a friendly town with a permanent population of 4,500 residents—many of whom work for Canada's largest railroad. Jasper is not tourist dependent, it's a real community.

Marmot Basin is 12 miles (19 km) south of Jasper town via Highway 93, 93A and the Marmot Basin Road, and has a base lodge called Caribou Chalet which houses the ticket office, ski and snowboard school, dining and restaurant facilities, the Marmot Shop, the daycare, guest services, and the rental and repair store.

ACCOMMODATIONS

If you're seeking on-hill accommodation you will not find it in Jasper; but there are 15 lodges, and some 1,800 beds, located in and around the town, including the Fairmont Jasper Park Lodge, situated on Lac Beauvert two miles (5 km) across the Athabasca River from the town of Jasper. Here there are 442 luxurious rooms in cedar chalets and original log cabins, and this is one of Jasper's oldest and most unique properties. Ice fishing, sleigh rides, cross-country skiing, and snowshoeing all happen from this resort. Other lodging options include the redecorated Amethyst Lodge with 97 oversized rooms. The Astoria Hotel is a cozy little Alpine hotel with 35 elegantly renovated guest rooms. The Tonquin Inn is located only blocks from downtown Jasper, and offers 136 spacious rooms, several with kitchenettes, saunas, and in-room wood-burning fireplaces. The Athabasca Hotel, located in the heart of Jasper with 61 rooms, is priced for all budgets and has a nightclub featuring live entertainment. At the

MOUNTAIN FACTS

Base	5,534 feet	(1,686 m)
Summit	8,534 feet	(2,601 m)
Elevation	3,000 feet	(915 m)
Easy		16%
Intermediate		25%
Advanced		44%
Expert		15%
Number of trails		75
Longest trail		3.5 miles (5.6 km)
Ski area		1,500 acres (608 ha)

SNOWFALL

Annual snowfall	160 inches (400 cm)
Snowmaking	1% of ski terrain

SKI LIFTS

Gondolas	-
High-Speed Quads	1
Fixed Grip Quads	1
Triple Chairs	1
Double Chairs	3
Surface Lifts	2
Total	8
Riders per hour	11,934

▼ **OPENING UP**
Marmot Basin has opened up 20 extra trails on the two huge mountain faces of Eagle Ridge.

▲ **A TALE OF TWO TERRAINS** **The higher you go at Marmot Basin the more open bowl terrain you hit. Lower down it stays mostly forested with tree-lined trails.**

budget end there are several Bed & Breakfast-style accommodations, without the breakfast, or the European equivalent of guesthouses via the Jasper Home Accommodation Association (check out www.visit-jasper.com). Or, if you really want to keep your accommodations costs very low, there is also a winter campsite.

SKI AREA

Located on the eastern slopes of the Rockies, Marmot Basin is a natural basin covered in very dry powder on its alpine bowls, while its lower slopes are tree-lined and more sheltered from the cold winds. Its northerly latitude—the most northerly ski resort in Canada—means it can get extremely cold with temperatures plummeting to 12°F (-11°C) in December. It can even be -40°F (-40°C) in January so be warned. The natural bowl area is dominated by Marmot Peak at 8,534 feet (2,601 m), linked to Caribou Ridge (7,525 feet/2,293 m) along one face, and to Marmot 2 at 8,300 feet (2,530 m) along another ridge called The Saddle. Beyond Marmot 2 is Peveril Peak at 8,793 feet (2,680 m). Marmot 2 then descends down to Cornice at 7,484 feet (2,281 m) to the newly opened Eagle Ridge. The latter development contains Eagle East and Chalet Slope, with 20 new trails created by selectively removing hundreds of trees from the two mountain faces on Eagle Ridge. These developments have significantly improved Marmot Basin's high-end terrain, and have opened up some of the best adventure terrain in the Rockies. Together, these faces make up 1,500 acres (608 ha) of skiable terrain, along 75 trails, and 3,000 feet (915 m) of vertical. Marmot offers an amazing variety of terrain for all levels of skier or rider—the terrain is

SKI SEASON
Late November to late April

◀ **WHERE EAGLES DARE**
Eagle Ridge has intermediate trails and exhilerating double black diamond terrain.

pretty evenly split between novice, intermediate, advanced, and expert trails—from high alpine, powder-filled bowls and immaculately groomed trails through to beautifully spaced gladed trails through the trees. The longest trail is 3.5 miles (5.6 km). However, not all the areas are lift-served. You have to hike and traverse some distance from the Knob chairlift (the highest) past the Saddle to gain access to Peak Run and other summit trails. But wherever you are on the mountain, you can see the whole basin from any single vantage point, and there are consistently spectacular vistas of Jasper National Park's surrounding mountain peaks, as well as the beautiful Athabasca Valley spread out below the ski area. Marmot also remains one of the least crowded resorts of its size and has one of the best lift-capacity-to-skier ratios in North America. The Day Lodge at Marmot is called Caribou Chalet and is located at 5,590 feet (1,704 m), while the highest lift ascends to approximately 8,200 feet (2,500 m) giving a vertical drop of 3,000 feet (914 m).

LIFT SYSTEM

Marmot Basin had the largest lift-serviced new terrain development in western Canada last season, with the addition of the new Eagle Ridge Quad Chair accessing two new mountain faces and 20 new trails. So Marmot now has a total of eight lifts: one high-speed detachable quad, one new fixed grip quad, one triple chair, three double chairs, and two T-bars. These can carry 11,934 skiers per hour. The lifts are open daily 9:00 AM to 4:00 PM and are spread across Marmot's terrain, allowing easy access to four linked areas within the entire ski terrain. The basin-shaped layout of the ski area creates a sense of openness the further up you go, and each lift accesses at least one trail suited to each level of skier or rider (i.e. green, blue and black). The new Eagle Ridge Quad Chair has spread out skier traffic in the upper area, and reduced lift lines at the nearby triple chair. As mentioned before, however, not all the mountain is reachable by lifts so advanced and expert skier especially have to be prepared to hike.

LIFT PASS

An adult one-day lift ticket will cost you Cdn$52 (Cdn$37 in low season, January 18 to February 2). There is a fractional saving on multi-day passes. Youth (13–17) and junior (6–12) and senior (65+) are all discounted, e.g. Cdn$20 per day for juniors. There are also reduced "Afternoon" rates if you kick off after 12:30 PM. For ski school novices, there is a Cdn$10 lift ticket using the School House T-bar only. Lift passes can be bought in Red Deer, Prince George, other sites from Edmonton to Jasper, and at Marmot Basin.

SKI SCHOOL

The Marmot Basin Ski & Snowboard School is located at the Base Day Lodge (Caribou Chalet) and runs from 9:00 AM to 4:30 PM. Largest class size is eight people. For kids aged four and over there are

ACCOMMODATIONS

AMETHYST LODGE
780-852-4431
www.mtn-park-lodges.com

ASTORIA HOTEL
780-852-3351
www.astoriahotel.com

ATHABASCA HOTEL
780-852-3386
www.athabascahotel.com

CHATEAU JASPER
780-852-5644
www.decorehotels.com

JASPER INN
780-852-4461
www.jasperinn.com

FAIRMONT'S JASPER PARK LODGE
780-852-6402
www.fairmont.com

LOBSTICK LODGE
780-852-4431
www.mtn-park-lodges.com

MALIGNE LODGE
780-852-3143
www.decorehotels.com

MARMOT LODGE
780-852-4431
www.mtn-park-lodges.com

MOUNT ROBSON INN
780-852-3327
www.mountrobsoninn.com

PYRAMID LAKE RESORT
780-852-4900
www.pyramidlakeresort.com

SAWRIDGE HOTEL
780-852-5111
www.sawridge.com

THE WHISTLERS INN
780-852-3361
www.whistlersinn.com

TONQUIN INN
780-852-4987
www.decorehotels.com

BARS & RESTAURANTS

A&W RESTAURANT
ANDI'S BISTRO
CALEDONIA GRILL
CANTONESE RESTAURANT
COCO'S CAFÉ
DENJIRO JAPANESE RESTAURANT
EARL'S RESTAURANT
EDITH CAVELL DINING ROOM
FIDDLE RIVER SEAFOOD CO
INN RESTAURANT & LOUNGE
KONTOS' RESTAURANT
L&W RESTAURANT
McDONALD'S
MISS ITALIA RISTAURANTE
MOUNTAIN FOODS & CAFÉ
O'SHEA'S RESTAURANT & BAR
PALISADES RESTAURANT
PAPA GEORGE'S
SUNRISE CAFÉ
SMITTY'S FAMILY RESTAURANT
SOFT ROCK CAFÉ
SOMETHING ELSE RESTAURANT
SPOONER'S CAFÉ
SUBWAY
TONQUIN PRIME RIB VILLAGE
TRUFFLES & TROUT
VILLA CARUSO STEAKHOUSE & BAR

Tiny Tots lessons, and arrangements can be made for supervised lunches for them. Little Rascals Nursery is a full seven days a week facility for children aged 19 months to seven years. Ski lessons are also available and concentrate on the very basics. An Adult Group Lesson (two hours) costs Cdn$29 and a Junior Group Lesson Cdn$22. A one-hour private lesson will cost Cdn$59.

BEGINNERS

The benefit for beginners is that each lift accesses at least one beginner (green) trail, which makes it great for family and mixed ability groups and means that beginners can get to the upper reaches of the mountain. There are three lifts at the base serving most of the lower-level terrain that beginners can use after they have mastered terrain from the School House T-bar. You can even head up to Caribou Ridge for an above-treeline thrill where a wide trail called Basin Run carries you back to the lower slopes. Novice trails called Easy Street and Sleepy Hollow (on Chalet Slope off Eagle Ridge) also take you down from some distance and with superb views from the top. Tranquilizer is another easy cruise lower down the mountain.

INTERMEDIATES

Good middling trails are provided by Show Off and Dromedary, and higher up any of the blue or black diamond trails off Chalet Slope are great gladed trails. Perhaps the most challenging trail at this level is Paradise—long and with a variety of fall-lines and terrain features above Marmot's mid-mountain

▲ **OFF THE BEATEN TRACK**
Freeriders will enjoy the Peak Run steeps and the Eagle Ridge powder.

Paradise Station. Basically every lift in the resort has an intermediate way down, even The Knob. Punch Bowl is another trail to try out at this level. The Knob Traverse below Marmot Peak takes you high on the mountain where you'll have incredible views. Fast intermediates will cover the groomed trails in under a day and will need to progress to ungroomed blacks otherwise they are likely to become bored.

ADVANCED & EXPERT

Head for Eagle East, Chalet Slope, and the Knob Area. The Knob Chair takes you to the highest lift-served terrain and from the top of that lift you have to hike the last part up to Marmot Peak. Peak Run awaits —or drop into the fine powder in the massive Dupres Bowl, with Dupres Chute dividing it from Charlie's Bowl and Wendy's Choice which is ludicrously steep and stays untracked longer. Chalet Slope and Eagle East are tough, due to their northeasterly aspect which holds the snow really well for powder skiing. Eagle Ridge is a mixture of open bowls (with even one long novice trail) cascading down into tree-lined gullies. The Chutes at the Knob and Charlie's Bowl are also challenging and most of this area is double black diamond terrain. Chalet Slope has several steep sections with lots of powder through the trees. Rope closures indicate the area boundary and there are only two points of access into the backcountry from the ski area. Snowcat and heliskiing are on offer also: the cat will take you to untracked powder on bowls and glades with trails to 3,000 feet (900 m) vertical for intermediate and advanced skiers. The heliski locations are some distance away: two hours from Jasper with Robson Helimagic (Valemount, B.C.) or three hours away at Mike Wiegele Helicopter Skiing.

▼ **HIGH & MIGHTY**
Marmot's high elevation and giant natural bowl shape ensure the driest natural powder. Its northerly latitude also means it gets cold, so wrap up warmly.

BOARDING & FREESTYLE

You have to hike to reach the best slopes, but the effort is well rewarded. It's a carver's paradise with excellent trails and different pitches, including the steep Dromedary and Spillway back to base. Eagle Ride with Eagle East and Chalet Slope will beckon with a real backcountry feel as you drop into vertigo-inducing traverses. But watch out for boundary signs funneling you back toward the trails or you'll have a long hike out. Marmot's Terrain Park on Marmot Run in the upper area of the mountain has nearly doubled in size and includes several man-made features including tabletops, spines and rails. It's very easy to get around with a significant amount of fall-line terrain reducing the need to walk, hike, or push your snowboard to the lifts (and all lifts and trails are open to boarders).

EATING ON THE MOUNTAIN

At Marmot there are two restaurants and two cafeterias in three day lodges. Marmot's Eagle Chalet is a beautifully designed log chalet located at mid-mountain that seats up to 60 people. The Eagle Lounge interior is one of the mountain's original chalets, and was used as the base day lodge throughout the 1960s when the base of the ski area was what is now the mid-mountain area. Paradise Chalet cafeteria is cool for late breakfasts and there's a balcony when the weather is warm enough. The Caribou Chalet (base lodge) has its own cafeteria and dining facilities for breakfast and lunch. All the day lodges are fully licensed and the sun decks on Marmot are big and also serve as bag lunch areas.

APRÈS SKI

After your last ride down, Marmot's Caribou Lounge has several bars, while back in Jasper there are over a dozen bars, plus two nightclubs—AthaB Nightclub and Pete's Bar. Whistle Stop in the Whistlers Inn has a good choice of beers with 10 ales on tap. Local musicians jam on Tuesday nights at the Athabasca Hotel, which also has a disco. Villa Caruso has a comfortable martini lounge with a fireplace and mountain views.

There are plenty of restaurants to choose from, most of them situated on Connaught Drive or Patricia Street. Andy's Bistro is popular, with very reasonable prices and a good wine list, while Edith Cavelle Dining Room at the Jasper Park Lodge is good for game. The Fiddle River serves fresh seafood and pasta dishes, while Papa George's Restaurant (Astoria Hotel) is casual and comfy and has Alberta steaks, buffalo, fresh trout and salmon, as well as burgers. There are also plenty of ethnic cuisines to sample—including Japanese sushi, Cantonese, Ukrainian, Italian and Spanish—despite being such a remote town.

OTHER ACTIVITIES

Jasper is recognized as a U.N.E.S.C.O. World Heritage Site and is one of the most pristine and protected environments in the world. There is no shortage of adventure activities. Recommended is a half-day railroad tour over Yellowhead Pass and along the Fraser River to Dunston. You stop by Mount Robson, the highest peak in the Canadian Rockies, and the ghost town of Lucerne.

There is skating; fishing for big northern pike; ice climbing; and walking through a palace of ice at Maligne Canyon. Dogsled rides, snowmobiling, at least five different cross-country skiing tours, and wildlife tours are also available.

Indoors, most hotels offer swimming pools, hot tubs and steam rooms. As for shopping, there is the usual selection of stores, and local galleries sell Canadian Indian and Inuit art and crafts.

USEFUL PHONE NUMBERS

Tourist Information Center	780-852-3858
Central Reservations Center	800-473-8135
Marmot Basin Ski & Snowboard School	780-852-3816
Ski Rescue Service	780-852-6162
Medical Center Seton General Hospital	780-852-3344
Jasper Taxi Service	780-852-3600

USEFUL WEBSITES & E-MAIL ADDRESSES

Official Website	www.skijaspercanada.com
Marmot Basin	www.skimarmot.com
Hotel & Other Information	www.discoverjasper.com
Jasper Attractions & Services	www.visit-jasper.com
Central Reservations Center	reservations@skijaspercanada.com
Weather Reports	www.wunderground.com
Snow Report & Web Cams	www.rsn.com/cams

▲ SPACE AND HAZARDS
The lower tree-lined slopes of the mountain they call the "Big Easy" make freeriding fast, furious with a real frontier feel. But tree-dwelling freeriders must be aware of 'dropping in' on trails already being used by their carving brothers and sisters!

▼ TIME-OUT
Eagle Ridge Chalet has a rustic indoors feel. Outside, the airy log cabin look is amplified by a large deck area with great views.

BANFF LAKE LOUISE IS CANADA'S LARGEST SKI AREA AND ONE OF THE MOST BEAUTIFUL SKI REGIONS IN THE WORLD, FEATURING THE BREATHTAKING BLUE-GREEN LAKE LOUISE, AWE-INSPIRING SUMMITS AND ENDLESS PRISTINE POWDER. THIS IS ALSO WHERE HELISKIING FIRST TOOK OFF AND THE ULTIMATE ALPINE DOWNHILL ADVENTURES ARE A CHOPPER RIDE AWAY.

BANFF LAKE LOUISE

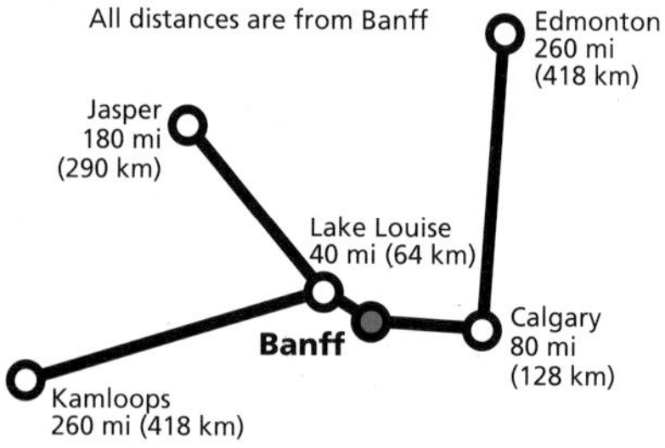

One of three friendly rival resorts near Banff, Alberta, Lake Louise is promoted as an "ensemble" world-class ski destination (via a tri-area lift ticket) along with Banff at Norquay, and Sunshine Village. It began with Mount Norquay in the early 1920s; Sunshine Village opened in the 1930s; and the Lake Louise ski area that exists today dates back to the 1930s. Mechanical lifts began appearing at the resorts in the early 1940s, with Canada's first chairlift installed at Norquay in 1948. Now there are over a million skier visitors each season, who are drawn by the jagged, majestic peaks, unforgettable natural beauty, and exceptional skiing and snowboarding.

Lake Louise has the largest and most varied terrain of the three resorts, with four mountain faces, thousands of acres of wide-open bowls and, critically, a beginner trail off every chairlift. Its centerpiece is the 1.5-mile (2.5-km) long, icy, blue-green lake fed by springs from the Victoria Glacier.

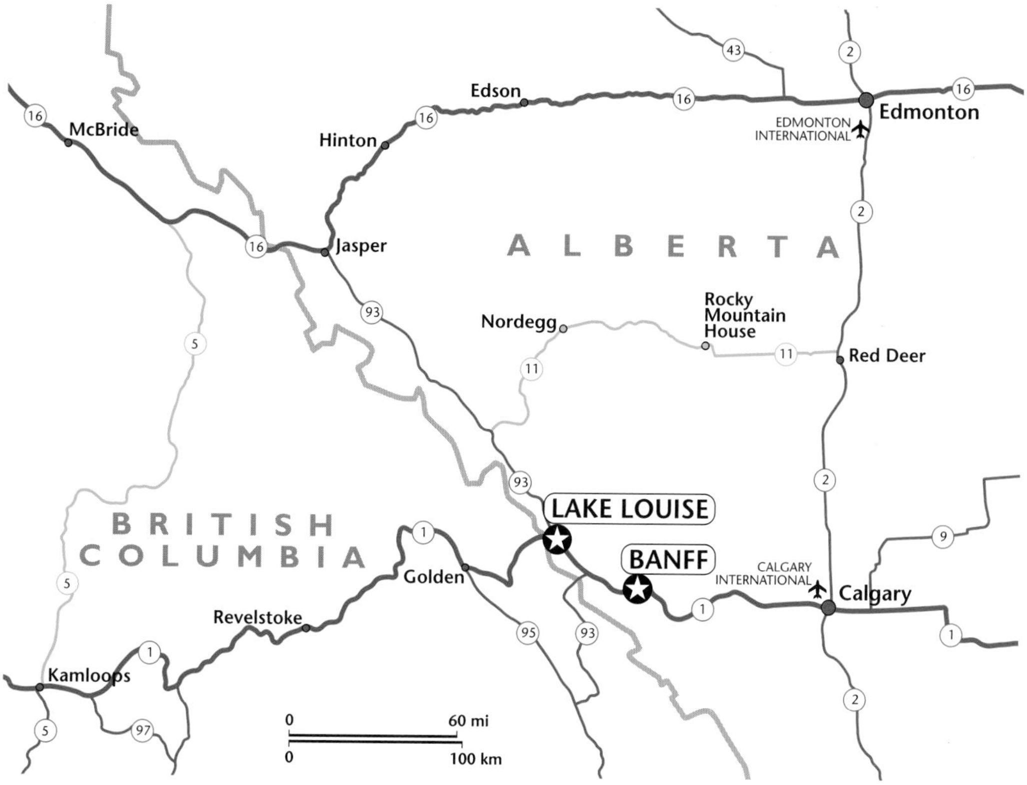

Originally settled in 1884 as a Canadian Pacific Railway logging camp and later designated Canada's first National Park and a U.N.E.S.C.O. World Heritage Side—Banff National Park—Banff is today consistently voted North America's Most Scenic Ski Area.

Sunshine Village, the highest resort, typically offers a blanket of superb powder snow on its wild and wide-open terrain and in 1999–2000 it pipped arch-rival Lake Louise as the No. 1 resort by attracting a record 595,000 visitors. Not to be outshone, Banff Mount Norquay is the locals' favorite, relying on its very easy reach from Banff and its very family-friendly image. It's also the only resort in the Canadian Rockies to offer night skiing.

GETTING THERE

The Lake Louise Ski Area is surrounded by the Canadian Rockies and lies approximately 115 miles (184 km) west of Calgary (the nearest international airport), in southern Alberta, Canada. The trip from Calgary to Banff takes 1.5 hours on a 4-lane highway, plus another half-hour to Lake Louise. Despite its railroad heritage there are, sadly, no passenger trains servicing the resort. There is however a regularly scheduled daily bus service to and from the Calgary Airport to both Banff and Lake Louise. All three resorts are linked by municipal bus services and there are shuttle buses between hotels and resorts. Lake Louise is furthest from Banff, 34 miles (56 km) away or a 45-minute drive (take that into account each way if you are thinking of "commuting" and there is parking at the ski hill itself to consider as well). Sunshine Village is 11 miles (18 km) out of Banff, and Banff Mount Norquay (formerly called Mystic Ridge) is just four miles (6 km) away.

THE VILLAGES

Louise "village" grew around the railroad station and the majestic Chateau Lake Louise Hotel still dominates. The station is no more but the hotel

◄ **FRIENDLY GIANT**
Skiers can set off from the Lodge of Ten Peaks on the Friendly Giant Express quad to the mid-mountain base at Whitehorn Lodge at 6,750 feet (2,057 m).

▼ **AIRY, MODERN BASE**
At Lake Louise's base, the 24,000 square foot (2,232 sq m) Lodge of Ten Peaks is a huge and impressive log-built complex with plenty of 'fuelling' options.

SKI SEASON
First week of November to first week of May

MOUNTAIN FACTS

	Lake Louise	Banff @ Norquay	Sunshine
Base	5,400 feet (1,646 m)	5,350 feet (1,631 m)	5,440 feet (1,658 m)
Summit	8,650 feet (2,637 m)	7,000 feet (2,134 m)	8,954 feet (2,730 m)
Elevation	3,250 feet (991 m)	1,650 feet (503 m)	3,514 feet (1,072 m)
Easy	25%	20%	22%
Intermediate	45%	36%	31%
Advanced/Expert	30%	44%	47%
Number of trails	113	31	103
Longest trail	5 miles (8 km)	0.7 mile (1.1 km)	3.1 miles (5 km)
Ski area	4,200 acres (1,700 ha)	190 acres (77 ha)	3,168 acres (1,283 ha)

SNOWFALL

	Lake Louise	Banff @ Norquay	Sunshine
Annual snowfall	140 inches (356 cm)	120 inches (305 cm)	408 inches (1,036 cm)
Snowmaking	1,700 acres (688 ha)	90% of ski terrain	None

ACCOMMODATIONS

BAKER CREEK CHALETS
403-522-3761

FAIRMONT CHATEAU LAKE LOUISE
403-522-3511

DEER LODGE
403-522-3747

LAKE LOUISE INN
403-522-3791

POST HOTEL
403-522-3989

certainly is. Development is tightly controlled by the Parks Service so the village is compact but has most amenities—gas station, bakery, grocery, liquor store, bus station, a wide range of lodgings, and over 20 restaurants and bars all linked by free shuttle buses.

The upper alpine Sunshine Village lies at 7,082 feet (2,160 m). Lodgings are found at the Sunshine Inn, and the village also has two licensed day lodges, nine food outlets, cocktail lounges, ski & snowboard school, rental store, daycare, snowboard park, outdoor hot pool, and reputedly Canada's best snow, and lots of it—408 inches (1,036 cm) a year!

At Banff Mt. Norquay families come out to play, but it is not a village *per se*. Because it's so close, you stay in the bustling town of Banff, with its hotels, B&Bs, lodges, restaurants, bistros, stores, galleries, boutiques, museums, and plenty of activities such as soaking in the natural hot springs. Mt. Norquay has a new base lodge with licensed lounge, dining, daycare, ski and snowboard schools, and rentals.

ACCOMMODATIONS

There is a wide choice of accommodations in and around Lake Louise village, only a 10-minute driving distance from the Lake Louise Ski Area. At the top end of the spectrum, the Fairmont Chateau Lake Louise, located at the shoreline of Lake Louise, in front of the Victoria Glacier, is a vast Victorian pile. Sumptuous it may be but pretty it isn't. However, it's not as expensive as it looks and group bookings can be attractively priced. In contrast, the International Youth Hostel has dorms, double rooms, a library and veggie café. There are plenty of other lodgings options—B&Bs, motels, and lodges—to suit all pockets in the town off Banff. There's even a winter camping site offering tent and trailer lodging. Sunshine's only accommodations are at the ski-in, ski-out Sunshine Inn.

SKI AREA

Lake Louise is the largest resort in the Canadian Rockies and the three ski resorts encompass 7,558 acres (3,060 ha) and 247 trails. And if you include the mountainous terrain reached only by helicopter then the skiable terrain is infinite. Lake Louise itself covers a vast 11 square miles (28 sq km). These are crisscrossed by 113 named trails and over 80 miles (128 km) of trails across four mountain faces covering 4,200 acres (1,700 ha) of ski area. That's not forgetting the six Back Bowls laying claim to the driest, lightest powder in the world in 2,500 acres (1,012 ha) of pristine, natural, wide-open wilderness. The dry, light snow that falls in the Canadian Rockies is classic "Champagne Powder." The best snow is usually found at higher elevations, in the Back Bowls, and on the trails with snowmaking. Most major Front Side trails have snowmaking and are generally in good shape throughout the season.

▼ BANFF MT. NORQUAY

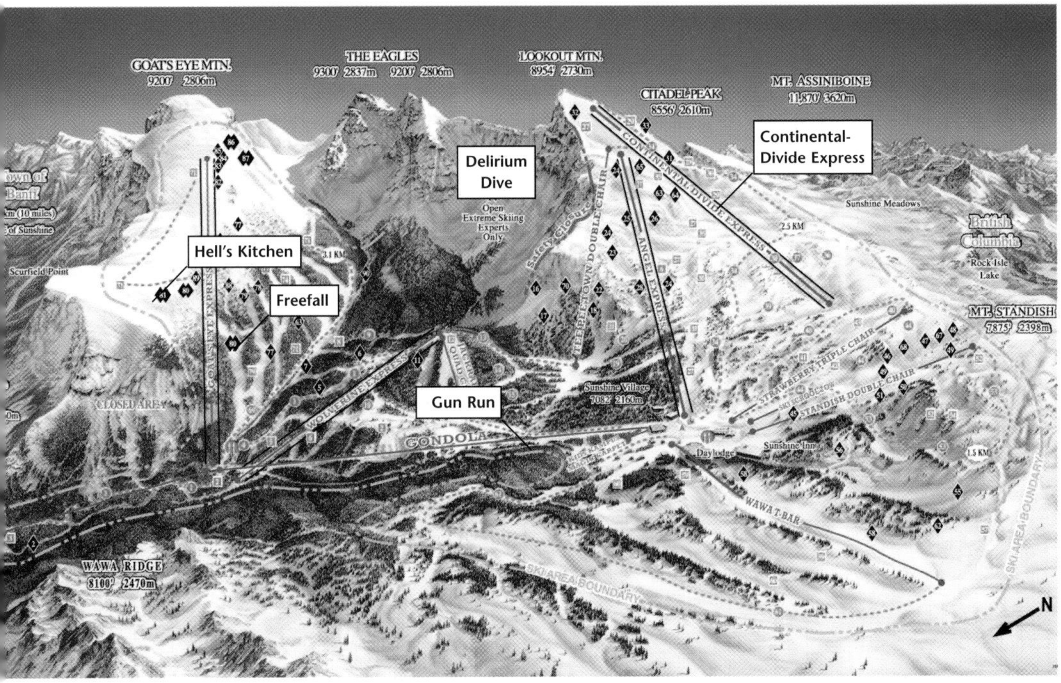

◄ SUNSHINE

Green and blue trails are groomed daily.

A key ingredient to Lake Louise's appeal is that there is a green, or easy trail, from every chairlift on the mountain: in other words all chairs have an easy and difficult way down and the varied terrain above and below the treeline appeals to all types of skiers. Even when visibility is poor, Lake Louise's long, tree-lined trails (making up 66 percent of the resort) offer protection and visibility. Boarders and freeriders will be impressed by "the Jungle," the largest terrain park in North America, which features a superpipe along with all the bumps, jumps, and lumps you can handle on this 2,000 feet (650 m) vertical ride.

Sunshine is a three-mountain resort offering everything from easy beginner slopes to some of the toughest expert terrain in North America. Mount Standish and Lookout Mountain are Sunshine's original two mountains, the latter having the ultimate hardcore backcountry face, Delirium Dive —40° or more at its gentlest—a mile-wide (1.6 km) cirque that is patrolled by the park service who won't let you in if you don't carry transceivers and shovels. But there are plenty of thrills on Sunshine's 103 trails without going near the Dive. Tons of snow, wicked freeriding and a natural terrain park on Mt. Standish make this a boarders' mecca. At Sunshine Village the vertical drop is 3,514 feet (1,072 m)—the biggest in the Canadian Rockies. The third and newest addition to the resort is Goat's Eye Mountain via a new 8-seat gondola taking skiers to the top in just six minutes. With 408 inches (10.2 m) of snow each winter, more than Lake Louise and Banff Mt. Norquay combined, Sunshine doesn't need snow machines.

▲ LAKE LOUISE

Banff Mount Norquay is a much smaller and more straightforward proposition: one mountain face, five lifts, 190 acres (77 ha) and a fair mix for all levels, over 31 tree-sheltered trails. Designed by skiers for skiers, it has plenty of carving and freeriding options. Night skiing and boarding are now on offer every Friday as well.

The ski season here is from the first week of November to first week of May, but be warned, the region is cold in winter, much colder than, say Colorado, with extreme lows in December and February of -22°F (-30°C) rising to 19°F (-7°C) in January. This can be tough on the less-seasoned skier and difficult for kids to handle—and when your not in the sun, it's even tougher.

▲ QUICKER ACCESS
Sunshine's high-speed gondola links skiers to the base of Goat's Eye Mountain and on to the base of Lookout Mountain. You can get from the valley to mid-mountain in around 13 minutes and lines are now rare.

LIFT SYSTEM

Lake Louise has a system of 11 interconnecting lifts, Sunshine Village has 12, and Banff Mount Norquay has five. At Lake Louise all the lifts are in strategic locations, making it easy to get around from frontside to backside and all four faces of the two mountains. You can ski all three areas with one ticket (the Tri-Area Pass) and get free transfers between hotels and resorts, plus an added-value coupon at Banff Mount Norquay. Ski Banff-Lake Louise-Sunshine offers multi-day tri-area lift tickets, including free roundtrip shuttle service between Banff or Lake Louise hotels and the ski areas. Ski Big Three Vacations offers customized ski vacation packages inclusive of lodgings, tri-area lift tickets and lesson programs.

LIFT PASSES

Lift pass prices vary but an adult day-pass will cost you Cdn$61. For kids aged 6–12 it costs Cdn$15, and under-sixes ski for free. Beginners can buy a T-bar ticket only, which they can upgrade later in the day for an all-mountain pass. Tickets can be bought in the base area at every ticket outlet and at Customer Service. There is no problem of waiting in lines at the Lake Louise Ski Area.

SKI SCHOOL

Each resort has a ski and snowboard school and Lake Louise Ski School—one of Canada's largest—is located at the base area, in the lower level of Whiskyjack Lodge. Group lessons start at age 13 and older, and lesson times are 10:00 AM to 12:30 PM, and 1:00 PM to 3:30 PM. There are excellent facilities for the younger skier with the Kid Ski & Shreddies for ages 5–12 (ski) and 7–12 (shreddies.) Lesson times are 10:00 AM–12:00 PM, and 1:15 PM–3:15 PM. The upper limit on a ski group size is eight. The Kinderski program for ages three and four has to be booked through daycare. Parents can book a supervised lunch for their children.

SKI LIFTS

	Lake Louise	Banff @ Norquay	Sunshine
Gondolas	1	-	1
High-Speed 6-Pack	1	-	-
High-Speed Quads	-	1	4
Fixed Grip Quads	4	2	2
Triple Chairs	1	-	1
Double Chairs	2	1	2
Surface Lifts	2	1	2
Total	11	5	12
Riders per hour	16,920	7,000	20,000

BEGINNERS

The best areas for beginners in Lake Louise is the base area, using Sunny T-bar, and on the main green Wiwaxy trail on the front side of the mountain. The Larch Area should not be missed as it has some easy trails like Marmot and Lookout. As every chair has an easy way down all four mountain faces, novices can enjoy a wide variety of access and the scenic vistas.

Beginners at Norquay should take the Cascade Quad lift, which gives access to a host of good trails. Easy trails are plentiful at Lake Louise: Saddleback and Pika; the long and open Wiwaxy; and—a personal favorite—the Cameron Way, are all ideal for gentle souls. Also, as a Lake Louise bonus, some trails down the mountain are pretty easy too – so no need to take the lift down at the end of the day.

While all resorts attempt to cater to every grade of skier, Sunshine is primarily an intermediate resort. Beginners, in or out of class, will take the Wheeler chair from the center station to the more open upper slopes, or take the longish uphill haul on the Strawberry-Standish chair combination; wrap up

▶ MODERATE CHALENGES
Mount Standish's summit is 7,875 feet (2,398) and somewhat in the shadow of its fellow Sunshine Village Peaks, but the groomed trails here off the Standish double chair and Strawberry triple chair are gentle and fun—ideal for beginners and intermediates.

well for the lift, it can be chilly. There are good trails all over the tops, and the nice long green run from the top of Lookout Mountain to finish off the day.

INTERMEDIATES

The bulk of Lake Louise trails—45 percent—are Intermediate. The longest trail is 5 miles (8 km) and the most challenging trail is Boomerang on the Back Bowls. Alternatively, take any frontside to backside circuit to enjoy an amazing variety of the open alpine terrain while also having easy access to lodges and facilities.

Those who just have to ski somewhere new each season can try Mystic Ridge (on Banff MT. Norquay) but otherwise stick to Lake Louise if you're an intermediate—you can ski almost everywhere but there are some great individual trails. Those who like wide open cruising trails will enjoy Larch, or the Skyline trail from the top station, but with 60 miles (100 km) of trails to explore, Lake Louise and Norquay is intermediate heaven.

Sunshine offers intermediate or moderate skiing in style and abundance; around 60 percent of Sunshine's trails are moderately long and moderately steep, and are fairly well enclosed by trees. All the trails are really within the grasp of any competent intermediate but Brewster's Chair, off the Great Divide chair, is a popular favorite.

ADVANCED & EXPERT

Higher level skiers head for the Back Bowls of Lake Louise: sustained pitch with big vertical. The toughest challenges are on the North Face of the Summit of Mount Whitehorn "1" and "2." Brown Shirt on the backside of Mt. Whitehorn is best for powder. Take the backside trails from the Summit Platter lift and back over to the front side trails via Paradise Triple Chair for a classic circuit. This chair takes you to a ridge where you are spoiled for choice—The Diamond Mine, as its name suggest, is an open bowl studded with diamond and double diamond black trails. From the top of the West Bowl on the front side of Mount Whitehorn there are spectacular views of the lake and the chateau.

Delirium Dive is the expert terrain area at Sunshine Village, located on the north and east aspects of Lookout Mountain with chutes, cliffs, and confined couloirs. Access is from the top of the Continental Divide high-speed quad through the check-in gate. Then it's a 130-foot (40-m) hike. There's usually a patroller around and a gate at the bottom with a key that reads your transceiver (which you need, along with shovel and probe) beep and lets you through. There's a ridge you can hike on the right-hand side, then take a set of stairs to the far right to reach the trail called Milky Way. If you traverse above Sweet and Low, there's a great little trail that faces Goat's Eye. Just below the summit there is a 15- to 20-foot (4–6 m) rock band that crowns the top of the Dive. You can negotiate entry into the Dive through the cliff's small weaknesses or simply drop in, but this gets skied out pretty quickly. Another more moderate way down is via access stairs that take you to tamer ground. Either way it's 2,000 vertical feet (610 m) of hardcore pleasure riding. It mellows out at the bottom and after fresh snow it's

▲ DROP DOWN
Lake Louise provides a vertical drop of 3,250 feet (991 m) and always a spectacular backdrop of serrated mountain peaks.

▲ **EXTREME SLOPES**
There is more inaccessible and unexplored (and out-of-bounds) ski terrain locked up in Canada's National Parks than in all the rest of the world. The intrepid expert can still find plenty of challenging off-piste skiing off the Back Bowls of Lake Louise and excellent untracked terrain at Sunshine's Delirium Dive.

especially awesome.

Those who like bouncing down moguls will enjoy the steep Lone Pine run at Norquay, or the Gun Run off the double chair. Those wanting off-piste—apart from paying close attention to avalanche warnings and stop signs—will find all they need in the Paradise and East Bowls at Lake Louise. The challenges at Sunshine are the trees and the ice. Trees cast shadow and Sunshine is not always sunny, so beware sudden patches of ice or hard crust. Testing runs here include the narrow Hell's Kitchen and Freefall mogul fields off Goat's Eye Mountain—which also has good off-piste—and the steep chutes off Lookout Mountain, notably the Big and Little Angel.

For the really adventurous, and nowadays that can include intermediates, there are three heliski operations: it's one to three hours from Lake Louise to Panorama, Golden, or Revelstoke in the majestic glaciated mountains of eastern British Columbia (out of Banff National Park.) It was in Banff that Austrian emigré Hans Gmoser established the first heliskiing over 30 years ago. The sensation of no lift pylons, no clanking or squealing, and no engines (apart from the beat of the helicopter leaving you) to spoil the environment is truly one of the pinnacles of the sport.

BOARDING & FREESTYLE

Lake Louise claims the largest terrain park in North America—The Jungle —featuring a 2,000-foot (6010-m) vertical ride with bumps, jumps, and a superpipe right under a chair. The Summit Platter Poma lift on the front side of Mt. Whitehorn is something of a challenge in itself for snowboarders, but there are some great hikes off the top to your left. For great powder head to the Back Bowls and keep far left to Brown Shirt. It's worth the detour, as are Upper Boomerang, North Cornice, and Wild Gully. For trees, head to Ptarmigan Chair and trails such as The Equalizer, Turn or Burn, or Ptarmigan Chute 2. Carvers should try Meadowlark, Home Run, and Gully on the Front Side, and Larch in the Larch Area for fresh corduroy on nicely groomed trails. There's good beginner terrain on the front side and in the Larch Area. Novice classes stick to the Sunny T-bar, which serves an excellent beginner area.

Banff at Norquay suits intermediate snowboarders best, but experts will find plenty of challenges here too. Excellent grooming and snowmaking makes it fun to cruise, whether to carve arcs or just go for it. Some trails are rolling rides with the odd lips for catching air. The snowboard park has a halfpipe and is groomed at least five nights a week. On Friday nights you can board under floodlights.

At Sunshine Village the lower Mount Standish is the place for riders. The Dell Valley makes a natural halfpipe near the Strawberry triple chair, and the area between the Wawa quad and the Standish Chairs is a natural terrain park with lots of natural hits, a quarterpipe, lips and drops. There is a halfpipe on Strawberry Face. If you like to hike for your turns, there are plenty of choices. You'll find lots of awesome cliffs, chutes and gullies, plus wide open bowls. Start off with a hike up from the tops of Standish Chair, Wawa quad, and Goat's Eye Express. The marked trails in these areas are also favorites with snowboarders. Be warned though—there are a few flats including one on Lookout Mountain when you're coming out of Bye Bye Bowl or South Divide. It requires a hoof up the last section, which is actually a little

► **FREERIDERS**
There is virtually limitless freeriding in the vast expanse of the Back Bowls and out-of-bounds area of Lake Louise with no trees to get in the way. But this ski terrain is both awesome and treacherous and freeriders should be aware of avalanche warnings and check with the ski patrollers about access and conditions.

hill that then drops you back into the main area so you can work your way to the lifts.

EATING ON THE MOUNTAIN

Lake Louise has four day lodges but the emphasis is on utilitarian rather than alluring. Having said that, at the base of the mountain in the beautiful log-built Lodge of the Ten Peaks you'll find the family-friendly Powderkeg Lounge and a cozy atmosphere. There's also a cafeteria here. At Whiskyjack Lodge, the Northface Restaurant serves up breakfasts and lunch, and there is also a cafeteria but not much else. Mid-mountain front side has the Whitehorn Lodge cafeteria, while Temple Lodge serves the Back Bowls, Ptarmigan, and Larch areas with a cafeteria and an attractive outdoor terrace. Sawyer's Nook, also in Temple Lodge, is probably the best full-service restaurant, with prime Alberta beef.

The choice at the smaller resorts is fairly limited too. Sunshine Village has eight places in which to refuel with Mad Trapper's as the place for lunch. The Sunshine Day Lodge has reputedly one of the best cafeterias going and upstairs a very fine dining room. The Alpine Grill and the Chimney Corner Lodge both serve reasonably priced pasta and plenty of it.

At Ski Banff at Norquay you can take your pick from the Timberline Lodge's steak house, or Cascade Lodge's mid-price deli and cafeteria, or its upstairs Lone Pine Pub-with-restaurant. The latter is affordable and attractive with good food and views.

APRÈS SKI

Nightlife in Lake Louise is quiet and centers around Glacier Saloon at Chateau Lake Louise, while the Sitzmark Lounge has live entertainment on the weekends. There are two après-ski outings in Lake Louise combining dinner with entertainment: the Torchlight Dinner and Ski at Whitehorn mid-mountain Lodge is a package including an après-ski party with appetizers, full buffet dinner, live entertainment, and a guided torchlight ski down the mountain. It takes place two or three times a week, starting right after skiing and lasting until 8:30 PM. Saturday nights features the Brewster Cowboy's Barbecue and Dance Barn, near the Fairmont Chateau, via a sleigh ride. Aside from this it's head for Banff if you want more choice with plenty of restaurants of every persuasion and bars from cowboy saloons, British-style pubs such as the Henry VIII, and at the Aurora an over-21s nightclub and restaurant. Downtown Banff has more than 100 bistros and fine restaurants including Japanese, Italian, steakhouses, Tex-Mex as well as cafés, pubs and delis.

▲ **HIGH MOUNTAIN LIVING**
At the top of a 13-minute gondola system, the Sunshine Village Inn provides Banff and Lake Louise's only on-mountain accommodation. Rooms are simple but comfortable. In walking distance are pubs, lounges, dining, live entertainment and day care serving this 7,082 feet (2,160 m) village.

OTHER ACTIVITIES

A host of outdoor activities are available at Lake Louise including cross-country, snowshoeing, ice walks, dog-sledding, skating, sleighrides, spas, and hot springs. Off-mountain there are plenty of family-oriented activities including swimming, bowling alleys, movie theaters, and shopping. Gym and pool facilities are available at various hotels. Shopping in Banff ranges from fashionwear to native crafts and specialty boutiques, along with the larger malls. Lake Louise has its own Samson Mall for shoppers. Art galleries and craft shops showcase Inuit, wildlife, landscape, and Native art along with ceramics and jewelry. There are also several museums and national historic sites in the neighborhood that highlight the natural history and man made heritage of the Rockies.

USEFUL PHONE NUMBERS

Lake Louise Ski Area	403-522-3555
Tourist Information Center	403-762-4561
Accommodation Reservation Centre	403-209-3321
Lake Louise Ski & Snowboard School	403-522-1333
Ski Patrol & Rescue Service	403-522-1311
Lake Louise Medical Clinic	403-522-2184
Taxi Lake Louise	403-522-2020

USEFUL WEBSITES

Three-Resorts Official Website	www.skibanfflakelouise.com
Lake Louise Website	www.skilouise.com
Banff at Norquay	www.banffnorquay.com
Sunshine Village	www.skibanff.com
Weather Reports	www.wunderground.com
Snow Report & Web Cams	www.rsn.com/cams

THERE ARE AROUND 90 SKI RESORTS IN THE VICINITY OF QUÉBEC CITY, AND ALTOGETHER THEY PROVIDE ABOUT 800 DOWNHILL TRAILS. THE CLOSEST TO THE CITY ARE STONEHAM AND MONT-SAINTE-ANNE, BOTH OF WHICH ARE UNDERSTANDABLY VERY POPULAR WITH LOCAL DAY SKIERS. REMEMBER THAT TEMPERATURES CAN BE BITTERLY COLD IN THE WINTER MONTHS, AND AS MOST OF THE RESORTS ARE RELATIVELY SMALL THEY CAN BE OVERCROWDED IN PEAK SEASON.

QUEBEC

The majority of Québec's population are of French extraction, which means that you need to expect manners, morals and customs, food and many other details to be thoroughly French Canadian. Canada became officially bilingual with the Official Languages Act of 1969, which made French equal in status to English, but Québec went a step further and in 1977 the famous Law 101 made French the province's official language. The Laurentians (Laurentides) extend between the hills, lakes and valleys north of Montréal between St-Jérome and Mont Tremblant. It is an area that has become home for many as it offers hiking trails, watersports, lively nightlife, fine restaurants and of course a vast and ever-expanding network of ski resorts. Very different from the days when Voltaire described Canada as "Quelques arpens de neige" ("a few acres of snow") in his work *Candide* (1759).

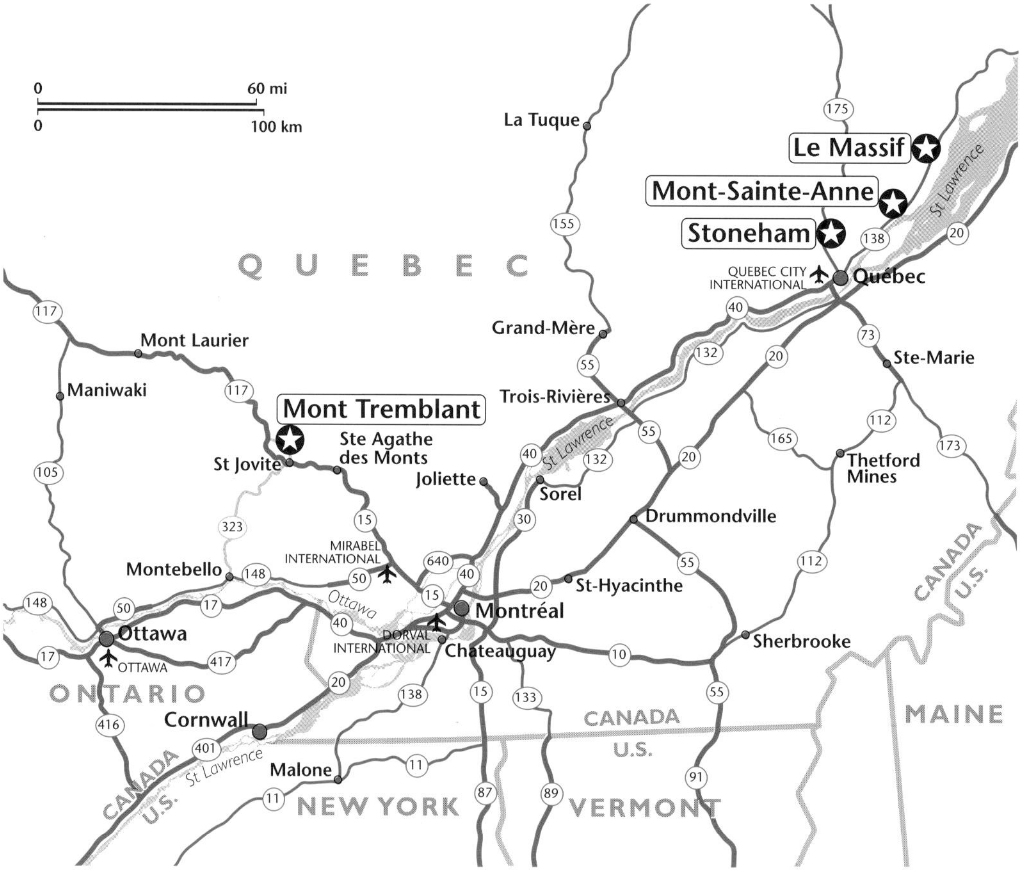

MONT TREMBLANT

MOUNTAIN FACTS

Base	870 feet (265 m)
Summit	3,000 feet (914 m)
Elevation	2,130 feet (649 m)
Easy	16%
Intermediate	32%
Advanced/Expert	52%
Number of trails	92
Number of terrain parks	2
Number of glades	121 acres (48 ha)
Longest trail	3.75 miles (6 km)
Ski area	610 acres (244 ha)

SNOWFALL

Snowmaking	76%
Annual snowfall	150 inches (380 cm)

SKI LIFTS

Gondolas	1
High-Speed Quads	6
Quads	1
Triple Chairs	2
Magic Carpets	3
Total	13
Riders per hour	27,230

SKI SEASON
Late November to mid-April

▲ **CHARMING CHOICE**
The pedestrian village combines chic boutiques and 5-star accommodation, as well as the welcome absence of vehicles.

In operation since 1939, Mont Tremblant is famous for wide open skies, fresh air, and natural beauty. The pedestrian village and uncrowded trails make it a very popular choice among Canadians and Americans, and a good choice for families, despite the typically very low temperatures of eastern Canada.

GETTING THERE

Located in the Laurentian Mountains, Mont Tremblant ski area is 75 miles (120 km) northwest of Montréal. The nearest international airport is at Montréal, 75 miles (120 km) away and a 90-minute drive. Ottawa International Airport is 94 miles (151 km) southwest and takes two hours by car, and Québec City International Airport is 169 miles (272 km) east and takes 3.5 hours by car. Skyport runs a shuttle service from all the airports to the resort, and the major car rental companies have desks at all the airports.

THE VILLAGE

The pedestrian village is charming. Restaurants offer everything from light snacks to gastronomical feasts, international, Mexican, Italian—the choice is yours. There are over 45 chic boutiques in the Place St. Bernard, at the foot of the slopes, along with gift stores, a photo center, art galleries, sporting goods, and a movie theater showing the latest releases. Hotels provide four- to five-star accommodations. The village is recommended as a place to bring the kids as it's free from cars and everyone is very welcoming.

SKIING & SNOWBOARDING

Tremblant has four skiing areas, each with a variety of green, blue, and black pistes: Versant Sud (Southside), Versant Nord (Northside), Versant Soleil, and Edge. Versant Soleil and Nord both have high-speed quads covering all the pistes, Sud has a high-speed heated gondola that takes nine minutes to get from the Place St. Bernard to the summit, and Edge has a quad chair. Beginners stay around Équilibre, a special two-acre (0.8-ha) area uniquely dedicated to beginner skiers and snowboarders, but Versant Sud also has green and some not too difficult blue trails from the top of the mountain, so the choice expands quite rapidly once you've mastered the basics. For intermediates the easier blues are on Versant Sud, while Versant Nord has some tougher challenges. More than half the trails are designated black or double black, making the going quite tough on any of the four ski areas. Dynamite, a double black on Versant Nord, is extremely steep. The Edge has some difficult trails, both steep and moguled, and often icy.

▶ **OUT OF THE COLD**
Escape the very low temperatures when staying in the cozy comfort of the lodges at the base of the mountain.

The terrain park, Parc Gravité, is on Versant Nord, accessed by a triple chair. It has 18 acres (7 ha) of ramps, curves, and jumps, an Olympic-sized 20-foot (6-m) superpipe, a quarterpipe, and the ubiquitous rollers and tabletops.

The Mont Tremblant Snow School has a great reputation. They limit class sizes to seven, and you'll always have a friendly bilingual instructor. Skiing classes are held for children aged three to 12, and snowboarding classes for children aged seven to 12. There are special ski weekends, ski weeks, and private lessons in skiing, snowboarding, cross-country skiing and telemarking. There are lots of added activities too, like First Track—be the first to make your mark on the slopes; Gliding Evenings; and night-time tubing.

Full-day lift passes cost Cdn$50 for adults (18–64), Cdn$37 for teens (13–17) and Seniors (65+), and Cdn$27 for children (6–12), with fives and under (Pee Wees) skiing free. A five-day pass costs Cdn$242 adults (18–64), Cdn$177 for teens (13–17) and seniors (65+), and Cdn$131 for children (6–12).

APRÈS SKI

The best bars are in Vieux Tremblant. The Café d'Époque has good music and a lively ambience. Le P'tit Caribou has been voted "Best Bar in eastern Canada" four consecutive times by *Ski Canada Magazine*. Octobar Rock in the Chalet des Voyageurs at the base of the Southside is a fun rock bar.

To help you relax after punishing those muscles, head for the Spa Le Scandinave, with a Finnish sauna, Norwegian steam bath, outdoor jacuzzi, and Swedish massage. Of if you want to keep on punishing those muscles, there are plenty of other sporting activities. Try forest dog-sledding, where you drive your own team of Husky dogs through the Laurentian wilderness, or traditional dog-sledding,

where you drive your own team of dogs through snow-covered fields, led by an experienced guide. Horseback riding in winter is a new experience for many and you can do it here.

Challenge yourself to some ice climbing (no experience necessary) or take an airplane tour and see Tremblant from a new perspective on board a Cessna snow plane. A quiet sleigh ride might be up your street—enjoy a cup of hot chocolate while a storyteller entertains you with legends of Tremblant. Take a guided snowshoe hike into the mountains to observe deer in their natural environment. Lightweight snowshoes are provided. Experience the thrill of snowmobiling along literally thousands of miles of forested trails and snow-covered fields. Visit Aventures Neige, and enjoy a whole day of tubing!

Cross-country skiing (*ski de fond* in French) is particularly good at Mont Tremblant as there is lots of undulating terrain and magnificent vistas along its 62-mile (100-km) network of trails.

ACCOMMODATIONS

FAIRMONT CHATEAU TREMBLANT	819-681-7000
LE WESTIN RESORT	819-681-2000
LE LODGE DE LA MONTAGNE	819-681-2000
LA TOURS DES VOYAGEURS	819-681-2000
LE SOMMET DES NEIGES	819-681-2000
CLUB TREMBLANT	819-425-8781
LE GRAND LODGE	819-425-2734

USEFUL PHONE NUMBERS

Tourist Information	819-425-2434
Central Reservations	800-567-6760
Skyport Shuttle Service	800-471-1155

USEFUL WEBSITES & E-MAIL ADDRESSES

Official Website	www.tremblant.com
Official Website	www.monttremblanttourism.com
Laurentians Website	www.laurentians.com
Official E-mail	reservations@intrawest.com
Official E-mail	tourism@mt-tremblant.com
Skyport Website	www.skyportinternational.com

▶ **THE EDGE**
Appropriate name for a trail that'll test even the most die-hard double black diamonders.

LE MASSIF

Le Massif is unique in that you park your car at the top of the mountain and access the trails from the summit rather than the base. It's tiny compared to most ski resorts, with just 240 acres (97 ha) of skiing, a mere fraction of the size of some of the resorts in the United States. And it's steep too, with the highest vertical drop east of the Canadian Rockies. There are fantastic views of the St. Lawrence River and out to the open sea from many of the trails.

GETTING THERE

Located in the Charlevoix region, 20 miles (33 km) east of Mont-Sainte-Anne and 45 miles (73 km), a 45-minute drive, from Québec City. Follow the 138 east from Québec to Le Massif and park your car directly at the top of the mountain. There's a regular train service to Québec City. To get to the resort from Québec by shuttle, take the Winter Express shuttle from any major Québec City hotel to Mont-Sainte-Anne and then the free shuttle service from Mont-Sainte-Anne to Le Massif (twice a day, once in the morning, once in the afternoon).

THE VILLAGE

Most of the lodgings, restaurants and other attractions are in nearby Petite-Rivière-Saint-François and Baie-Saint-Paul, on the St. Lawrence River. You can find cozy and comfortable lodging and distinctive regional cuisine (not a French fry in sight) as well as various local cultural attractions in these two charming villages. The Le Massif website has comprehensive information on all lodgings, restaurants and bars in both villages.

SKIING & SNOWBOARDING

With just 36 trails, Le Massif doesn't offer the same level of choice as other larger resorts, but it holds its own in terms of vertical thrills. Around 20 percent of the trails are for beginners, mostly clustered around the east side of the resort, which is good, as you don't get too many advanced skiers whizzing past you. Intermediates will focus mostly on the middle section of trails, where there are some good blues, and advanced and experts swap between the middle section and west section, where blacks and double blacks are scattered.

The National Alpine Ski Training Center has an excellent reputation and is the only facility of its kind in Québec. They train the Canadian ski team so you're in good hands. As well as programs and private lessons the Iniski-Inisurf is very popular, with a two-hour lesson, lift ticket and equipment rental all included—programs at 10:00 AM and 1:00 PM.

A full-day lift pass costs Cdn$38 for adults (17+), Cdn$30 for seniors (55+) and teens (17–23), and Cdn$21 for juniors (7–16). Children aged six and under ski free. Half-day passes (afternoon) cost Cdn$32 for adults (17+), Cdn$26 for seniors (55+) and teens (17–23), and Cdn$18 for juniors (7–16). A five-day pass costs Cdn$162 for adults (17+), Cdn$129 for seniors (55+) and teens (17–23), and Cdn$92 for juniors (7–16). The Carte-Blanche multipass allows skiers and boarders to ski at Stoneham, Mont-Sainte-Anne, and Le Relais as well.

APRÈS SKI

Two pubs at the resort, Le Chouenneux and Le Coteilleux, have a good selection of beers and a friendly après-ski atmosphere. For more choices of bars and restaurants, go to Petite-Rivière-Saint-François and Baie-Saint-Paul.

USEFUL PHONE NUMBERS

Tourist Information	418-632-5876 or 877-536-7743
Central Reservations	866-435-4160

USEFUL WEBSITES & E-MAIL ADDRESSES

Official Website	www.lemassif.com
Official E-mail	info@lemassif.com

MOUNTAIN FACTS

Base	118 feet (36 m)
Summit	2,645 feet (806 m)
Elevation	2,527 feet (770 m)
Easy	20%
Intermediate	36%
Advanced/Expert	44%
Number of trails	36
Longest trail	2.3 miles (3.7 km)
Ski area	240 acres (97 ha)

SNOWFALL

Snowmaking	70%
Annual snowfall	253 inches (643 cm)

SKI LIFTS

High-Speed Quads	2
Double Chairs	1
Surface Lifts	2
Total	5
Riders per hour	6,500

SKI SEASON
Early December to mid-April

▼ **ELITE DROP**
Le Massif de Petite-Rivière-Saint-François, as it is known, is located a short 45 miles (72 km) from Québec City in the beautiful Charlevoix region. With its 2,527-foot (770-m) vertical drop it attracts many of Canada's elite skiers.

MONT-SAINTE-ANNE

MOUNTAIN FACTS

Base	575 feet (175 m)
Summit	2,625 feet (800 m)
Elevation	2,050 feet (625 m)
Easy	23%
Intermediate	46%
Advanced/Expert	31%
Number of trails	56
Longest trail	3.6 miles (5.7 km)
Ski area	428 acres (173 ha)

SNOWFALL

Snowmaking	80%
Annual snowfall	160 inches (406 cm)

SKI LIFTS

Gondolas	1
High-Speed Quads	1
Quads	2
Triple Chairs	1
Double Chairs	2
Surface Lifts	5
Magic Carpets	1
Total	13
Riders per hour	18,650

ACCOMMODATIONS

CHATEAU MONT-SAINTE- ANNE
CHALETS MONT-SAINTE- ANNE
HOTEL VAL DES NEIGES

▼ TRAILS GALORE
Although it's small in terms of acreage, Mont-Sainte-Anne is perfectly formed, with 56 trails for all levels of skiing ability.

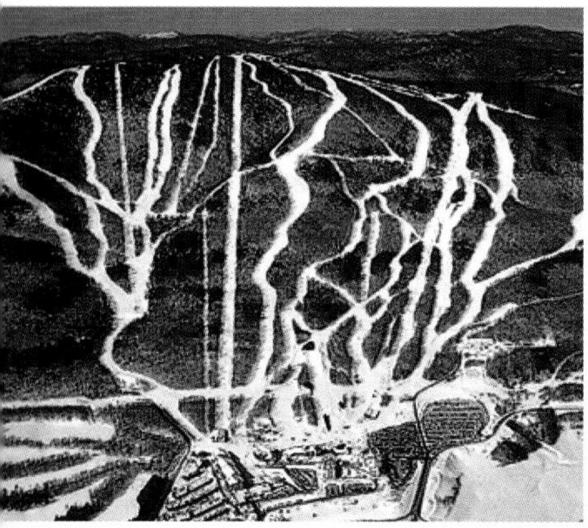

Overlooking the St. Lawrence River, just 30 minutes' drive from Québec City, Mont-Sainte-Anne is part of U.N.E.S.C.O.'s World Heritage list. Although renowned for its expert ski terrain, there are trails for all levels of skier over its 56 trails, which cover 428 acres (171 ha). Again, it is popular with families, even though it can get extremely cold in the depths of winter.

GETTING THERE

Mont-Sainte-Anne is located 25 miles (40 km) from Québec City, about 30 minutes' drive. The nearest international airport is Jean-Lesage, Québec City. There's a daily shuttle service from Québec City hotels to the resort on the Winter Express (four transfers per day). There's also a regular shuttle service between nearby hotels and the base of the mountain.

THE VILLAGE

The modern base area forms the village and has four restaurants/bars (there are three more on the mountain) and a few stores. There are more than 60 lodgings facilities either at the base of the mountain or in the vicinity of Mont-Sainte-Anne or in Québec City. The choice is varied, from inns and luxury hotels through to chalets and condos. Central Reservations will help you choose which one suits you best.

SKIING & SNOWBOARDING

The skiing is spread over three sides, with breathtaking scenery at every turn. The St. Lawrence River flows to the south and the impressive Laurentians are to the north. With 13 lifts serving 56 trails, there are never any lines and two of the lifts are covered, which is a bonus in the very cold winter months.

In a special beginners' area, beginners have a magic carpet and two other surface lifts that are free of charge for everyone at all times, for both those learning and those helping. There's a long beginner trail from the summit of the mountain to the base, which means that beginners can also enjoy the tremendous views over the St. Lawrence River. Intermediates have nearly half the trails for their enjoyment, all well groomed and some long. Most of the blue trails join up with each other. The famous expert trails cover about a third of the mountain and they are what has made Mont-Sainte-Anne famous. Watch your step, as the double blacks can be surprisingly steep. Off-piste skiing and boarding is allowed on the west side of the mountain.

Night skiing and boarding takes place daily from 3:00 PM to 10:00 PM on 15 lit trails, covering nine miles (15 km)—an unforgettable experience as they provide the highest vertical for night skiing in Canada.

There are two terrain parks, open to both skiers and boarders. The one on La Grande Allée trail is 0.6 mile (1 km) long, and off Le Court Vallon trail is a 1,900-foot (579-m) boardercross course. This fun park features obstacles, tabletops, and jumps. There are also two groomed halfpipes. Snowboarders have access to all trails and world-class boarders visit the resort every season for the F.I.S. Snowboard World Cup.

A free guiding service by experienced mountain hosts is offered daily at 10:00 AM and 1:30 PM, from the top of the mountain. There's also a team of 200 certified ski and snowboard instructors who provide private and group lessons for all levels. Disabled skiers are taught by C.A.D.S certified instructors and special equipment is provided free of charge.

Full-day lift passes cost Cdn$46 for adults (23–64), Cdn$37 for teens (14–22) and seniors (65+), and Cdn$25 for children (7–13), with sixes and under skiing free. A five-day pass costs Cdn$195 adults (23–64), Cdn$161 for teens (14–22) and seniors (65+), and Cdn$102 for children (7–13). The Carte-Blanche multipass allows skiers and boarders to ski at Stoneham, Le Massif and Le Relais as well.

APRÈS SKI

The Rendez-Vous restaurant and the Côté Jardin are in the Base Lodge at the base of the lifts and the Refuge à Charlie is at the base of the north side. All offer a good après-ski atmosphere. Within thirty minutes' drive, Québec City has a wide choice of restaurants, cafes, bars, and discos.

Other winter activities in the area include ice skating and snowshoeing in the woods at the base of the lifts.

USEFUL PHONE NUMBERS

Tourist Information	418-827-4561
Central Reservations	800-463-1568
Snowphone	418-827-4579

USEFUL WEBSITES & E-MAIL ADDRESSES

Official Website	www.mont-sainte-anne.com
Official E-mail	neige@mont-sainte-anne.com

STONEHAM

▼ **WELCOME SHELTER**
Sheltered from cold winds, Stoneham is popular with families coming for the day from Québec City, only 20 minutes away.

Stoneham is one of the three largest ski and snowboard areas in the province of Québec, although it is still quite small compared to U.S. resorts. Set in a horseshoe-shaped valley, it is well sheltered from the harsh eastern Canada winds, something you may well be grateful for. It's also known for having an extensive network of illuminated night-skiing trails, 17 in total, covering 184 acres (74 ha), and being so close to Québec City, people often come here for a night out.

GETTING THERE

Stoneham is located just 20 minutes' drive from Québec City. The Winter Express is a daily shuttle service from and to Québec City hotels, and there's a local bus shuttle on Saturday and Sunday from Sainte-Foy and Québec City.

THE VILLAGE

Stoneham Hotel, at the base of the mountain, is the only lodging in the vicinity, and offers 60 rooms and 120 fully equipped studios and condominiums. Otherwise the village is complete with five restaurants; ski and snowboard stores offering a wide variety of clothing and equipment; and Charlie's Grocery, including a bakery, a grocery, and video rentals. As Québec City is so near, many visitors either stay or eat out there.

SKIING & SNOWBOARDING

With 32 trails spread over four mountains, the resort caters to all levels of skier and snowboarder. At night it has 17 lit trails, the largest night-skiing network in Canada. Beginners have less choice than any of the other levels, with only 20 percent of trails dedicated to them. However, there are some long green trails that help beginners find their ski legs. Intermediate blue trails are dotted about the four ski areas, so you can ski from one mountain to another. Extreme skiing/boarding enthusiasts have access to the most trails, with the majority of double black diamond trails on mountain number 3. Three new trails have recently been designed specially for experts, forming an extreme zone on mountain number 4. The two terrain parks include a 0.6-mile (1-km) boardercross course and there's also a superpipe with 17-foot (5-m) walls, 15 rails, and 10 tabletops.

Stoneham Sports School has 150 fully qualified instructors, with private and group lessons offered daily, as well as programs with special equipment for skiers with disabilities.

Full-day (9:00 AM–6:00 PM) lift passes cost Cdn$37 for adults (23–64), Cdn$28 for teens (14–22) and seniors (65+), and Cdn$16 for children (7–13), with sixes and under skiing free. Day/night skiing from 12:30 PM–10:00 PM costs Cdn$33 for adults (23–64), Cdn$27 for teens (14–22) and seniors (65+), and Cdn$15 for children (7–13). Night skiing only for one day (3:00–10:00 PM) costs Cdn$21 for adults (23–64), Cdn$19 for teens (14–22) and seniors (65+), and Cdn$13 for children (7–13). A five-day pass costs Cdn$153 adults (23–64), Cdn$117 for teens (14–22) and seniors (65+), and Cdn$67 for children (7–13). The Carte-Blanche multipass allows skiers/boarders to ski at Mont-Sainte-Anne, Le Massif, and Le Relais too.

APRÈS SKI

Due to its popularity as a night out with the Québecois, Stoneham is surprisingly lively in the evenings. The base of the mountain has five restaurants, and several bars.

USEFUL PHONE NUMBERS

Tourist Information	418-848-2415
Central Reservations	800-463-1568
Stoneham Hotel	800-463-6888
Snowphone	418-848-2415

USEFUL WEBSITES & E-MAIL ADDRESSES

Official Website	www.ski-stoneham.com
Official E-mail	Info@ski-stoneham.com

MOUNTAIN FACTS

Base	695 feet (212 m)
Summit	2,075 feet (632 m)
Elevation	1,380 feet (420 m)
Easy	20%
Intermediate	23%
Advanced/Expert	57%
Number of trails	32 day; 17 night
Number of terrain parks	2
Longest trail	2 miles (3.2 km)
Ski area	326 acres (132 ha) day 184 acres (74 ha) night

SNOWFALL

Snowmaking	86%
Annual snowfall	140 inches (356 cm)

SKI LIFTS

High-Speed Quads	1
Quads	2
Double Chairs	1
Surface Lifts	5
Magic Carpets	-
Total	9
Riders per hour	14,200

ACCOMMODATIONS

STONEHAM HOTEL	418-848-2411

SIERRA-AT-TAHOE
(Photographer Grant Barta; Skier Matt Gold)

VAYU ZONE, TLH HELISKIING

When you're heading to ski country, why not fly on United, the airline the U.S. Ski and Snowboard Teams use? From around the world, you can fly to many ski destinations directly or via an easy connection in Denver. With the most flights and the most seats to 28 ski destinations, United gets you to the slopes quickly. Whether you want to get "big air" after your flight is entirely up to you.

US SKI TEAM US SNOWBOARD TEAM

WE ARE UNITED

www.unitedairlines.com

A STAR ALLIANCE MEMBER ™

CENTRAL RESERVATIONS

MOUNT BACHELOR
www.mtbachelor.com
+1 800 829 2442

SUN VALLEY
www.visitsunvalley.com
+1 800 634 3347

BIG SKY
www.bigskyresort.com
+1 800 548 4486

YELLOWSTONE CLUB
www.theyellowstoneclub.com
+1 888 700 7748

JACKSON HOLE
www.jacksonhole.com
+1 800 443 6931

NORTHSTAR AT TAHOE
www.skinorthstar.com
+1 800 466 6784

SQUAW VALLEY
www.skisquaw.com
+1 888 736 9775

ALPINE MEADOWS
www.alpinemeadows.com
+1 530 583 4232

HEAVENLY
www.skiheavenly.com
+1 800 HEAVEN

SIERRA-AT-TAHOE
www.sierratahoe.com
+1 530 659 7453

KIRKWOOD
www.kirkwood.com
+ 1 800 967 7500

MAMMOTH MOUNTAIN
www.mammothmountain.com
+1 800 MAMMOTH

SKI LAKE TAHOE
www.skilaketahoe.com
+1 800 588 SNOW

THE CANYONS
www.thecanyons.com
+1 877 698 0882

PARK CITY
www.parkcityinfo.com
+1 800 348 6759

DEER VALLEY
www.deervalley.com
+1 800 584 3337

ALTA
www.alta.com
+1 888 782 9258

SNOWBIRD
www.snowbird.com
+1 801 947 8220

SUNDANCE
www.sundanceresort.com
+1 801 225 4100

STEAMBOAT
www.steamboat.com/ski
+1 877 239 2628

WINTER PARK
www.skiwinterpark.com
+1 970 726 5587

VAIL
www.vail.com
+1 800 525 2257

BEAVER CREEK
www.beavercreek.com
+1 888 632 0073

KEYSTONE
www.keystoneresort.com
+1 888 254 4994

COPPER MOUNTAIN
www.coppercolorado.com
+1 888 539 7866

BRECKENRIDGE
www.breckenridge.com
+1 888 539 7866

ASPEN SNOWMASS
www.aspensnowmass.com
+1 800 290 1326

CRESTED BUTTE
www.crestedbutteresort.com
+1 888 463 6714

TELLURIDE
www.tellurideskiresort.com
+1 866 287 5016

TAOS
www.taosski.com
+1 866 836 9968

SMUGGLERS' NOTCH
www.smugs.com/ski
+1 800 451 8752

STOWE
www.stowe.com
+1 800 253 4754

KILLINGTON
www.killington.com
+1 888 764 2968

SUGARLOAF
www.sugarloaf.com
+1 800 843 5623

WHISTLER BLACKCOMB
www.whistlerblackcomb.com
+1 888 403 4727

FERNIE
www.skifernie.com
+1 877 333 2339

MIKE WIEGELE'S HELICOPTER SKIING
www.wiegele.com
+1 250 673 8381

TLH HELISKIING
www.tlhheliskiing.com
+1 250 558 5379

JASPER
www.skijaspercanada.com
+1 800 473 8135

BANFF LAKE LOUISE SUNSHINE
www.skibig3.com/ski
+1 877 754 7078

MONT TREMBLANT
www.Tremblant.com
+1 866 566 6873

QUEBEC CITY AREA
www.lemassif.com
+1 866 435 4160

MONT-SAINTE-ANNE
www.mont-sainte-anne.com
+1 800 463 1568

STONEHAM
www.ski-stoneham.com
+1 800 463 1568

SKI CANADA
www.skican.com
+1 888 4 SKICAN

TRAVEL INFORMATION

DISTANCES FROM NEAREST MAIN INTERNATIONAL AIRPORT

STATE	SKI RESORT	INTERNATIONAL AIRPORT	MILES	KM
OREGON	MOUNT BACHELOR	PORTLAND	170	272
IDAHO	SUN VALLEY	SALT LAKE CITY	340	544
MONTANA	BIG SKY	SALT LAKE CITY	346	554
	YELLOWSTONE CLUB	SALT LAKE CITY	349	558
WYOMING	JACKSON HOLE	SALT LAKE CITY	200	320
CALIFORNIA	NORTHSTAR AT TAHOE	RENO/TAHOE	40	64
	SQUAW VALLEY	RENO/TAHOE	42	67
	ALPINE MEADOWS	RENO/TAHOE	45	72
	HEAVENLY	RENO/TAHOE	55	88
	SIERRA-AT-TAHOE	RENO/TAHOE	72	115
	KIRKWOOD	RENO/TAHOE	80	128
	MAMMOTH MOUNTAIN	RENO/TAHOE	164	262
UTAH	THE CANYONS	SALT LAKE CITY	40	64
	PARK CITY	SALT LAKE CITY	37	59
	DEER VALLEY	SALT LAKE CITY	37	59
	ALTA	SALT LAKE CITY	33	53
	SNOWBIRD	SALT LAKE CITY	29	46
	SUNDANCE	SALT LAKE CITY	47	75
COLORADO	STEAMBOAT	DENVER	180	288
	WINTER PARK	DENVER	95	152
	VAIL	DENVER	120	192
	BEAVER CREEK	DENVER	126	202
	KEYSTONE	DENVER	100	160
	COPPER MOUNTAIN	DENVER	100	160
	BRECKENRIDGE	DENVER	104	166
	ASPEN SNOWMASS	DENVER	221	354
	CRESTED BUTTE	DENVER	231	370
	TELLURIDE	DENVER	330	528
NEW MEXICO	TAOS	ALBUQUERQUE	135	216
VERMONT	SMUGGLER'S NOTCH	MONTREAL	91	146
	STOWE	MONTREAL	140	224
	KILLINGTON	BOSTON	135	216
MAINE	SUGARLOAF	BOSTON	350	560
BRITISH COLUMBIA	WHISTLER BLACKCOMB	VANCOUVER	75	120
	FERNIE	CALGARY	150	240
	MIKE WIEGELE'S HELISKIING	VANCOUVER	232	371
	TLH HELISKIING	VANCOUVER	125	200
ALBERTA	JASPER	CALGARY	255	408
	BANFF LAKE LOUISE	CALGARY	115	184
QUEBEC	MONT TREMBLANT	MONTREAL	75	120
	LE MASSIF	QUEBEC CITY	45	72
	MONT-SAINTE-ANNE	QUEBEC CITY	25	40
	STONEHAM	QUEBEC CITY	15	24

MAJOR AIRLINES

AIR CANADA
www.aircanada.ca
US & Canada +1 888 247 2262
UK +44 (0) 8705 247226

AMERICAN AIRLINES
www.aa.com
US & Canada +1 800 433 7300
UK +44 (0) 208 572 5555

BRITISH AIRWAYS
www.british-airways.com
US & Canada +1 800 AIRWAYS
UK +44 (0) 845 77 333 77

CONTINENTAL AIRLINES
www.continental.com
US & Canada +1 800 525 0280
UK +44 0800 776464

DELTA AIRLINES
www.delta.com
US & Canada +1 800 221 1212
UK +44 0800 414767

UNITED AIRLINES
www.ual.com
www.unitedairlines.co.uk
US & Canada +1 800 864 8331
UK +44 (0) 845 844 4777

VIRGIN ATLANTIC AIRWAYS
www.virgin-atlantic.com
US & Canada +1 800 862 8621
UK +44 (0) 1293 450150

BAGGAGE ALLOWANCE

BE SURE TO CHECK YOUR AIRLINE'S BAGGAGE POLICIES, MANY OF WHICH APPEAR ON THEIR WEBSITES. POLICIES FOR INTERNATIONAL AND DOMESTIC FLIGHTS MAY DIFFER. SOME AIRLINES IMPOSE SUBSTANTIAL PENALTIES IF YOU EXCEED THE PERMITTED BAGGAGE ALLOWANCE.

ASSOCIATIONS

NORTH AMERICA

PROFESSIONAL SKI INSTRUCTORS OF AMERICA
www.psia.org
+1 303 988 0545

AMERICAN ASSOCIATION OF SNOWBOARD INSTRUCTORS
www.aasi.org
+1 303 988 0545

NATIONAL SKI PATROL
www.nsp.org
+1 303 988 1111

NATIONAL SPORTS CENTER FOR THE DISABLED
www.nscd.org
+1 970 726 1540

SNOWSPORTS INDUSTRIES AMERICA
www.snowsports.org
+1 703 556 9020

AMERICAN AVALANCHE ASSOCIATION
www.avalanche.org
+1 970 946 0822

UNITED KINGDOM

BRITISH ASSOCIATION OF SNOWSPORT INSTRUCTORS
www.basi.org.uk
+44 (0) 1479 861717

BRITISH SKI & SNOWBOARD FEDERATION
www.bssf.co.uk
+44 (0) 131 445 7676

WORLD SKI AND SNOWBOARD ASSOCIATION
www.worldski.co.uk
+44 (0) 114 279 7300

BRITISH SKI CLUB FOR THE DISABLED
www.bscd.org.uk
+44 (0) 1895 271104

THE UPHILL SKI CLUB FOR THE DISABLED
www.uphillskiclub.co.uk
+44 (0) 1479 861272

SKI CLUB OF GREAT BRITAIN
www.skiclub.co.uk
+44 (0) 845 458 0780

WEATHER FORECASTS & SNOW REPORTS

INTELLICAST.COM provides extensive specialized weather information to help plan all outdoor and weather sensitive activities, whether golfing, sailing, hiking, skiing or relaxing at the beach. Drawing on the meteorological knowledge of its staff, Intellicast.com now provides more free, accurate and up to date weather information on the Internet than ever before with over 250,000 pages of detailed weather information. With millions of visitors monthly, Intellicast.com is one of the largest and most successful sites on the internet. Website: www.intellicast.com

WEATHER UNDERGROUND is committed to delivering the most reliable, accurate weather information possible. State-of-the-art technology monitors conditions and forecasts for over 60,000 U.S. and international cities and 200 U.S. ski areas. Website: www.wunderground.com

RESORTS SPORTS NETWORK'S RSN.COM provides weather maps, reports on snow conditions and resort information, featuring the RSN Resort Cam® network, a collection of daily updated images from North America's top destination areas. Website: www.rsn.com.

THE AMERICAN AVALANCHE ASSOCIATION (AAA) is comprised of a collective group of dedicated professionals engaged in the study, forecasting, control and mitigation of snow avalanches. The association membership includes qualified researchers, professional avalanche forecasters, snow safety officers, snow rangers and qualified ski patrollers, technicians and other specialists. Website: www.avalanche.org

READERS' REPORTS–HOW YOU CAN HELP US

It is not possible for us to visit all of the resorts covered in this guide in the space of one season. And so to help keep Ski North America accurate and up-to-date, if you find anything in this book that is misleading or has changed please let us know.

Also, we encourage you to send us your own reports—good and bad—about your own experiences of the resorts featured in this guide.

What was it about the resort that you most liked, disliked and why? How did you find the ski area relative to your ability? Tell us your favorite trails and any particular ski tips that you feel would be helpful to others.

Your views about ski school, childcare, the lift system, accommodations, eating on the mountain, après-ski, restaurants and nightspots are especially helpful because when we visit a resort for just a few days (without children) it is impossible for us to match the vacation experience gained by you, your friends and family over a longer period.

In particular, we welcome your views about matters that are likely to be recurring and that we should know about. When reporting bad experiences, for example, about accommodations or restaurants, please be as specific as you can so we can check whether the particular problem has been remedied or not.

It is helpful if you structure your report using the same headings as we use in the resort sections of this book. Also remember to include with your report your full name, postal address and telephone number, the dates when you visited the resort, where you stayed and your ski experience.

Please send your report by e-mail to:
reports@ultimate-sports.co.uk
Or if you do not have access to a computer and e-mail you can send your report by mail to:
REPORTS, Ultimate Sports Publications Ltd, 42-44 Dolben Street, London SE1 0UQ

THE 100 BEST REPORTS EACH YEAR WILL EACH RECEIVE A FREE COPY OF THE NEXT EDITION OF SKI NORTH AMERICA

VISIT US ONLINE AT WWW.ULTIMATE-SPORTS.CO.UK FOR INFORMATION ABOUT SKI EUROPE AND OTHER NEW TITLES IN THE ULTIMATE SPORTS SERIES AND FOR DETAILS OF SPECIAL OFFERS AND PROMOTIONS

PICTURE CREDITS LIST

ALL PHOTOGRAPHS REPRODUCED BY PERMISSION OF BLACK DIAMOND, THE RESORTS AND/OR THE PHOTOGRAPHERS LISTED BELOW:

FRONT COVER – Pyramid Peak (also page 195) courtesy of Aspen Resort (Ultimate Sports Edition)
– Taking the Plunge (also page 101) courtesy of Mammoth Mountain Resort (Firefly Edition).

OPENING SPREADS – Rolo's (pages 2 and 3) Courtesy of Mike Wiegele's and Highland Bowl (page 5) courtesy of Aspen resort.

AVALANCHES & MOUNTAIN SAFETY – Halsted Morris; ALPINE MEADOWS – Courtesy of Alpine Meadows Resort; ALTA – Courtesy of Alta Ski Area; ASPEN SNOWMASS – Courtesy of Aspen Snowmass Resorts; BANFF LAKE LOUISE – Courtesy of Banff Lake Louise Resorts; BEAVER CREEK – Jack Affleck and courtesy of Vail Resorts; BIG SKY – Courtesy of Big Sky Resort; BRECKENRIDGE – Jack Affleck, Leisa Gibson, Carl Scofield and courtesy of Breckenridge Resort; COPPER MOUNTAIN – Courtesy of Copper Mountain Resort; CRESTED BUTTE – Tom Stillo and courtesy of Crested Butte Mountain Resort; DEER VALLEY – Courtesy of Deer Valley Resort; FERNIE – Henry Georgi; HEAVENLY – John Kelly, Scott Markewitz, Sherry McManus and courtesy of Heavenly Resort; JACKSON HOLE – David Gonzalez, John Layshock, Andrew McGarvy, Bob Woodall, Greg Von Doersten; and courtesy of Jackson Hole resort; JASPER – Courtesy of Marmot Basin, Jasper, Alberta; KEYSTONE – Jack Affleck, Leisa Gibson and courtesy of Keystone Resort; KILLINGTON – Courtesy of Killington Resort; KIRKWOOD – Courtesy of Kirkwood Resort; LE MASSIF – Courtesy of Le Massif Resort; MAMMOTH MOUNTAIN – Courtesy of Mammoth Mountain Resort; MIKE WIEGELE'S – Gary Brettnacher, John Kelly, Larry Prosor, Lorne Green, Josef Mallaun, Erich Schadinger, Don Cole Harvey, Frank Matson, Andy Aufschnaiter and courtesy of Mike Wiegele's Resort; MONT–SAINTE–ANNE – Jean Sylvain and courtesy of Mont–Sainte–Anne Resort; MONT TREMBLANT – Courtesy of Mont Tremblant Resort; MOUNT BACHELOR – Kaua/D'Vision, Bob Woodward and courtesy of Mount Bachelor Resort; NORTHSTAR AT TAHOE – Dan Coffey, Robbie Huntoon, Grafton Marshal Smith, Dave Norhad and courtesy of Northstar Resort; PARK CITY – Lori Adamski–Peek, Dan Campbell and courtesy of Park City Resort; SIERRA-AT-TAHOE – Grant Barta www.grantbartaphoto.com (also pages 298–299); SMUGGLERS' NOTCH – Courtesy of Smugglers' Notch Resort; SNOWBIRD – Courtesy of Snowbird Resort; SQUAW VALLEY – Eric Brandt, Nathan Kendall and courtesy of Squaw Valley Ski Corp; STEAMBOAT – Courtesy of Steamboat Resort; STONEHAM – Jean Vaudreuil and courtesy of Stoneham resort; STOWE – Dennis Curran and courtesy of Stowe Resort; SUGARLOAF – Courtesy of Sugarloaf Resort; SUN VALLEY – Courtesy of Sun Valley Resort; SUNDANCE – Courtesy of Sundance Resort; TAOS – Ken Gallard and courtesy of Taos Resort; TELLURIDE – Doug Berry, Tony Demin, Richard Durnan, Gus Gusciora, George Huey, Ron Kanter,Brett Schreckengost, Grafton Smith, T.R. Youngstrom and courtesy of Telluride Resort; TLH HELISKIING – Gordon Eshom, Randy Lincks, George Rosset and courtesy of TLH Heliski resort; THE CANYONS – Courtesy of The Canyons Resort; VAIL – Jack Affleck, Leisa Gibson, Jeff Potto, Ken Reddings, Sinuhe Shrecengost and courtesy of Vail Resort; WHISTLER BLACKCOMB – Courtesy of Whistler Blackcomb Resort; WINTER PARK – Courtesy of Winter Park Resort; YELLOWSTONE CLUB – Eric Kendall and Penny Kendall.

ALL TRAIL MAPS ARE REPRODUCED BY PERMISSION OF THE RESORTS.

ACKNOWLEDGEMENTS

SPECIAL THANKS TO:

Richard Watts for project management and for his invaluable assistance at all times.

Guy Chambers, Craig Johnson, Jim Odoire, Sam Stoyel, Charlie Witheridge and all at Black Diamond.

Editorial contributors Eric Kendall, Sarah Hudson, James Harrison, David Murdoch, Robin Neillands & Mike Allaby for their help in writing this book, Tim Williams for cartography, Duncan Kitson and Paul Kellett at PDK for design, Vannessa Morgan for proof reading and Clive Sparling for his help with production.

Photographer Grant Barta, and skiers Matt Gold and Ben Bleichman who hiked up Sierra-at-Tahoe on 15th May 2003 to shoot pictures for us (pages 84 – 89) after the 2003 season had ended.

AND THANKS ALSO TO:

Jenn Gleckman, Kris McKinnon, Gretchen Sproehule, Rachael Woods, Connie Marshall, Dwight Rimmasch, Mike Jette, Bob Bayliss, Mary Evans, Christina Schleicher, Emily Jacob, Dax Schieffer, Glenniss Indreland, Kate Wilson, Amanda McNally, Kelly Ladyga, Sandi Griffin, Ben Friedland, Beth Jahnigen, John Monson, Meredith Murphy, Diane Temple, Gina Kroft, Brian Brown, Chad Wassmer, Patti Denny, Diane Gillett, Melody Kultgen, Willo Rushfeldt, Kristen Aggers, Molly Cuffe, Tony Lyle, Anna Olson, Rob Ellen, Austin Clay, Dawn Doty, Helen Cospolich, Brian Halligan, Jen Anderson, Kim Jackson, Tania Pilkinton, Tracey Miller, Christine Grimble, Jose Reineking, David Ovendale, Joani Lynch, Lynn Carpenter, Melissa LaRose, Mike Wiegele, Carly Carmichael, Chris Johnson, Andre Jean Lauzon, Clauderic St Amand, Lyne Lortie, Marie Claude Renaud, Sebastien Dubois, Thomas Tellingson, Toby Baird, Nikki Brush, Shon Taylor, Kate McDonald Brown, Nicole Belt, Todd Majoris, Barbara Thomke, Jim Espey, Raelene Davis, Simon Diggins, Katja Dahl, Hayley Roper, Jenny O'Farrell, Mike Lane, Kirt Zimmer, Michael Colbourn, James Tabor, Angela Stone, Karen Greene, Shannon Besoyan, Maxine Jensen, Adriana Blake, Ana Karina Nilsson, Annie Kuhles, Kurt Metternick, Bob Hughes, Kate Gamblin, Alan Palmer, Leisa Gibson, Jen Brown, Sandi Griffin, Christopher Nicolson, Lauren Gehlen, Monica Leeck, D.B. Daugherty, Kate Roberts, Eric Ladd, Hank Kashiwa, Mike Watling, Maude Bedard, Nicholas Fournier, and all local skiers, riders and staff at each resort.

Mary Metz and Tim Warne at Mountaineers Books and Bruce Tremper at Utah Avalanche Institute for allowing us to excerpt and/or adapt text and tables from *Staying Alive in Avalanche Terrain* by Bruce Tremper.

Françoise Vulpé at Firefly Books.

And last, but not least, family, friends and anyone else who has helped in any way.

www.blackdiamond.co.uk

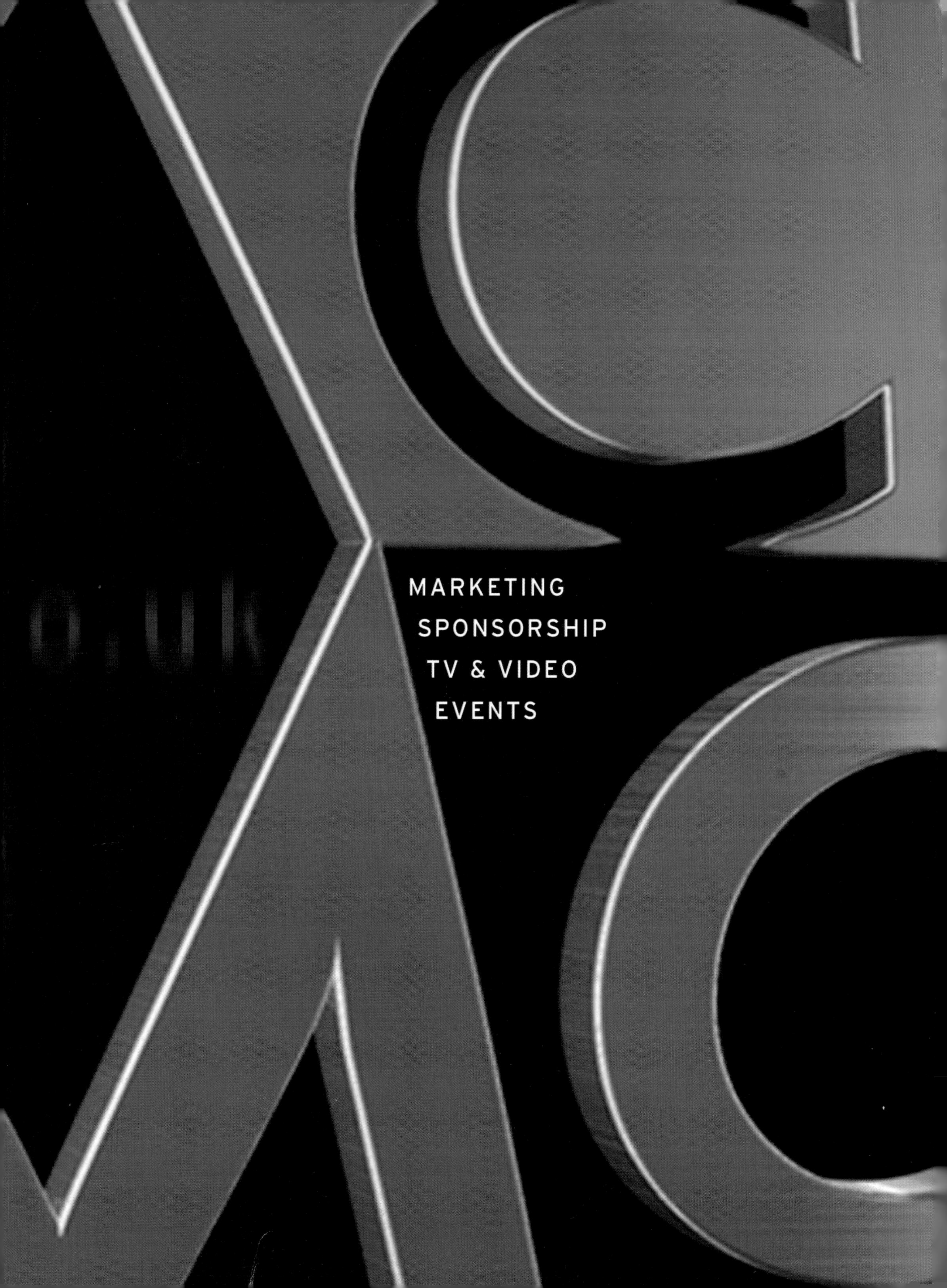
MARKETING
SPONSORSHIP
TV & VIDEO
EVENTS

INDEX